Contents

Unit 6 265

Detailed Table of Contents

Unit: Media and Social Issues

Issue: Do Media Reflect Contemporary Family Relationships?
Yes: Leigh H. Edwards, from "Reality TV and the American Family," University Press of Kentucky (2010)
No: Sarah Boxer, from "Why Are All the Cartoon Mothers Dead?" *The Atlantic* (2014)

Associate Professor Leigh H. Edwards examines how families are portrayed in television and discusses how certain narrative tropes, trends, and genres present us with real family relationships representative of American society and culture. She raises the important point that reality television in particular presents viewers with real conflicts to which many families can relate, because the programs portray real cultural problems that have no easy answers. She concludes her argument with an assessment that public debates about family and marriage often frame the content of the families we see on television. Sarah Boxer examines the content of animated movies and questions why so many mothers in fairy tales and children's films represent the absent mother. Since more American households are headed by married couples or single mothers, she questions the portrayals of mother figures, father figures, and step parents. Without mother figures, she claims, other characters have to step in to teach the lessons mothers often provide for their children, and audiences are left with questionable role models.

Issue: Have Media Representations of Minorities Improved?
Yes: Drew Chappell, from "'Better Multiculturalism' through Technology: *Dora the Explorer* and the Training of the Preschool Viewer(s)," Lexington Books (2013)
No: Elizabeth Monk-Turner, et al., from "The Portrayal of Racial Minorities on Prime Time Television: A Replication of the Mastro and Greenberg Study a Decade Later," *Studies in Popular Culture* (2010)

Professor Drew Chappell, in "Better Multiculturalism through Technology: *Dora the Explorer* and the Training of the Preschool Viewer(s)," juxtaposes facts about recent actions attempting to ban ethnic studies and restrict immigration in parts of the United States with the television show, *Dora the Explorer's* portrayal of a bilingual (English/Spanish) speaking girl, and discusses how the show introduces children to bilingualism, border identities, and multicultural discourse. Chappell discusses how the performance of identity in Dora's world can teach children about what brings all humans together. Elizabeth Monk-Turner, Mary Heiserman, Crystle Johnson, Vanity Cotton, and Manny Jackson, in "The Portrayal of Racial Minorities on Prime Time Television: A Replication of the Mastro and Greenberg Study a Decade Later," revisit what has become a classic study in the portrayal of minorities in media and finds that even though how minorities are represented have changed within context, no serious changes to stereotypes have really occurred. In this study of prime-time television programming, little has changed within the 10-year time span between the classic Mastro and Greenberg study, and the analysis provided by the authors.

Issue: Have More Women Become Involved as Decision Makers in Media Industries?
Yes: Hannah McIlveen, from "Web Warriors: The Women of Web Series," *Lydia Magazine* (2014)
No: Martha M. Lauzen, from "Boxed In: Portrayals of Female Characters and Employment of Behind-the-Scenes Women in 2014-15 Prime-time Television," Center for the Study of Woman in Television & Film (2015)

Hannah McIlveen challenges the dominant male culture of decision makers in television to discuss how women have been making inroads in nontraditional programming on the Web. Working in low-budget situations does not stop their creativity, and even television network executives are paying attention to new content from women creators on the Web. Every year, Professor Martha M. Lauzen, Ph.D., conducts a survey of the roles of women in prime-time television at the Center for the Study of Women in Television and Film at San Diego State University. In this report, she provides data for the 2014-2015 television season, and women are still underrepresented in prime-time television.

Issue: Do Media Distort Representations of Islam and Arab Cultures?
Yes: Wajahat Ali, et al., from "Fear, Inc.: The Roots of the Islamophobia Network in America," Center for American Progress (2011)
No: Gal Beckerman, from "The New Arab Conversation," *Columbia Journalism Review* (2007)

Wajahat Ali, Eli Clifton, Matthew Duss, Lee Fang, Scott Keyes, and Faiz Shakir discuss in Fear, Inc., a special report from the Center for American Progress, how the Muslim religion is among the most maligned stereotypes in popular culture, and how these images have fueled misperceptions about the Arab world. It explores how media have been an echo chamber for misinformation created by well-funded groups dedicated to spreading fear and misinformation. These images influence politicians and citizens and contribute to public opinion. Journalist Gal Beckerman discusses how Arab bloggers from the Middle

East are challenging popular stereotypes of Arab and Middle Eastern cultures. Because these bloggers are writing about their lives, the global public can read about their situations and understand them as individuals, rather than racial or ethnic group members.

Unit: A Question of Content

Issue: Do Media Cause Individuals to Develop Negative Body Images?
Yes: June Deery, from "The Body Shop," Palgrave Macmillan (2012)
No: Michael P. Levine and Sarah K. Murnen, from "'Everybody Knows That Mass Media Are/Are Not [*pick one*] a Cause of Eating Disorders': A Critical Review of Evidence for a Causal Link Between Media, Negative Body Image, and Disordered Eating in Females," *Journal of Social and Clinical Psychology* (2009)

June Deery examines the role of reality television and body makeover programs and concludes that these types of programs normalize the idea that bodies can and should be improved by plastic surgery, weight loss, and control programs, and that women in particular should subject themselves to all measures to find "success" and "happiness." She theorizes that these programs assume that women in particular do have negative body images, and that the real messages of these programs is that surgical steps can and should be taken to improve one's poor body image. Michael Levine and Sarah Murnen also investigate magazine ads, but find the assumption that media cause eating disorders to be too limited. Instead, they cite a wide range of social, behavioral, and cultural issues over time to understand the complex conditions under which girls begin to adopt negative body issues that result in eating disorders.

Issue: Do Video Games Encourage Sexist Behavior?
Yes: Anita Sarkeesian, from "Ms. Male Character—Tropes vs Women," *Feminist Frequency* (2013)
No: Kaitlin Tremblay, from "Intro to Gender Criticism for Gamers: From Princess Peach, to Claire Redfield, to FemSheps," *Gamasutra* (2012)

Anita Sarkeesian is a video game critic who also started a website called *Feminist Frequency*. In 2010, *Feminist Frequency* and *Bitch Media* put out a six-part series called "Tropes vs Women" in which Sarkeesian analyzes different tropes found in pop culture and the negative female stereotypes they perpetuate. This selection focuses on one of the tropes, the "Damsel in Distress," which Sarkeesian says is a theme that can be traced back to Greek mythology. Kaitlin Tremblay is an editor, a writer, and a video game maker who focuses primarily on topics that deal with horror, feminism, and mental illness. She says games are always a target for the best and the worst of gender criticism, and claims that when we play videogames you immerse yourself in the character, and therefore, you can overcome any negative victim-association that is so prevalent in many childhood games.

Issue: Is Product Placement an Effective Form of Advertising?
Yes: Kaylene Williams, et al., from "Product Placement Effectiveness: Revisited and Renewed," *Journal of Management and Marketing Research* (2011)
No: Ekaterina V. Karniouchina, Can Uslay, and Grigori Erenburg, from "Do Marketing Media Have Life Cycles? The Case of Product Placement in Movies," *Journal of Marketing* (2011)

Professors Kaylene Williams, Alfred Petrosky, Edward Hernandez, and Robert Page chronicle the evolution of product placement and define the term as incorporating "commercial content into noncommercial settings." They discuss the subtle differences between brand placement and product placement and raise the topic of how product placement is becoming more common in many media forms, including music and games. Professors Karniouchina, Uslay, and Erenburg analyzed 40 years of movies (1968–2007) to uncover the idea that product placement has become a tactic that no longer interests viewers of major motion pictures. As a result, they suggest that marketers should investigate other ways of trying to connect ideas and brand identities.

Issue: Is There Any Harm in Taking Selfies?
Yes: Elizabeth Day, from "How Selfies Became a Global Phenomenon," *The Guardian* (2013)
No: Jenna Wortham, from "My Selfie, Myself," *The New York Times Sunday Review* (2013)

British journalist Elizabeth Day thinks of selfies as modern-day self-portraits. Despite their popularity, she sides with critics who consider selfies to be narcissistic and expressions of our self-absorbed lifestyles. *New York Times* reporter Jenna Wortham claims that our predilection for responding to faces is just a part of a more technologized world, and that while we shouldn't discount the selfie phenomenon, we should also keep in mind that selfies are a type of visual diary.

Unit: News and Politics

Coronel, Coll and Kravitz of the Columbia School of Journalism conduct a painstakingly in-depth investigation of the process and decisions that led to the discredited story about rape and the University of Virginia. They re-create the reporter and editorial actions from first contact through retraction. Joe Strupp argues that the investigation encompassed failures in reporting, editing, editorial supervision and fact-checking. He suggests that it is time for journalists to begin to define best practices when reporting about rape cases.

Conservative author Thomas R. Eddlem makes the case that corporate media institutions influence the messages that the public sees and hears. As a result, the Supreme Court's 2010 *Citizens United* decision, which gives corporations the right to make political contributions and creates the possibility of the establishment of SuperPACs, also results in the exercise of freedom of speech. David Earley and Ian Vandewalker, two counsels at the Brennan Center for Justice at the New York University School of Law, argue that the rise of political spending that resulted from the Supreme Court's *Citizens United* decision has created a situation in which political elections can be "bought" by corporate donors. Because of the new law, they argue that the only way to ensure transparency is to create a situation in which all political donations are disclosed to the public.

In these sections of their longer study on the role of Twitter and politics, Professors Parmelee and Bichard examine how political leaders use Twitter to influence the public. While politicians establish personal relationships with followers, some tweets are intended to influence policy. They examine the potential for the one-way form of communication provided by Twitter to engage with the public. Shirky turns this issue around by asking about the use of social media to effect change within authoritarian regimes. He describes situations in which protests have been arranged by text. It is in the use of social media to coordinate actions and develop shared awareness that their power resides. But, he warns that these tools can be ineffective and cause as much harm as good.

Sheldon R. Gawiser and G. Evans Witt have a vast experience in developing polls and analyzing the results of polls. Their belief in the accuracy of polls to reflect public opinion is grounded in decades of experience, and in the scientific accuracy of the poll. They provide advice to journalists on how to measure the worth of a poll in terms of its scientific rigor as opposed to its casual approach toward accuracy. Herbert J. Gans discusses how news media personnel often portray public opinion through polls inaccurately. He makes an important distinction between the way people answer polls and the definition of public opinion.

Unit: Law and Policy

Issue: Does Technology Invade Our Privacy?
Yes: Daniel J. Solove, from "The All-or-Nothing Fallacy," Yale University Press (2011)
No: Stewart Baker, from "The Privacy Problem: What's Wrong with Privacy," *Tech Freedom* (2010)

Daniel J. Solove, Professor of Law at George Washington University and authority on privacy issues, argues that privacy is too often sacrificed for security concerns. He argues that there are often solutions that do not involve such sacrifices, but that they are dismissed by an all-or-nothing attitude. Stewart Baker, former Assistant Secretary for Policy at Homeland Security, argues vigorously for better collection and use of technological information. Its importance in preventing acts of terrorism, in tracking potential criminals, and in protecting the interests of the country far outweighs privacy concerns of individuals.

Issue: Does the Internet Change the Way We Think of Copyright and Plagiarism?
Yes: Marc Fisher, from "Steal This Idea," *Columbia Journalism Review* (2015)
No: Louis Menand, from "Crooner in Rights Spat," *The New Yorker* (2014)

Marc Fisher is a senior editor at *The Washington Post*, and recently held the position of Enterprise Editor for local news at the *Post*, where he led a team of writers who were experimenting with new forms of storytelling and journalism for both the print and online versions of the newspaper. Louis Menand is a Professor of History at Harvard University. He also is a past editor of *The New Yorker*, a contributing editor to *The New York Review of Books*, and a former associate editor at *The New Republic*. He was awarded the 2002 Pulitzer Prize for history for his book, *The Metaphysical Club* for which he also won the Francis Parkman Prize from the Society of American Historians.

Issue: Are Copyright Laws Effective in Curbing Piracy?
Yes: Brian R. Day, from "In Defense of Copyright: Creativity, Record Labels, and the Future of Music," *Seton Hall Journal of Sports and Entertainment Law* (2011)
No: Alex Sayf Cummings, from *Democracy of Sound: Music Piracy and the Remaking of American Copyright in the Twentieth Century*, Oxford University Press (2013)

Attorney Brian R. Day addresses the size of the recorded music industry which manufactures and distributes 85 percent of the recorded music in the United States today, and discusses the need for copyright protection and the different business models used by the music industry today. He argues that copyright is essential to the music industry and other media industries because it constitutionally protects the work of artists and their ability to profit from their talents. Alex Sayf Cummings writes from the perspective of the impact of piracy, bootlegging, and counterfeiting on the music industry and concludes that contemporary copyright legislation is just not adequate to circumvent the ease with which people can download unauthorized copies of musical performances. He warns that copyright is no longer adequate to meet the challenge of digital music today, and warns that the recorded music industry is in danger of becoming obsolete.

Unit: Media Business

Issue: Is Streaming the Future of the Music Industry?
Yes: Joan E. Solsman, from "Attention, Artists: Streaming Music Is the Inescapable Future. Embrace It." CNET News (2014)
No: Charles Arthur, from "Streaming: The Future of the Music Industry, Or It's Nightmare?" *The Guardian* (2015)

Journalist Joan E. Solsman discusses the rise of streaming services like Pandora and Spotify, and identifies three business models that are emerging for the number of streaming services. Her article shows how divergent the forms of distribution for music have become, and the impact on artist revenue for some of those new services. Journalist Charles Arthur discusses some of the same streaming services, but identifies how little profit many of them are making because consumer tendency to download free music cuts into the revenue of many of the emerging services.

Issue: Should We Oppose Media Consolidation?
Yes: Mark Cooper, from "Testimony before the U.S. Senate Judiciary Committee, Subcommittee on Antitrust, Competition Policy, and Consumer Rights," U.S. Senate (2010)
No: Brian L. Roberts and Jeff Zucker, from "Testimony before the U.S. Senate Judiciary Committee, Subcommittee on Antitrust, Competition Policy, and Consumer Rights," U.S. Senate (2010)

Mark Cooper, Director of the Consumer Federation of American Research, argues that allowing the merger of the largest cable network and the nation's premier video content producers and distribution outlets will alter the structure of the video marketplace, resulting in higher prices and fewer choices for the consumer. Such consolidation of the marketplace is not in the best interests of the American public. Brian L. Roberts and Jeff Zucker, then Presidents of Comcast and NBC, respectively, argue that the merged firms will benefit through the investment in innovation of both content and delivery mechanisms. Such a merger will allow this merged unit to compete more effectively in the increasingly global video market.

Unit: Life in the Digital Age

Issue: Do Social Media Enhance Real Relationships?

Yes: Zeynep Tufekci, from "Social Media's Small, Positive Role in Human Relationships," *The Atlantic* (2012)
No: Sherry Turkle, from "The Flight from Conversation," *New York Times Sunday Review* (2012)

Tufecki argues that social media is a counterweight to the many factors that separate people and a testament to peoples' ongoing desire to connect with each other. Rather than displacing connections, social media is enhancing it in more ways than were ever possible. With social media some become even more social; some have felt awkward, but more free online; others find communities of interest that go far beyond the limitations of their current environment. Social media adds, rather than subtracts, from connections. Turkle argues that social media provide the illusion of connection. Her perspective comes from hundreds of interviews that often describe a lonely environment in which technology trumps authentic communication. People can become confused about whether technology brings them closer together or moves them further apart. Her question can be paraphrased in the following manner: Is technology offering us the lives we want to lead?

Issue: Can Digital Libraries Replace Traditional Libraries?

Yes: Robert Darnton, from "A World Digital Library Is Coming True!" *The New York Review of Books* (2014)
No: Jill Lepore, from "The Cobweb: Can the Internet Be Archived?" *The New Yorker* (2015)

Harvard University Library Director Robert Darnton suggests that a new model of publishing scholarly work may need to be created to preserve ideas in electronic form. The traditional library, he says, relies on a financial model that is no longer sustainable. The result, he suggests, is to continue to convert scholarly research to digital data and for libraries to specialize, and cooperate in their lending processes. Historian and Harvard University Professor Jill Lepore examines the efforts to collect digital information—particularly Websites—through the Internet Archive, but provides frightening data on how incomplete the archive of digital data is, why that happens, and what consequences occur because of incomplete records of digital data.

Issue: Will the Benefit Be Worth the Cost for the Internet of Things?

Yes: Shawn Dubravac, from *Digital Destiny: How the New Age of Data Will Transform the Way We Work, Live, and Communicate*, Regnery Publishing (2015)
No: Federal Trade Commission, from "Internet of Things: Privacy and Security in a Connected World," FTC Staff Report (2015)

Dubravac sees a new era in which digital devices and services transform our lives. They will transform our individual lives, solve some major problems for humankinds, and improve our access to products and services. "The Internet of Things: Privacy and Security in a Connected World" contains reports of staff members who participated in an FTC workshop that discussed the potential security risks to personal safety inherent in the Internet of Things.

Preface

Communication is one of the most popular college majors in the country, suggesting that students are interested in the way in which messages are created and exchanged. We are surrounded by media and media technology today that continually mediate our experiences with ourselves, with others, and with the broader group we identify as "society." We've moved from traditional "mass" media that operated with large institutions sending messages to a large, heterogeneous audience to using media forms to interact in real-time with others, or just to amuse, entertain, or inform ourselves. Large-scale media producers have had to change business models to also cater to niche audiences, as well as to maintain their former practices and battle for the attention of audiences.

Today, people have the capacity to become producers of mediated content that can be shared online, through blogs, websites, social networking sites, and podcasts. Never before have we had the capacity to consume mass media, as well as produce our own forms of media and have a platform for low-cost or free distribution over the Internet.

This book addresses a number of controversial issues in media and society. The purpose of these readings and indeed of any course that deals with the social impact of media is to create a literate consumer of media—someone who can walk the fine line between a naive acceptance of all media and a cynical disregard for any positive benefits that media and media technologies may offer.

The study of media and society is very much a part of the way in which we live our lives by blending technologies and services, public and private media uses, and public and private behaviors. In the near future, many of the technologies we use today may be subsumed by yet newer technologies, or greater use of those that we already use. Film, television, music, radio, and print all come to us today over the Internet (through wired or wireless means), and smart phones are well on their way to replacing laptop computers as the "all-in-one" portable technology.

Since many of the topics for these readings are often in the news (or even constitute the news), you may already have opinions about them. We encourage you to read the selections and discuss the issues with an open mind. Even if you do not initially agree with a position or do not even understand how it is possible to make an opposing argument, give it a try. Remember, these problems often are not restricted to only two views; there may be many. We encourage you to discuss these topics as broadly as possible, and we believe that thinking seriously about media is an important goal.

These readings have been chosen to be used for students in introductory courses in media and society. We know that some instructors have found these selections useful for courses in writing about communication topics, ethics, and public speaking. The topics are such that they can be easily incorporated into any media course regardless of how it is organized—thematically, chronologically, or by media form.

Each issue includes an introduction to set the stage for debates argued in the YES and NO selections. We also pose a number of Learning Outcomes to help guide reading. We offer a starting point for discussion in the section titled, "Is There Common Ground?" We also offer suggestions for further reading on the issue and suggested Internet References to expand upon the material in each section. The introductions and the suggestions for additional resources and Internet sites do not preempt the reader's task: to achieve a critical and informed view of the issues at stake.

In reading an issue and forming your own opinion, you should not feel confined to adopt one or the other of the positions presented. Some readers may see important points on both sides of an issue and may construct for themselves a new and creative approach. Such an approach might incorporate the best of both sides, or it might provide an entirely new vantage point for understanding.

Acknowledgments

We wish to acknowledge the encouragement, support, and detail given to this project. We are particularly grateful to Debra Henricks, who has carefully and painstakingly worked with us to produce the best edition possible and who has guided us through a substantial revision of this book.

We would also like to extend our appreciation to the many professors who reviewed our previous edition, and we are grateful for the advice they have provided in the preparation of this edition. Alison would like to thank Anne Hurne at the University of Georgia for her continued support.

We would also like to thank our families and friends for their patience and understanding during the period in which we prepared this book.

Editors of This Volume

ALISON ALEXANDER is a Professor of Telecommunications and Senior Associate Dean at the Grady College of Journalism and Mass Communication at the University of Georgia. She is the past Editor of the *Journal of Broadcasting & Electronic Media,* and past President of the Association for Communication Administration and the Eastern Communication Association. She received her PhD in communication from Ohio State University. She is widely published in the area of media and family, audience research, and media economics.

JARICE HANSON is a Professor in the Department of Communication at the University of Massachusetts at Amherst. Her research focuses on the impact of new technology. She formerly held the Verizon Chair in Telecommunications at Temple University, and was the founding Dean of the School of Communications at Quinnipiac University. She received her MA and PhD at Northwestern University's Department of Radio-TV-Film. She is the author or editor of numerous books and articles, including *24/7: How Cell Phones and the Internet Change the Way We Live, Work and Play* (Praeger, 2007), *Constructing America's War Culture: Iraq, Media, and Images at Home* (coedited with Thomas Conroy) (Lexington Books, 2007), and *The Unconnected: Participation, Engagement, and Social Justice in the Information Society* (coedited with Paul M. A. Baker and Jeremy Hunsinger) (Peter Lang, 2013).

Academic Advisory Board Members

Members of the Academic Advisory Board are instrumental in the final selection of articles for the Taking Sides series. Their review of the articles for content, level, and appropriateness provides critical direction to the editor(s) and staff. We think that you will find their careful consideration reflected in this book.

Introduction

Ways of Thinking about Media and Society

Media are everywhere in the industrialized world today. It is likely that anyone reading this book has access to more forms of media than their grandparents could ever dream of. Many readers are probably adept at multitasking—a term unheard of when this book series began in 1987. Many readers are probably adept at using so many technologies that deliver content over tablets or smart phones that it almost seems strange to think that broadcast TV, cable TV, film, radio, newspapers, books and magazines, and the recording industry all once were thought of as different forms of media, all delivered in different ways, and all with different economic structures. The digital revolution has a price as many traditional or legacy media face this disruptive technology that has upended traditional business models. The convergence of these media over wired and wireless distribution forms now presents us with words, sounds, and images that often blur former distinctions among media forms and industries.

Media are also often scapegoats for the problems of society. Sometimes the relationship of social issues and media seems too obvious *not* to have some connection. For example, violence in the media may be a reflection of society, or, as some critics claim, violence in the media makes it seem that violence in society is the norm. But in reality, one important reason that the media are so often blamed for social problems is that media are so pervasive. Their very ubiquity gives them the status that makes them seem more influential than they actually are. If one were to look at the statistics on violence in the United States, it would be possible to see that there are fewer violent acts today than in recent history—but the presence of this violence in the media, through reportage or fictional representation, makes it appear more prevalent.

There are many approaches to investigating the relationships that are suggested by media and society. From an organizational perspective, the producers of media must find content and distribution forms that will be profitable, and therefore, they have a unique outlook on the audience as consumers. From the perspective of the creative artist, the profit motive may be important, but the exploration of the unique communicative power of the media may be paramount. The audience, too, has different use patterns and varying desires for information or entertainment, and

demonstrates a variety of choices in content offered to them, as well as what they take from the media. Whether the media reflect society or shape society has a lot to do with the dynamic interaction of many of these different components.

To complicate matters, the "mass" media have changed in recent years. Not long ago, "mass" media referred to messages that were created by large organizations for broad, heterogeneous audiences. This concept no longer suffices for the contemporary media environments. While the "mass" media still exist in the forms of radio, television, film, and general interest newspapers and magazines, many media forms today are hybrids of "mass" and "personal" media technologies that open a new realm of understanding about how audiences process the meaning of the messages. Audiences may be smaller and more diverse, but the phenomenon of using media to form a picture of the world and our place in it is still the fundamental reason for studying the relationship of media and society.

As we look at U.S. history, we can see that almost every form of media was first subject to some type of regulation by the government or by the media industry itself. This has changed over the years so that we now have a media environment in which the responsibility for the content of media no longer rests entirely in the hands of the FCC or the major corporations. We, as consumers, are asked to be critical of the media we consume. This requires that we become educated consumers, rather than relying on standards and practices of industry or government intervention into questionable content. While this may not seem like a big problem for adult consumers, the questions and answers become more difficult when we consider how children use the media to form judgments, form opinions, or seek information.

Our habits are changing as the media landscape grows. The average American still spends over three hours a day viewing television, which is in the average home over seven hours a day, but recent statistics indicate that the "average" American actually spends about 10 hours a day facing a screen of some sort—whether that is a TV screen, computer screen, tablet, or cell phone screen. That interaction with media clearly warrants some understanding of what happens in the process of the person/media interaction and relationship.

Politics and political processes have changed, in part, due to the way politicians use the media to reach voters. A proliferation of television channels has resulted from the popularity of cable, but does cable offer anything different from broadcast television? DVDs, Blu-Ray, and streaming services like Netflix deliver feature-length films to the home, changing the traditional practice of viewing film in a public place, and video distribution via cable or the Internet is now a practical option for anyone with transmission lines large enough and wireless broadband fast enough to download large files. The recording industry has been transformed by technology that allows consumers to sample, buy, or steal music online. The communications industry is a multibillion-dollar industry and the third fastest-growing industry in America. From these and other simple examples, it is clear that the media have changed American society, but our understanding of how and why remains incomplete.

Dynamics of Interaction

In recent years, the proliferation and availability of new media forms have changed on a global scale. In the United States, 98 percent of homes have at least one telephone, but by 2008 the number of cell phones outnumbered land phones. On a global scale, the number of cell phones nearly exceeds the world's population. In the United States, over 98 percent of the population has access to at least one television set, but in some parts of the world, televisions are still viewed communally or viewed only at certain hours of the day. The use of broadband and wireless connections continues to grow in the United States, while some other countries (usually smaller countries, with high GDP) are reaching saturation with broadband technologies, and other countries still have limited dial-up services for the Internet.

But apart from questions of access and available content, many fundamental questions about the power of media in any given society remain the same. How do audiences use the media available to them? How do message senders produce meaning? How much of the meaning of any message is produced by the audience? And increasingly important for discussion is, How do additional uses of media change our interpersonal environments and human interactions?

Progress in Media Research

Much of media research has been in search of theory. Theory is an organized refinement of everyday thinking; it is an attempt to establish a systematic view of a phenomenon

in order to better understand that phenomenon. Theory is tested against reality to establish whether or not it is a good explanation; so, for example, a researcher might notice that what is covered by news outlets is very similar to what citizens say are the important issues of the day. From such observations came agenda setting (the notion that the media confer importance on the topics they cover, directing public attention to what is considered important).

Much of the early media research was produced to answer questions of print media because print has long been regarded as a permanent record of history and events. The ability of newspapers and books to shape and influence public opinion was regarded as a necessity to the founding of new forms of governments—including the U.S. government—and a good number of our laws and regulations were originally written to favor print (like copyright and freedom of the press). But the bias of the medium carried certain restrictions. Print media necessarily were limited to those individuals who could read. The principles that emerged from this relationship were addressed in an often-quoted statement attributed to Thomas Jefferson, who wrote, "Were it left to me to decide whether we should have a government without newspapers, or newspapers without a government, I should not hesitate a moment to prefer the latter." But the next sentence in Jefferson's statement is equally important and often omitted from quotations: "But I should mean that every man should receive those papers and be capable of reading them." Today, however, the newspaper is no longer the primary distribution form for information that is critical to living in a democracy.

Today, media research on the relationships among media senders, the channels of communication, and the receivers of messages is not enough. Consumers must realize that "media literacy" and maybe even "technological literacy" are important concepts too. People can no longer take for granted that the media exist primarily to provide news, information, and entertainment. They must be more attuned to what media content says about them as individuals and as members of a society, and they need to be aware of how the ability for almost everyone to create media (like blogging or social networking) challenges traditional ownership and privacy laws and regulations. By integrating these various cultural components, the public can better criticize the regulation or lack of regulation that permits media industries to function the way they do.

The use of social science data to explore the effects of media on audiences strongly emphasized psychological and sociological schools of thought. It did not take long to move from the "magic bullet theory"—which proposed that media had a direct and immediate effect on the receivers of the message, and that the same message intended by the senders was the same when it was "shot" into the receiver—to other ideas of limited, or even indirect, means of influencing the audience.

Media research has shifted from addressing specifically effects-oriented paradigms to exploring the nature of the institutions of media production themselves, as well as examining the unique characteristics of each form of media and the ability of the media user to also produce media products. What most researchers agree upon today is that the best way to understand the power and impact of media is to look at context-specific situations to better understand the dynamics involved in the use of media and the importance of the content. Still, there are many approaches to media research from a variety of interdisciplinary fields: psychology, sociology, linguistics, art, comparative literature, economics, political science, and more. What these avenues of inquiry have in common is that they all tend to focus attention on individuals, families or other social groups, society in general, and culture in the broad sense. All of the interpretations frame meaning and investigate their subjects within institutional frameworks that are specific to any nation and/or culture.

Many of the questions for media researchers in the twenty-first century deal with the continued fragmentation of the audience, caused by greater choice of channels and technologies for traditional and new communication purposes. The power of some of these technologies to reach virtually any place on the globe within fractions of a second will continue to pose questions of access to media and the meaning of the messages transmitted. As individuals become more dependent upon the Internet for communication purposes, the sense of audience will further be changed as individual users choose what they want to receive, pay for, and keep. For all of these reasons, the field of media research is rich, growing, and challenging.

Questions for Consideration

In addressing the issues in this book, it is important to consider some recurring questions:

1. Are the media unifying or fragmenting? Does media content help the socialization process, or does it create anxiety or inaccurate portrayals of the world? Do people understand what they are doing when they post personal information online or open themselves to immediate criticism and feedback?

2. How are our basic institutions changing as we use media in new and different ways? Do media support or undermine our political processes? Do they change what we think of when we claim to live in a "democracy"? Do media operate in the public interest, or do media serve the rich and powerful corporations' quest for profit? Can media find a successful business model in the digital age? Can the media do both simultaneously?

3. Whose interests do the media represent? Do audiences actively work toward integrating media messages with their own experiences? How do new media technologies change our traditional ways of communicating? Are they leading us to a world in which interpersonal communication is radically altered because we rely on information systems to replace many traditional behaviors?

Summary

We live in a media-rich environment where almost everybody has access to some forms of media and some choices in content. As new technologies and services are developed, are they responding to the problems that previous media researchers and the public have detected? Over time, individuals have improved their ability to unravel the complex set of interactions that tie the media and society together, but they need to continue to question past results, new practices and technologies, and their own evaluative measures. When people critically examine the world around them—a world often presented by the media—they can more fully understand and enjoy the way they relate as individuals, as members of groups, and as members of a society.

Alison Alexander
University of Georgia

Jarice Hanson
University of Massachusetts—Amherst

Unit 1

UNIT

Media and Social Issues

Do media reflect the social attitudes and concerns of our times, or are they also able to construct, legitimize, and reinforce the social realities, behaviors, attitudes, and images of others? Do they operate to maintain existing power structures, or are they symbolic communication central to our culture? Do we use stereotypes to form ideas of appropriate ways of behaving, or to give us a sense of what we can do in the world? The ways media help us to shape a sense of reality are complex. How much do media influence us, versus how we use media to fit our already preconceived ideas? Should concern be directed toward vulnerable populations like children? If we truly have a variety of information sources and content to choose from, perhaps we can assume that distorted images are balanced with realistic ones—but is this a likely scenario in our society? Questions about the place of media within society, and within what many people call the "information age," are important for us to understand, whether we use media, or whether media use us.

Selected, Edited, and with Issue Framing Material by:
Alison Alexander, *University of Georgia*
and
Jarice Hanson, *University of Massachusetts—Amherst*

ISSUE

Do Media Reflect Contemporary Family Relationships?

YES: Leigh H. Edwards, from "Reality TV and the American Family," University Press of Kentucky (2010)

NO: Sarah Boxer, from "Why Are All the Cartoon Mothers Dead?" *The Atlantic* (2014)

Learning Outcomes

After reading this issue, you will be able to:

- Consider how children learn from media content.
- Understand the role different genres play in constructing a "mediated" world for audiences.
- Reflect on how often media distort images of real-world relationships.
- Think broadly about whether media reflect or distort sociological facts.
- Think about the images you see when you watch television or film, and consider whether these images have shaped your expectations.

ISSUE SUMMARY

YES: Associate Professor Leigh H. Edwards examines how families are portrayed in television and discusses how certain narrative tropes, trends, and genres present us with real family relationships representative of American society and culture. She raises the important point that reality television in particular presents viewers with real conflicts to which many families can relate, because the programs portray real cultural problems that have no easy answers. She concludes her argument with an assessment that public debates about family and marriage often frame the content of the families we see on television.

NO: Sarah Boxer examines the content of animated movies and questions why so many mothers in fairy tales and children's films represent the absent mother. Since more American households are headed by married couples or single mothers, she questions the portrayals of mother figures, father figures, and step parents. Without mother figures, she claims, other characters have to step in to teach the lessons mothers often provide for their children, and audiences are left with questionable role models.

Do media reflect social reality as though we were looking into a mirror, or do they frame the issues within social life so that we see them in a different way? Do we learn from the images we see in the media? Do we favor certain types of representations because they resonate with our own values? These basic questions support all studies that focus on the relationship of media and society. From early studies that suggested that the values portrayed in media would be immediately seized by the public, to models of limited and indirect effects, scholars, citizens, and students have grappled with the way media and society inform and relate to each other. Today we no longer question whether the media do affect our values—the question is now, *how* media affect our values.

Since television's early days, families have been represented as the focus of many genres and formats. The assumption that "everyone" can relate to domestic conflict and the roles family members play in their social lives seems to be a basic construct for drama as well as for comedy. Some theories support the idea that a "family structure" is such a basic social group with such universal understanding and appeal that every cast member in a show—whether representing members of a family or not—actually reflects an archetype of some member of a family unit. Some theorists even claim that we learn about the different roles each family member plays in a family unit, and we exhibit behaviors to fit those roles.

In these two selections, different genres are examined, but representation of real family members and situations families may encounter are the contexts for the authors' analyses of the impact media content has on the intended audience. The authors of these selections approach the topic of family representations in media with particular viewpoints. Professor Leigh H. Edwards's selection gives some history of the representations of the American family in television over the years, but she examines the genre of reality programming to suggest that four narrative structures have evolved: a nostalgia for the traditional nuclear family; representations of a new, modified nuclear family norm in which the husband and wife both work outside the home; an ideal of family pluralism; and a questioning of norms that give us a different sense of family diversity. She cites many contemporary reality television shows in which some semblance of "family" is represented, but claims that what unites all of these diverse family structures is the sense that people have to deal with cultural conflicts.

Sarah Boxer raises the question of why so many fairy tales and animated children's films seem to situate the mother outside of the picture. In most cases, she claims, the mother is dead, so who helps the children (or innocent characters of any species) learn about motherly love and guidance? When you consider the primary audience for this type of content—children—her observation of the dead mother becomes a more important factor to consider when we focus on how children learn from media, and what they learn from media.

Furthermore, Boxer examines the family relationships in animated films and finds that the father-figures sometimes take on mythic proportions. Is this presentation of gender roles (or lack of them) harmful to the development and socialization of some children? Are fathers in children's media content made to be superheroes? These are only some of the types of questions she raises.

In addition to examining representations of families (and changing families) in America, these selections remind us that media can often be an important form of entertainment that conditions audiences to have certain expectations, or teaches them about gender roles and social responsibilities. We know media are powerful, but their power is not always easy to understand, and we know that some of the early media content children see stays with them throughout their life. From ideas such as the "agenda setting theory" of communication, which posits that media do not tell us what to think, but rather, tell us what to think about, to studies of para-social interactions (the relationship we form with people whom we see in media), and ideas of *resonance*, which describes how we relate to the images we see in media, there are several assumptions and theories to guide an inquiry into the relationship of media content and its presentation of social values.

Some of the earliest television programs in the 1950s featured fathers who played the role of the "all knowing," eternally "understanding" parent. *Father Knows Best* was perhaps the quintessential glorification of fatherhood and the father as the "rock" of the family. Over the years, however, the "hapless" dad became more common in television. Homer Simpson is one such example, but even in the popular comedy *Modern Family*, all of the fathers are loving, and good providers, but occasionally helpless. Television mothers, though, have often played the roles of the "behind-the-scenes" fixer of problems, homemakers, and moral centers of the family.

For this reason, Sarah Boxer's observations of missing mother figures in children's animated features is a particularly interesting shift in media content. The overwhelming number of stories in which the mother is replaced by a strong father figure or even a helpful animal (!) suggests that mothers are expendable in these stories.

In general, however, the many representations of family roles and family relationships as portrayed in media suggest one of the most fundamental themes in all of media studies today. From fictionalized portrayals to shows that emulate "reality," we interpret media content according to our own experiences, beliefs, assumptions, and values. At the same time, we think of media portrayals as either "believable" or "unbelievable." Animation is a special category that presents viewers with a world that might or might not be true. The tension suggested by images that create assumptions about "reality" and representation gives us an "in between" place where we see how our favorite stories or portrayals of families provide a yardstick by which we gauge our own sense of what is "normal" or "abnormal." All in all, these media representations of families and family relationships provide a context by which we measure our own lives and experiences.

YES

Leigh H. Edwards

Reality TV and the American Family

Reality television shows are reframing ideas of the family in U.S. culture. The genre titillates by putting cultural anxieties about the family on display, hawking images of wife swapping, spouse shopping, and date hopping. Its TV landscape is dotted with programs about mating rituals, onscreen weddings, unions arranged by audiences, partners testing their bonds on fantasy dates with others, family switching, home and family improvement, peeks into celebrity households, parents and children marrying each other off on national television, and families pitching their lives as sitcom pilots. Though obviously not the only recurring theme pictured, family is one of the genre's obsessions. Scholars have begun to draw attention to certain questions surrounding family, gender, and sexuality, but we have yet to address fully how the genre debates . . . reshapes the family or to account for the centrality of that theme in reality programming. This discussion of the family is important, since TV has always played such a vital role in both shaping and reflecting fantasies of the American family.

Using historicized textual analysis, this essay demonstrates how the reality TV genre both reflects and helps shape changing "American family" ideals. A significant number of reality shows picture a seemingly newfound family diversity. For every traditional "modern nuclear family," with its wage-earning father, stay-at-home mother, and dependent children, we see a panoply of newer arrangements, such as post-divorce, single-parent, blended, and gay and lesbian families. What is the significance of this family diversity as a recurring theme in factual programming? Concurrent with images of demographic change, we also see a familiar rhetoric of the "family in crisis." Witness the emergency framework of *Nanny 911* (a British nanny must save inept American parents who are at their breaking point) or *Extreme Makeover: Home Edition* (a design team must renovate the home of a family otherwise facing disaster). Their premise is that the American family is in trouble. Many scholars have noted how the family has

constantly been described as being in crisis throughout its historical development—with the calamity of the moment always reflecting contemporaneous sociopolitical tensions. The idea of crisis has been used to justify "family values" debates, which usually involve public policy and political rhetoric that uses moral discourses to define what counts as a healthy family.

I would argue that reality programs focused on the familial settings and themes implicitly make their own arguments about the state of the American family, entering long-running family values debates. In their representation of family diversity (which different series laud or decry) and in their use of family crisis motifs, reality narratives capture a sense of anxiety and ambivalence about evolving family life in the United States. Reality TV market[s] themes about our current period of momentous social change: the shift from what sociologists term the "modern family," the nuclear model that reached its full expression in the context of Victorianera industrialization and peaked in the postwar 1950s, to the "postmodern family," a diversity of forms that have emerged since then. Indeed, a key theme in reality TV depictions is that family is now perpetually in process or in flux, open to debate. Social historians define the modern family as a nuclear unit with a male breadwinner, female homemaker, and dependent children; its gendered division of labor was largely only an option historically for the white middle class whose male heads of household had access to the "family wage." This form was naturalized as universal but was never the reality for a majority of people, even though it was upheld as a dominant cultural ideal. Diverse arrangements have appeared since the 1960s and 1970s, constituting what the historian Edward Shorter termed "the postmodern family." New familial forms have emerged, spurred by increases in divorce rates and single-parent households, women's entrance into the labor force in large numbers after 1960, the decline of the "family wage," and the pressures on labor caused by postindustrialism and by globalization.

Taken as a whole, reality series about the family alter some conventional familial norms while reinforcing others. I would agree with critics such as Tania Modleski and Sherrie A. Inness, who argue that popular culture texts that address issues such as gendered roles and the real contradictions in women's lives often both challenge and reaffirm traditional values. These reality programs picture some updated norms (frequently, the edited narratives validate wider definitions of familial relations or urge men to do more domestic labor). The genre's meditation on the shift in norms is not radical, however, because it occurs within TV's liberal pluralism framework. Various programs construct their own sense of the contradictions of family life, such as tensions involving women juggling work and child care, gender role renegotiations, further blurring of public and the private "separate sphere" ideologies, racialized family ideals, and fights about gay marriage. Such shows celebrate conflict, spectacularizing fraught kinship issues as a family circus in order to draw more viewers and advertising, but they most often resolve the strife into a liberal pluralist message by episode's end (for example, using the liberal discourse of individualism to represent racism as an interpersonal conflict that can be resolved between individuals through commonsense appeals rather than as a structural social issue).

I would contextualize these themes both in terms of television's long history as a domestic medium and in reference to ongoing family values battles. The new household models and demographic changes, such as increased divorce rates, sparked a political backlash beginning in the 1970s: the family values media debates that have intensified since the 1990s. These skirmishes, such as Dan Quayle's attack on the sitcom character Murphy Brown as a symbol of unwed motherhood in the 1992 presidential debates, are an important sociohistorical context for the current reality programming trend. For my purposes here, I date the full advent of the current genre to the premiere of MTV's *The Real World* in 1992, although related forerunners like police and emergency nonfiction series emerged in the late 1980s, and factual programming has, of course, been around since the medium's origins. Though critics debate the looseness of the term *reality TV* as a genre, I use it to refer to factual programming with key recurring generic and marketing characteristics (such as unscripted, low-cost, edited formats featuring a mix of documentary and fiction genres, often to great ratings success).

The links between TV and the family are foundational, as long-running research on television and the family has established. The television historian Lynn Spigel has shown how early TV developed coextensively with the postwar suburban middle-class families that the medium made into its favored topic and target audience. The historian Stephanie Coontz has noted how current nostalgia for the nuclear family ideal is filtered through 1950s domestic sitcoms like *Leave It to Beaver*. As critics have illustrated, family shows comment not only on society's basic organizing unit but also on demographic transformations by tracing their influence on the family. Ella Taylor traces a family crisis motif in 1970s series such as *All in the Family*, *The Jeffersons*, and *One Day at a Time*, noting network efforts to generate socially "relevant" programming to grab a targeted middle-class demographic as well as to respond to social changes prompted by the women's and civil rights movements. Herman Gray, likewise, in *Watching Race*, has detailed assimilationist messages, reflecting prevailing social discourses, in portraits of black families in the 1980s, like *The Cosby Show*. I demonstrate how reality TV opens a fresh chapter in TV's long-running love affair with the family—the medium has birthed a new genre that grapples with the postmodern family condition.

Reality TV mines quarrels about family life, producing, for example, gay dating shows (such as *Boy Meets Boy*, 2003) at the precise moment of national deliberations over gay marriage. The genre sinks its formidable teeth into these controversies. Much as domestic sitcoms did in the 1950s, it gives us new ways of thinking about familial forms in relationship to identity categories like gender and sexuality or to larger concepts like citizenship and national identity. It does so in part by illuminating the cultural tensions underlying family values debates, such as the family's contested nature as a U.S. institution that legitimates social identities, confers legal and property rights, and models the nation imagined as a family, whether a "house united" or a "house divided."

Tracing recurring tropes in reality programs about the family, I would argue for four key narrative stances toward social change: nostalgia for the traditional modern nuclear family; promotion of a new, modified nuclear family norm in which husband and wife both work outside the home; a tentative, superficial embrace of family pluralism in the context of liberal pluralism; and an open-ended questioning of norms that might include a more extensive sense of family diversity. These narrative trends are particularly evident in some specific reality subgenres: family-switching shows (*Trading Spouses, Wife Swap, Black. White, Meet Mister Mom*); observations of family life (*The Real Housewives of Orange County; Little People, Big World*); celebrity family series (*The Osbournes, Run's House, Meet the Barkers, Being Bobby Brown, Breaking Bonaduce, Hogan Knows Best*); home and family makeover programs (*Extreme Makeover: Home Edition, Renovate My Family*); family workplace series (*Dog the Bounty Hunter, Family Plots, Family*

Business); family gamedocs (*Things I Hate about You, Race to the Altar, Married by America, The Will, The Family*); parenting series (*Nanny 911, Supernanny, Showbiz Moms and Dads*); and historical reenactment programs with family settings (*Colonial House, Frontier House*).

These programs watch middle-class "average joes," perhaps the viewer's friends and neighbors, navigate the shoals of domesticity, grappling with cultural problems such as the tension between kinship and chosen bonds, the effect of the media on the family, and the state's efforts to define "family" as a matter of national concern and to legislate access to marriage rights. Ultimately, these shows convey a kind of emotional engagement, what Ien Ang would term "emotional realism," regarding changes in family structures in the United States, capturing a recent shift in middle-class attitudes toward the American family, a change in what Raymond Williams would call that group's "structure of feeling."

Narrative Tropes

Reality TV spectacularizes such issues as a family circus in order to draw viewers and sell advertising. Part of its vast ratings appeal stems from the fact that it portrays real people struggling with long-running cultural problems that have no easy answers: tensions in the ties that bind, between kinship and chosen bonds, between tradition and change; personal versus social identity; and competing moralities. The genre explores angst about what "the American family" is in the first place. Such widespread worries are not surprising, given that this unit is a social construction that is notoriously difficult to define, particularly since it has historically encoded gendered roles and hierarchies of class, race, and sexuality that define ideas of social acceptance, a crucible for selfhood and nationhood. Critics have noted the regulatory nature of the modern nuclear family model, and official discourse has traditionally framed that unit as a white, middle-class heterosexual norm to which citizens should aspire.

Reality TV does not explicitly solve those family values disputes. Instead, it concentrates on mining the conflict between the two familial forms, one residual and one emergent. Rather than answering questions about what the postmodern family will become, it rehearses sundry arguments about how the familial unit is getting exposed, built up, torn down, and redefined. Some programs offer wish-fulfillment fantasies, smoothing over rancorous public squabbles and social changes but not resolving those tensions.

For example, Bravo's *Things I Hate about You* (2004), reflecting this panoply, turns domesticity into a sport in which snarky judges determine which member of a couple is more annoying to live with and partners happily air their dirty laundry on TV (sometimes literally). One week we see an unmarried heterosexual couple with no children, the next a gay domestic partnership. No one model dominates. The series fits all these groupings into the same narrative framework: a story about family and the daily irritations of domesticity. . . .

Trends in Reality TV's Textual Representations of the Family

Drawing on the sociopolitical and media history of the family values debates, reality TV offers viewers the voyeuristic chance to peer into other people's households to see how all this cultural ruckus is affecting actual families. As the genre takes up the modern and postmodern family in various ways, it often explicitly engages with public policy and media discussions. The way reality serials address familial life illuminates an uneasy shift from modern nuclear family ideals to the postmodern reality of diverse practices.

One main trend in reality programming is for series to look backward with a nostalgia for the modern nuclear family that reveals the instability of that model. Some series revert to older concepts, such as the sociologist Talcott Parsons's mid-twentieth-century theories of functional and dysfunctional family forms. He argued that the modern nuclear family's function under industrialized capitalism was to reproduce and socialize children into dominant moral codes, as well as to define and promote norms of sexual behavior and ideas of affective bonds associated with companionate marriage. Dysfunctional families that deviated from norms were functionalism's defining "Other," and some critics argue that this paradigm still influences sociological research on family life (Stacey, *In the Name of the Family*). Pop psychology concepts of functionalism and dysfunctionalism certainly circulate widely in today's mass media, and we see their influence in reality shows.

A particularly apt example is the spouse-swapping subgenre, which includes shows like ABC's *Wife Swap*. The titillating title implies it will follow the wild exploits of swingers, but the show instead documents strangers who switch households and parenting duties for a short period. Similarly, on Fox's *Trading Spouses: Meet Your New Mommy* (the copycat show that beat ABC's to the air), two parents each occupy the other's home for several days. Both series focus on the conflict between households, revealing a fierce debate among participants as to whose family is healthier, more "normal," or more "functional."

On *Trading Spouses*, one two-part episode swaps mothers from white suburban nuclear families, each comprising a husband, a wife, two kids, and a dog ("Bowers/Pilek"). Both clans want to claim modern nuclear family functionality for themselves, but economic tensions ensue, even though each woman describes her family as middle class. A California mom with an opulent beach house judges her Massachusetts hosts, with their modest home and verbal fisticuffs, as unkempt, whereas her outspoken counterpart deems the beach household materialistic and emotionally disconnected. Each woman characterizes the other family as dysfunctional. Their conflict reveals not only the degree to which many people still use these older ideals as their own measuring sticks, here staged as issues such as tidiness or appropriate levels of emotional closeness, but also the tenuousness of those ideals, given the intense contradictions between two supposedly functional families.

Through the premise of swapping households or roles for several days, these programs explore Otherness by having participants step into someone else's performance of kinship behaviors. In so doing, they illuminate identity categories that are performed through the family. This dynamic was perhaps most notably executed on the series *Black. White,* which used makeup to switch a white and black family for several weeks and staged racial tensions between them. In this subgenre more generally, participants reproduce a version of their counterparts' social identity. Thus, the switch highlights the arbitrariness of such identity performances. Since the shows allow the participants to judge each other, family appears as a topic of open-ended debate.

These programs depend on conflict generated by social hierarchies of race, class, gender, and sexuality, and they privilege white male heteronormativity. Their narratives often focus on gender, encouraging men to take on more child care and domestic chores. Yet they still rely on ideologies of gender difference to explain household units and to reaffirm the mother's role as nurturer-caregiver. By absenting the mother, the wife-swap series imply that husbands and kids will learn to appreciate the woman of the house more.

These series encourage a liberal pluralist resolution to conflicts, one that upholds an easy humanist consensus, or what critics term "corporate multiculturalism," which markets diversity as another product rather than picturing and validating substantive cultural differences. The framing narratives resolve competing ideas, most often by defining as normal a modified modern nuclear family (two working parents). In shows about alternative households, for example, the narratives sympathize with the single mom or the lesbian couple but uphold the intact nuclear family as more rational and functional. Yet the narratives also often critique participants' overly intense nostalgia for the bygone modern nuclear ideal, and they sometimes allow for some validation of alternative models, such as an African American extended family. They depend on sensationalism and conflict over values to spark ratings.

This open warfare over functional and dysfunctional families includes a huge helping of nostalgia, as epitomized by a series like MTV's *The Osbournes*. This hit show supports the sense that if the modern nuclear ideal has been replaced by a diversity of family forms, U.S. culture still has an intense nostalgia for the older norm. Is nostalgia for the fantasy nuclear unit actually a defining characteristic of the postmodern family? It is for *The Osbournes*. Viewers flocked to the show because it juxtaposes a famously hard-living, heavy-metal family with classic sitcom family plotlines, edited to emphasize the irony of seeing the cursing, drug-abusing rock star Ozzy and his brood hilariously butchering *Ozzie and Harriet*–style narratives.

The entertainment press dubbed them "America's favorite family," and a series of high-profile magazine cover stories tried to explain the show's wild popularity by pointing to how the Osbournes "put the fun in dysfunctional." The show garnered MTV's highest-rated debut at that time and enjoyed some of the strongest ratings in the channel's history during its run from 2002 until 2005. Part of the appeal lies in how the Osbournes seem to capture on videotape a more accurate sense of the pressures of family life, ranging from sibling rivalry to teen sex and drug use to a serious illness (such as Sharon's cancer diagnosis and treatment). Even though their fame and fortune make them unlike home viewers, the family can be related to because of the struggles they confront openly. Likewise, they reflect current family diversity because they are a blended family; their brood includes their son and two daughters (one of whom declined to appear on the series), Ozzy's son from his first marriage, and their children's teen friend whom they adopted during the show after his mother died of cancer. Ozzy himself suggested that he did the series in order to expand understandings of the family: "What is a functional family? I know I'm dysfunctional by a long shot, but what guidelines do we all have to go by? *The Waltons*?" Ozzy here is both arbiter and agent; he notes TV's power to define a range of meanings for the family, whether through the Waltons or the Osbournes.

Yet even while the program's narrative meditates on entertaining dysfunctionality and new family realities, it also continuously tries to recuperate the Osbournes as a functional nuclear family. Story arcs are edited to frame them as dysfunctional (cursing parents, wild fights, teenage drug use), but also to rescue them as functional; there are sentimental shots of the family gathered together in their kitchen or clips of them expressing their love and loyalty despite the titillating fights. Even though Ozzy tells his family they are "all f—ing mad," in the same breath he says he "loves them more than life itself" ("A House Divided"). The edited narrative purposefully emphasizes the bonds of hearth and home, sometimes trying to establish functionality by cutting out serious family events that would have made Parsons blanch: Ozzy's drug relapse, severe mental illness, and nervous breakdown during taping; trips to rehab by Jack and Kelly, the son and daughter; and Sharon's temporary separation from Ozzy over these issues. Press coverage of the show and fan response likewise emphasized a recuperative dynamic, both looking for the loveable, reassuring nuclear family beneath the rough exterior. As an *Entertainment Weekly* cover story noted, Ozzy Osbourne went from being boycotted by parents' groups in the 1980s for bat biting and supposedly Satanic lyrics to being asked for parenting advice from men's magazines. Thus, even while registering the limitations of Parsons's model, the series still tries to rehabilitate this celebrity family as functional. As a result, this program and others like it explore the postmodern family, but at the same time they look back wistfully on the old modern nuclear paradigm.

The Osbournes is also a prime example of a program that explicitly comments on the influence of television on family ideals. Part of the show's insight comes from registering how much the media, whether the popular music industry or television, have shaped this family unit. Brian Graden, then president of MTV Entertainment, described the program's draw as "the juxtaposition of the fantastical rock-star life with the ordinary and the everyday"; summarizing one episode, he laughed, "Am I really seeing Ozzy Osbourne trying to turn on the vacuum cleaner?" Graden noted that after they collected footage on the Osbournes, producers realized that "a lot of these story lines mirrored classic domestic sitcom story lines, yet with a twist of outrageousness that you wouldn't believe." Watching footage of their daily experiences, Graden immediately views them through the lens of earlier TV sitcoms; everywhere he looks, he sees the Cleavers on speed. And the show Graden's company makes of this family's life might one day comprise the plotlines other viewers use to interpret their own experiences in some way. After their smash first season, the Osbournes were feted at the White House Correspondents' dinner and managed to parlay such national attention into more entertainment career opportunities, with a new MTV show, *Battle for Ozzfest* (2004–), hosted by Sharon and Ozzy and featuring bands competing to join their summer tour; Sharon's syndicated talk show that ran for one season (2003–2004); and their children's slew of TV, movie, and music ventures growing out of their exposure from the reality program.

Though most families could not follow the Osbournes into celebrity, what many do share with the rockers is the knowledge that TV significantly shapes familial ideals. This media awareness marks a parenting trend. In their recent audience study of family television-viewing practices, Stewart M. Hoover, Lynn Schofield Clark, and Diane F. Alters found that parents had a highly self-reflexive attitude toward the media. They were well conscious of how the mass media both reflect and shape social beliefs, and they worried about the daily influence of television in their children's lives. Hoover et al. identified this media anxiety as part of what they term "self-reflexive parenting" behaviors stemming from increased concerns about child rearing since the 1960s. They see this model of parenting as part of what Anthony Giddens calls the project of self-reflexivity in modernity, in which people are reflective about their interaction with the social world as they continually incorporate mediated experiences into their sense of self. . . .

Cultural Histories and Family Values Media Debates

I would argue that reality TV is the popular media form with the most to say about the current status of the American family. The television historian Lynn Spigel has shown that early TV developed coextensively with the post–World War II suburban middle-class family—a specific kind of modern nuclear family model the medium made into its favored subject and audience. As Spigel notes, while sociologists like Talcott Parsons were arguing in the 1940s and 1950s that the modern nuclear family is the social form best suited to capitalist progress, the new electronic TV medium targeted the postwar white, middle-class families flocking to the suburbs, encouraging the development of the modern family as a consumer unit.

As a new genre now exploring the self-conscious imbrication of family and the media as one of its main themes, reality TV raises vital issues of marketing and consumerism. If television enters the home to become, as Cecelia Tichi has shown, "the electronic hearth" around which the family gathers, so too does the family envision itself through the tube. TV addresses the family as ideal viewer, imagined community, and the basis for democracy mediated through mass communication; the nation is figured as a collective of families all watching their television sets (a collective that can now exercise its democratic rights by calling in to vote for a favorite singer on *American Idol*). If the domestic sitcom was like an electronic media version of a station wagon trundling the modern family along in the 1950s, reality TV is the hybrid gas-electric car of the postmodern family today. . . .

Not surprisingly, recent public arguments about family and marriage often turn reality TV into prime fodder. Conservative groups frequently protest reality fare. Most spectacularly, complaints made by conservative activists from the Parents Television Council prompted the Federal Communications Commission (FCC) to threaten Fox with a fine of $1.2 million, the largest to date, for *Married by America* when it was on the air. The show had audiences pick mates for couples who could have gotten married on air (though none did and all the arranged couples stopped dating after the show). The protestors found it a vulgar trivialization of the institution of marriage.

On the flip side of the coin, progressive thinkers have used reality TV to make public arguments advocating a greater diversity of marriage and household arrangements. The cultural theorist Lisa Duggan, in a 2004 *Nation* article, explores public policy about state-sanctioned marriage in the context of the debates over gay marriage, critiquing, for example, "marriage promotion" by both the Clinton and the Bush administrations as a way to privatize social welfare. Duggan calls for a diversification of democratically accessible forms of state recognition for households and partnerships, a "flexible menu of choices" that would dethrone the privileged civic status of sanctified marriage and "threaten the normative status of the nuclear family, undermining state endorsement of heterosexual privilege, the male 'headed' household and 'family values' moralism as social welfare policy." She uses reality TV as an example of current dissatisfaction with gendered, "traditional" marriage and a marker of its decline, describing "the competitive gold-digging sucker punch on TV's *Joe Millionaire*" (which tricked eager women into believing they were competing to marry a millionaire) as an entertainment culture indicator of the statistical flux in marriage and kinship arrangements. She argues that the franchise confirms social anxiety that "marriage is less stable and central to the organization of American life than ever." Notably, Duggan pairs her *Joe Millionaire* example with the pop singer Britney Spears's rapidly annulled 2004 Las Vegas wedding (to a high school friend, Jason Alexander) as similar social indexes; the celebrity life and the reality show plot

represent similar kinds of evidence, both equally real (or equally fake) in current entertainment media culture.

Regardless of the different ways the genre enters into existing political discussions, what is striking is that it continually becomes a site for family values debates. A case in point is how a couple competing on the sixth season of CBS's *The Amazing Race* (2005) made headlines because critics accused the husband of exhibiting abusive behavior toward his wife in the series footage. The couple, Jonathan Baker and Victoria Fuller, made the rounds of talk shows to protest that characterization, but the main dynamic of press coverage has been to turn them into a teaching moment. Both went on the entertainment TV newsmagazine *The Insider* and were asked to watch footage of themselves fighting and answer the charge that it looked abusive; Baker responded: "I'm a better person than that. I have to say I had a temper tantrum, you know, I pushed her, I never should have, and you know, I regret every moment of it and you know what, hopefully that experience will make me a better person. That's our story line, you know, that's who we were on television. That's not who we are in real life."

Such a framing of that reality TV footage is emblematic: the show is perceived as somewhat mediated and constructed but still real enough to warrant a press debate. Through a bit of internal network marketing, Dr. Phil actually made them the topic of one of his CBS prime-time specials on relationships. Noting that the show sparked reams of hate mail and even death threats toward the couple, Dr. Phil explicitly argues that America was watching the couple and wants to debate them in TV's public sphere. At the outset of the interview, he invokes and calls into being an imagined national public, saying, "America was outraged and appalled by what they've seen." After he exhorts the husband to correct his behavior, he concludes, "So America doesn't need to worry about you?" (*Dr. Phil Primetime Special*). Dr. Phil does not completely buy Baker's argument that he was only acting aggressively for the camera or that the editing heightened his behavior, and he admonishes the man for exhibiting bad behavior in any context, mediated or not. Dr. Phil is well aware of the construction of images that he himself perpetuates, and he even draws attention to how Baker tries to manipulate this on-camera interview by coaching his wife, yet he insists on a substantial component of actuality in all these depictions. In the press and popular response, the gamedoc show couple becomes a paradigmatic reality TV family example that can be used to analyze the state of the American family more generally.

Ultimately, reality programs add a new wrinkle to television's family ideas. The genre illuminates how the current definition of the family is up for grabs, and reality TV enters the debate arena in force. Instead of having nostalgia for the Cleavers as a model of the modern American family, viewers might one day have nostalgia for the Osbournes as a model of the postmodern American family. The amplified truth claims of reality TV comment on the social role of television itself as an electronic medium offering "public scripts" that, as the medium evolves, viewers increasingly want to interact with on the screen and participate in themselves.

LEIGH H. EDWARDS is an Associate Professor of English at Florida State University, where she specializes in nineteenth- and twentieth-century literature and popular culture.

Sarah Boxer

Why Are All the Cartoon Mothers Dead?

Bambi's mother, shot. Nemo's mother, eaten by a barracuda. Lilo's mother, killed in a car crash. Koda's mother in *Brother Bear*, speared. Po's mother in *Kung Fu Panda 2*, done in by a power-crazed peacock. Ariel's mother in the third *Little Mermaid*, crushed by a pirate ship. Human baby's mother in *Ice Age*, chased by a saber-toothed tiger over a waterfall.

I used to take the Peter Pan bus between Washington, D.C., and New York City. The ride was terrifying but the price was right, and you could count on watching a movie on the screen mounted behind the driver's seat. *Mrs. Doubtfire, The Man Without a Face*, that kind of thing. After a few trips, I noticed a curious pattern. All the movies on board seemed somehow to feature children lost or adrift, kids who had metaphorically fallen out of their prams. Gee, I thought, Peter Pan Bus Lines sure is keen to reinforce its brand identity. The mothers in the movies were either gone or useless. And the father figures? To die for!

A decade after my Peter Pan years, I began watching a lot of animated children's movies, both new and old, with my son. The same pattern held, but with a deadly twist. Either the mothers died onscreen, or they were mysteriously disposed of before the movie began: *Chicken Little, Aladdin, The Fox and the Hound, Pocahontas, Beauty and the Beast, The Emperor's New Groove, The Great Mouse Detective, Ratatouille, Barnyard, Despicable Me, Cloudy With a Chance of Meatballs*, and, this year, *Mr. Peabody and Sherman*. So many animated movies. Not a mother in sight.

The cartoonist Alison Bechdel once issued a challenge to the film industry with her now-famous test: show me a movie with at least two women in it who talk to each other about something besides a man. Here's another challenge: show me an animated kids' movie that has a named mother in it who lives until the credits roll. Guess what? Not many pass the test. And when I see a movie that does (*Brave, Coraline, A Bug's Life, Antz, The Incredibles, The Lion King, Fantastic Mr. Fox*), I have to admit that I am shocked . . . and, well, just a tad wary.

But I'm getting ahead of myself. The dead-mother plot has a long and storied history, going back past *Bambi* and *Snow White*, past the mystical motherless world of Luke Skywalker and Princess Leia, past Dickens's orphans, past Hans Christian Andersen's Little Mermaid, past the Brothers Grimm's stepmothers, and past Charles Perrault's Sleeping Beauty and Cinderella. As Marina Warner notes in her book *From the Beast to the Blonde*, one of the first Cinderella stories, that of Yeh-hsien, comes from ninth-century China. The dead-mother plot is a fixture of fiction, so deeply woven into our storytelling fabric that it seems impossible to unravel or explain.

But some have tried. In *Death and the Mother From Dickens to Freud: Victorian Fiction and the Anxiety of Origins* (1998), Carolyn Dever, a professor of English, noted that character development begins "in the space of the missing mother." The unfolding of plot and personality, she suggests, depends on the dead mother. In *The Uses of Enchantment* (1976), Bruno Bettelheim, the child psychologist, saw the dead mother as a psychological boon for kids:

> The typical fairy-tale splitting of the mother into a good (usually dead) mother and an evil stepmother . . . is not only a means of preserving an internal all-good mother when the real mother is not all-good, but it also permits anger at this bad "stepmother" without endangering the goodwill of the true mother.

You may notice that these thoughts about dead mothers share a notable feature: they don't bother at all with the dead mother herself, only with the person, force, or thing that sweeps in and benefits from her death. Bettelheim focuses on the child's internal sense of himself, Dever on subjectivity itself. Have we missed something here? Indeed. I present door No. 3, the newest beneficiary of the dead mother: the good father.

Take *Finding Nemo* (Disney/Pixar, 2003), the mother of all modern motherless movies. Before the title sequence, Nemo's mother, Coral, is eaten by a barracuda, so Nemo's father, Marlin, has to raise their kid alone. He starts out as an overprotective, humorless wreck, but in the course of the movie he faces down everything—whales, sharks, currents, surfer turtles, an amnesiac lady-fish, hungry seagulls—to save Nemo from the clutches of the evil stepmother-in-waiting Darla, a human monster-girl with hideous braces (vagina dentata, anyone?). Thus Marlin not only replaces the dead mother but becomes the dependable yet adventurous parent Nemo always wanted, one who can both hold him close and let him go. He is protector and playmate, comforter and buddy, mother and father.

In the parlance of Helen Gurley Brown, he has it all! He's not only the perfect parent but a lovely catch, too. (Usually when a widowed father is shown onscreen mooning over his dead wife's portrait or some other relic, it's to establish not how wonderful she was but rather how wonderful he is.) To quote Emily Yoffe in *The New York Times*, writing about the perfection of the widowed father in *Sleepless in Seattle*, "He is charming, wry, sensitive, successful, handsome, a great father, and, most of all, he absolutely adores his wife. Oh, the perfect part? She's dead." Dad's magic depends on Mom's death. Boohoo, and then yay!

In a striking number of animated kids' movies of the past couple of decades (coincidental with the resurgence of Disney and the rise of Pixar and DreamWorks), the dead mother is replaced not by an evil stepmother but by a good father. He may start out hypercritical (*Chicken Little*) or reluctant (*Ice Age*). He may be a tyrant (*The Little Mermaid*) or a ne'er-do-well (*Despicable Me*). He may be of the wrong species (*Kung Fu Panda*). He may even be the killer of the child's mother (*Brother Bear*). No matter how bad he starts out, though, he always ends up good.

He doesn't just do the job, he's fabulous at it. In *Brother Bear* (Disney, 2003) when the orphaned Koda tries to engage the older Kenai as a father figure (not knowing Kenai killed his mom), Kenai (who also doesn't know) refuses: "There is no 'we,' okay? I'm not taking you to any salmon run . . . Keep all that cuddly-bear stuff to a minimum." In the end, though, Kenai turns out to be quite the father figure. And they both live happily ever after in a world without mothers.

So desperate are these kids' movies to get rid of the mother that occasionally they wind up in some pretty weird waters. Near the beginning of *Ice Age*, (Blue Sky/20th Century Fox, 2002), the human mother jumps into a waterfall to save herself and her infant, drags herself to shore, and holds on long enough to hand her child to a woolly mammoth. To quote an online review by C. L. Hanson, "She has the strength to push her baby up onto a rock and look sadly into the eyes of the mammoth,

imploring him to steady her baby with his trunk," but—hold on—she doesn't have the strength to save herself? And by the way, if Manny the woolly mammoth is such a stand-up guy, why doesn't he "put his trunk around *both of them* and *save them both*" rather than watching her float downriver with a weary sigh? Because, as the reviewer noted, "the only purpose of her life was to set up their buddy adventure." Her work is done. Time to dispose of the body.

Many movies don't even bother with the mother; her death is simply assumed from the outset. In *Despicable Me* (Universal/Illumination, 2010), three orphaned girls, Margo, Edith, and Agnes, are adopted from an orphanage by Gru, a supervillain. Gru adopts them not because he wants children but because he plans to use them in his evil plot. He wants to shrink the moon and steal it. (Hey, wait, isn't the moon a symbol of female fertility?) But by the end of the movie, Gru discovers that his girls are more dear to him than the moon itself. And, as if this delicious father-cake needed some sticky icing, Gru gets to hear his own hypercritical mother—remember, it was *her* negativity that turned him evil in the first place!—admit that Gru's a better parent than she ever was. The supervillain becomes a superfather, redeemer of all bad mothers.

Quite simply, mothers are killed in today's kids' movies so the fathers can take over. (Of course, there are exceptions; in *Lilo and Stitch*, for instance, both of Lilo's parents die and it's her big sister who becomes the surrogate parent.) The old fairy-tale, family-romance movies that pitted poor motherless children against horrible vengeful stepmothers are a thing of the past. Now plucky children and their plucky fathers join forces to make their way in a motherless world. The orphan plot of yore seems to have morphed, over the past decade, into the buddy plot of today. Roll over, Freud: in a neat reversal of the Oedipus complex, the *mother* is killed so that the children can have the *father* to themselves. Sure, women and girls may come and go, even participate in the adventure, but mothers? Not allowed. And you know what? It looks like fun!

Dear reader, I hear your objection: So what? Hollywood has always been a fantasyland. Or, to quote the cat in *Bolt* (Disney, 2008), a kids' movie about a dog who thinks he's actually a superhero because he plays one on TV: "Look, genius . . . It's entertainment for people. It's fake! Nothing you think is real is real!" Get over it. It's just a movie. Or, to quote the empowerment anthem from *Frozen* (in which both parents die), "Let it go."

Okay, I will. But first, a brief dip into reality. Did you know that 67 percent of U.S. households with kids are headed by married couples, 25 percent by single mothers, and only 8 percent by single fathers (almost half of whom live with their partners)? In other words, the fantasy of the fabulous single father that's being served up in a theater near you isn't just any fantasy; it's close to the opposite of reality. And so I wonder: Why, when so many real families have mothers and no fathers, do so many children's movies present fathers as the only parents?

Is the unconscious goal of these motherless movies to paper over reality? Is it to encourage more men to be maternal? To suggest that fathers would be better than mothers if only they had the chance? To hint that the world would be better without mothers? Or perhaps we're just seeing a bad case of what the psychoanalyst Karen Horney called "womb envy." Or maybe an expression of the primal rage that the psychoanalyst Melanie Klein described as the infant's "uncontrollable greedy and destructive phantasies and impulses against his mother's breasts."

Consider *Barnyard* (Paramount/Nickelodeon, 2006), a deeply lame reworking of the *Lion King* plot, in which the father bull, Ben, teaches his reckless, motherless, goof-off son, Otis, how to be a man. ("A strong man stands up for himself; a stronger man stands up for others.") As pathetic as *Barnyard* is, there's something truly staggering in it. Whenever the bulls stand up on two hooves, they reveal pink udders right where their male equipment should be—rubbery teats that resemble, as Manohla Dargis described them in *The New York Times*, "chubby little fingers waving toodle-oo."

In the whacked-out, reality-denying world of animated movies, these chubby, wiggly four-fingered udders, which appear on both females and males, are my favorite counterfactuals, bar none. I love, love, love them. The first time I laid eyes on those honkers, my jaw dropped. Even Walt Disney himself, who cooked up pink elephants on parade, never tried *this*. It was as if the comical leather phalluses of ancient Greek theater had come back to life. As if the directors' very ids were plastered on the screen. Not only do *Barnyard*'s bulls have bizarre phallic teats, but Otis rudely swings his out the window of a speeding stolen car while drinking a six-pack of milk—yes, *milk*—and, as the police chase him, shouts, "Milk me!" Is he saying what I think he's saying? In a kids' movie? Could udder envy be any more naked?

When I finally shut my jaw, I realized that *Barnyard* isn't the only kids' movie with a case of udder confusion. (In the third *Ice Age*, Sid the Sloth, while trying to feed the three baby dinosaurs he's adopted, starts to milk a musk ox before discovering that it's a guy—ack!) But as far as I know, the *Barnyard* scene is the most violent instance; when the teated bull yells "Milk me!" it's like he's shouting

at women everywhere: "You think you're so hot with your tits and your babies. Well, suck on this! (And then die.)"

That's how I see it, anyway, and I don't think I'm alone.

In *How to Read Donald Duck* (1975), Ariel Dorfman, the Chilean American activist and writer, and Armand Mattelart, a Belgian sociologist, discuss the insidiousness of "the absence of woman as *mother* in Disney." Rather than presenting any really maternal figure, they say, Disney offers up only "the captive and ultimately frivolous woman," who lacks any tie to "the natural cycle of life itself"—Cinderella, Sleeping Beauty, Snow White. And in the natural mother's place, they note, Disney erects a "false mother Mickey," a creature of "chivalrous generosity" and "fair play" whose authority looks benign and cheery. The absence of a real mother thus makes way for a new authority, a new "natural" order. The road to social repression, in other words, is paved with Mickey Mouse.

In today's movie fathers, there's plenty of Mickey Mouse. They're magnanimous, caring, and fun. And I imagine these animated fathers look great to most kids. But let's call a spade a spade. The ineluctable regularity of the dead-mother, fun-father pattern is not just womb envy at work, and not just aggression against the breast; it's Mickey's glove displacing the maternal teat. It's misogyny made cute.

Dear reader, I hear you objecting again. Perhaps you're getting irritated. Perhaps you like Pixar. Perhaps you'd like to remind me of some living mothers in a few animated movies: Isn't that a single mother raising two kids in *Toy Story*? (Yes, she's the one who keeps trying to give away the toys.) And isn't that a mother at the end of *The Lego Movie*? (Yes, she's the one who cuts short the nascent father-son bonding moment in the basement by announcing that supper is ready.)

What about Fiona, the ogre-princess in *Shrek* (DreamWorks, 2001)? She certainly seems to be someone's caricature of a feminist—tough, competent, belching earthily with the boys. By *Shrek the Third* (2007), she's pregnant. At her baby shower, she makes all her beautiful, single friends—Snow White, Sleeping Beauty, Cinderella, and Rapunzel—seem like spoiled, materialistic wimps. But when it comes time for Fiona's own father, a frog king, to pass down the crown, he offers it not to *her* but to her ogre-husband, Shrek—who eventually turns it down because he has "something much more important in mind." (He's going to be a father!) That's right: the male gallantly refuses all that power (sweet old Mickey) while the female, who should have been next in line for the throne, isn't asked, and doesn't complain.

Patriarchy is slyly served. We've been slipped a Mickey!

A similar thing happens in *Ice Age: Dawn of the Dinosaurs* (2009). When Ellie, a sassy woolly mammoth, goes into labor, she's stuck on a cliff and her man, Manny, is off fighting predators. This leaves Diego, the saber-toothed tiger, to play birth coach. At one puzzling point, Ellie, the very picture of strength, yells to Diego, "You can do it! Push, push!" as if he were the one giving birth. He snaps back: "You have no idea what I'm going through!" (He's fending off vicious blue dinosaurs—more work than childbirth, from the looks of it.)

It's funny! The filmmakers, after all, don't *really* think Diego is working harder than Ellie. (Sexism always slides down better with a self-ironizing wink and giggle.) But once the baby pops out, we get patriarchy in earnest: the father, Manny, fresh from his own heroics, reenters the scene. Ellie hands him the baby, which he secures with his trunk and declares "perfect."

This cozy family scene reprises the original *Ice Age*, when Manny the woolly mammoth saved the human baby—and not the mother—with his trunk. This time, though, the mother is allowed to live. Why? Because she never upstaged the buddy plot. Her death would have been, well, overkill.

Have we moved beyond killing mothers, to a place where it no longer matters whether they live or die? From the newest crop of kids' animated movies, which are mostly buddy movies—*Planes, Turbo, Cloudy With a Chance of Meatballs 2, Monsters University, Free Birds, The Lego Movie*—it sure looks that way. It seems as if we have entered, at least in movie theaters, a post-mother world.

In March, when I took my son to see *Mr. Peabody and Sherman* (DreamWorks, 2014), I suspected that we'd be watching a buddy movie, pure and simple, in which the presence or absence of mothers was immaterial. I was wrong.

Apparently, it was finally time to blast mothers out of history. At the start of the movie, Mr. Peabody—a dog, a Harvard graduate, a Nobel laureate, and the inventor of Zumba, the fist bump, and the WABAC (pronounced "wayback") machine—says his dearest dream is to be a father. He adopts a human boy, Sherman; vows "to be the best father"; and is wildly successful at it. (He uses the WABAC to teach his son history by introducing him to figures like Benjamin Franklin, Vincent van Gogh, and William Shakespeare.)

The movie thus begins where other kids' movies end, with the perfect father-son relationship. Nothing can threaten them—except, alas, two gals, Ms. Grunion, an ugly social worker (the evil-stepmother figure), who wants to tear dog and boy apart, and Penny, a bratty girl who is jealous of Sherman's knowledge and gets him to take her on a trip in the WABAC. And there the adventure begins.

They go to Leonardo's Italy. (Why won't the Mona Lisa smile?) They go to ancient Troy. ("Don't even get me started about Oedipus. Let's just say that you do *not* want to be at his house over the holidays! It's awkward.") And they go to ancient Egypt, where Penny herself is inserted into history. Tellingly, she's not given the obvious, powerful role—Cleopatra—but instead becomes the bride of King Tut, who's destined to die early. (Her reaction to learning this bit of history? Vintage Valley Girl with a hint of gold digger: "Oh, trust me, I've thought it through. I'm getting everything!")

But the key moment comes at the end of the movie, when we get to see George Washington muttering about changing the Declaration of Independence. I held my breath. Would the Founding Father (yes, Father) correct one of the most famous, glaring faults of the document? I listened for the magic words, and this is what I heard: "We hold these truths to be self-evident, that all men—and *some dogs*—are created equal." What?!?! (Insert spit take.) Given the chance to rewrite history, the filmmakers give rights to *some dogs*? But not to the bitches (I mean to the women)? Sure, it's funny. Funny like udders on male cows. Funny sad. Funny infuriating. Funny painful.

The power of the WABAC to rewrite history, if only in fantasy, made me remember why I like animation so much. Just as time travel imagines the way things might have been, so does animation give the creator total omnipotence. With animation you can suspend the laws of physics and the laws of society and the laws of reason and the laws of biology and the laws of family. You can have a dog adopt a boy. You can turn a rat into a French chef. You can make male cows with big pink udders. You can change the Declaration of Independence. You can have a family in which every member is a doggone superhero.

As the Soviet film director and theorist Sergei Eisenstein wrote of Disney's early work, you can have "a family of octopuses on four legs, with a fifth serving as a tail, and a sixth—a trunk." You can do anything. Eisenstein marveled, "How much (imaginary!) divine omnipotence there is in this! What magic of reconstructing the world according to one's fantasy and will!"

And yet, in this medium where the creators have total control, we keep getting the same damned world—a world without mothers. Is this really the dearest wish of animation? Can mothers really be so threatening?

I'd like to end on a hopeful note, with a movie that passes my test with flying colors—*The Incredibles* (Disney/Pixar, 2004), which happens to feature not only three major female characters, including a great mother figure, Elastigirl (aka Helen Parr), who lives for the whole movie, but also a pretty credible father figure, Mr. Incredible (aka Bob Parr). Unlike just about every other movie dad, Mr. Incredible is far from perfect. He daydreams during dinner. He is more interested in getting back to hero-work (he has been forcibly retired, along with all the other heroes) than in how his kids are doing at school. He even lies to his wife about where he's going and what he's doing. He is super-angry. When his car door won't shut, he slams it so hard that the window shatters.

The hero of the movie isn't Mr. Incredible, but the mother, who turns back into Elastigirl, a really flexible, sexy, and strong superhero, in order to save her husband. ("Either he's in trouble or he's going to be!") At one point during the rescue mission, the plane that the mother is flying is hit by missiles and she and the kids have to eject. The mother uses her elasticity to reach out and grab her children and parachute them, with herself as the chute, to the ocean below. Then she transforms her body into a speedboat (her son, who has super-speed, is the motor) to reach the shore. It's a view of what animated movies could be—not another desperate attempt to assert the inalienable rights of men, but an incredible world where everyone has rights and powers, even the mothers.

I should point out that Elastigirl's superpower—flexibility, stretchiness, or what Eisenstein, back in the 1940s, termed "plasmaticness"—happens to be the very attribute he singled out as the most attractive imaginable in art, a universal sign of the ability to assume any form.

He found this elasticity not only in his beloved Mickey Mouse but also in Lewis Carroll's long-necked Alice, in the 18th-century Japanese etchings of "the many-metred arms of geishas," in the rubber-armed snake dancers of New York's black nightclubs, in Balzac's *La Peau de Chagrin*, in Wilhelm Busch's *Max und Moritz*, and in the stretched noses of the Tengu. Elastigirl, then, is not only a great character and a great mother, but the very picture of protoplasmic freedom.

For some reason, though, what really sticks in my mind is not Elastigirl stretching the limits of plasticity but rather a scene from *Ratatouille* (Disney/Pixar, 2007). Colette, the sole female in the kitchen of Gusteau's restaurant, is trying to teach the basics of cooking to Linguini, the bumbling orphan boy who gets a job in Gusteau's kitchen only because his mother slept with the great chef before she (yes) died.

As Colette chops away frenetically at some celery stalks, she shouts: "You think cooking is a cute job, eh? Like Mommy in the kitchen? Well, Mommy never had to face the dinner rush, when the orders come flooding in . . . Every second counts—and *you cannot be Mommy!*" Who is she shouting at? Linguini the lucky orphan? Herself? Men in general? Men who want to have it all? Women who want to have it all? Animators? Fathers? I really don't know, but it's a fantastic moment of pure rage. And it sure rings true.

SARAH BOXER is a writer and illustrator who has published two graphic novels, *In the Floyd Archives* and its sequel *Mother May I?*. She occasionally writes for *The Atlantic* on a wide range of subjects.

EXPLORING THE ISSUE

Do Media Reflect Contemporary Family Relationships?

Critical Thinking and Reflection

1. In what family portrayals in media do you most experience resonance? By that, we mean, which portrayals seem most similar to your own experience?
2. Do you think that the family relationships you observe in reality television are realistic?
3. Can you think of any fairy tales or children's films that feature a strong maternal birth mother?
4. Do you see family relationships in different media genres that you think "reflect reality" or those that might reflect the perspective of a "window on the world"?

Is There Common Ground?

Both of the authors of these selections ground their approach in a different way of seeing the world. They also primarily write about media content that targets different age groups. Professor Edwards is searching for the themes that media families portray, and Sarah Boxer examines content that is most often targeted toward children, though adults often see this content with children. But there is some common ground in the sense that we learn from the family portrayals we see, and we constantly measure our own experiences against the representations reflected in media content. Gender roles are particularly important issues for children to learn, so do children come away with different expectations when they view content that eliminates mothers, while fathers are portrayed as superheroes? Undoubtedly we reflect (consciously or unconsciously) on our own experiences as we consume media content, but do these extreme situations suggest other dynamics that you should consider?

Over decades, our society changes, but different people within our society judge these changes according to different criteria. There are a wider range of family units today than ever before. Nuclear families may not be the norm everywhere, but don't they still set the standard for the way families are represented in so many forms of media? Only 50 years ago, it might seem odd for a single person to adopt a child, but today families with only one parent, same sex parents, or extended families may live in the same household. By examining these questions and the authors' perspectives, you should gain a better sense of your own ideas about families and the representation of role models and gender relations, and how the two selections provide ideas about how media condition us to think of what is "normal" and what is not.

Additional Resources

Leigh H. Edwards, *The Triumph of Reality TV: The Revolution in American Television* (Praeger, 2013). Edwards examines a number of approaches to gauge the impact of reality television and the way it produces representations of social groups and individuals.

Richard M. Huff, ed., *Reality Television* (Praeger, 2006). This collection of essays includes additional perspectives on family portrayals in the media, reality television, and celebrity culture.

Dafnah Lemish, *Children and Media: A Global Perspective* (Wiley-Blackwell, 2014). By examining a wide range of media forms, the author takes an interdisciplinary approach to explaining how and why children perceive content in special ways.

Leonard Maltin, *The Disney Films*, 4th Edition (Disney Editions 2000). This collection of Disney films references plot, character, action, and impact of most of the cartoons produced by Disney Studios.

Internet References . . .

Animation World Network

www.awn.com

**Beyond Remote Controlled Childhood:
Teaching Young Children in the Media Age**

www.naeyc.org/books/beyond_remote_controlled
_childhood

Center for Media Literacy

www.medialit.org/media-values

Common Sense Media

www.commonsensemedia.org/blog/family-media

Henry J. Kaiser Family Foundation

www.kff.org/other/the-media-family-electronic-media
-in-the/

**Maria Konnikova, "What Grown Ups Can
Learn From Kids Books,"** *The Atlantic*,
August 6, 2012.

www.theatlantic.com/entertainment/archive/2012/08
/what-grown-ups-can-learn-from-kids-books/260738/

Selected, Edited, and with Issue Framing Material by:
Alison Alexander, *University of Georgia*
and
Jarice Hanson, *University of Massachusetts—Amherst*

ISSUE

Have Media Representations of Minorities Improved?

YES: Drew Chappell, from "'Better Multiculturalism' through Technology: *Dora the Explorer* and the Training of the Preschool Viewer(s)," in *Portrayals of Children in Popular Culture: Fleeting Images* (Lexington Books, 2013)

NO: Elizabeth Monk-Turner et al., from "The Portrayal of Racial Minorities on Prime Time Television: A Replication of the Mastro and Greenberg Study a Decade Later," *Studies in Popular Culture* (Spring 2010)

Learning Outcomes

After reading this issue, you will be able to:

- Think about the ways representation of race in the media affects our perceptions of individuals.
- Reflect on how what we see and hear in media influences our concept of self and others.
- Evaluate whether social change occurs through the images presented by media.
- Consider the role media play in the lives of different generations of users.

ISSUE SUMMARY

YES: Professor Drew Chappell, in "Better Multiculturalism through Technology: *Dora the Explorer* and the Training of the Preschool Viewer(s)," juxtaposes facts about recent actions attempting to ban ethnic studies and restrict immigration in parts of the United States with the television show, *Dora the Explorer's* portrayal of a bilingual (English/Spanish) speaking girl, and discusses how the show introduces children to bilingualism, border identities, and multicultural discourse. Chappell discusses how the performance of identity in Dora's world can teach children about what brings all humans together.

NO: Elizabeth Monk-Turner, Mary Heiserman, Crystle Johnson, Vanity Cotton, and Manny Jackson, in "The Portrayal of Racial Minorities on Prime Time Television: A Replication of the Mastro and Greenberg Study a Decade Later," revisit what has become a classic study in the portrayal of minorities in media and finds that even though how minorities are represented have changed within context, no serious changes to stereotypes have really occurred. In this study of prime-time television programming, little has changed within the 10-year time span between the classic Mastro and Greenberg study, and the analysis provided by the authors.

Intense controversy exists about how racial and ethnic groups are portrayed in the media. Many scholars argue that racial representations in popular culture help mold public opinion and set the agenda for public discourse on race issues in the media and society as a whole. Do members of an audience identify with the characters portrayed? Do expressions of images in the media communicate effectively about specific races, ethnicities, or cultures? How much can we learn about other cultures and personal difference through the portrayals of characters in the media? While there may not be one answer to each of the questions posed, we do know that some people are more highly influenced by images of the "other," and that for many people who live in homogeneous communities, their only exposure to people who are dif- ferent than themselves come through media. In this way, television (and other media forms) can be considered our "windows to the world" as we store the images from media, and make sense of them as we learn more about society.

Extrapolating the images portrayed in media to real life is a complicated process, but often involves some aspect of stereotyping. Despite such shows as the infamous *Amos'n'Andy,* portrayals of African Americans were for the most part absent from early television programming. In the 1970s, many all African American casts found their way to prime time television. Shows like *Good Times, The Jeffersons,* and in 1984, *The Cosby Show,* were all financially successful and showed that popular television, especially comedy, could portray loving families that had an appeal to a broad, multi-racial audience.

While the presence of minorities in television have increased with more shows targeting similar racial and ethnic groups, and many shows including members of minority groups within the cast, how those actors and actresses are portrayed still remain one of the most fundamental questions of examining television content. For example, what role does the character "Winston" plays in the popular prime-time comedy, *New Girl*? Does his race matter to the relationships within the show? Can race be represented without resorting to stereotypes, and if and when minority characters are portrayed in nonstereotypical ways, do viewers experience that character differently? Do the parasocial relationships we have with actors/characters in media influence our expectations of people we meet in real life?

The role of stereotyping in media has been a subject of intense study for scholars in media and society. Stereotypes are often thought about as primarily negative images, and yet, if more minorities were portrayed in positive roles, those stereotypes might actually suggest greater accomplishment and challenge negative stereotypes. At the same time, this question could also be extended to thinking about the stereotypes presented by women in the media, representations of age, body type, disability, and class. So the issue of stereotyping is a broad and important one for us to consider.

Many studies have been conducted to examine how minority ownership of programming outlets (like BET, or Telemundo, for example) influence the type of portrayals in media, and questions of ownership and decision making are central to understanding representation of minorities in general. But some larger questions still remain. How do news outlets portray people in the news? Is there a bias that might creep in and change the nature of the story being reported? Are minorities represented across the board in all media forms? What is the relationship of how any one of us learns about other people and difference, to those forms of media we consume?

Professor Drew Chappell takes an interesting approach from performance studies to examine how the animated character, in *Dora the Explorer,* engages in the performativity of multiculturalism. In so doing, the television show creates opportunities for young viewers to learn language, culture, and social values in a context of creating interactive experiences through the medium of television. Though programs like *Dora the Explorer* may not be the solution to introducing a more multicultural world, Chappell identifies issues that have heretofore been nonexistent in terms of how television can normalize relationships in a multicultural world.

In contrast, Elizabeth Monk-Turner, Mary Heiserman, Crystle Johnson, Vanity Cotton, and Manny Jackson adapt the methodology used in a study from 2000 by Mastro and Greenberg who examined representations of Caucasian, African American/Black, and Latino characters in primetime television to help us understand if, within a 10-year period, any significant difference could be discerned from prime-time representations of these groups. Comparing their data to the realities of the U.S. population by race, the authors demonstrate that minorities are still considerably underrepresented, and portrayed differently, and with different characteristics.

The issues represented by these selections should lead you to think broadly about the roles represented by racial and ethnic groups in media, and hopefully, the complex web of media content, ownership of media outlets, writers, actors, and directors. Furthermore, the number of cable channels and the increasing internationalization of media forms (especially film) should make you think more broadly about the issues of representation that go beyond your own school, community, and social relationships. Do you seek images that conform to your own preconceived notions about what is accepted in society? Can you think of situations or images in which some of your ideas about stereotypes have been challenged? How have you dealt with the deviation of what may, on the surface, seem "normal?"

It is also interesting to think about whether programs targeted to special groups, like children, have the potential to create social change, or whether these programs actually support more mainstream, prime-time media fare. Will *Dora the Explorer,* for example, be one of the television shows that shape a generation's expectations for life in the future when, according to the U.S. Census (2008), Latinos comprise one-fourth of the U.S. population? What shows did you watch when you were a child, and which ones do you remember most fondly? Did they all have representations of characters to whom you could relate? Or, did you learn some of your stereotypical reactions to "others" through those media you consumed?

Perhaps a basic question as you approach these two selections should be: how long does it take to change stereotypes? Intense controversy exists about how racial and ethnic groups are portrayed in the media. Many scholars argue that racial representations in popular culture help mold public opinion and set the agenda for public discourse on race issues in the media and society as a whole. Do members of an audience identity with the characters portrayed? Do expressions of images in the media communicate effectively about specific cultures? How much can we learn about other cultures and personal difference through the portrayals of characters in the media?

YES

Drew Chappell

"Better Multiculturalism" through Technology: *Dora the Explorer* and the Training of the Preschool Viewer(s)

By the late twentieth century, our time, a mythic time, we are all chimeras, theorized and fabricated hybrids of machine and organism; in short, we are cyborgs. This cyborg is our ontology; it gives us our politics.
—Haraway, 149

Arizona, April 23, 2010. Governor Jan Brewer, promoted from Secretary of State when Governor Janet Napolitano left office to serve as the Secretary of Homeland Security under Barack Obama, signs Senate Bill 1070, giving state police broad power to detain and question those people they suspect of being undocumented immigrants to the United States ("Arizona Enacts Stringent Law on Immigration," "Senate Bill 1070"). This legislation has touched off a firestorm of controversy, inspiring protest on both sides of the immigration issue. Emboldened by perceived support for such draconian policies, conservative lawmakers and education officials in Arizona followed up SB 1070 with a ban on ethnic studies ("Arizona Bill Targeting Ethnic Studies Signed into Law") and a crackdown on teachers who speak English with an accent ("Arizona Grades Teachers on Fluency"). In 2011 a bill denying birth certificates to children born in the United States to undocumented individuals is expected was introduced but defeated in Arizona (Rau 2011).

Four years earlier, in the 2006 midterm election, citizens in Arizona, Colorado, and New Mexico voted on measures aimed at discouraging "illegal immigration" from Mexico and South America. Among these measures were Arizona's Propositions 103, which would establish English as the official language of the state, and 300, which would deny public program eligibility to any person who was not a lawful resident of the United States (Arizona Secretary of State's Office). Both propositions passed into law. These were not the only attempts to respond to perceived abuses of immigration policy. Bilingual education had previously been targeted; in 2000, Arizona banned bilingual programs in schools and established English as the only instructional language.

In this politically charged climate, the Nickelodeon Jr. show *Dora the Explorer,* featuring a bilingual English/ Spanish speaking girl and her friends, remained a television hit, with 21.9 million viewers in November 2005 in

the United States (Wingett). Preschool children (who are approximately ages 2.5–5 in the United States) watched on television what they were discouraged from encountering in their daily lives: a Spanish speaking girl who, together with her diverse group of friends, leaves her home and family and crosses multiple borders with impunity in order to pursue various objectives.

Dora the Explorer (Dora) constitutes a cultural phenomenon; the television show's popularity has spawned a host of commercial products including toys, games, clothing, books, music albums, and home furnishings. In fact, in the 2006 holiday season, Dora was the number one toy license (Frenck 2). The show has won numerous awards, including a Peabody (for Broadcast Media) in 2003 and two Imagens (for positive portrayal of Latino characters/ culture) in 2003 and 2004 ("Awards for Dora" 1–4). It also spun off a second show featuring Dora's cousin Diego, called *Go, Diego, Go.* The show's reach and its cultural currency led me to choose *Dora* as a research site. Even before I had a preschool-age child, I could not escape the show's marketing and media coverage. I wondered what was behind its popularity. What specific narratives and performances did the show employ, and how did it construct dominant and subaltern identities that contribute to what I have elsewhere called "colonizing the imaginary": "an ideological process in which adults write their own culturally bound values, beliefs, and ideas onto narrative structures and performances intended for children's consumption (Chappell 18)?"

To interrogate this topic, I chose twelve episodes of the show that represented a cross-section of the show's storytelling strategies. I watched special double-length episodes ("Dora's Pirate Adventure," "Dora Saves the Mermaids," "Dora's World Adventure"), and standard episodes that reflected a number of tropes, ideas, and curricular goals. In watching these episodes, I paid close attention to the narratives created and the ways they called for children's embodiment—physically (speaking back to the show, moving with Dora), relationally (identifying with Dora and Boots's problems), and ideologically (grappling with the issues and values presented in the show, such as friendship). As I watched the program, with its deceptively simple formula and insistence on communicating directly to its audience, I became aware of subtle ways that the characters engage in an implicit dialog around multiculturalism (more on this term later). There is certainly more to *Dora* than there appears; the show cleverly uses surface-level representations to engage complex social and political concepts (perhaps without the viewer's awareness). Once I collected data, I used typologies and assertion development to analyze my findings. I created the typologies based on a semiotic reading of the *Dora* episodes in relation to contextual information found in the sites and spaces surrounding the show. This context included intended social use, promotional material, contemporary political discourse, and *Dora* merchandising outside the show itself. The typologies allowed for interpretation and analysis of the data (Bogdan and Biklen, Wolcott), and pointed toward a common theme put forth by the image of Dora as cultural traveler who bears the markings of a number of different subaltern identities, from a white middle-class U.S. perspective (non-white, female, child, Spanish speaker), and uses networks of friends and various technologies to solve each issue she faces. I then used assertion development (Erickson) to construct a theoretical understanding of the nature of embodiment and power in the show, as follows: *Dora the Explorer suggests that technology is the road to a multicultural society, and this society will focus on similarities rather than differences.*

Television as Performance

Children's television enters the child's own space; it "invades" the private sphere of the home via a broadcast signal, cable, or other device. To watch a program, young people must gather around a television screen, often located in a common area where parents can monitor their children's viewing. Watching television is a bit like a small-scale film screening; a screen becomes the center of focus, and images tell the story. Unlike in a movie theater, however, a child can feel free to move around as much as desired, take breaks, or "multitask," playing with toys, books, and so on while watching. Also, the characters on a television screen are (typically) miniaturized, easily controlled by the viewer (wielding a remote). This use of space may lead to a familiarity, an intimacy between viewer and television character(s). There is a sense that the program is "only for me," although I know there are many others watching the same program, not being able to see them "erases" their presence. Television uses time in specific, regimented ways; programs appear according to a schedule, thus allowing the practice of viewing to become routinized. On non public broadcasting channels (such as Nick Jr.—Dora's network) programs are "interrupted" for commercial content—product and service advertising. There is a "rhythm" to watching television shows and

waiting out commercials—an embodied sense of when the program will institute a twist or when a commercial is coming up. Like other media, TV trains users (starting in childhood) in its effective use.

Like film, television controls the viewer's gaze through its use of camera shots. These are typically more "claustrophobic" than in film, as many shows are filmed in studios using sets that are reused from week to week. Animated programs like *Dora* add another layer of mediation; they offer two-dimensional representations of people, places, and objects that the audience recognizes from outside experience. These referents, however, are recombined, exaggerated, and otherwise distorted through the animation process until they become more simulacra than simulations (Baudrillard). As in comic books, the tendency is for animated settings and events to transcend reality. In these worlds, extraordinary things may happen quite easily, as the animator's only limitation is what he or she can draw. Animation sets up a fantastic realm in which rules are malleable, conflict is explicitly handled, and objectives are clearly defined. Animated characters, again like their comic book counterparts, tend to be less psychologically complex and more emblematic. They bear only a passing resemblance to actual people, typically having one characteristic that defines and limits them.

As with film, television audiences are expected to sit relatively quietly and pay attention to what is happening on-screen. However, as mentioned above, television offers more opportunity for freedom of movement and "outside" actions. Typically, the viewing experience is framed as "passive," an engagement with the screen images connotes a detachment with the world at large. Much is made in the media of television's detrimental effects on children's health, as television replaces more "active" entertainment (I use quotes with active and passive to suggest that the dichotomous framing of these terms is troubling in light of the [potential] critical and semiotic activity performed while watching television). *Dora*'s creators specifically sought to get children's bodies moving when they view the program. They built in multiple opportunities for children to speak back to the characters and engage in other physical activities. The desired outcome of such a strategy is to make the viewer feel even closer to the characters, as if he or she is inhabiting and exploring Dora's world alongside her.

Most television programs have a two-pronged narrative strategy. They try to create stand-alone episode; so that viewers will have a complete experience during the half-hour or hour they spend watching. But producers also want to reward faithful viewing, and so they create larger narratives that build slowly over time. In the case of *Dora*, this larger story is not as explicitly handled; episodes are self-contained and similar, and the "rewards" for repeat viewing are a knowledge of minor characters and following Dora through multiple settings and genres and watching her persona flourish in each. The strategy of giving viewers a little at a time is part of the training process; like giving an animal a treat when it performs a desired action, a show that comes on at a specific time offers an anticipated and constant return. But children's knowledge of this predictable structure within an episode is also a form of power.

Dora, Her World, and Borders

Dora revolves around a young Latina girl and her friends traveling through various landscapes in search of missing articles or characters, or collaborating on a group objective. Each show follows a similar format, based around the narrative style and strategies of a computer game. Dora and Boots, her monkey best friend, introduce themselves, and a complication emerges. To achieve their objective, they call upon Map, a talking, rolled-up map who identifies a series of locations to which they must travel. Often during their journey, they encounter Swiper the Fox, who attempts to steal an item that Dora needs. Sometimes Swiper succeeds, and sometimes Dora and Boots foil him by chanting "Swiper, no swiping!" three times. Also on the journey, Dora utilizes her backpack (herself a character) to retrieve some necessary item from the myriad of objects she contains. Eventually, Dora and her friends achieve their objective, and sing a victory song: "We Did It." They then ask the viewer to recall his/her "favorite part" of the journey, before sharing their own. Every show follows this formula; elements such as locations, objects needed, and characters encountered may change, but the journey structure never alters.

Dora takes place in a borderland; its main character speaks two languages and Dora seems caught between Mexican and U.S. culture. Author/theorist Gloria Anzaldúa defines borders as more than physical boundaries: "Borders are set up to define the places that are safe and unsafe, to distinguish *us* from *them*. A border is a dividing line, a narrow strip along a steep edge. A borderland is a vague and undetermined space created by the emotional residue of an unnatural boundary" (3). I find this definition a useful space to begin talking about the discourse around Dora's explorations. Although Dora lives in a borderland, the only "borders" she encounters are spaces between locations, which are easily traversed. In her travels, she might be seen as a *border crosser*—someone who belongs to multiple cultures simultaneously and is able to move freely between and among them. Anzaldúa suggests that those who exist in this state are often feared, mocked, or seen as illegitimate, but Dora encounters no such prejudice. Although she holds several real-world markers of the historically subaltern or marginalized—female, nonwhite, child, Spanish speaker—she is centered in her own constructed society, and so represents the dominant identity (yet the audience has intertextual knowledge of her as a marginalized identity—at least in the U.S.).

By dominant identity, I mean that Dora represents a normative middle class U.S. childhood. She lives in a home, attends school, plays safely with her friends, and does not worry about money for meals (in fact, she sometimes gives Boots money when he doesn't have it available, as in "Ice Cream"). Her mother is an archaeologist, as we learn in "Job Day," but her father's employment (if any) is not addressed. He is mostly seen cooking and caring for Dora's younger siblings. As she is represented as a normative U.S. child, Dora also demonstrates the strategy of "selective incorporation of cultural elements from the various cultural worldviews and practices to which [she] has been exposed during . . . her life" (Chen, Benet-Martinez, and Bond 806). This reflects her positioning as bicultural within a globalized/mediatized environment. Could Dora's border identity point to a growing knowledge and expectation of multicultural identity? Educational theorists Cameron McCarthy and Greg Dimitriades describe the current social condition: "Indeed, if this is an era of the 'post,' it is also an era of difference—and the challenge of this era of difference is the challenge of living in a world of incompleteness, discontinuity, and multiplicity" (202). This paradigm organizes Dora's world, with its border-crossing protagonist and easy acceptance of various cultural backgrounds against an external lived backdrop of controversy over immigration policy and border politics. The show may aspire to Homi Bhabha's discursive "Third Space," with narratives and environments focused not around cultural distinction, but hybridity. In *Dora*, speaking more than one language is taken for granted and imparted as useful. In her world, various cultures (and even species) collaborate and celebrate their common goals and values. In fact, the show represents a liberal humanist societal outlook in which differences are minimized and unity centered.

Yet, the ethos of the *Dora* show also reflects some of the troubling discourse around the term "multiculturalism." Rusom Bharucha writes: "There is almost an in-built expectation written into the 'multi' which assumes that 'we *have* to get along and live together.' In short, it would seem to deny the 'right to exit' a particular society or to subvert the premises of 'living together'" (10). When presented to young people, is the ideology associated with use of this term a forward-looking worldview? Or, does it seek to establish a basic and official knowledge to which all cultures should be exposed in order to mold their cultural understandings while keeping their folkloric character (Torres 198)? In other words, is Dora's border crossing transgressive, challenging accepted notions of identity as "this" or "that," or is it monolithic, attempting to homogenize multiple blended identities into a singular "human" experience? Do the characters in *Dora* have the "right to exit" their common journeys and objectives, or to question the ways in which these objectives are pursued?

Bilingualism and Border Identities

At the beginning of most *Dora* episodes, she greets the audience: "Hola! Soy Dora!" Boots joins in: "And I'm Boots." This bilingual greeting sets the tone for the show, which includes dialogue in both Spanish and English. One of the stated goals of *Dora*'s creators was to teach Spanish vocabulary ("More about Dora" 1), and so episodes introduce Spanish words for numbers, greetings, and simple phrases. Some of these are translated into English, and some are not; the viewer must make meaning of the non-translated words through context. Yet, although the program includes bilingual elements, in its U.S. form, the "default language" is English. A child who spoke no Spanish at all would have no trouble following the narrative of Dora's journey.

Media and communications scholar Richard Popp suggests that the bilingual nature of *Dora* distinguishes the show within the field of educational programming. The focus on language learning becomes a motivation for parents to encourage their children to watch the show: "Language becomes a means of advancing into the upper echelons of education, work, and even taste groups. Bilingualism can open doors and act as a symbol of one's tolerance and refinement" (17). He points out, however, that parents of children watching the show must value the cultural capital associated with being bilingual. They must also have the means to "take the next step" and provide assistance to their children in order for them to progress beyond the simple words and phrases the show teaches (12). This attention to the *kind* of bilingualism being taught by *Dora* is important; the show's educative merit is in teaching English speaking children beginning Spanish, not in assisting Spanish speakers to maintain their language. (This is also true of dual-language schools in Arizona, which can only be attended by English-proficient students—there is no provision for using Spanish to develop English-speaking skills.) Essentially, Dora is a "helpful native," a guide whose purpose is to introduce her own language to outsiders, and to translate for them when they encounter unfamiliar contexts. But where does Dora "live"? What is the terrain the show guides the audience through?

Dora's home is not specifically located in a single country, but more of a borderland, a "no-place/everyplace." This home space is a verdant landscape with tropical trees and green hills. Dora's family's house has a Spanish tile roof, and the walls around its door and windows are painted with turquoise designs. The landscape and animal clues—Dora's friends include an iguana, monkey, and bull—seem to locate the show in Mexico or South America, but even this is a computer game-style simulation, a politically charged sedimentation of U.S. fantasies of travel/exploration/colonization. Because she lives in this borderland, Dora seems to be a cultural hybrid, a combination of multiple traditions and folkloric elements. She is drawn as a Latina girl, but plays out (for example) European fairy tale and transatlantic pirate narratives. In an interview, one of the show's writers stated: "We often combine a Latino character with a fable character. But really, it's all a legacy of imagery" (Sigler 43). The "legacy of imagery" the writer speaks of suggests a view of Dora as symbolically formed from multiple imaginary strains. She is a multicultural cipher, a hybrid in the most surface-level sense of Bhabha's

meaning. Without a specific racial or ethnic identity, each viewer can "download" his or her own cultural background onto Dora, molding her into whatever that child or adult needs or wants her to be. (Thus adding to her great cross-cultural appeal.)

Dora's family celebrates Christmas, with a tree in their living room and luminaria on the path outside ("A Present for Santa"). Yet the focus of the Christmas episode is on presents and their suitability for those who receive them, not on the religious or family-centered aspects of the holiday. When Swiper attempts to make off with their present for Santa, Boots hopes Christmas will bring out the fox's better nature: "Swiper wouldn't swipe on Christmas, would he, Dora?" In fact, Swiper takes the present, but returns it once he realizes it's for Santa. The present is "una guitarra" (a guitar), on which Santa serenades Boots and Dora with "Feliz Navidad." So Santa serves as a kind of universal bringer of good cheer rather than a Christian icon (this draws from his status in the culture at large, in which he has been largely stripped of religious context). Santa hails a liberal humanist/morality tale view of "Christmas" as unifying and peaceful—and yet, despite his secularization, he still represents Christian ideology; fully decontextualizing such a religious figure is not possible. In 2009, Nickelodeon premiered the episode "Dora Saves Three Kings Day,' which presents a surface treatment of Latino celebrations of Epiphany and the arrival of the three kings or magi (Reyes Magos). In the episode, Dora and her friends rescue animals which are to bring them to their village for the Three Kings celebration. . . .

When Dora travels, she does so almost instantaneously by stepping into a method of conveyance (that helpfully appears when she needs it) and then stepping off in a new location, usually after singing a brief song. These vehicles can take her across lakes, around the world, or even to another planet ("Journey to the Purple Planet"). She can also enter fairy tales by climbing into books ("Dora Saves the Prince") and breathe underwater using a magic crown to transform into a mermaid ("Dora Saves the Mermaids"). In her travels, Dora never buys a ticket or rides with other children. She has complete freedom to cross borders without documentation, and she never passes through any kind of immigration post. When she arrives at her destination, the local people and animals happily accept her. (One exception to this is when she enters Swiper's home space in "Berry Hunt" and picks berries—in this episode she is chased by a bear.) All this traveling suggests the space-bending possibilities of the Internet, a technology that allows communication and virtual travel across great distances. Because of its simulated nature, travel via the Internet does not require documentation or funds. Like Dora's transportation, it occurs instantaneously and whenever needed by the user. But, again like Dora, those who travel in this fashion are limited by the environments, people, and information available through the technology used. And these travelers must always return "home" to their physical bodies.

Although Dora may cross geographic borders, she cannot escape those of the television frame; she is at the mercy of her journey narrative and when her show ends, she disappears—or transitions into a Dora controlled by the child fan, assisted by branded dolls, clothing, and so on.

Children and Technology

Dora's narrative takes the form of a computer game, and Dora herself utilizes various technologies during her adventures. Thus, the show engages questions about the relationship of young people to technology such as: How is Dora's life structured as a computerized series of binary decisions? How does Dora's use of technology engage specific forms of embodiment and identities? And how does it reflect children's experience with technology in the "outside world"?

Theorists such as Neil Postman argue that children's use of media decreases their capacity for imaginative play and exposes them to harmful stimuli. On the other side of the continuum, David Buckingham argues that new media, such as computer software, the Internet, and text messaging, provide additional venues for communication and enhance young people's ability to extend their knowledge and influence. This utopic vision positions technology as generating new forms of learning, democratic literacy, liberation from bodily identity, and creative expression (Buckingham 44). Facility with multiple media also produces the ability to adapt to change, experiment creatively with different modalities, and learn to solve problems by "doing"—without rule books or manuals (McDonnell 115–16).

Through watching *Dora*, children learn the ritualized semiotic and performative aspects of machine use (Oravec 253). As they become accustomed to technology—through representations in entertainment or use of computers at home or school—children prepare to use machines in their daily lives. But cultural theorist Jo Ann Oravec cautions that: "Technology rituals can thus displace efforts to establish or participate in more human-centered rituals, rituals that involve higher levels of human response and permit more spontaneity, playfulness, and even magic" (Oravec 254). Notice the parallel here with Postman's view. As shows like *Dora* engage the binary structure of computer functions (calling for one right answer), might they curb children's creative use of the technology or ability to imagine alternative solutions and narratives?

When we use technology, we participate in an exercise of control over ourselves as users. We must use the technology in the way it demands; otherwise, it will not fulfill its function. Oravec suggests that adults have explored the "strategic use of technological ritual" to reinforce structure and establish discipline over children (262–263). Teaching such processes as launching a program, starting a file, saving work, researching on the Internet, etc. constitutes an imposition of structure, a discipline of children's minds and bodies focused toward particular uses

of machines. This discipline imposes a technological layer on top of other daily structures such as mealtimes, class schedules, and bedtimes. The process assists in socializing children to become technological workers in a modernist paradigm (Callahan). As Donna Haraway suggests in the quote I led with, such a process moves society into an ever closer, cyborglike relationship with its machines.

Another issue raised by Oravec is the purpose of introducing children to technology in a consumerist culture. She states: "Through these consumption rituals, children learn that technology is a consumer item, and that the purpose of human interaction with computers is to collect various devices and then follow the programmed instructions, experimenting within their affordances and constraints" (261). As children add more technological devices and media, they increase their cultural capital. Rather than calling on children to master a single program or tool, as a parent or teacher might, the consumer market suggests that diversifying one's technological portfolio provides a more direct key to success. This is reflected in the *Dora* program; Dora relies on a multitude of mechanical devices (transportation, tools, reference materials) to get where she needs to go and acquire necessary items. But she also consistently utilizes her map to access information and mark her progress. Indeed, having access to technology and exhibiting mastery in its use ensures Dora is able to complete her objectives successfully each episode. (Such consumerism/collection is also promoted through the proliferation of *Dora* merchandise, electronic and non-electronic.)

Technology in/as Dora's World

Dora makes extensive use of technology during her adventures. Some is "low tech" or magic, like the map that shows her the locations she needs to travel through to reach her objectives, or her backpack that magically holds whatever items she might need. And some is quite sophisticated—as mentioned, she has access to whatever mode of transportation she requires at any given time. In "Dora's World Adventure," she makes use of a collection of video screens that project images of her friends around the world and allow her to speak with them, as if on videophone. These screens, like Dora's instantaneous travel, suggest the possibilities of Internet communication. Dora's cousin Diego has a computerized "field journal" that he uses to collect information on animals ("Meet Diego"). The field journal seems to be linked not only to an information network about zoology, but also to a satellite feed—Diego can use it to locate any animal in seconds. The journal looks something like a Blackberry or GPS device, and its key function in the narrative gives it a "cool" factor that makes such devices attractive to the viewer.

Boots and Dora also like to "catch stars," reaching up and grabbing smiling stars that fly by them on their journey. Dora stores the stars in a special rainbow pocket on the side of her backpack. These "captive" stars, with diverse abilities and properties, prove useful as she applies them to various problems. Rocket Star, for example, can enable her to move more quickly. Glowy can light up dark places. In *Dora the Explorer: The Essential Guide,* a companion book to the television series aimed at emerging readers and their families, the author states that these small pieces of technology are "giggly star friends" (Bromberg 16), yet they seem unwilling to be caught and always fly away after being "helpful." The stars contribute to the framing of Dora's world as a video game, as they fly above the characters' heads and suggest the idea of "bonuses" when they are caught—they are objects, tools without any agency or function other than to aid Dora.

Other elements of the show suggest the mediated nature of Dora's world as well. In the original title sequence for the show, the camera zoomed in from outside a (non-animated) child's room and focused on a desktop computer. Dora and her friends appeared on that computer. In each episode, including those currently running, a mouse pointer clicks on Dora's name to transition from the title sequence to the main part of the program. This pointer then becomes the audience's avatar in Dora's world, allowing the assumed viewer to access ("click on") objects and elements in the landscape, as he or she would if playing a computer game. Once clicked, objects activate—they fly around the screen, or appear on Dora, or perform some other useful action. Of course, this "mouse pointer" access is not personalized to each viewer; there is one master narrative it portrays. This narrative is also centered around the "correct" answer; for example, if Dora asks for a flashlight, the pointer would choose the picture of a flashlight, not (for example) a maraca that, when shaken, could attract fireflies to light her way. In this way, Dora's technology maps onto Oravec's notion of technological rituals as discipline, as it prepares the viewer to interact with machines in a specific, linear, binary fashion. Rather than imagine multiple possibilities, preschoolers are taught to choose the most obvious, straightforward answer.

Behavioral Responses

As mentioned above, another stated objective of Dora's creators was that the show's audience "be active participants—not only by answering questions, but by getting off the couch and moving their bodies" ("More about Dora" 2). Several times each episode, the show calls for audience members to engage in various types of physical embodiment. In order to issue this call, Dora and the other characters speak directly to the audience, breaking the mediated fourth wall. Dora begins each episode by telling the viewers: "I need your help," and then asking if they will help her. Regardless of the children's response, Dora assumes an affirmative, and begins her journey with the viewer compelled alongside. This participation is touted by Nickelodeon executive Brown Johnson as empowering to the preschool viewers: "It makes them feel smart, and it makes them feel strong, and it makes them feel powerful . . . No one had ever asked for that degree of audience participation before" (Ralli C2). Yet, all of the participation is carefully choreographed to overlap with Dora's success along her journey.

After gaining the viewers' support, Dora, Boots, Map, and Backpack implicate them in their activities through various physical performances. Sometimes these are in the form of compelled speech—the characters tell the children watching that they "have to say" a key word, such as "backpack" or "map." Occasionally, Dora and Boots follow this demand with "louder!" Some of these speech acts engage learning through rote: viewers learn Spanish words by repeating them after Dora, for example. Often the characters employ close-ended questioning as a teaching strategy, asking children where a certain shape or animal is that Dora somehow is having trouble seeing. Sometimes the physical performance is focused on larger movements; children are asked to jump, or reach, or point to an object. Sometimes, viewers will "earn" some reward for engaging in these performances—a friendship bracelet, for example, at the end of the World Adventure story. When this happens, the reward is "given" to the viewers by passing it under (or around) the "camera" so that it appears to have been moved out of Dora's space and into the viewer's. The show thus establishes a token economy, based on following Dora's instructions, but the token is virtual and disappears as soon as the show is over. Yet, with all these compelled actions and rewards, the fourth wall is a blurry boundary—in many ways—in *Dora*.

In all these performances, as with the computer pointer avatar, there is one "right" answer, gesture, or other response, and it is assumed that the viewer embodies this correct performance. Thus, there is essentially only one way to engage with the program's narrative, except for interpretations of animal movements or other gestures called for in a general way. The major exception occurs at the end of each episode, when viewers are asked to tell Dora and Boots their favorite part of the day's journey. The characters leave a few seconds of time for children's open responses before validating them: "I liked that part, too." After this, Dora and Boots relate their favorite parts, which may be the same as the viewers'. Only here does the viewer get to express creativity, or break out of the binary right/wrong answer structure.

The interactivity in *Dora* functions as a metanarrative of the series as a whole, since it is structured as an interactive game—perform correct action, receive reward, progress along journey. But, because it is mediated, the interactivity is false, ultimately resulting in the audience's consumption of the "correct" performance. In the "bargain" of sitting down to watch *Dora,* viewers lose the ability to express themselves creatively, but gain the comfort of knowing they can never give the "wrong" answer. This is similar to technology use; a calculator cannot give a "wrong" answer, as long as the user inputs the question correctly. Is the bargain beneficial to the viewer? What are the right answers being imparted, and what alternate solutions are left out? Ultimately, Dora leaves little room for resistant viewing or "play."

Implications: Completing the Training

As Dora explores, she transmits specific ideologies regarding childhood and society. The viewers' assumed complicity with her actions places them at the center of debates over border identity and multiculturalism, and the place of technology. Dora's journeys are carefully constructed to serve as conduits for certain values, often having to do with being a "good" person—saving a friend, finding some useful or sentimental item, working as a team. As she travels, Dora sees her world not for what it *is*, but rather as a series of locations to be passed through. Locations serve less as significant journey markers than as staging points for challenges—the no places/every places of computer games. The objective matters most—again, a linear and structural standpoint—and the show cannot end until Dora meets that objective.

The way space is used in *Dora* also serves as a marker for how the show treats other concepts. As mentioned earlier, Dora's world is a simulacrum, a decontextualized version of real landscapes, a place that never was. Sociologist Henri Lefebvre suggests that space can be *abstract*, existing in the realm of the conceptual (we will use this kitchen to cook food), or *lived*, suggesting practical, material usage (the kitchen can also be used for playing with toys, or brushing the cat, or bandaging a cut). Literary theorist Nicholas Spencer argues: "Lefebvre describes abstract space as a homogenizing and fragmenting social force that seeks to destroy the potential for oppositional cultural space that lived space represents" (142). The flattening of space creates a unilateral expectation of how it will be used, disregarding possibilities for play. As Dora moves through her own abstract space, her possibilities for use of space are limited; she cannot bring her space to the realm of the material. Like a character in a novel who is similarly confined, "she cannot integrate her various spatial experiences into a social map of her world" (144). Since Dora cannot and does not bring her experience into the material, it is up to the children viewing the show to do it for themselves. They define their own sense of Dora's space, of who she is as a pretend or aspirational peer, and how her world culturally maps onto their own. Through this relational and ideological embodiment, the show imparts its training.

Multiculturalism—that contested term—is presented in *Dora* as a sort of extended series of friendships, a liberal humanist outlook exemplified by her team's cheer: "When we work together as a team, there's nothing we can't do. 'Cause being on a team means you help me and I help you" ("We're a Team"). Dora and her friends never encounter any hardships based on difference; they don't have difficulties understanding languages, traditions, gestures, or geographies. Their challenges are skills based: they search for objects, pass through locations, outwit Swiper the Fox, and cheer up a grumpy troll by making him laugh. The characters' differences easily coalesce into a network of abilities—accentuated by technological or magic objects that conveniently appear when needed, removing any struggle connected with building assemblages—that serve a common good. The *Dora* vision of community might thus be seen as an idealistic "happy multiculturalism." The characters share a common identity, even though they are of multiple species, cultural backgrounds, and genders. (Class is not specifically represented or addressed.) Dora and her friends are brought together by common, humanistic objectives that are supposed to transcend their perceived differences.

Educational theorist Carlos Alberto Torres proposes that under such a liberal humanist vision: "Unfortunately the tension between and among these differences is rarely interrogated, presuming a 'unity of difference'—that is, that all difference is both analogous and equivalent (201). This treatment of difference tends to reject radical notions and reproduce structure in its attempts to forge a unified "personhood" (Ladson-Billings and Tate 62). In its attempts to build a liberal humanistic third space—a hybridizing, democratic borderland—*Dora* defers conversation around issues of culture and power. Children do not learn about the relationships between injustice and common cause, or misunderstanding and friendship. Both contained and enabled by the technology that frames it, the show's multicultural discourse is ultimately imaginary and temporary. Everything in *Dora* comes too easily; it is decontextualized and abstracted from cultural and linguistic tensions. In the outside world, those who look like Dora may be stopped and detained by the police if they live in Arizona. Spanish speakers contend with a state system that enforces English as a sole mode of literacy, spoken and written. Yet, *Dora's* determination to exist in a highly simulated environment, with a mysterious avatar pointer and instantaneous travel, sets it apart from the outside world and ignores complex questions around the very issues it engages. The show colonizes the imaginary around the avoidance of cultural conflict and a false sense of unity, while outside, restrictive legislation is signed, protestors gather, and children respond in English when their parents speak to them in Spanish.

Works Cited

Anzaldúa, Gloria. *Borderlands: La Frontera*. San Francisco: Aunt Lute Books, 2007.

"Arizona Bill Targeting Ethnic Studies Signed into Law." *Los Angeles Times*, May 12, 2010. articles.latimes.com/2010/may/12/nation/la-na-ethnic-studies-20100512 (accessed April 29, 2012).

"Arizona Enacts Stringent Law on Immigration." *New York Times*, June 11, 2010. (accessed May 12, 2010). www.nytimes.com/2010/04/24/us/politics/24immig.html).

"Arizona Grades Teachers on Fluency." *Wall Street Journal,* June 11, 2010. online.wsj.com/article/SB10001424052 7487035725045752138832764275 28.html. (accessed April 29, 2012).

Arizona Secretary of State's Office. *2006 Proposition Guide: Proposition 103.* 16 October 2007. www.azsos .gov/election/2006/Info/PubPamphlet/Sun_Sounds/ english/Prop 103.htm (accessed April 29, 2012).

———. *2006 Proposition Guide: Proposition 300.* 16 October 2007. www.azsos.gov/election/2006/Info/ PubPamphlet/Sun_Sounds/english/Prop300.htm (accessed April 29, 2012).

"Awards for *Dora the Explorer.*" Internet Movie Database. www.imdb.com/title/tt0235917/awards (accessed April 29, 2012).

Baudrillard, Jean. *Simulacra and Simulation.* Ann Arbor: University of Michigan Press, 1994.

"Berry Hunt." *Dora the Explorer.* Nick Jr. 2000.

Bhabha, Homi. *The Location of Culture.* New York: Routledge, 1994.

Bharucha, Rusom. *The Politics of Cultural Practice.* London: Athlone Press, 2000.

Bogdan, Robert, and Sari Knopp Biklen. *Qualitative Research for Education: An Introduction to Theories and Methods,* fourth ed. Boston: Allyn and Bacon, 2003.

Bromberg, Brian. *Dora the Explorer. The Essential Guide.* London, New York: DK Publishing, Inc., 2006.

Buckingham, David. *After the Death of Childhood: Growing up in the Age of Electronic Media.* Cambridge, UK: Polity Press, 2000.

Callahan, Raymond. *Education and the Cult of Efficiency.* Chicago: University of Chicago Press, 1962.

Chappell, Andrew. *Colonizing the Imaginary: Children's Embodiment of Cultural Narratives.* Diss Arizona State University, 2008.

Chen, Sylvia Xiaohua, Veronica Benet-Martínez, and Michael Harris Bond. "Bicultural Identity, Bilingualism, and Psychological Adjustment in Multicultural Societies: Immigration-Based and Globalization-Based Acculturation." *Journal of Personality* 76, no. 4, 2008.

"Dora Saves the Mermaids." *Dora the Explorer.* Nick Jr. 2007.

"Dora Saves the Prince." *Dora the Explorer.* Nick Jr. 2002.

"Dora Saves Three Kings Day." *Dora the Explorer.* Nick Jr. 2009.

"Dora's Pirate Adventure." *Dora the Explorer.* Nick Jr. 2004.

"Dora's World Adventure." *Dora the Explorer.* Nick Jr. 2006.

Erickson, Frederick. "Qualitative Methods in Research on Teaching." In *Handbook of Research on Teaching.* 3rd ed, edited by. M. C. Wittrock, 119-161. Washington, DC: American Educational Research Association, 1986.

Fernández, Idy. "Go, Diego Go." *Hispanic* 18 (2005): 68.

Frenck, Moses. "Toy Treatment." *MediaWeek* 17, no. 8 (October 19, 2007): MyMl-MyM4.

Haraway, Donna. *Simians, Cyborgs and Women: The Reinvention of Nature.* New York: Routledge, 1991.

"Job Day." *Dora the Explorer,* Nick Jr. 2004.

"Journey to the Purple Planet." *Dora the Explorer.* Nick Jr. 2006.

Ladson-Billings, Gloria and William Tate. "Toward a Critical Race Theory of Education." *Teachers College Record* 97 (1995): 47–68.

McCarthy, Cameron and Greg Dimitriades. "Globalizing Pedagogies: Power, Resentment, and the Re-Narration of Difference." In *Globalization and Education: Critical Perspectives* edited by Nicholas C Burbules and Carlos Alberto Torres, 187–204. Lanham, MD: Rowman & Littlefield Publishers, 1998.

McDonnell, Kathleen. *Honey We Lost the Kids: Rethinking Childhood in the Multimedia Age.* Toronto, Canada: Second Story Press, 2001.

"Meet Diego." *Dora the Explorer.* Nick Jr. 2003.

"More about Dora." *Dora the Explorer.* Nick Jr. 2005. October 12, 2007. nickjr.co.uk/shows/dora/more. aspx#about (accessed April 29, 2012).

Oravec, Jo Ann. "From Gigapets to Internet: Childhood Technology Rituals as Commodities." In *Rituals and Patterns in Children's Lives,* edited by. Kathy Merlock Jackson, 252–268. Madison: University of Wisconsin Press, 2005.

Popp, Richard K. "Mass Media and the Linguistic Marketplace: Media, Language, and Distinction." *Journal of Communication Inquiry* 30 (2006): 5–20.

Postman, Neil. *The Disappearance of Childhood.* New York: Vintage, 1994.

"A Present for Santa." *Dora the Explorer.* Nick Jr. 2002.

Ralli, Tania. "The Mother of 'Blue' and 'Dora' Takes a Step Up at Nickelodeon." *New York Times,* February 28, 2005. www.nytimes.com/2005/02/28/business/ media/28kid.html (accessed April 29, 2012).

Rau, Alia Beard. "Arizona State Rejects 5 Major Immigration Bills." *The Arizona Republic.* February 2, 2012. http://www.azcentral.com/news/election/azelections/ articles/2011/03/17/20110317arizona-birthright-citizenship-bills-rejected.html?nclick_check=l (accessed October 24, 2012).

Salaňda, Johnny. *Fundamentals of Qualitative Research.* Oxford; New York: Oxford University Press, 2011.

"Senate Bill 1070." *State of Arizona Senate.* June 11, 2010. www.azleg.gov/legtext/491eg/2r/bills/sbl070s.pdf (accessed April 29, 2012).

Sigler, Eunice. "A Girl Named Dora." *Hispanic* 16 (2003): 42–5.

Spencer, Nicholas. *After Utopia: The Rise of Critical Space in Twentieth-Century American Fiction.* Lincoln: University of Nebraska Press, 2006.

"Sticky Tape." *Dora the Explorer.* Nick jr. 2001.

Torres, Carlos Alberto. *Democracy Education, and Multiculturalism: Dilemmas of Citizenship in a Global World.* Lanham, MD: Roman & Littlefield Publishers, 1998.

"We All Scream for Ice Cream." *Dora the Explorer. Nick Jr.* 2000.

"We're a Team." *Dora the Explorer.* Nick Jr. 2006.

Wingett, Yvonne. "'Dora' Unlocks Bilingual Treasure" *The Arizona Republic.* February 15, 2006. http://www.azcentral.corn/arizonarepublic/news/articles/0215earlyspanish0215.html (accessed April 29, 2012).

Wolcott, Harry F. *Transforming Qualitative Data: Description, Analysis, and Interpretation.* Thousand Oaks, CA: Sage, 1994.

Drew Chappell is a performance studies scholar who teaches at California State University, Fullerton. In addition to his research on play, globalization and visual and narrative research methods, he is also an award-winning playwright.

Elizabeth Monk-Turner et al.

 **NO**

The Portrayal of Racial Minorities on Prime Time Television: A Replication of the Mastro and Greenberg Study a Decade Later

Exploring how racial minorities are portrayed on television is valuable for two primary reasons (Mastro & Greenberg 2000). First, it is socially important to document how minorities are depicted on television as well as how such portrayals have changed over time. Second, as a cultural artifact, television reaches a wide audience. Many maintain that the way racial minorities are represented contributes to stereotypical images, whether positive or negative, that viewers develop (Potter, 1994; Potter & Chang, 1990; Bodenhausen et al., 1995; Devine & Baker, 1991; Persson & Musher-Eizenman, 2003; and Ford, 1997). As Signorielli (2001) observed, television has become the "nation's primary story-teller" (36).

This study replicates earlier work by Mastro & Greenberg (2000) who explored the representation and depiction of Caucasian, African American/black and Latino characters on prime time television. Mastro & Greenberg (2000) found that, compared to Caucasians and African Americans, Latinos were under-represented on primetime television, where they comprised only 3% of television characters. The Mastro & Greenberg (2000) study is important because they reported that Latino television characters were not as negatively stereotyped as African American television characters. While they found more African American representation on television, the roles and behaviors portrayed were negative characterizations (see too Weigel et al., 1995; Greenberg & Brand, 1994; Ford, 1997). Specifically, Latino characters were generally respected and the least lazy of any group, while African Americans were the laziest, least respected, and dressed most provocatively (see too Fyfe, 1999). The conversations of African American characters fared better in that they were most relaxed and most spontaneous, while the conversations of Latinos were least articulate, most accented, and least spontaneous. The work of this article replicates the earlier study by Mastro & Greenberg (2000) by exploring the representation, appearance, conversational characteristics and personal characteristics among Caucasian, Latino and African American characters on prime time television a decade later.

Mastro & Greenberg's (2000) work is notable because Latino representation was included in better understanding minority portrayal on prime time television. According to the U.S. Census, Latinos are the nation's largest ethnic or race minority as well as the fastest growing minority group (2008). Today, 15% of the U.S. population is Latino and one of every two people added to the population is Latino (U.S. Census, 2008). The U.S. Census estimates that by 2050, a fourth of the population will be Latino. While the size of the Latino population grows, research attention, notably representation and portrayal on television, lags. Therefore, it is important to track media images and how they have changed over time.

According to Nielsen Media, CBS, NBC, Fox, and ABC remained the top viewed networks on prime time television which were broadcast over the air (2009). CBS came in first place with 5.81 million prime time, with ABC trailing at 5.51 million prime time viewers. Over the period of this study, cable and satellite programs, as well as other niche networks, have competed for viewers; however, the major networks remain in the lead for the television viewing audience in general (Nielsen Media, 2009). Still, other outlets, such as the Spanish language network's Univision, which claims 3.21 million viewers, have changed the landscape of the media and television (Nielsen Media, 2009). Nevertheless, we argue that the images viewers see on major over-the-air channels continue to have the potential to impact how minority and majority group members are perceived in the wider society.

Background

Early work by Goffman (1974) posited that media images and messages work as a cognitive filter to help individuals make sense of the world. Others (Tan, Ling & Theng, 2002) have argued that television has the "potential to reach the most private realms of the human psyche" (853). If television images contribute to stereotypes, Graves' (1999) finding that racial minorities were generally negatively stereotyped on television is troublesome (see too Mastro & Robinson, 2000). Such negative stereotypes could shape how viewers think about racial minorities (see Graves, 1999).

Gerbner et al. (2002) argued that television continuously feeds "mainstream" views over a period of time.

Monk-Turner, Elizabeth; Heiserman, Mary; Johnson, Crystle; Cotton, Vanity; Jackson, Manny. From *Studies in Popular Culture*, vol. 32, no. 2, Spring 2010, pp. 101–114. Copyright © 2010 by Popular Culture Association in the South. Used with permission.

Proposing a cultivation hypothesis, Gerbner et al. (1994) posited that television images inform public opinions about the social world (see too Gerbner & Gross, 1976). Specifically, cultivation theory proposed that heavy exposure to media, television in particular, shaped how viewers saw the real world. What such viewers deem as appropriate role portrayals, values and ideologies are, over time, increasingly in line with those delivered on screen (Gerbner et al. 2007). Likewise, Robinson et al. (2007) argued that media images, along with lived experience, significantly shaped children's feelings of others.

Content analyzing animated Disney film images, Robinson et al. (2007) maintained that media images can "form, change, and reinforce stereotypes" (203; Editor's note: See Alexander M. Bruce, *Studies in Popular Culture* 30.1). Even if one does not accept the proposition that such images shape mental formations, Berg (1990) found that images seen on television validated existing stereotypes of the viewing audience and gave them additional credibility (see too Potter, 1994). Further, Greenberg (1988) suggested that certain images, particularly those that stand out to the viewing audience, may be more important in shaping racial attitudes than the mere number of minorities characters shown.

Bodenhausen et al. (1995) found that exposure to media images of successful African Americans may have positive effects on the racial attitudes of whites. Specifically, Vrij et al. (1996) argued that television images may change prejudiced racial attitudes. They found three characteristics were critical for such change to occur. First, television images needed to stress similarities between majority and minority group members. Further, these images needed to include multiple minority group members, not merely a token minority group member. Finally, the anti-discrimination message should be clear in the images shown (see Vrij et al., 1996). If minority characters were presented in a positive way, according to the fivepoint Likert scale used in our content analysis, we examined the explicitness of such positive characterizations. Again Vrij et al. (1996) argued that these factors were essential components of media portrayals of minority characters if negative racial stereotyping is to be lessened.

Method

Prime time television shows (8–10 p.m. EST) were content analyzed during a two-week period beginning in early March 2007. During this period, a one-week sample of all shows and characters shown on ABC, NBC, CBS and FOX was recorded and content analyzed (sports and news programs were excluded from the analysis). Thus, one complete prime time week (Monday to Friday) for each of the four networks was content analyzed. Our unit of analysis was the television character that appeared on these prime time shows, and both major and minor characters were included. The use of a one-week sample followed the pattern established by others who have maintained this type

of sample provides a reliable portrait of television portrayals (see Gerbner & Gross, 1976; Pfau, Muller & Garrow, 1995).

Coded variables replicated those used by Mastro & Greenberg (2000), who originally selected variables "to reflect the frequency and prominence of minority portrayals" (p. 693). These variables, they argued, were the attributes that past literature found "as primary components of image formation and stereotyping" (Mastro and Greenberg, 2000: p. 693; see also Berg, 1990). Coded variables included: race, age, network, income level, gender, and role prominence. If characters were major or main characters, those essential to the plot or story line, then their *role* prominence is coded as 1. Other characters were considered minor characters (0). Background characters who appeared on screen but were non-essential (people on the street or characters seen in the background in public areas) were excluded. *Race* is operationalized as Caucasian, African American, Latino/Hispanic, Asian American and all others. This categorization is in line with new Census race categories as well. *Age* is coded as less than 10, 10–20, 20s, 30s, and 40+. Perceived *income* level is coded as low (<$20,000 per year), middle ($20,000–$70,000), or high (over $70,000).

Next, we coded four sets of variables, again in line with Mastro and Greenberg (2000), on a five-point scale (bipolar adjective scales) (p. 694). Again, these items were originally selected because they reflected "an attribute or characteristic which has been associated with an ethnic stereotype" (p. 694). Five *physical characteristics* are content analyzed: weight (thin-obese), height (short-tall), hair color (blonde-black), skin color (fair-dark skin), and accent (no accent-heavy accent). A second set of six variables content analyzed *behavioral characteristics*: articulate-inarticulate, quiet-loud, passive-aggressive, lazy-motivated, ridiculed-respected and dumb-smart. Next, we coded a set of six variables to capture *appearance differences*: excessive makeup-no makeup, excessive accessories-no accessories, provocative attire-conservative attire, casual attire-professional attire, disheveled-well-groomed, and dirty-clean.

Finally, we note attributes that pick up *conversational characteristics*, whether the conversation was tense-relaxed and/or premeditatedspontaneous. To ensure reliability in coding, two coders content analyzed each television program. Intercoder reliability was high (89% agreement across all categories). When there was a disagreement with regard to coding, coders came to an agreement as to the best way to categorize the characterization. Clearly, coding television images is subjective as is how viewers see such images on screen.

Results

Most (74%) of our sample was comprised of Caucasian television actors, 16% of prime-time actors were African American, 5% were Latino, <2% were Asian Americans and <3% were of another racial category. In their work,

Mastro & Greenberg (2000) also found that 16% of prime-time television actors were African American; however, in their work only 3% of such actors were Latino. Over a period of ten years, the racial representation of television actors has not changed significantly. White actors continue to be in a distinct majority position, African American representation is in line with their percent of the U.S. population and the representation of Latinos continues to be in a distinct minority.

Like Mastro & Greenberg (2000), we did not find a significant difference by race, gender, or income. Mastro & Greenberg (2000) found that female characters, regardless of race, were in a minority position (around 37%) among prime time television actors. Our results show that female actors were better represented in prime time—especially among African American actors. Three fourths of African American actors on prime time, a decade later, were female, while 64% of Latino characters and 56% of white characters were female. The vast majority (74% and 73% respectively) of white and Latino characters fell in the middle income category; however, only 67% of African American characters were located here.

In their work, Mastro & Greenberg (2000) found Latinos were significantly younger than other characters. We did not observe significant age differences by race. In our sample, approximately a third of all characters were in their 30s. On the other hand, Mastro & Greenberg (2000) did not observe a significant difference by race and whether the television character was in a major or minor role. Our results show that the vast majority (91%) of Latino characters were portrayed in major television roles, along with 77% of white characters; however, only 61% of African American characters were observed in this role ($X^2 = 5.43$; p = .06).

Next, we explored differences in appearance, conversational style and personal attributes among racial groups. Mastro & Greenberg (2000) found significant differences by race in four of their six appearance characteristics. They found that Latinos wore more accessories and jewelry than whites and that they were the best groomed. Alternatively, African Americans were least well groomed and were more provocative in dress than white characters. A decade later, we found no significant differences by race on any of these six measures. Likewise, Mastro & Greenberg (2000) found significant conversational differences by race. They found that Latinos were most tense and least spontaneous especially compared to blacks. As was true for appearance characteristics, a decade later we found no significant differences by race with regard to these two conversational characteristics (tension and premeditation).

Finally, we content analyzed 11 personal characteristics. Mastro & Greenberg (2000) found significant differences by race for eight of these measures while we found significant differences for six personal characteristics. Mastro & Greenberg (2000) found significant race differences for height, hair, skin color, accent, articulation, respect, aggression, and laziness. We found significant differences for all

of these variables save height, aggression, and laziness; however, unlike Mastro & Greenberg (2000), we found significant race differences by intelligence. Mastro & Greenberg (2000) argued that significant race differences by these personal characteristics was an indication of straightforward stereotyping.

Our results show that Latinos continued to be portrayed as having a heavier accent than other racial groups. Most (64%) Latino characters have a heavy accent; however, few (<1%) white or black (3%) characters were portrayed in this way ($X^2 = 139.56$; p = <.0001). Likewise, the trend continues that Latino characters were portrayed as the least articulate of all television characters. A fourth of all black characters were depicted as most articulate along with 30% of white characters; however, no Latino characters fell in this category ($X^2 = 25.68$; p = .003). Not surprisingly, we noted that Latino and African American characters had the darkest hair ($X^2 = 79.66$; p = <.0001) and African Americans had the darkest skin color with Latinos intermediate and whites the fairest ($X^2 = 226.99$; p = <.0001). Unlike Mastro and Greenberg (2000), we found significant race difference by intelligence. Half (52%) of all African American actors were depicted as the most intelligent compared to 43% of whites and 27% of Latinos. At the same time, more African Americans (15%) and Latinos (18%) were depicted as least intelligent compared to <4% of whites ($X^2 = 23.86$; p = .02). This finding offers limited support for the idea of counter-stereotyping; however, the fact that so many more minority characters were deemed least intelligent compared to whites is of concern.

Mastro and Greenberg (2000) found three relationships that ran counter to traditional stereotypes. They found that Latinos were the least ridiculed (or most respected) characters shown on prime-time—a counter-stereotypical finding. A decade later; however, we found a reversal of fortune as Latino characters were most likely to be ridiculed and least likely to be respected compared to either white or black characters ($X^2 = 30.41$; p = .002). Mastro and Greenberg (2000) also found that Latino characters were least lazy and most motivated and that African American characters were least aggressive especially compared to whites. Our work found no significant differences by laziness or aggression. Thus, our work found no counter-stereotypical findings by race. In fact, with regard to being respected, our work shows that Latinos were negatively portrayed in this respect.

Finally, we content analyzed whether television actors were depicted as moral-immoral and whether or not they were portrayed as more admirable or despicable. Our work shows that significantly more African Americans and Latinos were shown as immoral (9% and 18% respectively) compared to only 2% of white television actors ($X^2 = 22.12$; p = .04). Likewise, significantly more African American and Latino characters were portrayed as despicable, rather than admirable, on television (9% and 18% respectively) compared to only 3% of white television actors ($X^2 = 22.93$; p = .02). This finding, coupled with the fading of counter-stereotypes observed by Mastro and Greenberg (2000) ten years ago, is troublesome.

Discussion

This work replicated the earlier work of Mastro and Greenberg (2000), who explored the portrayal of racial minorities on prime time television. Significant race differences in appearance and conversational style, observed by Mastro & Greenberg (2000), were not present a decade later. Unlike the earlier work, our results show that the vast majority of Latino (91%) and white (77%) characters were in main roles, while only 61% of African Americans were depicted in such a television role. Thus, the few Latino actors that appeared in prime time were in main roles. While African American characters were three times more likely than Latinos to appear on television, they were more likely to be depicted in minor roles. Still, the sheer representation of minority characters is lacking—especially Latino and other minority characters. Only 5% of all television actors observed were Latino, up only two percentage points from the prior study a decade earlier. The representation of African Americans remained constant over this time period at 16% of all television prime time actors. Thus, while some similarities appeared between characters, regardless of race, salient differences were present as well.

Mastro & Greenberg (2000) found counter-stereotypical images for three of the 11 personal characteristics they content analyzed. They found that their Latino characters were the least lazy and the least ridiculed (or most respected) among prime time television characters. Further, blacks were least aggressive, especially compared to white characters. Vrij et al. (1996) argued that such positive characteristics of minority characters were essential to diminish negative stereotyping by race. Unfortunately, we did not find such counter-stereotypes in our work. We found no significant differences by race with regard to being lazy or the display of aggression. Notably, we observed that more Latinos were ridiculed than was true for either whites or blacks (18%, <1%, and 0% respectively). Both African American and white characters were most likely to be respected and least likely to be ridiculed. Thus, if there was a counter-stereotype in our data, it was that black characters were frequently (45%) portrayed with the most respect along with white characters (36%). However, we posit that it is troubling that significantly more Latino (18%) and African American (9%) characters were portrayed as immoral compared to white (2%) characters. This coupled with the fact that significantly more Latino (18%) and black (9%) characters were viewed as despicable television characters, rather than admired ones, compared to white (3%) characters does nothing to counter negative racial stereotypes.

Like Mastro & Greenberg (2000) we found significant differences by race with regard to hair, skin color, accent and articulation. Notably, no Latino characters were portrayed as most articulate; however, approximately a fourth of black characters and 30% of white characters were shown in this way. Unlike Mastro and Greenberg (2000), we found that black and Latino characters were significantly more likely to be shown as being less intelligent compared to whites. Only 3% of all white characters were perceived as least intelligent compared to 15% of blacks and 18% of Latino characters. At the same time, the majority of African American television characters were portrayed as most intelligent (52% of all African American characters) compared to 43% of whites and only 27% of Latinos. One could argue that these images send mixed messages rather than the clear positive stereotype that Vrij et al. (1996) maintain is necessary to dismantle negative racial stereotyping.

The counter-stereotypical racial images Mastro and Greenberg (2000) observed were lacking in our sample. If positive characterizations are essential to lessening negative racial stereotyping, then prime time television is not providing such portrayals of minority characters. Rather, viewers still see Latinos as having heavy accents, with little articulation skills, and as generally not well respected—especially compared to either African Americans or whites. It seems that Latino representations have lost the most ground over this ten-year period. Viewers of prime-time television see few images to dent any negative stereotypes they may harbor about racial minorities; however, positive images of white characters continue. White prime-time television characters are solidly middle income, fair with regard to skin and hair color, devoid of a heavy accent, articulate, respected, viewed as moral and admirable characters.

Media images contribute to both positive and negative social stereotypes. Race differences in appearance and conversational style have significantly diminished over time; however, the representation of minorities on prime time has not changed over time. What message do viewers take away from media exposure when so few characters are Latinos? Do they notice that many of the African American characters on prime time appear in minor roles? Counter stereotypes observed by Mastro & Greenberg (2000) were not as marked ten years later. Now, of the few Latinos one sees on prime time, significantly more are ridiculed compared to other characters. On a positive note, African American characters were depicted, along with whites, as respected and intelligent characters. This is negated, though, by more minority characters, both Latino and African American, being portrayed as more immoral and despicable compared to whites.

Why, academics and viewers alike might ask, do significant differences remain in the depiction of prime time characters by race? Why hasn't the media done more in producing counter stereotypes of racial minorities to help diminish race stereotyping and social prejudices? Even if one does not accept that the media can reduce such social beliefs, why do the negative minority stereotypes continue? If Goffman (1974) correctly posited that such images are cognitive filters and shape popular meaning, what responsibility must the media accept in the creation and perpetuation of negative racial stereotyping? We argue that the depiction of minority characters on prime time has changed little over recent time. Counter stereo-typical images have faded for Latinos and mixed media messages exist for African American characters. Given that media images are viewed not only by a national but by a growing international audience, we argue that the media must wrestle with these constructed images.

References

Allan, K., & Coltrane, S. (1996). Gender Displaying Television Commercials: A Comparative Study of Television Commercials in the 1950s and 1980s. *Sex Roles*, 35, 185–204.

Atkin, D. (1992). An analysis of television series with minority-lead characters. *Critical Studies in Mass Communication*, 9, 337–349.

Bartsch, R., Burnett, R., Diller, T. & Rankin-Williams, E. (2000). Gender representation in television commercials. *Sex Roles*, 43,735–743.

Bazzini, D., McIntosh, W., Smith, S., Cook, S., & Harris, C. (1997). The aging woman in popular film. *Sex Roles*, 36, 531–543.

Berg, C. (1990). Stereotyping in films in general and of the Hispanic in particular. *The Howard Journal of Communications*, 2, 286–300.

Bodenhausen, G., Schwarz, N., Bless, H., & Wanke, M. (1995). Effects of Atypical Exemplars on Racial Beliefs: Enlightened Racism or Generalized Appraisals? *Journal of Experimental Social Psychology*, 31, 48–63.

Coltrane, S. & Adams, M. (1997). Work-Family Imagery and Gender Stereotypes. *Journal of Vocational Behavior*, 50, 323–347.

Coltane, S. & Messineo, M. (2000). The Perpetuation of Subtle Prejudice. *Sex Roles*, 42, 363–389.

Craig, R. (1992). The Effect of Television Day Part on Gender Portrayals in Television Commercials. *Sex Roles*, 26, 197–211.

Davis, D. (1990). Portrayals of women in prime-time television. *Sex Roles*, 23, 325–332.

Devine, P.G. & Baker, S.M. (1991). Measurement of racial stereotype subtyping. *Personality and Social Psychology Bulletin*, 17, 44–50.

Ford, T. (1997). Effects of stereotypical television portrayals of African-Americans on person perception. *Social Psychological Quarterly*, 60, 266–278.

Fyfe, J.J. (1999). Police use of deadly force: research and reform. In L.K. Gaines and G.W. Cordner (Eds.), *Policing Perspectives: An Anthology*. Los Angeles: Roxbury.

Gerbner, G. & Gross, L. (1976). Living with television: the violence profile. *Journal of Communication*, 26, 173–199.

Gerbner, G., Gross, L., Morgan, M. & Signorielli, N. (2002). Growing up with television: The cultivation perspective. In J. Bryant and D. Zillmann (Eds.), *Media effects: Advances in theory and research*. Hillsdale, NJ: Lawrence Erlbaum Associates.

Goffman, I. (1974). Frame analysis. Cambridge, MA: Harvard University Press.

Graves, S.B. (1999). Television and prejudice reduction: When does television as a vicarious experience make a difference? *Journal of Social Issues*, 55,707–725.

Greenberg, B. (1988). Some uncommon television images and the drench hypothesis. In S. Oskamp (Ed.), *Applied Social Psychology Annual* (Vol. 8) Television as a social issue. Newbury Park, CA: Sage.

Greenberg, B. & Brand, B. (1994). Minorities in the mass media: 1970s to 1990s. In J. Bryant and D. Zillmann (Eds.), Media Effects: *Advances in Theory and Research*. Hillsdale, NJ: Lawrence Erlbaum.

Greenberg, B. & Collette, I. (1997). The changing faces on TV: A demographic analysis of network television's new seasons. 1966–1999. *Journal of Broadcasting and Electronic Media*, 41, 4–13.

Hurtz, W. & Durkin, K. (1996). Gender role stereotyping in Australian radio commercials. *Sex Roles*, 36, 103–114.

Lauzen, M. & Dozier, D. (2005). Recognition and Respect Revisited. *Mass Communication and Society*, 8, 241–256.

Lee, E. & Li, K. (1997). The myth of the Asian American super-student. *A Magazine*, 1, 44–47.

Leslie, M. (1995). Slow Fade to ?: Advertising in Ebony Magazine, 1957–1989. *Journalism and Mass Communication Quarterly*, 72, 426–435.

Mastro, D. & Greenberg, B. (2000). The Portrayal of Racial Minorities on Prime Time Television. *Journal of Broadcasting and Electronic Media*, Fall, 690–703.

Mastro, D. & Robinson, A. (2000). Cops and crooks: images of minorities on primetime television. *Journal of Criminal Justice*, 28, 385–396.

Mayeda, D. (1999). From model minority to economic threat. *Journal of Sport and Social Issues*, 23, 203–217.

McArthur, L.Z. & Resko, B.G. (1975). The Portrayal of Men and Women in AmericanTelevision Commercials. *Journal of Social Psychology*, 97, 209–220.

Merlo, J. & Smith, K. (1994). The Portrayal of Gender Roles in Television Advertising. Society for the Study of Social Problems Paper.

Millard, J. & Grant, P. (2006). The Stereotypes of Black and White Women in Fashion Magazine Photographs. *Sex Roles*, 54, 659–673.

Nakayama, T.K. (1988). Model minority and the media. *Journal of Communication Inquiry*, 12, 65–73.

Nielsen Media. (2009). Nielsen Media Research Data. Most Watched Prime Time Televison.

Paek, H. & Shah, H. (2003). Racial Ideology, Model, Minorities, and the "No-So-Silent Partner." *The Howard Journal of Communications*, 14, 225–243.

Persson, A. & Musher-Eizenman, D. (2003). The impact of a prejudice-prevention television program on young children's ideas about race. *Early ChildhoodResearch Quarterly*, 18, 530–546.

Pfau, M., Mullen, L. & Garrow, K. (1995). The influence of television viewing on public perceptions of physicians. *Journal of Broadcasting and Electronic Media*, 39, 441–458.

Potter, W. (1994). Cultivation theory and research. *Journalism Monographs*, 147, 1–3.

Potter, W. & Chang, I. (1990). Television exposure measures and the cultivation hypothesis. *Journal of Broadcasting and Electronic Media*, 34, 113–333.

Robinson, M., Callister, M., Magoffin, D., & Moore, J. (2007). The portrayal of older characters in Disney animated films. *Journal of Aging Studies*, 3, 203–213.

Shim, D. (1998). From yellow peril through model minority to renewed yellow peril. *Journal of Communication Inquiry*, 22, 385–409.

Signorielli, N. (2001). The picture in the nineties. *Generations*, 25, 34–38.

Signorielli, N. (2004). Aging on television. *Journal of Broadcasting and Electronic Media*, 48, 279–301.

Steenland, S. (1990). *What's wrong with this picture:The status of women on screen and behind the camera in entertainment TV.* Washington, D.C.: National Commission on Working Women of Wider Opportunities for Women.

Stern, S. & Mastro, D. (2004). Gender Portrayals across the Life Span. *MassCommunication and Society*, 7, 215–236.

Tan, T.T., Ling, L.B., & Theng, E. (2002). Gender-role portrayals in Malaysian and Singaporean television commercials: an international advertising perspective. *Journal of Business Research*, 10, 853–861.

Tang, J. (1997). The model minority thesis revisited. *The Journal of Applied Behavioral Science*, 33, 291–315.

Taylor, C. & Lee, J. (1994). Not in vogue: Portrayals of Asian Americans in magazine advertising. *American Behavioral Scientist*, 38, 608–621.

Taylor, C. & Stern, B. (1997). Asian Americans: Television advertising and the model minority stereotype. *Journal of Advertising*, 26, 47–61.

U.S. Census. (2007, 2008). (Online). http://www.census.gov/population/projections/nation/nsrh/nprh0610.txt.

Vrij, A., van Schie, E. & Cherryman, J. (1996). Reducing ethnic prejudice through public communication programs. *Journal of Psychology*, 4, 413–420.

Weigel, R., Kim, E. & Frost, J. (1995). Race relations of prime time television reconsidered: patterns of continuity and change. *Journal of Applied Social Psychology*, 25, 223–236.

Wilkes, R. & Valencia, H. (1989). Hispanics and Blacks in Television Commercials. *Journal of Advertising*, 18, 19–25.

ELIZABETH MONK-TURNER, Mary Heiserman, Crystle Johnson, Vanity Cotton, and Manny Jackson all teach at Old Dominion University in Virginia.

EXPLORING THE ISSUE

Have Media Representations of Minorities Improved?

Critical Thinking and Reflection

1. Perhaps the best question is the one stated at the conclusion of the introduction; how long does it take to change stereotypes?
2. Do different generations have a different interpretation of what society is like, because of the media they consume?
3. Are representations of minorities in the media true to the minority—or is the minority actor/actress playing a role that could be played by someone of another race—and does it matter?
4. Should content in the media be broad enough to appeal to audiences of a range of backgrounds?
5. Should program providers conscientiously work toward reversing negative stereotypes?

Is There Common Ground?

The authors of both of these selections question the role of stereotypes and their real impact on audiences, but are less certain of what impact the images they discuss can have on actually creating change in society, or a change in the perceptions of minorities. While Monk-Turner, Heiserman, Johnson, Cotton, and Jackson all note that there are no major changes in the representation of minorities within a 10-year period, they do acknowledge some small changes in tone and the way minorities are represented. Chappell cites a great deal of evidence to show that *Dora the Explorer* creates opportunities for children to learn about multiculturalism, but he is still somewhat pessimistic about the long-term prospects for how such a program can normalize a major change in society.

For these authors, the impact of stereotyping and representations of minorities is of utmost importance, but what we still need to grapple with is how and why stereotypes persist, who pays attention to them, and how these images make a difference or confirm previously held beliefs by individuals. Examinations of content through these types of analysis are critical to understanding the realities of media content, but the multi-dimensions of how we make sense of these images are still more complex processes.

Create Central

www.mhhe.com/createcentral

Additional Resources

Simon Cottle, ed., *Ethnic Minorities and the Media: Changing Cultural Boundaries* (Open University Press, 2000).

Bradley S. Greenberg, Dana Mastro, and Jeffrey E. Brand, "Minorities and the Mass Media: Television into the 21st Century," in Jennings Bryant and Dolf Zillman, eds., *Media Effects: Advances in Theory and Research* (Taylor and Francis, 2008).

Mark Lloyd, "Remove the Barriers to Minorities in Media," *Center for American Progress* (August 5, 2005).

Internet References . . .

Center for American Progress, "Race and Beyond: The Media's Stereotypical Portrayals of Race"

www.americanprogress.org/issues/race/news/2013/03/05/55599/the-medias-stereotypical-portrayals-of-race/

Center for Media Literacy, "A Long Way to Go: Minorities and the Media"

www.medialit.org/reading-room/long-way-go-minorities-and-media

Moyers and Company, "Why Is Cable News So Obsessed with the Zimmerman Trial?"

http://billmoyers.com/2013/07/12/why-is-cable-news-so-obsessed-with-the-zimmerman-trial/

ReachingBlackConsumers.com, "Portrayal of Blacks in the Media"

www.reachingblackconsumers.com/2011/09/portrayal-of-blacks-in-the-media/

Smith, Aaron, "Explaining Racial Differences in Attitudes Toward Government Uses of Social Media," Pew Internet and American Life Project

www.pewinternet.org/Commentary/2010/May/Explaining-racial-differences-in-attitudes-towards-government-use-of-social-media.aspx

Selected, Edited, and with Issue Framing Material by:
Alison Alexander, *University of Georgia*
and
Jarice Hanson, *University of Massachusetts—Amherst*

ISSUE

Have More Women Become Involved as Decision Makers in Media Industries?

YES: Hannah McIlveen, from "Web Warriors: The Women of Web Series," *Lydia Magazine* (2014)

NO: Martha M. Lauzen, from "Boxed In: Portrayals of Female Characters and Employment of Behind-the-Scenes Women in 2014–15 Prime-time Television," Center for the Study of Women in Television & Film (2015)

Learning Outcomes

After reading this issue, you will be able to:

- Consider how new technologies present opportunities to groups of people who may have previously been marginalized from decision-making opportunities.
- Think about the unique contributions women bring to the workplace.
- Reflect on media content to consider whether the gender of decision makers really makes a difference.
- Assess opportunities in media industries for everyone in a changing media landscape.
- Think about whether different segments of society have equal opportunities in the workplace.

ISSUE SUMMARY

YES: Hannah McIlveen challenges the dominant male culture of decision makers in television to discuss how women have been making inroads in nontraditional programming on the Web. Working in low-budget situations does not stop their creativity, and even television network executives are paying attention to new content from women creators on the Web.

NO: Every year, Professor Martha M. Lauzen conducts a survey of the roles of women in prime-time television at the Center for the Study of Women in Television and Film at San Diego State University. In this report, she provides data for the 2014–2015 television season, and she states that women are still underrepresented in prime-time television.

For many years, the media industries have been referred to as "old boy industries," meaning that women rarely get the opportunity to make it to the executive, or decision-making level. Some claim that in time this will change, but many of the legacy industries have continued to slot women into some of the lower paid work that often features "soft" news, and women often are not given as many opportunities in media as men, though women make up 51 percent of the population in the United States. As Gloria Steinem stated in *The New York Times*, "It's hard to think of anything except air, food and water that is more important than the media. . . . Especially for groups that have been on the periphery for whatever reason: If we can't see it, we can't be it." Studies over many years continue to show that women are often stereotyped in legacy media content, and that opportunities for women in programs as well as behind the scenes are relatively few. In Professor Martha M. Lauzen's annual report, we see that women remain underrepresented in prime-time television content as well as in executive and creative jobs behind the camera.

But Hannah McIlveen, writing in the online magazine *Lydia Magazine*, says that the emerging world of Web television is still open to women, and that many of the most creative series that are emerging are from women who write, produce, direct, and occasionally, star in original Web series. Furthermore, the Web platform allows a wider range of stories to be told, so there are more images of underrepresented groups, like Latino/Latina characters, characters with disabilities, and Lesbian, Gay, Bisexual, Transgender, and Queer (LGBTQ) characters. The creative opportunities for women on the Web then are far more open to women's creativity and choices. These series have been so successful that even the traditional legacy media are sitting up and taking notice. But even though the Web gives women an opportunity to explore their creative voices, the money to be made in Web television is significantly less than in traditional media forms. Still, the Web can provide an excellent training ground for women and all marginalized groups to learn about the craft of media content construction, and possibly benefit from their own creative initiatives.

Gender inequities in the workplace have a long tradition, and media industries are no exception. From representation of women in media content to opportunities for women to get jobs in media industries, the problem has been long acknowledged as contributing to the perpetuation of distorted representations of American society. This topic cuts across topics of social standards of beauty, expectations of womanhood, role models available to young girls, and many more aspects of our social world that consider media as a reflection of reality. At the same time, we should be aware that gender discrepancies are not the only problems in media industries, and some of the other selections in Taking Sides bring to the discussion of equity and balance in media and in the media industries additional issues such as ethnicity, race, and class diversity.

It is always difficult for people who have been marginalized (for whatever reason) to break the barriers of entry to jobs that have long been held by certain gender groups that may also reflect gender and class biases. But one might feel justified in assuming that in the twenty-first century, it's time for a change. Over the years many good intentions have backfired or completely stalled. In 1963 the Equal Pay Act was supposed to level the discrepancies in men's and women's pay when both were doing the same work, but a "gender gap" in pay persists. In most career- or job-related areas, full-time women workers' earnings are only about 78 percent of their male counterparts' earnings. The gender gap for pay gets even worse for African American and Latina women, with African

American women earning approximately 64 cents and Latina women earning 56 cents for every dollar earned by a white, non-Hispanic man. These problems are shared by every country in the world, where pay equity for women always falls behind that of their male counterparts.

In media industries, the pay gaps not only often exist, but opportunities for traditionally male dominated jobs are rare. This raises an important question for anyone who hopes to work in the media industries: will you be compensated fairly? Furthermore, if you are successful in getting a job in the media industries, can you be an agent of change? Will your generation be the one that shifts male domination to equal opportunity for men and women, as well as other marginalized groups, no matter what their gender? Practically, what can anyone do to be an agent of change?

These issues are not confined to media industries. Discrimination can exist in any profession, but it is often a secret that is hidden from prospective employees. Some companies have rules prohibiting employees from discussing their salaries, and others ask potential employees to sign documents that restrict what they can talk about with other employees on a number of issues that might come up in the workplace. These rules and practices, while not illegal, may tip you off to a situation in which the value of one's labor (and opportunities afforded to them) are steeped in corporate culture that might hide internal inequities.

Before embarking on a career, every individual should do as much homework as possible to see whether the salaries in the field are competitive and fair. Women often have to learn how to be better negotiators in early salary talks, because the longer you stay with one company, the more likely you are to make incremental leaps in salary that are still predicated on your initial salary. Perhaps as people become more aware of the inequities that exist in traditional companies, the more they may be willing to take some risks on lesser known opportunities where job satisfaction and creative control are important.

A number of online sources are now available to help potential employees have a better sense of what starting salaries are in different fields, and women in particular may want to explore some books and training courses on negotiating salary and benefits. Unfortunately, many of the opportunities in new media, like Web television production, may not be compensated. If this is the case, maybe it will be necessary to think about how you might raise the money you need to create an online show or series. Crowdfunding through Kickstarter or Indiegogo, or any one of the online fundraising campaigns, may be helpful to get you over a production budget hurdle or pay for living expenses while you create content for an alternative platform. New media distribution platforms may actually be a means of creating an important wedge in traditional business models and practices, but anyone entering this field should be aware of the potential problems for long-term employment from the start.

These selections raise a number of important points for discussion and hopefully will prompt you to examine your own belief system about equity and balance in the workplace. They also ask us to be more critical about looking at bylines in media, thinking about the gatekeepers of traditional and emerging content, and considering whether there are "women's issues" that are actually more attuned to issues that affect everyone. The media landscape is changing quickly. Does this mean that old problems will persist, or might these problems offer some alternatives to the way media has reflected society in the past?

YES ↵

Hannah McIlveen

Web Warriors: The Women of Web Series

Imagine this: every television network has a team of people dedicated to finding the next Tina Fey (or, at the slightly edgier networks, the next Lena Dunham); the next female powerhouse who has the kind of talent, charisma and chutzpah they can really build a show on.

These imaginary people sit around a table into the wee hours, drinking too much coffee and wracking their brains, the walls behind them lined with white boards, names frantically scribbled and circled and crossed out. They're looking for the next big woman to shake up TV comedy.

As much as we wish this fantasy team dedicated to finding the next "funny femme" actually existed, comedy TV is still mostly a man's game. And for every Tina Fey, Amy Poehler or Mindy Kaling, there are countless other men making it in lieu of women.

But there is hope. Rather than continue to struggle to make it in traditional comedy television, many women are heading online to make their own opportunities in digital TV.

Through online video sharing and streaming sites, female creators, screenwriters, directors, producers and actors are telling exciting stories from viewpoints that Hollywood tends to marginalize—not only sharing their own experiences as women but exploring the viewpoints of racial minorities, people with disabilities and LGBTQ individuals, proving that web is the home of inclusive comedy that television just isn't ready for.

In bypassing Hollywood's structured institution of television production, the women of web series are able to worry less about getting permission, following rules and fighting sexism. Instead, they can put all of their creative energy into telling stories, many of which touch on deeply personal subject matter (embarrassing sex and struggles with prejudice, anyone?) that reach out to a very specific and dedicated audience. Furthermore, these women always retain a commitment to bringing something new—something that matters and that isn't being seen elsewhere—to TV culture.

Take web series *East WillyB,* co-created and executive produced by star Julia Ahumada Grob, which features a cast of Latino characters of all shapes, sizes and ages. Telling the stories of gentrification in Bushwick, Brooklyn (dubbed East Williamsburg in an effort by realtors to sell the neighborhood, traditionally known as crime-heavy, to new, often White, tenants) the show features singing, fighting, loving and everything in between. Not only does *East WillyB* tell a story that a massive portion of the American population can relate to, it does so without the stereotypical portrayal of Latino culture that is often seen on network television.

Then there is Teal Sherer's *My Gimpy Life*. The series explores the prejudices, exploitation and condescension that the disabled face daily.

Sherer asks people to re-examine their assumptions about disabilities, but she does so in such a fun and self-deprecating way that it never sounds like preaching; just like damn good comedy. Sherer's goal with *My Gimpy Life* is to represent people who deserve a voice in television, but who aren't getting one.

"As a disability advocate," says Sherer, "I want to share my perspective and broaden people's minds. Disabled people are out in the real world, but we're underrepresented in films and on TV. I want producers and casting people to consider disabled actors for any role, not just ones that are written as disabled characters. It's so important to have people in the media that you can relate and connect to."

Another marginalized demographic that's flourishing in web series is a group that has been perhaps inelegantly titled "the uncool LGBTQ" set. While lesbian, gay, bisexual, and transgender characters and storylines gain more attention on network shows like

FOX's *Glee* and HBO's *Looking*, the focus still remains squarely on the young, hip and impossibly beautiful. Meanwhile, on the web, women like Ingrid Jungermann and Amy York Rubin are telling the less glamorous (read: more realistic) stories of LGBTQ life. For Rubin, the game is all about celebrating life's wonderfully awkward and painfully relatable moments in a way that feels authentic.

For Jungermann, the act of bringing verisimilitude to lesbian storylines also has everything to do with relatability—most notable in the age of her characters.

She's dubious about traditional television's interest in LGBTQ people past a certain age saying, "I don't know if networks or cable are ready for a lesbian show about a gay lady approaching 40."

But she's used her two web series, *The Slope* and *F to the 7th*, to represent a broader range of gay characters. While networks continue to employ mustachioed hipsters and Naya Rivera-lookalikes in gay and lesbian roles, women like Rubin and Jungermann cast a refreshingly matter-of-fact (and touchingly amusing) light on LGBTQ culture.

On the lighter, though no less meaningful, side of women bringing innovative comedy to digital television are series like *Ghost Ghirls* and *Seeking the Web Series*. The women behind (and starring in) these shows each bring their own exciting additions to TV culture.

When Amanda Lund and Maria Blasucci co-wrote, executive produced and co-starred in *Ghost Ghirls* for Yahoo! Screen, they brought a whole new genre of comedy to the table: the ghost hunter spoof. Their deadpan delivery, sharp dialogue, and seamless rapport with impressive guest stars like Molly Shannon and Bob Odenkirk shot this Jack Black co-production to viral fame and made many wonder how something like it had never been done before.

With her own series, *Seeking*, up-and-comer Ronit Aranoff is also bringing something undeniably refreshing to comedy by updating the stale genre of rom-coms through crowdsourcing.

She wanted to tell what she calls "real life dating stories" by pulling from strangers' lives; to make an engaging comedy by using stories that literally happened to real, live people—and not just the oft-bland fictional people whose stories you're used to hearing.

"I was tired of watching shows that told stories of a very small cross-section of the population," says Aranoff, "So I decided to ask everyone across age, race, ethnicity, socioeconomic background, [and] religion what their dating experiences were. We're so proud that it's a show about everyone's story." Because of this deeply human framework, *Seeking* never feels contrived. Even when the storylines are silly, it somehow manages to make the silliness ring true—freaky Confederate hipsters and all.

The individual reasons women head online to exert their creative energy may vary, but they usually fall into two broad categories: accessibility and creative freedom.

The most obvious benefit of going digital (as every film school student with a sock puppet and a borrowed Handycam knows) is the low barrier for entry. Anyone who can rent a camera and sign up for a YouTube account is free to start a show—though, of course, it helps if you've got something interesting to say. The lower barrier of entry for web series has a lot to do with money, of course, but it also has to do with rules and permission.

Making a network TV show is one giant rule-following, permission-seeking party. The process of how to submit spec scripts and proofs of concept, the political back-and-forth with executives and all the spoken and unspoken rules to follow before you even go so far as to make that first exploratory contact can stop creators before they've even begun. If you hear back at all from a network, what you hear will probably be a "no."

But as Aranoff so blithely puts it, with digital content, "the only person you have to wait for a yes from is yourself."

When it comes down to it, many women creators get into digital content because it feels like the only option, which is hard to believe considering they're bringing us some of the most exciting, hilarious, and emotionally brave content out there. Even Jack Black's main gals, Lund and Blasucci, fell into this camp before they got hooked up with Black's production company.

"We started writing and making web shorts because we couldn't get any auditions," says Lund. "It was kind of a last resort that we also really enjoyed."

With self-directed digital content, the "yes's and no's" and rules of Hollywood are moot, fostering an environment that's a lot more comfortable to many creatives.

Jungermann remarks that "the web series form is perfect for people who are comfortable making their own rules." Many of the women in web series are excited about finally being able to do their own thing, playing by their own rules.

"*Seeking* is on my terms and I'm really proud of that," says Aranoff.

Jungermann's personal tactic for making content (which seems like something that applies to many web series creators) is to "reshape ideas in a way I can understand them, rely on humility and honesty and hope that whatever I put out there will be understood." A decidedly more zen approach to content creation than you would find from any network executive.

The digital realm is not only a creatively fulfilling place for writers and producers, but for whole casts and crews. The deeper sense of ownership and creative control that comes with going independent and digital can also lead to a greater sense of community for everyone on set. According to Grob, the set of *East WillyB* really felt this impact.

"There was a real family, community energy to the series," she says. "Everyone felt like they were contributing to something very special, a series that was unlike anything that ever existed before, so they gave everything to [it]."

Rubin also experienced the innate sense of community that comes with independent productions on the set of *Little Horribles*.

"Anything indie—which is more the defining factor than it being for web or TV—[is] a really collaborative environment," she says. "There's no client, no studio—it's just about making something everyone feels good about." And that's something viewers can in turn feel good about, too.

Of course, for every benefit of going digital, there's a corollary negative aspect; nothing as beautiful as creative control and freedom of expression comes without a cost. While digital content is inclusive, democratic, and exhilarating in its endless possibilities, it's also unstable. Web series are rarely lucrative and the format is still struggling to gain the recognition it deserves from advertisers and TV's power players.

"I think the web is a great place to explore your creative voice, experiment artistically, learn, and show 'proof of concept' of what you are capable of," says Grob. "It's a very hard place to make money, though. That is the largest challenge indie creators face."

Money continues to be a big issue for web series producers, even as the medium gains popularity among viewers and consideration among critics. Sure, web series are easier to make on the cheap than a multi-cam sitcom, but there's still the need for capital to get that Handycam recording. The trouble with digital content and the almighty dollar isn't just a concern for starving artists who need to pay their rent, either; it's also something viewers should be worried about. As Jungermann is quick to caution, "No matter what anyone says, making work without enough money is detrimental to creativity."

But as the struggles increase for these women, so do the rewards, which is what will keep the creative juices flowing through the web series genre for as long into the future as people have stories to tell. Lund puts it most eloquently when she remarks that holding all the creative power on a series is "way more rewarding . . . You just have this adrenaline kick when you're super passionate about a project. Like when a mother lifts a car up because her child is stuck under it. It's *exactly* like that."

In a way, though, all the common limits of web series are also a big part of what make them so special. A tiny budget, low space allotments, and limited mobility of a production can lead to appealingly intimate results. As creators like Jungermann have no choice but to "keep it small and focus on characters and writing," viewers get the benefit of seeing thoughtful, tightly written, and carefully pared down episodes that encompass only what they really need to. Nothing is stretched to fill time or cut down to allow for commercial breaks. Things just are the way they need to be, with a compelling story front and center. It's a refreshing departure from bombastic network shows with their extraneous sets and scene-stealing CGI. In contrast, an episode of a web series that takes place exclusively in someone's living room—but that feels as emotionally grand as any pearl-clutching scene from *Game of Thrones*—feels fresh.

And that freshness is leading to great strides for women in content creation. Issa Rae, unofficial queen of the web series genre, has built a digital content empire for herself, proving that it *is* possible to have a career in web content as a female minority. And though it feels a little bit like saying every computer science major has the ability to be the next Mark Zuckerberg (not quite realistic) the inclusivity of the space will continue to foster creative growth—and the hope is that financial sustainability isn't too far off. Rae, creator and star of *Awkward Black Girl*, believes this is the case.

"The corporate world has started to embrace digital content in a major way," Rae says. "Companies and networks alike are scrambling to try to figure out the digital world and advertisers are putting out *a lot* more money toward digital content than they were before. The first web series I took seriously (*Fly Guys present The 'F' Word*) was back in 2009, and I remember asking a colleague about trying to get sponsorships and hopefully taking the series to television. She told me nobody was checking for the web, and that there was no money there. She said my best bet was to go the traditional route. That was only five years ago and things have done a 180."

Hollywood's gender and diversity gaps, both in front of and behind the camera, narrow year by year. And though the stats have a long way to go before they're anything close to equal, it's not unreasonable to question how much longer network executives can ignore all of the incredibly talented women out there (though Comedy Central's adoption of Abbi Jacobson and Ilana Glazer's web series, *Broad City*, was a step in the right direction.)

As much as this is about feminism and equality and fairly recognizing talent where recognition is due

("It shouldn't be a newsflash in 2014 that we are hilarious!" jokes Aranoff), the truth is that traditional TV production is largely about money—and good talent and good content lead to good money.

Perhaps this will come as digital content continues to gain respect and raise its profile with critics and the general viewing public. Lund agrees, "I think digital content and traditional TV are eventually going to be indistinguishable. Digital content is now equal to, if not far beyond, the quality of TV. Shows that Netflix does like *Orange is the New Black* and *House of Cards* are better than most shows on TV."

Rubin's also optimistic that the distinction between digital and traditional television is on the way out. She says, bluntly, "It's all just content." If the critics are behind it, and the creators, screenwriters, and actors are behind it, then digital content is well on its way.

As frustrating as it can be for creatives trying to make their voices heard online (according to Grob, to sustain a web series financially you need to aim for at least 100,000 views per episode—no small feat), the tides are indeed changing. Maybe the eventual financial success of web series will rely on the continued expansion of streaming services like Netflix, Hulu, Amazon Prime, and *Ghost Ghirls'* home base Yahoo! Screen. The global takeover of these services does seem kind of impending. Netflix's subscribership gains points each year while HBO's and Amazon Prime's original content gets sharper and more critically acclaimed with each new pilot season.

Techno-financial wizards are working on new ways to eek dollars out of online video, and general awareness about the high quality of web content continues to grow. Perhaps in ten years' time, it'll be possible for new digital content creators to skip the aspiration of traditional television altogether and spend their time appealing to the likes of Reed Hastings instead of Richard Plepler.

In the meantime, these women's work is smart, hilarious and often brave, and it's going to shape the TV landscape of the future in big ways. These are the women the networks need to watch.

Hannah McIlveen writes on a wide range of topics for *Lydia Magazine*, an online journal targeted to women in their 20s and early 30s. All articles are by women and about women, and McIlveen's articles span a range of popular culture topics.

Martha M. Lauzen

Boxed In: Portrayals of Female Characters and Employment of Behind-the-Scenes Women in 2014–15 Prime-time Television

In 2014–15, female characters comprised 42% of all speaking characters on broadcast television programs and 40% of all characters on broadcast, cable, and Netflix programs.

Behind the scenes, women accounted for 27% of creators, directors, writers, producers, executive producers, editors, and directors of photography working on broadcast programs and 25% of those working in these key roles on broadcast, cable, and Netflix programs.

Programs with at least one woman executive producer or creator featured a higher percentage of female characters and employed substantially greater percentages of women writers, directors, and editors than programs with exclusively male executive producers or creators. For example, on broadcast programs with no women executive producers, females accounted for 37% of major characters. On programs with at least one woman executive producer, females comprised 43% of major characters.

On broadcast programs with no women executive producers, women accounted for 6% of writers. On programs with at least one woman executive producer, women comprised 32% of writers.

The findings in this year's report are divided into two major sections. The first section provides the on-screen and behind-the-scenes findings for the broadcast networks, offering historical comparisons for 2014–15 with figures dating from 1997–98. This section also includes an overview of important relationships between women in key behind-the-scenes roles such as executive producers and creators, and the representation of female characters and employment of women as writers, directors, and editors.

The second section provides the behind-the-scenes and on-screen findings for the total sample of programs appearing on the broadcast networks, basic and pay cable (A&E, AMC, FX, History, TNT, USA, HBO, Showtime), and

Netflix, and includes a summary of important on-screen and behind-the-scenes relationships.

The study examines one randomly selected episode of every series. Random selection is a frequently used and widely accepted method of sampling episodes from the population of episodes in a season.

Findings for Broadcast Networks

Females on Screen

- 42% of all speaking characters and 42% of major characters were female in 2014–15. This represents no change from 2013–14, but an increase of 3 percentage points from 1997–98.
- Programs airing on ABC featured the highest percentage of female characters (45%), followed by CW (43%), NBC and Fox (40%), and CBS (39%).
- Reality programs were more likely to feature female characters than programs in other genres. Females comprised 47% of characters on reality programs, 41% of characters on situation comedies, and 40% of characters on dramas.
- Female characters continue to be portrayed as younger than their male counterparts. The majority of female characters were in their 20s and 30s (60%), whereas the majority of male characters were in their 30s and 40s (55%).
- Female characters experience a precipitous decline in numbers from their 30s to their 40s. 31% of female characters were in their 30s but only 18% were in their 40s. Male characters also experience a decline but it is not as dramatic (from 30% to 25%).
- Few female or male characters age past 60. Only 2% of female and 4% of male characters were in their 60s or above.

- 77% of female characters were white, 15% were African-American, 3% were Latina, 4% were Asian, and 1% were of some other race or ethnicity.
- Viewers were less likely to know the occupational status of female characters than male characters. 35% of female characters but only 24% of male characters had an unknown occupational status.

Women Behind the Scenes

- In 2014–15, women comprised 27% of all individuals working as creators, directors, writers, producers, executive producers, editors, and directors of photography. This represents no change from 2013–14 and an increase of 6 percentage points since 1997–98.
- Overall, women fared best as producers (38%), followed by writers (26%), executive producers (26%), creators (23%), editors (21%), directors (14%), and directors of photography (2%).
- 45% of programs employed 4 or fewer women in the roles considered. Only 4% of programs employed 4 or fewer men.
- Women comprised 23% of creators. This represents an increase of 3 percentage points from 2013–14 and an increase of 5 percentage points from 1997–98.
- Women accounted for 26% of executive producers. This represents an increase of 3 percentage points from 2013–14 and an increase of 7 percentage points since 1997–98.
- Women comprised 38% of producers. This represents a decrease of 5 percentage points from 2013–14, and represents an increase of 9 percentage points since 1997–98.
- Women accounted for 26% of writers. This represents an increase of 1 percentage point from 2013–14 and an increase of 6 percentage points since 1997–98.
- Women comprised 14% of directors. This represents an increase of 1 percentage point from 2013–14, and an increase of 6 percentage points since 1997–98.
- Women accounted for 21% of editors. This represents an increase of 4 percentage points from 2013–14, and an increase of 6 percentage points since 1997–98.
- Women comprised 2% of directors of photography. This represents no change from 2013–14 and an increase of 2 percentage points since 1997–98.
- 70% of the episodes considered had no female creators, 86% had no female directors, 70% had no female writers, 78% had no female editors, and 98% had no female directors of photography.

Important Relationships

- Broadcast programs with at least one woman executive producer featured more female characters and employed more women directors, writers, and editors than programs with no women executive producers.
- On programs with at least one woman executive producer, females comprised 43% of major characters. On programs with no women executive producers, females accounted for 37% of characters.
- On programs with at least one woman executive producer, women accounted for 32% of writers, compared to 6% of writers on programs with no women executive producers.
- On programs with at least one woman executive producer, women accounted for 15% of directors, compared to 9% of directors on programs with no women executive producers.
- On programs with at least one woman executive producer, women accounted for 25% of editors. On programs with no women executive producers, women comprised 13% of editors.
- Programs with at least one woman creator featured more female characters and employed more women directors, writers, and editors than programs with no women creators.
- On programs with at least one woman creator, females accounted for 45% of major characters. On programs with no women creators, females comprised 41% of major characters.
- On programs with at least one woman creator, women accounted for 50% of writers. On programs with no women creators, women comprised 15% of writers.
- On programs with at least one woman creator, women accounted for 23% of directors. On programs with no women creators, women comprised 10% of directors.
- On programs with at least one woman creator, women accounted for 36% of editors. On programs with no women creators, women comprised 14% of editors.

Findings for Broadcast Networks, Cable & Netflix Programs

On Screen Females

- Females accounted for 40% of all speaking characters and 40% of major characters.
- 78% of female characters were white, 13% were African American, 4% were Latina, 4% were Asian, and 1% were of some other race or ethnicity.

- The majority of female characters (60%) were in their 20s and 30s. The majority of male characters (57%) were in their 30s and 40s. The percentage of female characters drops dramatically from their 30s to their 40s. 32% of female characters were in their 30s but only 19% of female characters were in their 40s. Male characters experienced only a slight decline in numbers (from 29% to 28%).
- Male characters were much more likely than female characters to be seen working. 55% of male characters and 43% of female characters were seen at work and working.

Behind-the-Scenes Women

- Women comprised 25% of individuals in key behind-the-scenes roles on programs airing on the broadcast networks and cable channels, and available through Netflix in 2014–2015. This figure represents no change from 2013–14 and a decline of 1 percentage point from 2012–13.
- Women fared best as producers (38%), followed by writers (25%), executive producers (23%), creators (22%), editors (20%), directors (12%), and directors of photography (1%).
- 57% of the programs employed 4 or fewer women. Only 5% of programs employed 4 or fewer men.
- Women comprised 22% of creators. This represents an increase of 3 percentage points from 2013–14.
- Women accounted for 23% of executive producers. This represents an increase of 2 percentage points from 2013–14.
- Women comprised 38% of producers. This represents a decline of 2 percentage points from 2013–14.
- Women accounted for 25% of writers, a decline of ƒ1 percentage point from 2013–14.
- Women comprised 12% of directors. This represents a decrease of 1 percentage point from 2013–14.
- Women accounted for 20% of editors. This represents an increase of 4 percentage points from 2013–14.
- Women comprised 1% of directors of photography. This represents no change from 2013–14.

Important Relationships

- Broadcast and cable programs with at least one woman executive producer featured more female characters and employed more women directors, writers, and editors than programs with no women executive producers.
- On programs with at least one woman executive producer, females comprised 42% of major characters. On programs with no women executive producers, females accounted for 35% of major characters.
- On programs with at least one woman executive producer, women comprised 12% of directors, compared with 11% of directors on programs with no women executive producers.
- On programs with at least one woman executive producer, women accounted for 32% of writers, compared with 8% on programs with no women executive producers.
- On programs with at least one women executive producer, women comprised 24% of editors, compared with 12% on programs with no women executive producers.
- Broadcast and cable programs with at least one woman creator featured more female characters and employed more women directors, writers, and editors than programs with no female creators.
- On programs with at least one woman creator, females accounted for 46% of major characters. On programs with no women creators, females comprised 39% of major characters.
- On programs with at least one woman creator, women comprised 49% of writers, compared with 15% on programs with no women creators.
- On programs with at least one woman creator, women accounted for 18% of directors, compared with 10% on programs with no women creators.
- On programs with at least one woman creator, women accounted for 37% of editors, compared with 13% of editors on programs with no women creators.

Martha M. Lauzen is a professor in the School of Theatre, Television, and Film at San Diego State University. Her annual report, *Boxed In*, has been providing current data on women in prime-time television in front of and behind the camera for over 18 years.

EXPLORING THE ISSUE

Have More Women Become Involved as Decision Makers in Media Industries?

Critical Thinking and Reflection

1. What harm is there, and who is harmed by perpetuating media images of society that focus on men and marginalize women or other groups?
2. Can new distribution forms of technology change the way marginalized groups get access to audiences?
3. Can new business models be created that disrupt traditional career opportunities and result in a greater range or equitable distribution of upper-level decision-making jobs in media?
4. How might issues of the "pay gap" among different groups be addressed more systematically in society?
5. What can women do to become better advocates for themselves, and what can men do to support greater equity for women in the workplace?

Is There Common Ground?

The authors of these two selections agree that the status quo is not acceptable for women in the workplace, but differ on the possibilities for the future. Martha M. Lauzen's *Boxed In* study for 2014–2015 shows that there is still a huge gender gap in the creative jobs in television, and that women still remain underrepresented in prime-time television.

Hannah McIlveen focuses on a specific emerging form of media in terms of Web content, and describes how dynamic women are becoming in this new medium. She also asserts that when women are creative and productive, traditional media executives sit up and take notice, thereby offering some hope that alternative distribution forms for media may be the way change ultimately comes about. It may be too soon to see how Web content disrupts the media industries, but at least she offers some hope for change.

Gender and pay inequity is a problem in all fields, and the media industries are no exception, but the media industries are in a prime position to publicize change in terms of what they produce. Both women and men have to be aware of these problems and make concerted efforts to create opportunities for everyone in a media landscape that is increasingly serving niche audiences. Awareness of the problem is the first hurdle to tackle.

Additional Resources

Linda Babcock and Sara Laschever, *Women Don't Ask: Negotiation and the Gender Divide* (Bantam, 2007). This book provides useful tips to women on negotiating salary and job opportunities.

Andrew Dawson and Sean P. Holmes, *Working in the Global Film and Television Industries: Creativity, Systems, Space, Patronage,* (Bloomsbury Academic, 2012). This survey of labor opportunities in media reflects cultural values that influence how, why, and when women are treated fairly.

Suzanne Franks, *Women and Journalism* (Reuters Institute for the Study of Journalism at Oxford University, 2013). This study examines opportunities for women in the field of journalism, and discusses the gender pay gap.

Lois P. Frankel, *Nice Girls Don't Get the Corner Office: Unconscious Mistakes Women Make That Sabotage Their Careers* (Business Plus, 2014). This is a self-help book that shows behaviors that keep women from being assertive in male-dominated workplaces.

Internet References . . .

Geena Davis Institute on Gender in Media

http://seejane.org/

Half the Sky Movement

www.halftheskymovement.org/

International Women's Media Center

www.iwmf.org/

Journalism and Women Symposium (JAWS)

www.jaws.org/

Nieman Reports, "Where Are the Women?"

http://niemanreports.org/articles/where-are-the-women/

Selected, Edited, and with Issue Framing Material by:
Alison Alexander, *University of Georgia*
and
Jarice Hanson, *University of Massachusetts—Amherst*

ISSUE

Do Media Distort Representations of Islam and Arab Cultures?

YES: Wajahat Ali et al., from "Fear, Inc.: The Roots of the Islamophobia Network in America," Center for American Progress (August 2011)

NO: Gal Beckerman, from "The New Arab Conversation," *Columbia Journalism Review* (January/February, 2007)

Learning Outcomes

After reading this issue, you will be able to:

- Discuss the misrepresentation of Arab culture.
- Evaluate the possibility of blogs and other social media to combat stereotypes.
- Describe the ways in which journalistic practices promote stereotypes.
- Apply these concepts to stereotyping in society.

ISSUE SUMMARY

YES: Wajahat Ali, Eli Clifton, Matthew Duss, Lee Fang, Scott Keyes, and Faiz Shakir discuss in Fear, Inc., a special report from the Center for American Progress, how the Muslim religion is among the most maligned stereotypes in popular culture, and how these images have fueled misperceptions about the Arab world. It explores how media have been an echo chamber for misinformation created by well-funded groups dedicated to spreading fear and misinformation. These images influence politicians and citizens and contribute to public opinion.

NO: Journalist Gal Beckerman discusses how Arab bloggers from the Middle East are challenging popular stereotypes of Arab and Middle Eastern cultures. Because these bloggers are writing about their lives, the global public can read about their situations and understand them as individuals, rather than racial or ethnic group members.

Stereotypes and distorted images of racial, ethnic, and gender groups abound in the media, but can these images distract the public so severely that they influence political ideology? Our history of understanding the impact of racial profiling, based on stereotypes that distort what is commonly called "the Other," indicates that these stereotypes can have multiple harmful effects. Throughout American popular culture, we have seen how different groups portrayed in the media contribute to public opinion of groups for whom we have little or no firsthand understanding.

It has been said that despite recent sensitivity to multiculturalism and a growing call for respect for people of other races and ethnicities, the image of the Arab still represents evil. No doubt our multiyear wars with people in Iraq and Afghanistan have contributed to a misunderstanding of who or what our military troops are fighting, and for what purpose, but the conflation of the people of the Middle East with "the enemy" is an example of how powerful stereotypes can be.

Journalist Gal Beckerman focuses on the impact of bloggers and the ability of these individuals to get personal messages out to others beyond geographic borders. Despite the Arab world's limited Internet access, Beckerman finds blogs represent humane voices in a sea of confusion. The contrast of the individual bloggers' messages compared to the mainstream Arab media provides one point of departure for getting to know "the Other" in a more intimate way, but at the same time, as Beckerman writes, "the Middle East is a region where the historical and the personal slam up against each other daily in a way they do only once a decade or so in America." In the voices of bloggers, we get to know the daily beliefs, frustrations, and humanity of "the Other." In knowing "the Other," simplistic stereotypes become harder to maintain.

If stereotypes could be managed by simply coming to know the people behind the image, perhaps social media could erase the misperceptions. The Center for American Progress fears that powerful forces are at work that will prevent that resolution. Fear, Inc. argues that misrepresentations and stereotypes are encouraged in the United States by a small group of anti-Muslim organizations and individuals. Quoted elsewhere in the article is a report on the organization Stop Islamization of America, which the Anti-Defamation League concluded "promotes a conspiratorial anti-Muslim agenda under the guise of fighting radical Islam." Much of the power of these groups comes from what Fear, Inc. describes as a well-developed right-wing media echo chamber that amplifies a few marginal voices. Explicitly, this report names *The Rush Limbaugh Show, The Sean Hannity Show*, and the Fox Network among others.

In evaluating this claim, it is important to understand some of the internal practices of news organizations. Classically, *balance* in news stories is achieved by representing both sides of an issue. To display balance in a newspaper story, stories on controversial issues may often be represented by quotes from both supporters and dissenters. Fairness can also be achieved by presenting both sides in a news story. This is a traditional journalistic practice. Editorials are a different matter in that they typically state an opinion and build an argument for that opinion's validity. Currently, television and radio are full of talk shows that highlight certain points of view or focus on bringing opposing voices together. Why are there so many of these types of shows? Quoted elsewhere in this volume is a telling phrase, "News is expensive, opinion is cheap." Shows that bring in politicians and pundits are not expensive. In addition, they function to allow those with a point of view to build their argument for the American public. To promote robust and hard-hitting debate, hosts look for individuals with controversial points of view. When the show itself has a point of view, hosts again look to controversial figures to challenge prevailing opinion and to perhaps shape it in their direction. These are the conditions under which a few voices promote anti-Muslim sentiment in America.

This issue brings up more than the question of the power of stereotyping in the media: It asks us to determine the underlying intent that is creating these stereotypes. It makes us ask whether the images in media really matter to us, where these images come from, and whether different types of media can communicate more effectively than others depending upon the content. Anytime we are challenged to question our own beliefs, and how those beliefs may be influenced by media, we get one step closer to understanding the complexity of media images, media forms, and how we, individually and collectively, understand our place and role in society.

Whenever we deal with issues of stereotypes and whether they do or do not influence our perceptions of people in society, we broach the uncomfortable area of human biases and prejudices. We know that media do indeed shape our sense of self and how we "fit" our own culture, but what if you are a person who does not see images of people who look like you, or who share your traditions, heritage, race, ethnicity, gender, or religion in media? The people who are not portrayed and the images we don't see are just as important as the distorted images that we do see. Absence of accurate images can be as harmful as the presence of distorted images. Gaye Tuchman, a sociologist of media, called it "symbolic annihilation."

The most insidious thing about stereotypes is that we seldom question whether they are accurate or not, and yet questioning the images we see in media is one of the most important features of understanding media's relationship to society. There is evidence that U.S. media have improved in terms of portrayals of African Americans, Hispanics, and Asians, and images of gays and lesbians are starting to improve; but as these selections show, accurate representations of Arabs in the mainstream media still have a long way to go.

Perhaps blogging or alternative media will lead the way.

YES

Wajahat Ali et al.

Fear, Inc.: The Roots of the Islamophobia Network in America

Introduction and Summary

On July 22, a man planted a bomb in an Oslo government building that killed eight people. A few hours after the explosion, he shot and killed 68 people, mostly teenagers, at a Labor Party youth camp on Norway's Utoya Island.

By midday, pundits were speculating as to who had perpetrated the greatest massacre in Norwegian history since World War II. Numerous mainstream media outlets, including *The New York Times*, *The Washington Post*, and *The Atlantic*, speculated about an Al Qaeda connection and a "jihadist" motivation behind the attacks. But by the next morning it was clear that the attacker was a 32-year-old, white, blond-haired and blue-eyed Norwegian named Anders Breivik. He was not a Muslim, but rather a self-described Christian conservative.

According to his attorney, Breivik claimed responsibility for his self-described "gruesome but necessary" actions. On July 26, Breivik told the court that violence was "necessary" to save Europe from Marxism and "Muslimization." In his 1,500-page manifesto, which meticulously details his attack methods and aims to inspire others to extremist violence, Breivik vows "brutal and breathtaking operations which will result in casualties" to fight the alleged "ongoing Islamic Colonization of Europe."

Breivik's manifesto contains numerous footnotes and in-text citations to American bloggers and pundits, quoting them as experts on Islam's "war against the West." This small group of anti-Muslim organizations and individuals in our nation is obscure to most Americans but wields great influence in shaping the national and international political debate. Their names are heralded within communities that are actively organizing against Islam and targeting Muslims in the United States. . . .

While these bloggers and pundits were not responsible for Breivik's deadly attacks, their writings on Islam and multiculturalism appear to have helped create a world view, held by this lone Norwegian gunman, that sees Islam as at war with the West and the West needing to be defended. According to former CIA officer and terrorism consultant Marc Sageman, just as religious extremism "is the infrastructure from which Al Qaeda emerged," the writings of these anti-Muslim misinformation experts are "the infrastructure from which Breivik emerged." Sageman adds that their rhetoric "is not cost-free." . . .

This network of hate is not a new presence in the United States. Indeed, its ability to organize, coordinate, and disseminate its ideology through grassroots organizations increased dramatically over the past 10 years. Furthermore, its ability to influence politicians' talking points and wedge issues for the upcoming 2012 elections has mainstreamed what was once considered fringe, extremist rhetoric.

And it all starts with the money flowing from a select group of foundations. A small group of foundations and wealthy donors are the lifeblood of the Islamophobia network in America, providing critical funding to a clutch of right-wing think tanks that peddle hate and fear of Muslims and Islam—in the form of books, reports, websites, blogs, and carefully crafted talking points that anti-Islam grassroots organizations and some right-wing religious groups use as propaganda for their constituency.

The Right-Wing Media Enablers of Anti-Islam Propaganda

Spreading anti-Muslim hate in America depends on a well-developed right-wing media echo chamber to amplify a few marginal voices. The think tank misinformation experts and grassroots and religious-right organizations profiled in this report boast a symbiotic relationship with a loosely aligned, ideologically-akin group of right-wing blogs, magazines, radio stations, newspapers, and television news shows to spread their anti-Islam messages and myths. The media outlets, in turn, give members of this network the exposure needed to amplify their message, reach larger audiences, drive fundraising numbers, and grow their membership base.

Some well-established conservative media outlets are a key part of this echo chamber, mixing coverage of alarmist threats posed by the mere existence of Muslims in America with other news stories. Chief among the media partners are the Fox News empire, the influential conservative magazine National Review and its website, a host of right-wing radio hosts, *The Washington Times* newspaper and website, and the Christian Broadcasting Network and website.

Members of the Islamophobia network published articles or hit the airwaves this year and in 2010 to misinform our nation about Muslim American congregations. Here's a sampling.

- David Yerushalmi in *Middle East Quarterly* misinforms America that more than 80 percent of U.S. mosques advocate or promote violence.
- Frank Gaffney of the Center for Security Policy writes in *The Washington Times*:

"Most mosques in the United States are actually engaged in—or at least supportive of—a totalitarian, seditious agenda they call Shariah. Its express purpose is undermining and ultimately forcibly replacing the U.S. government and its founding documents. In their place would be a "caliph" governing in accordance with Shariah's political-military-legal code."

- Islamophobia grassroots organizer Pamela Geller says that "4 out of 5 mosques preach hate" on CNN Sunday Morning.
- Fox News commentator Bill O'Reilly, in an interview with Rep. Keith Ellison (D-MN) on the O'Reilly Factor, cites Frank Gaffney to charge that "violent extremism and sharia law is being condoned in 75 percent of the American Muslim mosques."
- Rep. Peter King (R-NY) says that "over 80 percent of the mosques in this country are controlled by radical Imams" on the Laura Ingraham Show. . . .

Let's look at each in turn.

Hate Radio

Anti-Muslim websites work in tandem with popular radio talk-show hosts who repeat and amplify the alarmist threats and conspiracy theories promoted by the blogs and their supporters. The industry of "hate radio" includes nationally known personalities such as Rush Limbaugh, Michael Savage, Glenn Beck, and others. Together, they use their programs as bully pulpits to preach anti-Muslim messages of intolerance and hate.

'The Rush Limbaugh Show'

Rush Limbaugh hosts the most popular radio talk show in America. "The Rush Limbaugh Show" is carried by more than 600 radio stations nationwide and is broadcast to more than 15 million listeners a week. Limbaugh, age 60, calls himself "America's anchorman" and "America's truth detector." He uses his highly influential radio pulpit to spread the word, and one of his favorite messages is casting suspicion on President Obama's religious identity. Limbaugh has called Obama "Imam Obamadinejad," said the president is into caliphate building, and that he might think of himself as the 12th imam.

Such claims have an effect. In 2010, nearly 18 percent of Americans incorrectly believed that President Obama was a Muslim, due in no small part to the media orchestration of such claims.

Limbaugh joins Pamela Geller and others as a vociferous critic of the Park51 community center in New York City. During the protests last summer, he compared Muslims building the community center to the Klu Klux Klan establishing a "memorial at Gettysburg." Limbaugh also charged that the community center was a "recruiting tool for foreign extremists," and repeated the talking point that organizers want the center to be a "victory monument at Ground Zero." Unfortunately Limbaugh's microphone will stay on for years to come. In 2008, he signed an eight-year, $400 million renewal contract with Clear Channel.

'The Sean Hannity Show'

The nation's second most popular talk show is "The Sean Hannity Show," a nationally syndicated talk-radio show that airs on Premiere Radio Networks and is hosted by Sean Hannity. Hannity, age 49, also hosts a cable-TV news show, "Hannity," on Fox News. Nearly 14 million listeners tune into Hannity's radio show each week to hear guests repeat the same talking points and conspiracy theories that can be heard on Limbaugh, Fox News, and other places. Questions abound about President Obama's religious affiliation, the Muslim Brotherhood infiltrating the Conservative Political Action Committee, and threats of homegrown terrorism in our midst. Listening to Hannity, one could hear Rep. Peter King (R-NY) agree with his host that 85 percent of mosques in America are run by Islamic fundamentalists after Hannity cited Steven Emerson and Daniel Pipes to prove his point.

'The Savage Nation'

Mike Savage hosts "The Savage Nation," another top-rated national radio program, which is syndicated through Talk Radio Network. More than 350 radio stations broadcast his show to nearly 9 million weekly listeners, putting him just behind Rush Limbaugh and Sean Hannity in ratings. Savage, 69, is known for his angry diatribes against minorities, including Muslims. On April 17, 2006, for example, he told listeners that Americans should "kill 100 million" Muslims. In October 2007 he said, "I don't wanna hear one more word about Islam. Take your religion and shove it up your behind. I'm sick of you." He then suggested that American Muslims be deported.

Along with Limbaugh, Savage promotes the myth that President Obama could be a secret Muslim. Before Obama was elected, Savage called him "Senator Barack Madrassas Obama." During the 2008 campaign, Savage said, "Now we have an unknown stealth candidate who went to a madrassa in Indonesia and, in fact, was a Muslim." Seeking to get "the facts," Savage insisted that "[w]e have a right to know if he's a so-called friendly Muslim or one who aspires to more radical teachings."

'The Glenn Beck Program'

Glenn Beck also has a popular radio show that is broadcast by more than 400 stations and syndicated by Premiere Radio

Networks. Beck's show ties with Savage's show for third place for national radio talk shows with more than 9 million listeners weekly. Beck, 47, conjures fears equating Muslims with terrorists and brings religion into the mix. Last December, he speculated on his show about the number of American Muslims who might be terrorists, saying: "Let's say it's half a percent of the U.S. population. That's being generous. What's that number? What is the number of Islamic terrorists, 1 percent? I think it's closer to 10 percent."

In February, one of Beck's guests was Joel Richardson, the apocalyptic author of the book *The Islamic Antichrist*. Richardson was on the show to discuss "Islam's Mahdi, the Antichrist, the Middle East and Bible prophecy." According to Richardson, the "Antichrist" will be a Muslim and Islam will be Satan's "primary vehicle" to usher the end of times. . . .

The Right-Wing Mainstream News Enablers of Islamophobia

Fox News has one of the biggest and most influential megaphones in TV news. It uses this megaphone to amplify anti-Muslim alarmist threats and conspiracy theories on a regular basis. Virtually all the leading Islamophobia players have made recurring appearances on popular Fox News programs, such as "Hannity," "The O'Reilly Factor," and "Fox & Friends." The cable news network also featured former Speaker of the House of Representatives Newt Gingrich as a commentator, which he uses to promote his increasingly Islamophobic opinions, such as his call for curbs on freedom of speech to keep terrorists from spreading their message after six imams were mistakenly removed from a Minneapolis flight in 2006.

On these shows, players echo one another's warnings and repeat with serious certainty the same threats they warned about on radio shows and in blogs, newspapers, online magazines, and more. Their staple threats include: Muslims imposing Sharia in America, Muslims establishing a global caliphate, Muslims engaging in homegrown jihad, and Muslims infiltrating President Obama's administration to promote dangerous Islamist agendas.

Gingrich in particular has made Sharia law his hobby horse. In September last year, for example, he told the audience at a Value Voters Summit in Washington, D.C., "We should have a federal law that says sharia law cannot be recognized by any court in the United States." Such a law will let judges know, Gingrich went on, that "no judge will remain in office that tried to use sharia law." These words prompted a standing ovation from the crowd.

Gingrich, age 68, is helping shift this once-fringe conspiracy about Sharia into the mainstream. He's doing so not just by spouting the network's talking points but also by endorsing their products: For instance, Gingrich narrated the fearmongering documentary "America at Risk," produced by the conservative Citizens United Productions, which warns of the threat of Sharia and Islamic extremism infiltrating America. Unsurprisingly, the documentary features Center for Security Policy's Frank Gaffney. Gingrich screened the movie at David Horowitz's Restoration Weekend in November 2010.

Gingrich's rhetoric has escalated to levels to where it is no longer logically consistent. In March, Gingrich bizarrely worried aloud that his two children would grow up in a "secular atheist country, potentially dominated by radical Islamists," suggesting that the country would be simultaneously run by Islamists and atheists.

Sadly, these scare tactics are working. It is not surprising that when alarmist threats are repeated with enough frequency through multiple outlets to millions of people with no rebuttal by like-minded leaders, that those threats become conventional wisdom. And so, the nonpartisan Public Religion Research Institute found in a recent poll that there was a strong correlation between holding erroneous views about Muslims and Islam and watching Fox News. These are correlative, not necessarily causative findings, but they are striking.

Specifically, the poll found that:

- Americans who most trust Fox News are more likely to believe that Muslims want to establish Sharia law, have not done enough to oppose extremism, and believe investigating Muslim extremism is a good idea.
- Nearly twice as many Republicans as Democrats believe that Muslims want to establish Sharia law in America, 31 percent to 15 percent. One-third of white evangelical Christians believe this compared to 20 percent of white protestants and 22 percent of white Catholics.
- More than three-quarters of those who most trust Fox News believe that Rep. Peter King's congressional hearings on Muslim radicalization were a good idea, compared to just 45 percent of those who most trust CNN, and 28 percent of those who most trust public television. . . .

National Review

National Review is a biweekly magazine founded in 1955 by influential conservative William F. Buckley Jr. It calls itself "America's most widely read and influential magazine and website for conservative news, commentary, and opinion." While *National Review* speaks to a more mainstream conservative audience than many of the media outlets described in this chapter, it also features writers and articles that raise alarmist warnings and threats about Muslims and Islam, though often in less apocalyptic language. . . .

National Review publishes pieces by Daniel Pipes in the magazine and on the website. In 1990 Pipes wrote: "Western European societies are unprepared for the massive immigration of brown-skinned peoples cooking strange foods and maintaining different standards of hygiene . . . All immigrants bring exotic customs and attitudes, but Muslim customs are more troublesome than most."

The Washington Times **and the Clarion Fund**

Then there is *The Washington Times*—a conservative daily newspaper and website created by Sun Myung Moon, founder of the Unification Church. *The Washington Times* promotes socially and politically conservative views and often features members of the Islamophobia network profiled in this report.Despite its small readership, *The Washington Times* punches well above its weight in the national media because many of the views it raises and voices it carries are picked up by media outlets with powerful megaphones, such as Fox News and conservative talk-radio shows, helping spread anti-Muslim messages into the larger public sphere. *The Washington Times*, for example, helped promote a flawed study about U.S. mosques written by David Yerushalmi. The newspaper's editorial page added to attacks against Park51 in August of 2010. And columnists from *The Washington Times* have contributed to the myth that President Obama is a Muslim.

The Clarion Fund is a New York City-based nonprofit organization that aims "to educate Americans about issues of national security" by focusing on "the threats of Radical Islam." The organization was founded by Canadian-Israeli film producer and Rabbi Raphael Shore. Although very little is known about its funding sources, evidence suggests that Chicago businessman Barre Seid may have contributed $17 million to the Clarion Fund to help bankroll the production and dissemination of the inflammatory anti-Muslim movie, "Obsession: Radical Islam's War on the West." The film "reveals an 'insider's view' of the hatred the Radicals are teaching, their incitement of global jihad, and their goal of world domination," according to the movie's own website. During the 2008 presidential campaign, 28 million DVDs of the movie were sent to 28 swing states. In addition, the film was cited in Breivik's manifesto.

The Clarion Fund also produced a documentary, "The Third Jihad," narrated by Zudhi Jasser and briefly used to train NYPD officers on counterterrorism. After seeing the video, a police officer said, "It was so ridiculously one-sided. It just made Muslims look like the enemy. It was straight propaganda."

How the Anti-Muslim Media Work Together

These right-wing media outlets play a major role in pushing out a playlist of nonexistent Sharia threats, Islamic takeovers of the world, extremist Muslim infiltration into society and government, and more. As we demonstrate in the next chapter of this report, politicians at the national, state, and local levels rely on these media enablers to spread their anti-Muslim messages to conservative grass-roots and religious-right groups, helping them to raise campaign funds and get voters to the polls.

By taking extreme anti-Islam views from fringe blogs to radio shows all the way to national television shows, anti-Muslim voices and views gain legitimacy and credibility. [A] network of anti-Muslim forces created a set of false facts to raise a national controversy over the establishment of a Muslim community center in lower New York City—the so-called Ground Zero mosque. [T]he Islamophobia network's media outlets successfully manufactured hysteria surrounding the community center in the summer of 2010.

Pamela Geller introduced the controversy on December 8, 2009, in her blog, Atlas Shrugs. Within two weeks Geller was calling the community center the "mosque at Ground Zero," even though it was not a mosque and was not located at Ground Zero.

Interestingly, Fox News was not initially opposed to the project. On Dec. 21, 2009, Fox News host Laura Ingraham invited Daisy Khan, the wife of Imam Feisal Abdul Rauf, one of the center's lead organizers, to discuss the proposed community center. Ingraham said, "I can't find many people who really have a problem with it." She added, "I like what you're trying to do."

Even so, Geller continued to manufacture hysteria around the center and its alleged proximity to Ground Zero. At a May 2010 Tea Party convention in Tennessee, Geller called the center "the ultimate flag of conquest" and "a shrine to the very ideology that inspired the jihadist attacks at Ground Zero." A few days later, she posted "Vote on Mega Mosque at Ground Zero" on her blog.

Geller claimed the Park51 organizers planned to "leverage" the mosque's proximity to Ground Zero to proselytize and "grow the Muslim community." She also said that Imam Rauf "embraced" Sharia, which she described as "brutal policies that discriminate against women, gays, and religious minorities."

Throughout the summer, the Islamophobia network was amplifying Geller's accusations and pushing them out via radio shows and other outlets. On his radio show in August, Glenn Beck called the Park51 center "the 9-11 mosque." That same month, Rush Limbaugh told millions of listeners that the community center was a "recruiting tool for foreign extremists," and a "victory monument at Ground Zero." And Geller went on Hannity's Fox News show to declare the center a "provocative mega mosque" that aimed to "trample on the grief of 9-11 families and all Americans.

Islamophobia leaders added to the frenzy, appearing on mainstream TV news channels to hold forth about the community center. Brigitte Gabriel, founder of ACT! for America, did her part when she appeared on Sean Hannity's Fox News show and said the center was a "project to advance Islam" and a "slap in the face." Gabriel also claimed that the "Muslim world operates on symbols, everything has to be symbolic. And this—they chose this place in particular because of the symbol it represents to the Arabic world."

In December 2010, well after the summer had ended and plans for the community center were being revised, Frank Gaffney went on Fox News and scolded the network for underestimating the threat of "stealth jihad" that mosques were introducing in America. Gaffney linked the "Ground Zero Mosque" to his favorite threat, Sharia, claiming that "a mosque that is used to promote a seditious program, which is what Sharia is . . . that is not a protected religious practice, that is in fact sedition."

This example of how the Islamophobia network's leaders and media enablers turned a local zoning case into a national controversy provides a reason as to why many right-wing politicians are so eager to parrot anti-Muslim attacks: They raise funds and get conservative voters to the polls. . . .

WAJAHAT ALI is a Researcher at the Center for American Progress and a Researcher for the Center for American Progress Action Fund.

ELI CLIFTON is a Researcher at the Center for American Progress and a National Security Reporter for the Center for American Progress Action Fund and ThinkProgress.org.

MATTHEW DUSS is a Policy Analyst at the Center for American Progress and the Director of the Center's Middle East Progress.

LEE FANG is a Researcher at the Center for American Progress and an Investigative Researcher/Blogger for the Center for American Progress Action Fund and ThinkProgress.org.

SCOTT KEYES is a Researcher at the Center for American Progress and an Investigative Researcher for ThinkProgress.org at the Center for American Progress Action Fund.

FAIZ SHAKIR is a Vice President at the Center for American Progress and serves as Editor-in-Chief of ThinkProgress.org. Faiz has previously worked as a Research Associate for the Democratic National Committee, as a Legislative Aide to Sen. Bob Graham (D-FL) on the Senate Veterans Affairs Committee, and as a Communications Aide in the White House Office of National Drug Control Policy.

Gal Beckerman

The New Arab Conversation

Bombs don't discriminate between combatants and children. This sad fact became an inconvenient one last summer [2006] for Israel, which had maintained that its bombing of Lebanon was solely an attack on Hezbollah, the Shiite militia that had kidnapped two Israeli soldiers and menaced the Jewish state's northern border. To an anxious Lebanese population who'd seen most of their country's south reduced to a parking lot, Israel's persistent message—We are doing this for your own good—rang increasingly hollow.

By the beginning of August, the French and American ambassadors to the United Nations had finally hammered out a cease-fire resolution. But as the Security Council prepared to vote, the Lebanese government and the Arab League declared that the agreement was too favorable to Israel. A tense and edgy delegation arrived in New York on August 8 to plead the Arab case.

Dan Gillerman, the Israeli ambassador to the UN, didn't have to do much at those deliberations—simply listen to the complaints, appear to be the least obstructionist in the room, and restate his country's position, as absurd as it may have sounded by that point, that Israel's bombs were in fact helping the Lebanese people to free themselves from the "cancer" of Hezbollah that had metastasized in their midst. In this last task, he had an unusual ally: "I believe that one courageous Lebanese youngster was speaking for many when he wrote in his Internet blog, and I quote, 'It is not only Israeli soldiers that the Hezbollah has taken hostage. It is us, the people of Lebanon.'"

This "Lebanese youngster" was, of course, a blogger, and maybe the first to have his words bounce off the solemn walls of the United Nations. And though he probably would not have appreciated being deployed as a weapon in Israel's public-relations war, the presence of his independent voice, a counterintuitive opinion not filtered through any official source, said a lot about the power of Middle Eastern Web logs to expose a hidden trove of multiple perspectives in a world that the West often imagines as having only one perspective—that of the "Arab Street," a place of conformity, of mass acquiescence to singular passions, be they blind support for a dictator or seething hatred of Israel.

Last summer was, in fact, a watershed moment for the Middle Eastern blogosphere. The conflict between Israel and Hezbollah not only brought attention to the many different Arab conversations that had taken place on homemade Web sites in the past two or three years, but also launched thousands more of them. And they were more than just a handful of aberrant voices. They reflected a new culture of openness, dialogue, and questioning. And unlike the neoconservative notion that these ideals can be dropped on a foreign population like so many bomblets, the push for change here is coming from within. Whether it is a Jordanian student discussing the taboo subject of the monarchy's viability or a Saudi woman writing about her sexual experiences or an Egyptian commenting with sadness at an Israeli blogger's description of a suicide bombing, each of these unprecedented acts is one small move toward opening up these societies.

The Arab blogosphere has been growing for a few years now, though not at a particularly quick pace. Only 10 percent of the Arab world has Internet access, yet that is a five-fold increase from 2000. Of course, not all Arab blogs are about liberalizing Arab society. Some use the technology as another front in the jihad against the West being waged by groups like Al Qaeda. One, Irhabi 007, who was recently profiled in *The Atlantic Monthly,* created Web sites to disseminate videos of beheadings and insurgent attacks on U.S. forces in Iraq. Most analysts and bloggers put the number of Arab bloggers at fewer than 25,000. Of those, a majority blog in Arabic. And though there are surely interesting discussions happening on those sites, Arab bloggers themselves say that a particularly interesting alternative space is being formed on the sites composed in English. Now aggregated on blogging portals like iToot.net and enhanced by the YouTube-like Web site Ikbis, it is in this community of people who are self-consciously half-turned toward the West that one can feel the breathing becoming easier.

Those bloggers are people like Roba Al-Assi, a twenty-one-year-old design student in Amman, Jordan, who recently wrote about her opposition to the death penalty for Saddam Hussein:

> It is the premeditated and cold-blooded killing of a human being by the state in the name of justice (I know he killed thousands, but it is in my moral fabric to be better than others. Throw him in jail for the rest of his life, that's a lot worse than death).

Or the Egyptian blogger who calls himself Big Pharaoh, a twenty-seven-year-old graduate of the American University in Cairo, who expressed his support for the Egyptian culture minister who was criticized for stating that he thought the hijab, the traditional woman's head covering worn by some Muslim women, was "regressive":

> There are numerous things that make me proud of this country. How the country descended into such stupidity, ignorance, and darkness is definitely not among them. I feel like vomiting every time I think about how this man was virulently attacked for merely stating his opinion on a thing as stupid as the hair cover.

Or Laila El-Haddad, who, on her blog, "Unplugged: Diary of a Palestinian Mother," describes herself as a "journalist, mom, occupied Palestinian—all packed into one," and posted this account of crossing at Rafah from Egypt back into Gaza, after waiting in limbo for weeks for the border to open:

> Some wailed in exhaustion, others fainted; still others cracked dry humor, trying to pass the time. We stood, thousands of us, packed together elbow to elbow like cattle, penned in between steel barriers on one end, and riot-geared Egyptian security guards on the perimeter, who were given orders not to allow anyone through until they hear otherwise from the Israelis—and to respond with force if anyone dared.

In the American blogosphere, opinions and life tales blossom a millionfold every day. But against the background of a largely party-line mainstream local Arab media, and the absence of avenues for national conversation, these Arab bloggers, most of whom are anonymous for their own safety, commit small acts of bravery simply by speaking their minds. It should be said that most of the people maintaining blogs do come out of the highest strata of society, economically and educationally, so their opinions can seem at times to represent no wider a circle than the upper crust of any given country. But, as Ammar Abdulhamid, a Syrian blogger who was forced into exile in September 2005 for his democracy activism, which included blogging about his eight-month interrogation by Syrian security services, put it: "There is nothing wrong with admitting that we represent a certain elite. It's not exclusively an economic elite, though economics surely plays a large factor. These are people who are comfortable, who have more time to blog. But in itself this is not the problem. The importance of this technology at this stage is to connect the elites better, to network the elites, to make them able to share more ideas and organize." The power of the medium, Abdulhamid says, will come when those bloggers find a way to "cross the bridge between the elite and the grass roots"—a process that is already beginning, through a few organized demonstrations coordinated by

bloggers, online campaigns, and the posting of information about police brutality or sexual harassment.

Blogs can serve two functions: they are diaries, where the minutiae of a life are spelled out in 500-word posts, and they are a personal op-ed page, in which a writer comments at will about news articles and daily political developments, rambles in anger or appreciation, or promotes ideas. All of this happens every day on American blogs. But the context in the Arab blogosphere is different. For one thing, it is so much smaller. In the U.S., political blogs tend to split off into separate spheres of left and right that rarely touch—call them Huffingtonville and Hewittland—each with its predictable response to any political event. But the small size of the Arab blogosphere forces people with contrary opinions, or even more mildly divergent viewpoints, to engage each other. As one Arab blogger said, "We're not big enough to preach to the choir yet. There is no choir."

But the more compelling reason for the singularity of the Arab blogosphere is that the Middle East is a region where the historical and the personal slam up against each other daily in a way they do only once a decade or so in America. This gives even mundane musings elevated significance. Bloggers are writing about their lives. But those lives are taking place in environments in which politics and history cannot be perceived as mere elements on the margins. For the twentysomething growing up in Riyadh, writing resentfully about the power of the religious authorities, the questions are fundamental ones about the state of her society. For the Egyptian blogger, the brutal suppression of a demonstration can make the difference in whether he chooses to stay in the country or leave. This urgency makes the commentary more complex and interesting than the us-versus-them combat of so many American blogs. "We see it's the whole country at stake," said a well-known Lebanese blogger who goes by the nom de blog Abu Kais. "For us, watching politics is not like watching a football game. It's existential."

●◆●

Salam Pax is widely acknowledged as the Adam of Middle East bloggers. The blogging revolution that first began to spread through America in the late 1990s (the first "online diary," as a blog was then known, was created by a Swarthmore student in January 1994) reached the Middle East three or four years ago, and it was only with Pax's quirky and insightful dispatches in 2003 from a prewar and then postwar Iraq that Americans were made aware that the phenomenon had arrived there, too.

His blog, "Where is Raed?" had all the hallmarks of those that would follow in its wake. A twenty-nine-year-old recently graduated architecture student who had spent time in the West, Pax wrote in fluent English, observing the chaos that was quickly accumulating around him. At first, he was writing for himself, using the blog as a diary, but then he became aware of the scarcity of Arab bloggers writing in English about anything other than religious matters. As he told *The Guardian* in 2003, "I was saying, 'Come on, look, the Arabs here: sex, alcohol, belly dancers, TV shows, where are they?' All you saw was people talking about God and Allah. There was nothing about what was happening here." Then the war began, and that impulse to expose the parts of his world that the West was not seeing took on an even greater urgency. By the time of the invasion, 20,000 people were reading Pax regularly. His posts captured an emotional, lived experience of the war, one that evaded most journalists covering the conflict. . . .

The dynamism of the blog posts, as well as the string of comments that usually follow each of them, can best be appreciated when viewed against a backdrop of the mainstream Arab media. With the exception of a few papers in Lebanon (notably, the English-language *Daily Star*) and a handful of publications in Egypt and Jordan, most local media in the Arab world are still either directly state-controlled or subject to such intimidation by the government that journalists and editors rarely challenge authority. Each country's media have their red lines that cannot be crossed. In Jordan, it is the monarchy. In Egypt, it's the Mubarak regime. Any criticism of fundamentalist Islam's growing role in Arab society is off limits to everyone. And in much of the Arab local media Israel is portrayed as the ultimate evil. Israel, in fact, can be a tool of state control in Arab media. A high level of anti-Israel rhetoric serves the purpose of directing anger and scrutiny away from the regimes in power.

That was mitigated somewhat by the advent in recent years of satellite channels like Al-Jazeera and Al-Arabiya, which offer at least the potential of a more independent analysis and criticism of Arab governments. But by some accounts, both channels, though Al-Jazeera more so, have taken on a tone and a content that plays, as one Syrian blogger put it, "to the largest common denominator, drawing on the same language of victimhood, the tired Arab nationalist line. It is Fox news. Many people compare it to CNN. I think it has to be compared to Fox." (The Israeli media, for their part, though certainly free and open to criticizing the government and not averse by any means to plastering the country's problems on the front page, also resort most often to simple narratives and well-known generalizations when it comes to depicting the Arab enemy, not giving serious attention to the aspiration of the Palestinians, for example.)

The bloggers have stood out against this background. Some of them have even used the Web for political action. Bloggers led an Arab movement to support products from Denmark in the aftermath of the Danish cartoon riots and the Arab boycott that followed. They have also organized demonstrations and, much like American bloggers, used their Web sites as forums to expose injustices. Egyptian bloggers recently circulated video of men wilding in the streets of Cairo, sexually assaulting women at random, eventually bringing the incident to the world's attention.

Jordanian bloggers, angry that the government regulators had decided to block access to Skype, a phone service that allows users to communicate freely over the Internet, started a campaign that led to the decision's reversal. And then there was the war, in which bloggers organized donations for the displaced of Lebanon.

Still, there are good reasons why most of the Arab blogosphere remains anonymous. Just this past year, several bloggers were jailed in Egypt, including Abdel Karim Sulaiman Amer, who was arrested in November and charged with "spreading information disruptive of public order," "incitement to hate Muslims," and "defaming the President of the Republic." Earlier last year, another Egyptian blogger, Alaa Ahmed Seif al-Islam, was arrested and given three consecutive fifteen-day detentions in prison, largely for his blogging activity. Other countries, like Bahrain and Saudi Arabia, don't arrest bloggers, but they aggressively block blogs they find subversive.

The Committee to Protect Bloggers, a now defunct U.S. organization that monitored bloggers who found themselves in danger, kept track of the various forms of intimidation and suppression. Curt Hopkins, who was the group's director, says there are three basic methods that countries employ to suppress bloggers: technical filtering, the law, and direct intimidation. Though it is fairly easy to track down bloggers using IP addresses, bloggers have an easier time evading the authorities than do journalists working for a newspaper. "When it comes to shutting down a publication, it's pretty easy," says Hopkins. "You just send some goons with baseball bats and suddenly you don't have a publication. It's that simple. Also it's easier to find people because they are in the offices when you come to arrest them. And though it's true that if you have enough money and time, you can find almost anyone, you've got to remember that most governments don't have enough money and enough time." Abdulhamid, the Syrian blogger who continued to update his blog every day, even while the state police were interrogating him, also noticed such limitations. "During my interrogation, I saw that, one, most security apparatus really don't have access to the Internet; two, they don't know how to use that technology very well to begin with, even if they did have access." Still, enough bloggers have either been arrested or, as in Abdulhamid's case, had their lives threatened, for the fear to be well founded. . . .

Maybe the most dramatic way in which this blogosphere is affecting the Arab world is by breaking down that ultimate taboo. Even in a place like Lebanon, with a large portion of the population striving to create a liberal, modern society, Israel is the last barrier. That is rooted in Lebanon's history, including recent history. Yet there is so much investment in seeing Israel as the source of all its problems that it has become a mindless reflex for many.

There are, of course, plenty of bloggers who use the Internet as a way to disseminate more hate and misunderstanding, many of whom also gained attention last summer during the war. One case, infamous among Arab and

Israeli bloggers, is Perpetual Refugee, a Lebanese business-man who had occasion to visit Israel a few times, social-ized with Israelis . . . and subsequently wrote friendly posts about making peace. As soon as the war came, he made what was described as a "360-degree turn," becoming vir-ulently hateful about Jews, about how Israel "massacred innocent souls to fulfill its biblical destiny." But Perpetual Refugee was something of a high-profile anomaly among the English-language bloggers.

"I always say there are two kinds of arguments," says Sandmonkey. "There are the arguments in which you hope to find the truth and the arguments in which you want to defend an established truth." It's the first type of argument that seems to be prevailing. Take this post by Charles Malik (also a pseudonym), a Lebanese blogger, who found himself exploring the Israeli blogosphere last April, by chance on Holocaust Remembrance Day. He asks questions that would seem almost blasphemous consider-ing the climate in the Middle East:

> Think about what Israelis deal with on a daily basis: frequent suicide bombs, support for such attacks by the popularly elected Palestinian gov-ernment, threats of annihilation from a country arming itself with nuclear weapons, constant words of hate from the Arabic speaking world, and remembrances of the Holocaust. . . . Not knowing about "them" is the worst crime we can commit. It invalidates them as humans, as if they don't even matter. They are Stalin's faceless enemy, the rabid dog, the evil bloodsuckers whom it is righteous to kill. Our papers definitely need to start cover-ing more than major political events in Israel. We should remember their tragedies.

If the Arab bloggers tend to be those who have been exposed to the West, many of the Israelis interacting with them are recent immigrants like Lisa Goldman, who arrived six years ago, and Lirun Rabinowitz, who has been living in Israel for a year and a half. Rabinowitz shares his blog with a Lebanese woman and was recently invited to be a co-author on the United Arab Emirates community blog and, even more surprisingly, on an annual Ramadan blog, in which various bloggers write about how the Mus-lim holiday is celebrated in their countries. Recently, on the UAE blog, he was accused in the comments section of being needlessly provocative for putting the words "Tel Aviv" after his name at the end of his posts. To his sur-prise, a number of Arab readers rushed to his defense in the comments section.

Rabinowitz says that perusing the Arab blogosphere has deepened his understanding of what is happening inside Arab society. "When I go to them, I see what are they worrying about, what are they wondering, how they are feeling, what level of analysis they are putting on things, how keen they are to see my side, and when they are only prepared to see their own. Is there room for bridging? And

I learn a lot about what their knee-jerk reaction looks like, what their analysis looks like, what their fears look like." And to him, that added layer of knowledge is a rebuke to the other forces in Israeli society that he feels are trying to define the "enemy" for him. "You want to tell me that these people are stupid? Well, they're not," says Rabinow-itz. "You want to tell me that these people want to live in a dictatorship? Well, they don't. You want to tell me that they can't be Muslim and tolerant and friendly at the same time? Well, it's wrong. You want to tell me that they hate me just because they're Muslim and I'm Jewish? Well that's wrong, too. And they prove that to me every day. And I get this amazing opportunity to dispel every demonic myth and every stupid stereotype that I could have ever thought of, and that's amazingly liberating."

Is this hopeful? Yes, as long as one keeps in mind, once again, what a small segment of the population, both Arab and Israeli, is sitting in front of glowing screens and reaching out to the "other." The bloggers will say, univer-sally, that revolutions almost always start with a tiny elite. But we are a long way from this revolution's doorstep. Instead, this blogosphere feels more like a small commu-nity of open-minded young people who have discovered pathways that were previously closed.

Still, seeds do grow. The grass-roots student wing of the civil rights movement, born at Shaw University in Raleigh, North Carolina, in 1960, in what evolved into the Student Nonviolent Coordinating Committee (or SNCC), was made up of young people, privileged enough to be attending college but not content with the pace of inte-gration in America. They made themselves into a van-guard, tearing holes in walls so that others could then pass through after them. Someone had to take the first step, and who better than they—young, educated, and sensitive to the restrictions that were going to be placed on their personal and communal advancement.

The young insider-outsiders of the Middle East, blog-ging openly about their frustrations with the Arab world, about its persistent prejudices and limitations, as a way of liberalizing their societies, are doing what the front line of any social movement does—they say the unspeak-able, they form the bonds that were previously unthink-able, they stand in the places that they are not supposed to stand. The Arab world will reform only when mindsets begin to change and a culture of dissent burgeons where it has never been allowed to exist openly before. If there is a way to kick-start this process, it is surely in the post of a twentysomething blogger wondering out loud why things can't be more open, more transparent—more different.

GAL BECKERMAN is a reporter for *Columbia Journalism Review*. He was the New York bureau chief of the *Jerusalem Post* and has been researching and writing a history of the movement to free the Jews from the Soviet Union during the Cold War.

EXPLORING THE ISSUE

Do Media Distort Representations of Islam and Arab Cultures?

Critical Thinking and Reflection

1. What are the possibilities for social media to create more balanced perceptions of others? Are there other ways in which the Internet could foster better relationships globally?
2. How are stereotypes created and maintained, particularly where there is little ability to interact with others directly? What part do the media play? And, how is the media influenced by the agendas of different groups?
3. Do journalistic practices of balance encourage oppositional thinking and enhance the power of marginal groups?
4. How can these concepts be applied to issues of stereotyping overall in the media and in society?

Is There Common Ground?

Over the years both media and society in general have become more aware of stereotyping. Groups who feel they have been stereotyped have sought more realistic portrayals, the limitations of roles in entertainment programming, and a recognition that one attribute does not define the individual. Progress has been made; more is needed. Yet when a group or a country is defined as the enemy, it is hard to remember that it still is composed of a diverse set of people and attitudes. It was a humorous sidebar when French Fries were renamed Freedom Fries in the House of Representatives cafeteria, as a result of anti-French sentiment when France protested the 2003 invasion of Iraq. It was much less humorous when friends were denied service at a D.C. fast food restaurant because they had been overheard speaking French.

Anti-Muslim sentiment is widespread as indicated by the chilling attack in Norway recounted in Fear, Inc. The tragedy of 9/11 made it all too easy to conflate Muslim and terrorism. Yet, there were many voices after 9/11 that urged us to not overgeneralize to an entire religion the actions of a few. We have many examples of where common ground has been found among previous disparate groups; we have other examples of great tragedies when relegating a group to "the Other" status has contributed to repression and even genocide. In all cases, common ground is found in ethical and thoughtful responses to overgeneralized stereotypes.

Create Central

www.mhhe.com/createcentral

Additional Resources

Brigitte Lebens Nacos and Oscar Torres-Reyna, *Fueling Our Fears: Stereotyping, Media Coverage, and*

Public Opinion of Muslim Americans (Rowman & Littlefield, 2007)

This book discusses the Arab/Muslim controversy, particularly for Muslims born in America, and considers how Americans look at Arabs and Muslims at home and abroad.

Edward Schiappa, *Beyond Representational Correctness: Rethinking Criticism of Popular Media* (State University of New York Press, 2008)

The book addresses the role of stereotyping in general in the media, and the parasocial relationships we have with people in the media.

The Journal of Arab and Muslim Media

An online source that often focuses on content and images within media and can be accessed through most academic libraries.

Peter Morey and Amina Yagin, *Framing Muslims: Stereotyping and Representation after 9/11* (Harvard University Press, 2011)

In this volume, the authors display the ways in which stereotypes that depict Muslims as an inherently problematic presence in the West are constructed and create a gulf between representations and reality.

Edward Said, *Covering Islam: How the Media and the Experts Determine How We See the Rest of the World* (Vintage Books, 1997)

In this seminar work, Edward Said, an influential professor and a cultural critic, looked at how American popular media have used and perpetuated a narrow and unfavorable image of Islamic peoples, and how this has prevented understanding while providing a fictitious common enemy for the diverse American populace.

Internet References. . .

Center for Media and Public Affairs

www.cmpa.com

Project Censored

www.projectcensored.org

The Center for Media and Democracy

www.prwatch.org/

Unit 2

UNIT

A Question of Content

*W*e no longer live in a world in which all of our media are directed toward mass audiences. Today we have both mass media and personal media, like video games, iPods, and cell phones. Because people use media content in very different ways, and so much of how we make sense of media depends on our own ages and life experiences, the issue of media content that is appropriate for certain audiences takes on a new importance. In this section, we deal with issues that often influence people from all ages, ethnic groups, and all walks of life—but the questions for discussion become more pointed when we consider that different audiences may perceive different things in the content of some forms of media. In this section, we consider issues that affect our sense of body, behavior, and expression of self to others.

Selected, Edited, and with Issue Framing Material by:
Alison Alexander, *University of Georgia*
and
Jarice Hanson, *University of Massachusetts—Amherst*

ISSUE

Do Media Cause Individuals to Develop Negative Body Images?

YES: June Deery, from "The Body Shop" in *Consuming Reality: The Commercialization of Factual Entertainment* (Palgrave Macmillan, 2012)

NO: Michael P. Levine and Sarah K. Murnen, from "'Everybody Knows That Mass Media Are/Are Not [*pick one*] a Cause of Eating Disorders': A Critical Review of Evidence for a Causal Link Between Media, Negative Body Image, and Disordered Eating in Females," *Journal of Social and Clinical Psychology* (January 2009)

Learning Outcomes
After reading this issue, you will be able to: <ul><li>Evaluate the media messages about body image in a better way.</li><li>Analyze how the images influence children and people who may have a particular viewpoint about standards of beauty and attractiveness.</li><li>Understand the power of advertising and marketing lifestyle to a range of age groups.</li><li>Apply the critical skills to other aspects of your lives.</li></ul>

ISSUE SUMMARY

YES: June Deery examines the role of reality television and body makeover programs and concludes that these types of programs normalize the idea that bodies can and should be improved by plastic surgery, weight loss, and control programs, and that women in particular should subject themselves to all measures to find "success" and "happiness." She theorizes that these programs assume that women in particular do have negative body images, and that the real messages of these programs is that surgical steps can and should be taken to improve one's poor body image.

NO: Michael Levine and Sarah Murnen also investigate magazine ads, but find the assumption that media cause eating disorders to be too limited. Instead, they cite a wide range of social, behavioral, and cultural issues over time to understand the complex conditions under which girls begin to adopt negative body issues that result in eating disorders.

Often media are accused of representing images that result in people's negative behaviors. Sometimes, media are so present in our lives that it seems apparent that there is, or should be, a direct link between media images and real-life manifestations of those images. We know that media have some influence over the way some people construct their ideas of reality, but the most difficult considerations have to do with who is affected, and under what conditions. The authors of these two selections look at the impact of reality television and the assumptions so many shows make about the normalization of a negative body image, and how magazines send mixed messages to readers.

The authors of the selections for this issue examine the content of reality television shows and magazines, but

start from different perspectives. June Deery focuses on reality shows and basic assumptions about body image, while Michael P. Levine and Sarah K. Murnen start with the question of whether images in magazines foster eating disorders and concepts of body image in general. What both selections have in common though is the idea that mediated images assume that there is an ideal body type, and that we as media consumers, measure our own bodies in comparison to the images we see.

We have evidence that plastic surgery for body sculpting is a growing business for both women and men, so the representations in the makeover and reality shows discussed by Deery suggest that television can play an extraordinary role in fostering one's own body image and sense of control over their body. We also know that in extreme cases, some people develop eating disorders based on the ideal body image as superthin, and that extreme measures can harm health. Professors Levine and Murnen evaluate the literature on what causes girls (in particular) to develop eating disorders, and find out that other cultural, social, and psychological issues play a much larger role in causing girls to actually harm themselves by extreme behaviors. Their perspective examines how behavior and self-image are formed over time, and in a world that has several competing causes for why someone psychologically succumbs to extreme eating behavior. Since the Levine and Murnen articles were written, much more evidence has come to light concerning the growing problem of adolescent boys with eating disorders too.

The complexities between media images and self-image are many indeed, and we know that not everyone is influenced by media in the same way. Socialization, family pressures and expectations, the type of media one consumes, and how peers talk about media images all have the potential to influence us in different ways, and still, probably all of us at some time know that something we saw in media made us feel a certain way, or think about something in a special way. When it comes to internalizing those images, our minds often register reactions in ways which we may not be aware.

Advertisers often seek to understand the underlying motivations that cause us to respond—especially for buying products, but sometimes we look to support from other people to confirm what we want to believe. Celebrities also tend to project body images that are often significantly underweight, thereby providing role models that may influence conscious or unconscious desires to be "like them." American culture is rife with stories about the perils of obesity and unhealthy lifestyles. As a result, it is difficult to seek one particular cause that could be the definitive answer to why anyone develops the self-image that he or she does. But the process of trying to understand the range of psychological and sociological processes that come along with media images is fascinating, and sometimes, frightening.

There have been occasional stories of how product manufacturers have tried to overcome the typical media image of body type. For example, in 2004 Dove soap's "Campaign for Real Beauty" featured girls and women who did not have the media-ideal body type. The campaign used real people and identified them as beautiful for being who and what they were, but in 2008, Unilever (Dove's parent company) and Ogilvy and Mather, the product's advertising company, came under fire for retouching the pictures of the real people in the ads. In a May 12, 2008 article in *Advertising Age*, it was reported that the alleged retouching had created a "ruckus" that was one of the largest scandals in the history of advertising.

The issues of body image and media image are closely aligned to the question of whether advertising is ethical. The social role of advertising suggests that the consumers are suggestible, and that they are motivated to improve themselves, their lifestyles, and attitudes by consuming the products and images they see in media. Often people make assumptions that ads reflecting body type are primarily a female-only issue, but as these authors allude, there are increasing similarities to female and male advertising, especially when it comes to body image and health.

Today we often hear about the problem of obesity—particularly for children. This is a particularly pointed problem for children in school who may not get the type of physical fitness they need, and who often play videogames rather than cultivating an active lifestyle. If these children are influenced by the images in reality TV and as portrayed in magazines, will they look to surgical solutions, or find answers in creating lifestyles that allow them to be comfortable with their own bodies, and concerned about their health? These cultural realities are difficult to reconcile with the idea that the products we buy actually can help us look or feel a certain way, but advertisers know that by praying on our weaknesses, we are often tempted to buy more. But along with our own consumption habits, body modification can also become a way of buying what we think of as the ideal, despite the physical consequences.

YES ⬅

June Deery

The Body Shop

...

For some time, people have accepted the responsibility of maintaining and making fashionable their living space. Surgical makeovers mainstream the idea that we should do the same for our bodies—not just by arranging hair and clothing but by altering the body's very architecture. While some superficial body modification is as old as human culture (piercings, tattoos), recent technologies render the body more radically malleable than ever before. Thanks to surgical techniques, the body's flaws are fixable: therefore, says a consumerist society, they ought to be fixed. Exactly what motivates any given individual to request a surgical makeover is impossible to fully determine—even for the subject involved—but there is no question that media-advertising has already played a significant role before anyone lines up for their makeover audition. My aim in examining on-screen transformations is to follow the logic presented in each series and offer an interpretation of its cultural significance.

Although it has been exported around the world, the surgical makeover is another particularly American form of reality television which appeals to this culture's intense and early interest in physical appearance, in glamour, in self-improvement, and in what amounts to a cult of youth. In other countries cosmetic surgery is less socially acceptable, as in many parts of Europe (Franco 2008), or people are more reserved when it comes to showing the body in general, as in China or other parts of Asia. My account will consider a variety of mostly American formats, including *Extreme Makeover, The Swan, 10 Years Younger, Bridalplasty,* and the docusoap *The Real Housewives*. These programs put into popular view rarefied postmodern discourses about the fluidity of the self, about sex and gender, and about the self as a project; however, they are generally noncommittal about whether this project involves multiple selves or the linear evolution of one core self. . . .

Every culture has taboos and prohibitions about which body parts may be subject to another's view, when, and in what circumstances—taboos that are often understood as a matter of ethics but also signal underlying economic arrangements (e.g., the female body as property in capitalist patriarchy). On surgical makeovers, shots of nipples and genitalia are conventionally blurred but otherwise makeover subjects have to display and discuss with a doctor, while on camera, what they perceive to be their specific physical flaws. Ordinarily, this filming of a patient consultation would of course be judged highly unprofessional. The fact that the critique of the body comes largely from the subject herself, a lifelong witness of media images, rather than from another judge, is at this stage a fairly minor distinction. The scenario is uncomfortable for the patient and this is, of course, the point, for their humiliation is the price they have to pay for securing a media audience/surgery. The patients are exposed according to the producers' stipulations in a process that has no medical use or justification. The inappropriateness of this voyeurism was particularly flagrant on *Bridalplasty* when the surgery candidates had to bare all not only to the surgeon or anonymous others (TV audience) once the episode aired, but also to a small, face-to-face group of rival brides on the show. Having their disgraced body parts displayed as they sit in a known group has a particular note of impropriety and it made one candidate burst out with: "No one should have to do this!" accompanied by an awkward laugh. Sue Tait suggests that such sequences are in part designed to get viewers on board with the surveillance and its normative judgments in order to justify the upcoming surgery. The audience is "to share the candidate's assessing and disciplinary gaze and assent with the identification of the aberrant features of the displayed body. This ostensibly 'proves' that surgical intervention is warranted. . .". That may be the plan anyway.

The Temple

The typical makeover has a female patient seeking help from a male surgeon. His bending over her mute and supine body in the operation room brings to mind the old narrative of the male scientist dissecting Nature depicted as a female body. Or his incisions could be seen in purely sexual terms as a male penetration. A more pecific account which dominated Western thought for centuries is Aristotelian reproduction. Without benefit of empirical research, this most influential natural philosopher forthrightly asserted that during reproduction the male shaped formless matter that lay within the female and so he was likened to, among other things, a carpenter creating objects out of wood. So here we have at least fragments of the tropes of body as house and male as builder embedded in early Western patriarchal thought. In the case of the modern makeover, the surgeon resembles a builder not of another body within a woman's body but of the woman herself. Indeed, one of the most striking and repeated images on televised surgeries is of the male surgeon marking up with ink areas of the patient's body that he will be work upon, like a carpenter marking up a piece of wood before he cuts into it. Aristotle's account reflected the tradition of according superiority to form over matter, to intellect and skill over dull substance. The modern makeover does not deviate significantly from this account. . . .

Yet while it is an intimate space, the body is also potentially a site of separation and alienation. Having a body is why subjects can be taken as objects or as things and one could argue that this is the stance being advocated on TV shows that solve problems by fixing the body's material and surface—a glib conclusion, perhaps, but an understandable one. For example, during their initial consultation both surgeons and patients tend to distance themselves from body identity and personal biography by agreeing on the importance of general principles of design such as proportion and symmetry, as one would when working on an architectural project. We saw in style makeovers a similar invocation of principles in order to impress upon subjects that there can and should be an objective assessment of body topology. This is even more the case in surgical makeovers where redesigning the body is presented as an objective task based on neutral factors such as geometric space and proportion, a sublimation most noticeable on *Extreme Makeover* when a photo of the patient's body is displayed like a blueprint, either static on the UK edition or rotating against a geometric grid in the American. In both instances, graphics label problem areas that need to be fixed, an early mapping which reinforces the idea that the person has become part of the object world. In actual fact, surgery is a violent act involving the breaking, tearing, and sawing of human bone and tissue, but on makeover shows clean spatial graphics largely overshadow blood and gore. Contrast this with procedural crime dramas such as CBS's *CSI* (2000–), another popular strain of television that focuses on the narratives that bodies reveal but that relies on sadistic violence and trauma. The surgical makeover focuses on more containable abstract images which suggest that its procedures are almost a matter of mathematical measurement and redistribution of mass: for women, the redistribution involves smaller waists, larger breasts, smaller noses, bigger lips, while for men the results are "stronger" chins, wider chests, and straighter noses. In addition, one effect of surgery is to make these bodies more like buildings by being static and taut.

In common parlance, patients employ phrases such as "getting work done" or having "a nose job" to euphemistically attach their cosmetic surgery to the more impersonal notion of commercial construction and there may be a form of relief or even liberation in this transaction as depicted on television makeovers. For seeing their body as an object to be worked upon perhaps removes culpability from these subjects, especially as their assessment of their body's flaws is not challenged by sympathetic doctors who simply ratify that their concerns are justified

and deserving of attention. Hosts on house makeovers are often careful to avoid blaming inhabitants for the dilapidated condition of their home, stressing financial and time constraints for lack of upkeep and repair. Similarly, blaming subjects is not part of the discourse of *Extreme Makeover* or *Bridalplasty*. Patients simply hand over their body as an unsatisfactory project for someone else to fix. Surgeons say little about the reasons for excess flesh: they simply suck the offending matter out (avoiding phrases like "you are fat"). However, culpability does emerge on *10 Years Younger* where being put on public display in a glass box has a whiff of the village stocks. This time subjects are held accountable for their state of disrepair: usually the problem is lack of prevention (sunscreen) or bad habits (diet, smoking). Blame and personal accountability are at the forefront of weight loss programs such as *The Biggest Loser*, programs that do not resort to surgery and instead encourage people to modify their bodies themselves over time. Programs that focus on surgery incorporate diet and exercise guides to some extent, but their emphasis is on promoting the rapid transformation achieved by putting one's body in someone else's hands, and the magic happens when the patient is not even conscious of being worked upon by others (under anesthetics). . . .

No one calculates more closely how to make the most of this synthetic narcissism than the women of *The Real Housewives* franchise, whose extrovert behavior exposes the more muted transactions occurring in a series like *Extreme Makeover* or *The Swan*. On *The Real Housewives*, making the body look good is a serious business and while cosmetic surgery is not a central narrative focus it is a vital element in the lives of those being filmed. It appears that most of the women have had some "work" done and increasingly they acknowledge this on camera. Unlike the modest "ugly ducklings" of charitable makeovers, the housewives rely fairly heavily on cosmetic surgery to advance their ambitions, which for many of these women is circumscribed by the finding and keeping of a wealthy husband. For others, an attractive body is also good for their professional careers (e.g., models, realtors, marketers, designers). In either case, these women recognize that body upgrades are essential for maintaining their market value and so for them cosmetic surgery is calculated and routine. In one scene, a husband rewards his wife for having her breasts augmented by surprising her in the recovery room with a gift of diamond earrings. Drowsy but gratified, she gets the message and says (with a laugh of sorts) that she should have cosmetic surgery more often, presumably because of the immediate financial gain.

So much is surgery normalized that one mother and daughter go in for a cozy surgery together (Lynne and daughter in *The Real Housewives of Orange County*) and another woman has almost a drive-thru experience when she has her fourth breast augmentation at a "Same Day Surgery" clinic in a strip mall (Danielle in *The Real Housewives of New Jersey*). The casual nature of the clinic and its setting is one reason why other medical practitioners look aghast at some cosmetic surgeons because they don't legally have to operate within hospitals and can conduct business anywhere. Several other *Real Housewives* women are filmed having minor cosmetic procedures as a fairly regular part of their lives and sometimes they bring friends along as though on a shopping trip. Botox parties are especially popular, both in home and work settings: for example, Vicki (*The Real Housewives of Orange County*) thinks it a nice reward for her employees to have a surprise office Botox party where she coerces them into getting injected, while also acknowledging that having an attractive appearance is good for (her) business. This brings office management into a new (and possibly illegal) area. But her intentions are pure to the extent that she, like the other women in this series, are convinced that working on physical appearance is a sound investment in one's financial future and so she is mentoring others in how best to succeed. Some of the housewives openly discuss how much they paid for various procedures and whether it was a good deal. Certainly they are not shy about displaying the results.

For many of these glamorous, sexualized, postfeminist women, turning their bodies into objects of desire is their chief career and it is their success at this self-commodification that allows them to spend most of their lives consuming other goods and services. Those who secure and rely on a wealthy husband's money are shown working hard to "maintain their body" and keep their side of the bargain. They may not work but they "work out," a distinct form of labor usually undertaken by those who don't otherwise have to exert themselves manually. In societies of abundance, part of being beautiful is being toned and slim. This signals discipline and has become an indication of prestige, of success, even of class. *The Real Housewives* series do not depict charity makeovers but those who are able to afford surgery (mostly thanks to their husbands) and who come across, for the most part, as irredeemably superficial and hollow. Their harping on about how it is their choice to trade physical attraction for money (or, less bluntly, achieve a "successful" marriage) hardly masks their subordinate position or the fragility of that marital arrangement. For all their faith in improvement through consumption, there is still an unease and a defensive attitude about their body's status as a commodity, even if within a marriage contract. The specter of being a "prostitution whore" looms over these well-groomed and surgically enhanced women who are in many ways caricatures, but, as caricatures, effectively illustrate some of the negotiations, ambivalences, and even hypocrisies of many other contemporary women and men who similarly invest in their body's appearance. In one sense it seems these women trade their bodies for real estate and in this way one property is exchanged for another. The wealthy husbands become a means to an end, the end being a luxurious home. At least this is where editors often focus their attention; for example, outside shots of each opulent dwelling is ritualistically used to identify the person who

will be featured next. Only to the extent that they are wedded to the house (as a signifier of economic position) are they "house-wives," for certainly there is little evidence of the housewifery that is traditionally associated with this term given that many of these women employ nannies, maids, and personal assistants. However, as the various series have evolved, an unintended consequence of the franchise's success is that several of these women are growing more financially and socially independent (for them it appears the two are connected). . . .

On *The Swan* even the subject was not permitted to see her transformed body until it was simultaneously revealed to viewers. Prior to the reveal ceremony, the show's "mirror police" forbade every candidate from looking in any reflecting surfaces on penalty of being thrown out. When she is first allowed to see herself in a staged ceremony in front of a mirror, each subject's re-imaging of her new body is, in Foucauldian terms, a quite literal internalization of the mechanisms of surveillance and the gaze of the Other. She is now not only an object, but "an object of vision: a sight" a sight that seems to both fascinate and alienate her. The fact that her body is the product of others' work is perhaps why the subject is not usually modest about expressing delight in how it looks: in praising her appearance she is praising those who created it. On the more punitive *10 Years Younger* subjects who request a makeover have to stand in a glass box in the equivalent of the town square while passing strangers (literally the-person-on-the-street) are polled about the subject's age and physical appearance. Their appearance (i.e., market value) is assessed while on display, as though a retail object. To compound their status as a thing, they are deaf and mute while in the box and are unable to hear what these casual others are saying about them.

Here is how the *Queer Eye* website describes their style makeovers:

> With help from family and friends, the Fab Five treat each new guy as a head-to-toe project. Soon, the straight man is educated on everything from hair products to Prada and Feng Shui to foreign films. At the end of every fashion-packed, fun-filled lifestyle makeover, a freshly scrubbed, newly enlightened guy emerges—complete with that "new man" smell

Each episode, we are told, boils down to a "one-hour guide to building a better man." This description of a person in terms of an industrial product like an automobile is intended to be comic because it is not exactly appropriate. But it is not entirely inapplicable either. The made-over person does resemble a product to the extent that his new identity is produced and produced by others. This is especially the case with surgical makeovers where some surgeons refer to the post-op body as, indeed, "the final product." Moreover, when these made-over bodies conform to a fairly narrow range of looks this homogeneity increases the sense that they have not been born but produced: like any manufacturing process, it is a matter of finding cheap raw material ("ordinary" subjects), processing and designing it in line with market forces, and then packaging the results. . . .

In any society, the treatment of the body indicates some of the ways power circulates. Crucially observed in the modern era a shift away from obviously coercive legal and militaristic control of the body to today's more commonly administrative, medical and psychocultural mechanisms. We witnessed the producers' attempts at coercion on style makeovers but on surgical makeovers their control tends to be more firm. On these shows just about all of the patient's movements are dictated in another example of private, commercial forces being acceptable where public and government overtures are not. Rather than formal, institutional restrictions, there is a therapeutic imperative distributed through private channels (media-advertising) urging the subject to conform. To a deeper extent than with shopping makeovers, this handing over of the body for surgery creates an alienation in the labor of self-reproduction. However, television shows such as *Extreme Makeover* and *The Swan* have also helped create a new relationship between patient and surgeon beyond the TV screen. When these series were being filmed they reflected the still authoritarian relationship between uninformed patient and all-knowing doctor where the patient does not question, negotiate, or critique. But since most of these shows have aired and the Internet has opened up further sources of information, patients are more likely to shop around for a surgeon who will best perform what they already judge needs to be done. Meredith Jones observes that, in part because of information circulating through popular channels like reality television, cosmetic surgery patients are now more inclined to approach their doctors as customers looking for a good service provider. So the commercial basis of the transaction is more marked today despite the public relations exercise of makeover TV that tried to erase these finances. In an era when such surgery has become another thing you buy, surgeons report a loss of status but an increase in business.

Attractive bodies attract and very attractive bodies attract even more, so it is no surprise that media-advertising skews toward representations of ideal beauty. More than this, advertising enjoins us to aspire to achieve the extraordinary appearance it uses to capture our attention. As numerous studies have suggested, one of the strongest effects of the media's daily parade of ideal beauty is that this alters what viewers regard as normal and what they aspire to be. That the logic of television prioritizes the superficial and the visual has had profound and still evolving cultural ramifications. For instance, if our models of ideal beauty were textual only there would be more room for our own standards and input, whereas a visual model fixes and imposes the image in exact detail. This opens up an almost infinite market for selling products to those who will never meet this image. On surgical makeovers we witness a diligent and procrustean chopping of bodies to meet a beauty ideal, but there is no suggestion that media representations should instead be altered. The previously unmediated become fulfilled not just by being mediated but by being *mediatized*, meaning conforming to media images. Surgical candidates appear to have little interest in media exposure as an end in itself, but this kind of programming teaches them, and by extension us, that being mediated can be very beneficial and life transforming and therefore something to be desired.

What particularly struck Fredric Jameson about Guy Debord's depiction of the "society of the spectacle" was the latter's observation that the ultimate form of commodity reification in contemporary society is the image itself. With surgical makeovers, the media image is reified "in the subject and then resold as a TV image. In other words, if ever discourse impacted the material realm it is at this point, the human body. As Baudrillard observed, today we find not only "the forced extraversion of all interiority"—which almost any reality series pushes to the limit—but also the "forced introjection of all exteriority", meaning the internalizing of media imagery. RTV makeovers don't just display the ideal bodies we see everywhere else in the media, they show people imposing this ideal on real bodies: so that they become a simulation of an ideal. In some instances, as in MTV's *I Want a Famous Face* or TV Guide Channel's (nonsurgical) *Look-a-Like*, participants wish to resemble specific media products such as Brad Pitt or Pamela Anderson. Others wish to emulate an iconic figure who is not human, as in Cindy Jackson's 29 plastic surgeries to make her look like Barbie. (Cindy, incidentally, is the name of a British version of the Barbie doll.) RTV's mainstreaming of surgical procedures that offer to realize a hyperbolic image raises the bar for what people are expected to do and to spend in order to achieve a satisfactory status. Producers are tapping into a media effect (the near obsessive desire for an attractive body) within a media product (the makeover series) in order to create a media product of the body.

But it is not an internal feedback loop entirely. Nor is the significance of physical attractiveness an illusion arbitrarily impressed upon us by a cynical media simply in order to secure its own profits. People pay heed to media images, to what the culture deems attractive, because there are real-world consequences. We observe anecdotally and through more formal study that those who look attractive are admired and rewarded. Some of this response may be due to biological mechanisms and some to more socially constructed and culturally variant preferences, but whatever the origins of our attitudes there is little dispute that in real life being judged attractive has distinct advantages. On the biological front, certain body types may be favored because they signal fertility and virility while, for example, symmetrical features may indicate freedom from harmful genetic mutations, traumas, or residual effects of disease. Sociological studies suggest that the physically attractive are more likely to be promoted and to achieve other forms of success in all stages of life. In any case, whatever the validity of such results, the perception that appearance matters becomes important and largely self-fulfilling, a logic at least reinforced on makeover TV.

Gender Construction

One of the most compelling roles played by media-advertising is that of defining what is feminine or masculine, and it is striking how often female makeover patients report that they wish to be "more feminine," a concept that is almost always tied to being more "sexy." The men's desire for masculinity is generally more muted and indeed there is a possibility that their seeking surgical enhancement will be coded as feminine. Whatever the case, on-screen doctors treat anyone's desire to accentuate their gender as natural and are happy to support heterosexist and sexist norms. As Brenda Weber notes, they appear to support the idea that "sex or biology is malleable while gender is constant," and so the former is shaped to match the latter. One pragmatic advantage of invoking "feminine" or "masculine" in a surgical context is that if doctors and patients have a similar understanding of what this means then it will provide a commonly agreed upon diagram of what an improved body should look like, and so doctors, patients, and presumably viewers will be similarly impressed by the results. But two things are being communicated here: that being strongly gender-marked is a desirable goal and that this effect can be produced through fairly rapid and superficial changes in bodily appearance. As though upholding, and in fact enacting, Judith Butler's notion that biological matters, too, are culturally determined, surgeons redesign the patient's body in order to better meet their culture's gender template. This is a remarkable process since it is only in recent times that there been such an opportunity for a culture to not only interpret but also to physically carve the body and to do so radically, swiftly, and with reasonable safety. In this manner, discourse physically shapes materiality and, if we maintain a gender/ sex distinction, then cosmetic surgery imposes notions of gender (femininity) on to sex (the female body).

The women on some of these shows emerge not just as feminine but as hyperfeminine, most notably on *The Swan* and *The Real Housewives* where the glamour version of femininity produces women who hark back to more patriarchal times: big hair, high heels, lots of "curves," and so on. These shows appear to offer enclaves of "enlightened sexism" where it is deemed acceptable to resurrect retrograde stereotypes and diffuse offense to more progressive viewers with mockery and ironic amusement. The matter takes an absurd turn when what seems like sexism is extended even to the design of teeth. *Extreme Makeover's* Dr. Bill Dorfman is of the opinion that a woman gets what she wants by "flashing her pearly whites" and that a "feminine smile is bright, soft, and beguiling.... Not unlike a feminine-looking body, a feminine-looking smile is all about curves." Masculine teeth, on the other hand, should appear "more angular" with the central incisors "square,

strong, and more powerful" than the surrounding teeth. If biology doesn't mark gender in this way, then the surgeon is there to help fix this oversight.

One main reason for the surgical redesign of the body is that it is a place that exists in time, and there are two things that we have always known about aging: that it is inevitable and that it is universal. Both of these facts enhance the profitability of addressing nature's planned obsolescence. Fighting time's effects on the flesh is, indeed, a billion dollar segment of the "fashion-beauty complex" in which scientific-sounding ingredients and techniques (with adjectives like bio and molecular) are marketed as powerful "defense" mechanisms, often incorporating but reengineering natural substances. For example, Garnier offers "Ultra-LiftPro gravity defying cream" (Newton, never mind NASA, would be impressed). But this is the essence of commodification: adding value by offering the techné (craft, technology) that works on and even against nature. In many consumer cultures women of any age, despite other accomplishments, are expected to look as slim and adolescent as when they first started out in the market (or as they never did). The fat deposits and stretch marks that are natural testaments to the nurturance of others are matters for self-loathing, while wrinkles are pathologized as a disease that must be cured. As its title suggests, *10 Years Younger* makes reversing the signs of aging its particular focus. On the British version of this format the host walks the subject through a gallery of blown-up photos each sitting on its own easel and each documenting the subject's gradual physical deterioration over time: as they penetrate this spatialization of time's passing, the sense of failure and public condemnation could not be more bleak. Aging, or rather allowing the signs of aging to go uncorrected, is treated as at least a misdemeanor if not a larger crime. But as Sadie Wearing points out, there is a contradiction about the attitude to aging in this and other makeover programming that reflects an ambivalence in postfeminist thinking. On the one hand, postfeminism suggests that aging need not mean loss of femininity, of fun, of self, and so on. But, on the other hand, it insists that people take on the responsibility of making the body look as young as possible by making the right consumer choices.

We have seen how makeover TV, in conjunction with media-advertising, supports what sociologists have identified as a shift in postindustrial society to where "The body is less and less an extrinsic 'given'. . . but becomes itself reflexively mobilized". The extent to which surgical work on this self is either empowering or a sign of victimhood has for some time been a polarizing topic and has given rise to some debate among feminist scholars. There are those such as Naomi Wolf, Susan Bordo, and Germaine Greer who assert that opting for cosmetic surgery cannot be reconciled with feminism and that the practice is little more than a reprehensible effect of patriarchy.[22] Even when an individual feels they are freeing themselves, "In fact, what is happening is a more intense policing of the body" Then there is Kathy Davis who argues that such scholars need to respect the fact that for any individual the option may be empowering and rational given the sociopolitical conditions under which they act. However, it seems the majority of scholars today have adopted a more mixed or ambivalent approach which recognizes both empowerment and oppression. They are unwilling to dismiss cosmetic surgery patients as deluded or vain or victimized, but they underline that individual choice is constrained by the larger sociopolitical structure within which the decision to have surgery is made. As we have seen, makeover TV presents an upbeat narrative of individual empowerment with no serious acknowledgment of social pressures or constraints. Almost invariably TV subjects maintain that their surgery confers on them more "self-esteem," a term that is today very much in vogue (though, remarkably, only since the late 1990s). This benefit is regarded as deeply and individually empowering, though it could be considered a disingenuous claim since this self-esteem is so clearly yoked to the esteem of others (the reveal) and the frequent assertion that "I am doing it for myself" becomes almost meaningless since they are clearly improving their appearance in such a way as to better impress others. In any case, one of the problems with research in this area is that so much depends on self-reporting from patients and this can only take us so far. Even if this input is genuine and reliable, people tend to repeat the available repertoires (self-esteem, I'm doing it for myself) without necessarily realizing how they are being influenced and it is difficult to see how anyone else could prove influence either. However, this much we can say: that reality shows provide some insight into what people say (publicly) about why they want surgery, that they provide information about what surgeons can accomplish, that there appears to be an interest (on television and in real life) in accentuating sexual differences, and that according to both patients and surgeons these series have contributed to an increase in requests for various procedures. Deeper psychological or collective reasons why people elect for surgery are worth speculating about but are not easily proven.

Seeking surgery could, for example, be another form of compensation symptomatic of large sociopolitical trends. This was the opinion of Christopher Lasch and has been implied by others since. When studying narcissistic behavior in the 1970s, Lasch suggested that the focus on the self and on self-improvement was a reaction to the individual's feeling of helplessness in a wider sphere (in his own period, the failure to effect political change after the 1960s and the ever-present threat of nuclear warfare). Lasch believed that the self-empowerment that comes from working on the self was acting as a palliative for larger forces bearing down on individuals which they could not alter. Noting the recent intense focus on body improvement, Anthony Giddens similarly traces its origins to a deeper unease and further institutional unraveling. "What might appear as a wholesale movement towards the narcissistic cultivation of bodily appearance is," he maintains, "an expression of a concern lying much deeper actively to 'construct' and control the body". It may be that the body is targeted because it is a malleable material whose change is feasible and evident, and whose alteration produces both social and financial benefits. As we have seen, improving one's body can be presented as a pragmatic way to prosper in a climate of instability and job insecurity in which individuals are being urged to make the most of their own public relations. More broadly, it may be a comfort in a society of increasing complexity and risk to focus on something one can control. Sociologist Chris Shilling backs this up when he identifies a contemporary reaction where "if one feels unable to exert influence over an increasingly complex society, at least one can have some effect on the size, shape and appearance of one's body". If we accept this explanation, then the accelerated embrace of cosmetic surgery is a sign of a cultural and political ill health that goes far beyond somatic concerns.

Whatever the reasons—and no doubt they are diverse and complex—what is clear is that record numbers of people in Western nations report dissatisfaction with their body image, even in childhood. In this context, TV's surgical fixes are likely to lead to increased pressure to change, which statistics suggest is already happening. As surgery becomes more widespread, we can speculate that the end result will be a form of commercial eugenics linking beauty, money, and rank even more firmly than in epochs past; for if, as these makeovers insist, we can fix our body image but we don't, then an unimproved body would signal either indolence or lower socioeconomic status. Beyond this, if the focus rests on body as the locus for change this inward turn promises to provide little political counterbalance to the prioritization of public image, whether of the individual or of larger social bodies, thus contributing to a future when both micro and macro politics could implode entirely to media-advertising and PR.

. . . .

June Deery is an Associate Professor at Rensellaer Polytechnic Institute. Her research focuses on television and the Internet, and her primary areas of study are gender, class, commercialization, and politics.

Michael P. Levine and
Sarah K. Murnen

"Everybody Knows That Mass Media Are/Are Not [*pick one*] a Cause of Eating Disorders": A Critical Review of Evidence for a Causal Link Between Media, Negative Body Image, and Disordered Eating in Females

Numerous professionals, parents, and adolescents find the media's status as a cause of body dissatisfaction, drive for thinness, and eating disorders to be self-evident: *"Of course,* mass media contribute to unhealthy beauty ideals, body dissatisfaction, and disordered eating—haven't you seen the magazine covers in the supermarket newsstands lately? No wonder so many girls have body image issues and eating disorders." On the contrary, a growing number of parents, biopsychiatric researchers, clinicians, and cynical adolescents find proclamations about media as a *cause* of any disorder to be an irritating distraction. Their contention is, in effect: *"Of course,* we know now that eating disorders, like mood disorders and schizophrenia, are severe, self-sustaining psychiatric illnesses with a genetic and biochemical basis. So, *of course,* no scientist seriously thinks that mass media and the escapades of actors, models, and celebrities have anything to do with causing them." . . .

The relationships between mass media, negative body image, and unhealthy behaviors (e.g., use and abuse of steroids and food supplements) in males are receiving increasing attention. The gender differences (conservatively, 6 to 8 females for each male) in the prevalence of anorexia nervosa, bulimia nervosa, and eating disorder not otherwise specified (EDNOS) other than Binge Eating Disorder are among the largest reported for mental disorders.

Although the matter of dimensions and/or categories is complex and unresolved, substantial evidence suggests that the serious and frequently chronic conditions recognized as the "Eating Disorders" are composite expressions of a set of dimensions, such as negative emotionality, binge eating, and unhealthy forms of weight and shape management. The latter includes restrictive dieting, self-induced vomiting after eating, and abuse of laxatives, diuretics, diet pills, and exercise.

The adhesive drawing together and framing these intertwined continua is negative body image. In most media effects research the multidimensional construct of body image is represented by various measures of what are essentially perceptual-emotional conclusions (e.g., "I look too fat to myself and others" + "I am disgusted by and ashamed of this" = "I hate how fat I look and feel"). For females "body dissatisfaction" results from—and feeds—a schema that integrates three fundamental components: idealization of slenderness and leanness; an irrational fear of fat; and a conviction that weight and shape are central determinants of one's identity. . . .

Researchers in many fields have stopped thinking about "the" cause of a disorder as "the agent" that directly brings about the undesirable outcome. Instead, there is an emphasis on variables that are reliably and usefully associated with an increase over time in the probability of a subsequent outcome. Such variables are called risk factors.

Thinking in terms of risk factors has two major implications for investigating mass media as a "cause" of eating disorders. The first concerns the oft-heard "relative rarity" argument: How could mass media be a cause when the vast majority of girls and young women are exposed to ostensibly toxic influences, but only a small percentage develop eating disorders? This critique dissolves when one considers multiple risk factors as multiplicative probabilities. Assume, conservatively, that 35% of adolescent girls are engaged with those mass media containing various unhealthy messages. Assume also that three other risk factors—such as peer preoccupation with weight and shape; family history of overweight/obesity; and being socialized by parents and older siblings to believe firmly that a female's identity and worth are shaped primarily by appearance—each have a probability of .35 of occurring in the population. . . .

Second, if mass media constitute a *causal risk factor* for the spectrum of negative body image and disordered

From *Journal of Social and Clinical Psychology,* vol. 28, no. 1, January 2009, pp. 9–16, 19–26, 30–34 (excerpted, refs. omitted). Copyright © 2009 by Guilford Publications. Reprinted by permission via Copyright Clearance Center.

eating, then the following will be the case. *Cross-sectional studies* will show that the extent of exposure to mass media, or to various specific forms of mass media, is a correlate of that spectrum. *Longitudinal studies* will demonstrate that exposure to mass media precedes and predicts development of negative body image and disordered eating. *Laboratory experiments* should show that well-controlled manipulation of the media risk factor (independent variable) causes the hypothesized changes in "state" body satisfaction and other relevant dependent variables, while *controlled analog (laboratory) or field experiments* should demonstrate that prevention programs designed to combat known risk factors do indeed reduce or delay the onset of disordered eating.

These criteria are demanding in and of themselves. Nevertheless, it is also important to incorporate the contributions to knowledge of two further sources: common sense and people's "lived experience." Specifically, if mass media are a causal risk factor, then *content analyses* should document that media provide the raw material from which children and adolescents could *readily* extract and construct the information, affective valences, and behavioral cues necessary to develop the components of disordered eating. Similarly, *surveys and ecological analyses* will reveal that engagement with mass media is frequent and intensive enough to provide multiple opportunities for this type of social-cognitive learning. Finally, *surveys and qualitative studies* should find that, beginning at the age where they can think critically about themselves in relation to personal and outside influences, children and adolescents will report that mass media are sources of influence, and even pressure, on themselves, their peers, and others. . . .

Appearance, status, sexuality, and buying and consuming are, for many reasons (including the power of mass media), very important aspects of life throughout many countries. Consequently, the content of mass media provides daily, multiple, overlapping, and, all too often, unhealthy messages about gender, attractiveness, ideal body sizes and shapes, self-control, desire, food, and weight *management*. These messages sometimes intentionally, sometimes incidentally indoctrinate developing girls and boys with the following easily extracted themes: (a) being sexually attractive is of paramount importance; (b) the sources of ideals about attractiveness ("being 'hot'!"), style, and the best, most competitive practices for becoming and staying beautiful are obviously located outside the self; and (c) mass media are the most important and inherently enjoyable "external" source of the information, motivation, and products necessary to be attractive and fashionable.

Mass Media and the Thinness Schema

Thus, with respect to the cultural foundations of negative body image and disordered eating, even girls (and boys) as young as 4 or 5 have no trouble finding in mass media the

raw materials for various maladaptive but *entirely normative* media-based *schemata* concerning gender and attractiveness. The *"thinness schema"* for females is a set of assumptions, "facts," and strong feelings that are organized so as to establish a readiness to think and respond in terms of, for example, the following themes: (1) Women are "naturally" invested in their beauty assets and thus beauty is a woman's principal project in life; (2) a slender, youthful attractive "image" is really something substantive, because it is pleasing to males and it demonstrates to females that one is in control of one's life; and (3) learning to perceive, monitor, and indeed experience yourself as the object of an essentially masculine gaze is an important part of being feminine and beautiful.

Transnational Idol: The Exaltation of Thinness and the Vilification of Fat

There is a wealth of evidence from content analyses that the ideal female body showcased on television, in movies, in magazines, and on the internet reflects, indeed embodies, the proposition that "thin is normative and attractive." While (because?) American girls and women are becoming heavier, the current body *ideal* (idol) for women has become and remains unrealistically thin. In fact, mass media are one of many sociocultural sources for the normative prejudice that fat is "horrible and ugly," and that "getting fatter" is a sign of at least 4 of the classic "*7 deadly sins*"—extravagance, gluttony, greed, sloth, and, maybe, pride. . . .

The presence of a positive correlation between level of exposure to mass media, or to certain types of mass media, and the spectrum of disordered eating is a necessary but not sufficient condition for determination of causal agency. However, absence of a positive correlation negates the argument for causality. . . .

Longitudinal Correlates of Exposure to Mass Media

. . . Compared to cross-sectional studies, longitudinal research linking media exposure with body image is sparse. The few published studies do suggest that early exposure to thin-ideal television predicts a subsequent increase in body-image problems. For a sample of Australian girls aged 5 to 8, viewing of appearance-focused television programs (but not magazines) predicted a decrease in appearance satisfaction 1 year later. For European American and African American girls ages 7 through 12 greater overall television exposure predicted both a thinner ideal *adult* body shape and a higher level of disordered eating 1 year later. The results of both studies were valid regardless of whether the children were heavy, or perceived themselves to be thin or heavy, at the outset of the research. The thrust of these two studies is consistent with Sinton and Birch's finding that, among the 11-year-old American girls they studied, awareness of media messages about thinness was related to the strength of appearance schemas a year later.

The importance of a longitudinal design is revealed in recent studies of older children and young adolescents conducted by Tiggemann and by Field and colleagues. In a sample of 214 Australian high school girls (mean age = 14), Tiggemann found that the only measure of television exposure, including total hours of exposure, to produce meaningful cross-sectional and longitudinal correlations was the self-reported extent of watching soap operas. Cross-lagged correlational analyses showed that Time 1 exposure to soap operas predicted, to a small but significant degree, internalization of the slender ideal and level of appearance schema at 1-year follow up (Time 2). Time spent reading appearance-oriented magazines, but not other magazines, at Time 1 predicted, also to a small but significant degree, Time 2 levels of internalization, appearance schema, and drive for thinness. However, none of the media exposure variables was a significant longitudinal predictor of body dissatisfaction. Moreover, hierarchical regressions controlling for Time 1 level of each of the four criterion variables (e.g., internalization) found that none of the media exposure measures added significantly to prediction of the Time 2 criteria.

Although Field and colleagues used only single-variable measures of media exposure, their longitudinal research also casts doubt on exposure as a causal risk factor for older children and younger adolescents. Field et al. investigated a sample of over 6900 girls who were ages 9 through 15 at the 1996 baseline. Preliminary cross-sectional work did produce the expected positive linear association between frequency of reading women's fashion magazines and intensity of weight concerns. However, subsequent longitudinal research revealed that over a 1-year period the key predictor of the *development* of weight concerns and frequent dieting was "making a lot of effort to look like same-sex figures in the media." A 7-year follow-up showed that initiation of binge-eating, but not purging, in (now) adolescent and young adult females was predicted independently by frequent dieting and by Time 2 level of attempting to look like persons in the media.

The only longitudinal investigation of young adult women we could locate was Aubrey's 2-year panel study of college-age women. In support of Criterion 4, the extent of exposure to sexually objectifying media at Time 1 predicted level of self-objectification at Time 2, especially in women with low self-esteem. Measures of the tendency to self-objectify are positively correlated with eating disorder symptoms such as misperceptions of weight and shape, body shame, drive for thinness, and restrictive dieting.

Conclusion

Evidence from a very small number of longitudinal studies indicates that for children and very young adolescents, extent of media exposure does appear to predict increases in negative body image and disordered eating. Tiggemann's suggests that by early adolescence the causal risk factor is not media exposure, or even internalization of the slender beauty ideal, but rather the intensity and extent of "core beliefs and assumptions about the importance, meaning, and effect of appearance in an individual's life." . . .

Multimethod studies by Hargreaves and Tiggemann in Australia produced compelling evidence for the contention that mass media have negative and cumulative effects on body image in girls and young women. The adolescent girls whose body image was most negatively affected by experimental exposure to 20 television commercials featuring the thin ideal tended to have greater levels of body dissatisfaction and drive for thinness 2 years later, even when initial level of body dissatisfaction was controlled statistically.

The most vulnerable girls may well have a self-schema dominated by the core importance of physical appearance. In a study of girls ages 15 through 18 Hargreaves and Tiggemann found that appearance-focused TV commercials did activate an appearance-related self-schema, as reflected in several measures of cognitive set. Moreover, as predicted, appearance-focused commercials generated greater appearance dissatisfaction for those girls who began the study with a more extensive, emotionally charged, self-schema for appearance. Interestingly, the negative impact of the thin-beauty ideal in television commercials was, unlike previous findings with magazine images, unaffected by either the girls' initial level of body dissatisfaction or whether their viewing style was more personal (self-focused) or more detached (image-focused).

Positive (Assimilation) Effects. Durkin and Paxton found that 32% of the 7th grade girls and 22% of the 10th grade Australian girls who were exposed to images of attractive models from magazines exhibited an *increase* in state body satisfaction. Similarly, two studies of Canadian college students found that restrained eaters showed moderate to large increases in body satisfaction following exposure to similar magazine images, whereas unrestrained eaters had very large decreases in body satisfaction.

Two studies in the United States by Wilcox and Laird suggest that young women who focus on the slender models in magazines while defocusing attention on themselves are more likely to identify with the models and thus to feel better about their own bodies. Conversely, women who self-consciously divide their attention between the models and themselves are more likely to evaluate themselves and reach a conclusion that leaves them feeling inferior and worse. This finding is supported by research showing that self-evaluative processes, as opposed to self-improvement motives, are more likely to reflect and activate "upward" social comparison processes, which themselves tend to generate negative feelings about one's body.

Pro-Ana Web Sites. The internet offers many pro-anorexia (pro-ana) and pro-bulimia (pro-mia) web sites. Some of the most prominent pro-ana sites defiantly and zealously promote AN as a sacred lifestyle rather than a debilitating psychiatric disorder. Their "thinspirational" images of emaciation and their explicit behavioral instructions for attaining and sustaining the thin ideal are intended to reinforce the identity and practices of those already entrenched in AN or BN.

If concentrated exposure to typical images of slender models have negative experimental effects, then we might well expect the images and messages from pro-anorexia web sites to have even more negative effects. Two recent experiments by Bardone-Cone and Cass examined the effects of a web site that they constructed to feature the prototypical content of pro-ana sites. As predicted, exposure to this site had a large number of negative effects on young women, independent of their dispositional levels of thin ideal internalization and disordered eating. At present, we do not know what effects pro-ana and pro-mia sites have on the adolescent girls and young women who avidly seek them out because they already have a full-blown eating disorder. . . .

Media Literacy: Laboratory Investigations

. . . Media literacy (ML) is a set of knowledge, attitudes, and skills that enable people to work together to understand, appreciate, and critically analyze the nature of mass media and one's relationships with them. Systematic investigations of ML can be categorized into analog laboratory studies, brief interventions, and longer, more intensive programs.

. . . Several controlled experiments show that very brief written or video interventions can inoculate college-age women, including those who already have a negative body image, against the general tendency to feel worse about their bodies and themselves after viewing slides or video containing media-based images of the slender beauty ideal. The most effective ML "inoculation" highlights the clash between the artificial, constructed nature of the slender, flawless, "model look" versus two stark realities: (1) the actual shapes and weights of females (and males) naturally vary a great deal across a population; and (2) dieting to attain an "ideal" and "glamorous" weight/shape that is unnatural for a given individual has many negative effects, including risk for an eating disorder. . . .

Several programs for high-school and college-age females used slide presentations or Jean Kilbourne's video *Slim Hopes* (www.mediaed.org/videos/MediaAndHealth/SlimHopes) to help participants consider the history of changing, but consistently restrictive, beauty ideals and then to answer some fundamental questions: Do *real* women look like the models in advertising? Will buying the product being advertised make me look like this model? These programs emphasize how fashion models, working with the production staffs of magazines and movies, use "cosmetic" surgery, computer graphics, and other technologies to *construct* idealized *images*. Participants

are encouraged to explore how these manipulations are carefully orchestrated to stir up the desire to purchase products, many of which will supposedly reduce the discrepancy between such unreal, "perfect" images versus the body shapes and weights of normal, healthy females.

These ML programs are brief, so positive effects are necessarily limited. Nevertheless, it is noteworthy that they tend to reduce, at least in the short run, one important risk factor for disordered eating: internalization of the slender beauty ideal.

Well-controlled studies of multi-lesson, multifaceted media literacy programs that unfold over 1 to 2 months have shown that media literacy training can help girls *and* boys ages 10 through 14 to reduce risk factors such as internalization of the slender or muscular ideal, while increasing the potentially protective factors of self-acceptance, self-confidence in friendships, and confidence in their ability to be activists and thus affect weight-related social norms. In addition to spending considerable time working on the same components as those in the analog and brief interventions, intensive ML programs address the process and costs of social comparison. They also get participants involved in working within their ML groups, their school, and their larger community to translate their increasing literacy into peer education, consumer activism, and creating and promoting new, healthier media.

Recent investigations with college students also show ML to be a promising form of prevention. For example, Watson and Vaughn developed a 4-week, 6-hour intervention consisting of psychoeducation about the nature and sources of body dissatisfaction; group-based content analysis of beauty ideals in popular women's magazines; discussion of media ideals and beauty enhancement techniques; and a brief cognitive intervention designed to help participants dispute negative beliefs and feelings activated by media images of the thin ideal. Compared to a 1-day, 90-min version of this intervention, a one-time viewing of a 34-min media literacy film, and a no-intervention control, the extended intervention was the most successful in reducing the following risk factors for disordered eating: unhealthy social attitudes, internalization of the slender ideal, and body dissatisfaction. . . .

Presumed Influences on Others

In thinking about the subjective experiences of media pressures and influences, it is worth examining more closely the construct of "awareness" of the thin ideal. The perception that peers and people in general (e.g., employers) are influenced by thin-ideal media can itself be a form of subjective pressure that motivates young people to diet in an attempt to meet that ideal. In fact, it appears that the mere presumption of media effects on others may exert its own effect, at least on older females. Park's analytic study of over 400 undergraduates found that the more issues of beauty and fashion magazines a young woman reads per month, the greater the perceived prevalence of the thin ideal in those magazines. The greater this perceived prevalence, the greater the presumed influence of that ideal on *other women;* and in turn the greater the perceived influence on *self,* which predicted the desire to be thin. More research of this type with younger samples is needed to test this "cultivation of perceived social norms" hypothesis: Greater consumption of beauty and fashion magazines or of appearance-focused TV and internet content will foster stronger, more influential beliefs that the slender ideal is ubiquitous and normative for peers. This logic will, in turn, be a source of pressure and inspiration for the person's own desire to be thin(ner). . . .

And, yet, in light of the important research by Tiggemann and by Field et al. there remains a need to demonstrate more conclusively that either (1) direct engagement with mass media or (2) media effects that are mediated by parents and/or peers *precede* development of the more proximal risk factors such as negative body image. Similarly, despite the preliminary but encouraging evidence from media literacy interventions of varying intensities, to date no studies have tested the deceptively simple proposition that prevention programs can increase media literacy and thereby reduce or eliminate negative media influences—and in turn reduce or delay development of proximal risk factors (e.g., internalization of the thin ideal, social comparison tendencies) *and* attendant outcomes such as EDNOS.

What We Need to Know but Don't Know Yet

This review suggests five principal gaps in our knowledge about mass media as a potential causal risk factor for the spectrum of disordered eating. The first three are derived from the conclusion immediately above. First, there is a need for longitudinal research that examines the predictive validity of media exposure, motives for media use, and the subjective experience of media influences. Second, as noted by an anonymous reviewer of this manuscript, there remains a dearth of information about whether it is the thinness-depicting aspects of magazine, TV, and other media content that exert negative effects. Thus, survey-based longitudinal investigations of media exposure should strive to determine as precisely as possible not only frequency and intensity of consumption, but also the nature of the images, articles, programs, and such to which participants are exposed. Third, there is a need for prevention research that capitalizes on and extends the promising findings of extended media literacy interventions.

The fourth research direction concerns the relationship, particularly from a developmental perspective, between engagement with mass media and other causal risk factors. We need to learn much more about the ways in which body image disturbance and disordered eating are influenced by perceived social norms, by the confluence of media, family, and peer messages about weight and *shape,* and by *indirect* media exposure, such as acquisition of body

ideals and eating behaviors via interactions with family, peers, and significant adults (e.g., coaches) who learned them directly from television and magazines. Direct media effects may be small to modest, but the combination of direct and indirect effects, that is, the cumulative media effect, may be substantial.

Finally, the transactions between the developing child (or adolescent) and media constitute another set of important research questions to address. A cross-sectional study by Gralen, Levine, Smolak, and Murnen (1990) indicated that the correlates of negative body image and disordered eating in young adolescents tended to be more concrete and behavioral (e.g., onset of dating, pubertal development, teasing about weight and shape), whereas the predictors in middle to later adolescence were more psychological, such as the experience of a discrepancy between perception of one's own shape versus an internalized ideal shape. More recently, a longitudinal study by Harrison found that the number of hours that children ages 6 through 8 watched television per week predicted an increase in disordered eating without predicting idealization of a slender body. This raises the interesting and testable proposition that exposure to various salient media messages, including those contained in the onslaught of advertisements for diet-, fitness-, and weight-related products, might have little effect on the "thinness beliefs" of young children, while leading them to vilify fat, glamorize dieting as a grown-up practice, and yet still think of fattening, non-nutritious foods as desirable in general and useful for assuaging negative feelings.

With respect to the transformation of relevant psychological processes over late childhood, early adolescence, and later adolescence, Thompson and colleagues have developed and validated various features of the Tripartite Model in which media, family, and peers influence directly internalization of the slender beauty ideal and social comparison processes. This valuable model reminds us that, after nearly 25 years of research on media and body image, we still know relatively little about the automatic, intentional, and motivational processes involved in the role of *social comparison* in media effects. Basic questions remain: What dispositional and situational factors determine when people will make upward social comparisons with highly dissimilar fashion models whose "image" has been constructed by cosmetic surgeons, photographers, and computer experts? And under what circumstances will such comparisons result in negative effects (contrast) or positive effects (assimilation)?

Multidimensional models such as Thompson's also emphasize the need to determine when and how in the developmental process a number of important mechanisms such as appearance schematicity, thin-ideal internalization, social comparison processes, and self-objectification begin to play key roles. Further experimental and longitudinal studies of these mediators will be a very positive step toward understanding the emergence, particularly around puberty, of attentiveness and vulnerability to thin-ideal media images *and* to the many other potentially negative influences that emanate from family, peers, and influential adults such as coaches.

MICHAEL P. LEVINE is the Samuel B. Cummings Jr. Professor of Psychology at Kenyon College, where he teaches and conducts research on abnormal psychology, eating disorders, body image, and the development of personality.

SARAH K. MURNEN is Professor and Chair of the Department of Psychology at Kenyon College. Her research focuses on gender-related issues from a feminist, sociocultural background.

EXPLORING THE ISSUE

Do Media Cause Individuals to Develop Negative Body Images?

Critical Thinking and Reflection

1. What media celebrities or personalities do you emulate? What type of body image do they portray? Do you see your own sense of self influenced by the standards media people exemplify?
2. How are stories about eating disorders framed in the media? Are we told that eating disorders are a choice or that they are detrimental to our health?
3. How would you identify a healthy lifestyle for children and adults?
4. What evaluative measures do you have to assess beauty, health, or eating disorders? How do you describe each? What does your description say about your own views on each of these topics?
5. How do you form standards of what is "appropriate" and what do you do to measure your own behaviors? For example, do you have a weak self-image because you feel you can't measure up to mediated standards of health or beauty? What types of control do you exercise (if you do exercise control) to make you feel that you have a healthy attitude about body image?

Is There Common Ground?

June Deery's analysis of reality television programs that include extreme measures such as plastic surgery, and Michael P. Levine and Sarah K. Murnen's research that sees "two sides of the coin" in response to magazine advertising and body image each make assumptions about the impact of media in our lives, but the perspectives they offer give us much to think about.

The psychology of how one thinks of their body is an important and worthy subject for contemplation. Many books and articles have been written to untangle the many possible threads that lead to how self-image is constituted and maintained. For many years, self-improvement and self-help books have been among the best sellers in bookstores. Critical self-reflection about how one sees themselves and how one judges others is one of the most complex, but important subjects in examining the relationship of media and society.

Create Central

www.mhhe.com/createcentral

Additional Resources

Naomi Wolf, *The Beauty Myth: How Images of Beauty Are Used Against Women* (William Morrow and Company, 1991)

This book crafted a persuasive argument that the concept of beauty was a political issue that kept women stuck in a patriarchal system. By media and social issues preying on women's insecurities about their bodies, women's ability to fully participate in the labor force and in the social world was undermined. In 2002, Wolf published the second edition of the book with a new introduction, and in reviewing the new version, critic Emily Wilson, writing for *The Guardian* in the U.K., noted, "The world has changed—a bit—over the past decade and a half, but not enough."

Vickie Rutledge Shields and Dawn Heinecken, *Measuring Up: How Advertising Affects Self-Image* (University of Pennsylvania Press, 2002), or Ellen Cole and Jessica Henderson Daniel, eds., *Featuring Females: Feminist Analyses of Media* (American Psychological Association, 2005)

For more reading on images of ideal bodies in the media and the impact on consumers who may find their own bodies lacking, check out the above-mentioned books.

Arnold E. Andersen, *Making Weight: Men's Conflicts with Food, Weight, Shape & Appearance* (Gurze Books, 2000)

For a study of body image from the male perspective, the above-mentioned book is a helpful analysis of men's increasing sensitivity to issues of weight and appearance.

The U.S. Department of Health and Human Services has posted a Healthy Weight Chart on the Internet:

www.nhlbisupport.com/bmi

The popular magazine, *Psychology Today* occasionally writes about self-esteem issues. One such article that can be helpful to consult is

www.psychologytoday.com/basics/self-esteem

Internet References . . .

The U.S. Department of Health and Human Services

www.womenshealth.gov/body-image/

Selected, Edited, and with Issue Framing Material by:
Alison Alexander, *University of Georgia*
and
Jarice Hanson, *University of Massachusetts—Amherst*

ISSUE

Do Video Games Encourage Sexist Behavior?

YES: Anita Sarkeesian, from "Ms. Male Character—Tropes vs Woman," *Feminist Frequency* (2013)

NO: Kaitlin Tremblay, from "Intro to Gender Criticism for Gamers: From Princess Peach, to Claire Redfield, to FemSheps," *Gamasutra* (2012)

Learning Outcomes

After reading this issue, you will be able to:

- Consider the impact of the images in video games and other forms of media.
- Develop an opinion about those who threaten people who produce criticism of the media.
- Think more holistically about the nature of gaming and who plays video games.
- Consider the impact of immersive technology on behavior.
- Explore the power of images and actions in gaming scenarios.

ISSUE SUMMARY

YES: Anita Sarkeesian is a video game critic who also started a website called *Feminist Frequency*. In 2010, *Feminist Frequency* and *Bitch Media* put out a six-part series called "Tropes vs Women" in which Sarkeesian analyzes different tropes found in pop culture and the negative female stereotypes they perpetuate. This selection focuses on one of the tropes, the "Damsel in Distress," which Sarkeesian says is a theme that can be traced back to Greek mythology.

NO: Kaitlin Tremblay is an editor, a writer, and a video game maker who focuses primarily on topics that deal with horror, feminism, and mental illness. She says games are always a target for the best and the worst of gender criticism, and she claims that when we play video games we immerse ourselves in the character, and therefore, we can overcome any negative victim association that is so prevalent in many childhood games.

One of the first research questions in media studies was whether seeing violence in film would provoke audience members to be violent. As more research was conducted, the "direct" effects of the impact of media on behavior began to be better understood. A model of "indirect" effects emerged, suggesting that although sometimes violence in the media might provoke to violence people who were predisposed to look for violent images and think of them as validation for violent urges, the more common result is that the viewers of violent images have a complex ideological reaction to media violence that makes them look at the issue of violence in a more nuanced way. The entire area of media effects deals with the relationships that emerge between content and individuals within the broader audience.

Today there are still many studies that focus on the subtle relationships that prompt antisocial behavior as a reaction to media content. In this issue we explore sexism in video games, but in the cases we examine, *some* video gamers have gone to extremes and have created a gender war between feminists who advocate for stronger roles for women in video games and men who insist on perpetuating extreme female images that offend a number of women. The "gamergate" controversy that began in 2014 involves the harassment of many women video game designers, critics, and players, who have been threatened, stalked, and even threatened with death. This issue brings up questions about the images of women in video games, but because of the current controversy surrounding the harassment of so many women developers and critics, we should be mindful of the way violence and gender politics are played out in social media too.

Anita Sarkeesian is a video game critic who started a blog called Feminist Frequency in 2009 in which she critiqued a number of forms of popular culture. She began a YouTube series called "Tropes vs Women in Video Games" to examine the plot devices and representations of women in a wide range of video games. In this multipart series, she explores a wide variety of interpretive frames for understanding not only the meaning of the images we see in video games—especially in terms of the portrayal of women—but also how and why many video game developers have chosen to use these images in their games. This selection is from Sarkeesian's "Damsels in Distress (Part 1)," which was originally released on March 7, 2013. The term "tropes" refers to a recurring theme or motif in media. Sarkeesian makes the argument by continually stressing that video games use objectified, stereotypical images of women as helpless, dumb, and needing a man to "save" the woman. This type of sexism, she contends, insults both women and men.

Video game developer Kaitlin Tremblay approaches the problem of sexism from a slightly different perspective by outlining gender criticism and the performativity of gender in media. She claims that the cathartic values of playing video games in which any player can assume any gender they wish are part of the joy of gameplaying, and that in the act of becoming the protagonist of a game, we actually learn about other genders and about the fluidity of gender identity. She doesn't say there is no sexism in video games—rather, she says it isn't going away so we had better figure out how to cope with it.

In many ways, Sarkeesian and Tremblay are outlining traditional arguments in media studies that seek to understand the effects of media on our behaviors and in our culture. But their positions are exacerbated by the reality that some of the actions being taken to silence cultural critics are offensive, intimidating, and antisocial. In the case of videogaming, the role of social media that have no gatekeepers raises questions about media that incite antisocial behavior. Much like the studies of cyberbullying, the impact of online communication can be extremely threatening and unsettling for those targeted by uncivil participants in the gamer community. The controversy

caused by gamergate has been described as a culture war, and has been called a right-wing backlash against the progressive video game industry, which seeks to be more inclusive. While the industry undoubtedly has financial motives for being more inclusive, the identities many gamers seem to want to protect are complex social images of performed masculinity and dominance over others.

Video games have been around since the 1950s, but home-consoles and more portable devices became available in the 1970s and 1980s and extended the availability of games to many. At first, it seemed as though young men were most often the gamers, but today, games are played by people of all ages and are almost equally balanced by the number of women players (approximately 40%) to men. The number of women who design games has also grown, though the major game developers are still, for the most part, made up of designers who are men.

There are currently dozens of studies being conducted to find out why some male gamers seem threatened by women gamers, and why the presence of women who advocate for more gender-friendly games are the objects of online harassment. Sometimes women play with a pseudonym or a gender-neutral avatar to avoid becoming the subject of another gamer's hostility, and law enforcement is beginning to pay greater attention to issues of online harassment in commercial gaming. Some traditional studies pose the question of why some individuals (male or female) feel that communicating online entitles one to be a bully or exhibit obnoxious behavior, and these studies often cite the issue of gaming as something that is played in the privacy of one's home where usual, social behavior is not expected. Other studies focus on the shock factor that some people like to exhibit when they think they are anonymous online.

This issue brings together some very important issues for discussion. How and why is sexism perpetuated in different media forms? By whom, and for whom? Would people exhibit antisocial behavior online if their identities were known? Does the violence inherent in so many games lead a gamer to exhibit more violent behavior, even toward people who are commenting on games or designing them for gamers who have other interests? Also important, are social media vehicles for harassment and intimidation? In this very hotly debated topic, we see a number of social issues that extend from legacy media to social media, and a number of questions related to media effects and cultural politics.

YES ↵

Anita Sarkeesian

Ms. Male Character—Tropes vs Woman

Welcome to our multi-part video series exploring the roles and representations of women in video games. This project will examine the tropes, plot devices and patterns most commonly associated with women in gaming from a systemic, big picture perspective.

This series will include critical analysis of many beloved games and characters, but remember that it is both possible (and even necessary) to simultaneously enjoy media while also being critical of it's more problematic or pernicious aspects.

So without further ado let's jump right in to the Damsel in Distress.

Let's start with a story of a game that no one ever got to play.

Back in 1999 game developer RARE was hard at work on a new original title for the Nintendo 64 called "Dinosaur Planet." The game was to star a 16 year old hero named Krystal as one of the two playable protagonists. She was tasked with traveling through time, fighting prehistoric monsters with her magical staff and saving the world. She was strong, she was capable and she was heroic.

Well it would have been, except the game never got released. As development on the project neared completion, legendary game-designer Shigeru Miyamoto joked about how he thought it should be the 3rd installment in his Star Fox franchise instead. Over the next two years he and Nintendo did just that. They re-wrote and re-designed the game, and released it as Star Fox Adventures for the Game Cube in 2002.

In this revamped version the would-be protagonist Krystal has been transformed into a damsel in distress and spends the vast majority of the game trapped inside a crystal prison, waiting to be rescued by the game's new hero Fox McCloud.

The in-game action sequences that had originally been built for Krystal were converted to feature Fox instead. Krystal is given a skimpier more sexualized outfit.

And yes, [that is] cheesy saxophone music playing to make sure it "crystal clear" that she is now an object of desire even while in suspended animation—to add insult to injury Fox is now using her magic staff to fight his way through the game to save her.

The tale of how Krystal went from protagonist of her own epic adventure to passive victim in someone else's game illustrates how the Damsel in Distress trope disempowers female characters and robs them of the chance to be heroes in their own rite.

The term "damsel in distress" is a translation of the French "demoiselle en detresse." Demoiselle simply means "young lady" while detresse means roughly "Anxiety or despair caused by a sense of abandonment, helplessness or danger."

As a trope the damsel in distress is a plot device in which a female character is placed in a perilous situation from which she cannot escape on her own and must be rescued by a male character, usually providing a core incentive or motivation for the protagonist's quest.

In video games this is most often accomplished via kidnapping but it can also take the form of petrification or demon possession for example.

Traditionally the woman in distress is a family member or a love interest of the hero; princesses, wives, girlfriends and sisters are all commonly used to fill the role.

Of course the Damsel in Distress predates the invention of video games by several thousand years. The trope can be traced back to ancient greek mythology with the tale of Perseus.

According to the myth, Andromeda is about to be devoured by a sea monster after being chained naked to a rock as a human sacrifice. Perseus slays the beast, rescues the princess and then claims her as his wife.

In the Middle Ages the Damsel in Distress was a common feature in many medieval songs, legends and fairy tales. The saving of a defenseless woman was often portrayed as the raison d'être—or reason for existence—in romance tales or poems of the era involving a 'Knight-errant' the wandering knight adventuring to prove his chivalry, prowess and virtue.

At the turn of the 20th century, victimized young women become the cliche of choice for the nascent American film industry as it provided an easy and sensational plot device for the silver screen. A famous early example is the 1913 Keystone Kops short "Barney Oldfield's Race for a Life" which features the now iconic scene of a woman being tied to the railroad tracks by an evil mustache twirling villain.

Around the same time, the motif of a giant monkey carrying away a screaming woman began to gain widespread popularity in media of all kinds. Notably, Tarzan's love interest Jane is captured by a brutish primate in Edgar Rice Burroughs' 1912 pulp-adventure "Tarzan and the Apes." In 1930, Walt Disney used the meme in an early Mickey Mouse cartoon called "The Gorilla Mystery."

The imagery was even exploited by the US Military [a] recruitment poster for World War I.

But it was in 1933 that two things happened which, 50 years later, would set the stage for the Damsel in Distress trope to become a foundational element in video games as a medium. First, Paramount Pictures introduced their animated series "Popeye the Sailor" to cinema audiences.

The formula for most shorts involves Popeye rescuing a kidnapped Olive Oyl.

Second, in March of that year, RKO Pictures released their groundbreaking hit film "King Kong" in which a giant ape abducts a young woman and is eventually killed while trying to keep possession of her.

Fast forward to 1981 when a Japanese company named Nintendo entrusted a young designer named Shigeru Miyamoto with the task of creating a new arcade game for the American market.

Originally, the project was conceived of as a game starring Popeye the Sailor, but when Nintendo wasn't able to secure the rights, Miyamoto created his own characters to fill the void, heavily influenced by the movie, King Kong.

The game's hero "Jump Man" is tasked with rescuing a damsel, named "The Lady" after she is carried off by a giant ape. In later versions she is renamed "Pauline."

Although Donkey Kong is perhaps the most famous early arcade game to feature the Damsel in Distress it wasn't the first time Miyamoto employed the trope. Two years earlier, he had a hand in designing a 1979 arcade game called Sheriff.

In it a vague female-shaped collection of pixels, referred to as "The Beauty," must be rescued from a pack of bandits. The hero is then rewarded with a "smooch of victory" for his bravery in the end.

A few years later Miyamoto recycled his Donkey Kong character designs; Pauline became the template for a new damsel named Princess Toadstool and "Jump Man" became a certain very famous plumber.

Super Mario Bros: The Great Mission to Save Princess Peach

Princess Peach is in many ways the quintessential "stock character" version of the Damsel in Distress. The ill-fated princess appears in 14 games of the core Super Mario Brothers platformer games and she's kidnapped in 13 of them.

The North American release of Super Mario Brothers 2 in 1988 remains the only game in the core series in where Peach is not kidnapped and also the only game where she is a playable character. Though it should be noted it wasn't originally created to be a Mario game at all. The game was originally released in Japan under a completely different title called Yume Kōjō: Doki Doki Panic which roughly translates to "Dream Factory: Heart-Pounding Panic."

Nintendo of America thought that the original Japanese release of Super Mario Brothers 2 was too difficult and too similar to the first game so they re-skinned and re-designed Doki Doki Panic to star Mario and Luigi instead.

However the Japanese game already had 4 playable characters, so the designers opted to include Toad and the Princess to fill the two remaining slots, building directly on top of the older pre-existing character models. So really, if we're honest, Peach is kinda, accidently [sic] playable in this one.

Still, she had the awesome ability to float for short distances, which came in really handy especially in the ice levels.

Sadly Peach has never been a playable character again in the franchise. Even with newer games that feature 4 player options, like New Super Mario Brothers Wii and Wii U, the Princess is still excluded from the action. She's been replaced with another Toad instead as to allow Nintendo to force her back into the damsel role again and again.

Peach does of course appear in many spin-offs such as the Mario Party, Mario Sports and Mario Kart series as well as the Super Smash Brothers Nintendo Universe crossover fighting games. However all of these spins-offs fall well outside the core Super Mario series of platformers. She is the star of only one adventure and we will get to that a little later.

One way to think about Damsel'd characters is via what's called the subject/object dichotomy. In the simplest terms, subjects act and objects are acted upon. The subject is the protagonist, one the story is centered on and the one doing most of the action. In video games this is almost always the main playable character and the one from whose perspective most of the story is seen.

So the damsel trope typically makes men the "subject" of the narratives while relegating women to the "object." This is a form of objectification because as objects, damsel'ed women are being acted upon, most often becoming or reduced to a prize to be won, a treasure to be found or a goal to be achieved.

The brief intra sequence accompanying many classic arcade games tends to reinforce the framing of women as a possession that's been stolen from the protagonist.

The hero's fight to retrieve his stolen property then provides lazy justification for the actual gameplay.

At its heart the damsel trope is not really about women at all, she simply becomes the central object of a competition between men (at least in the traditional incarnations). I've heard it said that "In the game of patriarchy women are not the opposing team, they are the ball." So for example, we can think of the Super Mario franchise as a grand game being played between Mario and Bowser. And Princess Peach's role is essentially that of the ball.

Even though Nintendo certainly didn't invent the Damsel in Distress, the popularity of their "save the princess" formula essentially set the standard for the industry. The trope quickly became the go-to motivational hook for developers as it provided an easy way to tap into adolescent male power fantasies in order to sell more games to young straight boys and men.

Throughout the 80s and 90s the trope became so prevalent that it would be nearly impossible to mention them all. There are literally hundreds of examples showing up in platformers, side scrolling beat-em ups, first person shooters and role-playing games alike.

Many of these games drew inspiration from the historical myths that we discussed earlier. Medieval legends, Greek mythology and Arabic folk tales were all popular themes.

Let's take a quick moment to clear up some common misconceptions about this trope. As a plot device the damsel in distress is often grouped with other separate tropes: including the designated victim, the heroic rescue and the smooch of victory. However it's important to remember that these associated conventions are not necessarily a part of the damsel in distress trope itself.

So the woman in question may or may not play the victim role for the entire game or series while our brave hero may or may not even be successful in his rescue attempt. All that is really required to fulfill the damsel in distress trope is for a female character to be reduced to a state of helplessness from which she requires rescuing by a typically male hero for the benefit of his story arc.

This brings us to the other famous Nintendo Princess. In 1986 Shigeru Miyamoto doubled down on his Damsel in Distress formula with the NES release of The Legend of Zelda. This was the first in what would become one of the most beloved action adventure game franchises of all time.

Over the course of more than a dozen games, spanning a quarter century, all of the incarnations of Princess Zelda have been kidnapped, cursed, possessed, turned to stone or otherwise disempowered at some point.

Zelda has never been the star in her own adventure, nor been a true playable character in the core series.

However it must be said that not all damsels are created equal and Zelda is occasionally given a more active or integral role to play than her counterpart in the Mushroom Kingdom. Unlike Peach, Zelda is not completely defined by her role as Ganondorf's perpetual kidnap victim and in a few later games she even rides a line between damsel and sidekick. Remember the Damsel in Distress as a plot device is something that happens to a female character, and not necessarily something that the character is from start to finish.

Once in awhile she might be given the opportunity to have a slightly more active role in facilitating the hero's quest—typically by opening doors, giving hints, power-ups and other helpful items. On rare occasions she might even offer a last minute helping hand to the hero after all is said and done at end of the journey. I call this variant on the theme "The Helpful Damsel."

Indeed Zelda is at her best when she takes the form of Sheik in Ocarina of Time (1998) and Tetra in The Wind Waker (2003).

In Ocarina of Time, Zelda avoids capture for the first three quarters of the game. Disguised as Sheik she is a helpful and active participant in the adventure and is shown to be more than capable, however as soon as she transforms back into her more stereotypically feminine form of Princess Zelda, she is kidnapped within 3 minutes. Literally 3 minutes, I timed it. Her rescue then becomes central to the end of Link's quest.

Similarly, in The Wind Waker (2003), Tetra is a feisty and impressive young pirate captain. But as soon as she is revealed to be, and transformed into her more stereotypically feminine form of Princess Zelda, she is told that she's no longer allowed to accompany Link on the adventure because it's suddenly "too dangerous" for her. She is ordered to wait in the castle, which she does until she is eventually kidnapped, while waiting obediently in the same spot. It is noteworthy that in the very last stage of the boss battle, she does help Link fight Ganondorf, for a few brief minutes, which is a refreshing change.

However the next time Tetra's incarnation appears in 2007's The Phantom Hourglass she is kidnapped immediately during the intra. Later she is turned to stone and then kidnapped for a second time.

It's disappointing that even with her moments of heroism, Zelda is still damsel'ed—she is removed from the action, pushed aside, and made helpless at least once in every game she appears in.

This brings us to one of the core reasons why the trope is so problematic and pernicious for women's representations. The damsel in distress is not just a synonym for "Weak," instead it works by ripping away the power from female characters, even helpful or seemingly capable ones. No matter what we are told about their magical abilities, skills or strengths they still ultimately captured or otherwise incapacitated and then must wait for rescue.

Distilled down to its essence, the plot device works by trading the disempowerment of female characters FOR the empowerment of male characters.

Let's compare the damsel to the archetypal Hero Myth, in which the typically male character may occasionally also be harmed, incapacitated or briefly imprisoned at some point during their journey.

In these situations, the character relies on their intelligence, cunning, and skill to engineer their own escape— or, you know, just punching a hole in the prison wall works too.

The point is they are ultimately able to gain back their own freedom. In fact, that process of overcoming the ordeal is an important step in the protagonist's transformation into a hero figure.

A Damsel'ed woman on the other hand is shown to be incapable of escaping the predicament on her own and then must wait for a savior to come and do it for her.

In this way the Damsel's ordeal is not her own, instead it's framed as a trial for the hero to overcome. Consequently, the trope robs women in peril of the opportunity be the architects of their own escape and therefore prevents them from becoming archetypal heroes themselves.

Today many old-school damsel games are being resurrected for modern platforms, services or mobile devices

as publishers are in a rush to cash in on gaming nostalgia and capitalize on any recognizable characters from years gone by.

For example—SEGA's 1993 platformer Sonic CD featuring a damsel'ed Amy Rose has been enhanced and made available for download on a wide variety of modern platforms.

Jordan Mechner's famous (1984) Karateka and Prince of Persia (1989), originally released for the Apple ii home computer in the 1980s, have both seen modern HD remakes.

And the 1983 animated Laserdisc game Dragon's Lair with ditzy Princess Daphne has been ported to just about every system imaginable.

Remember Pauline, damsel from the classic Donkey Kong arcade?

Well she has also been revived, first in 1994's Donkey Kong for the Gameboy and later in the Mario vs Donkey Kong series for the Nintendo DS. Each game features a re-hashing of the old excuse plot with Pauline is whisked away by the giant ape during the opening credits.

The now iconic opening seconds of the 1987 beat-em up arcade game Double Dragon has Marian being punched in the stomach, throwen over the shoulder of a thug and carried away. In several versions her panties are clearly shown to the player while being abducted.

The game has been remade, re-released and ported to dozens of systems over the last 25 years, ensuring that Marian will continue to be battered and damseled for each new generation to enjoy. Most recently Double Dragon Neon in 2012 re-introduced new gamers to this repressive crap yet again, this time is full HD.

The pattern of presenting women as fundamentally weak, ineffective or entirely incapable also has larger ramifications beyond the characters themselves and the specific games they inhabit. We have to remember that these games do not exist in a vacuum, they are an increasingly important and influential part of our larger social and cultural ecosystem.

The reality is that this troupe is being used in a real-world context where backwards sexist attitudes are already rampant. It's a sad fact that a large percentage of the world's population still clings to the deeply sexist belief that women as a group need to be sheltered, protected and taken care of by men.

The belief that women are somehow a "naturally weaker gender" is a deeply ingrained socially constructed myth, which of course is completely false—but the notion is reinforced and perpetuated when women are continuously portrayed as frail, fragile, and vulnerable creatures.

Just to be clear, I am not saying that all games using the damsel in distress as a plot device are automatically sexist or have no value. But it's undeniable that popular culture is a powerful influence in or lives and the Damsel in Distress trope as a recurring trend does help to normalize extremely toxic, patronizing and paternalistic attitudes about women.

Now I grew up on Nintendo, I've been a fan of the Mario and Zelda franchises for most of my life and they will always have a special place in my heart, as I'm sure is true for a great number of garners out there. But it's still important to recognize and think critically about the more problematic aspects especially considering many of these franchises are as popular as ever and the characters have become worldwide icons.

ANITA SARKEESIAN is a Canadian-American cultural critic who started the website Feminist Frequency to focus on critiques of how women are portrayed in media. She has gained attention for her work on the roles women play in video games, and is a controversial public speaker who has been targeted in the "gamergate" controversy that is notable for harassment against several feminists in the video game industry.

Kaitlin Tremblay  **NO**

Intro to Gender Criticism for Gamers: From Princess Peach, to Claire Redfield, to FemSheps

As much as we all love Dead or Alive Xtreme Beach Volleyball—wait, do we?—we have to admit it brings to light some pretty unsettling ideas about women and video games: namely, that representation of women has fought a long, hard (no pun intended, of course) fight to be more than characters with spectacular tits.

This isn't to say that video games are evil and vehicles of patriarchy, because quite honestly, I think that video games, more than any other medium, are capable of achieving a thoughtful and progressive gender politic. It just needs to be conscious of gender criticism in order to do so, and to avoid the mentality of: "She has tits and she knows how to use a gun, what else do you want?" There has been resistance to approaches that criticize gender in games (albeit largely in comments threads), but I think that a lot of that resistance stems from a misunderstanding of what gender criticism is *about*. This article in an introduction to the major ideas that govern this mode of criticism, and how it applies to games.

How to Be: A Brief Introduction to Gender and Performance

Gender criticism is about identifying, exploring and bringing into focus stereotypical representations of gender. We challenge stereotypes of gender because ultimately, there is no innate, natural link between gender and sex, yet culture has imposed a hierarchy of roles based on these social, gendered constructs. Like the inevitable damsel in distress, Princess Peach. Peach, we all love you, but goddamn girl, get yourself some pepper spray.

In video games, the major stereotyped myths of women are typically the damsel in distress, hyper-sexualized villain (Sylvia Christel from No More Heroes) and the sexy/strong best friend (Tifa from Final Fantasy VII). Oh,

and let's not forget that pointy-haired Cloud has his eyes on the more feminine Aeris, so Tifa's not even in the running as a viable love-interest because she wears drab clothing rather than a bright pink dress. In all of these instances, the female character is, more likely than not, in love with the male protagonist or trying desperately to bang him.

See the problem?

What we need to take away from gender criticism in order to appease us feminist-gamer-girls frothing at the mouths is that stereotypes are harmful and alienating. We need to understand what Judith Butler, one of the foremost gender critics of our time, means when she says that gender is a societal construct and is therefore being performed.

Performance theory is the conception that we have internalized or been socially conditioned into "becoming" our gender. or instance, femininity is performed (via our clothes, our posture, our attitude et cetera) the way an actor would perform a role: we are given a script and told to act. Except, unlike actors, we're all exposed to the memory-erasing flash from Men In Black, and aren't consciously aware that we are performing what it means to be feminine or what it means to be masculine; we assume that they are "natural."

In saying that gender is a performance, I don't mean that it's not as simple as staring at your closet and deciding if you want to be feminine or masculine today; we don't have an active choice about how our genders are performed. The signifiers of femininity (clothing, attitude, manner of speech and so forth) are all pre-scripted, and we receive the script from society and cultural indoctrination. This is why so many people cry out against stereotypical portrayals of gender, because this social conditioning on the performance of gender actually influences both the way an individual relates to themselves and the way society relates to them.

How to Play: Gender Possibilities in Games

Here's where video games become brilliant. Especially in the light of such extreme character customization as with the Mass Effect franchise, we're allowed to expose these traits, mix them up, pick and choose and perform however/whoever we want. Freed from societal concerns (and ultimately consequences, because gender performativity is reinforced through negative societal pressure), we can pick *whatever traits/characteristics we want to play with*. Not only do we get to choose if we want to be dude or not, we get to pick their attitude, their alignment, their history and proficiencies.

Video games are so much . . . fun and can also offer the arena for the best—or worst—gender criticism. We need to remember that video games are one of the top forms of entertainment for children and therefore one of the most insistence avenues for receiving cultural information about ourselves. We need video games to be mindful of what they are teaching. This is part of why is it's so much fun to play as Princess Peach in MarioKart: getting to throw a red shell at Bowser is cathartic as all hell, and it does a lot to disrupt the narrative of victim hood that was so common in the games we played growing up.

The other major takeaway from Butler is that not only are these constructs, they are political constructs as well. Representation of gender is never neutral. The danger is that these stereotypes are vehicles for cultural conditioning of these societal constructs. And we need to keep this in mind for games that aren't character customizable.

Here comes our second major issue identified by gender criticism: that is, the issue of representation and objectification. Let's not forget that these stereotyped female characters are usually smoking hot. Which isn't necessarily a problem, but tends to be. We're drawn to beauty naturally, but the problem is that women tend to only serve the purpose of being beautiful and sexy, and this has always been a tool of suppression: "don't you worry your pretty little head about this, this is a man's problem." When a women is primarily defined by her sexiness, then it's as if that's the only thing she can be.

Gods and Goddesses: Addressing Some Myths

I'd like to address this myth that sexualization in video games is necessarily bad—because it isn't all the time. The trick is to sexualize, while at the same develop the character as a dynamic person, and not just a curvy woman who can only afford dominatrix clothing. Because let's be honest: sexualisation and video games is never going to go away, for either gender. *Nor should it.* The characters we play become basically extensions of ourselves—and when I'm feeling sick and exhausted and don't have the energy to change out of the same clothes I've worn for the past three days, it's a pleasure to have my character to be sexy for me.

One argument offered against this criticism of women in games is that men, especially in RPGs [role-playing games], are just as sexualized as women. While this is true, the difference tends to be that when men are sexy, there tends to be more to them. While I cited Sylvia Christel earlier as an example of the hyper-sexualized villain, I want to add a caveat: I also would say she has a fair amount of characterization added to her, especially in No More Heroes 2. She becomes more than just the hot bitch pulling the strings.

But when women are just sexualized and offer nothing else to the story arc, we run into the issue of objectification. Mary Ann Doane, using theories developed by Laura Mulvey, tackles female spectatorship in regards to film, but her theory is helpful here, because she states that cinema (essentially a spectator art) evicts the female spectator by virtue of creating her as the object of desire for the male gaze, despite the fact that the video game is creating a narrative about females. The problem is that if females are presented as only objects for sexual consumption, a large portion of women are left alienated by this—and the ones that aren't, are forced into the same spectatorial role as men. All the while, this eviction is creating a narrative about women, that is predicated on their exclusion.

The point here is that we need to make this theory of spectatorship obsolete: there has to be a way for gamer girls to identify with video games without being either the sex-kitten or aligned with masculinity.

Here's where things get touchy: in video games, male characters are also sexualized and depicted with extreme machismo and presented as ideals (Mario notwithstanding). But that isn't all they are. They're dynamic. And when we play games that offer only male characters as the lead, we're all aligning ourselves with that character. In feminist criticism, the masculine subject is often regarded as "the universal," relegating female characters to the position of "other"—they're something other than the standard, active subject.

The issue with gender criticism in video games is that female characters have had a hell of a time escaping this othered position. And it's a crime, because the gaming industry and nerd culture has faced it's own share of being "othered" within society. While this stereotyping of gender within video games is definitely shifting, it is always imperative to be conscious of what is being said about gender through the representations and narrativization of all characters involved. And we can't stop interrogating these stereotypes and gendered roles, because the only way to achieve subversion is through constant questioning and revitalizing of our concepts of gender.

This leads me to a final myth I'd like to address: that men won't enjoy playing as a female character. According to this, women identify easier with male characters, than men do with female characters. If this is the case, then it's only because men are conditioned to be aversive to identifying with femininity (and the violence and cultural bias against drag queens illustrates this). Back to Doanne and Mulvey: if a female spectator is going to identify with anybody, it has to be with the male spectator because there is no such thing as the female spectator, because females are only ever objects to be looked at. Why else all the super sexy, yet weather-inappropriate outfits female characters don?

The difference is that in video games, it is not mere spectatorship. We become the protagonist, and thus are necessarily in an active position. Video games become a way of bridging the distance between what we see and what this image culturally represents. Resident Evil: Code Veronica serves as an example of how gender does not change the game play of video games. The game play is divided between Claire and Chris Redfield. And while Claire does get saved by Steve, who professes his love for her as he dies, this doesn't change the fact that the immediate connection made with the game is through her: you won't make it to the Chris part, unless you succeed as Claire. You become either character fluidly and enjoy the game on the exact same level.

While video games have fallen victim to the same cultural traps in their gender politics, they also serve as a venue for an incredible amount of subversion and change. But in order to achieve this subversion of stereotypical gender norms, we need to be consciously aware and constantly challenging the images, representations and characterizations that are handed to us.

KAITLIN TREMBLAY is a game designer and writer. She is best known for her games that focus on eating disorders—"Stop Me If You've Heard This One Before"—and on depression; "There Are Monsters Under Your Bed." She calls her games "interactive fiction."

EXPLORING THE ISSUE

Do Video Games Encourage Sexist Behavior?

Critical Thinking and Reflection

1. Do you, or does anyone you know, relate to video game characters as representatives of real-world women and men?
2. Do you feel that the images in media, especially interactive forms of media, engage users who might respond to stereotypes?
3. Do you think that violence in any form of media serves to justify more violence in real life?
4. The gamergate controversy has resulted in some people threatening those who critique sexist images in video games. Should their threats be taken seriously?
5. Are children influenced by the images they see when they play video games?

Is There Common Ground?

Both of the writers in this issue agree that gender is often a highly controversial issue when discussing and critiquing video games, but both disagree on the significance of representations in gender when people play. Sarkeesian discusses the misogynistic nature of many games and the people (primarily men) who play them, but Tremblay feels that the immersive nature of playing videogames can be cathartic. Both also agree that when there are more women game designers, the current sexist issues are likely to recede.

This issue relates to one of the most fundamental questions: the relationship of media content to the way individuals internalize media images to form attitudes toward others. Very similar critiques have been aimed at images of women in advertising who have been objectified (largely by males who have created those images) with the assumption that men like them, and women, are intrigued by them. The issue also raises the question about whether any form of content is solely the purview of one gender or another. The assumption made by many of the staunchest advocates for the status quo is that video games are a male bastion that shuns women players. But the increasing number of players of both genders and of all ages refutes this misguided position.

Additional Resources

John Banks, *Co-Creating Videogames* (London: Bloomsbury, 2013). This book examines how authors and game players negotiate gender boundaries and understanding.

Jens Eder, Fotis Jannidis, and Ralf Schneider, *Characters in Fictional Worlds: Understanding Imaginary Beings in Literature, Film, and Other Media* (New York: De Gruyter, 2010). Authors examine familiar tropes from a variety of media forms and discuss their social impact.

Adrienne Shaw, *Gaming At the Edge: Sexuality and Gender at the Margins of Gamer Culture* (University of Minnesota Press, 2014). In this book, Shaw discusses a number of strategies gamers use. She discusses the gamergate controversy and the role of feminism in understanding the meaning of games.

Dimitri Williams, Mia Consolvo, Scott Caplan, and Nick Yee, "Looking for Gender: Gender Roles and Behaviors Among Online Gamers," *Journal of Communication* Vol 59 Issue 4, 2009: 700–725. In this article the authors look at the points of intersection between gamers and the games they play, and how gender is manifested.

Eileen L. Zurbriggen and Tomi-Ann Roberts, *The Sexualization Of Girls and Girlhood : Causes, Consequences, and Resistance* (New York University Press, 2013). This book discusses the range of issues that contribute to the ongoing victimization of girls and women, and the way girls and women can resist patriarchal behaviors and attitudes.

Internet References . . .

Bitch Media An online magazine and website focusing on Women in the Media

https://bitchmedia.org/

Gender and Education Association

http://www.genderandeducation.com/resources/

Inquisitr.com "What do Boys Think of Over Sexualized Women in Video Games?"

http://www.inquisitr.com/2244672/what-boys-think-of
-over-sexualized-women-in-video-games/

Media Watch "Challenging Racism, Sexism, and Violence in Media"

http://www.mediawatch.com/

Jesse Meixsell, *VentureBeat* (April 14, 2014) "Female Sexualization In Gaming: A Male Gamer's Perspective"

http://venturebeat.com/community/2014/04/14
/female-sexualization-in-gaming-a-male
-gamers-perspective/

Selected, Edited, and with Issue Framing Material by:
Alison Alexander, *University of Georgia*
and
Jarice Hanson, *University of Massachusetts—Amherst*

ISSUE

Is Product Placement an Effective Form of Advertising?

YES: Kaylene Williams et al., from "Product Placement Effectiveness: Revisited and Renewed," *Journal of Management and Marketing Research* (2011)

NO: Ekaterina V. Karniouchina, Can Uslay, and Grigori Erenburg, "Do Marketing Media Have Life Cycles? The Case of Product Placement in Movies," *Journal of Marketing* (2011)

Learning Outcomes

After reading this issue, you will be able to:

- Consider the role of product placement as an advertising tool.
- Critically think about the ethics of product placement.
- Evaluate how advertising techniques influence media content.
- Think more carefully about how persuasive advertising in general can be, and product placement in particular.
- Understand the range of influences that shape media content.

ISSUE SUMMARY

YES: Professors Kaylene Williams, Alfred Petrosky, Edward Hernandez, and Robert Page chronicle the evolution of product placement and define the term as incorporating "commercial content into noncommercial settings." They discuss the subtle differences between brand placement and product placement and raise the topic of how product placement is becoming more common in many media forms, including music and games.

NO: Professors Karniouchina, Uslay, and Erenburg analyzed 40 years of movies (1968–2007) to uncover the idea that product placement has become a tactic that no longer interests viewers of major motion pictures. As a result, they suggest that marketers should investigate other ways of trying to connect ideas and brand identities.

In May 2007, the United States House of Representatives' Committee on Energy and Commerce held sessions on the "Digital Future of the United States." Among the invited speakers was Philip Rosenthal, an actor/writer who had created and became the executive producer of the popular television series *Everybody Loves Raymond,* which ran on CBS from 1996 to 2005. Rosenthal was speaking on behalf of the Writers Guild of America—West, and the Screen Actors' Guild, so his comments on product placement were particularly relevant to the way product placement has become a part of the production process of television, in particular. While he acknowledged the subtle ways product placement influences shot composition in media, such as the actor's taking a drink out of a can with the label prominently displayed so that the camera can record the product, he cautioned; "Some of these commercial insertions could be dismissed as trivial . . . . This often subtle but always insidious blurring of the line between content and commerce is an issue not just for the creative community, but for the American viewing public as well."

Rosenthal continued to identify how product placement—a seemingly insignificant feature of underwriting the cost of media production by advertisers who pay for the use of their products in media content—has influenced the way writers write, how children learn to consume, and how the public has been exposed to media messages that exploit their emotional connection to shows and characters for the purpose of selling merchandise. The most egregious forms of product placement, he cautioned, occur when business deals between advertisers and production companies make the product a part of the storyline, which forces characters to talk about the product in what then becomes a long infomercial.

The Representatives in the room were shocked to learn that product placement has become such a component of our media landscape. This leads us to question whether the public too would be shocked to learn about the prevalence of product placement, and the potential of this technique to influence our thoughts and behaviors.

Both selections in this issue start with the perspective that product placement is neutral and natural—a change in the discourse about the prevalence in society, as well as a comment on how the public seemingly accepts the content presented to them by media producers. The authors of the two positions focus on more fundamental questions, concerning the effectiveness of product placement rather than the moral or ethical dimensions of whether product placement may be good, bad, or both.

Professors Williams, Petrosky, Hernandez, and Page approach the issue through the lens of advertisers who are seeking to understand the conditions under which product placement may be most effective. Professor Cowley and marketing executive Barron examine the same approach, but go in-depth to uncover a theoretical perspective that integrates social psychology with the act of product placement to show that some of the same techniques can have negative consequences. These two selections help us understand the power of product placement in terms of its history, practice, and how it influences the various media industries, but we have to inject the moral dimensions of questioning whether product placement contributes to our consumer society in positive or negative ways, and, we can ask the question, "Do we really need product placement?"

Historically, questions concerning advertising and techniques used to persuade or influence the public have made the assumption that misleading or deceiving the public is generally something that should be discouraged.

If product placement is normalized through the "behind the scenes" business of raising money for media production, the possibility of the public being misled is hidden from plain view. If product placement has become so prevalent that it is no longer a part of the discourse of advertising and the way the public is "manipulated" by media, perhaps we're really saying that we've lost the fight to make our media industries more ethical.

Some people might say that they don't mind, or don't consciously notice when the judges of *American Idol* all sip from cans of Coca-Cola, but the fact that the judges do shows that product placement has become big business. Similarly, popular television shows like *Biggest Loser*, make-over shows, and many genres of reality television blatantly call attention to products and product placement. What is really at stake, however, is the recurring question of whether advertising makes us buy things, and whether it matters at all, and that's why the normalization of product placement in media matters to us all.

In the United States our media industries grew as primarily commercial entities, but this is not the case in many other countries. Certainly, an argument could be made that the more "international" media become in their distribution arrangements, the more of a "global" norm develops and influences the type of content that can be created, but isn't this also a justification for multinational firms that seek to expand their product sales to other countries? Can consumer desire for a product develop by seeing the product represented in media, over and over? It's not enough to just say "that's the way it is." The real questions are: (a) how did media business get this way? and (b) are there other options for the way businesses operate that might be in the public's interest?

Our media institutions are changing constantly as producers look for ways to attract viewers, and product placement is just one example of how both advertising and television (or advertising and film, music, or video industries) are blurring the distinctions between industries and commercial activity. The power of the media industries, their practices, and the way in which media and society are connected through dozens, if not hundreds, of threads make us more aware of the power of media to influence the way we think, behave, develop attitudes, and function in society.

While this issue and the two selections pose a specific question for discussion, perhaps the bigger questions are all about what this specific example says about how the media and society have evolved over time.

YES

Kaylene Williams et al.

Product Placement Effectiveness: Revisited and Renewed

Product placement is the purposeful incorporation of commercial content into noncommercial settings, that is, a product plug generated via the fusion of advertising and entertainment. Product placement—also known as product brand placement, in-program sponsoring, branded entertainment, or product integration—is a marketing practice in advertising and promotion wherein a brand name, product, package, signage, or other trademark merchandise is inserted into and used contextually in a motion picture, television, or other media vehicle for commercial purposes. In product placement, the involved audience gets exposed to the brands and products during the natural process of the movie, television program, or content vehicle. That is, product placement in popular mass media provides exposure to potential target consumers and shows brands being used or consumed in their natural settings. Ultimately, the product or brand is seen as a quality of the association with characters using and approving of the product placement, for example, Harold and Kumar on a road trip to find a White Castle, Austin Powers blasting into space in a Big Boy statue rocket, Will Ferrell promoting Checkers and Rally's Hamburgers in the NASCAR comedy *Talladega Nights*, MSN appearing in Bridget Jones' Diary, BMW and its online short films, Amazon.com's Amazon Theatre showcasing stars and featured products, Ford and *Extreme Makeover*, Tom Hanks and FedEx and Wilson, Oprah giving away Buicks, Curious George and Dole, Herbie and VW, Simpsons' and the Quik-E-Mart, *Forrest Gump* and the Bubba Gum Shrimp Co. restaurants, Jack Daniels and *Mad Men*, and LG phones in *The Office*, just to name a few. In addition, Weaver gives numerous examples of product placements related to tourism, for example, the film *Sideways* promoting wine tourism in California's Napa Valley, the Ritz-Carlton hotel chain selling Sealy mattresses on the Internet, Holiday Inn Express selling Kohler's Stay Smart shower head, Showtime and HBO in many hotels and motels, and Southwest Airlines serving Nabisco products.

Even though product placement was named and identified formally only as recently as the 1980s, product placement is not new. Originally, product placement served as a way for movie studios and television networks to reduce the cost of production through borrowed props. Brand/product placement first appeared in Lumiere films in Europe in 1896. In the early years of U.S. product placements, the idea of connecting entertainment with consumption messages showed up in the entertainment films of Thomas Edison featuring shots of products from the Edison factory and Edison's industrial clients. Beginning in the 1930s, Procter & Gamble broadcasted on the radio its "soap operas" featuring its soap powders. Also, television and film were used by the tobacco companies to lend glamour and the "right attitude" to smoking. However, due to poorly organized efforts and negative publicity about the surrender of media content to commercialization, product placements were relatively dormant after the Depression. Product placements were recatalyzed in the 1960–70s with a growth spurt during the 1980s and 1990s.

Movies and programs are watched many times, accordingly, product placements are not limited in time to the original filmed item. In addition, today's technology can insert product placements in places they were not before. This digital product integration is a new frontier for paid product placement. As a result, consumers will see more and more product placements that are strategically placed in the media. Most product placements are for consumer products, yet service placements appear more prominently. Service placements tend to be woven into the script and are probably more effective than product placements that are used simply as background props.

Product placements may be initiated by a company that suggests its products to a studio or TV show, or it might work the other way around. Intermediaries and

Williams, Kaylene; Petrosky, Alfred; Hernandez, Edward; Page Jr, Robert. From *Journal of Management and Marketing Research*, vol. 7, April 2011, pp. 132–155. Copyright © 2011 by Kaylene Williams. Used with permission by the author.

brokers also match up companies with product placement opportunities. Costs for product placements can range from less than $10,000 to several hundred thousand dollars. However, television and movie producers routinely place products in their entertainment vehicles for free or in exchange for promotional tie-ins.

In terms of the Internet, consumers want to communicate with companies and brands so that they can get the information they want or need. So, companies need to listen to online conversations and establish what interests their online community. Then, they can provide that information in an engaging format including storytelling, articles, images, and video. For example, Yahoo! has produced branded video content—5–10 minute "webisodes" that usually feature story lines around a specific product such as a show about someone driving cross country in a Toyota Hybrid, sponsored by Toyota. "Being able to creatively brand interesting and valuable online content that attracts readers and viewers might just turn out to be the shortest way to consumer's hearts and minds."

While product placements have been used prolifically to target ultimate household consumers, they are beginning to expand into the business-to-business domain. In general, buying-center participants find the practice to be acceptable for a wide array of B2B products and services. In particular, when buying-center participants are exposed to experimental B2B influence through placement within major motion picture products, participants demonstrate an impressive level of recall and a modestly favorable attitude and purchase intention.

Use of Product Placement

Even though measures of its effectiveness have been problematic, product placement is a fast growing multi-billion dollar industry. According to the research company PQ Media, global paid product placements were valued at $3.07 Billion in 2006 with global unpaid product placements valued at about $6 Billion in 2005 and $7.45 Billion in 2006. Global paid product placement spending is expected to grow at a compounded annual rate of 27.9% over 2005–2010 to $7.55 Billion. Consequently, product placement growth is expected to significantly outpace that of traditional advertising and marketing. By 2010, the overall value of paid and unpaid product placement is expected to increase 18.4% compounded annually to $13.96 Billion. Television product placements are the dominant choice of brand marketers, accounting for 71.4% of global spending in 2006. Advertisement spending on product placement in games in the U.S. is likely to reach $1 Billion by 2010.

The U.S. is the largest and fastest growing paid product placement market, $1.5 Billion in 2005, $2.9 Billion in 2007, and $3.7 Billion in 2008. Marketers increased the dollars spent on branded content in 2009, double the 2008 figures. Branded content comprised 32% of overall marketing, advertising, and communications budgets. These numbers are expected to jump significantly in 2010. Some 75% of U.S. prime-time network shows use product placements. This number is expected to increase due to the fact that 41% of U.S. homes are expected to have and use digital video recorders that can skip through commercials. Hence, communicating core marketing messages is vital and difficult. Consider the following data:

- "90% of people with digital video recorders skip TV ads."
- "To be seen, brands now have to get inside the content."
- "Consumer consumption of entertainment increases when economic times get tough."
- "ITV reported an increase of 1.1% in TV viewing in the first quarter of 2009."
- "Cinema admissions for 2009 to April 30 stand at 55.2 million, a 14.2% increase on the same periods in 2008."
- "Research shows product placement in content boosts brand awareness, raises brand affinity and encourages prospective purchasers."
- "60% of viewers felt more positive about brands they recognized in a placement."
- "45% said they would be more likely to make a purchase."

Product placements can be a cost-effective method for reaching target customers. Because of this, product placements are likely to eclipse traditional advertising messages.

In terms of specific numbers, U.S. product placement occurrences for January 1–November 30, 2008 broadcast network programming for the Top 10 programs featured 29,823 product placements. *Biggest Loser* was the leader in terms of the number of product placements (6,248 occurrences), followed by *American Idol, Extreme Makeover Home Edition, America's Toughest Jobs, One Tree Hill, Deal or No Deal, America's Next Top Model, Last Comic Standing, Kitchen Nightmares,* and *Hells Kitchen.* The Top 10 brands that featured product placements for January 1–November 30, 2008 were CVS Pharmacy, TRESemme, El, Pollo Loco, Bluefly.com, Sears, Glad, Whole Foods Market, Food & Wine Magazine, GQ Magazine, and Hugo Boss.

The use of product placements in recorded music also is growing. As noted by Plambeck

> "According to a report released last week by PQ Media, a research firm, the money spent on product placement in recorded music grew 8 percent in 2009 compared with the year before, while overall paid product placement declined 2.8 percent, to $3.6 Billion."

> "The money is often used to offset the video's cost, which is usually shared by the artist and label."

> "Patrick Quinn, chief executive of PQ Media, said that revenue from product placement in music videos totaled $15 million to $20 million last year, more than double the amount in 2000, and he expected that to grow again this year."

> "The Lady Gaga video, which has been viewed 62 million (updated: 91.8 million as of November 14, 2010) times on YouTube, included product placements from Miracle Whip and Virgin Mobile."

Another area of growing product placements is placed-based video ads in stores, shopping malls, restaurants, medical offices, bars, airports, or health clubs. Approximately 29.6% of U.S. adults or 67.4 million adults have viewed these types of video ads in the last 30 days. Both young men and young women, in general, are more likely than the population as a whole to report they viewed place-based video ads. Young men aged 18–34 are 28% more likely (young women are 13% more likely) than the population as a whole to have viewed a placebased video ad in the last 30 days. This is important because these young consumers are difficult to reach via traditional media. "Video advertising in stores and shopping malls garnered the largest audience, at nearly 19% and 15% of the U.S. adult population, respectively. This was followed by nearly 11% of U.S. adults who saw a video ad in the last 30 days in a restaurant or medical office, nearly 9% who saw a video ad in a bar/pub or at an airport, and 7% who saw a video ad while at the gym or health club."

Generally, U.S. product placement markets are much more advanced than other countries such that other countries often aspire to the U.S. model. The next largest global markets are Brazil, Australia, France, and Japan. China is forecast to be the fastest growing market for product placements this year, up 34.5%. Product placement methods differ widely by country given varying cultures and regulations. Most product placements are in five product areas: transportation and parts, apparel and accessories, food and beverage, travel and leisure, and media and entertainment.

Purposes of Product Placement

Product placement can be very useful. Ultimately, product placements among entertainment firms, corporate brands, and agencies are all monetarily driven, either directly or indirectly. At the very least, entertainment firms and independent production companies are hoping to reduce their budgets so that more dollars can be invested elsewhere. Its purposes include achieving prominent audience exposure, visibility, attention, and interest; increasing brand awareness; increasing consumer memory and recall; creating instant recognition in the media vehicle and at the point of purchase; changing consumers' attitudes or overall evaluations of the brand; changing the audiences' purchase behaviors and intent; creating favorable practitioners' views on brand placement; and promoting consumers' attitudes towards the practice of brand placement and the various product placement vehicles. As noted by van Reijmersdal, Neijens, and Smit, a substantial part of the effects and interactions of product placement is still unknown.

(1) To achieve prominent audience exposure, visibility, attention, and interest

Product placements can have a significant effect on message receptivity. The sponsor of product placements is likely to gain goodwill by associating itself with a popular program targeted to a specific audience. The more successful the program, the longer shelf life of the product placement. Interest in advertising appearing in product placement in movies is reported to be of "considerable" or "some" interest to 31.2% of consumers. More frequent viewers and viewers who enjoy the program pay more attention to product placements. Brands need to be visible just long enough to attract attention, but not too long to annoy the audience.

(2) To increase brand awareness

Nielsen Media Research has shown that product placement in television shows can raise brand awareness by 20%. Tsal, Liang, and Liu found that higher brand awareness results in a greater recall rate, more positive attitudes, and a stronger intention of buying. When brand awareness is high, a positive attitude toward the script leads to a higher recall rate. Also, when a brand gains a certain level of awareness, the more positive the attitude toward product placement, the stronger its effect on recall rate, attitude, and intention of buying. However, when product/brand awareness is not high enough, consumers typically fail even to remember the names of the advertised products.

(3) To increase consumer memory and recall of the brand or product

Product placements can have a significant effect on recall. For example, memory improves when visual/auditory modality and plot connection are congruent. Pokrywczynski has found that viewers can correctly recognize and recall placed brands in movies, using aided recall measures and free recall measures. Also, brands placed prominently in a movie scene enjoy higher brand recall than those that are not. Verbal and visual brand placements are better recalled than placements having one or the other. In addition, showing the brand early and often with at least one verbal mention enhances brand recall. Also, sitcoms rather than reality shows tend to spark better recall for product placements. Hong, Wang, and de los Santos, found that product placement upholds brand salience or the order in which brands come to mind. They note that to build brand salience, product placement strategies should focus on how a product can explicitly convey the product's superiority, durability, performance, and specification. That is, marketers should focus on how a product can be noticed, even if it is perceived as artificially inserted for commercial purpose. As such, marketers need to give as much attention to product placements as they do to the insertion of commercials into a television program. To achieve higher brand salience, they also found that products should be placed more in negative-context programming than in positive ones and should not excessively interfere with the plot. In addition, Gupta and Gould found that greater recall can be obtained by smart placement of product placements in game shows, in particular, placements that appear at the beginning of a game show command higher recall. Brand recall is typically no higher than 30%. Or, as summarized by van Reijmersdal, "Prominent brand placement affects memory positively, but affects attitudes negatively when audiences are involved with the medium vehicle, when they like the medium vehicle, or when they become aware of the deliberate brand placement (selling attempt)."

(4) To create instant recognition of the product/brand in the media vehicle and at the point of purchase

Product placement can have a significant effect on recognition. Familiar brands achieve higher levels of recognition than unfamiliar brands. In addition product or brand placement recognition levels received from audio-visual prominent placements exceed the recognition rates achieved by visual-only prominent placements. Some 57.5% of viewers recognized a brand in a placement when the brand also was advertised during the show. That number is higher than the 46.5% of viewers who recognized the brand from watching only a television spot for the brand. While prominence of the placement leads to increased recognition, if the placement is too long or too prominently placed,

viewers might become suspicious, elaborate on the commercial purpose of the placement, counter-argue, and form negative attitudes or behaviors. In addition, star liking, cognitive effect, and pleasure affect recognition for product placements. Specifically, brand recognition due to product placements increased 29% during highly enjoyable programs.

(5) To bring desired change in consumers' attitudes or overall evaluations of the brand

The influence of product placement on attitudes, preferences, and emotions toward a product or brand has not been researched very much. With this in mind, however, no differences have been found in viewers attitudes toward a product or brand. On the other hand, initial evidence suggests that consumers align their attitudes toward products with the characters' attitudes to the products. In addition, this process is driven by the consumers' attachment to the characters. Argan, Velioglu, and Argan suggest that the audience pays attention to and accepts brand placement in movies and takes celebrities as references when shopping. However, the movie should not be over commercialized. At the same time, initial studies find that attitudes toward product placements do not differ based on gender, age, income, or education. However, as discussed later, more recent studies have found differences. Authors van Reijmersdal, Neijens, and Smit have found that as consumers watch more episodes, the brand image becomes more in agreement with the program image. This confirms that learning and human association memory are important to brand placement. It also has been noted that product placements on emotionally engaging programs were recognized by 43% more viewers.

(6) To bring a change in the audiences' purchase behaviors and intent

Product placements are associated with increased purchase intent and sales, particularly when products appear in sitcoms, for example *Ally McBeal* in Nick and Nora pajamas, *Frasier and Friends* in Starbucks and New World Coffee, and Cosmopolitan martinis in *Sex and the City*. In one example, Dairy Queen was featured on *The Apprentice*. The contestants needed to create a promotional campaign for the Blizzard. During the week of the broadcast, Blizzard sales were up more than 30%. Website hits also were up significantly on the corporate and Blizzard Fan Club sites as well as the Blizzard promotional site. While DQ had six minutes of screen time, the overall tone was a little harsh with two contestants arguing. So, it was not the most positive environment for good, old-fashioned DQ. However, it cost DQ in the "low seven figures" to appear on the show and run its supporting promotion. Not bad for a 30% increase in sales. Controversy does seem to generate attention.

(7) To create favorable practitioners' views on brand placement

Practitioners' views on product placement generally are favorable or else the product placement market would not continue to increase. Practitioners remain positive about product placements as long as no harm is done, sales and brand image go up, and consumers are positive about the product and brand. Also, product placements help the practitioner make up for an increasingly fragmented broadcast market due to technology such as TiVo and DVD recorders.

(8) To promote consumers' attitudes towards the practice of brand placement and the various product placement vehicles

In general, attitudes toward product placement are favorable across media types. Additionally, viewers tend to like product placements as long as they add realism to the scene. Snoody has found that viewer enjoyment of product placements actually increased for media vehicle versions of product placements where products were an integral part of the script. He conjectures that peoples' lives are so saturated with brands that the inclusion of identifiable products adds to the sense of reality, that is, validates the individual's reality. Also, product placements are preferred to fictitious brands and are understood to be necessary for cost containment in the making of programs and movies. About half of respondents said that they would be more likely to buy featured products. People with more fashionable and extroverted lifestyles typically have more positive attitudes toward product placement. Sung and de Gregorio found that college students' attitudes toward brand placement are positive overall across media, but that brand placements in songs and video games are less acceptable than within films and television programs. So, marketers need to take into account the appropriateness of the specific genre of the particular media program into which they intend to place brands. Non-students are more neutral toward the practice than students. In general, consumers are positively disposed toward product placement, value the realism of the ad, and do not consider the ad to be unethical or misleading as long as the product is not ethically charged, for example, alcohol. Also, while there is a generally positive perception of the practice overall, there are reservations regarding the insertion of certain ethically charged products such as firearms, tobacco, and alcohol. Also, if brand image is positive, then consumers' brand evaluations toward the product placement seem to be more positive. Older consumers are more likely to dislike product placements and more likely to consider the practice as manipulation.

Overall, the managerial implications have been stated eloquently and succinctly by van Reijmersdal, Neijens, and Smit:

'To create brand placements that are positively evaluated, they should be placed within programs, movies, games, or magazines that are involving for the audience. Placements are also positively evaluated when the placement format is more editorial rather than commercial.

"To increase brand memory, brands should be prominently placed and be accompanied by an actor in films or television programs. Brand evaluations can become more positive when the placement is more editorial instead of commercial and when non-users of the brand are reached. Behavior and behavioral intentions are influenced best when the audience has positive evaluations of brand placement, when placements are presented in editorial formats, and when placements are repeated."

Use of Product Placement in Specific Media

Researchers have studied product placement in various media advergames, computer/video games, digital games, movies, television, television magazines, novels, online games, simulation games, sporting events, game shows, radio, physical environments such as hotel rooms, rental cars, or ships (Weaver, 2007), virtual/online environments, and songs. Most product placement studies have focused on film (33.87%), television (32.25%), and video games (20.21%). In actuality, most product placement is done through television, film, and video games. However, regardless of the media used, the brand's image and the content vehicle need to fit in such a way that the product/brand image will not be harmed and that attention will be brought to the product or brand. Also, because advertisers continue to look for ways to stay in touch with consumers, they easily could follow their audiences into less-regulated media such as the Internet and 3-G mobile phones. As web-connected television becomes a practical reality, a user-driven environment and peer-to-peer file swapping is being reinforced. While new platforms such as 4G and MPEG-4 create greater opportunities for interactivity, successful product placement still must be relevant to its host content.

Television

Television viewing is complicated with the use of zipping, zapping, TiVo, and DVRs. That is, the audience can shift the channel, change the program, and slow down or fast-forward the program to avoid advertising. In addition, media clutter, similarity of programming across channels, and channel switching behavior all compound the advertising effectiveness of television. As a result, top-rated television shows are not necessarily the best places for product placements. Product placements depend on a number of factors, including length of the time on air, when and how products are woven into the story line, and targeted audience.

Plot connection (Russell, 1998) is the degree to which the brand is woven into the plot of the story. Lower plot placements do not contribute much to the story. Higher plot placements comprise a major thematic element. Essentially, verbally mentioned brand names that contribute to the narrative structure of the plot need to be highly connected to the plot. Lower plot visual placements need to serve an accessory role to the story that is lower in plot connection. Visual placements need to be lower in plot connections, and audio and visual placements need to be even higher in plot connection. Also, prominent brand placements in television have a more significant advantage than subtle brand placements.

Film

What is the effect of Tom Cruise chewing Hollywood gum or Agent 007 using a BMW? These are typical examples of product placement in movies. Higher involvement is required to view a movie than for viewing television. Television viewers can multi-task in the home setting thereby reducing their attention span and brand retention. Moviegoers actively choose the experience, movie, time, and cost. As such, they are much more receptive to the brand communication during the movie. A majority of movie watchers have a positive attitude toward this form of marketing communication, feeling it is preferable to commercials shown on the screen before the movie. More frequent viewers and viewers who enjoy the movie more, pay attention to product placements in the movie.

Shapiro has classified four types of product placements in movies: (1) provides only clear visibility of the product or brand being shown without verbal reference, for example, a bottle of Coca-Cola sitting on the counter; (2) used in a scene without verbal reference, for example, actor drinks a Coca-Cola but does not mention anything about it; (3) has a spoken reference, for example, "Boy, I'm thirsty for a Coke"; and (4) provides brand in use and is mentioned by a main star, for example, actor says "This Coke tastes so refreshing" while drinking the Coke. The star using and speaking about the brand in the film is assumed to have higher impact than the mere visual display of the brand. That is, meaningful stimuli become more integrated into a person's cognitive structure and are processed deeply and generate greater recall. Yang and Raskos-Ewoldsen found that higher levels of placements influence recognition of the brand and attitudes toward the brand. However, single placement of the brand within the movie influenced implicit memory and the implicit choice task. To gain greater audience recognition, the brand needs to be used by the main character or needs to play a role in the unfolding story. That is, prominence and plot connection are important. Product placements may have a long-term effect on implicit memory and perceptions of familiarity.

Computer/Video Games

Products and brands are expanding into video games and even creating their own games. Active product placement in computer games can have positive effects. For example, exposure to a particular brand in a computer game can increase the brand attitude among consumers whose original attitude toward the brand is fairly low. Product placement within computer games has been found to be an effective means of building high spontaneous brand recall and even of influencing consumers less positively predisposed towards a brand, that is, non-users. Product placements in computer/video games are becoming powerful marketing tools that form an active part of the gamers' play experience. In particular, they can be used to target the elusive younger male consumer segment with brands woven into near real-life situations that provide a means of interacting with the brand. Lee and Faber note that the location or proximity of the brand messages in the game, game involvement, and prior-game experience interact to influence brand memory. A highly incongruent brand Is better recalled than either a moderately incongruent brand or a highly congruent brand. As experienced players' involvement increases, brand recognition decreases, that is, they are paying attention to the game. Also, product placement seems to grow on the second exposure, that is, when a consumer sees the movie, then the DVD comes out, and in actually playing the game. The multiple viewings may reduce the intrigue in the storyline and give more time to notice the props.

Essentially, there are three general approaches to game advertising: (1) traditional product placements, signs, and billboard ads that are just in the games from the beginning and cannot be changed later, (2) dynamic advertising wherein new ads can be inserted at anytime via the Internet, and (3) advergames or rebranded versions of current games that blatantly promote a single product throughout, Until now, advergames and product placements have been the leading forms of in-game advertising. For example, Burger King created three games suitable for the whole family: racing, action, and adventure, featuring The King, Subservient Chicken, and Brooke Burke. Their target market of young males meshes well with the Xbox audience, given that 18–34 year old men have been a hard group for marketers to get their product or name in front of.

However, dynamic advertising is taking off and is probably the wave of the future. In dynamic advertising, a marketer can specify where ads are put, can set times when ads will run, can choose which audience type your ad goes to, and can get the tracking available for Internet ads. Approximately 62% of gamers are playing online at least some of the time. Researchers can track how long each ad is on the screen, how much of the screen the ad occupies and from what angle the gamer is viewing the ad. Companies pay for ad impressions—one ad impression constitutes 10 seconds of screen time. For example, about half of video games are suitable for ads and could be contextually relevant to the game. More than 50 games already are receiving dynamic ad content, with another 70 set to go by year-end.

Another wave of the future is 3D ads that are twice as powerful as billboards. Also, the latest version of digital video standard MPEG-4 offers the possibility to personalize storylines or even hyperlink from tagged content, so viewers can click on objects they want to buy. Whatever the future brings, advertising and product placements need to fit with the game. That is, video game developers need to incorporate advertising in an ambient way that will not distract players. In addition, the center of the screen gets the most attention based on eye-tracking research.

Summary

Product placement has become an increasingly popular way of reaching potential customers who are able to zap past commercials. To reach these retreating audiences, advertisers use product placements increasingly in clever, effective ways that do not cost too much. The result is that the average consumer is exposed to 3,000 brands a day including billboards, T shirts, tattoos, schools, doctor's office, ski hills, and sandy beaches. While some preliminary conclusions with regard to product placements have been reached, the industry is far from a comprehensive analysis and testing of all the antecedents and consequences of product placement. In the interim, however, a wise caveat to consider for product and brand placement is "Our philosophy is if the brand doesn't make the show better, the brand doesn't make the show. People must not notice the integration, but they must remember it. That's the test." The ideal product placement situation is win-win-win-win: customer gets to know about new and established products and their benefits, client gets relatively inexpensive branding of their product, media vehicle gets a brand for free or can reduce its production budget, and the product placement agency gets paid for bringing the parties together.

KAYLENE WILLIAMS, **ALFRED PETROSKY**, and **EDWARD HERNANDEZ** are all professors at California State University, Stanislaus, and **ROBERT PAGE, JR.,** is a professor at Southern Connecticut State University, New Haven, CT.

Ekaterina V. Karniouchina, Can Uslay, and
Grigori Erenburg

 **NO**

Do Marketing Media Have Life Cycles? The Case of Product Placement in Movies

For better or worse (e.g., more than four dozen brands in *The Departed* [2006]), product placement in the movies has become a part of the contemporary marketing arsenal, lending its power to offerings ranging from pregnancy tests to luxury cars. Gupta and Gould (1997, p. 37) define product placement as a marketing strategy that "involves incorporating brands in movies in return for money or for some promotional or other consideration." Industry sources boast that it can do wonders and significantly boost sales of featured brands. For example, Ray-Ban considered the lifespan of its Wayfarer model sunglasses to be almost over when it placed them in *Risky Business* (1983). Before the release of the movie, the declining sales were at approximately 18,000 units a year; following the movie release, the annual sales of the revived product jumped to 360,000 units. By 1989, following a number of successive placements (e.g., *Top Gun* [1986]), sales reached 4 million units. Despite the abundance of such success stories, the evidence for the tangible benefits of product placement is mostly anecdotal, and studies that empirically demonstrate its economic worth are scant at best. Nevertheless, firms can take extreme measures to establish strategic dominance in branded entertainment. At the peak of the "cola wars" in the early 1980s, Coca-Cola went as far as purchasing Columbia Pictures to control the entertainment arena.

Product placement originally fell under the umbrella of covert marketing because viewers were often unaware of the commercial persuasion effort. Many early marketing research efforts concentrated on the subliminal and covert nature of this marketing medium. However, as consumers have become more marketing savvy and the technique more prominent, it has shifted closer to the realm of conventional marketing. At present, the question remains whether this tactic is still as effective as it was in the past; it is commonly believed that when advertisers cross the line and overwhelm the audience with blatant product placements, their efforts will backfire.

In this article, we adopt a longitudinal perspective and examine the evolution of the effectiveness of product placement in the movies over a 40-year time frame. . . . We conclude with managerial implications, future research directions, and limitations.

An Historical Perspective on Product Placement

Although many researchers believe that product placement was born when a little boy made an extraterrestrial friend by laying a trail of Reese's Pieces in *E.T.* (1982), other sources are starkly divided on its true origins. For example, Karrh, McKee, and Pardun (2003) argue that product placement originated in the 1940s, while others suggest that this marketing medium can be traced back to the end of nineteenth century, when Lever Brothers' Sunlight soap was placed in several films. However, most sources agree that the practice emerged as a legitimate marketing instrument in the mid-1970s and has been rapidly expanding since that time. The biggest surge has arguably been during first decade of the twenty-first century. Product placement spending in the United States grew at an annual rate of almost 34% to $2.9 billion in 2007 and was projected to reach $5.6 billion in 2010.

In the early stages of its development, product placement was governed by ad hoc decisions and intuition. Branded placement was a casual process, in which branded items were donated, loaned, or purchased at a discount for particular scenes. However, in the new millennium, the process of placing branded consumer products in feature films has gained mass appeal, becoming orderly and institutional, with clearly defined roles involving multiple parties and intermediaries. For example, Next Medium has propelled itself as a leader in the product placement arena by automating the process of product placement in the movies, television shows, and video games and even allowing product placement needs to be filled using an auction-based platform. With more than 80% of national marketers using branded placement, the practice is certainly a part of today's mainstream marketing arsenal.

Because of the proliferation of this marketing medium, consumers are becoming aware of product placement tactics and have started to show evidence of resistance to persuasion. In addition, in an ironic twist, product placements have now created a cluttered environment, which marketers initially designed the tactic to avoid. Furthermore, consumers and industry participants are beginning to question whether the overabundance of placements detracts from the viewing experience and interferes with filmmakers' creative vision (e.g., Writers Guild of America West 2005). Numerous Internet blogs are devoted to dissecting and mocking placement-heavy films (e.g., http://www.brandspotters.com). Multiple consumer advocacy groups are calling on the Federal Trade Commission and other government agencies to curb and/ or regulate product placement practices (e.g., Commercial Alert 2003). . . .

Product Placement Efficacy

Researchers have traditionally attributed the efficacy of product placement as a marketing medium to its ability to cut through advertising clutter by relying on transference mechanisms. Instead of competing against a plethora of competitive advertisements in more traditional advertising channels, product placement acts in a more unobtrusive way by evoking the positive associations, aspirations, and symbolic meanings connected with the underlying movie content. Excitation transfer theory also suggests that the excitement associated with film sequences can be transferred to other subsequently presented objects, including embedded products. Labeled by the industry as "the anti-TiVo," product placements are also believed to be more effective in reaching the target audience than traditional advertising spots because they are immune to ad skipping. Finally, product placements might circumvent consumer resentment by blurring the lines between commercial content and entertainment, thereby providing "advertainment." . . .

At present, the consensus is that, despite the large spectrum of research on product placement, the economic value of a placement remains a pressing research question. We are aware of only one study that has attempted to evaluate the effect of product placement in movies on firm value: In a cross-sectional study, Wiles and Danielova

(2009) investigate price reactions for stocks of publicly traded companies that placed their brands in the 24 most popular movies of 2002. Their daily event study indicates that product placement in these movies resulted in .89% positive abnormal return over the (–2, 0) movie release event window. Surprisingly, the cumulative abnormal return (CAR) over the (–2, 1) time window was not significant, indicating a possible price reversal that takes place immediately after the movies' release. Therefore, additional research on the efficacy of such a heavily used marketing medium is warranted. In this study, we examine both blockbuster and non-blockbuster movies and extend this emerging research stream with a longitudinal examination of the value of product placements and related tie-in campaigns (i.e., concurrent advertisement campaigns marketers use to accentuate the effect of placements).

Conceptual Framework

A possible explanation why so little research has been done to estimate the financial worth of product placements is the complex lagged effects of product placement on firms' cash flows. Moreover, other concurrent activities affect cash flows and revenues, making it difficult to tease out the value product placement adds specifically. We attempt to overcome this problem by analyzing stock market reaction to product placement.

The efficient market theory (EMT) stipulates that stock prices reflect available information regarding a firm's future cash flows. According to this theory, once information about the product placement is available to investors, the resulting change in stock price should reflect investors' expectations of the total change in future cash flows due to the product placement. Our conceptual framework builds on the EMT, which posits that investors' responses to product placements are contingent on their expectations regarding customer behavior. By measuring stock price reaction to the release of the movie in which the company's brand is featured, we estimate the incremental value that the investors place on that product placement. We introduce several factors related to the placements' ability to resonate with moviegoers, and produce the desired effect. In addition, we introduce information-processing effects and market-related controls because they can influence investors' willingness and ability to invest in brands that are placed in feature films and our ability to detect abnormal returns. Next, we discuss the conceptual framework and its key factors in more detail. . . .

Srinivasan and Hanssens (2009) note that product innovation has a greater impact on firm value when coupled with greater advertising support. It is possible that product placements that are tied to concurrent traditional advertising/sales promotion campaigns also generate higher returns because they can create more traction with consumers. To control for this, we incorporate promotional tie-in campaigns into the framework. The framework also recognizes that the effectiveness of the tie-in campaigns can follow a certain trajectory over time and be affected by additional drivers such as A-list celebrity participation.

To account for the awareness of the movie before its release, we incorporate adjusted production budget, which research has found to be highly correlated with advertising spending because advertising data are not available for the majority of time frame covered by our study. Moreover, the framework includes brand familiarity because it can influence the awareness and acceptance of the placement effort.

Acceptance

In addition to exposure, consumers should also be receptive to buying the products placed in the movies. More prominent placements could be more memorable; at the same time, consumers can show resistance to over-the-top marketing efforts and exhibit general anticonsumption tendencies in various settings. Some placements can be so overt (e.g., repeated placements of the same brand within the film) that the centrality of the brand/product to the plot can alert the viewers to the placement effort and even cause resentment. Therefore, we incorporate overtness of the placement in our framework.

Meanwhile, growing resentment of product placements could give rise to negative time effects, and familiarity with the medium and increased product placement expertise of marketers could give rise to positive time effects. We also include the actors' star power in the framework because it can influence the acceptance level of the placed brands if the stars are perceived as endorsers. The degree of annoyance might be greater when placements are embedded in poor-quality films. In addition, we anticipate that certain movies and movie genres are less suitable for product placement. . . .

Data and Methods

In this study, we employ the Brand Hype Movie Mapper data set. Brand Hype (University of Concordia) is an educational resource that includes a searchable movie/brand placement data set starting with 1968. Our investigation is based on the 1968–2007 time frame and uses 928 product placement observations (linked to 159 films) that have sufficient financial data for our analysis. The average opening box office revenue in our sample is $18.3 million, which is significantly lower than the $44.8 million average Wiles and Danielova (2009) report. Therefore, the sample used in this study represents a broader cross-section of small and blockbuster films. . . .

Discussion of Findings
Event Study Results

[Event study results] reveal a gradual stock price buildup that begins approximately ten days before the movie release and continues for approximately three business weeks (i.e., 16 days) after the release date, followed by price stabilization. Over the price buildup period (i.e., the [−10, 16] event window), the stocks gain .75% on average. The returns to product placements in the movies are positive and significant. . . .

In line with recent marketing research, the documented price pattern suggests that investors' new information processing takes time; delayed stock market response to marketing-related information may be a more common phenomenon than previously believed. For example, Pauwels et al. (2004) find that it takes six weeks in the automobile sector to absorb new product introductions. This finding is also consistent with traditional finance literature that notes that it takes time for the information to be fully reflected in stock prices.

Although stock prices can be driven by informed trading, they can also be affected by uninformed noise trading. If the latter is the case, stock price reaction would only be temporary, and the change in stock prices would not be a good measure of the value of product placement. . . . We also note the potential presence of noise trading, which results in a minor price adjustment in the post event window. . . .

Other Significant Findings

The variable (NUMBER OF APPEARANCES WITH MAIN CHARACTER) has a significant negative coefficient. (An alternative measure of overtness using time on screen with the main character generated qualitatively the same results.) There is anecdotal evidence suggesting that blatant product placements can be detrimental. For example, FedEx drew criticism for the relentless abundance of FedEx references in the movie *Cast Away* (2000). Our result is consistent with the literature that suggests that "in your face," overt placements may not be as effective as their more subtle counterparts. . . .

Differences Across Movies and Industries

The results indicate that our sample has significant movie and industry specific heterogeneity ($p < .01$). The implication is that picking appropriate films for placement is a relevant managerial concern. Further examination of the industry-related random effects revealed additional dynamics associated with industry differences. . . .

Two industries are characterized by large positive residuals and low posterior variance: electronics and automotive placements enjoy .8% and .2% higher returns, respectively, when compared with other placements. At the same time, other popular placements, such as those for soft and alcoholic drinks, media and entertainment, and food processing, do not enjoy similar advantages. Alcoholic beverages lag almost half a percentage point behind average placements. Although it is possible that some of the alcohol-related placements do not present the product in a positive light, the examination of our sample offers another explanation. The vast majority of placements are for inexpensive domestic beer, a relatively mundane product category. We also note that, across the board, the "unexciting" product categories (e.g., food processing; telecom; retail, which captures retail "super-chains" and large box stores) have lower returns. . . .

[D]ynamics of the prices around the movie release date separately for the three groups of movies. The significant price increases for the high-grossing films start 30 trading days before the release of the film, with most of the CARs taking place before Day 4; then, a period of insignificant price movements are followed by the downward adjustment. The price reaction for the movies with lower box office revenues starts later (right after the release date) but takes less time to complete. Prices stabilize on the new level within two weeks. The price pattern for the blockbuster films suggest that, while the investors' reaction to the placements in such movies reaches a higher magnitude than the reaction to the lower-grossing films, some of the initial reaction may be driven by uninformed trading and, to that degree, is not indicative of the potential increase in companies' future revenues. The earlier prerelease price run-up for high-grossing movies is consistent with this explanation because hype among the noise traders could be driven by the intense prerelease advertising campaigns associated with these high-grossing/high-budget films. Nevertheless, the permanent price impact of the placement in high-grossing movies does not seem to be different from that in low-grossing movies.

The combined results from this study and that of Wiles and Danielova (2009) indicate that blockbuster films may be associated with higher initial CARs to product placements in films but also with a strong downward adjustment that takes place when the movie opens. Blockbuster films may generate more hype, encouraging noise trading. However, this increased hype does not lead to an additional sustainable increase in the firm's economic value.

Finally, we considered the possibility that longitudinal changes in advertising spending at both film and brand level could influence the relationship between time and placement effectiveness. We performed this robustness check with the 1994–2007 subsample by including advertising expenditure across all media for brands and total advertising budget for films. (Our source, ACNielsen, began collecting both types of data in 1994.) The quadratic curve produced similar estimates to the linear trend (also similar to results for the full sample). . . .

Including both advertising related variables (i.e., movie and brand related advertising spending) did not affect the inverted U-shaped trend or the timing of the peak in the effectiveness of the tie-in campaigns. First-order conditions indicated that the peak in effectiveness of the tie-in campaigns took place in 2000 (as we found in the full data set results). Although inclusion of advertising-related variables did not affect the underlying time related trends, it enriches our understanding of tie-in effectiveness. For example, negative and significant interaction between the tie-ins and brand-level advertising spending suggest that tie-ins are more effective for brands with lower advertising intensity. . . .

Implications for Managers

Our findings suggest that, just as products go through a life cycle, so too do the instruments used to market them. When a new technique shows promise, innovators and early adopters expand its use and start perfecting its application, which lead to growth and increased effectiveness. In the case of product placement in the movies, it seems this happened before the 1990s. However, as a new marketing technique gains wider acceptance, lack of novelty may diminish its effectiveness and consumers may start showing resistance to persuasion. They turn to consumer advocacy groups (e.g., Media Awareness Network, Commercial Alert) and technologies that enable them to avoid exposure to advertising (e.g., DVR) and even lobby for blanket legislation (e.g., do-not-call lists). Even in the absence of regulatory action, consumers seem to learn to tune out the messages, or they become savvy and impervious to the new type of marketing media. It is also possible that the costs of effective forms of marketing media increase, rendering them less profitable. Regardless of the exact mechanism, our findings indicate the presence of inverted U-shaped relationship over time in the returns for a new marketing practice and reinforce the need for the marketing industry to reinvent itself as new tactics lose their luster. The inverted U-shaped relationship holds true not only for product placements themselves but also for promotional tie-in campaigns used to support them.

DeLorme, Reid, and Zimmer (1994) report negative attitudes toward placements involving overexposed brands. Our results suggest that overexposing the brand within the same film (as measured by the number of appearances with the main character) can be detrimental. Furthermore, we find that tie-in campaigns are less effective for brands with larger advertising budgets. Counterintuitively, lower-intensity, fleeting placements can be more profitable than repetitive and potentially more expensive marquee placements with main characters. This finding is consistent with previous literature that suggests that "visual-only placements, typically the lower-priced placements, are processed by viewers at a low level of cognition and therefore may lead to stronger emotional and purchase intent effects than more elaborate placements that mention the product by name or show the product in use." Moreover, romance movies in particular seem to be less suitable for placements. This finding suggests that movies that require deep emotional involvement do not necessarily make the best platforms for placements, because they could be perceived as disruptive.

Previous literature has suggested that too many brand placements can result in less attention devoted to each individual placement due to clutter and information overload. Surprisingly, it seems that this insight from traditional advertising research does not transfer to the product placement arena. . . . Perhaps movies that are more suitable for placements attract more placements, potentially masking the underlying relationship. We considered other functional forms representing various types of curvilinear relationships but failed to detect any significant empirical regularity. Therefore, more product placement in a movie does not necessarily affect the value of a given placement in a negative way. Marketers may actually benefit from aligning themselves with a movie with other placements: Given the confirmed importance of selecting the movie for placement, existing placement agreements can signal suitability and serve as qualifiers.

Future Research Directions and Limitations

It is an ongoing challenge for marketers to constantly develop, identify, experiment with, and adopt novel media and techniques to reach and persuade their audiences. Meanwhile, marketers must gauge, decrease, and abandon

less effective media activity just to remain competitive. Is it inevitable that all marketing media ultimately succumb to a life cycle (introduction, growth, maturity, and decline), just as products do? To our knowledge, this study represents a first attempt to investigate the longitudinal effectiveness of a successful marketing medium through its life cycle and could be viewed as a building block toward a theory of marketing medium life cycle. We advocate the longitudinal examination of the economic worth of both traditional and emerging media.

Extant literature has primarily concentrated on product placements in the movies consistent with Gupta and Gould's (1997) definition. However, product placements have found several additional outlets, such as traditional television shows, reality shows, newscasts, video games, music videos, lyrics, catalogs, comic strips, novels, live broadcasts, Internet casting, and even magazine editorials. There is a need to develop an integrated definition that incorporates the variety of current and emerging product placement domains and forms. It would be of interest to examine the extent to which such alternative placement media registers abnormal returns and whether they are also subject to a curvilinear relationship (i.e., life cycle). If so, what would be the expected trajectory of their effectiveness over time? Future studies would also benefit from incorporating various placement-related factors that have been shown to have an impact on advertising effectiveness, such as brand/plot/genre congruity, execution-related factors, and attitude toward sponsor, which we did not explore in this study. These factors may explain how some companies manage to achieve success through placements despite life-cycle considerations.

Although the data set we used in this study represents a great resource for product placement researchers, it is not without limitations. For example, because the data collection was led by film scholars, critically acclaimed and mature content movies were overrepresented in the data set. Although most differences are relatively mild, the high critical acclaim of the movies included in the Brand Hype data set may have led to more conservative estimates of the economic worth of product placements because Wiles and Danielova's (2009) and our findings suggest that the placements in such films are associated with lower CARs.

Despite the tremendous growth and volume of product placements in recent years, Balasubramanian, Karrh, and Patwardhan (2006) note that only 29% of these placements are paid. It seems to be important to examine the antecedents and consequences of barter, gratis, and hybrid forms of product placements to improve the return on investment of this marketing medium and to determine best practices. An interesting caveat is that the Federal Communication Commission currently requires the disclosure of paid product placements but does not penalize the omission of such disclosures unless there is a deliberate nonobjective claim or deception related to the product. This means creative room for the interpretation of regulation regarding barter and gratis placements. It is likely that nonpaid product placements (which do not have to be disclosed) not only offer greater return on investment but also can be more effective. Still, nonpaid placements can come at a cost: It is not uncommon for a marketer to pay six-figure fees to product placement agencies for annual service contracts. It would be worthwhile to distinguish between paid and nonpaid forms of product placements in further research.

Our focus in this study was on assessing the effect of product placement in the movies on the value of the companies that owned the advertised brands. An interesting research question is the flip side of this issue: What is the impact of product placements on the movie's success? In the context of print advertising, it has been shown that too much advertising relative to editorial content can be detrimental to consumers' perceptions of editorial quality and can have a negative impact on circulation. Mandese (2006, p. 3) cites industry sources who argue that in the television context, "when consumers grow wary of product placement . . . they may not simply react negatively about the brands involved but may actually turn the shows off." Consistent with the literature on distrust, Wei, Fischer, and Main (2008) find that audience members who recognized a paid placement not only lowered their evaluations of the placed brand but also lowered their evaluations of the hosts, show, and radio station. We did not find any evidence of such a relationship in our sample. Organically integrated brands in a movie may actually enhance a film's artistic qualities by creating a more realistic setting and providing a connection between the story and the "real world." A more detailed investigation that considers endogeneity between movie quality, placement volume, and placement quality is warranted.

This article draws generalizations regarding the effectiveness of product placements over time. However, other areas of longitudinal exploration remain to be addressed. For example, is there a value in lasting relationships between movie stars and brands? For example, Will Smith seems to have a long-standing relationship with Ray-Ban (e.g., *Men in Black* [1997]; *Men in Black II* [2002]; *Bad Boys II* [2003]; *Hancock* [2008]). Do these continuous relationships benefit advertisers by allowing the brand to adhere to the star's persona and capitalize on celebrity appeal, thereby enhancing the realism of the placement? Similar questions could be asked about the enduring relationships between the brands and movie franchises. For example, the James Bond franchise has had a long engagement with the Rolex brand since the 1960s; however, starting with *Golden Eye* (1995), the franchise switched to Omega. Whether the effective formation and management of such relationships can result in tangible benefits to firms' bottom lines remains to be explored. . . .

References

Balasubramanian, Siva K., James A. Karrh, and Hemant Patwardhan (2006), "Audience Response to Product Placements: An Integrative Framework and Future Research Agenda," *Journal of Advertising*, 35 (3), 115–27.

DeLorme, Denise E., Leonard Reid, and Mary R. Zimmer (1994), "Brands in Films: Young Moviegoers' Experiences and Interpretations," in *Proceedings of the 1994 Conference of the American Academy of Advertising*, Karen W. King, ed. Athens, GA: American Academy of Advertising, 60.

Gupta, Paula B. and Stephen J. Gould (1997), "Consumers Perceptions of the Ethics and Acceptability of Product Placements in Movies: Product Category and Individual Differences," *Journal of Current Issues and Research in Advertising*, 19 (1), 37–50.

Mandese, Joe (2006), "When Product Placement Goes Too Far," *Broadcasting and Cable*, (January 1), (accessed January 10, 2011), [available at http://www.broadcastingcable.com/article/102250-When_Product_Placement_Goes_Too_Far.php].

Pauwels, Koen, Jorge M. Silva-Russo, Shuba Srinivasan, and Dominique M. Hanssens (2004), "New Products, Sales Promotions, and Firm Value: The Case of the Automobile Industry," *Journal of Marketing*, 68 (October), 142–56.

Wei, Mei-Ling, Eileen Fischer, and Kelley J. Main (2008), "An Examination of the Effects of Activating Persuasion Knowledge on Consumer Response to Brands Engaging in Covert Marketing," *Journal of Public Policy & Marketing*, 27 (Spring), 34–44.

Wiles, Michael A. and Anna Danielova (2009), "The Worth of Product Placement in Successful Films: An Event Study Analysis," *Journal of Marketing*, 73 (July), 44–63.

Writers Guild of America West (2005), "Entertainment Guilds Call for Industry Code of Conduct of FCC Regulation for Product Integration in Programming and Film: Guilds Issue White Paper Report on the Runaway Use of Stealth Advertising in Television and Film," (accessed May 1, 2010), [available at http://www.wga.org/subpage_newsevents.aspx?id=1422].

EKATERINA V. KARNIOUCHINA and **CAN USLAY** are both assistant professors of marketing at the Argyros School of Business and Economics, Chapman University.

GRIGORI ERENBURG is an assistant professor of finance at King's University College, University of Western Ontario, Canada.

EXPLORING THE ISSUE

Is Product Placement an Effective Form of Advertising?

Critical Thinking and Reflection

1. Though product placement has become more common, do you think advertisers are operating ethically when they pay to have certain products featured in media content?
2. How and in what way(s) can product placement influence the flow of a media program or media content?
3. Is product placement as popular in new media as it has been in traditional television and film content?
4. Would you be willing to pay more for media content that did not include subsidized images through product placement? Would the production company/companies have to change their business models?
5. Over time, do audiences become anaesthetized to this type of advertising?

Is There Common Ground?

For the authors of the two selections in this issue, product placement is an accepted advertising technique, but the authors differ in how deeply one can examine the functionality or dysfunctionality of the way product placement achieves its desired result—which is to blur the difference between advertising and program content. These authors do not involve themselves with questions of morality, ethics, or whether product placement actually could harm the public, but rather, keep their eyes on the success of the advertising campaign through this technique.

The common ground these authors tread upon is the normalization of advertising and advertising techniques that are so prominent in our society today. As such, they avoid problems that the advertising industry has had to deal with for decades—and those questions deal with whether advertising operates in the public good or not.

What are your perspectives on the role of advertising techniques to attract audiences, and the role of advertising in our society?

Additional Resources

Scott Donaton, *Madison and Vine: Why the Entertainment and Advertising Industries Must Converge to Survive* (Crain Communications, 2004).

Mary-Lou Galician, ed., *Handbook of Product Placement in the Mass Media: New Strategies in Marketing Theory, Practice, Trends, and Ethics* (Best Business Books, 2004).

Jean-Marc Lehu, *Branded Entertainment: Product Placement & Brand Strategy in the Entertainment Business* (Kogan-Page, 2009).

Internet References . . .

American Marketing Association, Statement of Ethics

http://www.marketingpower.com/AboutAMA/Pages
/Statement%20of%Ethics.aspx

American Psychological Association, "Advertising to Children: Is It Ethical?"

http://www.apa.org/monitor/sep00/advertising.aspx

An Ethical Evaluation of Product Placement—A Deceptive Practice?

http://www.academia.edu/600330/An_ethical
_evaluation_of_product_placement
_a_deceptive_practice

Selected, Edited, and with Issue Framing Material by:
Alison Alexander, *University of Georgia*
and
Jarice Hanson, *University of Massachusetts—Amherst*

ISSUE

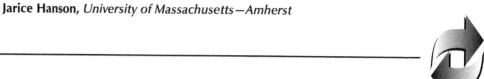

Is There Any Harm In Taking Selfies?

YES: Elizabeth Day, from "How Selfies Became a Global Phenomenon," *The Guardian* (2013)

NO: Jenna Wortham, from "My Selfie, Myself," *New York Times Sunday Review* (2013)

Learning Outcomes

After reading this issue, you will be able to:

- Consider the many aspects of taking selfies as a cultural phenomenon.
- Think about how one presents one's self to others.
- Consider whether some selfies divulge too much personal information to others.
- Explore how one creates a digital persona and digital identity in online form.
- Reflect on the meaning of self-portraiture over time.

ISSUE SUMMARY

YES: British journalist Elizabeth Day thinks of selfies as modern-day self-portraits. Despite their popularity, she sides with critics who consider selfies to be narcissistic and expressions of our self-absorbed lifestyles.

NO: *New York Times* reporter Jenna Wortham claims that our predilection for responding to faces is just a part of a more technologized world, and that while we shouldn't discount the selfie phenomenon, we should also keep in mind that selfies are a type of visual diary.

On the surface, selfies—those self-portraits often taken with a cell phone camera and posted online—seem innocuous, but in recent years the number of selfies taken and the possible meaning that those images have for the person in the picture and the social statement he or she makes have begun to stir the interests of social scientists and cultural critics. Certainly, the taking of self-portraits is nothing new, but the frequency with which they are taken and posted for others to see has resulted in a popular activity. When Ellen DeGeneres took a selfie at the 2014 Oscar Awards with Jared Leto, Jennifer Lawrence, Meryl Streep, Bradley Cooper, Peter Nyong'o Jr., Channing Tatum, Julia Roberts, Kevin Spacey, Brad Pitt, Lupita Nyong'o, and Angelina Jolie (how did they all fit on that small screen?), Twitter crashed as the image was simultaneously sent to 37 million people worldwide. Of course, this action made Samsung, a sponsor of the Oscar Awards, very happy! The word "selfie" became one of the "words of the

year" in *Time* magazine's 2012 annual collection of new, trending topics. In 2013, the Oxford English Dictionary also added the word to its compendium of words in the English language.

The photo capabilities of cell phones have fueled interest in selfies, and a number of social media outlets—Instagram in particular—have helped selfies become a part of our culture. Some selfies are carefully crafted, and some follow the style of Kim Kardashian, who introduced the pouty mouthed, head turned classic selfie image. Though celebrity selfies are popular and help the celebrity stay in the media spotlight (think of how often Justin Bieber tweets selfies of himself), selfies themselves have become cultural icons of self-representation.

Some scholars have focused on the types of problems selfies address, such as the narcissistic desire to be seen, and the denigration of one's body image when one compares their selfies to those that have been carefully crafted by celebrities and their publicists, but once you get beyond the fun of a quick snap of the camera, selfies may well make a number of statements about the subject, and the way the subject thinks of himself/herself in relationship to friends, and others in society. The Pew Internet and American Life Project conducted a study in 2014 and found that people of all ages say they have posted a selfie of themselves at some time, but that millennials (people who reached young adulthood around the year 2000) post significantly more than any other age group. And, as social media usage increases among all ages every year, we can expect the selfie to become even more apparent in the next few years as cell phone manufacturers make better cameras, and social networks make it easier to upload and distribute selfies on a variety of platforms.

In this issue, the two authors cite different evidence to argue the question of whether selfies can be harmful. Elizabeth Day discusses how and why selfies caught on, and suggests that we project a good deal of biographical information about ourselves when we take and post selfies. In arguing that selfies are a prime example of a narcissistic age, she outlines the statement selfies make about our sexuality and our sense of worth in society. She quotes many selfie takers who justify their actions based upon wanting to look good when they go out, or who actually contribute to a "pornification" of our culture in terms of constructing images that suggest that people create images that self-objectify themselves. These questions she raises ask us to think twice about why we take selfies, and the way other people may "read" those images.

On the other hand, Jenna Wortham discusses how selfies mediate a person's sense of self and the outer environment. She is less willing to examine the rise of sexual selfies and those that create objectified images, and instead discusses some of the ways that selfies connect people to others. As components of "visual diaries," selfies reflect how visual our culture has become, and how we've begun to rely on our impressions of faces as modes of communication.

Selfies themselves have been grouped into a number of subgroups. After-sex selfies, selfies with celebrities and politicians, selfies in different geographical regions, and selfies that mimic the positions of statues and public exhibitions have been collected on some social media sites and tend to elicit a number of responses from viewers. For many of these types of selfies, comments can range from admiration to disgust. Though neither of our authors discusses the number of "likes" people may get from posting their pictures, this quasi-measure of popularity has a lot to do with the way selfie-posters think about their behaviors when they do post pictures on social media platforms.

The ease of snapping a selfie with a cell phone that requires no special lighting and gives instant results is also a factor in thinking about how technology today is often used for purposes for which it was not originally intended. For many people, the selfie is a type of mirror that lets them see how they might be perceived by others. As a result, many selfie-snappers openly talk about how much time they devote to getting just the right look, and expressing the mood they want to the world. A number of websites exist that discuss the aesthetics of taking a good selfie so that the self-portrait has the right look and the right tone to express one's personality and elicit the desired effect.

Among some of the most recent academic studies of selfies, we learn that men may actually exhibit more antisocial traits than women when taking selfies. With the headline, "Hey, Guys: Posting a Lot of Selfies Doesn't Send a Good Message," researchers at Ohio University conducted a large study that shows that men who posted a number of online photos of themselves often scored more highly on measures of narcissism and psychopathy. In other research, men's selfies were grouped according to the selfie "type," suggesting that expressions of masculinity and competition were often the subtexts for the types of selfies men take, and post. Yet another study discussed how selfies actually annoy friends, who feel that they have to look at pictures that make them see their friends as more self-absorbed than they want to believe. Undoubtedly, the longer we live with the selfie phenomenon, the more studies will emerge that delve into the behavior of those who take and post selfies.

YES ↵

Elizabeth Day

How Selfies Became a Global Phenomenon

. . .

It starts with a certain angle: a smartphone tilted at 45 degrees just above your eyeline is generally deemed the most forgiving. Then a light source: the flattering beam of a backlit window or a bursting supernova of flash reflected in a bathroom mirror, as preparations are under way for a night out.

The pose is important. Knowing self-awareness is conveyed by the slight raise of an eyebrow, the sideways smile that says you're not taking it too seriously. A doe-eyed stare and mussed-up hair denotes natural beauty, as if you've just woken up and can't help looking like this. Sexiness is suggested by sucked-in cheeks, pouting lips, a nonchalant cock of the head and a hint of bare flesh just below the clavicle. Snap!

Afterwards, a flattering filter is applied. Outlines are blurred, colours are softened, a sepia tint soaks through to imply a simpler era of vinyl records and VW camper vans.

All of this is the work of an instant. Then, with a single tap, you are ready to upload: to Twitter, to Facebook, to Instagram, each likeness accompanied by a self-referential hashtag. Your image is retweeted and tagged and shared. Your screen fills with thumbs-up signs and heart-shaped emoticons. You are "liked" several times over. You feel a shiver of—what, exactly? Approbation? Reassurance? Existential calm? Whatever it is, it's addictive. Soon, you repeat the whole process, trying out a different pose. Again and again, you offer yourself up for public consumption.

This, then, is the selfie: the self-portrait of the digital age. We are all at it. Just type "selfie" into the Twitter search bar. Or take a look at Instagram, where over 90m photos are currently posted with the hashtag #me.

Adolescent pop poppet Justin Bieber constantly Tweets photos of himself with his shirt off to the shrieking delight of his huge online following. Rihanna has treated her fans to Instagrammed selfies of her enjoying the view at a strip club, of her buttocks barely concealed by a tiny denim thong and of her posing with two oversize cannabis joints while in Amsterdam. Reality TV star Kim Kardashian overshares to the extent that, in March, she posted a picture of her own face covered in blood after undergoing a so-called "vampire facial." In the same month, the selfie-obsessed model and actress Kelly Brook banned herself from posting any more of them (her willpower lasted two hours).

The political classes have started doing it too. President Obama's daughters, Sasha and Malia, took selfies at his second inauguration. In June, Hillary Clinton got in on the act after her daughter, Chelsea, tweeted a joint picture of them taken on her phone at arm's length. Earlier this month, three sisters from Nebraska stormed the field of a college baseball match and filmed themselves while doing so, eventually being removed by security guards. Stills from the six-second Vine video clip became known as "the most expensive selfie of all time" after it emerged that the sisters were facing a $1,500 fine.

. . .

"The selfie is revolutionising how we gather autobiographical information about ourselves and our friends," says Dr Mariann Hardey, a lecturer in marketing at Durham University who specialises in digital social networks. "It's about continuously rewriting yourself. It's an extension of our natural construction of self. It's about presenting yourself in the best way . . . [similar to] when women put on makeup or men who bodybuild to look a certain way: it's an aspect of performance that's about knowing yourself and being vulnerable."

. . .

Although photographic self-portraits have been around since 1839, when daguerreotype pioneer Robert Cornelius took a picture of himself outside his family's store in Philadelphia (whether he had the help of an assistant is not known), it was not until the invention of the compact digital camera that the selfie boomed in popularity. There was some experimentation with the selfie in the 1970s—most notably by Andy Warhol—when the Polaroid camera came of age and freed amateur photographers from the tyranny of the darkroom. But film was expensive and it wasn't until the advent of digital that photographs became truly instantaneous.

The fact that we no longer had to traipse to our local chemist to develop a roll of holiday snaps encouraged us to experiment—after all, on a digital camera, the image could be easily deleted if we didn't like the results. A selfie could be done with the timer button or simply by holding the camera at arm's length, if you didn't mind the looming tunnel of flesh dog-earing one corner of the image.

As a result, images tagged as #selfie began appearing on the photo-sharing website Flickr as early as 2004. But it was the introduction of smartphones—most crucially the iPhone 4, which came along in 2010 with a front-facing camera—that made the selfie go viral. According to the latest annual Ofcom communications report, 60% of UK mobile phone users now own a smartphone and a recent survey of more than 800 teenagers by the Pew Research Centre in America found that 91% posted photos of themselves online—up from 79% in 2006.

Recently, the Chinese manufacturer Huawei unveiled plans for a new smartphone with "instant facial beauty support" software which reduces wrinkles and blends skin tone.

"A lot of the cameras on smartphones are incredibly good," says Michael Pritchard, the director general of the Royal Photographic Society. "The rise of digital cameras and the iPhone coincided with the fact that there are a lot more single people around [than before]. The number of single-occupancy households is rising, more people are divorcing and living single lives and people go on holiday by themselves more and don't have anyone else to take the picture. That's one reason I take selfies: because I do actually want to record where I am."

But if selfies are simply an exercise in recording private memories and charting the course of our lives, then why do we feel such a pressing need to share them with hundreds and thousands of friends and strangers online? To some, the selfie has become the ultimate symbol of the narcissistic age. Its instantaneous nature encourages superficiality—or so the argument goes. One of the possible side-effects has been that we care more than ever before about how we appear and, as a consequence, social acceptance comes only when the outside world accepts the way we look, rather than endorsing the work we do or the way we behave off-camera.

The American writer John Paul Titlow has described selfie-sharing as: "a high school popularity contest on digital steroids." In an article published on the website ReadWrite earlier this year, Titlow argued that selfie users "are seeking some kind of approval from their peers and the larger community, which thanks to the internet is now effectively infinite."

Indeed, although many people who post pictures of themselves on the internet do so in the belief that it will only ever be seen by their group of friends on any given social network, the truth is that the images can be viewed and used by other agencies. There are now entire porn sites devoted to the "amateur" naked selfie and concerns have recently been raised that jilted lovers can seek their revenge by making explicit images of their ex publicly available online.

The preponderance of young women posing for selfies in a state of undress is a potentially worrying issue. When the model Cara Delevingne Instagrammed a picture of her nipples poking through a black lace top, it rapidly got over 60,000 "Likes."

According to Gail Dines, the author of *Pornland: How Porn Has Hijacked Our Sexuality*: "Because of porn culture, women have internalised that image of themselves. They self-objectify, which means they're actually doing to themselves what the male gaze does to them."

Dines argues that although men can "gain visibility" in a variety of ways, for women the predominant way to get attention is "fuckability." And it is true that a lot of female selfie aficionados take their visual vernacular directly from pornography (unwittingly or otherwise): the pouting mouth, the pressed-together cleavage, the rumpled bedclothes in the background hinting at opportunity.

But Rebecca Brown, a 23-year-old graduate trainee from Birmingham, believes her penchant for selfies is neither degrading nor narcissistic. Instead, she explains, it is a simple means of self-exploration.

"It's almost like a visual diary," she says. "I can look back and see what I looked like at a particular time, what I was wearing. It's exploring your identity in digital form. To me it's not about nudity or having a raunchy or raw kind of look . . . People think if you take pictures of yourself, you're self-obsessed but that's like saying if you write a diary or an autobiography, you're self-obsessed. Not necessarily. A selfie is a format and a platform to share who you are."

Does she feed off the social approval that a selfie can generate?

"I suppose you take photos to see what you look like," Brown concedes. "Before I go out, I'll take a couple of pictures almost to see how I look in other people's eyes.

In the same way that if you wrote a really good piece of work and had people commenting about how good it was, or if you put something on Twitter that people retweeted, if people start liking your selfie, then obviously you're going to get a natural buzz. It gives you a nice boost and you can walk with that little bit more confidence."

· · ·

The popularity of the selfie is, says Mariann Hardey, "an extension of how we live and learn about each other" and a way of imparting necessary information about who we are. By way of an example, Hardey says that when her father died suddenly last year, she took refuge in her Instagram feed.

"I couldn't bear the conversations but one way to prove to friends that I was OK was to take a picture of myself," she says. "That revealed something very important to my friends—one, that I was still functioning and, two, I was out doing stuff. An image can convey more than words."

The idea that young women are self-objectifying by posing semi-pornographically for selfies is, she believes, a dangerous one.

"When we're talking about what is acceptable for women in terms of constructing an image, we need to be very careful of not heading down into the territory of 'she was wearing a short skirt, so she was asking to be raped'. We should avoid that argument because it's probably an extension of more patriarchal demands."

"Women should be allowed to portray themselves in a way they feel enhanced by. Who didn't experiment with cutting their hair off and dying it pink when they were younger? This is just a natural progression of experimenting with the changing interfaces of being young and one of these interfaces, yes, is sexual identity."

A selfie can, in some respects, be a more authentic representation of beauty than other media images. In an article for *Psychology Today* published earlier this year, Sarah J Gervais, an assistant professor of psychology, wrote that: "Instagram (and other social media) has allowed the public to reclaim photography as a source of empowerment . . . [it] offers a quiet resistance to the barrage of perfect images that we face each day. Rather than being bombarded with those creations . . . we can look through our Instagram feed and see images of real people—with beautiful diversity."

"Instagram also allows us the opportunity to see below the surface. We capture a glimpse into the makings of people's daily lives. We get a sense of those things that make the everyday extraordinary."

The appeal for celebrities like Bieber, Kardashian et al is connected to this. The expansion of social networking has enabled them to communicate directly with their fanbase and to build up large, loyal followings among people who believe they are getting a real glimpse into the lives of the rich and famous.

· · ·

The key is the idea of "manageable reality": celebrities can now exercise more control than ever over the dissemination of their image. The paradox at the heart of the selfie is that it masquerades as a "candid" shot, taken without access to airbrushing or post-production, but in fact, a carefully posed selfie, edited with all the right filters, is a far more appealing prospect than a snatched paparazzo shot taken from a deliberately unflattering angle.

"It's about self-exposure and control," says artist Simon Foxall, whose work questions the parameters of individuality and self-expression. "A selfie blurs the line between 'reality' and the performance of a fantasy self, so one collapses into the other."

Beyond that, a judicious use of selfies can make good business sense too: Alexa Chung and Florence Welch have both used selfies to post daily updates on what they are wearing, thereby cementing their position as modern style icons and guaranteeing, no doubt, the continuation of a series of lucrative fashion deals. (Chung, for one, has designed a womenswear line for the fashion brand Madewell for the last three years.)

The website What I Wore Today began as a site that featured young entrepreneur Poppy Dinsey posing for a daily selfie, in a different outfit for every day of the year. It became an internet hit and has now expanded to allow users to upload their own images, as well as generating advertising revenue by featuring online links to clothing retailers.

"People like the control selfies give them," says Dinsey. "Sometimes it's just a practical matter of not having anyone around to shoot you and that's why I always took my own pictures in mirrors for WIWT. But you're deciding how to frame yourself—you're not trusting someone else to make you look good. With front-facing cameras on iPhones, and so on, you can see the picture you're taking and frame it perfectly to show yourself off as best as possible—your mate isn't going to make the same effort when taking your picture. Plus, you can retake and retake without anyone having to know how much vanity has gone into that 'casual' pose."

In some ways, of course, the notion of control is disingenuous: once a selfie is posted online, it is out there for public delectation. Future employers can see it. Marketers can use it. A resentful former lover could exploit it.

You can use digital technology to manipulate your own image as much as you like. But the truth about selfies is that once they are online, you can never control how other people see you.

ELIZABETH DAY is a British journalist, broadcaster, and novelist. Since 2007, she has been a feature writer for *The Observer*. She has also written three novels: *Scissors, Paper, Stone*; *Home Fires*; and *Paradise City*.

Jenna Wortham

My Selfie, Myself

RECENTLY, I came across a great find in a Vermont antiques store: an old black-and-white photograph of a female pilot on a mountaintop, her aviator glasses pushed up on her forehead, revealing a satisfied, wind-burned face, the wings of her plane just visible behind her. But the best part of the discovery was the slow realization that she was holding the camera herself. It was, for lack of a better word, a "selfie."

It reminded me of another self-portrait of sorts, one I've been watching evolve online of the mysterious Benny Winfield Jr.

I don't know Mr. Winfield personally, but I've seen his face most days for the past few months, in dozens of photographs he shares on the social networking application Instagram. He calls himself the "leader of the selfie movement" and each image is hypnotically the same—his grinning face fills the frame, and is usually accompanied by a bit of inspirational text.

The self-portraits are worlds—and decades—apart. But they are threaded together by a timeless delight in our ability to document our lives and leave behind a trace for others to discover.

"There is a primal human urge to stand outside of ourselves and look at ourselves," said Clive Thompson, a technology writer and the author of the new book "Smarter Than You Think: How Technology Is Changing Our Minds for the Better."

Selfies have become the catchall term for digital self-portraits abetted by the explosion of cellphone cameras and photo-editing and sharing services. Every major social media site is overflowing with millions of them. Everyone from the pope to the Obama girls has been spotted in one. In late August, Oxford Dictionaries Online added the term to its lexicon. One of the advertisements for the new Grand Theft Auto V video game features a woman in a bikini taking a photograph of herself with an iPhone. In a recent episode of Showtime's "Homeland," one of the main characters snaps and sends a topless selfie to her boyfriend. Snapchat, a photo-based messaging service, is processing 350 million photos each day, while a recent project on Kickstarter raised $90,000 to develop and sell a small Bluetooth shutter release for smartphones and tablets to help people take photographs of themselves more easily.

It is the perfect preoccupation for our Internet-saturated time, a ready-made platform to record and post our lives where others can see and experience them in tandem with us. And in a way, it signals a new frontier in the evolution in social media.

"People are wrestling with how they appear to the rest of the world," Mr. Thompson said. "Taking a photograph is a way of trying to understand how people see you, who you are and what you look like, and there's nothing wrong with that."

At times, it feels largely performative, another way to polish public-facing images of who we are, or who we'd like to appear to be. Selfies often veer into scandalous or shameless territory—think of Miley Cyrus or Geraldo Rivera—and at their most egregious raise all sorts of questions about vanity, narcissism and our obsession with beauty and body image.

But it's far too simplistic to write off the selfie phenomenon. We are swiftly becoming accustomed to—and perhaps even starting to prefer—online conversations and interactions that revolve around images and photos. They are often more effective at conveying a feeling or reaction than text. Plus, we've become more comfortable seeing our faces on-screen, thanks to services like Snapchat, Skype, Google Hangout and FaceTime, and the exhilarating feeling of connectedness that comes from even the briefest video conversation. Receiving a photo of the face of the person you're talking to brings back the human element of the interaction, which is easily misplaced if the interaction is primarily text-based.

"The idea of the selfie is much more like your face is the caption and you're trying to explain a moment or tell a story," said Frédéric della Faille, the founder and designer of Frontback, a popular new photo-sharing application that lets users take photographs using both front- and rear-facing cameras. "It's much more of a moment and a story than a photo." And more often than not, he added, "It's not about being beautiful."

In other words, it is about showing your friends and family your elation when you're having a good day or opening a dialogue or line of communication using an image the same way you might simply text "hi" or "what's up?"

And selfies strongly suggest that the world we observe through social media is more interesting when people insert themselves into it—a fact that many social media sites like Vine, a video-sharing tool owned by Twitter, have noticed. Dom Hofmann, one of the founders of Vine, said the first iteration of the application didn't let people shoot videos using the front-facing camera, partly because of technical constraints. His co-founder, Rus Yusupov, was in favor of adding the feature to the service, but Mr. Hofmann had concerns that it might denigrate the quality of the content people were sharing through the service.

"Rus felt that it would open up a lot of creative possibilities," said Mr. Hofmann. "But I thought it would be a lot of vanity. I didn't see much value in it."

But after some discussion, and repeated requests from users, the company decided to release the front-camera capability as an update. It turned out that his partner was right. Users loved it, Mr. Hofmann said.

"It wasn't really about vanity at all," he said. "It's not really about how you look. It's about you doing something else, or you in other places. It's a more personal way to share an experience."

The feedback loop that selfies can inspire doesn't hurt, either. As an early Instagram user, I rarely turned the camera on myself. I preferred sharing pictures of sunsets, crazy dance parties and bodega cats to showing off a new haircut or outfit. But over the last year or so, I've watched as all my peers slowly began turning their cameras inward on themselves. It's made my feed more interesting and entertaining. And I'd much rather see my friends' faces as they prepare food than a close-up photo of the finished meals instead. The rare occasion when I feel bold enough to post a full-face frontal, I see spikes in comments and feedback, the kind that pictures of a park or a concert photo rarely get.

In fact, I've even noticed that the occasional selfie appears to nudge some friends who I haven't seen in a while to get in touch via e-mail or text to suggest that we meet for a drink to catch up, as if seeing my face on a screen reminds them it's been awhile since they've seen it in real life.

Dr. Pamela Rutledge, director of the nonprofit Media Psychology Research Center, says that's how the human brain works.

"We are hard-wired to respond to faces," she said. "It's unconscious. Our brains process visuals faster, and we are more engaged when we see faces. If you're looking at a whole page of photos, the ones you will notice are the close-ups and selfies."

As for the well-worn assertion that selfies foster vanity and somehow court stalkers, "There are some people who put themselves at a certain amount of risk by exposing too much," Dr. Rutledge said. "But that's not about the selfie. That's about someone who is not making good choices."

Rather than dismissing the trend as a side effect of digital culture or a sad form of exhibitionism, maybe we're better off seeing selfies for what they are at their best—a kind of visual diary, a way to mark our short existence and hold it up to others as proof that we were here. The rest, of course, is open to interpretation.

JENNA WORTHAM is a technology writer for the *New York Times*. She specializes in stories that focus on the way people use technology, on start-ups, and digital culture. Prior to writing for the *Times*, she was a writer with *Wired* magazine.

EXPLORING THE ISSUE

Is There Any Harm in Taking Selfies?

Critical Thinking and Reflection

1. Consider whether selfies are more culturally important than just snapping a picture for fun.
2. Think about the way celebrities have used selfies for self-promotion, and measure our own behavior against theirs.
3. Reflect on the digital trail we leave by posting selfies and personal information online.
4. Think of whether selfies are a reflection of self-indulgence that may actually reflect a person's attitudes toward others.

Is There Common Ground?

Both authors represented in this issue discuss the rise of the visual image and the role selfies play in the long history of self-portraiture. They differ, though, on the range of cultural readings that selfies sometimes prompt. Undoubtedly, selfies are a part of a culture that is obsessed with taking and sharing pictures, and the excellent cameras that come with today's cell phones and file sharing apps and social networks help spread those images.

We might question whether selfies are just popular forms of expression that will die out over time, or whether they really do constitute a new art form. Perhaps someday there will be great collections of selfies exhibited in museums, or collected in books and journals. If that happens, we can be sure that cultural critics will continue to examine selfies and what they say about the people who take them and share them.

Additional Resources

Jack Linshi, "Men Who Share Selfies Online Show More Signs of Psychopathy, Study Says," *Time Magazine*, January 11, 2015. This report addresses

the Ohio University study that reports on men's use of selfies.

Kate Losse, "The Return of the Selfie," *The New Yorker*, May 31, 2013. Taking the position that the selfie is becoming a cultural reference point, Losse discusses what selfies say about a person's self-image.

Gwendolyn Seidman, Ph.D. "Are Selfies a Sign of Narcissism and Psycopathy?" *Psychology Today* (January 15, 2015). In this short article, Seidman examines some of the more common assumptions supporting academic research in the effects of selfies.

P. Sorakowski, A Sorokawska, A. Oleszkiewics, T. Frackowiak, A. Huk, and K. Pisanski, "Selfie Posting Behaviors are Associated with Narcissism Among Men," *Personal Individual Differences*, 85 (2015), pp. 123–127. This article focuses on men and narcissism in particular, and discusses how male behavior may be influenced by issues of masculinity.

Internet References . . .

BBC News, Self-portraits and Social Media: The Rise of the 'Selfie'

www.bbc.com/news/magazine-22511650

Heriot Watt University, "Sharing Photographs on Facebook Could Damage Relationships, New Study Shows" (October 26, 2015)

www.hw.ac.uk/news/sharing-photographs-facebook
-could-damage-13069.htm

Jerry Saltz (2014) "At Arm's Length: The History of the Selfie," *Vulture.com*

www.vulture.com/2014/01/history-of-the-selfie.html#

Selfiecity (a comparison of selfies taken in five major cities)

http://selfiecity.net/

The Selfies Research Network is an international group of academics studying the social and cultural implications of the selfie.

www.selfiesresearchers.com

Unit 3

UNIT

News and Politics

*A*t one time, one of the most hotly debated questions about media was whether media content demonstrated a liberal or conservative bias. In recent years, this question has receded, while other, more important issues have risen to the fore. Among those new questions, we ask whether privacy should be protected in important, stressful situations, such as the reporting of rape on campus; the relationship of power and influence in corporate funding of political campaigns; whether Twitter is a serious form of media that helps us understand politics and political issues; and whether polls accurately reflect public opinion. Although all of these issues have been debated for years—and, in some cases, decades—we approach this set of questions with a contemporary lens that focuses on the meaning of these issues as the nature of what is political expands.

Selected, Edited, and with Issue Framing Material by:
Alison Alexander, *University of Georgia*
and
Jarice Hanson, *University of Massachusetts—Amherst*

ISSUE

Will the *Rolling Stone* "Rape on Campus" Story Change Journalism for the Better?

YES: Sheila Coronel, Steve Coll, and Derek Kravitz, from "*Rolling Stone*'s Investigation: 'A Failure That Was Avoidable'," *Columbia Journalism Review* (2015)

NO: Joe Strupp, from "How the *Rolling Stone* Rape Story Failure Has—and Hasn't—Changed Media Coverage," *Media Matters* (2015)

Learning Outcomes

After reading this issue, you will be able to:

- Discuss what went wrong with the *Rolling Stone* article.
- Describe the journalistic norms that were violated.
- Evaluate the consequences.
- Speculate on how this may change rape coverage.

ISSUE SUMMARY

YES: Coronel, Coll, and Kravitz of the Columbia School of Journalism conduct a painstakingly in-depth investigation of the process and decisions that led to the discredited story about rape and the University of Virginia. They re-create the reporter and editorial actions from first contact through retraction.

NO: Joe Strupp argues that the investigation encompassed failures in reporting, editing, editorial supervision, and fact-checking. He suggests that it is time for journalists to begin to define best practices when reporting about rape cases.

On November 19, 2014, *Rolling Stone* published "A Rape on Campus: A Brutal Assault and Struggle for Justice at UVA." It caused a sensation, ultimately drawing 2.7 million viewers to the online story, more than any other non-celebrity story ever. The story detailed a horrific rape and the subsequent actions of the survivor and UVA authorities. From the beginning, the author, Sabrina Erdely, planned on using this as an example of the difficulties of dealing with campus assaults, where university administrations are hampered by privacy laws and conflicting jurisdictions of university and local police. For reasons that are discussed extensively in the YES selection, Erdely became concerned about her chief informant, "Jackie." On December 4, 2014, *Rolling Stone* retracted the reporting on Jackie's allegations of gang rape at the University of Virginia.

As it should, this incident precipitated soul-searching within the journalistic profession. *Rolling Stone* came under attack and was the object of much outrage. In late December 2014, *Rolling Stone* asked the Columbia School of Journalism to conduct an independent review of the editorial process that resulted in the retracted article. In the midst of the furor, a series of questions about journalism ethics and practice began to emerge. What went wrong? What practices were ignored or omitted that might have prevented these mistakes? Rape has long been a difficult area for reporters. Was concern about the survivor allowed to overrule best journalistic practices? A few began to hope that this Pulitzer's situation might lead to better coverage of sexual assault cases.

Covering rape stories has always been difficult. It is still the case that newspapers and television news rarely release the names of rape victims. While laws vary across states as to whether or not the name is redacted or released, journalists generally do not print these names because of the social stigma that is still attached to rape. There are extenuating circumstances where names might be released, such as when a rape is involved in news for another reason, such as a rape/kidnapping scenario. Also names may be revealed when the rape involves prominent people, for example, celebrities. (It may come as a surprise to you that celebrities are given fewer rights to privacy than are private citizens. Celebrities are regarded as public figures and thus their lives are considered to be matters of public concern. In issues involving contentious relationships between the press and celebrities, freedom of the press usually wins in the United States.) Other standards for reporting rape have changed over the years. It used to be accepted to refer to individuals as rape "victims." Contemporary norms often refer to individuals as rape "survivors." One reporter indicated that these labels are both still used in different situations. Hard news reporters are more likely to use the term *victim*, whereas feature stories that might, for example, portray coping strategies after the attack are more likely to use the term *survivor*. One of the themes of the YES selection is whether *Rolling Stone* was too accommodating to Jackie's requests because of the traumatic rape allegations.

Exposés have another set of norms for journalistic practice. There are a number of "rules" to be followed. Perhaps the most important is "one source never works." You may not know much about the Watergate investigation. If not, see *All the President's Men* starring Robert Redford and Dustin Hoffman as Bob Woodward and Carl Bernstein, *The Washington Post* Pulitzer Prize-winning reporters who broke the story of the botched burglary of the Democratic Party Headquarters at the Watergate complex. Their informant, Deep Throat, helped them make the connection with the White House. Their work provided the information that was crucial in the ultimate resignation of President Richard Nixon. Throughout the movie you will see Woodward and Bernstein's editor, Bill Bradlee, refusing to publish unless they have two sources to confirm.

One of the most significant failures of *Rolling Stone* editing was that they let the lure of a good story get ahead of the evidence. The blinders of a good story meant that they did not pursue the fundament question: How do we know that this is true? How could they, for example, not make the call to the fraternity house to get their reaction? Back to the fundamentals: One source is never enough. Verifying information is a tenet of journalism that most outside the field do not understand. Journalists have a strong commitment to accuracy, but how do journalists verify? Checking information with other sources, consulting pubic records, double checking basic facts, verifying quotes, verifying attribution, and sometimes even allowing sources to have pre-publication review are a number of strategies that reporters assert are part of their verification processes. Unfortunately, it seems that few journalists have standard routines for verification. It is the failure of many news organizations to have defined verification processes that makes Joe Strupp pessimistic about permanent changes resulting from the *Rolling Stone* case.

In our NO selection, Joe Strupp argues that the investigation encompassed failures in reporting, editing, editorial supervision, and fact-checking. He suggests that it is time for journalists to begin to define best practices when reporting about rape cases. Media outlets from *The New York Times* to *USA Today* indicated they would adjust their procedures in light of this episode. Others indicated that their guidelines on sourcing and fairness mean that they did not need to change their practices. While the *Rolling Stone*'s failure with this story and the analysis by the Columbia Journalism School faculty draws a map for how to do better, Joe Strupp fears that the failure of major media organziations to affirmatively respond to this issue will mean that little will change.

The consequences of this story are still emerging. The associate dean of students at UVA is suing *Rolling Stone*. Three members of Phi Kappa Psi, the fraternity of the article, have filed suit. Will Dana, managing editor of *Rolling Stone*, has stepped down. The implications of this debacle are not limited to our focus on discussions of ethics and editorial practices. In this case, the implications could have serious repercussions for the financial status of the company.

YES ⬅

Sheila Coronel, Steve Coll, and Derek Kravitz

Rolling Stone's Investigation: 'A Failure That Was Avoidable'

Last JULY 8, SABRINA RUBIN ERDELY, a writer for *Rolling Stone*, telephoned Emily Renda, a rape survivor working on sexual assault issues as a staff member at the University of Virginia. Erdely said she was searching for a single, emblematic college rape case that would show "what it's like to be on campus now . . . where not only is rape so prevalent but also that there's this pervasive culture of sexual harassment/rape culture," according to Erdely's notes of the conversation.

. . .

Renda put the writer in touch with a rising junior at UVA who would soon be known to millions of *Rolling Stone* readers as "Jackie," a shortened version of her true first name. Erdely said later that when she first encountered Jackie, she felt the student "had this stamp of credibility" because a university employee had connected them. Earlier that summer, Renda had even appeared before a Senate committee and had made reference to Jackie's allegations during her testimony—another apparent sign of the case's seriousness.

"I'd definitely be interested in sharing my story," Jackie wrote in an email a few days later.

On July 14, Erdely phoned her. Jackie launched into a vivid account of a monstrous crime. She said, according to Erdely's notes, that in September 2012, early in her freshman year, a third-year student she knew as a fellow lifeguard at the university's aquatic center had invited her to "my first fraternity party ever." After midnight, her date took her upstairs to a darkened bedroom. "I remember looking at the clock and it was 12:52 when we got into the room," she told Erdely. Her date shut the door behind them. Jackie continued, according to the writer's notes:

> *My eyes were adjusting to the dark. And I said his name and turned around. . . . I heard voices and I started to scream and someone pummeled into me and told me to shut up. And that's when I tripped and fell against the coffee table and it smashed underneath me*

> *and this other boy, who was throwing his weight on top of me. Then one of them grabbed my shoulders. . . . One of them put his hand over my mouth and I bit him—and he straight-up punched me in the face. . . . One of them said, 'Grab its motherfucking leg.' As soon as they said it, I knew they were going to rape me.*

The rest of Jackie's account was equally precise and horrifying. The lifeguard coached seven boys as they raped her one by one. Erdely hung up the phone "sickened and shaken," she said. . . . (Jackie declined to respond to questions for this report. Her lawyer said it "is in her best interest to remain silent at this time." The quotations attributed to Jackie here come from notes Erdely said she typed contemporaneously or from recorded interviews.)

Between July and October 2014, Erdely said, she interviewed Jackie seven more times. The writer was based in Philadelphia and had been reporting for *Rolling Stone* since 2008. . . . Will Dana, the magazine's managing editor, considered her "a very thorough and persnickety reporter who's able to navigate extremely difficult stories with a lot of different points of view."

Jackie proved to be a challenging source. At times, she did not respond to Erdely's calls, texts and emails. . . . Also, Jackie refused to provide Erdely the name of the lifeguard who had organized the attack on her. . . . That led to tense exchanges between Erdely and Jackie, but the confrontation ended when *Rolling Stone*'s editors decided to go ahead without knowing the lifeguard's name or verifying his existence. After that concession, Jackie cooperated fully until publication.

. . .

Rolling Stone published "A Rape on Campus: A Brutal Assault and Struggle for Justice at UVA" on Nov. 19, 2014. It caused a great sensation. . . . The online story ultimately attracted more than 2.7 million views, more than any other feature not about a celebrity that the magazine had ever published.

A week after publication, on the day before Thanksgiving, Erdely spoke with Jackie by phone. "She thanked me many times," Erdely said. Jackie seemed "adrenaline-charged . . . feeling really good."

Erdely chose this moment to revisit the mystery of the lifeguard who had lured Jackie and overseen her assault. . . .

Jackie gave Erdely a name. But as the reporter typed, her fingers stopped. Jackie was unsure how to spell the lifeguard's last name. . . .

"An alarm bell went off in my head," Erdely said. How could Jackie not know the exact name of someone she said had carried out such a terrible crime against her—a man she professed to fear deeply?

Over the next few days, worried about the integrity of her story, the reporter investigated the name Jackie had provided. . . . She discussed her concerns with her editors. Her work faced new pressures. The writer Richard Bradley had published . . . doubts about the plausibility of Jackie's account. . . . She also learned that T. Rees Shapiro, a *Washington Post* reporter, was preparing a story . . . that would raise serious doubts about *Rolling Stone*'s reporting.

Late on Dec. 4, Jackie texted Erdely, and the writer called back. It was by now after midnight. "We proceeded to have a conversation that led me to have serious doubts," Erdely said.

She telephoned her principal editor on the story, Sean Woods, and said she had now lost confidence in the accuracy of her published description of Jackie's assault. Woods . . . "was just stunned," he said. He "raced into the office" to help decide what to do next. Later that day, the magazine published an editor's note that effectively retracted *Rolling Stone*'s reporting on Jackie's allegations of gang rape at the University of Virginia. "It was the worst day of my professional life," Woods said.

Failure and Its Consequences

Rolling Stone's repudiation of the main narrative in "A Rape on Campus" is a story of journalistic failure that was avoidable. The failure encompassed reporting, editing, editorial supervision and fact-checking. The magazine set aside or rationalized as unnecessary essential practices of reporting. . . . The published story glossed over the gaps in the magazine's reporting by using pseudonyms and by failing to state where important information had come from.

In late March, after a four-month investigation, the Charlottesville, Va., police department said that it had . . . concluded, "There is no substantive basis to support the account alleged in the *Rolling Stone* article." The story's blowup comes as another shock to journalism's credibility amid head-swiveling change in the media industry. The particulars of *Rolling Stone*'s failure make clear the need for a revitalized consensus in newsrooms old and new about what best journalistic practices entail, at an operating-manual-level of detail.

As at other once-robust print magazines and newspapers, *Rolling Stone*'s editorial staff has shrunk in recent years as print advertising revenue has fallen and shifted online. . . . Yet *Rolling Stone* continues to invest in professional fact-checkers and to fund time-consuming investigations like Erdely's. The magazine's records and interviews with participants show that the failure of "A Rape on Campus" was not due to a lack of resources. The problem was methodology, compounded by an environment where several journalists with decades of collective experience failed to surface and debate problems about their reporting or to heed the questions they did receive from a fact-checking colleague.

Erdely and her editors had hoped their investigation would sound an alarm about campus sexual assault and would challenge Virginia and other universities to do better. Instead, the magazine's failure may have spread the idea that many women invent rape allegations. . . .

The university has also suffered. *Rolling Stone*'s account linked UVA's fraternity culture to a horrendous crime and portrayed the administration as neglectful. . . .

In retrospect, Dana, the managing editor, who has worked at *Rolling Stone* since 1996, said . . . "Every single person at every level of this thing had opportunities to pull the strings a little harder, to question things a little more deeply, and that was not done."

Yet the editors and Erdely have concluded that their main fault was to be too accommodating of Jackie. . . . "Ultimately, we were too deferential to our rape victim; we honored too many of her requests in our reporting," Woods said. "We should have been much tougher, and in not doing that, we maybe did her a disservice."

. . .

Yet the explanation that *Rolling Stone* failed because it deferred to a victim cannot adequately account for what went wrong. Erdely's reporting records and interviews with participants make clear that the magazine did not pursue important reporting paths even when Jackie had made no request that they refrain. The editors made judgments about attribution, fact-checking and verification that greatly increased their risks of error but had little or nothing to do with protecting Jackie's position.

It would be unfortunate if *Rolling Stone*'s failure were to deter journalists from taking on high-risk investigations of rape in which powerful individuals or institutions may wish to avoid scrutiny but where the facts may be underdeveloped. There is clearly a need for a more considered understanding and debate among journalists and others about the best practices for reporting on rape survivors, as well as on sexual assault allegations that have not been adjudicated. This report will suggest ways forward. It will also seek to clarify, however, why *Rolling Stone*'s failure with "A Rape on Campus" need not have happened, even accounting for the magazine's sensitivity to Jackie's position. That is mainly a story about reporting and editing.

'How Else Do You Suggest I Find It Out?'

By the time *Rolling Stone*'s editors assigned an article on campus sexual assault to Erdely in the spring of 2014, high-profile rape cases at Yale, Harvard, Columbia, Vanderbilt and Florida State had been in the headlines for months. . . .

There were numerous reports of campus assault that had been mishandled by universities. . . . The facts in these cases were sometimes disputed, but they had generated a wave of campus activism. "My original idea," Dana said, was "to look at one of these cases and have the story be more about the process of what happens when an assault is reported and the sort of issues it brings up."

Jackie's story seemed a powerful candidate for such a narrative. Yet once she heard the story, Erdely struggled to decide how much she could independently verify the details Jackie provided without jeopardizing Jackie's cooperation. . . .

[T]hree failures of reporting effort stand out. They involve basic, even routine journalistic practice—not special investigative effort. And if these reporting pathways had been followed, *Rolling Stone* very likely would have avoided trouble.

Three Friends and a 'Shit Show'

During their first interview, Jackie told Erdely that after she escaped the fraternity where seven men, egged on by her date, had raped her, she called three friends for help. . . . She described the two young men and one woman . . . as Ryan, Alex and Kathryn. . . . She said they met her in the early hours of Sept. 29, 2012, on the campus grounds. Jackie said she was "crying and crying" at first and that all she could communicate was that "something bad" had happened. She said her friends understood that she had been sexually assaulted. . . .

On Sept. 11, Erdely traveled to Charlottesville and met Jackie in person for the first time, at a restaurant near the UVA campus. With her digital recorder running, the reporter again asked about speaking to Ryan. "I did talk to

Ryan," Jackie disclosed. . . . Jackie went on to quote Ryan's incredulous reaction: "No! . . . I'm in a fraternity here, Jackie, I don't want the Greek system to go down, and it seems like that's what you want to happen. . . . I don't want to be a part of whatever little shit show you're running."

. . .

If Erdely had reached Ryan Duffin—his true name—he would have said that he had never told Jackie that he would not participate in *Rolling Stone*'s "shit show." . . . If Erdely had learned Ryan's account that Jackie had fabricated their conversation, she would have changed course immediately, to research other UVA rape cases free of such contradictions, she said later. . . .

The episode reaffirms a truism of reporting: Checking derogatory information with subjects is a matter of fairness, but it can also produce surprising new facts.

'Can You Comment?'

Throughout her reporting, Erdely told Jackie and others that she wanted to publish the name of the fraternity where Jackie said she had been raped. . . . Last October, as she was finishing her story, Erdely emailed Stephen Scipione, Phi Kappa Psi's local chapter president. "I've become aware of allegations of gang rape that have been made against the UVA chapter of Phi Kappa Psi," Erdely wrote. "Can you comment on those allegations?"

It was a decidedly truncated version of the facts that Erdely believed she had in hand. She did not reveal Jackie's account of the date of the attack. She did not reveal that Jackie said . . . that prospective pledges were present or that the man who allegedly orchestrated the attack was a Phi Kappa Psi member who was also a lifeguard at the university aquatic center. . . .

On Oct. 15, Scipione replied to Erdely's request for comment. He had learned, he wrote to her by email, "that an individual who remains unidentified had supposedly reported to someone who supposedly reported to the University that during a party there was a sexual assault." He added, "Even though this allegation is fourth hand and there are no details and no named accuser, the leadership and fraternity as a whole have taken this very seriously."

. . .

Even if *Rolling Stone* did not trust Phi Kappa Psi's motivations, if it had given the fraternity a chance to review the allegations in detail, the factual discrepancies the fraternity would likely have reported might have led Erdely and her editors to try to verify Jackie's account more thoroughly.

The Mystery of "Drew"

In her interviews, Jackie freely used a first name—but no last name—of the lifeguard she said had orchestrated her rape. On Sept. 16, for the first time, Erdely raised the possibility of tracking this man down.

. . .

"How would you feel if I reached out to him for a comment?" Erdely asked, the notes record.

"I'm not sure I would be comfortable with that."

That exchange inaugurated a six-week struggle between Erdely and Jackie. For a while, it seemed to Erdely as if the stalemate might lead Jackie to withdraw from cooperation altogether.

On Oct. 20, Erdely asked again for the man's last name.

. . .

"I don't want to give his last name," Jackie replied. "I don't even want to get him involved in this. . . . He completely terrifies me. I've never been so scared of a person in my entire life, and I've never wanted to tell anybody his last name. . . . I guess part of me was thinking that he'd never even know about the article."

. . .

After this conversation, Jackie stopped responding to Erdely's calls and messages. "There was a point in which she disappeared for about two weeks," Erdely said, "and we became very concerned" about Jackie's well-being.

. . .

Erdely did try to identify the man on her own. She asked Jackie's friends if they could help. They demurred. She searched online to see if the clues she had would produce a full name. This turned up nothing definitive. . . .

By October's end, with the story scheduled for closing in just two weeks, Jackie was still refusing to answer Erdely's texts and voicemails. Finally, on Nov. 3, after consulting with her editors, Erdely left a message for Jackie proposing to her a "solution" that would allow *Rolling Stone* to avoid contacting the lifeguard after all. The magazine would use a pseudonym; "Drew" was eventually chosen.

. . .

If *Rolling Stone* had located him and heard his response to Jackie's allegations, including the verifiable fact that he did not belong to Phi Kappa Psi, this might have led Erdely to reconsider her focus on that case. In any event, *Rolling Stone* stopped looking for him.

'What Are They Hiding?'

"A Rape on Campus" had ambitions beyond recounting one woman's assault. . . . The systems colleges have put in place to deal with sexual misconduct have come under intense scrutiny. These systems are works in progress, entangled in changing and sometimes contradictory federal rules that seek at once to keep students safe, hold perpetrators to account and protect every student's privacy.

. . .

Erdely's choice of the University of Virginia as a case study was well timed. . . . The university had by then endured a number of highly visible sexual assault cases. The Department of Education's Office of Civil Rights had placed the school, along with 54 others, under a broad compliance review.

"The overarching point of the article," Erdely wrote in response to questions from *The Washington Post* last December, was not Jackie, but "the culture that greeted her and so many other UVA women I interviewed, who came forward with allegations, only to be met with indifference."

. . .

'A Chilling Effect'

After she heard Jackie's shocking story, Erdely zeroed in on the obligation of universities under federal law to issue timely warnings when there is a "serious or continuing" threat to student safety. Erdely understood from Jackie that eight months after the alleged assault, she had reported to UVA about being gang-raped at the Phi Kappa Psi house. . . . The university, *Rolling Stone* reported in its published story, was remiss in not warning its students about this apparently predatory fraternity.

. . .

Over the years, the Department of Education has issued guidelines that stress victim confidentiality and autonomy. This means survivors decide whether to report and what assistance they would like. "If she did not identify any individual or Greek organization by name, the university was very, very limited in what it can do," said S. Daniel Carter, a campus safety advocate and director of the nonprofit 32 National Campus Safety Initiative.

As *Rolling Stone* reported, at their May 2013 meeting, Eramo presented Jackie her options: reporting the assault to the police or to the university's Sexual Misconduct Board. The dean also offered counseling and other services. She checked with Jackie in succeeding weeks to see whether she wanted to take action. . . .

Between that time and April 2014, the university received no further information about Jackie's case, according to the police and UVA sources.

On April 21, 2014, Jackie again met with Eramo, according to the police. . . .

Once more, the University of Virginia did not issue a warning. Whether the administration should have done so, given the information it then possessed, is a question under review by the University of Virginia's governing Board of Visitors. . . .

The day after her meeting with the dean, Jackie met with Charlottesville and UVA police in a meeting arranged by Eramo. Jackie reported . . . her assault at the Phi Kappa Psi house. The police later said that she declined to provide details about the gang rape because "[s]he feared retaliation from the fraternity if she followed through with a criminal investigation." . . .

'I'm Afraid It May Look Like We're Trying to Hide Something'

In early September, Erdely asked to interview Eramo. The request created a dilemma for UVA. Universities must comply with a scaffold of federal laws that limit what they can make public about their students. The most important of these is the Family Educational Rights and Privacy Act, or FERPA, which protects student privacy and can make it difficult for university staff members to release records or answer questions about any enrollee.

Eramo was willing to talk if she wasn't asked about specific cases, but about hypothetical situations, as Erdely had cleverly suggested as a way around student privacy limitations.

. . .

. . . Vice President for Student Life Patricia Lampkin vetoed the idea [in an e-mail]. . . . Lampkin said she felt that given FERPA restrictions, there was nothing Eramo could say in an interview that would give Erdely "a full and balanced view of the situation."

The distrust was mutual. "I had actually gone to campus thinking that they were going to be very helpful," Erdely said. Now she felt she was being stonewalled. . . .

. . .

To Erdely, UVA looked as if it was in damage control mode. "So I think that instead of being skeptical of Jackie," she said, "I became skeptical of UVA. . . . What are they hiding and why are they acting this way?"

. . .

On Oct. 2, Erdely interviewed UVA President Teresa Sullivan. The reporter asked probing [questions] . . . about allegations of gang rapes at Phi Kappa Psi. Sullivan said that a fraternity was under investigation but declined to comment further about specific cases.

. . .

Erdely concluded that UVA had not done enough. "Having presumably judged there to be no threat," she wrote in her published story, UVA "took no action to warn the campus that an allegation of gang rape had been made against an active fraternity." Overall, she wrote, "rapes are kept quiet" at UVA in part because of "an administration that critics say is less concerned with protecting students than it is with protecting its own reputation from scandal."

. . .

The Editing: 'I Wish Somebody Had Pushed Me Harder'

Sean Woods, Erdely's primary editor, might have prevented the effective retraction of Jackie's account by pressing his writer to close the gaps in her reporting. . . . Investigative reporters working on difficult, emotive or contentious stories often have blind spots. It is up to their editors to insist on more phone calls, more travel, more time, until the reporting is complete. Woods did not do enough.

. . .

[T]he detailed editorial supervision [was up] to managing editor Will Dana, who has been at the magazine for almost two decades. Dana might have looked more deeply into the story drafts he read, spotted the reporting gaps and insisted that they be fixed. He did not. "It's on me," Dana said. "I'm responsible."

In hindsight, the most consequential decision *Rolling Stone* made was to accept that Erdely had not contacted the three friends who spoke with Jackie on the night she said she was raped. That was the reporting path, if taken, that would have almost certainly led the magazine's editors to change plans.

. . .

"In retrospect, I wish somebody had pushed me harder" about reaching out to the three for their versions, Erdely said. "I guess maybe I was surprised that nobody said, 'Why haven't you called them?' But nobody did, and I wasn't going to press that issue." Of course, just because an editor does not ask a reporter to check derogatory information with a subject, that does not absolve the reporter of responsibility.

Woods remembered the sequence differently. After he read the first draft, he said, "I asked Sabrina to go reach" the three friends. "She said she couldn't. . . . I did repeatedly ask, 'Can we reach these people? Can we?' And I was told no." He accepted this because "I felt we had enough." The documentary evidence provided by *Rolling Stone* sheds no light on whose recollection—Erdely's or Wood's [sic]—is correct.

Woods said he ultimately approved pseudonyms because he didn't want to embarrass the three students by having Jackie's account of their self-involved patter out there for all their friends and classmates to see. "I wanted to protect them," he said.

. . .

'We Need to Verify This'

None of the editors discussed with Erdely whether Phi Kappa Psi or UVA, while being asked for "comment," had been given enough detail about Jackie's narrative to point out holes or contradictions. Erdely never raised the subject with her editors.

As to "Drew," the lifeguard, Dana said he was not even aware that *Rolling Stone* did not know the man's full name and had not confirmed his existence. . . .

[Woods recalls noting,] "If you've got to go around Jackie, fine, but we need to verify this," meaning Drew's identity. He remembered having this discussion "at least three times."

But when Jackie became unresponsive to Erdely in late October, Woods and Dana gave in. They authorized Erdely to tell Jackie they would stop trying to find the lifeguard. Woods resolved the issue as he had done earlier with the three friends: by using a pseudonym in the story.

'I Had a Faith'

It is not possible in journalism to reach every source a reporter or editor might wish. A solution is to be transparent with readers about what is known or unknown at the time of publication.

. . .

- *Rolling Stone*'s editors did not make clear to readers that Erdely and her editors did not know "Drew's" true name, had not talked to him and had been unable to verify that he existed. That was fundamental to readers' understanding. . . .
- Woods allowed the "shit show" quote from "Randall" into the story without making it clear that Erdely had not gotten it from him but from Jackie. . . . Not only did this mislead readers about the quote's

origins, it also compounded the false impression that *Rolling Stone* knew who "Randall" was. . . .

The editors invested *Rolling Stone*'s reputation in a single source. . . .

Woods and Erdely knew Jackie had spoken about her assault with other activists on campus, with at least one suitemate and to UVA. They could not imagine that Jackie would invent such a story. Woods said he and Erdely "both came to the decision that this person was telling the truth." They saw her as a "whistle blower" who was fighting indifference and inertia at the university.

The problem of confirmation bias—the tendency of people to be trapped by pre-existing assumptions and to select facts that support their own views while overlooking contradictory ones . . . is a well-established finding of social science. It seems to have been a factor here. Erdely believed the university was obstructing justice. She felt she had been blocked. Like many other universities, UVA had a flawed record of managing sexual assault cases. Jackie's experience seemed to confirm this larger pattern. Her story seemed well established on campus, repeated and accepted. "If I had been informed ahead of time of one problem or discrepancy with her overall story, we would have acted upon that very aggressively," Dana said. . . .

No such doubts came to his attention, he said. As to the apparent gaps in reporting, attribution and verification that had accumulated in the story's drafts, Dana said, "I had a faith that as it went through the fact-checking that all this was going to be straightened out."

Fact-Checking

At *Rolling Stone*, every story is assigned to a fact-checker. . . . Their job is to review a writer's story after it has been drafted, to double-check details like dates and physical descriptions. They also look at issues such as attribution and whether story subjects who have been depicted unfavorably have had their say. Typically, checkers will speak with the writer's sources . . . to verify facts within quotations and other details. . . .

In this case, the fact-checker assigned to "A Rape on Campus" had been checking stories [for years]. She relied heavily on Jackie, as Erdely had done. She said she was "also aware of the fact that UVA believed this story to be true." That was a misunderstanding. What *Rolling Stone* knew at the time of publication was that Jackie had given a version of her account to UVA and other student activists. . . . UVA had placed Phi Kappa Psi under scrutiny. None of this meant that the university had reached a conclusion about Jackie's narrative. . . .

The checker did try to improve the story's reporting and attribution of quotations concerning the three friends. She marked on a draft that Ryan . . . had not been interviewed, and that his "shit show" quote had originated with Jackie. "Put this on Jackie?" the checker wrote. "Any way we can confirm with him?" She said she talked about this problem of clarity with Woods and Erdely. "I pushed. . . . They came to the conclusion that they were comfortable" with not making it clear to readers that they had never contacted Ryan.

. . .

Looking Forward

For Rolling Stone: An Exceptional Lapse or a Failure of Policy?

The collapse of "A Rape on Campus" does not involve . . . fabrication. . . . There is no evidence in Erdely's materials or from interviews with her subjects that she invented facts; the problem was that she relied on what Jackie told her without vetting its accuracy.

. . . *Rolling Stone*'s senior editors are unanimous in the belief that the story's failure does not require them to change their editorial systems. . . .

Yet better and clearer policies about reporting practices, pseudonyms and attribution might well have prevented the magazine's errors. . . .

Stronger policy and clearer staff understanding in at least three areas might have changed the final outcome:

Pseudonyms
Dana, Woods and McPherson said using pseudonyms at *Rolling Stone* is a "case by case" issue that requires no special convening or review. Pseudonyms are inherently undesirable in journalism. . . . Their use in this case was a crutch—it allowed the magazine to evade coming to terms with reporting gaps. *Rolling Stone* should consider banning them. . . .

Checking Derogatory Information
Erdely and Woods made the fateful agreement not to check with the three friends. If the fact-checking department had understood that such a practice was unacceptable, the outcome would almost certainly have changed.

Confronting Subjects With Details
When Erdely sought "comment," she missed the opportunity to hear challenging, detailed rebuttals from Phi Kappa Psi before publication. . . . If both the reporter and

checker had understood that by policy they should routinely share specific, derogatory details with the subjects of their reporting, *Rolling Stone* might have veered in a different direction.

For Journalists: Reporting on Campus Rape
Rolling Stone is not the first news organization to be sharply criticized for its reporting on rape. Of all crimes, rape is perhaps the toughest to cover. . . . Reporting on a case that has not been investigated and adjudicated, as *Rolling Stone* did, can be even more challenging.

There are several areas that require care and should be the subject of continuing deliberation among journalists:

Balancing Sensitivity to Victims and the Demands of Verification
Because questioning a victim's account can be traumatic, counselors have cautioned journalists to allow survivors some control over their own stories. This is good advice. Yet it does survivors no good if reporters documenting their cases avoid rigorous practices of verification. That may only subject the victim to greater scrutiny and skepticism.

. . .

Corroborating Survivor Accounts
Walt Bogdanich, a Pulitzer Prize-winning investigative reporter for *The New York Times* who has spent the past two years reporting on campus rape, said he tries to track down every available shred of corroborating evidence—hospital records, 911 calls, text messages or emails that have been sent immediately after the assault. In some cases, it can be possible to obtain video, either from security cameras or from cellphones.

. . .

Holding Institutions to Account
Given the difficulties, journalists are rarely in a position to prove guilt or innocence in rape. "The real value of what we do as journalists is analyzing the response of the institutions to the accusation," Bogdanich said. This approach can also make it easier to persuade both victims and perpetrators to talk. . . .

To succeed at such reporting, it is necessary to gain a deep understanding of the tangle of rules and guidelines on campus sexual assault. There's Title IX, the Clery Act and the Violence Against Women Act. There are directives from the Office of Civil Rights and recommendations from the White House. Congress and state legislatures are proposing new laws.

The responsibilities that universities have in preventing campus sexual assault—and the standards of performance they should be held to—are important matters of public interest. *Rolling Stone* was right to take them on. The pattern of its failure draws a map of how to do better.

. . .

Sheila Coronel is Dean of Academic Affairs at the Columbia Journalism School and Director of the Stabile Center for Investigative Journalism.

Steve Coll is the Dean of Columbia Journalism School.

Derek Kravitz is a postgraduate research scholar at the Columbia Journalism School.

Joe Strupp

 **NO**

How the *Rolling Stone* Rape Story Failure Has—And Hasn't—Changed Media Coverage

Three months after a Columbia University investigation found major journalistic errors in a *Rolling Stone* report on campus sexual assault at the University of Virginia, major news outlets say they have not adjusted their approach to covering similar stories. But rape survivor advocates say they have seen less coverage of the issue since the failures of the *Rolling Stone* report came to light, and, in some cases, an increased hesitancy in trusting survivors' accounts.

The November 2014 *Rolling Stone* article "A Rape on Campus" prominently featured the story of "Jackie," a pseudonymous University of Virginia student who told the outlet she was gang-raped in 2012 at a fraternity party.

After initially receiving praise, the article came under fire for an apparent failure to seek comment from the alleged suspects. Other factual questions arose, prompting *Rolling Stone* to commission an investigation with the Columbia University Graduate School of Journalism and its dean, Steve Coll.

That investigation, released in early April, found the *Rolling Stone* story was a "journalistic failure that was avoidable. The failure encompassed reporting, editing, editorial supervision and fact-checking. The magazine set aside or rationalized as unnecessary essential practices of reporting that, if pursued, would likely have led the magazine's editors to reconsider publishing Jackie's narrative so prominently, if at all."

Though the report outlined specific failures in the *Rolling Stone* editorial process (while declining to adjudicate exactly what happened to "Jackie"), it also pointed to broader problems in how all outlets cover sexual assault, and offered some suggestions on "how journalists might begin to define best practices when reporting about rape cases on campus or elsewhere." It recommended, for example, that journalists spend time further deliberating how best to balance sensitivity to victims with the demands of verification, and how best to corroborate survivor accounts.

In interviews with *Media Matters*, editors from *The New York Times*, *The Washington Post*, *USA Today* and other outlets said they have not adjusted their approach to covering the stories of rape survivors in light of the *Rolling Stone* mess and the resulting Columbia report.

Several editors said that the *Rolling Stone* saga would not cause them to believe survivors less or hesitate to publicize their stories.

"I don't think that story holds any larger lessons about rape coverage, or whether one should believe alleged assault victims," *New York Times* executive editor Dean Baquet told *Media Matters* via email. "It was a poorly-done story . . . It doesn't make me any more or less likely to believe a source. We always verify, get the other side, and report the heck out of a story, no matter the subject."

Other editors who spoke with *Media Matters* maintain their coverage will be unaffected.

"It hasn't, or won't change how we view these stories," said David Callaway, editor of *USA Today*. "I always thought the idea that news organizations would cut back on their coverage because of one poor example seemed a bit far-fetched. We still get people coming to us with stories or requests for coverage many times a day, and the ones we choose to go after we only pursue if we can verify. We have detailed guidelines on sourcing and fairness in coverage and we have no plans to change those in the wake of the *Rolling Stone* debacle."

He added, "Verification is the key. Reporters get lots of tips and listen to lots of tales. Some are true. Some are not. None should be published unless they can be verified and all sides contacted. That hasn't changed."

For Martin Baron, editor of *The Washington Post*, the same is true: "Nothing has changed in our coverage. We always try to be both sensitive and careful, and to report such stories thoroughly."

Colleen Schwartz, a spokesperson for *The Wall Street Journal*, responded to a request for comment to *Journal* editor-in-chief Gerard Baker with this statement:

Our journalists take very seriously our tradition at *The Wall Street Journal* of vetting assertions before they are published, whatever the topic. We discuss and debate journalism practices, standards and ethics as a matter of course at the Journal, but the high bar we set for ourselves for being accurate and fair existed here long before the publication of the *Rolling Stone* story. We will continue to uphold our same rigorous standards, irrespective of the *Rolling Stone* article.

Robert Rosenthal, executive director of the Center for Investigative Reporting, said via email, "This is very sensitive and difficult reporting and the *Rolling Stone* incident did not teach us anything except to rely on the standards and practices CIR has maintained for 37 years when it comes to verification for all of our work. And to do everything we can to make sure we are fair in our conclusions and that they are based on facts and sources who are named, not anonymous."

Asked specifically if the *Rolling Stone* story would prompt his reporters to question rape survivors more, he said, "I think the issue of veracity with any source is something we discuss and think about on any story. Understanding the potential motivations of any source on any story is something I was taught very early on in my career and we think about it at CIR especially if someone is alleging negative or damaging things about an individual or an organization. Allegations about sexual abuse brought by a victim are painful to hear and deal with but bring a great responsibility to do the right thing for all who might be touched by the story."

Greg Moore, editor of *The Denver Post,* said the *Rolling Stone* episode is a "cautionary tale."

"*The Rolling Stone* debacle is not going to affect how we deal with allegations of rape," Moore said, calling it, "a reminder that journalists need to always verify information before publishing. That is our practice in print and online. Things like what happened to *Rolling Stone* occur when you don't follow your reporting and editing procedures." He concluded, "If anything, we have reminded people to question how we know what we think we know. Regarding allegations of rape, we always want to be sensitive and fair and we will continue to be."

Audrey Cooper, editor-in-chief of the *San Francisco Chronicle*, said the focus should be on the treatment of anonymous sources, not "whether to believe alleged victims."

"It's about how you treat and prosecute (for lack of a better term) anonymous sources," she said. "We have strong and longstanding policies on anonymous sources, and I am confident those policies would prevent publication of similarly flawed stories."

Ed Wasserman, dean of the Graduate School of Journalism at the University of California, Berkeley, remains concerned.

"It would be unrealistic to say this doesn't cast a shadow over cases like this," he told *Media Matters*. "The danger there is that these will be viewed as squalid, inconclusive and very difficult to report with a whole lot of institutional downsides. There are realities that are very difficult to report on while respecting evidentiary standards that journalists adhere to. You can't read the Columbia account of what *Rolling Stone* did without wincing at the failure to follow rudimentary journalist standards."

"I think that some news organizations will definitely shy away from these stories," he concluded, "because they don't have the chops to handle them and they are mindful that they will end up with something that is both squalid and inconclusive."

While most outlets were confident the *Rolling Stone* fiasco would not change coverage, some rape survivor advocates and support groups contend the *Rolling Stone* failures have created a backlash against survivors' stories that is already being felt.

One lawyer who handles such cases for survivors said fewer reporters are coming to her for comment and perspective on campus rape, and that she has also seen journalists scrutinize cases and survivor accounts more than in the past.

"It went from three calls a day to maybe three calls a week, we are seeing a big downturn, less interest in covering it," said Laura Dunn, an attorney and founder of SurvJustice. "It is not completely devastating to the movement, but you are seeing more focus on the accused."

Dunn said she has seen a clear impact on reporting: "It has changed how some news media report on the story. I have had one journalist [for whom] it did not matter that I was a lawyer and I had documentation, he wanted someone to independently verify my involvement [in a particular case]. I ended up not working with that journalist."

Jamia Wilson, executive director of Women Action and the Media, another advocacy group, claimed she has seen a decline in overall media coverage of the issue since the *Rolling Stone* debacle. "I have not seen as much coverage on the issue. I don't think the volume of coverage has been as much."

Wilson was also critical of media outlets for not seeking to change their approach for the better. "It's really sad and disappointing to hear them say there won't be changes," she said.

Karin Roland, organizing director of UltraViolet, a women's rights group that focuses on such issues, said *Rolling*

Stone's "shoddy journalism" hurt survivors' believability, adding "that is a grave disservice to the survivor in question, to all survivors and all students at that school who had a chance to shine a light on a major problem."

She said the fallout is being felt: "In the back of people's minds there is a question of whether they can believe survivors or not."

Part of the problem, according to some women's advocacy groups, are the stories of rape news outlets choose to investigate in the first place.

"To me, the worst aspect of the *Rolling Stone* article was the fact that the magazine and the author insisted on telling the most salacious story they could find, the most outrageous, the most sensationalistic story of rape they could find," said Terry O'Neill, president of the National Organization for Women. "They worked directly with the head of the student group that advocates around sexual assaults, but they didn't [use many of those stories] and my understanding is that the less sensationalist stories were abundant. I think that right there tells you what's wrong with coverage of sexual assault in the United States today."

Sharmili Majmudar, executive director of Rape Victim Advocates, said the lesson from *Rolling Stone* should be how rape and sexual assault are handled by law enforcement and campus officials.

"Lost in the aftermath is the fact that universities routinely discourage reporting of sexual violence, and respond poorly to such reporting when it does occur, as evidenced by the Title IX investigations currently underway at over 100 colleges and universities," she said. "Unfortunately, the focus of coverage has become about 'Jackie' specifically rather than the widespread issue of sexual violence at educational institutions."

Media Matters has previously documented how media's failings and inconsistencies when it comes to reporting on sexual assault—particularly in conservative media, though the trend extends to the mainstream—can reinforce the stigmas against survivors and discourage victims from reporting these crimes in the first place. Survivors have repeatedly said that the fear that no one will believe them keeps them from speaking out, while some feel re-victimized by the suggestion from media figures that they are lying about the traumatic events they experienced.

As the Columbia report explained, "journalists are rarely in a position to prove guilt or innocence in rape." But it is a matter of public interest to report on how institutions handle—or mishandle—the accusations, and *Rolling Stone*'s failure "draws a map of how to do better."

JOE STRUPP is a veteran journalist who has been with Media Matters For America since 2010. He is an investigative reporter who has written for *The Washington Post*. He has spoken about media issues on media ranging from Fox News, NPR, and Voice of America.

EXPLORING THE ISSUE

Will the *Rolling Stone* "Rape on Campus" Story Change Journalism for the Better?

Critical Thinking and Reflection

1. Could you provide advice to media organizations on how to best handle sensitive and potentially explosive material?
2. Given what you now know, can you deconstruct what went wrong in the *Rolling Stone* article?
3. How would you integrate appropriate guidelines and safeguards in a newsroom?
4. Is there a need for a national conversation among journalists on this issue?
5. Would you advise rape survivors to talk with the press? Why or why not?

Is There Common Ground?

You could look at these two articles and say that there is very little disagreement across the divide of this issue. Journalistic norms for verification, accuracy, and truth telling are not in question. Everyone agrees that these are foundational to practicing journalists. In a time when citizen journalism has become a staple in many media outlets and when bloggers refer to themselves as journalists, it is the adherence to standards such as those above that should separate the working journalist from the citizen blogger.

The issue is not standards; it is practices. These standards are normative. How could such a breach occur? You can be sure that everyone at *Rolling Stone* is very sorry about this article, from the author to the managing editor(s). Where there is little common ground is between those who feel that the lessons have been learned and those who argue for creating a defied verification process within their newsrooms. Have the lessons been learned or will it happen again the next time a great story begins to founder on lack of verification?

Additional Resources

Clifford G. Christians, Mark Fackler, Kathy Richardson, Peggy Kreshel, and Robert H. Woods , Media *Ethics: Cases and Moral Reasoning*, 9th ed. (Routledge, 2011).

Kate Harding, *Asking for It: The Alarming Rise of Rape Culture and What We Can Do about It.* (DeCapo Books, 2015).

Bill Kovach and Tom Rosenstiel, *The Elements of Journalism: What Newspeople Should Know and the Public Should Expect,* 3rd ed. (Three Rivers Press, 2014).

Roger Simpson and William Coté, *Covering Violence: A Guide to Ethical Reporting About Victims & Trauma.* (Columbia University Press, 2006).

Internet References . . .

The Washington Post

https://www.washingtonpost.com/news
/volokh-conspiracy/wp/2015/04/05/libel-law-and
-the-rolling-stone-uva-alleged-gang-rape-story
-an-update-in-light-of-the-columbia-school-of
-journalism-report/

Poynter Institute

www.poynter.org/opinion/my-take/307585/rape-and
-anonymity-a-fateful-pairing/

RAINN: Rape, Abuse & Incest National Network

https://rainn.org/get-help/national-sexual-assault
-hotline

Reporters Committee on Freedom of the Press

www.rcfp.org/browse-media-law-resources/news
-media-law/news-media-and-law-spring-2015/clash
-ethics-and-law

Selected, Edited, and with Issue Framing Material by:
Alison Alexander, *University of Georgia*
and
Jarice Hanson, *University of Massachusetts - Amherst*

ISSUE

Should Corporations Be Allowed to Finance Political Campaigns?

YES: Thomas R. Eddlem, from "Citizens United Is Breaking Up Corporate Dominance of Elections," *The New American* (June 26, 2012)

NO: David Earley and Ian Vandewalker, from "Transparency for Corporate Political Spending: A Federal Solution," Brennan Center for Justice at New York University School of Law (2012)

Learning Outcomes

After reading this issue, you should be able to:

- Consider the impact of money and freedom of speech in political campaigns.
- Evaluate the impact of political campaign donations.
- Compare the way media industries and special interest groups influence what we know and their influence in the democratic process.

ISSUE SUMMARY

YES: Conservative author Thomas R. Eddlem makes the case that corporate media institutions influence the messages that the public sees and hears. As a result, the Supreme Court's 2010 *Citizens United* decision, which gives corporations the right to make political contributions and creates the possibility of the establishment of SuperPACs, also results in the exercise of freedom of speech.

NO: David Earley and Ian Vandewalker, two counsels at the Brennan Center for Justice at the New York University School of Law, argue that the rise of political spending that resulted from the Supreme Court's *Citizens United* decision has created a situation in which political elections can be "bought" by corporate donors. Because of the new law, they argue that the only way to ensure transparency is to create a situation in which all political donations are disclosed to the public.

The 2012 presidential election, which pitted incumbent Barack Obama against Mitt Romney, was the most costly in history. According to most reports, the two candidates spent over 2 billion dollars on their campaigns. When added to the cost of all other campaigns in the 2012 congressional elections, the sum total reached 8 billion dollars. These historic figures were largely the result of changes to traditional campaign finance practices, and attributed to the 2010 Supreme Court's *Citizens United* decision, which lifted restrictions on the amount of money corporate donors and special interest groups could donate to political candidates, issues, and campaigns, and allowed the formation of SuperPACs (political action committees).

The relationship of campaign donors and the cost of running a political campaign have always been controversial. In the United States, at the federal level, Congress has the responsibility of enacting campaign finance laws, and they are enforced by an independent federal agency called the Federal Election Commission (FEC). Traditionally, individual donors could contribute to a political candidate's campaign, but were restricted by certain dollar amounts. Typically, an individual could give up to $2,500 to a candidate. But in 2008, an independent organization called Citizens United wanted to air a film that was critical of Hillary Clinton, who was then a candidate for president. The film was called *Hillary: The Movie*, and Citizens United wanted to advertise the film during television broadcasts close to a Democratic primary, which was prohibited by the 2002 Bipartisan Campaign Reform Act (known as the McCain-Feingold Act).

Though the U.S. District Court for the District of Columbia originally prohibited Citizens United from advertising their film within 30 days of the convention, the case was appealed to the Supreme Court, and in 2010 the court overturned the District Court's decision (on a vote of 5-4) and found that the First Amendment prohibited the government from restricting political expenditures by corporations and unions. Many people criticized the Court for giving corporations the same freedom of speech that individual citizens are guaranteed, but the end result of the *Citizens United* decision was that the amount of money raised for candidates or to oppose candidates or certain positions could now be raised through organizations of donors, called political action committees (PACs), or very large organizations called SuperPACs that can accept unlimited amounts of money from corporations, unions, and associations. In the 2012 campaigns, it was found that much of the SuperPAC money was spent on negative advertising, and major criticism was leveled at millionaire and billionaire donors who appeared to be trying to "buy" political influence by backing certain candidates, and certain issues.

The controversy even found its way to Comedy Central, where Stephen Colbert used his show *The Colbert Report* to announce that by following the new FEC rules, he could start his own SuperPAC, Americans for a Better Tomorrow, Tomorrow, which raised 1.2 million dollars from viewers in 15 months. By publicizing the weaknesses in the new system, Colbert's SuperPAC demonstrated how weak the new decision was, and how it could be subject to manipulation. In 2012, Colbert was awarded a Peabody Award for how well he had used his SuperPAC parody as an "innovative means of teaching American viewers about the landmark court decision."

No doubt, some people like the idea of contributing to organizations that support their views, but in the case of the *Citizens United* decision and the increased power of SuperPACs, many say that the Supreme Court made a terrible decision because it equates corporate power with freedom of speech, in effect, giving the loudest megaphone to those who have the most money. John McCain, former candidate for president called it the "worst decision ever," and President Obama criticized the decision in his 2010 State of the Union address. In the YES and NO selections, conservative author Thomas R. Eddlem equates the *Citizens United* decision with the same power that media industries have been exerting over what the public knows, and claims that if we really want to see who influences politics, we should look to the news media and the members of the Council on Foreign Relations, a group of high-powered members of the media who influence politics in their own ways. Two attorneys, David Earley and Ian Vandewalker, who work for the Brennan Center for Justice at the New York University School of Law, remind us that even though the Citizens United organization supported the idea of disclosure laws to make campaign donations more transparent for the public, the Supreme Court and Congress did not act to make those disclosure rules a part of the practice of the decision, and as a result, opened the door to misuse and manipulation.

YES ⬅

Thomas R. Eddlem

Citizens United Is Breaking Up Corporate Dominance of Elections

With the 2012 political season heating up, many people are calling for a ban on the SuperPacs created in the wake of the 2010 Supreme Court *Citizens United* decision. A few on the left have even called for a constitutional amendment to ban corporations from making political advertisements, for fear that corporations have come to dominate elections in the United States.

In one sense, they are right. But it's not the Super-Pacs. The corporations that have been dominating the public debate for decades are the media empires. Right now, six corporations control most of the television, radio, and print publishing networks that Americans see on a daily basis. They drive the debate, and the social issues behind the debate.

- **ABC/Disney** runs ABC News, as well as a large number of local and cable television stations, theme parks, and movie studios.
- **Time-Warner** owns CNN, TNT, and a whole slew of cable television stations, Warner Brothers movie studios, plus a large number of magazines, including *Time, People,* and *Sports Illustrated.*
- **NewsCorp** runs Fox News, a radio news network, 20th Century Fox movie studios, and dozens of newspapers and book publishers.
- **NBCUniversal** is jointly owned by Comcast and General Electric, one of the largest corporations in America. It runs the NBC network, MSNBC, a large selection of cable channels, Universal theme parks, and digital media.
- **Viacom** owns a variety of cable television channels and Paramount Pictures movie studios.
- **CBS Corporation** owns CBS television network, Showtime, a number of cable television stations, and a radio news network.

Even the Left admits that a few corporations control the message most Americans see.

What they don't talk about is that these few corporations are associated with each other in the New York-based Council on Foreign Relations, and that they have a tight relationship with government and establishment corporate leadership across the country. The Council on Foreign Relations has only 4,500 members, out of a national population of some 300 million. But they boast some of the most powerful media personalities and media corporate leaders in the country.

Corporate Members of the CFR include NewsCorp, Google, Time-Warner, Verizon, Microsoft, McGraw-Hill (publishing), General Electric (49 percent of NBC), and Thomson-Reuters (publishing/news network). And many of the personalities that Americans see every day on television are CFR members. For *example*:

NBC/MSNBC: Brian Williams (NBC anchor), Mika Brzezinski (MSNBC anchor), Maria Bartiromo (CNBC anchor), Tom Brokaw (former anchor), and Jonathan Alter (NBC News/*Newsweek* magazine)

CBS: Bob Schieffer (anchor) and Dan Rather (former anchor)

CNN: Fareed Zakaria (CNN anchor), Erin Burnett (CNN anchor), and commentators David Gergen, Jonathan Karl, and Jeffrey Toobin

ABC/Disney: George Stephanopoulos (anchor), Diane Sawyer (anchor), Katie Couric (former anchor), and commentators Peggy Noonan and George Will

Fox/NewsCorp: Rupert Murdoch (CEO of News-Corp) and commentators Morton Kondracke and Charles Krauthammer

Even movie stars are CFR members, such as Angelina Jolie, Warren Beatty, and George Clooney.

But it's not just full-time journalists and Hollywood bigshots from the CFR that get network airtime. The CFR member/anchors call CFR member/"experts" to affirm their positions. CFR President Richard Haass *boasted* in the CFR's 2011 Annual Report that the "CFR has been active on the full range of U.S. foreign policy concerns. Experts published five hundred and seventy op-eds and articles in the *New York Times, Washington Post, Wall Street Journal, Financial Times, Newsweek, Time,* and the *Atlantic,* among others, and made nearly five hundred media appearances on major U.S. and international news networks. CFR experts also testified before Congress fourteen times and briefed U.S. and foreign government officials over four hundred times."

So go ahead: Change the channel and pretend you can get a different perspective. In reality, it doesn't matter what channel you flip to; the CFR limits on acceptable debate are evident on every national channel, something that many freedom-lovers witnessed with the media ignoring or—later—demeaning Ron Paul in the presidential race. There's no national debate on eliminating all foreign aid, even though some *three-fourths of Americans want to do it*. Why not? Because it's not on the CFR talking points. There's no debate about bringing Americans home from hundreds of military bases abroad, even though a clear majority of Americans want it. Why not? Because it's not on the CFR talking points.

Imagine if such a concentration of top media personalities were found to be members of the National Rifle Association or the Teamsters Union, both of which have a membership nearly 1,000 times that of the Council on Foreign Relations. Wouldn't there be an outcry about bias or corruption?

We also saw the mainstream media coalesce around the idea that we had to bail out the banks in 2008 and 2009. Why was that? The CFR and its members led the people to bail out companies that were headed by their fellow CFR members. CFR corporate membership includes major banks such as Goldman Sachs, Morgan Stanley, Citibank, Bank of America—and did include AIG—until it went bankrupt despite the bailouts.

And it's not surprising that they got the bailouts either, since the CFR was *holding policy discussions* with Treasury Department officials throughout the conference. They *still are*.

Of course, it's easy to get a *phone-in from the Treasury Secretary* before he heads out to the G-20 conference if he's already a member. Indeed, it's not just Timothy Geithner who's a member, but just about all the past Treasury secretaries have been members of the Council on Foreign Relations for 50 years—from Bush's Hank Paulson to Clinton's Lawrence Summers and Robert Rubin (the latter a former CEO of Goldman Sachs).

This is true across the spectrum of government. Obama's Secretary of State Hillary Clinton is a member, just as Condi Rice and Colin Powell were under the Bush administration, and Madeleine Albright and Warren Christopher were under the Clinton administration.

The point of all this discussion is not to beat up on the Council on Foreign Relations, though its members probably deserve it. It's to point out that our media and our elections are already tightly controlled by a handful of well-connected multi-billion-dollar media corporations. And they were controlled that way long before the *Citizens United* decision. That's how they've been able to get the bailout deals done at the expense of the middle-class taxpayers—despite protests by the Tea Party and the Occupy movement. In this battle, it's a fight not just between the 99 percent and the one percent, but between the 99.999 percent and the 0.001 percent, who are practiced and very good at robbing the 99.999 percent through the agency of government authority.

But the stranglehold of these five corporations is breaking. The Internet started the breakup, but *Citizens United* tore that media oligopoly wide open. Under *Citizens United*, people have only to find one millionaire to fund their views and they can get around the mainstream media with grass-roots campaigning, Internet ads, or even conventional television advertisements. This happened with Liberty For All SuperPac, which helped guide Ron Paul fan Thomas Massie to a Republican primary win in an open Kentucky congressional district. And FreedomWorks SuperPac has shaken up Utah politics with its "Retire Hatch" campaign to stop TARP bailout Republican Orrin Hatch. A six-term senator, Hatch would never have had to have been in a run-off election against Dan Liljenquist without FreedomWorks SuperPac's help.

The Left implores the nation to repeal *Citizens United* in order to "take money out of politics." But the only way to do this is to ban freedom of the press. The *New York Times* condemned the *Citizens United* decision when it came out in 2009, complaining that corporations should not be involved in politics. This was just days after the *Times'* corporate subsidiary, the *Boston Globe*, had *endorsed* the Democrat in the Massachusetts U.S. Senate race to replace the late Ted Kennedy.

No corporations involved in politics?

. . . except themselves.

As James Madison noted in *Federalist #10*, political disagreements can be decided by either government censorship or allowing everyone to broadcast their views and trusting the people to make the right decisions at the ballot box. He chose the latter, stating:

> There are two methods of curing the mischiefs of faction: the one, by removing its causes; the other, by controlling its effects.
>
> There are again two methods of removing the causes of faction: the one, by destroying the liberty which is essential to its existence; the other, by giving to every citizen the same opinions, the same passions, and the same interests.
>
> It could never be more truly said than of the first remedy, that it was worse than the disease. Liberty is to faction what air is to fire, an aliment [element] without which it instantly expires. But it could not be less folly to abolish liberty, which is essential to political life, because it nourishes faction, than it would be to wish the annihilation of air, which is essential to animal life, because it imparts to fire its destructive agency.

Destroying essential liberty is precisely what the critics of *Citizens United* want to do. The attitude of the repeal-*Citizens-United* crowd can be summed up accurately as "totalitarian paternalism." They don't trust the people to come to the right conclusions. The people must be safely shepherded by the guardians of acceptable opinion, as represented by the five or six giant corporations that run the establishment media. Or perhaps they remain blissfully unaware that repealing *Citizens United* would put the same old establishment back in charge.

In the end it is an attitude of censorship worthy of Joseph Stalin. More importantly, it is flatly contradictory to the *First and Tenth Amendments* to the U.S. Constitution.

The cry on the Left is that corporations are not people. That's true; corporations and SuperPacs are associations of people. And this too was part of the First Amendment, which protected the right of the people to assemble and associate.

During congressional debate on the Bill of Rights in 1789, Connecticut Congressman Theodore Sedgwick *opposed* the First Amendment because he thought adding freedom of assembly to freedom of speech and press was redundant. According to the Annals of Congress, Sedgwick "feared it would tend to make them appear trifling in the eyes of their constituents; what, said he, shall we secure the freedom of speech, and think it necessary, at the same time, to allow the right of assembling? If people freely converse together, they must assemble for that purpose; it is a self-evident, unalienable right which the people possess; it is certainly a thing that never would be called in question; it is derogatory to the dignity of the House to descend to such minutiae. . . ."

The right to band together for a political cause and spend money was well-entrenched in the American constitutional system by the 1830s, when Alexis de Tocqueville *noted* in his *Democracy in America* that:

> In no country in the world has the principle of association been more successfully used or applied to a greater multitude of objects than in America. Besides the permanent associations which are established by law under the names of townships, cities, and counties, a vast number of others are formed and maintained by the agency of private individuals. . . . An association consists simply in the public assent which a number of individuals give to certain doctrines and in the engagement which they contract to promote in a certain manner the spread of those doctrines. The right of associating in this fashion almost merges with freedom of the press, but societies thus formed possess more authority than the press.

While the Left demonizes the label "corporations," it's nothing more than a label, a bogeyman. Call them associations of Americans exercising their rights to freedom of the press and freedom of speech, and the bogeyman is banished. The *Citizens United* decision allows more speech, not less. And for that reason, the Founding Fathers were probably smiling down from heaven when the decision was released.

Thomas R. Eddlem is a freelance writer and former newspaper editor who often writes for *The New American,* a conservative magazine. A native of Boston, he also contributes to other magazines and blogs, and has a radio show in the southeastern region of Massachusetts.

David Earley and
Ian Vandewalker

 **NO**

Transparency for Corporate Political Spending: A Federal Solution

American elections are awash in cash as never before. Spending in the 2012 presidential election will shatter all historic records, as will spending in Congressional races. But the most significant money won't be in the candidates' campaign coffers. The money transforming contemporary elections is that flowing into—and being spent by—outside groups that are legally independent of the candidates. Many of these outside groups are able to raise funds in unlimited amounts from wealthy individuals, unions, and corporations.

As the law stands today, corporations and unions can spend unlimited amounts of money in order to influence the outcome of elections. If individuals, unions, or corporations choose to spend political money directly—by producing television advertising and buying air time, for example—they must publicly disclose the expenditures and their contributors. But it is easy to evade such disclosure by simply routing political contributions through intermediary groups that purchase the ad time. The end result is that wealthy individuals, corporations, and unions can spend millions on political advertising to influence voters' choices at the ballot box, without disclosing this spending to the public.

After the Supreme Court decided *Citizens United v. FEC*, Americans were outraged at the invitation extended to corporations to spend unlimited sums to influence elections. But in addition to expanding corporations' ability to make political expenditures, *Citizens United* strongly approved of disclosure requirements. The court emphasized the importance of such disclosure, explaining that through it "[s]hareholders can determine whether their corporation's political speech advances the corporation's interest in making profits, and citizens can see whether elected officials are 'in the pocket' of so-called moneyed interests."

Unfortunately, a disclosure regime that would accomplish these goals did not exist at the time *Citizens United* was decided. Nor does it exist now: more than two years after *Citizens United*, Congress has done nothing to improve our nation's disclosure laws. The DISCLOSE Act of 2012, which would have required groups spending more than $10,000 during an election cycle to identify donors of more than $10,000, was filibustered in the Senate.

But the failure of Congress to act does not necessarily mean that Americans' calls for accountability in political spending must go unanswered. Instead, the Securities and Exchange Commission ("SEC") can take action, having both the authority and the responsibility to protect shareholders and the public by mandating the disclosure of political expenditures by publicly-traded corporations. Indeed, one of the SEC commissioners, Luis Aguilar, recently came forward in support of disclosure rules and urged the full Commission to act. The rest of the Commission should follow his lead. . . .

The Pressure on Corporate Decision Makers to Engage in Political Spending Has Risen with the Increasing Cost of American Elections

The Supreme Court's 2010 decision in *Citizens United v. FEC* ushered in a new era of spending in our nation's elections. The Court opened the door for unions and corporations to spend unlimited amounts to influence the outcomes of elections. While *Citizens United* enabled companies to spend treasury funds on political advertisements, lower court decisions expanded the ruling to strike down contribution limits on outside groups that exist solely to air political advertisements. Most significant was a decision by the United States Court of Appeals for the D.C. Circuit, *SpeechNow.org v. FEC*, which permitted individuals, corporations, and unions to give unlimited amounts to groups called independent-expenditure-only committees, more commonly known as "super PACs." Super PACs can accept unlimited contributions and spend unlimited sums on political advertisements.

The capacity to raise and spend unlimited sums on elections has ratcheted up the demand for political dollars—and political fundraisers have increasingly targeted corporate managers. In a 2010 Zogby International poll of business leaders, almost half of respondents said that pressure has increased to give to politicians since 2008. Seventy-two percent of respondents explained that their businesses gave money to either "gain access to influence the legislative process (55 percent) or to avoid adverse legislative consequences (17 percent)." Indeed, "members of the business community . . . face 'shake downs' for political contributions" from aggressive politicians.

For example, in a 2010 meeting with 80 corporate PAC leaders, one Republican Party official candidly put these leaders on notice by stating, "we're evaluating giving patterns." He admitted that he tells corporate donors, "I understand you have to give money to Democrats. But I want to be back in the majority. You don't have to give [this Democrat] $5,000. Give them $2,000. You can give $3,000 elsewhere. Now let me show you some open seats where you can make an investment" in a suitable candidate.

Businesses face real pressure from politicians to make political expenditures, a problem made worse by *Citizens United.*

Given these increased pressures on corporate leaders, it is unsurprising that corporate political spending is growing along with the costs of elections. In recent years, spending in federal elections has exploded. Contributions to federal candidates have more than doubled from $781 million in 1998 to an astounding $1.9 billion in 2010. As a result of *Citizens United* in particular, outside spending in the 2010 federal elections quadrupled relative to the last midterm elections held in 2006. . . .

Even though the cash flowing into elections after *Citizens United* has the potential to determine winners and losers at the polls, Americans are often in the dark about who controls the spigot. Current law offers various avenues by which corporations can engage in political spending without public disclosure. Closing these loopholes, and bringing transparency to corporate political activities, would yield benefits to shareholders, investors, and voters.

There are several ways under current law for corporations to engage in political electioneering without revealing their donors. *First,* although super PACs must report their donors, donations can be veiled by shunting them through shell corporations. For example, journalists investigating two corporations that each gave $1 million to the super PAC supporting Mitt Romney discovered that the corporations had the same address, but neither seemed to actually have an office there, and neither appeared to engage in any business. Both companies were tied to a Utah multimillionaire, Steven Lund, who later acknowledged using them to donate in support of Romney.

Second, corporations can pass their political spending through nonprofit "social welfare" groups organized under section 501(c)(4) of the tax code. Many of these organizations are spending large sums on elections, and there is no requirement that they publicly disclose their donors. At least some of these groups appear to have little social purpose aside from spending to influence elections. One 501(c)(4), Crossroads GPS, has spent tens of millions of dollars on television ads in swing states attacking President Obama: it announced a $25 million ad campaign in May and another $25 million blitz in July. Among its donations, Crossroads GPS has reported two valued at $10 million each, but the group did not publicly disclose the source of either donation.

Third, corporations underwrite substantial amounts of political advertising by routing donations through nonprofit trade organizations organized under section 501(c)(6) of the tax code. One of the largest 501(c)(6) spenders on elections is the U.S. Chamber of Commerce. Corporations donate millions to the Chamber, which is not required to report the identities of its donors. The Chamber is then able to leverage huge sums of corporate money to influence electoral outcomes, and intends to spend more $100 million in the 2012 elections. After a court decision required the disclosure of donors who support the type of political ad on which the Chamber has historically relied, the organization announced that it would no longer sponsor that type of advertising and would switch to another that allows it to keep its donors secret.

Disclosure of corporate political spending protects both shareholders and the proper functioning of American democracy. Corporate managers are currently largely free to make political expenditures according to their own interests because shareholders have little or no control over such spending; without disclosure, shareholders don't know about political spending, and so are unable to use corporate democracy to rein it in.

Half of American households own shares in major corporations—many through mutual funds, pensions, 401 (k) accounts, and the like. An increase in oversight of corporate political spending by shareholders, as well as the sunshine of public disclosure, would act as a democratizing influence on that spending. It would give a larger and more diverse portion of Americans influence over the financing of elections. That oversight cannot be exercised without information about spending. . . .

Corporate disclosure of political expenditures presents a number of benefits, both to investors and to the market broadly. As an example of the latter, it can shed light on companies' practice of securing market advantages by cashing in on elected officials' gratitude for donations. This practice distorts the operation of the marketplace and can create a suboptimal distribution of capital because advantage is gained through political influence rather than genuine market value. Disclosure can also help to ensure that corporations do not violate campaign finance laws; violations would be far easier to detect if details about companies' spending were publicly available.

In addition to these broader benefits, disclosure of political expenditures by corporations would directly protect investors in two ways: (1) empowering investors' oversight concerning political spending and its effect on profits, and (2) allowing shareholders to ensure their money is not used to support candidates or causes that conflict with their personal beliefs. Both issues are clearly relevant to those who own stock in a given company, who have various ways to react to actions by corporate management, including voting against retention of the board and divesting their shares. But these issues also matter to *potential* investors who are deciding whether to buy stock in a particular company and seek to make an informed decision. Responsible investors learn about the companies whose stock they are considering buying as they attempt to ensure a return on their investment.

As an initial matter, transparency in political spending by corporations allows current and potential shareholders to monitor whether spending choices by corporate managers benefit a firm's bottom line. An example involving News Corporation illustrates how this dynamic plays out. In June 2010, News Corporation—which owns Fox News among many other media entities—donated $1 million to the Republican Governors Association. Rupert Murdoch, the founder, chairman, and CEO of the company, at first explained: "It had nothing to do with Fox News. The RGA [gift] was actually [a result of] my friendship with John Kasich." Kasich had previously hosted his own program on Fox News and, at the time, was a Republican candidate for governor of Ohio; Kasich went on to narrowly defeat Democratic incumbent Ted Strickland by a two point margin. Murdoch later explained that the donation was "in the interest of the country and of all the shareholders" and that his previous explanation was a "foolish throwaway line." When asked whether shareholders might be permitted to be involved in the process of choosing political expenditures, Murdoch dismissed the possibility, saying: "No. Sorry, you have the right to vote us off the board if you don't like that."

News Corporation's conduct is a glaring example of a manager acting in his own interest rather than the company's. Managers have considerable decision-making power regarding how to spend money, and shareholders have an interest in decisions about spending being made in the pursuit of corporate returns. Some political scientists have concluded that companies that spend money on elections have lower returns, and that their returns decrease as political spending rises. Corporations making political donations may come close to—or venture over—the lines demarcating violations of campaign finance laws or prohibited pay-to-play activities. Criminal liability would obviously affect profits. In order to make well-informed decisions, investors must have information about actions by corporate management so they can assess whether a corporation's political spending helps or hurts the company's bottom line.

Distinct from their financial interest in the company's profit, shareholders also have a political or expressive interest in refraining from financially supporting political activities with which they disagree. Robust disclosure of corporate political spending gives shareholders the tools to ensure they invest only in companies with whose political spending they agree. In 2010, Target Corporation contributed $150,000 to MN Forward, a PAC "that backs pro-business candidates in [Minnesota] statewide races, including a candidate for governor who opposes same-sex marriage." As a result of the contribution, Target was the subject of boycotts and extensive negative publicity. Beyond having concern with how political expenditures could harm Target's corporate image and profitability, shareholders asked the company to consider when contributing to political candidates "whether a candidate espouses policies that conflict with the company's values." At least one Target shareholder, a foundation that funds groups fighting against prejudice against gay, lesbian, bisexual, and transgender people, liquidated its stock in protest. As Target Chairman, President, and CEO Gregg Steinhafel later explained in an apology letter to "Target Leaders," he was "genuinely sorry" because the "decision affected many . . . in a way [he] did not anticipate." At the 2011 annual shareholder meeting, Steinhafel was so exasperated from receiving questions about Target's political contributions that he said, "Does anybody have a question relating to our business that is unrelated to political giving? I would love to hear any question related to something else."

Target was not the only company to receive negative feedback as a result of its political activities. Replacements, Ltd., a North Carolina company that sells china, silver, and glassware, lobbied legislators, made monetary contributions, and even sold T-shirts in its showroom in an effort to oppose the state's Amendment One, which would ban same-sex marriage. Numerous customers expressed disagreement with the company's actions and vowed to conduct no further business with the company. As this example shows, harm to a company's bottom line can occur for engaging in any political activity, regardless of the viewpoint expressed. . . .

The informational interest. As the Supreme Court noted, voters have an interest in knowing "where political campaign money comes from and how it is spent by the candidate in order to aid the voters in evaluating those who seek . . . office." Knowing who is speaking allows voters to better understand the messages they receive and "to place each candidate in the political spectrum more precisely than is often possible solely on the basis of party labels and campaign speeches."

Outside political spenders have a storied history of hiding behind deceptive organization names to obfuscate the true source of funds. A few years ago in Colorado, an organization named "'Littleton Neighbors Voting No' spent $170,000 to defeat a restriction that would have prevented Wal-Mart from coming to town." While the name of this organization might evoke images of a grassroots group of people coming together in the small Colorado town of about 41,000 people, it was later revealed that the organization was funded exclusively by Wal-Mart. Indeed, this is just one of the latest examples in a long line of misleading monikers that has been extensively documented, including by the Supreme Court. In rejecting an earlier challenge to a disclosure law, the Court explained:

> Curiously, Plaintiffs want to preserve the ability to run these advertisements while hiding behind dubious and misleading names like: 'The Coalition—Americans Working for Real Change' (funded by business organizations opposed to organized labor) [and] 'Citizens for Better Medicare' (funded by the pharmaceutical industry). . . . Given these tactics, Plaintiffs never satisfactorily answer the question of how 'uninhibited, robust, and wide-open' speech can occur when organizations hide themselves from the scrutiny of the voting public.

Disclosure prevents companies from masking their spending, allowing the public to know the sources of electoral advertising. . . .

How to Achieve Disclosure of Corporate Political Spending

Requiring disclosure of corporate political spending would produce numerous benefits for the investor community and the body politic. *How* to achieve full transparency around corporate political spending, however, presents a separate question. Various solutions are available at least in theory: disclosure policies could be adopted by companies voluntarily, through regulation by the states, or through federal regulation. Federal regulation is the superior option because of the nationwide application that federal rules would have and the uniformity they would bring to a system of disclosure. . . .

Federally Mandated Disclosure: The Best Solution

Federal regulation would not suffer from the same limitations as state-by-state regulation. The federal government already engages in significant oversight of publicly held corporations through federal securities laws. Given the keen interest of investors and the public in the issue, the SEC clearly has the statutory authority to add political spending to the disclosures required of publicly held corporations. The Securities Exchange Act of 1934 created the SEC and gives it "complete discretion . . . to require in corporate reports . . . such information as it deems necessary or appropriate in the public interest or to protect investors." A "philosophy of full disclosure" is the "fundamental purpose" of the Securities Exchange Act; disclosure is necessary "to achieve a high standard of business ethics in the securities industry." . . .

The SEC should promulgate regulations requiring public corporations to disclose all of their political expenditures on a periodic basis. As SEC Commissioner Aguilar has said, "[a]rming investors with the information they need to facilitate informed decision-making is a core responsibility of the SEC. In fact, it is one of the factors that led to the creation of the SEC." In particular, such disclosures should include political contributions, independent expenditures, electioneering communications, and contributions to organizations that undertake these activities. Political expenditures at all levels of government—federal, state, and local—should all be reported. Each entry should include specific information, including the identity of any candidates involved, whether the payment supports or opposes the candidate, the amount of the expenditure, and the date of the expenditure. Similar information should be collected with regard to ballot initiatives, referenda, and other issues put to a public vote.

Political expenditures should be reported quarterly on a company's Form 10-Q filing with the SEC. A central database that included all disclosures nationwide would be far easier for shareholders and voters alike to navigate than fifty separate databases maintained by the states. Reviewing disclosure forms can be an involved, labor-intensive process. While private efforts have been made to consolidate state disclosures into one central database, regulation that created a nationwide database would be uniform and dependable. The SEC can easily incorporate the collection of this information into its preexisting EDGAR filing system, which already receives thousands of electronic filings daily. This information would then be freely available to shareholders and voters through the Internet, with many filings being posted on the same day they are submitted.

Recent legal changes have created an electoral environment fraught with new risks for shareholders and voters alike. Corporate spending on elections may impact the fiscal health of corporations and has the potential to distort the operation of the market. Shareholders may unknowingly fund activity that conflicts with their political beliefs. Voters can be kept in the dark about the sources of advertisements designed to influence their votes. Disclosure, however, would minimize these risks: shareholders would know how their companies are spending money and voters would know who is funding political speech.

While *Citizens United* prompted increased corporate spending on politics, the decision also contained the seeds of the solution. The Supreme Court strongly approved of laws requiring disclosure of political expenditures and noted the importance of well-functioning corporate democracy. As the Court succinctly put it, "prompt disclosure of expenditures can provide shareholders and citizens with the information needed to hold corporations and elected officials accountable for their positions and supporters." Such prompt disclosure is not required by current law, but an SEC rule would change that. In the words of SEC Commissioner Aguilar, "Investors are not receiving adequate disclosure, and as the investors' advocate, the Commission should act swiftly to rectify the situation by requiring transparency."

DAVID EARLEY is an attorney at the Brennan Center for Justice at the New York University School of Law where he focuses on campaign finance reform. He is a former article editor for the *New York University Annual Survey of American Law*.

IAN VANDEWALKER works on issues of voting rights and campaign finance reform at the Brennan Center for Justice at the New York University School of Law. An attorney, he graduated from the NYU School of Law where he was senior article editor for the *New York University Review of Law and Social Change*.

EXPLORING THE ISSUE

Should Corporations Be Allowed to Finance Political Campaigns?

Critical Thinking and Reflection

1. Does our political process give too much power to those who can make large campaign donations?
2. What arguments are there for giving corporations the same rights as individuals, and should corporations or special interest groups be subject to caps on how much money they can contribute?
3. Do negative political ads really work?
4. How complex are the relationships of campaigns, democracy, and using media to inform the public?

Is There Common Ground?

Several groups, like the ACLU, have put pressure on the Supreme Court to reverse the *Citizens United* decision, and several citizens groups have started grassroots campaigns to have the decision changed, but even if the Court revisits the decision, most pundits are expecting that elections in the near future will continue to raise exorbitant amounts of money, and that campaigning is likely to become even more negative in the future. At the same time, members of Congress have offered additional modifications to campaign finance reform, and we can expect to see this debate heating up in the future.

Other countries have different ways of dealing with the relationship of money and influence; some limit the amount of time before an election for media coverage, while some have specific limits of what parties can spend on elections. If the United States were to radically overhaul the way campaigns are run, and how they are run, the negotiations would very likely take years. Perhaps the best we can expect is that voters become educated to understand the process and impact of the money spent on political campaigns.

Create Central

www.mhhe.com/createcentral

Additional Resources

The American Civil Liberties Union (ACLU) has long been concerned with the relationship of money and politics. Their website focuses on their interpretation of the history of campaign finance reform, and provides periodic updates to keep the public informed of their efforts to monitor political money flow:

www.aclu.org/free-speech/campaign-finance-reform

Stephen Colbert of *The Colbert Report* has an online archive of his efforts to start and maintain his own SuperPAC, Americans for a Better Tommorow, Tomorrow, which includes updates of his financial filings:

www.colbertsuperpac.com/home.php

The Washington Post kept a running total of the money spent in the 2012 presidential campaign by month:

**www.washingtonpost.com/wp-srv/special/politics/
campaign-finance/**

Greg Palast with illustrations by Ted Rall, *Billionaires & Ballot Bandits: How to Steal an Election in 9 Easy Steps* (Seven Stories Press, 2012). In this collection of previously published essays from a variety of publications, the author takes a light-hearted, but nonetheless, serious approach to understanding how the 2012 election unfolded.

Internet References . . .

The Conference Board

www.conference-board.org/politicalspending/

Selected, Edited, and with Issue Framing Material by:
Alison Alexander, *University of Georgia*
and
Jarice Hanson, *University of Massachusetts—Amherst*

ISSUE

Are Twitter and Other Social Media a Good Source of Political Information?

YES: John H. Parmelee and Shannon L. Bichard, from *Politics and the Twitter Revolution: How Tweets Influence the Relationship between Political Leaders and the Public,* Lexington Books (2012)

NO: Clay Shirky, from "The Political Power of Social Media: Technology, the Public Sphere and Political Change," *Foreign Affairs* (2011)

Learning Outcomes

After reading this issue, you will be able to:

- Consider how social media, especially Twitter, is being used for political purposes.
- Reflect on how individuals use forms of media for political information.
- Think about the range of activities that constitute democratic participation.
- Consider how Twitter may persuade users to examine their own civic participation.

ISSUE SUMMARY

YES: In these sections of their longer study on the role of Twitter and politics, Professors Parmelee and Bichard examine how political leaders use Twitter to influence the public. While politicians establish personal relationships with followers, some tweets are intended to influence policy. The authors examine the potential for the one-way form of communication provided by Twitter to engage with the public.

NO: Shirky turns this issue around by asking about the use of social media to effect change within authoritarian regimes. He describes situations in which protests have been arranged by text. It is in the use of social media to coordinate actions and develop shared awareness that their power resides. But, he warns that these tools can be ineffective and cause as much harm as good.

Twitter may be a unique form of media in that it is intended to be short-form communication (limited to 140 characters) and immediate (anyone with a Twitter account can send or receive messages). These messages are not filtered through the traditional "gatekeeper" of editor or production process and therefore can appear to be very personal. As we've learned over time, Twitter messages credited to an individual might actually be written and disseminated by someone else—either a public relations person, or someone else employed by (or posing as) the sender of the tweet. At the same time, much of Twitter is retweeted by the receivers of messages and passed on from one person to another. So, how is information via Twitter used and understood, and does this form of communication really matter?

There are many different approaches to understanding the power and impact of a new medium like Twitter. A number of people look at social networking in general as a boon to the democratic process of information sharing and exchange, while many others remain skeptical of short-form communications, like Twitter. The authors of both of these selections agree that studies investigating the real impact of Twitter and other social media's communicative potential in political life are only starting to emerge. Parmelee and Bichard focus on one aspect of Twitter use, to help us understand not only the potential for Twitter and politics, but also illuminate a number of realities and misconceptions about how prominent Twitter is, or how prominent it may become, in political life. Shirky looks at the life and death situations in which social media play a role.

One of the underlying premises of the use of any social network is the question of whether social media operate in the public sphere or not. Do social media, and Twitter in particular, contribute to a more democratic society by bypassing big media and allowing users a more direct form of communication from sender to receiver? Are tweets and retweets a form of political information dissemination, or are they public relations opportunities? Who tweets, and why? And most importantly, as our media landscape grows to encompass social media as well as legacy media, can short-form communications like tweets really influence the way the public thinks and behaves?

The selection from Parmelee and Bichard is taken from the Introduction and the Conclusion of their book, *Politics and the Twitter Revolution: How Tweets Influence the Relationship between Political Leaders and the Public*. It could be said that their position is an optimistic one. In this selection we learn who uses political tweets, and who, within the U.S. public, pays attention to them. The authors take the perspective that in the realm of political communication in the United States, Twitter followers tend to be from an older and more professional demographic than groups who use other forms of social media. They discuss the issues of followers' political ideologies, demographics, and the relative influence of Twitter vis-à-vis traditional media and interpersonal sources of information. They also warn that there is little research to date on whether Twitter actually influences political beliefs. They conclude that even though Twitter essentially operates as one-way communication from political leaders to the public, the relationship between political leaders and their followers is quite powerful.

Shirky takes an entirely different approach to examining the impact of social media use across a variety of protest situations. Rather than looking at how politicians use social media for political support, Shirky's article examines how those challenging authoritarian governments use social media and the consequences. He does not see social media as a good tool for immediate change, and particularly is concerned that social media campaigns can expose protesters. He argues that access to information is not a primary way that social media constrains government action. Social media are useful for coordinating action and creating social awareness, but they also can do as much harm as good. Shirky argues that the Internet and social media are much better at promoting long-term change, and argues instead for the support of local public speech and assembly to effect shorter-term change.

Together these selections help us understand the range of issues behind Twitter as a medium of information, and its role in the very important process of using media forms for democratic purposes such as understanding political information, changing political structure, and influencing users' beliefs, attitudes, and behaviors. Will Twitter and other social media evolve over time, and will more people gravitate to messages from political leaders as Twitter use spreads? Will new ways of using Twitter evolve to capture the attention of users, and ultimately make Twitter an even more important medium of information dissemination? What are the limits of Twitter as a medium? Will social media be able to foster social change, rather than just promote immediate protest?

Like many "new" forms of communication, we have a lot to learn as the technology and social use of the medium grow over time. For those Twitter users as well as those who contemplate using Twitter, it will be important to think of Twitter (and other social media) as elements within our larger media landscape.

For students and scholars who wish to pursue the persuasive capacity of the medium, there is a strong desire to compare Twitter to other forms of media; because Twitter continues to evolve, the potential for examining Twitter's impact on our society and in the world is a fascinating social phenomenon. Shirky's warning that we should remember that not every culture adopts technology and uses it in the way we do in the United States is an important point.

YES ⬅

**John H. Parmelee and
Shannon L. Bichard**

Politics and the Twitter Revolution: How Tweets Influence the Relationship between Political Leaders and the Public

. . . **P**olitical tweeting raises many questions for those who study political communication. For example, to what degree do political tweets influence follower's political views and behavior? . . . Do followers have certain characteristics that make some followers more easily influenced than others? Who can be most easily influenced may rest on characteristics such as demographics, ideology, interest in politics, trust in government, and followers' motives for using Twitter. To measure the impact of tweets, it is possible to find these connections by constructing a detailed profile of the people who choose to follow political leaders on Twitter. Measuring the impact of tweets also means comparing the effects of political tweets with more traditional forms of political influence: friends, family, acquaintances, and co-workers. Are tweeted messages from political leaders (whom most followers have usually never met) more or less politically influential than messages that are communicated by family or acquaintances?

. . .

Now is a good time to examine how Twitter is used in politics. . . . Twitter has enjoyed an exponential increase in popularity that compares only to social networking sites such as Facebook and YouTube. Twitter is used by more than 175 million people worldwide, and more than 30 billion tweets have been sent. Politicians are increasingly using it, too. Today, the president and most governors, members of Congress, and mayors of large metropolitan areas have Twitter accounts. President Barack Obama has the most Twitter followers of any political leader, with more than 7 million. Other political leaders tend to have between 10,000 and 100,000 followers, though some governors, mayors, and other officials have more

than 1 million followers. The number of followers that a political leader has varies considerably and often does not depend on the size of the leaders' constituency. For example, the mayor of New York (which has a population of 8 million), has about 83,000 followers. In comparison, the mayor of Newark, New Jersey (which has a population of less than 300,000), has more than 1 million followers.

When political leaders and their followers engage on Twitter, they are part of the power and promise of Web 2.0, which refers to websites and social networking platforms that enable users to create their own content and share it with other users. Just one example of Web 2.0 is the video-sharing site YouTube, a service where anyone can post video messages to be seen, commented on, and forwarded by millions of viewers literally overnight. In terms of politics, the participatory and interactive nature of Web 2.0, including Twitter, has the potential to promote a more open exchange of ideas across a wide audience concerning key issues.

. . .

Twitter's Features

While Twitter messages can be only 140 characters, a lot can be communicated in that small space. Tweets can include links to websites that provide additional information. Political leaders often use this linking function to direct followers to sites such as the following:

- online news sites or blogs that validate their policies
- websites for their campaign or an ally's campaign
- petitions
- photos of themselves on the job
- government-based sites that provide services to constituents

The following is an example of a tweet from Massachusetts Governor Duval Patrick that includes such a link:

- MassGovernor: Before grabbing your helmet, learn how the rules of the road have changed. http://cot.ag/dCnemg

Clicking the link sends the user to an official Commonwealth of Massachusetts site that explains a new law regarding vehicle safety. As can be seen in this example, a link's Web address often is shortened on Twitter to save valuable space.

Hashtags are another important aspect of political tweets. A *hashtag* is a word or abbreviation (designated in a tweet by the "#" sign) that can be searched on Twitter's website. The tweets of anyone who includes that hashtag are grouped together on Twitter. Hashtags have political value because political leaders, or anyone else, can spark dialog on an issue by giving the issue a hashtag in their tweets. Twitter users can search the hashtag, see what has been said about the issue, and they can also contribute to the conversation. The following tweet from the White House Twitter account shows how hashtags are used:

- whitehouse: President Obama: "the long battle to stop the leak and contain the oil is finally close to coming to an end" "#oilspill

Clicking (or searching for) the hashtag "#oilspill" directs users to hundreds of tweets from a wide cross-section of people who are talking about the 2010 British Petroleum (BP) oil spill in the Gulf of Mexico. Often, those tweets include additional links to websites and hashtags, which allow users to learn and discuss even more about BP, oil drilling, and the environmental impact of the spill.

Leaders also can spread their influence beyond their band of followers if they are included on "lists" that are made by Twitter users. Any user can create a list, which is simply a grouping of other Twitter users that is based on some commonality: a hobby, a musical taste, or an interest in politics. Users who click a list that is labeled, say, "influential political leaders," see a stream of tweets from the leaders on that list, regardless of whether the users are followers. Also, users can add leaders to a list even if the users are not the leaders' followers.

. . .

Since its founding in 2006, Twitter's popularity and use has skyrocketed. The service went from about 5 million users at the end of 2008 to 75 million users one year later. In addition, users are becoming increasingly active. Users went from sending 1 billion tweets a month in the fall of 2008, to 2 billion tweets per month during the summer of 2010. According to media commentator Jolie O'Dell "Twitter's growth curve is clearly accelerating." Twitter is considered important enough that the Library of Congress is archiving every public tweet since the company's inception.

. . .

Some applications are designed especially to help political leaders and followers to be more influential (and influenced). The website TweetCongress displays the tweets of all congressional members, shows trending keywords and hashtags, and provides a directory to find which members tweet and how frequently. TweetCongress calls its site "a grass-roots effort to get our men and women in Congress to open up and have a real conversation with us." GovTwit, which focuses on the tweets of government agencies, has many of the same features as TweetCongress.

Twitter's early success also has come with some problems. The service has occasionally crashed due to the high volume of tweets. Also, hackers have had some success in hijacking user accounts. The most high-profile example came in January 2009, when hackers were able to send a phony tweet from the account of then-President-elect Obama. Other people simply set up a Twitter account and pretend to be somebody famous. As a result, Twitter now does "verified accounts" for celebrities and other high-profile users, including political leaders. This process requires a background check to establish the authenticity of the user. Despite some setbacks, Twitter has grown considerably since its founding and it attracts an audience that political leaders find valuable.

. . .

The Content of Political Tweets

What goes into leaders' tweets? There is research on that question. So far, the findings suggest that political leaders use tweets primarily to broadcast information about their policies and their personality. Interacting with followers is a secondary priority. One analysis of more than 6,000 tweets of members of Congress showed these results:

Congresspeople are primarily using Twitter to disperse information, particularly links to news articles about themselves and to their blog posts, and to report on their daily activities. These tend not to provide new insights into government or the legislative process or to improve transparency: rather, they are vehicles for self-promotion.

Political leaders at the state level also focus heavily on disseminating information to followers about themselves and about their issues. A case study of one particularly prolific tweeter, Minnesota State Representative Laura Brod, found mentions of policy issues to be the most frequently occurring category of tweet. In second place were tweets she made that dealt with what the study called "personal life and musings."

Those politicians who are particularly successful at using Twitter make an effort to have more than one-way communication with followers. By replying to and retweeting followers' tweets, leaders are able to create a conversation on Twitter that keeps existing followers satisfied and attracts more followers. That strategy is one reason why Newark's Mayor Booker has more than twice as many followers as there are residents in the city he runs. Booker's tweets often include two-way communication with followers, and he does not focus solely on policy. A study by Donia found that his tweets are designed to meet the needs of a busy social media audience:

> Mayor Booker realizes that there are literally hundreds of thousands of people reading what he says on a daily basis and they likely give his page or profile a quick scroll before moving on to something else, so his information has to captivate them, if even for a few seconds. He is able to captivate them by mixing up his types of posts—not just events or quotations—but also links, videos, pictures, and stories.

Some other political leaders conduct two-way communication on Twitter. Congressman Michael Burgess of Texas invited the public to ask questions via Twitter during a health policy forum that was being broadcast online. In another example, to field questions about budgetary issues, Democrats conducted a "Twitter town hall" in which members of Congress responded to comments sent to the hashtag #AskDems.

The "personality" of the writing in political tweets can range considerably. Some messages are formal and read like short press releases, such as the following from New York Mayor Michael Bloomberg:

- MikeBloomberg: Dangerous heat forecast for NYC this weekend. For info on cooling centers call 311, visit http://nyc.gov/oem or follow @notifyNYC

Others tweets have a homespun, personal style. Missouri Senator Claire McCaskill is an exemplar of this approach, as can be seen in her response to a followers' tweet:

- Clairecmc: Yes @tigeranniemac that was me at Target in the soap aisle. You shoulda said hi. Was with my daughter Lily. We're very friendly.

Still others' tweets include humor or sarcasm to get the point across. Senator John McCain, who has long been known for fighting what he sees as wasteful federal spending, uses sarcasm frequently when tweeting about such spending:

- SenJohnMcCain: $1,427,250 for genetic improvements of switchgrass—I thought switchgrass genes were pretty good already, guess I was wrong.

Sometimes the content in political tweets has gotten political leaders in trouble, and the following are some famous illustrations of that fact. For example, New York Congressman Anthony Weiner was forced to resign after he tweeted a lewd photo. Michigan Congressman Peter Hoekstra caused a security risk when he tweeted that his congressional delegation had just landed in Iraq. Missouri Senator Claire McCaskill had to apologize after being criticized, even by her own mother, for tweeting on the House floor during Obama's first State of the Union address. Problems sometimes arise because of the speed and ease at which leaders can send a tweet, combined with the desire to make their followers feel connected.

. . .

Reasons to Tweet

Tweeting serves several purposes for political leaders. The main purpose is that Twitter allows leaders to communicate directly to a mass audience. Politicians are always looking for ways to get their message across without having it filtered and potentially altered by others, such as news media. Twitter, along with other social networks, can fill that need. That reason is why many inside and outside politics, such as former House Speaker Newt Gingrich, encourage its use: "Using Twitter to bypass traditional media and directly reach voters is definitely a good thing." Some political leaders are unable to get as much press coverage as they desire, or go through periods of limited power. Spreading the word on Twitter is essential for these politicians. One media consultant noted that Republicans (GOP) used Twitter far more than Democrats in the months after Obama's inauguration solidified Democratic control of the legislative and executive branches of government.

Because the GOP's power was at low ebb, they found that their ideas and issues were not being covered; thus Twitter became an alternate venue to disseminate their message. In addition, strategic use of Twitter can increase the amount of press coverage that a politician gets. Journalists often follow the politicians they cover, so tweets that include newsworthy information can lead to a story in traditional media outlets.

Tweeting can serve to mobilize action. Many political tweets include requests for followers to take some action, such as contributing to a campaign or signing a petition. A leader's tweet followers are an ideal group to contact to take part in such action because they may be more likely to be motivated to do what they are asked than the average person. The very act of choosing to be a follower suggests a significant interest and commitment to that leader.

The rise of the Tea Party is one case study of how Twitter can be used to mobilize political activists. Members of the Tea Party (whose main cause is to reduce federal spending) are part of a movement that has little centralized authority and is spread across the country. Yet without the organizational structure and resources of a major political party, they have staged numerous large protests and elected candidates to office. Sarno found that Tea Party members' use of Twitter was instrumental in their ability to share ideas on how to build up the movement and attract people to their protests:

> Much of the sharing is now facilitated by the fast-growing messaging site Twitter, where today the keyword "teaparty" was one of the most frequently used terms. Users sent out a flurry of updates about attendance, links to photos on Flickr and Photobucket, and videos on YouTube and other sites.

Mobilizing activists to sign petitions is regularly done on Twitter. Act.ly is one such site that has found success among progressives who want to sway political leaders. After creating a petition on act.ly and tweeting it, anyone who receives the petition can "sign" it by retweeting. The petition tweets are then sent via Twitter to the political leaders being targeted. Leaders can respond to the petitions if they choose. Speed and the ability to reach out to many people are two great advantages of using Twitter for political petitions (further, it is free). "You can go from outrage to petition idea to people signing in about 2 minutes," according to Gilliam, the site's creator. "There is huge potential to tweet change." One environmental interest group used the Twitter petition concept

to pressure Massachusetts Senator Scott Brown to vote its way on pending energy legislation.

Speed of idea dissemination is why many politicians use Twitter. When the then House Speaker Nancy Pelosi wanted to call back Congress early from a recess to vote on Medicaid and education funding, she broke the news on Twitter. In the modern 24-hour news cycle, there is no faster way to transmit information. According to journalist Michael O'Brien,

> Her office said they opted to use Twitter to break the news, instead of a conventional press release, because of the intense interest in the vote. "We wanted to get the word out quickly on the decision that the House will be voting to keep teachers on the job. The Senate cloture vote was a major topic that was being followed closely on Twitter, the blogs, online news site, newspapers, TV, and wires," said Nadeam Elshami, a spokesman for the speaker. "So that is why we used Twitter, and we e-mailed the news release within minutes."

Twitter is used differently by the major political parties. Republicans took an early lead over Democrats in terms of joining Twitter, tweeting frequently, and attracting followers. In Congress, for example, the list of members who send the most tweets per day includes few Democrats. The Democrats also lag behind Republicans when it comes to the number of followers and amount of influence. Republicans hold 70 of the 100 most influential congressional Twitter accounts. However, the Democrats are beginning to use Twitter more. In fall of 2009, fewer than 60 Democratic members used Twitter; but 156 used it as of the summer of 2011. In comparison, 229 Republican members tweet.

. . .

The Impact of Twitter: Research Results

Now that billions of tweets are being sent by more than 100 million people worldwide, some researchers and companies are devoted to measuring the ways in which Twitter use influences politics and other facets of society. One of the most difficult aspects of this research work is determining what constitutes "influence" on Twitter. There are many possible definitions of the concept of influence. In terms of politics, for example, one measure of influence is to simply count the number of followers that leaders have and then conclude that those politicians with the most followers have the most influence. By that measure, Obama's 7 million followers make him the most influential leader. However, this measure ignores many important features of Twitter that, if used effectively, can increase a leader's influence. Features such as retweeting, replying, and linking to URLs are especially useful to examine. For example, a leader with 10,000 followers may be able to spread his or her ideas further than a leader with 20,000 followers, depending on how actively the two leaders' messages are retweeted by followers. In addition, leaders who often reply to followers' tweeted questions and comments can create an appreciative and loyal group of followers who may be more willing to fulfill leaders' requests for action. One of those actions is clicking links; these links direct followers to websites that a leader deems politically useful. Such links often are embedded in a leader's tweets.

Because of the different ways in which influence can be measured, some social media analytics companies (such as Sysomos, Twitalyzer, and Klout) have examined the concept of influence by using a variety of definitions. For instance, Sysomos looked at the Twitter influence of political leaders such as Obama, celebrities such as Britney Spears, and news organizations such as *The New York Times*. Sysomos found that a follower count is not as meaningful a measure of influence as one would think. Sysomos's calculation of influence, which is called an *authority ranking,* was based on several factors, including these characteristics: number of followers, frequency of updates, and retweets. By this measure by Sysomos, Obama has less influence than *The New York Times,* even though the news organization has far fewer followers than the president. In another example, in measuring the amount of replying that leaders do to followers' tweets, Twitalyzer found that many politicians, including senators McCain and McCaskill, took more time to address questions and comments than Obama. Klout has still other ways to measure the impact of leaders on the microblog. One of Klout's calculations of influence is called *true reach,* a measure that reveals how many of a leader's followers are paying attention to the tweets they receive. Another Klout calculation of influence is called a *network influence score,* which takes into account that some followers are more important to a leader than other followers. Some followers are highly influential in terms of who follows them and how engaged they are. A leader whose network of followers is highly influential is likely to find Twitter a more valuable political tool than a leader with followers who have a low network influence score.

. . .

Who Follows Political Leaders on Twitter—And Why?

Research shows that followers who use Twitter for general purposes are from an older and more professional demographic than those who use other forms of social media. But no studies [to date] have examined the demographic makeup of those who follow political leaders on Twitter. This lack of studies is important because certain demographic and psychographic groups, such as those who are highly educated and interested in politics, are potentially more politically influential and valuable to leaders than other groups. Even more fundamental is to discover what types of people and organizations are considered to be political leaders who are worth following. Certain individuals, such as elected public officials, are an obvious choice of who might be worth following. But to what degree do followers choose to follow people who fall outside that narrow definition? Today some of the most politically influential people hold no office. Al Gore (a former U.S. vice president) and Sarah Palin (a former candidate for U.S. vice president) are two good examples. Gore is arguably more powerful today in terms of environmental politics than when he was vice president. As a private citizen, Palin has reached a larger audience and influenced the national agenda more than when she was governor of Alaska.

In addition to finding out who is being followed, it also would be helpful to know what motivates users in choosing which political leaders to follow. Do they follow leaders primarily as a means to receive political information? If so, that would be an information-seeking motive. Or do they follow leaders because they want to interact with leaders or fellow political junkies? If so, that would be a social and self-expressive motive. Further, does a follower's motivation affect how much influence a leader's tweets have?

How Influential Are Political Tweets?

Political leaders tweet for many reasons, including going over the heads of the mass media (such as television) to reach the public. By tweeting, they wish to generate media coverage. At other times, these leaders want to mobilize their political "troops" of followers to take action on their behalf. Leaders could suggest to followers a wide variety of actions: take part in a petition or protest, read a recommended blog post or news story, spread the word to others to vote for a candidate, or support legislation. Spreading the word is especially easy on Twitter because of its features such as retweeting, mentioning, hashtags, and website linking. While previous research has found that Twitter users are eager to share opinions and often do so regarding brands they like or dislike it is not clear whether followers of political tweets are as willing to spreading the word about politicians and policies. Because there is no research on how influential political tweets are on followers, it is impossible to know how often followers take actions that are requested by leaders. In addition, it is not clear how much influence political tweets have on shaping followers' political views. Is that influence greater than more traditional sources of political influence, such as friends, family, and co-workers? It may even be that the influence of political tweets varies depending on a follower's ideology or demographic makeup.

. . .

How Twitter Influences the Relationship between Political Leaders and the Public

. . . Because of the number of people using the microblogging service for politics, how they use it, and how they are affected by it, Twitter influences how political leaders and the public relate in a number of crucial ways:

- The relationship that followers have with their leaders is quite powerful. Political leaders' tweets regularly cause followers to look up information and take other actions that the leaders request. In addition, the relationship that followers have with the leaders often influences followers' political views as much as or more than their family and friends.
- From the followers' perspective, the relationship goes beyond receiving information from leaders; it is about sharing leaders' information with others. Leaders tweet political information to followers, and followers pass that information along. Leaders' tweets give followers something to talk and tweet about with others, which is a popular activity among followers. This relationship is beneficial for followers and leaders. Followers now have access to more political information to share, and leaders have their views spread by followers to an increasingly wide audience.
- From the leaders' perspective, the relationship is based on using Twitter mainly as a one-way communication vehicle to transmit their policies and ideas. However, their followers want to use Twitter as a forum for two-way communication with

leaders and other politically interested individuals. As a result, many followers crave engagement with leaders but often are left disappointed.
- One of Twitter's great strengths is that it forces political leaders (and anyone else) to quickly get to the point. Politicians, for example, are notoriously longwinded in their speeches, press releases, and other forms of communication. Those followers who receive politicians' brief tweets, however, are able to see elected officials in a new light. The 140-character limit of tweets means that politicians and other leaders must be succinct in their writing, and that brevity is a refreshing change. As writing teacher William Zinsser noted: "Clutter is the disease of American writing. We are a society strangling in unnecessary words, circular construction, pompous frills and meaningless jargon. . . . The secret of good writing is to strip every sentence to its cleanest components." Twitter imposes that kind of brevity.
- While the average political Twitter user often seeks a politically diverse range of leaders to follow, those who are extremely ideological tend to avoid diverse viewpoints on Twitter. This practice may not be healthy.

. . .

So what makes political leaders' tweets so influential? Participants in the in-depth interviews said there are nine elements that cause leaders' tweets to be acted upon: clarity, a call to action, personal relevance, professional usefulness, helpful links and hashtags, including a political counterpoint, humor, interactivity, and outrageousness. Some of these elements are important for fairly obvious reasons; for example, tweets that are written clearly and include politically useful information have a better chance to persuade than tweets that are confusing or irrelevant. Other elements, however, deserve further discussion. The fact that participants said they were looking for political counterpoints indicates they are open to having their political views influenced by an ideologically wide range of leaders. The desire for humorous political tweets dovetails with the finding that many followers have an entertainment motivation in following political leaders. Also, other research has found humor to be quite persuasive. One study on why some e-mail messages are forwarded frequently found that humor was a key determinant because humor can "spark strong emotion." Interactivity, as has been noted previously, is an important element because followers like to see their leaders engaging with their audiences (not merely transmitting to them). One form of interactivity happens when leaders solicit advice from their followers. The last element mentioned, outrageousness, underscores the point that leaders' tweets can have unintended consequences. A tweet that seems exaggerated or false often causes followers to react, sometimes by criticizing the leader who sent it.

Taken together, the findings add to what is known about the persuasiveness of word-of-mouth communication. While past research shows that companies can harness the power of WOM to create buzz marketing campaigns around their products, far less is known about whether political leaders can use Twitter to create political buzz. Surveys and in-depth interviews with followers indicate that political leaders can be proactive in using their tweets to generate a lot of interest in an issue. What leaders want to avoid, however, is using Twitter to do political "astroturf" campaigns, which are "campaigns disguised as spontaneous, popular 'grassroots' behavior that are in reality carried out by a single person or organization." Astroturfers achieve this effect on Twitter by creating many fake user accounts to initially spread a leader's message. However, such a practice is not necessary on Twitter because followers seem quite willing to spread leaders' ideas without any deception needed.

Followers' motives play a major role in how influential political leaders' tweets can be. Those followers with social and self-expressive motives were the most likely to respond to leaders' tweets by retweeting, looking for recommended information, or taking suggested actions. With that knowledge in mind, it becomes even clearer why political leaders can benefit by interacting more with their followers. Those followers with social and self-expressive motives are the individuals who interact the most on Twitter and expect engagement with the leaders they follow. As a result, leaders who engage in two-way communication on Twitter stand the best chance of attracting and keeping those followers with social and self-expressive motives—the very individuals most influenced by leaders.

JOHN H. PARMELEE is an associate professor in the Department of Communication at the University of North Florida. Most of his research involves political communication and journalism in emerging democracies.

SHANNON L. BICHARD is an associate professor in the College of Mass Communications at Texas Tech University. She teaches advertising, and her research interests focus on public opinion and consumer behavior.

Clay Shirky

 **NO**

The Political Power of Social Media: Technology, the Public Sphere and Political Change

On January 17, 2001, during the impeachment trial of Philippine President Joseph Estrada, loyalists in the Philippine Congress voted to set aside key evidence against him. Less than two hours after the decision was announced, thousands of Filipinos, angry that their corrupt president might be let off the hook, converged on Epifanio de los Santos Avenue, a major crossroads in Manila. The protest was arranged, in part, by forwarded text messages reading, "Go 2 EDSA. Wear blk." The crowd quickly swelled, and in the next few days, over a million people arrived, choking traffic in downtown Manila.

The public's ability to coordinate such a massive and rapid response—close to seven million text messages were sent that week—so alarmed the country's legislators that they reversed course and allowed the evidence to be presented. Estrada's fate was sealed; by January 20, he was gone. The event marked the first time that social media had helped force out a national leader. Estrada himself blamed "the text-messaging generation" for his downfall.

Since the rise of the Internet in the early 1990s, the world's networked population has grown from the low millions to the low billions. Over the same period, social media have become a fact of life for civil society worldwide, involving many actors—regular citizens, activists, nongovernmental organizations, telecommunications firms, software providers, governments. This raises an obvious question for the U.S. government: How does the ubiquity of social media affect U.S. interests, and how should U.S. policy respond to it?

As the communications landscape gets denser, more complex, and more participatory, the networked population is gaining greater access to information, more opportunities to engage in public speech, and an enhanced ability to undertake collective action. In the political arena, as the protests in Manila demonstrated, these increased freedoms can help loosely coordinated publics demand change.

The Philippine strategy has been adopted many times since. In some cases, the protesters ultimately succeeded, as in Spain in 2004, when demonstrations organized by text messaging led to the quick ouster of Spanish Prime Minister José María Aznar, who had inaccurately blamed the Madrid transit bombings on Basque separatists. The Communist Party lost power in Moldova in 2009 when massive protests coordinated in part by text message, Facebook, and Twitter broke out after an obviously fraudulent election. Around the world, the Catholic Church has faced lawsuits over its harboring of child rapists, a process that started when The Boston Globes 2002 expose of sexual abuse in the church went viral online in a matter of hours.

There are, however, many examples of the activists failing, as in Belarus in March 2006, when street protests (arranged in part by e-mail) against President Aleksandr Lukashenko's alleged vote rigging swelled, then faltered, leaving Lukashenko more determined than ever to control social media. During the June 2009 uprising of the Green Movement in Iran, activists used every possible technological coordinating tool to protest the miscount of votes for Mir Hossein Mousavi but were ultimately brought to heel by a violent crackdown. . . .

The use of social media tools—text messaging, e-mail, photo sharing, social networking, and the like—does not have a single preordained outcome. Therefore, attempts to outline their effects on political action are too often reduced to dueling anecdotes. If you regard the failure of the Belarusian protests to oust Lukashenko as paradigmatic, you will regard the Moldovan experience as an outlier, and vice versa. Empirical work on the subject is also hard to come by, in part because these tools are so new and in part because relevant examples are so rare. The safest characterization of recent quantitative attempts to answer the question, Do digital tools enhance democracy? (such as those by Jacob Groshek and Philip Howard) is that these tools probably do not hurt in the short run and might help in the long run—and that they have the most dramatic effects in states where a public sphere already constrains the actions of the government.

Despite this mixed record, social media have become coordinating tools for nearly all of the world's political movements, just as most of the world's authoritarian governments (and, alarmingly, an increasing number of democratic ones) are trying to limit access to it. In response, the U.S. State Department has committed itself to "Internet freedom" as a specific policy aim. Arguing for the right of people to use the Internet freely is an appropriate policy for the United States, both because it aligns with the strategic goal of strengthening civil society worldwide and because it resonates with American beliefs about freedom of expression. But attempts to yoke the idea of Internet freedom to short-term goals—particularly ones that are country-specific or are intended to help particular dissident groups or encourage regime change—are likely to be ineffective on average. And when they fail, the consequences can be serious.

Although the story of Estrada's ouster and other similar events have led observers to focus on the power of mass protests to topple governments, the potential of social media lies mainly in their support of civil society and the public sphere—change measured in years and decades rather than weeks or months. The U.S. government should maintain Internet freedom as a goal to be pursued in a principled and regime-neutral fashion, not as a tool for effecting immediate policy aims country by country. It should likewise assume that progress will be incremental and, unsurprisingly, slowest in the most authoritarian regimes.

The Perils of Internet Freedom

In January 2010, U.S. Secretary of State Hillary Clinton outlined how the United States would promote Internet freedom abroad. She emphasized several kinds of freedom, including the freedom to access information (such as the ability to use Wikipedia and Google inside Iran), the freedom of ordinary citizens to produce their own public media (such as the rights of Burmese activists to blog), and the freedom of citizens to converse with one another (such as the Chinese public's capacity to use instant messaging without interference).

Most notably, Clinton announced funding for the development of tools designed to reopen access to the Internet in countries that restrict it. This "instrumental" approach to Internet freedom concentrates on preventing states from censoring outside Web sites, such as Google,

YouTube, or that of The New York Times. It focuses only secondarily on public speech by citizens and least of all on private or social uses of digital media. According to this vision, Washington can and should deliver rapid, directed responses to censorship by authoritarian regimes.

The instrumental view is politically appealing, action-oriented, and almost certainly wrong. It overestimates the value of broadcast media while underestimating the value of media that allow citizens to communicate privately among themselves. It overestimates the value of access to information, particularly information hosted in the West, while underestimating the value of tools for local coordination. And it overestimates the importance of computers while underestimating the importance of simpler tools, such as cell phones.

The instrumental approach can also be dangerous. Consider the debacle around the proposed censorship-circumvention software known as Haystack, which, according to its developer, was meant to be a "one-to-one match for how the [Iranian] regime implements censorship." The tool was widely praised in Washington; the U.S. government even granted it an export license. But the program was never carefully vetted, and when security experts examined it, it turned out that it not only failed at its goal of hiding messages from governments but also made it, in the words of one analyst, "possible for an adversary to specifically pinpoint individual users." . . . The challenges of . . . Haystack demonstrate how difficult it is to weaponize social media to pursue country-specific and near-term policy goals.

New media conducive to fostering participation can indeed increase the freedoms Clinton outlined, just as the printing press, the postal service, the telegraph, and the telephone did before. One complaint about the idea of new media as a political force is that most people simply use these tools for commerce, social life, or self-distraction, but this is common to all forms of media. Far more people in the 1500s were reading erotic novels than Martin Luther's "Ninety-five Theses," and far more people before the American Revolution were reading Poor Richard's Almanack than the work of the Committees of Correspondence. But those political works still had an enormous political effect.

Just as Luther adopted the newly practical printing press to protest against the Catholic Church, and the American revolutionaries synchronized their beliefs using the postal service that Benjamin Franklin had designed, today's dissident movements will use any means possible to frame their views and coordinate their actions; it would be impossible to describe the Moldovan Communist Party's loss of Parliament after the 2009 elections without discussing the use of cell phones and online tools by its opponents to mobilize. Authoritarian governments stifle communication among their citizens because they fear, correctly, that a better-coordinated populace would constrain their ability to act without oversight.

Despite this basic truth—that communicative freedom is good for political freedom—the instrumental mode of Internet statecraft is still problematic. It is difficult for outsiders to understand the local conditions of dissent. External support runs the risk of tainting even peaceful opposition as being directed by foreign elements. Dissidents can be exposed by the unintended effects of novel tools. A government's demands for Internet freedom abroad can vary from country to country, depending on the importance of the relationship, leading to cynicism about its motives.

The more promising way to think about social media is as long-term tools that can strengthen civil society and the public sphere. In contrast to the instrumental view of Internet freedom, this can be called the "environmental" view. According to this conception, positive changes in the life of a country, including pro-democratic regime change, follow, rather than precede, the development of a strong public sphere. This is not to say that popular movements will not successfully use these tools to discipline or even oust their governments, but rather that U.S. attempts to direct such uses are likely to do more harm than good. Considered in this light, Internet freedom is a long game, to be conceived of and supported not as a separate agenda but merely as an important input to the more fundamental political freedoms.

The Theater of Collapse

Any discussion of political action in repressive regimes must take into account the astonishing fall of communism in 1989 in eastern Europe and the subsequent collapse of the Soviet Union in 1991. Throughout the Cold War, the United States invested in a variety of communications tools, including broadcasting the Voice of America radio station, hosting an American pavilion in Moscow (home of the famous Nixon-Khrushchev "kitchen debate"), and smuggling Xerox machines behind the Iron Curtain to aid the underground press, or samizdat. Yet despite this emphasis on communications, the end of the Cold War was triggered not by a defiant uprising of Voice of America listeners but by economic change. As the price of oil fell while that of wheat spiked, the Soviet model of selling expensive oil to buy cheap wheat stopped working. As a result, the Kremlin was forced to secure loans from the West, loans that would have been put at risk had the government intervened militarily in the affairs of non-Russian states. In 1989, one could argue, the ability of citizens to communicate, considered against the background of macroeconomic forces, was largely irrelevant.

. . .

The ability of these groups to create and disseminate literature and political documents, even with simple photocopiers, provided a visible alternative to the communist regimes. For large groups of citizens in these countries, the political and, even more important, economic bankruptcy of the government was no longer an open secret but a public fact. This made it difficult and then impossible for the regimes to order their troops to take on such large groups.

Thus, it was a shift in the balance of power between the state and civil society that led to the largely peaceful collapse of communist control. The state's ability to use violence had been weakened, and the civil society that would have borne the brunt of its violence had grown stronger. When civil society triumphed, many of the people who had articulated opposition to the communist regimes—such as Tadeusz Mazowiecki in Poland and Vaclav Havel in Czechoslovakia—became the new political leaders of those countries. Communications tools during the Cold War did not cause governments to collapse, but they helped the people take power from the state when it was weak.

The idea that media, from the Voice of America to samizdat, play a supporting role in social change by strengthening the public sphere echoes the historical role of the printing press. As the German philosopher Jürgen Habermas argued in his 1962 book, The Structural Transformation of the Public Sphere, the printing press helped democratize Europe by providing space for discussion and agreement among politically engaged citizens, often before the state had fully democratized, an argument extended by later scholars, such as Asa Briggs, Elizabeth Eisenstein, and Paul Starr.

Political freedom has to be accompanied by a civil society literate enough and densely connected enough to discuss the issues presented to the public. In a famous study of political opinion after the 1948 U.S. presidential election, the sociologists Elihu Katz and Paul Lazarsfeld discovered that mass media alone do not change people's minds; instead, there is a two-step process. Opinions are first transmitted by the media, and then they get echoed by friends, family members, and colleagues. It is in this second, social step that political opinions are formed. This is the step in which the Internet in general, and social media in particular, can make a difference. As with the printing press, the Internet spreads not just media consumption but media production as well—it allows people to privately and publicly articulate and debate a welter of conflicting views.

A slowly developing public sphere, where public opinion relies on both media and conversation, is the core of the environmental view of Internet freedom. As opposed to the self-aggrandizing view that the West holds the source code for democracy—and if it were only made accessible, the remaining autocratic states would crumble—the environmental view assumes that little political change happens without the dissemination and adoption of ideas and opinions in the public sphere. Access to information is far less important, politically, than access to conversation. Moreover, a public sphere is more likely to emerge in a society as a result of people's dissatisfaction with matters of economics or day-to-day governance than from their embrace of abstract political ideals.

To take a contemporary example, the Chinese government today is in more danger of being forced to adopt democratic norms by middle-class members of the ethnic Han majority demanding less corrupt local governments than it is by Uighurs or Tibetans demanding autonomy. Similarly, the One Million Signatures Campaign, an Iranian women's rights movement that focuses on the repeal of laws inimical to women, has been more successful in liberalizing the behavior of the Iranian government than the more confrontational Green Movement.

For optimistic observers of public demonstrations, this is weak tea, but both the empirical and the theoretical work suggest that protests, when effective, are the end of a long process, rather than a replacement for it. Any real commitment by the United States to improving political freedom worldwide should concentrate on that process—which can only occur when there is a strong public sphere.

The Conservative Dilemma

Disciplined and coordinated groups, whether businesses or governments, have always had an advantage over undisciplined ones: they have an easier time engaging in collective action because they have an orderly way of directing the action of their members. Social media can compensate for the disadvantages of undisciplined groups by reducing the costs of coordination. The anti-Estrada movement in the Philippines used the ease of sending and forwarding text messages to organize a massive group with no need (and no time) for standard managerial control. As a result, larger, looser groups can now take on some kinds of coordinated action, such as protest movements and public media campaigns, that were previously reserved for formal organizations. For political movements, one of the main forms of coordination is what the military calls "shared awareness," the ability of each member of a group to not only understand the situation at hand but also understand that everyone else does, too. Social media increase shared awareness by propagating messages through social networks. . . .

The Chinese anticorruption protests that broke out in the aftermath of the devastating May 2008 earthquake in Sichuan are another example[s] of such ad hoc synchronization. The protesters were parents, particularly mothers, who had lost their only children in the collapse of shoddily built schools, the result of collusion between construction firms and the local government. . . . The consequences of government corruption were made broadly visible, and it went from being an open secret to a public truth.

The Chinese government originally allowed reporting on the post-earthquake protests, but abruptly reversed itself in June. Security forces began arresting protesters and threatening journalists when it became clear that the protesters were demanding real local reform and not merely state reparations. From the government's perspective, the threat was not that citizens were aware of the corruption, which the state could do nothing about in the short run. Beijing was afraid of the possible effects if this awareness became shared: it would have to either enact reforms or respond in a way that would alarm more citizens. After all, the prevalence of camera phones has made it harder to carry out a widespread but undocumented crackdown.

This condition of shared awareness—which is increasingly evident in all modern states—creates what is commonly called "the dictator's dilemma" but that might more accurately be described by the phrase coined by the media theorist Briggs: "the conservative dilemma," so named because it applies not only to autocrats but also to democratic governments and to religious and business leaders. The dilemma is created by new media that increase public access to speech or assembly, with the spread of such media, whether photocopiers or Web browsers, a state accustomed to having a monopoly on public speech finds itself called to account for anomalies between its view of events and the public's. The two responses to the conservative dilemma are censorship and propaganda. But neither of these is as effective a source of control as the enforced silence of the citizens. The state will censor critics or produce propaganda as it needs to, but both of those actions have higher costs than simply not having any critics to silence or reply to in the first place. But if a government were to shut down Internet access or ban cell phones, it would risk radicalizing otherwise pro-regime citizens or harming the economy.

The conservative dilemma exists in part because political speech and apolitical speech are not mutually exclusive. Many of the South Korean teenage girls who turned out in Seoul's Cheonggyecheon Park in 2008 to protest U.S. beef imports were radicalized in the discussion section of a Web site dedicated to Dong Bang Shin Ki, a South Korean boy band. DBSK is not a political group, and the protesters were not typical political actors. But that online community, with around 800,000 active members, amplified the second step of Katz and Lazarsfeld's two-step process by allowing members to form political opinions through conversation.

Popular culture also heightens the conservative dilemma by providing cover for more political uses of social media. Tools specifically designed for dissident use are politically easy for the state to shut down, whereas tools in broad use become much harder to censor without risking politicizing the larger group of otherwise apolitical actors. Ethan Zuckerman of Harvard's Berkman Center for Internet and Society calls this "the cute cat theory of digital activism." Specific tools designed to defeat state censorship (such as proxy servers) can be shut down with little political penalty, but broader tools that the larger population uses to, say, share pictures of cute cats are harder to shut down.

For these reasons, it makes more sense to invest in social media as general, rather than specifically political, tools to promote self-governance. The norm of free speech is inherently political and far from universally shared. To the degree that the United States makes free speech a first-order goal, it should expect that goal to work relatively well in democratic countries that are allies, less well in undemocratic countries that are allies, and least of all in undemocratic countries that are not allies. But nearly every country in the world desires economic growth. Since governments jeopardize that growth when they ban technologies that can be used for both political and economic coordination, the United States should rely on countries' economic incentives to allow widespread media use. In other words, the U.S. government should work for conditions that increase the conservative dilemma, appealing to states' self-interest rather than the contentious virtue of freedom, as a way to create or strengthen countries' public spheres.

Social Media Skepticism

There are, broadly speaking, two arguments against the idea that social media will make a difference in national politics. The first is that the tools are themselves ineffective, and the second is that they produce as much harm to democratization as good, because repressive governments are becoming better at using these tools to suppress dissent.

The critique of ineffectiveness, most recently offered by Malcolm Gladwell in The New Yorker, concentrates on examples of what has been termed "slacktivism," whereby casual participants seek social change through low-cost activities, such as joining Facebook's "Save Darfur" group, that are long on bumper-sticker sentiment and short on any useful action. The critique is correct but not central to the question of social media's power; the fact that barely committed actors cannot click their way to a better world does not mean that committed actors cannot use social media effectively. Recent protest movements . . . have used social media not as a replacement for real-world action but as a way to coordinate it. As a result, all of those protests exposed participants to the threat of violence, and in some cases its actual use. In fact, the adoption of these tools (especially cell phones) as a way to coordinate and document real-world action is so ubiquitous that it will probably be a part of all future political movements.

This obviously does not mean that every political movement that uses these tools will succeed, because the state has not lost the power to react. This points to the second, and much more serious, critique of social media as tools for political improvement—namely, that the state is gaining increasingly sophisticated means of monitoring, interdicting, or co-opting these tools. The use of social media, the scholars Rebecca MacKinnon of the New America Foundation and Evgeny Morozov of the Open Society Institute have argued, is just as likely to strengthen authoritarian regimes as it is to weaken them. The Chinese government has spent considerable effort perfecting several systems for controlling political threats from social media. The least important of these is its censorship and surveillance program. Increasingly, the government recognizes that threats to its legitimacy are coming from inside the state and that blocking the Web site of The New York Times does little to prevent grieving mothers from airing their complaints about corruption.

The Chinese system has evolved from a relatively simple filter of incoming Internet traffic in the mid-1990s to a sophisticated operation that not only limits outside information but also uses arguments about nationalism and public morals to encourage operators of Chinese Web services to censor their users and users to censor themselves. Because its goal is to prevent information from having politically synchronizing effects, the state does not need to censor the Internet comprehensively; rather, it just needs to minimize access to information.

Authoritarian states are increasingly shutting down their communications grids to deny dissidents the ability to coordinate in real time and broadcast documentation of an event. This strategy also activates the conservative dilemma, creating a short-term risk of alerting the population at large to political conflict. When the government of Bahrain banned Google Earth after an annotated map of the royal family's annexation of public land began circulating, the effect was to alert far more Bahrainis to the offending map than knew about it originally. So widely did the news spread that the government relented and reopened access after four days.

. . .

In the most extreme cases, the use of social media tools is a matter of life and death, as with the proposed death sentence for the blogger Hossein Derakhshan in Iran (since commuted to 19 and a half years in prison). . . . Indeed, the best practical reason to think that social media can help bring political change is that both dissidents and governments think they can. All over the world, activists believe in the utility of these tools and take steps to use them accordingly. And the governments they contend with think social media tools are powerful, too, and are willing to harass, arrest, exile, or kill users in response. One way the United States can heighten the conservative dilemma without running afoul of as many political complications is to demand the release of citizens imprisoned for using media in these ways. Anything that constrains the worst threats of violence by the state against citizens using these tools also increases the conservative dilemma.

Looking at the Long Run

To the degree that the United States pursues Internet freedom as a tool of statecraft, it should de-emphasize anti-censorship tools, particularly those aimed at specific regimes, and increase its support for local public speech and assembly more generally. Access to information is not unimportant, of course, but it is not the primary way social media constrain autocratic rulers or benefit citizens of a democracy. Direct, U.S. government—sponsored support for specific tools or campaigns targeted at specific regimes risk creating backlash that a more patient and global application of principles will not.

This entails reordering the State Departments Internet freedom goals. Securing the freedom of personal and social communication among a state's population should be the highest priority, closely followed by securing individual citizens' ability to speak in public. This reordering would reflect the reality that it is a strong civil society—one in which citizens have freedom of assembly—rather than access to Google or YouTube, that does the most to force governments to serve their citizens.

As a practical example of this, the United States should be at least as worried about Egypt's recent controls on the mandatory licensing of group-oriented text-messaging services as it is about Egypt's attempts to add new restrictions on press freedom. The freedom of assembly that such text-messaging services support is as central to American democratic ideals as is freedom of the press. Similarly, South Korea's requirement that citizens register with their real names for certain Internet services is an attempt to reduce their ability to surprise the state with the kind of coordinated action that took place during the 2008 protest in Seoul. If the United States does not complain as directly about this policy as it does about Chinese censorship, it risks compromising its ability to argue for Internet freedom as a global ideal.

More difficult, but also essential, will be for the U.S. government to articulate a policy of engagement with the private companies and organizations that host the networked public sphere. Services based in the United States, such as Facebook, Twitter, Wikipedia, and YouTube, and those based overseas, such as QQ. (a Chinese instant-messaging service), WikiLeaks (a repository of leaked documents whose servers are in Sweden), Tuenti (a Spanish social network), and Naver (a Korean one), are among the sites used most for political speech, conversation, and coordination. And the world's wireless carriers transmit text messages, photos, and videos from cell phones through those sites. How much can these entities be expected to support freedom of speech and assembly for their users?

The issue here is analogous to the questions about freedom of speech in the United States in private but commercial environments, such as those regarding what kind of protests can be conducted in shopping malls. For good or ill, the platforms supporting the networked public sphere are privately held and run; Clinton committed the United States to working with those companies, but it is unlikely that without some legal framework, as exists for real-world speech and action, moral suasion will be enough to convince commercial actors to support freedom of speech and assembly.

It would be nice to have a flexible set of short-term digital tactics that could be used against different regimes at different times. But the requirements of real-world statecraft mean that what is desirable may not be likely. Activists in both repressive and democratic regimes will use the Internet and related tools to try to effect change in their countries, but Washington's ability to shape or target these changes is limited. Instead, Washington should adopt a more general approach, promoting freedom of speech, freedom of the press, and freedom of assembly everywhere. And it should understand that progress will be slow. Only by switching from an instrumental to an environmental view of the effects of social media on the public sphere will the United States be able to take advantage of the long-term benefits these tools promise—even though that may mean accepting short-term disappointment.

Reference

Shirky [CC]. The Political Power of Social Media: Technology, the Public Sphere and Political Change. *Foreign Affairs-New York-*, 2011[;] *90*(1)[:] 28–41.

CLAY SHIRKY is Professor of New Media at New York University and the author of *Cognitive Surplus: Creativity and Generosity in a Connected Age.*

EXPLORING THE ISSUE

Are Twitter and Other Social Media a Good Source of Political Information?

Critical Thinking and Reflection

1. How pervasive is Twitter (and the Internet) in different regions of the world? Does the public's trust in the forms of media available to them provide any insight into whether Twitter is considered important within that culture, or not?
2. How is Twitter similar to or different from other forms of social media? Do these similarities or differences suggest different ways of thinking about Twitter's role within specific cultural contexts?
3. How might Twitter become an even more powerful medium of dissemination of information? Who would benefit from this/these change(s)?
4. When other forms of media were new, were they also subject to the same questions that Twitter poses? What is the next step in social media as a political tool?

Is There Common Ground?

The authors of these two selections examine the use of Twitter for political purposes, but they ask significantly different questions to contextualize Twitter within the public sphere. It should be stressed that the first selection comes from a longer, more theoretically and methodologically rigorous study, so to be fair to the authors we should remember that their book provides many more details than can be encapsulated in a short, edited segment. However, both selections examine emerging media for the purpose of helping us understand the power of Twitter and other social media as unique forms of political communication. They help us understand that as an emerging phenomenon, Twitter and other social media are likely to be used differently in different cultural settings, and that they should be viewed with respect to the communication and information infrastructure available in any specific country.

As more studies emerge we can expect to see that there is not one uniform use or understanding of how social media communicate political information or are used for political purposes that are easily applied to different cultures or regions. History, economy, and technological availability influence how Twitter, and any form of medium, is perceived by the people within a country or region and quite often, as the research in *Taking Sides* clearly illuminates, there are often multiple ways of understanding media use, and many different individual perspectives on using media and technology for purposes of communication. Both the technology and social use of Twitter will evolve, and though we can't project how the medium may change over the years, we can be sure there will be multiple perspectives on how it is used, by whom, and for what purpose.

Additional Resources

Jason Gainous and Keven M. Wagner, *Tweeting to Power: The Social Media Revolution in American Politics* (Oxford University Press, 2013).

Jurgen Habermas, *The Structural Transformation of the Public Sphere: An Inquiry Into a Category of Bourgeois Society* (MIT Press, 1989).

Eric Schmidt and Jared Cohen, "The Digital Disruption: Connectivity and the Diffusion of Power," *Foreign Affairs* (November 2010)

Shanto Iyengar, M*edia Politics: A Citizen's Guide*, 3rd ed. (W. W. Norton and Company, 2015)

Internet References . . .

E-Democracy.org

forums.e-democracy.org/about

Lindsay Hoffman, "Reflecting on Twitter and its Implications for Democracy"

www.huffingtonpost.com/lindsay-hoffman/twitter
-elections_b_2568989.html

Pew Research Center

Amy Mitchell and Pul Hitlin, "Twitter Reaction to Events Often at Odds with Overall Public Opinion"

www.pewresearch.org/2013/03/04/twitter-reaction-to
-events-often-at-odds-with-overall-public-opinion/

Marc A. Smith, Lee Rainie, Ben Shneiderman, and Itai Himelboim, "Mapping Twitter Topic Networks: From Polarized Crowds to Community Clusters"

www.pewinternet.org/2014/02/20/mapping-twitter
-topic-networks-from-polarized-crowds-to
-community-clusters/

Kentaro Toyama, "Twitter Isn't Spreading Democracy—Democracy Is Spreading Twitter"

www.theatlantic.com/technology/archive/2013/11
/twitter-isnt-spreading-democracy-democracy-is
-spreading-twitter/281368/

Selected, Edited, and with Issue Framing Material by:
Alison Alexander, *University of Georgia*
and
Jarice Hanson, *University of Massachusetts—Amherst*

ISSUE

Are Polls an Accurate Assessment of Public Opinion?

YES: Sheldon R. Gawiser and G. Evans Witt, from "20 Questions a Journalist Should Ask About Poll Results," *National Council of Public Polls* (2012)

NO: Herbert J. Gans, from "Public Opinion Polls Do Not Always Report Public Opinion," *Nieman Journalism Lab* (2013)

Learning Outcomes
After reading this issue, you will be able to:
• Consider the type of poll, become aware of the size of the population sampled, and think about the credibility of the pollster.
• Become more aware of how media use polls for their intended effects.
• Think about alternative or minority viewpoints that are not reflected in polls.
• Reflect on whether poll reports further the agenda of the news organization.

ISSUE SUMMARY

YES: Sheldon R. Gawiser and G. Evans Witt have a vast experience in developing polls and analyzing the results of polls. Their belief in the accuracy of polls to reflect public opinion is grounded in decades of experience, and in the scientific accuracy of the poll. They provide advice to journalists on how to measure the worth of a poll in terms of its scientific rigor as opposed to its casual approach toward accuracy.

NO: Herbert J. Gans discusses how news media personnel often portray public opinion through polls inaccurately. He makes an important distinction between the way people answer polls and the definition of public opinion.

The rise of public opinion polling owes a debt to the technologies that facilitated many of the techniques that are still used in polling today. The telephone certainly made it possible to call someone and ask his or her opinion, and in the days of phone books that listed names, addresses, and phone numbers of people who had phones, this treasure of a resource was invaluable for conducting polls that were randomized (every fifth name might be called, for example), or for those who lived in geographic proximity, as could be detected by the telephone exchange numbers. Radio was a medium that often distributed national newscasts, prior to television and the Internet, and some of the earliest polling companies polled public opinion based on what people

either read in the newspapers, or perhaps heard on radio. Therefore, the entire history of polling is conditioned by the technologies that made survey sampling possible.

Politicians have always wanted to understand what the public thinks, and how policies can be crafted to gain favor by an electorate. Public opinion polling in the United States owes much to the pioneering work of George Gallup, who founded the American Institute of Public Opinion in 1936. Princeton University started the academic journal *Public Opinion Quarterly* in 1937 to focus on emerging techniques and applications of polling criteria. Soon, the Roper, Crossley, and Harris Polls were also established to help monitor public opinion about a wide range of things, from politics to product marketing. The

National Opinion Research Center was founded in 1941 and was the first noncommercial polling company. Today, however, many colleges and universities provide homes to polling companies, and it is not unusual for major companies to use any number of commercial marketing firms to test their products and ideas.

The authors of these selections have insider knowledge about what it takes to conduct a good, scientifically rigorous poll, and all of them criticize the types of polls that are conducted using nonscientific models. In general, the authors agree that polls that reflect rigorous methodological standards can be scientifically and statistically important, but that when methods are distorted by the sponsor's desire to find what it is looking for, or when good social science is not being applied, the results can be very misleading.

Understanding public opinion has long been a critical component of considering the relationship between the press and the public. In 1922, Walter Lippmann, himself a journalist and keen observer of the way media shaped the images in the minds of the audience, wrote a very influential book called *Public Opinion*. In this book he called for the principle of objectivity to be a value that every journalist should strive for, but at the same time, he knew that the words of journalists often influenced what he called the "manufacture of consent," which created images for the audience that influenced audience members' psychological interpretation of meaning. Lippmann's pioneering work helped create the academic study of the media, and provided both a philosophical and moral imperative for the training of journalists.

Today, however, the number of communication technologies we use and have access to has changed the nature of some types of polling. Have you ever been asked for your opinion online, and once you start a questionnaire, you wonder who this poll is for, and what the polling organization might do with your information? Online polls are often "click bait" for companies that may be trying to find out more information about you, rather than what answers you provide to a simple, easy-to-use interactive online service. And yet, there seems to be something compelling about offering our perspective. Sometimes we want to air our viewpoints. Other times we find ourselves caught up in answering questions because they are constructed to really seem as though our opinions matter. The problem with the number of nonscientific polls, though, is that they sometimes diminish what a poll really means and affect the interpretation of the meaning of the responses elicited by the poll.

In a recent *New Yorker* article, journalist Jill Lepore wrote that "From the late 1990s to 2012, twelve hundred polling organizations conducted nearly 37,000 polls by making more than three billion phone calls" (Lepore, November 16, 2015). These numbers are staggering, and we can probably assume that not all of these polls were conducted scientifically, or with rigorous methods. Interestingly, she provides the history of polls that once equated the "poll" to mean the top of a person's head; therefore, when people went to be polled, the result was a head-count. Eventually, "the polls" were the places where voting would take place. As Lepore develops the thesis of her article, she explains how, over time, "polling" began to mean both surveys of opinions as well as forecasts of election results.

Certainly what constitutes a poll has changed over the years, but today, there are also many kinds of polls. "Push polls" use terms that might sway a person's response toward a calculated result so that the "pollster" manipulates the result. "Straw polls" are unofficial expressions of tendencies to lean certain ways in discussions, or toward political "votes" or expressions of opinion. "Benchmark polls" are often done to provide insights on how a candidate's popularity is tracked over time, and "entrance" or "exit" polls ask voters what they think they will vote on, or for whom, and later, on what they said they did (which may not always be what they really did).

One problem with the reporting of public opinion is that sometimes respondents say what they think the pollster wants to hear, whether they really believe the statement or not. For example, a person might be asked how she intends to vote, and she may want to provide an answer even though she is not registered to vote. The assertion actually hides the fact that the person is not political, but she doesn't want to be perceived as not being politically active. Many psychological studies have focused on why people sometimes respond by telling someone what they think that person wants to hear. The actual measurement of public opinion often is blurred by a number of psychological and sociological factors.

But despite the wide range of interpretations and applications of polls today, the authors of the selections in this issue remind us that there are a host of issues that should be addressed when we rely on polls for information. It is ultimately the responsibility of the reader or viewer of poll data to ask important questions about the validity of the poll, and what it means in the larger context of things.

YES ⤶

Sheldon R. Gawiser and G. Evans Witt

20 Questions a Journalist Should Ask About Poll Results

Polls provide the best direct source of information about public opinion. They are valuable tools for journalists and can serve as the basis for accurate, informative news stories. For the journalist looking at a set of poll numbers, here are the 20 questions to ask the pollster before reporting any results. This publication is designed to help working journalists do a thorough, professional job covering polls. It is not a primer on how to conduct a public opinion survey.

The only polls that should be reported are "scientific" polls. A number of the questions here will help you decide whether or not a poll is a "scientific" one worthy of coverage—or an unscientific survey without value.

Unscientific pseudo-polls are widespread and sometimes entertaining, but they never provide the kind of information that belongs in a serious report. Examples include 900-number call-in polls, man-on-the-street surveys, many Internet polls, shopping mall polls, and even the classic toilet tissue poll featuring pictures of the candidates on each roll.

One major distinguishing difference between scientific and unscientific polls is who picks the respondents for the survey. In a scientific poll, the pollster identifies and seeks out the people to be interviewed. In an unscientific poll, the respondents usually "volunteer" their opinions, selecting themselves for the poll.

The results of the well-conducted scientific poll provide a reliable guide to the opinions of many people in addition to those interviewed—even the opinions of all Americans. The results of an unscientific poll tell you nothing beyond simply what those respondents say.

By asking these 20 questions, the journalist can seek the facts to decide how to report any poll that comes across the news desk.

. . .

1. Who Did the Poll?

What polling firm, research house, political campaign, or other group conducted the poll? This is always the first question to ask.

If you don't know who did the poll, you can't get the answers to all the other questions listed here. If the person providing poll results can't or won't tell you who did it, the results should not be reported, for their validity cannot be checked.

Reputable polling firms will provide you with the information you need to evaluate the survey. Because reputation is important to a quality firm, a professionally conducted poll will avoid many errors.

2. Who Paid for the Poll and Why Was It Done?

You must know who paid for the survey, because that tells you—and your audience—who thought these topics are important enough to spend money finding out what people think.

Polls are not conducted for the good of the world. They are conducted for a reason—either to gain helpful information or to advance a particular cause.

It may be the news organization wants to develop a good story. It may be the politician wants to be re-elected. It may be that the corporation is trying to push sales of its new product. Or a special-interest group may be trying to prove that its views are the views of the entire country.

All are legitimate reasons for doing a poll.

The important issue for you as a journalist is whether the motive for doing the poll creates such serious doubts about the validity of the results that the numbers should not be publicized.

Private polls conducted for a political campaign are often unsuited for publication. These polls are conducted solely to help the candidate win—and for no other reason. The poll may have very slanted questions or a strange sampling methodology, all with a tactical campaign purpose. A campaign may be testing out new slogans, a new statement on a key issue or a new attack on an opponent. But since the goal of the candidate's poll may not be a straightforward, unbiased reading of the public's sentiments, the results should be reported with great care.

Likewise, reporting on a survey by a special-interest group is tricky. For example, an environmental group trumpets a poll saying the American people support strong measures to protect the environment. That may be true, but the poll was conducted for a group with definite views. That may have swayed the question wording, the timing of the poll, the group interviewed and the order of the questions. You should carefully examine the poll to be certain that it accurately reflects public opinion and does not simply push a single viewpoint.

3. How Many People Were Interviewed for the Survey?

Because polls give approximate answers, the more people interviewed in a scientific poll, the smaller the error due to the size of the sample, all other things being equal. A common trap to avoid is that "more is automatically better." While it is absolutely true that the more people interviewed in a scientific survey, the smaller the sampling error, other factors may be more important in judging the quality of a survey.

4. How Were Those People Chosen?

The key reason that some polls reflect public opinion accurately and other polls are unscientific junk is how people were chosen to be interviewed. In scientific polls, the pollster uses a specific statistical method for picking respondents. In unscientific polls, the person picks himself to participate.

The method pollsters use to pick interviewees relies on the bedrock of mathematical reality: when the chance of selecting each person in the target population is known, then and only then do the results of the sample survey reflect the entire population. This is called a random sample or a probability sample. This is the reason that interviews with 1,000 American adults can accurately reflect the opinions of more than 210 million American adults.

Most scientific samples use special techniques to be economically feasible. For example, some sampling methods for telephone interviewing do not just pick randomly generated telephone numbers. Only telephone exchanges that are known to contain working residential numbers are selected, reducing the number of wasted calls. This still produces a random sample. But samples of only listed telephone numbers do not produce a random sample of all working telephone numbers.

But even a random sample cannot be purely random in practice as some people don't have phones, refuse to answer, or aren't home.

Surveys conducted in countries other than the United States may use different but still valid scientific sampling techniques, for example, because relatively few residents have telephones. In surveys in other countries, the same questions about sampling should be asked before reporting a survey.

5. What Area (Nation, State, or Region) or What Group (Teachers, Lawyers, Democratic Voters, etc.) Were These People Chosen From?

It is absolutely critical to know from which group the interviewees were chosen. You must know if a sample was drawn from among all adults in the United States, or just from those in one state or in one city, or from another group. For example, a survey of business people can reflect the opinions of business people—but not of all adults. Only if the interviewees were chosen from among all American adults, can the poll reflect the opinions of all American adults.

In the case of telephone samples, the population represented is that of people living in households with telephones. For most purposes, telephone households are similar to the general population. But if you were reporting a poll on what it was like to be homeless, a telephone sample would not be appropriate. The increasingly widespread use of cell phones, particularly as the only phone in some households, may have an impact in the future on the ability of a telephone poll to accurately reflect a specific population. Remember, the use of a scientific sampling technique does not mean that the correct population was interviewed.

Political polls are especially sensitive to this issue.

In pre-primary and pre-election polls, which people are chosen as the base for poll results is critical. A poll of all adults, for example, is not very useful for a primary race where only 25 percent of the registered voters actually turn out. So look for polls based on registered voters, "likely voters," previous primary voters and such. These distinctions are important and should be included in the story, for one of the most difficult challenges in polling is trying to figure out who actually is going to vote.

The ease of conducting surveys in the United States is not duplicated around the world. It may not be possible or practical in some countries to conduct surveys of a random sample throughout the country. Surveys based on a smaller group than the entire population—such as a few larger cities—can still be reliable if reported correctly—as the views of those in the larger cities, for example, but not those of the country—and may be the only available data.

6. Are the Results Based on the Answers of All the People Interviewed?

One of the easiest ways to misrepresent the results of a poll is to report the answers of only a subgroup. For example, there is usually a substantial difference between the opinions of Democrats and Republicans on campaign-related matters. Reporting the opinions of only Democrats in a poll purported to be of all adults would substantially misrepresent the results.

Poll results based on Democrats must be identified as such and should be reported as representing only Democratic opinions.

Of course, reporting on just one subgroup can be exactly the right course. In polling on a primary contest, it is the opinions of those who can vote in the primary that count—not those who cannot vote in that contest. Primary polls should include only eligible primary voters.

7. Who Should Have Been Interviewed and Was Not? Or Do Response Rates Matter?

No survey ever reaches everyone who should have been interviewed. You ought to know what steps were undertaken to minimize non-response, such as the number of attempts to reach the appropriate respondent and over how many days.

There are many reasons why people who should have been interviewed were not. They may have refused attempts to interview them. Or interviews may not have been attempted if people were not home when the interviewer called. Or there may have been a language problem or a hearing problem.

In recent years, the percentage of people who respond to polls has diminished. There has been an increase in those who refuse to participate. Some of this is due to the increase in telemarketing and part is due to Caller ID and other technology that allows screening of incoming calls. While this is a subject that concerns pollsters, so far careful study has found that these reduced response rates have not had a major impact on the accuracy of most public polls.

Where possible, you should obtain the overall response rate from the pollster, calculated on a recognized basis such as the standards of the American Association for Public Opinion Research. One poll is not "better" than another simply because of the one statistic called response rate.

8. When Was the Poll Done?

Events have a dramatic impact on poll results. Your interpretation of a poll should depend on when it was conducted relative to key events. Even the freshest poll results can be overtaken by events. The President may have given a stirring speech to the nation, pictures of abuse of prisoners by the military may have been broadcast[ed], the stock market may have crashed or an oil tanker may have sunk, spilling millions of gallons of crude on beautiful beaches.

Poll results that are several weeks or months old may be perfectly valid, but events may have erased any newsworthy relationship to current public opinion.

9. How Were the Interviews Conducted?

There are four main possibilities: in person, by telephone, online or by mail. Most surveys are conducted by telephone, with the calls made by interviewers from a central location. However, some surveys are still conducted by sending interviewers into people's homes to conduct the interviews.

Some surveys are conducted by mail. In scientific polls, the pollster picks the people to receive the mail questionnaires. The respondent fills out the questionnaire and returns it.

Mail surveys can be excellent sources of information, but it takes weeks to do a mail survey, meaning that the results cannot be as timely as a telephone survey. And mail surveys can be subject to other kinds of errors, particularly extremely low response rates. In many mail surveys, many more people fail to participate than do. This makes the results suspect.

Surveys done in shopping malls, in stores or on the sidewalk may have their uses for their sponsors, but publishing the results in the media is not among them. These approaches may yield interesting human-interest stories, but they should never be treated as if they represent public opinion.

Advances in computer technology have allowed the development of computerized interviewing systems that dial the phone, play taped questions to a respondent and then record answers the person gives by punching numbers on the telephone keypad. Such surveys may be more vulnerable to significant problems including uncontrolled selection of respondents within the household, the ability of young children to complete the survey, and poor response rates.

Such problems should disqualify any survey from being used unless the journalist knows that the survey has proper respondent selection, verifiable age screening, and reasonable response rates.

10. What About Polls on the Internet or World Wide Web?

The explosive growth of the Internet and the World Wide Web has given rise to an equally explosive growth in various types of online polls and surveys.

Online surveys can be scientific if the samples are drawn in the right way. Some online surveys start with a scientific national random sample and recruit participants while others just take anyone who volunteers. Online surveys need to be carefully evaluated before use.

Several methods have been developed to sample the opinions of those who have online access. The fundamental rules of sampling still apply online: the pollster must select those who are asked to participate in the survey in a random fashion. In those cases where the population of interest has nearly universal Internet access or where the pollster has carefully recruited from the entire population, online polls are candidates for reporting.

However, even a survey that accurately sampled all those who have access to the Internet would still fall short of a poll of all Americans, as about one in three adults do not have Internet access.

But many Internet polls are simply the latest variation on the pseudo-polls that have existed for many years. Whether the effort is a click-on Web survey, a dial-in poll or a mail-in survey, the results should be ignored and not reported. All these pseudo-polls suffer from the same problem: the respondents are self-selected. The individuals choose themselves to take part in the poll—there is no pollster choosing the respondents to be interviewed.

Remember, the purpose of a poll is to draw conclusions about the population, not about the sample. In these pseudo-polls, there is no way to project the results to any larger group. Any similarity between the results of a pseudo-poll and a scientific survey is pure chance.

Clicking on your candidate's button in the "voting booth" on a Web site may drive up the numbers for your candidate in a presidential horse-race poll online. For most such efforts, no effort is made to pick the respondents, to limit users from voting multiple times or to reach out for people who might not normally visit the Web site.

The dial-in or click-in polls may be fine for deciding who should win on *American Idol* or which music video is the *MTV Video of the Week*. The opinions expressed may be real, but in sum the numbers are just entertainment. There is no way to tell who actually called in, how old they are, or how many times each person called.

Never be fooled by the number of responses. In some cases a few people call in thousands of times. Even if 500,000 calls are tallied, no one has any real knowledge of what the results mean. If big numbers impress you, remember that the *Literary Digest*'s non-scientific sample of 2,000,000 people said Landon would beat Roosevelt in the 1936 Presidential election.

Mail-in coupon polls are just as bad. In this case, the magazine or newspaper includes a coupon to be returned with the answers to the questions. Again, there is no way to know who responded and how many times each person did.

Another variation on the pseudo-poll comes as part of a fund-raising effort. An organization sends out a letter with a survey form attached to a large list of people, asking for opinions and for the respondent to send money to support the organization or pay for tabulating the survey. The questions are often loaded and the results of such an effort are always meaningless.

This technique is used by a wide variety of organizations from political parties and special-interest groups to charitable organizations. Again, if the poll in question is part of a fund-raising pitch, pitch it—in the wastebasket.

11. What Is the Sampling Error for the Poll Results?

Interviews with a scientific sample of 1,000 adults can accurately reflect the opinions of nearly 210 million American adults. That means interviews attempted with all 210 million adults—if such were possible—would give approximately the same results as a well-conducted survey based on 1,000 interviews.

What happens if another carefully done poll of 1,000 adults gives slightly different results from the first survey? Neither of the polls is "wrong." This range of possible results is called the error due to sampling, often called the margin of error.

This is not an "error" in the sense of making a mistake. Rather, it is a measure of the possible range of approximation in the results because a sample was used.

Pollsters express the degree of the certainty of results based on a sample as a "confidence level." This means a sample is likely to be within so many points of the results one would have gotten if an interview were attempted with the entire target population. Most polls are usually reported using the 95% confidence level.

Thus, for example, a "3 percentage point margin of error" in a national poll means that if the attempt were made to interview every adult in the nation with the same questions in the same way at the same time as the poll was taken, the poll's answers would fall within plus or minus 3 percentage points of the complete count's results 95% of the time.

This does not address the issue of whether people cooperate with the survey, or if the questions are understood, or if any other methodological issue exists. The sampling error is only the portion of the potential error in a survey introduced by using a sample rather than interviewing the entire population. Sampling error tells us nothing about the refusals or those consistently unavailable for interview; it also tells us nothing about the biasing effects of a particular question wording or the bias a particular interviewer may inject into the interview situation. It also applies only to scientific surveys.

Remember that the sampling error margin applies to each figure in the results—it is at least 3 percentage points plus or minus for each one in our example. Thus, in a poll question matching two candidates for President, both figures are subject to sampling error.

12. Who's on First?

Sampling error raises one of the thorniest problems in the presentation of poll results: For a horse-race poll, when is one candidate really ahead of the other?

Certainly, if the gap between the two candidates is less than the sampling error margin, you should not say that one candidate is ahead of the other. You can say the race is "close," the race is "roughly even," or there is "little difference between the candidates." But it should not be called a "dead heat" unless the candidates are tied with the same percentages. And it certainly is not a "statistical tie" unless both candidates have the same exact percentages.

And just as certainly, when the gap between the two candidates is equal to or more than twice the error margin—6 percentage points in our example—and if there are only two candidates and no undecided voters, you can say with confidence that the poll says Candidate A is clearly leading Candidate B.

When the gap between the two candidates is more than the error margin but less than twice the error margin, you should say that Candidate A "is ahead," "has an advantage" or "holds an edge." The story should mention that there is a small possibility that Candidate B is ahead of Candidate A.

When there are more than two choices or undecided voters—virtually in every poll in the real world—the question gets much more complicated.

While the solution is statistically complex, you can fairly easily evaluate this situation by estimating the error margin. You can do that by taking the sum of the percentages for each of the two candidates in question and multiplying it by the total respondents for the survey (only the likely voters if that is appropriate). This number is now the effective sample size for your judgment. Look up the sampling error in a table of statistics for that reduced sample size, and apply it to the candidate percentages. If they overlap, then you do not know if one is ahead. If they do not, then you can make the judgment that one candidate has a lead.

And bear in mind that when subgroup results are reported—women or blacks or young people—the sampling error margin for those figures is greater than for results based on the sample as a whole. Be very careful about reporting results from extremely small subgroups. Any results based on fewer than 100 respondents are subject to such large sampling errors that it is almost impossible to report the numbers in a meaningful manner.

13. What Other Kinds of Factors Can Skew Poll Results?

The margin of sampling error is just one possible source of inaccuracy in a poll. It is not necessarily the source of the greatest possible error; we use it because it's the only one that can be quantified. And, other things being equal, it is useful for evaluating whether differences between poll results are meaningful in a statistical sense.

Question phrasing and question order are also likely sources of flaws. Inadequate interviewer training and supervision, data processing errors and other operational problems can also introduce errors. Professional polling operations are less subject to these problems than volunteer-conducted polls, which are usually less trustworthy. Be particularly careful of polls conducted by untrained and unsupervised college students. There have been several cases where the results were at least in part reported by the students without conducting any survey at all.

You should always ask if the poll results have been "weighted." This process is usually used to account for unequal probabilities of selection and to adjust slightly the demographics in the sample. You should be aware that a poll could be manipulated unduly by weighting the numbers to produce a desired result. While some weighting may be appropriate, other weighting is not. Weighting a scientific poll is only appropriate to reflect unequal probabilities or to adjust to independent values that are mostly constant.

14. What Questions Were Asked?

You must find out the exact wording of the poll questions. Why? Because the very wording of questions can make major differences in the results.

Perhaps the best test of any poll question is your reaction to it. On the face of it, does the question seem fair and unbiased? Does it present a balanced set of choices? Would most people be able to answer the question?

On sensitive questions—such as abortion—the complete wording of the question should probably be included in your story. It may well be worthwhile to compare the results of several different polls from different organizations on sensitive questions. You should examine carefully both the results and the exact wording of the questions.

15. In What Order Were the Questions Asked?

Sometimes the very order of the questions can have an impact on the results. Often that impact is intentional; sometimes it is not. The impact of order can often be subtle.

During troubled economic times, for example, if people are asked what they think of the economy before they are asked their opinion of the president, the presidential popularity rating will probably be lower than if you had reversed the order of the questions. And in good economic times, the opposite is true.

What is important here is whether the questions that were asked prior to the critical question in the poll could sway the results. If the poll asks questions about abortion just before a question about an abortion ballot measure, the prior questions could sway the results.

16. What About "Push Polls"?

In recent years, some political campaigns and special-interest groups have used a technique called "push polls" to spread rumors and even outright lies about opponents. These efforts are not polls, but political manipulation trying to hide behind the smokescreen of a public opinion survey.

In a "push poll," a large number of people are called by telephone and asked to participate in a purported survey. The survey "questions" are really thinly-veiled accusations against an opponent or repetitions of rumors about a candidate's personal or professional behavior. The focus here is on making certain the respondent hears and understands the accusation in the question, not in gathering the respondent's opinions.

"Push polls" are unethical and have been condemned by professional polling organizations.

"Push polls" must be distinguished from some types of legitimate surveys done by political campaigns. At times, a campaign poll may ask a series of questions about contrasting issue positions of the candidates—or various things that could be said about a candidate, some of which are negative. These legitimate questions seek to gauge the public's reaction to a candidate's position or to a possible legitimate attack on a candidate's record.

A legitimate poll can be distinguished from a "push poll" usually by:

The number of calls made—a push poll makes thousands and thousands of calls, instead of hundreds for most surveys; The identity of who is making the telephone calls—a polling firm for a scientific survey as opposed to a telemarketing house or the campaign itself for a "push poll"; The lack of any true gathering of results in a "push poll," which has as its only objective the dissemination of false or misleading information.

17. What Other Polls Have Been Done on This Topic? Do They Say the Same Thing? If They Are Different, Why Are They Different?

Results of other polls—by a newspaper or television station, a public survey firm or even a candidate's opponent—should be used to check and contrast poll results you have in hand.

If the polls differ, first check the timing of the interviewing. If the polls were done at different times, the differing results may demonstrate a swing in public opinion.

If the polls were done about the same time, ask each poll sponsor for an explanation of the differences. Conflicting polls often make good stories.

18. What About Exit Polls?

Exit polls, properly conducted, are an excellent source of information about voters in a given election. They are the only opportunity to survey actual voters and only voters.

There are several issues that should be considered in reporting exit polls. First, exit polls report how voters believe they cast their ballots. The election of 2000 showed that voters may think they have voted for a candidate, but their votes may not have been recorded. Or in some cases, voters actually voted for a different candidate than they thought they did.

Second, absentee voters are not included in many exit polls. In states where a large number of voters vote either early or absentee, an absentee telephone poll may be combined with an exit poll to measure voter opinion. If in a specific case there are large numbers of absentee voters and no absentee poll, you should be careful to report that the exit poll is only of Election Day voters.

Third, make sure that the company conducting the exit poll has a track record. Too many exit polls are conducted in a minimal number of voting locations by people who do not have experience in this specialized method of polling. Those results can be misleading.

19. What Else Needs to Be Included in the Report of a Poll?

The key element in reporting polls is context. Not only does this mean that you should compare the poll to others taken at the same time or earlier, but it also means that you need to report on what events may have impacted on the poll results.

A good poll story not only reports the results of the poll, but also assists the reader in the interpretation of those results. If the poll shows a continued decline in consumer confidence even though leading economic indicators have improved, your report might include some analysis of whether or not people see improvement in their daily economic lives even though the indicators are on the rise.

If a candidate has shown marked improvement in a horse race, you might want to report about the millions of dollars spent on advertising immediately prior to the poll.

Putting the poll in context should be a major part of your reporting.

20. So I've Asked All the Questions. The Answers Sound Good. Should We Report the Results?

Yes, because reputable polling organizations consistently do good work.

However, remember that the laws of chance alone say that the results of one poll out of 20 may be skewed away from the public's real views just because of sampling error.

Also remember that no matter how good the poll, no matter how wide the margin, no matter how big the sample, a pre-election poll does not show that one candidate has the race "locked up." Things change—often and dramatically in politics. That's why candidates campaign.

If the poll was conducted correctly, and you have been able to obtain the information outlined here, your news judgment and that of your editors should be applied to polls, as it is to every other element of a story.

In spite of the difficulties, the public opinion survey, correctly conducted, is still the best objective measure of the state of the views of the public.

SHELDON R. GAWISER, PH.D., is the Director of Elections at NBC News. G. Evans Witt is the CEO of Princeton Survey Research Associates International. Both Gawiser and Witt are the cofounders of the Associated Press/NBC News Poll.

Herbert J. Gans **NO**

Public Opinion Polls Do Not Always Report Public Opinion

Polls have long been newsworthy, but never more so than when their conclusions can be compared to contrary politician behavior, the recent gun control debate being a particularly dramatic example. The pollsters' finding that 90 percent of their respondents said they favored universal background checks for guns was juxtaposed (except by Fox News) with the Senate's filibustered rejection of such legislation.

More interesting and important, the news media turned poll respondents' answers to pollsters' questions into the expression of public opinion. In effect, the news media, and later many politicians, including President Obama, seemed to imply that the Republicans refused to listen to *vox populi*. Some may even have been thinking that the polls were sometimes a better instrument of American democracy than its elected officials.

In one respect, the polls *are* more democratic; they report the opinions of a random sample of the entire population, while elected officials have been chosen by an electorate which at best includes 60 percent of the eligible voters and at worst many fewer. Thus, when 90 percent of poll respondents agree on the answers to polling questions, the polls are sending a message about majoritarian democracy.

In other respects, however, polls are not the best representative of the popular will, for people's answers to pollster questions are not quite the same as their opinions—or, for that matter, public opinion.

The pollsters typically ask people whether they favor or oppose, agree or disagree, approve or disapprove of an issue, and their wording generally follows the centrist bias of the mainstream news media. They offer respondents only two sides (along with the opportunity to say "don't know" or "unsure"), thus leaving out alternatives proposed by people with minority political views. Occasionally, one side is presented in stronger or more approving

language—but by and large, poll questions maintain the balanced neutrality of the mainstream news media.

The pollsters' reports and press releases usually begin with the asked question and then present tables with the statistical proportions of poll respondents giving each of the possible answers. However, the news media stories about the polls usually report only the results, and by leaving out the questions and the don't knows, transform answers into opinions. When these opinions are shared by a majority, the news stories turn poll respondents into the public, thus giving birth to public opinion.

Normally, the news story tells what proportion of that public favors the legislation being questioned or rejected by the Beltway politicians. Indeed, such polls are newsworthy in large part because the reportage is framed as a conflict between majoritarian opinions and politicians' rejection of the popular will.

To be sure, poll respondents favor what they tell the pollsters they favor. But still, poll answers are not quite the same as their opinions. While their answers may reflect their already determined opinions, they may also express what they feel, or believe they ought to feel, at the moment. Pollsters should therefore distinguish between respondents with previously determined opinion and those with spur-of-the-moment answers to pollster questions.

However, only rarely do pollsters ask whether the respondents have thought about the question before the pollsters called, or whether they will ever do so again. In addition, polls usually do not tell us whether respondents have talked about the issue with family or friends, or whether they have expressed their answer *cum* opinion in other, more directly political ways.

In fact, respondents incur no responsibilities with their answers, no subsequent obligation to vote or do anything else. Conversely, politicians can lose the next election with a vote that angers their base.

If poll results can be interpreted as opinion, they are pollster-evoked or *passive* opinions. They are not the *active* opinions of citizens who feel strongly about, or participate in some way in the debates about forthcoming legislation or a presidential decision.

Elected officials may take passive opinions into account but they pay far more attention to active opinions. Above all, however, politicians listen most closely to the usual suspects with power: influential citizens, Congressional leaders and whips, lobbies, and campaign funders.

Jennifer Steinhauer of *The New York Times* was right on target when she described the poll results as an expression of "national sentiment," which she then contrasted with the Senate's "political dynamic."

Some Corrective Fixes

Since polls will continue to be used as indicators of public opinion, the news media should be adding some context to their reporting of the results. From time to time, they should remind the news audience that polls are answers to questions rather than opinions, just as they now remind audiences of the polls' error margins.

In addition, the pollsters should be urged to pose and report intensity questions, telling the politicians and the public how strongly respondents feel about what they tell pollsters, and whether they have been politically active in behalf of these feelings.

At the same time, the news media should keep track of other kinds of intensity measures. For about 30 years, the Pew Research Center has been reporting what news stories a national sample says it follows very closely. Some respondents may exaggerate that closeness, but not many stories are followed closely by more than 50 percent of the sample. Over the years, stories that touch people emotionally and personally relevant ones have always scored highest.

In 2012, the Sandy Hook tragedy was followed very closely by 57 percent, and rising gas prices by 52 percent. In late January 2013, the gun control debate reached a high of 42 percent and stood at 37 percent in early April. The debates over the debt limit and immigration were followed very closely by just under 25 percent of the Pew sample, but 63 percent followed the Boston Marathon bombing very closely.

Better ways the news media can put the passivity of poll opinions into context include the following:

- Report news about active citizen expressions of opinion, at local town halls, organized debates, demonstrations, teach ins, and the like. Gatherings involving predominantly adult and older mainstream Americans are particularly important; and some politically conscientious websites could be counting and reporting the number of such active expressions, large and small, all across the country.
- Keep track of the number, content, and tone of phone calls, letters, and other communications to elected officials, particularly those directly involved in an issue. Spontaneous communications have priority over organized ones, notably the now ubiquitous petitions requiring only single clicks on a website.

  In fact, the mainstream news media, journalistic websites, and other enterprising fact-finders should regularly be asking elected and appointed officials about communications and visits from citizens on currently debated political and social issues.
- Plan follow-up stories after legislation dealing with major problems and issues has been approved or disapproved. Such stories are already being reported, but for the purpose of putting poll results in context, they should emphasize what citizen communications politicians received and try to find out which ones they took into account.

  Regular reporting of such stories would add to public understanding of which kinds of citizen participation and active opinion the politicians consider. That would also help people understand the place of polls in democratic politics, and perhaps lead to debates about whether they can or should play a larger role in politics. Such debates might even stimulate journalistic and other discussions of the pros and cons of majoritarian democracy.

HERBERT J. GANS is a distinguished sociologist from Columbia University who conducts work in urban affairs, policy research, and the use of news media, particularly as the decisions about what constitute news become manifest in news content.

EXPLORING THE ISSUE

Are Polls an Accurate Assessment of Public Opinion?

Critical Thinking and Reflection

1. Think about how often you hear polls reported and consider the sponsor of the poll as well as the results.
2. Consider whether polls become the focus of news stories or are used to set our agenda (agenda setting theory) about what is important.
3. Reflect on the rigor of conducting a strong, statistically relevant poll.
4. Understand the difference between public opinion and public statements reflecting a topic.
5. Develop a more critical eye to understanding how public opinion influences public policy.

Is There Common Ground?

The authors of these two selections agree that some polls, when carefully constructed to measure public opinion, can be accurate, but they differ on how news media report the results of polls and on whether polls are scientifically or casually constructed. The potential for measuring public opinion is important, but the application and use of polls sometimes skew the real meaning of the data that appear to represent public opinion.

The authors of both selections believe that with care, polls can be more accurate, and with a critical eye, journalists and the public can understand the authority of the pollsters and their products. They also agree that when polls are conducted correctly, they play an important role in the democratic process.

Additional Resources

James N. Druckman and Lawrence R. Jacobs, *Who Governs?: Presidents, Public Opinion and Manipulation* (University of Chicago Press, 2015). The authors of this book examine the way Presidents largely ignore public opinion of the masses and cater instead, to the whims of a few affluent citizens and political insiders.

Patrick Fisher, *Demographic Gaps in American Political Behavior* (New York: Westview Press, 2014). In this book, the author discusses how different political groups influence public opinion and the creation of policy.

Arthur S. Hayes, *Press Critics Are the Fifth Estate: Media Watchdogs in America* (Westport, CT and London: Praeger, 2008). Hayes discusses the rise of new media that make bloggers and other press critics a part of the political system by influencing public opinion through their roles as critics of mainstream media.

Jill Lepore, "Politics and the New Machine: What the Turn from Polls to Data Science Means for Democracy," *The New Yorker* (November 16, 2015). The author provides a rich history of polling and talks about how the methods of polling have not kept up with new technology.

Stacey Margolis, *Fictions of Mass Democracy in Nineteenth-Century America* (New York: Cambridge University Press, 2015). Before there were polls, public opinion was measured in very different ways. Margolis explores the impact of this type of governance, so predominant in the nineteenth century, and how that has affected today's belief in understanding public opinion.

Internet References . . .

Gallup Polls

www.gallup.com/home.aspx

Pew Internet Research

www.pewinternet.org/

Polling Report

http://www.pollingreport.com/

Rassmusen Reports

www.rasmussenreports.com/

Unit 4

UNIT

Law and Policy

*N*ew technology influences the interpretation of laws and policies that were crafted in earlier times. In many cases we use private technology in public places. When we do that, do we willingly give up personal privacy? When we transport our communication technologies to different places, are we violating our own right to privacy, or influencing the privacy of others? The issues in this section deal with important topics, such as privacy and security, copyright, and plagiarism.

Selected, Edited, and with Issue Framing Material by:
Alison Alexander, *University of Georgia*
and
Jarice Hanson, *University of Massachusetts - Amherst*

ISSUE

Does Technology
Invade Our Privacy?

YES: Daniel J. Solove, from "The All-or-Nothing Fallacy," in *Nothing to Hide: The False Tradeoff between Privacy and Security* (Yale University Press, 2011)

NO: Stewart Baker, from "The Privacy Problem: What's Wrong with Privacy," in *The Next Digital Decade: Essays on the Future of the Internet* (Tech Freedom, 2010)

Learning Outcomes

After reading this issue, you will be able to:

- Explain the limitations of the "nothing to hide"and the "all-or-nothing" fallacies.
- Identify the trade-offs of security versus privacy from the point of view of each author.
- Describe the definitions of privacy used by these authors.
- Evaluate the solutions suggested by both authors.
- Agree or disagree: You have zero privacy anyway. Get over it.

ISSUE SUMMARY

YES: Daniel J. Solove, Professor of Law at George Washington University and authority on privacy issues, argues that privacy is too often sacrificed for security concerns. He argues that there are often solutions that do not involve such sacrifices, but that they are dismissed by an all-or-nothing attitude.

NO: Stewart Baker, former Assistant Secretary for Policy at Homeland Security, argues vigorously for better collection and use of technological information. Its importance in preventing acts of terrorism, in tracking potential criminals, and in protecting the interests of the country far outweighs privacy concerns of individuals.

New technologies allow unprecedented invasions of privacy. We are familiar with some of the concerns: Can employers really make us open our Facebook page before they hire us? What if I end up on-screen in one of the views captured by Google Street View technology? What if an unflattering picture taken by a friend or in a public space goes viral before I even know about it? What if a stalker uses the Internet to track down information about me? What if my search for medical information is used by Google to target ads to me—and anyone who might see those ads?

What unites these concerns? All these "what if" questions are about the control of personal information. Although there is a great agreement on the importance of privacy, there is little agreement on how it can be accomplished. The most effective way of controlling privacy comes from efforts to exercise control over personal information. The Electronic Frontier Forum (EFF.org) has

several web pages dedicated to explaining that anonymity is a right, conferred by the U.S. Constitution, and it criticizes many organizations for challenging or violating rights. In 2011, EFF criticized Facebook's new policy on selling personal information of Facebook users to advertisers, and claimed that it violated the trust of users. Others are less concerned. Scott McNealy, cofounder of Sun Microsystems, is famously reported saying, "You have zero privacy anyway. Get over it."

An important feature of this issue is that often people leave "trails" of information that can actually identify them, even when users assumed they were anonymous. We rarely consider the technological structures of news media (such as the Internet and cell phones), nor do we realize that the idea of using technology in public places actually records our use, including the time, and often, our identifying information. Think for a moment of a situation in which someone who was using a public computer terminal in a library types in his or her password, perhaps a credit card number, and the many websites he or she visited. If the person forgets to logoff or to clear the cache of the computer, this information is easily accessible to the next user who can easily view the recent history of the computer's use. In *I Know Who You Are and I Saw What You Did*, Lori Andrews tells a chilling story of a school district that activated webcams on school-issued laptops using software designed to help recovery if the laptops were stolen. Instead district personnel collected screenshots of the room where the laptop was located, often a bedroom, where these high school students were studying, dressing, or sleeping.

As you can see, the issues go far beyond overhearing someone on a cell phone in a public place or accidentally hitting "reply all" on an indiscrete email. There is always the possibility of someone forwarding electronic messages to others, as we have seen recently in the scandals surrounding political figures using cell phones for sexting, or in the British *News of the World* cell phone-hacking scandals—both situations in which their perpetrators thought they could hide behind their online anonymity, only to be disgraced and humiliated once the information so easily came to light.

The problems of privacy become even more important when we move from the realm of the personal control of information to public or governmental uses of that information. Digital technologies have created surprisingly robust pictures of our lives. At this time, the National Security Agency (NSA) is embroiled in a global scandal surrounding data collection of information about U.S. and international figures. Much of this emerges from the loosening of restrictions and the subsequent cover activities that emerged after 9/11 and the Patriot Act. Although this scandal is much too complex to unravel in this issue, the result has put the issue of governmental surveillance in the spotlight.

In this digital world, how do we weight the benefits and the consequences of government surveillance of its citizens, as well as its allies? Daniel Solove argues that privacy is too often sacrificed in the name of security. His book is titled *Nothing to Hide*, a phrase that is used to minimize the violation of privacy. "I've got nothing to hide. Only if you're doing something wrong should you worry." Solove attacks these and other arguments about the value of security and the negligible loss of privacy in times of crisis or when national security is threatened. He deplores the "all-or-nothing" governmental approach that implies that every security measure must be taken, no matter what the personal cost or the possibility of other less invasive solutions.

Stewart Baker asks "What's Wrong with Privacy" and proceeds to tell us just exactly what concerns about privacy do to disable national security. He argues that privacy groups discourage actions that could prevent terrorist activity such as occurred on 9/11/2001. Baker talks about the early establishment of right to privacy doctrine and the spirit of the privacy movement today, which he describes as reactionary, Luddite, and anti-technology. He is particularly concerned about efforts to narrow the ability of databases to "talk" to one another, thus preventing the creation of big data sources that can amass incredible amounts of information about the objects of surveillance. Baker also discusses his solutions to these privacy concerns. He dismisses several ideas that don't work, and argues finally for accountability: investigations and punishment of those who misuse data.

We are used to thinking about privacy as a concern for personal information. And, we are used to thinking about big data as something that scientists collect or perhaps the 24/7 information that Nielsen can collect about viewing habits with recent technological advances. The stakes are much higher when we talk about combating terrorism or protecting the security of our country. Certainly, the current NSA scandals make it clear that careful judgment is required; loosening the constraints on surveillance can result in highly unfavorable outcomes. These authors will challenge you, with highly contrasting points of view, to envision the solutions to these concerns.

YES

Daniel J. Solove

The All-or-Nothing Fallacy

"I'd gladly give up my privacy if it will keep me secure from a terrorist attack." I hear this refrain again and again. The debate is often cast as an all-or-nothing choice, whether we should have privacy or a specific security measure. Consider the way the government defended the NSA surveillance program, which involved secret wiretapping of phone calls without any oversight. In a congressional hearing, Attorney General Alberto Gonzales stated: "Our enemy is listening, and I cannot help but wonder if they are not shaking their heads in amazement at the thought that anyone would imperil such a sensitive program by leaking its existence in the first place, and smiling at the prospect that we might now disclose even more or perhaps even unilaterally disarm ourselves of a key tool in the war on terror."

Notice his language. He's implying that if we protect privacy, it will mean that we must "disarm" ourselves of some really valuable security measures. He's suggesting that even terrorists would consider us crazy for making such a tradeoff.

I constantly hear arguments like this when officials justify security measures or argue that they shouldn't be regulated. They point to the value of the surveillance and the peril we'd be in without it. "We're hearing quite a lot of chatter about terrorist attacks," they say. "Do you want us to stop listening? Then the terrorists could talk about how they plan to blow up a plane, and we won't know about it. Is a little privacy really worth that cost?"

Those defending the national-security side of the balance often view security and liberty as a zero-sum tradeoff. The legal scholars Eric Posner and Adrian Vermeule contend that "any increase in security requires a decrease in liberty." The argument is that security and civil liberties such as privacy can never be reconciled. Every gain in privacy must be a loss in security. Every gain in security must be a loss in privacy.

But this argument is flawed. The argument that privacy and security are mutually exclusive stems from what I call the "all-or-nothing fallacy." Sacrificing privacy doesn't automatically make us more secure. Not all security measures are invasive of privacy. Moreover, no correlation has been established between the effectiveness of a security measure and a corresponding decrease in liberty. In other words, the most effective security measures need not be the most detrimental to liberty. . . .

Security and privacy need not be mutually exclusive. For example, one security response to the September 11 attacks was to lock the cockpit doors on airplanes. This prevents a terrorist from gaining control of the plane. Does it invade privacy? Hardly at all. . . .

The all-or-nothing fallacy causes tremendous distortion in the balance between privacy and security. In fact, I believe that many courts and commentators who balance security measures against privacy rights conduct the balance wrongly because of this fallacy. . . . On one side of the scale they weigh the benefits of the security measure. On the other side they weigh privacy rights.

At first blush, this seems like a reasonable approach—balance the security measure against privacy. Yet it is quite wrong. Placing the security measure on the scale assumes that the *entire security measure, all-or-nothing, is in the balance.* It's not. Protecting privacy seldom negates the security measure altogether. Rarely does judicial oversight or the application of the Fourth Amendment prohibit a government surveillance activity. Instead, the activity is allowed subject to oversight and sometimes a degree of limitation.

Most constitutional and statutory protections work this way. The Fourth Amendment, for example, allows all sorts of very invasive searches. Under the Fourth Amendment, the government can search your home. It can search your computer. It can do a full body-cavity search. It can search nearly anything and engage in nearly any kind of surveillance. How can this be so? Because the Fourth Amendment doesn't protect privacy by stopping the government from searching; it works by requiring judicial oversight and mandating that the government justify its measures. So under the Fourth Amendment, the government can engage in highly invasive searches if it justifies the need to do so beforehand to a judge.

Like the Fourth Amendment, electronic-surveillance law allows for wiretapping, but limits the practice by mandating judicial supervision, minimizing the breadth of the wiretapping, and requiring law-enforcement officials to report back to the court to prevent abuses. Thus the protection of privacy might demand the imposition of oversight and regulation but need not entail scrapping an entire security measure. . . .

Solove, Daniel J. From *Nothing to Hide: The False Tradeoff between Privacy and Security*, 2011, pp. 33–37, 62–64, 66–69, 182–183, 185–191 193–194. Copyright © 2011 by Yale University Press. Used with permission.

Far too often, however, discussions of security and liberty fail to assess the balance this way. Polls frequently pose the question as an all-or-nothing tradeoff. A 2002 Pew Research poll asked American citizens:

> Should the government be allowed to read e-mails and listen to phone calls to fight terrorism?

A 2005 poll from Rasmussen Reports posed the question:

> Should the National Security Agency be allowed to intercept telephone conversations between terrorism suspects in other countries and people living in the United States?

Both these questions, however, neglect to account for warrants and court orders. Few would contend that the government shouldn't be allowed to conduct a wide range of searches when it has a search warrant or court order. So the questions that *should* be posed are:

> Should the government be allowed to read emails and listen to phone calls *without a search warrant or the appropriate court order required by law* to fight terrorism?

> Should the National Security Agency be allowed to intercept telephone conversations between terrorism suspects in other countries and people living in the United States *without a court order or judicial oversight?*

The choice is not between a security measure and nothing, but between a security measure with oversight and regulation and a security measure at the sole discretion of executive officials. In many cases, oversight and regulation do not diminish a security measure substantially, so the cost of protecting privacy can be quite low. Unfortunately, the balance is rarely assessed properly. When the balance is measured under the all-or-nothing fallacy, the scale dips dramatically toward the security side. The costs of protecting privacy are falsely inflated, and the security measure is accorded too much weight.

The National-Security Argument

Many people argue that the government should be regulated much less when it pursues matters of national security than when it investigates ordinary crime. They contend that national-security threats are quite different from the dangers of crime. For example, as Andrew McCarthy, senior fellow of the Foundation for the Defense of Democracies and former federal prosecutor, testified to Congress:

> We want constitutional rights to protect Americans from oppressive executive action. We do not, however, want constitutional rights to be con-

verted by enemies of the United States into weapons in their war against us. We want courts to be a vigorous check against overbearing governmental tactics in the investigation and prosecution of Americans for ordinary violations of law; but we do not—or, at least, we should not—want courts to degrade the effectiveness of executive action targeted at enemies of the United States who seek to kill Americans and undermine their liberties.

Those who maintain the exceptionalism of national-security threats propose weaker Fourth Amendment requirements or none at all. They contend that matters involving national security must be kept secret and should be insulated from close scrutiny. Should matters of national security be given special treatment? I argue that the distinction between matters of national security and regular crime is too fuzzy and incoherent to be workable.

The Law of National Security

In 1969 the three founding members of a group called "the White Panthers" bombed a CIA office in Michigan. The group wasn't a white supremacist group; in fact, they supported the goals of the Black Panther Party. They also advocated radical anarchist goals, arguing that everything should be free and that money should be abolished. The group's manifesto stated: "We demand total freedom for everybody! And we will not be stopped until we get it. . . . ROCK AND ROLL music is the spearhead of our attack because it is so effective and so much fun."

During its investigation of the crime, the government wiretapped calls made by one of the bombers. The wiretapping was conducted without warrants supported by probable cause required by the Fourth Amendment.

The case made its way up to the U.S. Supreme Court in 1972. The Nixon administration argued that because the bombing involved a threat to national security, the government wasn't bound by the Fourth Amendment. The administration argued the U.S. Constitution grants the president special national-security powers to "preserve, protect and defend the Constitution of the United States," and these powers trump the regular protections of the Fourth Amendment.

The Supreme Court rebuffed President Nixon's claim that he could ignore Fourth Amendment rights in the name of national security:

> [W]e do not think a case has been made for the requested departure from Fourth Amendment standards. The circumstances described do not justify complete exemption of domestic security surveillance from prior judicial scrutiny. Official surveillance, whether its purpose be criminal investigation or ongoing intelligence gathering, risks infringement of constitutionally protected privacy of speech. Security surveillances are especially sensitive because of the inherent vagueness of the domestic security concept, the necessarily broad and continuing nature of intelligence

gathering, and the temptation to utilize such surveillances to oversee political dissent. We recognize, as we have before, the constitutional basis of the President's domestic security role, but we think it must be exercised in a manner compatible with the Fourth Amendment. In this case we hold that this requires an appropriate prior warrant procedure.

The Court noted that the Fourth Amendment might require slightly different procedures for matters of national security depending upon practical considerations. Thus Fourth Amendment regulation is flexible to the particular needs of the situation.

Despite the Supreme Court's rejection of the argument that national security should entail a dramatic departure from constitutional protections, the national-security argument is still invoked. The legal scholar Stephen Vladeck notes that the concept of national security has a distorting effect on the law: "[O]ne can find national security considerations influencing ordinary judicial decision making across the entire gamut of contemporary civil and criminal litigation." Although claims of national security don't directly eliminate rights or civil liberties, they severely weaken them. National-security claims are often accompanied by calls for deference, as well as demands for secrecy. . . .

Improper Invocations of "National Security"

"National security" has often been abused as a justification not only for surveillance but also for maintaining the secrecy of government records as well as for violating the civil liberties of citizens. The Japanese internment during World War II, as well as many other abuses, was authorized in the name of national security. As the court noted in *United States v. Ehrlichman,* the Watergate burglary was an example of the misuse of national-security powers: "The danger of leaving delicate decisions of propriety and probable cause to those actually assigned to ferret out 'national security' information is potent, and is indeed illustrated by the intrusion undertaken in this case."

The government has often raised national-security concerns to conceal embarrassing and scandalous documents from the public—documents which often turned out to be harmless, such as the Pentagon Papers, a study of the U.S. military and political involvement in Vietnam. Daniel Ellsberg, an analyst who worked on the study, gave the Pentagon Papers to the *New York Times*. The government sought to prevent publication by claiming that disclosing the Pentagon Papers would create a "grave and immediate danger to the security of the United States." But this claim was false. The U.S. Supreme Court rejected the government's attempt to stop the Pentagon Papers from being disclosed, and national security wasn't harmed after they were published. Solicitor General Edwin Griswold, who wrote the government's brief, later recanted, stating that he hadn't seen "any trace of a threat to national security" in the Pentagon Papers. The dire claims the government made about national security were bogus, just a way to cover up what the Pentagon Papers revealed—that the government had made deceptive claims about the Vietnam War.

After the September 11 attacks, the government began using a tactic called the "state secrets privilege" to exclude evidence in a case if it will reveal a classified secret. Even if the government isn't a party to the case, it can swoop in and invoke the privilege. Many times, the case gets dismissed because a person can't prove her case without the evidence. Tom Blanton, director of George Washington University's National Security Archive, says that the state secrets privilege acts like a "neutron bomb" on a case, effectively wiping it out. . . .

Ironically, the case that gave rise to the state secrets privilege involved an improper use of secrecy. In *United States v. Reynolds,* a U.S. Air Force plane exploded in flight, killing nine people. Only four people were able to parachute to safety. The widows of three civilians who died in the accident sued the government for negligence. In a civil lawsuit, plaintiffs are ordinarily entitled to see documents pertaining to an accident, and the plaintiffs in this case wanted to see the Air Force's accident report and other evidence surrounding the incident But the government withheld these documents due to national-security concerns. The government wouldn't even allow the trial judge to examine the documents to evaluate the government's claim that their disclosure would undermine national security.

The U.S. Supreme Court upheld the government's actions under the state secrets privilege, declaring that "when the formal claim of privilege was filed by the Secretary of the Air Force, under circumstances indicating a reasonable possibility that military secrets were involved, there was certainly a sufficient showing of privilege to cut off further demand for the document." The Court deferred to the government's assertions; indeed, it even refused to examine the accident report. When the report was eventually declassified forty-seven years later, it revealed no state secrets. Instead, it showed that the government had been negligent. In his book about the case, Louis Fisher, a senior scholar at the Library of Congress, concludes that the government "falsely described" the documents and "misled" the courts.

Certainly, there are times where the government has a compelling reason to keep information secret, But it is currently far too easy for the government to cry "national security" to conceal unseemly information. Claims of secrecy in the name of national security must be subjected to rigorous scrutiny. . . .

Should the Government Engage in Data Mining?

I like to shop on Amazon.com. Every time I visit Amazon.com, they say to me: "Welcome, Daniel." They know me by name! And then they say: "We've got recommendations for you." I love their recommendations. They suggest various books and products I might like, and they're pretty good at it.

Amazon.corn's recommendations are the product of a form of "data mining." Data mining involves creating profiles by amassing personal data and then analyzing it for nuggets of wisdom about individuals. Amazon looks at my buying pattern and compares it to similar patterns of other people. If I bought a *Lord of the Rings* movie, it might recommend a *Harry Potter* movie. Why? Because a high percentage of people buying a *Lord of the Rings* movie also bought a *Harry Potter* movie. Despite our desire to be authentic and unique, we're often similar to other people, and we're frequently quite predictable.

Some government officials think that if data mining works so well for Amazon and other companies, then it might work well for law enforcement. If data mining can predict whether I'm likely to buy a *Harry Potter* movie, maybe it can also predict whether I'm likely to commit a crime or engage in terrorism.

Generally, law enforcement is investigative, focusing on apprehending perpetrators of past crimes. When it comes to terrorism, law enforcement shifts to being more preventative, seeking to identify terrorists before they act. This is why the government has become interested in data mining—to predict who might conduct a future terrorist attack.

Proponents of data mining argue that examining information for patterns will greatly assist in locating terrorists because certain characteristics and behaviors are likely to be associated with terrorist activity. As Judge Richard Posner argues, in "an era of global terrorism and proliferation of weapons of mass destruction, the government has a compelling need to gather, pool, sift, and search vast quantities of information, much of it personal."

Data mining supporters contend that because it involves computers analyzing data, the information is rarely seen by humans, so there's no privacy harm. They also argue that there's no privacy harm because much of the data already exists in databases, so nothing new is being disclosed. And as the law professor Eric Goldman argues, in many cases people don't even know their data is being analyzed. He declares: "This situation brings to mind the ancient Zen parable: if a tree falls in a forest and no one is around to hear it, does it make a sound?". . .

The Problems of Data Mining

Defenders of data mining insist that it causes only minimal privacy harms. As Richard Posner argues:

> The collection, mainly through electronic means, of vast amounts of personal data is said to invade privacy. But machine collection and processing of data cannot, as such, invade privacy. Because of their volume, the data are first sifted by computers, which search for names, addresses, phone numbers, etc., that may have intelligence value. This initial sifting, far from invading privacy (a computer is not a sentient being), keeps most private data from being read by any intelligence officer.

The potential harm from data mining, according to Posner, is use of the information to blackmail an "administration's critics and political opponents" or to "ridicule or embarrass." This argument defines the privacy problems with data mining in narrow ways that neglect to account for the full panoply of problems created by the practice. Posner focuses on the problems of disclosure and the threat of disclosure (blackmail). But data mining involves many other kinds of problems, which I'll now discuss.

Inaccuracy

Data mining isn't very accurate in the behavioral predictions it makes. The difficulty is that while patterns repeat themselves, they don't do so with perfect regularity. We can be fairly confident in predicting that gravity will still work tomorrow. But predicting the weather isn't as easy—and certainly, human behavior is far more unpredictable than the weather.

Consider the following profiles:

1. "John" was a young man who was born and raised in Egypt. His parents were Muslim, though not strongly religious. His father was a successful attorney and his mother came from a wealthy family. He had two sisters, one of whom became a doctor, the other a professor. John studied architecture at Cairo University. He later lived in Germany and worked at an urban-planning firm. He had a number of close friends, and he lived with roommates. He increasingly became more religious, eventually founding a prayer group. After five years in Germany, he came to the United States. He decided to enroll in flying school to learn how to fly airplanes.
2. "Matt" was a young man who was born and raised near Buffalo, New York. His parents were Catholic, but Matt later became an agnostic. He had two sisters. His parents were middle class, and his father worked at a General Motors factory. He was a good student in high school, but he dropped out of college. He liked to collect guns, and he strongly believed in gun rights. Matt enjoyed computer programming. He enlisted in the U.S. Army. After leaving the army, he worked as a security guard. He maintained close ties with several friends he met in the army.
3. "Bill" was a middle-aged man born in Chicago to middle-class parents. He was admitted at an early age to Harvard. He received a Ph.D. in math from Michigan, and then became a professor at Berkeley. He later quit the professorship and moved to a cabin in the woods. He enjoyed reading history books, riding his bike, and gardening.

"John" is Mohammed Atta, the ringleader of the September 11 attacks. "Matt" is Timothy McVeigh, who bombed the Alfred P. Murrah Federal Building in Oklahoma City in 1995, killing 168 people. "Bill" is Theodore Kaczynski, the Unabomber, who mailed bombs to people for a period of nearly twenty years. These three individuals had very different backgrounds and beliefs. Atta had radicalized Islamic beliefs, McVeigh was an agnostic who believed the power of the U.S. government was running amok, and Kaczynski was an atheist who hated modern technology and industry.

Terrorists come not in just one flavor but in many, making it more difficult to construct an accurate profile. Atta, McVeigh, and Kaczynski had vastly different political beliefs, childhoods, families, socioeconomic backgrounds, levels of intelligence, and religions. Interestingly, all came from apparently normal families. Many other individuals have similar backgrounds, similar religious and political beliefs, and similar behavior patterns, but no desire to commit terrorist acts.

The things terrorists of the future do may be similar to the things done by terrorists of the past, but they, also may be different. By focusing on patterns based on past experience, we may ignore new characteristics and behaviors of the terrorists of the future.

Data mining proponents might reply that although not all terrorists repeat the past, they nonetheless might have some things in common, so looking at behavior patterns might still help us identify them. The problem is that even if data mining identifies some terrorists correctly, it is effective only if it doesn't have too many "false positives"—people who fit the profile but who aren't terrorists.

More than two million people fly each day worldwide. A data mining program to identify terrorists with a false positive rate of 1 percent (which would be exceptionally low for such a program) would flag more than twenty thousand false positives every day. This is quite a large number of innocent people who will be wrongly snagged by the system.

Why is the government so interested in data mining when the accuracy and workability of the practice remain uncertain? Part of the government's interest in data mining stems from the aggressive marketing efforts of database companies. After September 11, database companies met with government officials and made a persuasive pitch about the virtues of data mining. The technology, which often works quite well in the commercial setting, can sound dazzling when presented by skillful marketers.

The problem, however, is that just because data mining might be effective for businesses trying to predict customer behavior, it isn't necessarily effective for government officials trying to predict who will engage in terrorism. A high level of accuracy is not essential when data mining is used by businesses to target marketing for consumers, because the cost of error to individuals is minimal. If Amazon.com makes a poor book recommendation to me, there's little harm. I just move on to the next recommendation. But the consequences of government data mining are vastly greater: being singled out for extra investigation, repeatedly being subjected to extra screening at the airport, being stranded while on a no-fly list, or even being arrested.

First Amendment Concerns

Another potential threat posed by data mining is that it can target people based on their First Amendment–protected activities. . . . Suspicious profiles might involve information about people's free speech, free association, or religious activity. Singling people out for extra investigation, for denial of the right to travel by plane, or for inclusion in a suspicious-persons blacklist is more troubling if the action is based even in part on protected First Amendment activities. How do we know that the profiles aren't based on a person's free expression? What if a person is singled out for extra investigation based on his unpopular political views? How do we know that the profiles aren't based upon a person's religious activity? If people are members of unpopular political groups, do they get singled out for extra screening at the airport?

Information gathering about First Amendment-protected activities involving people's reading habits and speech might chill the exercise of these rights. There doesn't need to be a leak to deter people from reading unpopular books or saying unpopular things. People might be deterred by the fact that the government can readily learn about what a person reads and says—and that the government might mine this data to make predictions about a person's behavior.

Suppose I perform the following searches on Google about ricin, a poison made from castor beans that can be lethal if ingested or inhaled:

> obtain ricin
> where to buy castor beans
> lethal dosage of ricin
> how to administer ricin
> how to make ricin from castor beans

Suppose I also buy a book on Amazon called *The Idiot's Guide to Using Poison*. Looks quite suspicious, doesn't it? But I have an innocent explanation: I'm 'writing a novel about a character who murders someone with ricin. Although I have no intent to do evil, I certainly wouldn't want some nervous government law-enforcement officials to see my activities. Nor would I want some computer to start beeping because of my odd buying and Web-surfing behavior. Even though there's an innocent explanation, I shouldn't have to worry about explaining myself or being subjected to an investigation or extra scrutiny at the airport.

Perhaps I might be undeterred and still do the searches and buy the book. But not everyone would feel as comfortable. Some people might refrain from researching ricin or other things because of a fear of potential consequences, and that's a problem in a society that values robust freedom to speak, write, and read.

Equality

Data mining also implicates the principle that people should be treated equally under the law regardless of their race, ethnicity, or religion. How do we know the extent to which race or ethnicity is used in the profiles?

Some argue that data mining helps to eliminate stereotyping and discrimination. Computers can minimize the human element, thus preventing bias and racism from entering into the process. Whereas some data mining techniques involve a human-created profile of a terrorist and seek to identify people who match the profile, other data mining techniques ostensibly let the computer compose the profile by analyzing patterns of behavior from known terrorists. Even this technique, however, involves human judgment. Somebody has to make the initial judgment about who qualifies as a known terrorist and who does not. Profiles can contain pernicious assumptions hidden in the architecture of computer code and embedded in algorithms so that they appear to be the decision of neutral computers.

On the other hand, one might argue, profiling via data mining might be better than the alternatives. The legal scholar Frederick Schauer aptly notes that there is no escape from profiling, for without data mining, officials will be making their own subjective judgments about who is suspicious. These judgments are based on an implicit profile, though one that isn't overt and articulated. "[T]he issue is not about whether to use profiles or not but instead about whether to use (or to prefer) formal written profiles or informal unwritten ones." Although it is true that formal profiles constructed in advance have their virtues over discretionary profiling by officials, formal profiles contain some disadvantages. They are more systematic than the discretionary approach, thus compounding the effects of information tied to race, ethnicity, religion, speech, or other factors that might be problematic. Those profiling informally are subject to scrutiny, as they have to answer in court about why they believed a person was suspicious. Data mining, however, lacks such transparency. . . . Formal written profiles cease to have an advantage over informal unwritten ones if they remain hidden and unsupervised. . . .

Transparency
The key problem with data mining is that it is hard to carry out with transparency. Transparency, or openness, is essential to promote accountability and to provide the public with a way to ensure that government officials are not engaging in abuse. "Sunlight is said to be the best of disinfectants," Justice Brandeis declared, "electric light the most efficient policeman." As James Madison stated: "A popular government without popular information or the means of acquiring it is but a prologue to a farce or a tragedy or perhaps both. Knowledge will forever govern ignorance. And a people who mean to be their own governors must arm themselves with the power which knowledge gives."

One problem with many data mining programs is that they lack adequate transparency. The programs are secret because revealing the patterns that trigger identification as a possible future terrorist will tip off terrorists about what behaviors to avoid. This is indeed a legitimate concern. . . . Without public accountability, unelected bureaucrats can administer data mining programs in ways often insulated from any scrutiny at all. For example, the information gathered about people for use in data mining might be collected from sources that don't take sufficient steps to maintain accuracy. Without oversight, it is unclear what level of accuracy the government requires for the information it gathers and uses. . . . If a person is routinely singled out based on a profile and wants to challenge the profile, there appears to be no way to do so unless the profile is revealed.

The lack of transparency in data mining programs makes it nearly impossible to balance the privacy and security interests. Given the significant potential privacy issues and other constitutional concerns, combined with speculative and unproven security benefits as well as the availability of many other alternative means of promoting security, should data mining still be on the table as a viable policy option? One could argue that data mining at least should be investigated and studied. There is nothing wrong with doing so, but the cost must be considered in light of alternative security measures that might already be effective and present fewer potential problems. . . .

Daniel J. Solove is a Research Professor of Law at George Washington University. He is an expert in Privacy Law, and the author of several books on privacy and over 40 law review articles.

Stewart Baker

 **NO**

The Privacy Problem:
What's Wrong with Privacy?

Why are privacy groups so viscerally opposed to government action that could reduce the risks posed by exponential technologies? The cost of their stance was made clear on September 11, 2001. That tragedy might not have occurred if not for the aggressive privacy and civil liberties protection imposed by the Foreign Intelligence Surveillance Court and the Department of Justice's Office of Intelligence; and it might have been avoided if border authorities had been able to use airline reservation data to screen the hijackers as they entered the United States.

But even after 9/11, privacy campaigners tried to rebuild the wall and to keep the Department of Homeland Security (DHS) from using airline reservation data effectively. They failed; too much blood had been spilled.

But in the fields where disaster has not yet struck—computer security and biotechnology—privacy groups have blocked the government from taking even modest steps to head off danger.

I like to think that I care about privacy, too. But I had no sympathy for privacy crusaders' ferocious objection to any new government use of technology and data. Where, I wondered, did their objection come from?

So I looked into the history of privacy crusading. And that's where I found the answer.

The Birth of the Right of Privacy

In the 1880s, Samuel Dennis Warren was near the top of the Boston aristocracy. He had finished second in his class at Harvard Law School. He founded a law firm with the man who finished just ahead of him, Louis Brandeis, and they prospered mightily. Brandeis was a brilliant, creative lawyer and social reformer who would eventually become a great Supreme Court justice.

But Samuel Dennis Warren was haunted. There was a canker in the rose of his life. His wife was a great hostess, and her parties were carefully planned. When Warren's cousin married, Mabel Warren held a wedding breakfast and filled her house with flowers for the event. The papers described her home as a "veritable floral bower."

No one should have to put up with this. Surely you see the problem. No? Well, Brandeis did.

He and Warren both thought that, by covering a private social event, the newspapers had reached new heights of impertinence and intrusiveness. The parties and guest lists of a Boston Brahmin and his wife were no one's business but their own, he thought. And so was born the right to privacy.

Angered by the press coverage of these private events, Brandeis and Warren wrote one of the most frequently cited law review articles ever published. In fact, "The Right to Privacy," which appeared in the 1890 Harvard Law Review, is more often cited than read—for good reason, as we'll see. But a close reading of the article actually tells us a lot about the modern concept of privacy.

Brandeis, also the father of the policy-oriented legal brief, begins the article with a candid exposition of the policy reasons why courts should recognize a new right to privacy. His argument is uncompromising:

> The press is overstepping in every direction the obvious bounds of propriety and of decency. Gossip is no longer the resource of the idle and of the vicious, but has become a trade, which is pursued with industry as well as effrontery ... To occupy the indolent, column upon column is filled with idle gossip, which can only be procured by intrusion upon the domestic circle. The intensity and complexity of life, attendant upon advancing civilization, have rendered necessary some retreat from the world, and man, under the refining influence of culture, has become more sensitive to publicity, so that solitude and privacy have become more essential to the individual; but modern enterprise and invention have, through invasions upon his privacy, subjected him to mental pain and distress, far greater than could be inflicted by mere bodily injury ... Even gossip apparently harmless, when widely and persistently circulated, is potent for evil ... When personal gossip attains the dignity of print, and crowds the space available for matters of real interest to the community, what wonder that the ignorant and thoughtless mistake its relative importance ... Triviality destroys at once robustness of thought and delicacy of feeling.

What does Brandeis mean by this? To be brief, he thinks it should be illegal for the newspapers to publish harmless information about himself and his family. That, he says, is idle gossip, and it distracts "ignorant and thoughtless" newspaper readers from more high-minded subjects. It also afflicts the refined and cultured members of society—like, say, Samuel Dennis Warren and his wife—who need solitude but who are instead harassed by the fruits of "modern enterprise and invention."

What's remarkable about "The Right to Privacy" is that the article's title still invokes reverence, even though its substance is, well, laughable.

Is there anyone alive who thinks it should be illegal for the media to reveal the guest-list at a prominent socialite's dinner party or to describe how elaborate the floral arrangements were? . . .

Equally peculiar is the suggestion that we should keep such information from the inferior classes lest they abandon self-improvement and wallow instead in gossip about their betters. That makes Brandeis sound like a wuss and a snob.

He does sound quite up-to-date when he complains that "modern enterprise and invention" are invading our solitude. That is a familiar complaint. It's what privacy advocates are saying today about Google, not to mention the National Security Agency (NSA). Until you realize that he's complaining about the scourge of "instantaneous photographs and newspaper enterprise." Huh? Brandeis evidently thinks that publishing a private citizen's photo in the newspaper causes "mental pain and distress, far greater than could be inflicted by mere bodily injury."

If we agreed today, of course, we probably wouldn't have posted 5 billion photographs of ourselves and our friends on Flickr.

Spirit of the Privacy Movement Today

Anachronistic as it seems, the spirit of Brandeis's article is still the spirit of the privacy movement. The right to privacy was born as a reactionary defense of the status quo, and so it remains. Then, as now, new technology suddenly made it possible to spread information more cheaply and more easily. This was new, and uncomfortable. But apart from a howl of pain—pain "far greater than . . . mere bodily injury"—Brandeis doesn't tell us why it's so bad. I guess you had to be there—literally. . . .

We should not mock Brandeis too harshly. His article clearly conveys a heartfelt sense of invasion. But it is a sense of invasion we can never share. The sensitivity about being photographed or mentioned in the newspapers, a raw spot that rubbed Brandeis so painfully, has calloused over. So thick is the callous that most of us would be tickled, not appalled, to have our dinner parties make the local paper, and especially so if it included our photos.

And that's the second thing that Brandeis's article can tell us about more contemporary privacy flaps. His brand of resistance to change is still alive and well in privacy circles, even if the targets have been updated. Each new privacy kerfuffle inspires strong feelings precisely because we are reacting against the effects of a new technology. Yet as time goes on, the new technology becomes commonplace. Our reaction dwindles away. The raw spot grows a callous. And once the initial reaction has passed,

so does the sense that our privacy has been invaded. In short, we get used to it.

At the beginning, of course, we don't want to get used to it. We want to keep on living the way we did before, except with a few more amenities. And so, like Brandeis, we are tempted to ask the law to stop the changes we see coming. There's nothing more natural, or more reactionary, than that.

Most privacy advocates don't see themselves as reactionaries or advocates for the status quo, of course. Right and left, they cast themselves as underdogs battling for change against the entrenched forces of big government. But virtually all of their activism is actually devoted to stopping change—keeping the government (and sometimes industry) from taking advantage of new technology to process and use information.

But simply opposing change, especially technological change, is a losing battle. At heart, the privacy groups know it, which may explain some of their shrillness and lack of perspective. Information really does "want to be free"—or at least cheap. And the spread of cheap information about all of us will change our relationship to the world. We will have fewer secrets. Crippling government by preventing it from using information that everyone else can get will not give us back our secrets.

In the 1970s, well before the personal computer and the Internet, privacy campaigners persuaded the country that the FBI's newspaper clipping files about U.S. citizens were a threat to privacy. Sure, the information was public, they acknowledged, but gathering it all in one file was viewed as vaguely sinister. The attorney general banned the practice in the absence of some legal reason for doing so, usually called an investigative "predicate."

So, in 2001, when Google had made it possible for anyone to assemble a clips file about anyone in seconds, the one institution in the country that could not print out the results of its Google searches about Americans was the FBI. This was bad for our security, and it didn't protect anyone's privacy either.

The privacy campaigners are fighting the inevitable. The "permanent record" our high school principals threatened us with is already here—in Facebook. Anonymity, its thrills and its freedom, has been characteristic of big cities for centuries. But anonymity will also grow scarce as data becomes easier and easier to gather and correlate. We will lose something as a result, no question about it. The privacy groups' response is profoundly conservative in the William F. Buckley sense—standing athwart history yelling, "Stop!" . . .

That might work if governments didn't need the data for important goals such as preventing terrorists from entering the country. After September 11, though, we can no longer afford the forced inefficiency of denying modern information technology to government. In the long run, any effective method of ensuring privacy is going to have to focus on using technology in a smart way, not just trying to make government slow and stupid.

The Evolution of Technology & the "Zone of Privacy"

That doesn't mean we have to give up all privacy protection. It just means that we have to look for protections that work with technology instead of against it. We can't stop technology from making information cheap and reducing anonymity, but we can deploy that same technology to make sure that government officials can't misuse data and hide their tracks. This new privacy model is partially procedural—greater oversight and transparency—and partly substantive—protecting individuals from actual adverse consequences rather than hypothetical informational injuries.

Under this approach, the first people who should lose their privacy are the government workers with access to personal data. They should be subject to audit, to challenge, and to punishment if they use the data for improper purposes. That's an approach that works with emerging technology to build the world we want to live in. In contrast, it is simple Luddism to keep government from doing with information technology what every other part of society can do.

The problem is that Luddism always has appeal. "Change is bad" is a slogan that has never lacked for adherents, and privacy advocates sounded alarm after alarm with that slogan as the backdrop when we tried to put in place a data-based border screening system.

But would we really thank our ancestors if they'd taken the substance of Brandeis's article as seriously as its title? If, without a legislature ever considering the question, judges had declared that no one could publish true facts about a man's nonpolitical life, or even his photograph, without his permission?

I don't think so. Things change. Americans grow less private about their sex lives but more private about financial matters. Today, few of us are willing to have strangers living in our homes, listening to our family conversations, and then gossiping about us over the back fence with the strangers who live in our friends' homes. Yet I'll bet that both Brandeis and Warren tolerated without a second thought the limits that having servants put on their privacy.

Why does our concept of privacy vary from time to time? Here's one theory: Privacy is allied with shame. We are all ashamed of something about ourselves, something we would prefer that no one, or just a few people, know about. We want to keep it private. Sometimes, of course, we should be ashamed. Criminals always want privacy for their acts. But we're also ashamed—or at least feel embarrassment, the first cousin of shame—about a lot of things that aren't crimes.

We may be ashamed of our bodies, at least until we're sure we won't be mocked for our physical shortcomings. Privacy is similar; we are often quite willing to share information about ourselves, including what we look like without our clothes, when we trust our audience, or when the context makes us believe that our shortcomings will go unnoticed. . . .

The things that Brandeis considered privacy invasions are similar. Very few of us are happy the first time we see our photograph or an interview in the newspaper. But pretty soon we realize it's just not that big a deal. Our nose and our style of speech are things that the people we know have already accepted, and no one else cares enough to embarrass us about them. The same is true when we Google ourselves and see that a bad review of our dinner-theater performance is number three on the list. Our first reaction is embarrassment and unhappiness, but the reaction is oddly evanescent.

If this is so, then the "zone of privacy" is going to vary from time to time and place to place—just as our concept of physical modesty does. The zone of privacy has boundaries on two sides. We don't care about some information that might be revealed about us, probably because the revelation causes us no harm—or we've gotten used to it. If the information is still embarrassing, we want to keep it private, and society may agree. But we can't expect privacy for information that society views as truly shameful or criminal.

Over time, information will move into and out of the zone of privacy on both sides. Some information will simply become so unthreatening that we'll laugh at the idea that it is part of the privacy zone. . . .

The biggest privacy battles will often be in circumstances where the rules are changing. The subtext of many Internet privacy fights, for example, is whether some new measure will expose the identities of people who download pornography or copyrighted music and movies. Society is divided about how shameful it is to download these items, and it displaces that moral and legal debate into a fight about privacy.

Divorce litigation, for instance, is brutal in part because information shared in a context of love and confidence ends up being disclosed to the world in a deliberately harmful way. Often the activity in question (like making a telephone call or a credit card purchase) is something that the individual does freely, with clear knowledge that some other people (his bank or his phone company) know what he is doing. . . .

In those cases, the privacy concern is not that the bank or the phone company (or our spouse) actually has the information, but rather what they will do with the information they have—whether they will use the data in ways we didn't expect or give the data to someone who can harm us. We want to make sure the data will not be used to harm us in unexpected ways.

And that helps explain why privacy advocates are so often Luddite in inclination. Modern technology keeps changing the ways in which information is used. Once, we could count on practical obscurity—the difficulty of finding bits of data from our past—to protect us from unexpected disclosures. Now, storage costs are virtually nil, and processing power is increasing exponentially. It is no longer possible to assume that your data, even though technically public, will never actually be used. It is dirt cheap for data processors to compile dossiers on individuals, and to use the data in ways we didn't expect.

Some would argue that this isn't really "privacy" so much as a concern about abuse of information. However it's defined, though, the real question is what kind of protection is it reasonable for us to expect. Can we really write a detailed legislative or contractual pre-nup for each disclosure, setting forth exactly how our data will be used before we hand it over? I doubt it. Maybe we can forbid obvious misuses, but the more detailed we try to get, the more we run into the problem that our notions of what is private, and indeed of what is embarrassing, are certain to change over time. If so, does it make sense to freeze today's privacy preferences into law?

In fact, that's the mistake that Brandeis made—and the last lesson we can learn from the odd mix of veneration and guffawing that his article provokes. Brandeis wanted to extend common law copyright until it covered everything that can be recorded about an individual. The purpose was to protect the individual from all the new technologies and businesses that had suddenly made it easy to gather and disseminate personal information: "the too enterprising press, the photographer, or the possessor of any other modern device for rewording or reproducing scenes or sounds." . . .

Every year, information gets cheaper to store and to duplicate. Computers, iPods, and the Internet are all "modern devices" for "reproducing scenes or sounds," which means that any effort to control reproduction of pictures, sounds, and scenes becomes extraordinarily difficult if not impossible. In fact, it can't be done.

There is a deep irony here. Brandeis thought that the way to ensure the strength of his new right to privacy was to enforce it just like state copyright law. If you don't like the way "your" private information is distributed, you can sue everyone who publishes it. One hundred years later, the owners of federal statutory copyrights in popular music and movies followed this prescription to a T. They began to use litigation to protect their data rights against "the possessor[s] of any other modern device for . . . reproducing scenes or sounds," a class that now included many of their customers. The Recording Industry Association of America (RIAA) sued consumers by the tens of thousands for using their devices to copy and distribute songs.

Unwittingly, the RIAA gave a thorough test to Brandeis's notion that the law could simply stand in front of new technology and bring it to a halt through litigation. There aren't a lot of people who think that that has worked out well for the RIAA's members, or for their rights. . . .

It's one thing to redirect the path of technological change by a few degrees. It's another to insist that it take a right angle. Brandeis wanted it to take a right angle; he wanted to defy the changes that technology was pressing upon him. So did the RIAA.

Both were embracing a kind of Luddism—a reactionary spasm in the face of technological change. They were doomed to fail. The new technologies, after all, empowered ordinary citizens and consumers in ways that could not be resisted. If the law tries to keep people from enjoying the new technologies, in the end it is the law that will suffer.

But just because technologies are irresistible does not mean that they cannot be guided, or cannot have their worst effects offset by other technologies. The solutions I'm advocating will only work if they allow the world to keep practically all the benefits of the exponential empowerment that new technology makes possible.

Privacy for the Real World: Proposed Solutions

So what's my solution to the tension between information technology and our current sense of privacy? . . .

But before talking about what *might* work, let's take a closer look at some of the ideas that don't.

Ownership of Personal Data

The first privacy solution is one we've already seen. It's the Brandeisian notion that we should all "own" our personal data. That has some appeal, of course. If I have a secret, it feels a lot like property. I can choose to keep it to myself, or I can share it with a few people whom I trust. And I would like to believe that sharing a secret with a few trusted friends doesn't turn it into public property. It's like my home. Just because I've invited one guest home doesn't mean the public is welcome.

But in the end, information is not really like property. Property can only be held by one person at a time, or at most by a few people. But information can be shared and kept at the same time. And those with whom it is shared can pass it on to others at little or no cost. If you ever told a friend about your secret crush in junior high, you've already learned that information cannot be controlled like property. As Ben Franklin is credited with saying, "Three may keep a secret if two of them are dead." . . .

The recording and movie industries discovered the same thing. If these industries with their enormous lobbying and litigation budgets cannot control information that they own as a matter of law, the rest of us are unlikely to be able to control information about ourselves. Gossip is not going to become illegal simply because technology amplifies it. . . .

In fact, so transformed is Brandeis's privacy doctrine that it is now described, accurately, as a "right of publicity," which surely would have him turning in his grave. Currently, most states honor Brandeis by allowing lawsuits for unauthorized commercial use of a person's likeness, either by statute or judge-made law. . . .

Judges began shrinking the [property] right until it only had bite in the one set of circumstances where the right to control one's image actually feels like a property right—when the image is worth real bucks. Thus, the courts require disgorgement of profits made when a celebrity's name, face, voice, or even personal style is used without permission to sell or endorse products. As a result, the right to exploit a celebrity's image really is property today; it can be sold, transferred, and even inherited.

There's only one problem with this effort to turn privacy into property: it hasn't done much for privacy. It simply protects the right of celebrities to make money off their fame. In fact, by monetizing things like celebrity images, it rewards those who have most relentlessly sacrificed their privacy to gain fame.

The right of publicity is well named. It is the right to put your privacy up for sale. Not surprisingly, a lot of people have been inspired to do just that. Ironically, Brandeis's doctrine has helped to destroy the essence of what he hoped to preserve.

Oh, and in the process, Brandeis's approach has stifled creativity and restricted free speech—muzzling artists, social commentators, and businesspeople who want to make creative use of images that are an essential part of our cultural environment. It's a disaster. Slowly, courts are waking up to the irony and limiting the right of publicity.

The same "private information as property" approach has also made a modest appearance in some consumer privacy laws, and it's worked out just as badly. At bottom, consumer privacy protection laws like the Right to Financial Privacy Act treat a consumer's data like a consumer's money: You can give your data (or your money) to a company in exchange for some benefit, but only if you've been told the terms of the transaction and have consented. Similarly, the Cable Communications Policy Act of 1984 prevents cable providers from using or releasing personal information in most cases unless the providers get the customer's consent. The fruit of this approach is clear to anyone with a bank account or an Internet connection. Everywhere you turn, you're confronted with "informed consent" and "terms of service" disclosures; these are uniformly impenetrable and non-negotiable. No one reads them before clicking the box, so the "consent" is more fiction than reality; certainly it does little to protect privacy. Indeed, it's turning out a lot like the right of publicity. By treating privacy as property, consumer privacy protection law invites all of us to sell our privacy.

And we do. Only for most of us, the going price turns out to be disconcertingly cheap.

Mandatory Predicates for Information Access

The second way of protecting privacy is to require what's called a "predicate" for access to information. That's a name only a lawyer could love. In fact, the whole concept is one that only lawyers love.

Simply put, the notion is that government shouldn't get certain private information unless it satisfies a threshold requirement—a "predicate" for access to the data. Lawyers have played a huge role in shaping American thinking about privacy, and the predicate approach has been widely adopted as a privacy protection. But its value for that purpose is quite doubtful.

The predicate approach to privacy can be traced to the Fourth Amendment, which guarantees that "no Warrants shall issue, but upon probable cause." Translated from legalese, this means that the government may not search your home unless it has a good reason to do so. When the government asks for a search warrant, it must show the judge "probable cause"—evidence that the search will likely turn up criminal evidence or contraband. Probable cause is the predicate for the search.

When a flap arose in the 1970s over the FBI practice of assembling domestic security dossiers on Americans who had not broken the law, the attorney general stepped in to protect their privacy. He issued new guidelines for the FBI. He was a lawyer, so he declared that the FBI could not do domestic security investigations of Americans without a predicate.

The predicate wasn't probable cause; that was too high a standard. Instead, the attorney general allowed the launching of a domestic security investigation only if the bureau presented "specific and articulable facts giving reason to believe" that the subject of the investigation may be involved in violence.

Actually, the story of the FBI guidelines shows why the predicate approach often fails. The dossiers being assembled by the FBI were often just clippings and other public information. They usually weren't the product of a search in the classic sense; no federal agents had entered private property to obtain the information. Nonetheless, the FBI guidelines treated the gathering of the information itself as though it were a kind of search.

In so doing, the guidelines were following in Brandeis's footsteps—treating information as though it were physical property. The collection of the information was equated to a physical intrusion into the home or office of the individual. Implicitly, it assumes that data can be locked up like property.

But that analogy has already failed. It failed for Brandeis and it failed for the RIAA. It failed for the FBI guidelines, too. As clippings became easier to retrieve, clippings files became easier to assemble. Then Google made it possible for anyone to assemble an electronic clips file on anyone. There was nothing secret about the clippings then. They were about as private as a bus terminal.

But the law was stuck in another era. Under the guidelines, only the FBI and CIA needed a predicate to do Google searches. You have to be a pretty resilient society to decide that you want to deny to your law enforcement agencies a tool that is freely available to nine-year-old girls and terrorist gangs. Resilient, but stupid. (Not surprisingly, the guidelines were revised after 9/11.)

That's one reason we shouldn't treat the assembling of data as though it were a search of physical property. As technology makes it easier and easier to collect data, the analogy between doing that and conducting a search of a truly private space will become less and less persuasive. No one thinks government agencies should have a predicate to use the White Pages. Soon, predicates that keep law enforcement from collecting information in other ways will become equally anachronistic, leaving law enforcement stuck in the 1950s while everyone else gets to live in the twenty-first century.

Limits on Information Use

That leaves the third approach to privacy, one we've already seen in action. If requiring a predicate is the lawyer's solution; this third approach is the bureaucrat's solution. It is at heart the approach adopted by the European Union: Instead of putting limits on when information may be collected, it sets limits on how the information is used.

The European Union's data protection principles cover a lot of ground, but their unifying theme is imposing limits on how private data is used. Under those principles, personal data may only be used in ways that are consistent with the purposes for which the data were gathered. Any data that is retained must be relevant to the original purposes and must be stored securely to prevent misuse.

The EU's negotiating position in the passenger name records conflict was largely derived from this set of principles. The principles also explain Europe's enthusiasm for a wall between law enforcement and intelligence. If DHS gathered reservation data for the purpose of screening travelers when they cross the border, why should any other agency be given access to the data? This also explains the EU's insistence on short deadlines for the destruction of PNR data. Once it had been used to screen passengers, it had served the purpose for which it was gathered and should be promptly discarded.

There is a core of sense in this solution. It focuses mainly on the consequences of collecting information, and not on the act of collection. It doesn't try to insist that information is property. It recognizes that when we give information to others, we usually have an expectation about how it will be used, and as long as the use fits our expectations, we aren't too fussy about who exactly gets to see it. By concentrating on how personal information is used, this solution may get closer to the core of privacy than one that focuses on how personal information is collected.

It has another advantage, too. In the case of government databases, focusing on use also allows us to acknowledge the overriding importance of some government data systems while still protecting against petty uses of highly personal information.

Call it the deadbeat-dad problem, or call it mission creep, but there's an uncomfortable pattern to the use of data by governments. Often, personal data must be gathered for a pressing reason—the prevention of crime or terrorism, perhaps, or the administration of a social security system. Then, as time goes on, it becomes attractive to use the data for other, less pressing purposes—collecting child support, perhaps, or enforcing parking tickets. No one would support the gathering of a large personal database simply to collect unpaid parking fines; but "mission creep" can easily carry the database well beyond its original purpose. A limitation on use prevents mission creep, or at least forces a debate about each step in the expansion.

That's all fine. But in the end, this solution is also flawed.

It, too, is fighting technology, though less obviously than the predicate and property approaches. Data that has already been gathered is easier to use for other purposes. It's foolish to pretend otherwise. Indeed, developments in information technology in recent years have produced real strides in searching unstructured data or in finding relationships in data without knowing for sure that the data will actually produce anything useful. In short, there are now good reasons to collate data gathered for widely differing purposes, just to see the patterns that emerge.

This new technical capability is hard to square with use limitations or with early destruction of data. For if collating data in the government's hands could have prevented a successful terrorist attack, no one will congratulate the agency that refused to allow the collation because the data was collected for tax or regulatory purposes, say, and not to catch terrorists.

What's more, use limitations have caused great harm when applied too aggressively. The notorious "wall" between law enforcement and intelligence was at heart a use limitation. It assumed that law enforcement agencies would gather information using their authority, and then would use the information only for law enforcement purposes. Intelligence agencies would do the same. Or so the theory went. But strict enforcement of this use limitation was unimaginably costly. In August 2001, two terrorists were known to have entered the United States. As the search for them began, the government's top priority was enforcing the wall—keeping intelligence about the terrorists from being used by the "wrong" part of the FBI. Government lawyers insisted that law enforcement resources could not be used to pursue intelligence that two known al Qaeda agents were in the United States in August 2001.

This was a fatal blunder. The criminal investigators were well-resourced and eager. They might have found the men. The intelligence investigators, in contrast, had few resources and did not locate the terrorists, at least not until September 11, when the terrorists' names were discovered on the manifests of the hijacked planes. It was a high price to pay for the modest comfort of "use" limitations.

Like all use limitations, the "wall" between law enforcement sounded reasonable enough in the abstract. While no one could point to a real privacy abuse arising from cooperation between the intelligence and law enforcement agencies in the United States, it was easy to point to the Gestapo and other totalitarian organizations where there had been too much cooperation among agencies.

So, what might have been a sensible, modest use restriction preventing the dissemination of information without a good reason became an impermeable barrier.

That's why the bureaucratic system for protecting privacy so often fails. The use restrictions and related limits are abstract. They make a kind of modest sense, but if they are enforced too strictly, they prevent new uses of information that may be critically important.

And often they are enforced too strictly. You don't have to tell a bureaucrat twice to withhold information from a rival agency. Lawsuits, bad press, and Congressional investigations all seem to push against a flexible reading of the rules. If a use for information is not identified at the outset, it can be nearly impossible to add the use later, no matter how sensible the change may seem. This leads agencies to try to draft broad uses for the data they collect, which defeats the original point of setting use restrictions.

It's like wearing someone else's dress. Over time, use restrictions end up tight where they should be roomy—and loose where they should be tight. No one is left satisfied.

The Audit Approach: Enforced Accountability

So what will work? Simple: accountability, especially electronically-enforced accountability.

The best way to understand this solution is to begin with Barack Obama's passport records—and with "Joe the Plumber." These were two minor flaps that punctuated the 2008 presidential campaign. But both tell us something about how privacy is really protected these days.

In March of 2008, Barack Obama and Hillary Clinton were dueling across the country in weekly primary showdowns. Suddenly, the campaign took an odd turn. The Bush administration's State Department announced that it had fired or disciplined several contractors for examining Obama's passport records.

Democrats erupted. It wasn't hard to jump to the conclusion that the candidate's files had been searched for partisan purposes. After an investigation, the flap slowly deflated. It soon emerged that all three of the main presidential candidates' passport files had been improperly accessed. Investigators reported that the State Department was able to quickly identify who had examined the files by using its computer audit system. This system flagged any unusual requests for access to the files of prominent Americans. The fired contractors did not deny the computer record. Several of them were charged with crimes and pleaded guilty. All, it turned out, had acted purely out of "curiosity."

Six months later, it was the Republicans' turn to howl about privacy violations in the campaign. Samuel "Joe" Wurzelbacher, a plumber, became an overnight hero to Republicans in October 2008 after he was practically the only person who laid a glove on Barack Obama during the campaign. The candidate made an impromptu stop in Wurzelbacher's Ohio neighborhood and was surprised when the plumber forced him into a detailed on-camera defense of his tax plan. Three days later, "Joe the Plumber" and his taxes were invoked dozens of times in the presidential debates.

The price of fame was high. A media frenzy quickly stripped Wurzelbacher of anonymity. Scouring the public record, reporters found that the plumber had been hit with a tax lien; they also found government data that raised doubts about the status of his plumbing license.

Reporters weren't the only ones digging. Ohio state employees also queried confidential state records about Wurzelbacher. In all, they conducted eighteen state records checks on Wurzelbacher. They asked whether the plumber owed child support, whether he'd ever received welfare or unemployment benefits, and whether he was in any Ohio law enforcement databases. Some of these searches were proper responses to media requests under Ohio open records laws; others looked more like an effort to dig dirt on the man.

Ohio's inspector general launched an investigation and in less than a month was able to classify all but one of the eighteen records searches as either legitimate or improper. Thirteen searches were traced and deemed proper, but three particularly intrusive searches were found improper; they had been carried out at the request of a high-ranking state employee who was also a strong Obama supporter. She was suspended from her job and soon stepped down. A fourth search was traced to a former information technology contractor who had not been authorized to search the system he accessed; he was placed under criminal investigation.

What do these two flaps have in common? They were investigated within weeks of the improper access, and practically everyone involved was immediately caught. That's vitally important. Information technology isn't just taking away your privacy or mine. It's taking away the privacy of government workers even faster. Data is cheap to gather and cheap to store. It's even getting cheap to analyze.

So it isn't hard to identify every official who accessed a particular file on a particular day. That's what happened here. And the consequences for privacy are profound.

If the lawyer's solution is to put a predicate between government and the data and the bureaucrat's solution is to put use restrictions on the data, then this is the auditor's solution. Government access to personal data need not be restricted by speed bumps or walls. Instead, it can be protected by rules, so long as the rules are enforced.

What's new is that network security and audit tools now make it easy to enforce the rules. That's important because it takes the profit motive out of misuse of government data. No profit-motivated official is going to take the risk of stealing personal data if it's obvious that he'll be caught as soon as people start to complain about identity theft. Systematic misuse of government databases is a lot harder and more dangerous if good auditing is in place.

If the plight of government investigators trying to prevent terrorist attacks doesn't move you, think about the plight of medical technicians trying to keep you alive after a bad traffic accident.

The Obama administration has launched a long-overdue effort to bring electronic medical records into common use. But the privacy problem in this area is severe. Few of us want our medical records to be available to casual browsers. At the same time, we can't personally verify the bona fides of the people accessing our records, especially if we're lying by the side of the road suffering from what looks like brain or spine damage.

But the electronic record system won't work if it can't tell the first responders that you have unusual allergies or a pacemaker. It has to do that quickly and without a lot of formalities. Auditing access after the fact is likely to be our best answer to this problem, as it is to the very similar problem of how to let law enforcement and intelligence agencies share information smoothly and quickly in response to changing and urgent circumstances.

These technologies can be very flexible. This makes them especially suitable for cases where outright denial of data access could have fatal results. The tools can be set to give some people immediate access, or to open the databases in certain situations, with an audit to follow. They can monitor each person with access to the data and learn that person's access patterns—what kinds of data, at what time, for how long, with or without copying, and the like. Deviations from the established pattern can have many consequences. Perhaps access will be granted but the person will be alerted that an explanation must be offered within twenty-four hours. Or access could be granted while a silent alarm sounds, allowing systems administrators to begin a real-time investigation.

There's a kind of paradox at the heart of this solution. We can protect people from misuse of their data, but only by stripping network users of any privacy or anonymity when they look at the data. The privacy campaigners aren't likely to complain, though. In our experience, their interest in preserving the privacy of intelligence and law enforcement officers is pretty limited.

In the end, that's the difference between a privacy policy that makes sense and one that doesn't. We can't lock up data that is getting cheaper every day. Pretending that it's property won't work. Putting "predicates" between government and the data it needs won't work, and neither will insisting that they may only be used for purposes foreseen when it was collected.

What we *can* do is use new information technology tools to deter government officials from misusing their access to that data.

As you know by now, I think that some technology poses extraordinary risks. But we can avoid the worst risks if we take action early. We shouldn't try to stop the trajectory of new technology. But we can bend it just a little. Call it a course correction on an exponential curve.

That's also true for privacy. The future is coming—like it or not. Our data will be everywhere. But we can bend the curve of technology to make those who hold the data more accountable. Bending the exponential curve a bit—that's a privacy policy that could work. And a technology policy that makes sense.

STEWART BAKER was the first Assistant Secretary for Policy at the Department of Homeland Security. He has served as counsel for the National Security Agency and is currently a partner in the law office of Steptoe & Johnson.

EXPLORING THE ISSUE

Does Technology Invade Our Privacy?

Critical Thinking and Reflection

1. Analyze a situation in which technology leads us to think one thing (providing an illusion of anonymity or privacy) while creating a situation in which anonymity/privacy can be easily violated. Should new laws be created to solve these problems?
2. Consider the varying definitions of privacy presented by these authors. Can you create one of your own?
3. Is privacy becoming less "important" in a society in which we use so many technologies in public places?
4. Should the NSA have warrantless access to digital records?

Is There Common Ground?

The selections on this issue are just the tip of the iceberg when it comes to considering the implications of surveillance access to the many ways in which we communicate digitally every day. Wiki Leaks, the NSA scandals, even the attention you are likely to attract if you begin searching the net for information on building bombs reveals that we have no real understanding of the information that can and has been created about any of us. This is an issue that goes far beyond protecting our personal information.

The rights of the individual will often suffer in times of crisis. It is only through constant vigilance that such rights can be protected. Traditionally, we have invoked the Fourth Amendment to the Constitution as providing us our right to personal privacy in our own home, but how does that hold up when we use technologies to communicate in public settings? Warrants are required to search our homes and must show probable cause for the search. What is the appropriate level of legal requirements to gain access to our personal communications? It seems unlikely that these opposing viewpoints will easily find common ground.

Create Central

www.mhhe.com/createcentral

Additional Resources

Lori Andrews, *I Know Who You Are and I Saw What You Did: Social Networks and the Death of Privacy* (Free Press, 2011)

James Bamford, *The Shadow Factory: The NSA from 9/11 to the Eavesdropping on America* (Anchor, 2009)

Yves-Alexandre de Montjoye, César A. Hidalgo, Michel Verleysen, and Vincent D. Blondel. "Unique in the Crowd: The Privacy Bounds of Human Mobility," *Nature* (March 2013)

Erik Sofge and Davin Coburn, *Popular Mechanics: Who's Spying on You? The Looming Threat to Your Privacy, Identity, and Family in the Digital Age* (Hearst, 2012)

Siva Vaidhyanathan, *The Googlization of Everything (And Why We Should Worry)* (University of California Press, 2011)

Internet References . . .

American Civil Liberties Union (ACLU)

http://aclu-wa.org/student-rights-and-responsibilities-digital-age-guide-public-school-students-washington-state

Pew Internet & American Life Project: Anonymity, Privacy and Security Online

www.pewinternet.org/Reports/2013/Anonymity-online.aspx

Privacy.Org: The Site for News, Information and Action

http://privacy.org/

Privacy Rights Clearinghouse

www.privacyrights.org/fs/fs18-cyb.htm

Shorenstein Center's Journalist's Resource

http://journalistsresource.org/studies/society/internet/the-state-of-internet-privacy-in-2013-research-roundupissue

Selected, Edited, and with Issue Framing Material by:
Alison Alexander, *University of Georgia*
and
Jarice Hanson, *University of Massachusetts—Amherst*

ISSUE

Does the Internet Change the Way We Think of Copyright and Plagiarism?

YES: Marc Fisher, from "Steal This Idea," *Columbia Journalism Review* (2015)

NO: Louis Menand, from "Crooner in Rights Spat," *The New Yorker* (2014)

Learning Outcomes

After reading this issue, you will be able to:

- Think about whether some laws become outdated, and what is necessary to change them.
- Realize how easy it is to alter original content with digital technology.
- Think about how often you, or people you know, use material without attribution.
- Think about remix culture, mash-ups, and derivative content.
- Reflect on the impact of digital technology as it changes traditional ideas of what is "right."

ISSUE SUMMARY

YES: Marc Fisher is a senior editor at *The Washington Post* and recently held the position of Enterprise Editor for local news at the *Post*, where he led a team of writers who were experimenting with new forms of storytelling and journalism for both the print and online versions of the newspaper.

NO: Louis Menand is a Professor of History at Harvard University. He also is a past editor of *The New Yorker*, a contributing editor to *The New York Review of Books*, and a former associate editor at *The New Republic*. He was awarded the 2002 Pulitzer Prize for history for his book *The Metaphysical Club*, for which he also won the Francis Parkman Prize from the Society of American Historians.

Copyright and plagiarism are closely aligned. While there may be laws that specifically reflect the history of copyright and the ownership of intellectual property, plagiarism is an action that builds upon other people's ideas. Often it is fairly easy, especially with the tools Fisher describes, to check on original content to see if plagiarism occurs, but at the same time, when do the thoughts or writings of others influence someone to think differently? In that situation, what moral imperative is there to cite original ideas as new ideas are developed? As the authors for these two selections indicate, current issues of copyright and plagiarism go beyond ideas into thinking about new, digitally produced remix or mashup cultural products.

Both of the authors in these selections focus on the practice of plagiarism and copyright in professionally produced media content, but the issues they raise go beyond the professional world and affect our decisions daily. Most films, television shows, and photocopies of printed materials all are easy to copy in digital format today. It is often hard to tell the difference between an original media artifact and a duplicated one, and, as the authors show, the Internet is largely responsible for distributing content that is easily appropriated by others. While there are many stories of professional communicators who have violated copyright and are responsible for their plagiarized material, we should also consider our own behaviors and whether we are more willing to accept violations of practices when we engage in them ourselves. If we—willingly or unwittingly—violate copyright or we knowingly or unknowingly plagiarize something—does our own sense of entitlement influence the way we think laws and practices should be realized in the larger social context?

Undoubtedly, copyright laws have become tangled in a web of technological change and the changing social mores about ownership. You might clearly state that taking someone's car without his knowledge is stealing, but is that the same thing as when you borrow a friend's DVD or CD and burn a copy for your own use? The media industries are understandably concerned about protecting their products and profits. New artists hope to make a living off of their music or the films, videos, or games they create. And yet, there is something about the ephemeral nature of digital media that seems to encourage illegal behavior in many situations. Many people claim they can't afford to buy music or pay for the films they want to see, so they share passwords with friends to "borrow" services, but this is a hollow argument. The Recording Industry Association of America acknowledges that when music files can be purchased inexpensively, the amount of illegal copyright violations go down, but the problem is a sticky one for those industries that would like to retain control of the products they distribute and the profits that allow them to continue to operate.

Several alternatives have been suggested to deal with updating copyright and clarifying plagiarism and the practice of unauthorized use of original material. Fair use is a category of copyright law that allows some use of copyrighted materials for purposes of education, parody, commentary, or other noncommercial purposes, but still, correct attribution should be given to the original material. The Electronic Frontier Foundation and the GNU Project both advocate an idea called "copyleft," which is an alternative to copyright and allows people to use original content that is licensed (through a copyleft license) to manipulate the original data to develop something new; but still, attributing the original content to the authors is required, and fulfills a moral and ethical imperative to give credit where credit is due. The Creative Commons is another alternative to copyright, and it too allows for sharing of materials that does not result in payment to the original author, but the original author agrees to allow others to use the material. This is very much the ethical imperative of "freeware" or "open source" models of sharing content that go beyond traditional legal definitions of copyright and/or plagiarism.

Despite the alternatives, copyright is a deeply engrained legal concept that has consequences for individual authors and the nations that sometimes have different copyright laws that affect international distribution of content. Despite many countries' general adherence to the Berne Convention guidelines, some countries have laws about copyright that are very different from U.S. law. For example, Sweden has much more flexibility in copyright law, and companies that have their base there (like The Pirate Bay) or originally were based in Sweden (like Spotify), have more legal protection to distribute digital content than in other countries where copyright law protects original authors of media content.

In the United States, one of the most important legal precedents dealing with a technology that could potentially violate copyright occurred in 1984 when the Supreme Court heard a case officially called *Sony Corp. of America v. Universal City Studios, Inc.,* 464 U.S. 417. This became known as "the Betamax Case" and dealt with the capability of the new video cassette recorder (VCR) to download television programs to a video cassette for later viewing. While Universal City Studios claimed that people were violating their copyright by recording programs on their VCRs, the Court decided that since the VCR could be used for other purposes than just downloading television content, the technology would be legal. That precedent has influenced many other court decisions in the United States dealing with the capacity of a new technology to challenge a previous application of law. In this case, as long as VCRs could be used for personal uses to view content recorded on home camcorders, or rented videos, the technology was allowed to be marketed and used for other purposes, including the home recording of television program—as long as the user did not sell those recordings for personal profit.

But when professional practices are considered, it is easier to see how professionals—like journalists who ostensibly do original research for their stories—can be caught and discredited for passing off stories that are not true. These people are not only expected to act ethically, but can also damage their own credibility and the credibility of their employers when they do violate copyright through plagiarism. But in today's world, journalism is not confined to mainstream media. Anyone with a blog, or who "publishes" content online, or creates remixes or mashups of digital content also falls into the category of potentially plagiarizing the work of someone else.

Both of the authors in these selections acknowledge that copyright is more than just a set of laws, and that plagiarism is a practice that becomes more difficult to detect in an age of technology that allows consumers to also become producers of content. Is this the time to reflect on the meaning of ownership and the legal, moral, and ethical practices that are evolving? How far should the debate take us? Do we need an overhaul of older laws, or can those laws (and practices) be modified so that they are more in line with the times? This issue is certain to give you plenty to think about, talk about, and, hopefully, it should require you to think about your own use of contemporary media.

YES

Marc Fisher

Steal This Idea

Why Plagiarize When You Can Rip Off a Writer's Thoughts?

I COULD FRAME THIS PIECE about plagiarism by starting with a little verse about a renowned professor who won his fame by appropriating the work of another:

> *Let no one else's work evade your eyes*
> *Remember why the good Lord made your eyes*
>
> *So don't shade your eyes*
>
> *But plagiarize, plagiarize, plagiarize . . .*
>
> *Only be sure always to call it please 'research.'*

I might credit the author of those lines, the satirist and folk singer Tom Lehrer, but you'd likely think me less clever for merely quoting someone when I could have used an idea of my own.

Perhaps I should start off with what put plagiarism back in journalism's center court—a series of allegations against prominent writers such as CNN's Fareed Zakaria, *The New Yorker's* Malcolm Gladwell, and BuzzFeed's Benny Johnson. Surely I could get away with quoting from the allegations without any attribution because the two bloggers who investigated the journalists have remained anonymous. They don't even want credit for their work!

To get at the meta-ness at the heart of journalism's plagiarism problem—the basic question of how we define plagiarism right now—I could pierce through the jabber with this bit of provocation: Substantially all ideas are secondhand, consciously and unconsciously drawn from a million outside sources. The actual and valuable material of all human utterances is plagiarism.

Those last two sentences, I admit, are not mine. The novelist Jonathan Lethem wrote them in *Harper's* (and, actually, he didn't come up with those sentences, either—he took them from Mark Twain). He's so critical of the rigid way most journalists think about plagiarism that he probably wouldn't mind if I took his words and used them

here, so long as I added an additional thought of my own, a bit of a remix.

I'd start with his two sentences and attach a fillip of my own, something like this: Journalists are so fragile right now, so damaged by years of newsroom cuts and diminishing impact, that we're more intent than ever on proving our purity, to ourselves and to our readers. We will therefore land ferociously on any miscreant who borrows even four or five words from another source. We will turn ourselves into the plagiarism police, vainly straining to show that our work is original, when, in fact, nearly all journalism is second-order—that is, we discover, report, and interpret the ideas and actions of others.

The conventions of this profession require that I give Lethem credit for his words, both because simply appropriating his language would be theft of a sort, and because I'd be mucking with the basic compact between writer and reader—the idea that in journalism, credibility is our all.

Both journalism and plagiarism have fallen into a murky new reality in which there's no clear consensus about the old rules. Even the authorities who make the rules disagree over basic definitions. What is plagiarism in a world in which musicians appropriate digital samples of other people's work into their own creations, only to be praised as innovators? What is plagiarism to an audience that grew up believing it's okay to appropriate—really, steal—movies, music, and chunks of written work from the internet? What is plagiarism when prominent lawyers and public policy advocates argue that excessive restraints on the reuse of intellectual content inhibit Americans' creativity?

Artists, musicians, novelists, and even lawyers now debate whether strict old rules about plagiarism unduly restrict what the Constitution calls "the Progress of Science and useful Arts"—the basis for laws of copyright. But is journalism so different from other creative terrain that we must hew to standards that are being relaxed in so many other parts of our culture? Must journalistic rules established way back when cut and paste was a literal instruction now be considered immutable?

This all used to seem so simple: Plagiarism, our high school teachers taught us, is wrong. The Society of Professional Journalists' position paper on the topic is blunt: "Never plagiarize," it says. "Whether inadvertent or deliberate, there is no excuse for plagiarism."

But plagiarism is not that simple. Many old-school purists would agree that if I reworked Lethem's sentences, I would not be a plagiarist—even if my new wording made liberal use of his idea. Why are we stricter about the use of someone else's words than we are about claiming his ideas, when the underlying idea is usually more important than the specific wording? In music, visual art, and an increasing number of other fields, lifting a passage or image from another author can be an honorable act. Call it remix, call it sampling—it's a communal path toward creativity. Yet lifting even a few words from someone else can still get a reporter sacked. How can that be right?

At the risk of exacerbating the generational divide engulfing journalism, let's start by recognizing that some of the current conflict about plagiarism does trace to the year you were born. Things are shifting so quickly that when Susan Drucker teaches journalism and media ethics courses at Hofstra University in New York, she sees a significant gulf between, say, 23-year-olds and 17-year-olds.

"The graduate students still see literary theft as stealing," she says, "but the 17- and 18-year-old undergraduates don't see this as wrong. 'It's so easy to copy material on the internet,' they say. 'How can it be wrong?'"

Drucker doesn't buy into the idea that the undergrads will come to see that the rules are the rules, and that they make sense. "Just look at the language: People don't even say 'copying' or 'theft;' they say 'borrowing' or 'inserting.' As the language changes, so does the sense of guilt. We're becoming comfortable as a culture with the idea that if we add any value at all, we can take credit and authorship. That may seem offensive to older journalists, but in a way, the young people are right, because digital technologies dis-embed: They make it harder to identify the real source of origin. If I mention an article I saw in *The New York Times*, my students will say they read it on Reddit or through Twitter. By the time it reaches them, they're not aware of the original source, and they don't care."

. . .

Still, that's the classroom, not the newsroom, where one would think the dictates of the marketplace and the traditions of the craft would help maintain a useful distinction between work that is new and that which is recycled.

Not so. The same technology that has softened the definition of plagiarism has also made it radically easier to plagiarize, intentionally or not. "I just cut and pasted and then I forgot," say many reporters who have been caught using lifted language. Copied material gets inserted into a reporter's draft and before you know it, the reporter is saying, "I forgot to change the wording," or "I forgot to insert attribution."

"Building on others' stories is nothing new," says Steve Buttry, a longtime editor, most recently at Digital First Media, who teaches and coaches journalists at Louisiana State University. "There was always a genre of story we called the 'clip job,' where a reporter parachuted in, did some original reporting to advance the story, but mainly relied on a whole lot of stuff from other sources that wasn't credited. What's new is that there are people out there being plagiarism cops."

Two prominent members of that new breed of wording police are so much a product of the digital age that they are known only by their Twitter handles, @blippoblappo and @crushingbort, authors of the blog Our Bad Media. Since last summer, the two word cops have used digital technology to level detailed allegations of plagiarism against foreign affairs columnist Zakaria of CNN and *The Washington Post*; Johnson, a master of the listicle at BuzzFeed; and *The New Yorker*'s Gladwell.

Zakaria was previously accused of lifting language from books and articles by other writers; CNN suspended and then reinstated him. His bosses defended him against a second wave of allegations, with [The] *Washington Post* editorial page editor Fred Hiatt saying it's hardly plagiarism to use the same facts that someone else has cited.

Johnson was caught pasting into his own work phrases and sentences from Wikipedia, Yahoo Answers, and a slew of magazines and newspapers. He was immediately sacked at BuzzFeed but quickly landed a job as a social media editor at *National Review*, with Politico's Mike Allen noting that the plagiarist was getting a "surprisingly quick shot at redemption." In February, Johnson joined Independent Journal Review as creative content director.

Since the authors of the blog Our Bad Media won't say who they are or what they do for a living (they say they are not working journalists), we know nothing about their motives, ideological or otherwise. But whether you view the duo as vigilantes or the vanguard of a consumer-driven era of accountability, they have forced editors to consider their allegations and provide answers. Yet despite Our Bad Media's exhaustive detailing of similarities between their targets' stories and the sources they failed to cite, all of the alleged plagiarists are still gainfully employed.

Gladwell's editor, David Remnick, responded to the case against his writer with a statement wondering how best to credit a source: "The issue is an ongoing editorial challenge known to writers and editors everywhere—to what extent should a piece of journalism, which doesn't have the apparatus of academic footnotes, credit secondary sources? It's an issue that can get complicated when there are many sources with overlapping information."

The violations that Our Bad Media seeks to chronicle are the old-fashioned kind: Writers incorporating someone else's work into their own. But a major contributor to the haze around plagiarism these days is a different and rapidly growing kind of journalism—aggregation.

Many editors I spoke to say a disproportionate number of recent plagiarism cases result from the growing practice of producing articles based entirely or mostly on the work of others. Aggregation, many say, makes journalists—especially young ones—especially susceptible to word larceny.

At new media outlets such as BuzzFeed and Mashable as well as at old-line print and broadcast operations, aggregation has emerged as a cheap and effective way to cover a far broader array of news than current staff levels might otherwise support. Aggregation is hardly new; "from combined sources" is a line that ran over countless news stories in papers for upwards of a century, as editors cobbled together accounts using wires and files from major newspapers. But the new aggregators are under increasing pressure to produce fresh copy in the moment to take advantage of whatever's trending on social media.

"With aggregation, there's definitely an erosion of attribution," says Jonathan Bailey, 34, a consultant who blogs at Plagiarism Today and investigates plagiarism allegations for clients, including some news organizations. "The people doing the copying and pasting think they're just sharing the way they would on Facebook. And employers sometimes look the other way because there is money in the added traffic: If I aggregate your story, I'm capturing some of your search traffic and that can cost you tens of thousands in revenue."

Julie Westfall runs the Real-Time News Desk at the *Los Angeles Times*, where she and five reporters try to keep the *Times'* site at the leading edge of events. Their goal is to do as much original reporting as they can, but the nature of breaking and trending news is that the first accounts often come from elsewhere.

"Our job is to help get confirmed stuff on all of our platforms as quickly as possible," says Westfall, 34. "We aggregate when someone has something confirmed that we can't get right away." Although there's no written rule, Westfall tells her staff that "we need to say where

stuff comes from," as in "police told the Associated Press that. . ."

But in the moment, such decisions aren't always simple. "My team and *The Washington Post*'s and Gawker and BuzzFeed are all figuring out when to attribute," Westfall says. "That's where there could be a generational difference. Young people are more likely to say the information is out there and you can't ignore it. Sometimes it's not efficient to keep trying to get hold of a person to essentially say the same thing that they've already said to another reporter."

. . .

In the cultural battles over aggregation, the word "plagiarism" gets bandied about all too loosely. Often, the grumbling about aggregation is really more about basic courtesy. In January, an editor at *The Guardian*, Erin McCann, tweaked BuzzFeed on Twitter for publishing a story based almost entirely on a *Guardian* reporter's account of the opening of Paul Revere's time capsule at a Boston museum. The journalistic infraction was not plagiarism—after all, the BuzzFeed piece was made up primarily of the *Guardian* reporter's tweets, prominently including his name. But nowhere did BuzzFeed acknowledge *The Guardian*, at least not until McCann complained, after which BuzzFeed added a hat tip to the bottom of its piece.

"It would have been nice if they'd said in the text of the BuzzFeed piece that a *Guardian* reporter was on the scene and reported the story," Westfall says. "The fact that that's not done in every single story is the result of the shades of gray"—the lingering uncertainty about when to attribute.

The rule is simple for Buttry, who says he saw several cases of aggregation that crossed the line into plagiarism when he worked at Digital First Media, the newspaper chain that experimented with a heavy emphasis on aggregation for its national and foreign coverage. "They all resulted in discipline, typically a stern rebuke and suspension," he says.

Buttry offers a four-word solution: When in doubt, attribute. "Sometimes you don't remember where you got an idea, or it's a mash-up," he says. "But when you know the source of your inspiration, you should acknowledge it, maybe in the story or maybe in a social media post or even an email to the original reporter. Then that person feels flattered, not ripped off."

That solution, however, assumes that the plagiarist knows he's doing something considered morally wrong. How do you defend against a misdeed when its perpetrators don't think they've broken any rules?

I called a bunch of people who had been caught plagiarizing and had lost their jobs because of it. Some didn't return my messages; those who did said the last thing they wanted to do was freshen up the Google references to the worst episode in their lives.

"The best thing is to just be honest about it," says one former reporter who got caught and never found another job in journalism. "The conversation about plagiarism needs to happen. I'd just rather not be defined by it. All I can say is that anytime you make a mistake like that, it has a short-term and a long-term impact, and both of them are huge."

As a young reporter at a small newspaper, this man lifted a chunk of a press release and put it directly into his story about a local business. The reporter says he thought what he did was considered okay—he was getting the same information across either way, and there wasn't anything special about the news release's wording.

Hearing that he was going to be fired, he quit. Later, he told prospective employers that he'd done "something really, really stupid" and wanted to redeem himself.

Now, he says, he realizes he broke the rules, but he believes plenty of others in his position do the same thing without the slightest notion that they are jeopardizing their jobs.

Kelly McBride spends a lot of her time working with editors who've caught plagiarists and with reporters who've been found out. McBride, who for many years has taught ethics at the Poynter Institute, has no doubt that people who intentionally steal others' work should be fired. Still, she has a root empathy for those who get caught, especially for those she considers petty plagiarists—that is, those with no pattern of abuse.

Often, she says, those cases involve people who panic. Three plagiarists I spoke to blamed their infractions on moving too quickly under pressure to produce, an excuse for which many editors have zero patience, since journalism has always valued speed.

But McBride says the combination of a stepped-up pace of production and a sharp decrease in supervision is producing many more infractions. "These are mostly young people who struggle with the mechanics of writing," she says, "and when you struggle with mechanics, you are much, much more likely to plagiarize."

Add the thinning ranks of editors and you have a problem. "I started out sitting next to editors who showed me, okay, let's find the subject and the verb in this sentence, editors who stuck with me," McBride says. "Without the grace of those editors, I don't know that I'd have made it. In most newsrooms right now, that doesn't happen."

On top of the lack of guidance, there's the shift toward a remix culture and the resulting confusion about what constitutes honest aggregation. "As journalism institutions, we are not clear about standards when we ask people to aggregate," McBride says. "When those young people who start out as aggregators move into original reporting, they will be confused."

Amid that jumble of standards, under the crushing power of the scarlet P, is it time for a ceasefire in the war on plagiarism? Some notorious plagiarists are serial offenders—con artists and fabulists such as Jayson Blair or Stephen Glass—but should there be different penalties for those who broke rules that were never clear to them in the first place?

No one argues for wholesale theft of others' work, but a growing chorus of academics and others find it counterproductive to focus on rooting out scofflaws. As far back as the 19th century, the German poet Heinrich Heine, citing literary stealing by Goethe and Shakespeare, wrote that "Nothing is sillier than this charge of plagiarism . . . The poet dare help himself wherever . . . he finds material suited to his work."

In all forms of art and culture, appropriation of others' work is essential to creativity, Lethem contends. The American mistake, he says, has been to adopt a mercantile, legalistic ethic in which a piece of writing is a commercial product rather than a way to advance ideas and spread information for the public good.

Lawrence Lessig, a Harvard law professor, takes the notion that ideas want to be free a step farther. In his books, Free *Culture* and *Remix*, Lessig says it's wrong to apply to writing the same rules we use to protect against theft. "Ideas released to the world are free," he writes. "I don't take anything from you when I copy the way you dress." He quotes Thomas Jefferson: "He who receives an idea from me, receives instruction himself without lessening mine; as he who lights his taper at mine, receives light without darkening me."

Gladwell, responding to Our Bad Media's allegations, directed readers to a piece he wrote for *The New Yorker* in 2004 about his reaction when a playwright used, without attribution, passages from one of his own articles. Initially miffed, Gladwell examined why plagiarism has become such an ethical tripwire. When he finally confronted the playwright, Bryony Lavery, about why she hadn't credited him for the material, she told him: "I thought it was OK to use it . . . I thought it was news."

Gladwell found some merit in that notion. "When I worked at a newspaper," he wrote, "we were routinely dispatched to 'match' a story from the Times: to do a new version of someone else's idea. But had we 'matched' any of the *Times'* words—even the most banal of phrases—it could have been a firing offense."

That notion of originality, Gladwell concluded, is "the narcissism of small differences: Because journalism cannot own up to its heavily derivative nature, it must enforce originality on the level of the sentence." He decided to let go of his offense over his words being appropriated; he would no longer pretend "that a writer's words have a virgin birth and an eternal life."

Does that mean Gladwell wouldn't mind if I took one of his elegant [The] *New Yorker* pieces and published it under my byline in *The Washington Post*, where we were once colleagues? Of course not, because by merely stealing his words, I would not be doing anything creative. If, however, I published an annotated version of his story, challenging or building upon his reporting and thinking, Gladwell might feel honored.

Even among journalism's purists, there's a growing sense that although giving credit to others is essential, the remix culture has enriched a creative person's toolkit. "Before the internet, I don't think we appreciated the way borrowing and sampling informed original work," McBride says. "I'm a parent of an actress/comedian and a musician and I see how their work is built on other stuff. We in journalism developed this false pride where journalists feel diminished giving credit to others who've done similar work. It's so silly."

Even the man who sells software designed to catch plagiarists recognizes that nailing people for lifting a few words is a misdemeanor compared to the felony of stealing someone else's ideas. But prosecuting misdemeanors has a larger purpose, says Chris Harrick, an executive of Turnitin, a purveyor of plagiarism detection software that's popular among universities and has a few media clients as well.

"Plagiarizing ideas is abstract," he says, "so people go after text matches." It's analogous to the controversial "broken windows" idea in criminal justice: By attacking the little infractions, you set the bar, diminishing the likelihood that bad guys will attempt more severe crimes. Letting low-level violators slip away by making excuses about the nature of digital culture is buying into moral and ethical decline, Harrick says.

"People still care about fairness, about maintaining social and moral barriers against dishonesty," he says. "There's a lot of worry that the lines of originality have been blurred with retweeting, sharing, and sampling, so kids from middle school to college often don't have a good sense of what it means to be original."

This strikes Gene Weingarten as hokum. I called my longtime editor and friend because he had written a piece contending, in his usual genteel manner, that the sacking of Benny Johnson for serially plagiarizing BuzzFeed listicles was "petty bull-poo."

Weingarten, who writes a column in *The Washington Post Magazine*, says using a hair-trigger definition of plagiarism in the brave new world of aggregation and digital sweatshops mocks the real thing. "In the public mind, real plagiarism is conflated with trivial stuff," Weingarten says. "Nobody expects an aggregated story to be entirely original work. If you're reading a listicle on BuzzFeed about North Korea, do people think the writer produced nine pieces in one day and went to Pyongyang in his spare time?"

Weingarten sees an important difference between deliberate stealing of someone's creative work and careless copying of boilerplate information. "I would be happy to join my tut-tutting brethren and denounce this sort of lazy, crappy writing so long as we don't call it 'plagiarism,'" he says. The lesser infraction is "a failure of creativity and diligence, not a serious ethical flaw."

So, I ask, what material is okay to copy? A couple of grafs from a routine police story? "No, that's the reporter's own work," he replies. "He went out and put himself in a dangerous situation to get that."

Fine, how about a quote from the president's speech? "That's not stealing," Weingarten says. Even if I pick up some other reporter's transcribing error? "That's bad, but it's laziness, not plagiarism," he says.

We go on like this for a while before Weingarten grumbles that I've dragged him into exactly what he objects to about the new gotcha plagiarism-hunting: "It's this kindergarten game of 'what's okay?'"

So where does that leave us? How do we focus on real, pernicious, trust-busting plagiarism without spending undue energy sniffing out people who fail to reword a smart phrase they ran across in their reporting?

"I feel certain there is a way to define what's real plagiarism and what's trivial," Gene says. "The way is to ask me on a case-by-case basis."

A funny notion now, in the age of Our Bad Media and Turnitin, when the entire world has been deputized as the plagiarism police. But what Weingarten suggests is exactly the way it worked Before Google. Editors decided, period.

The world has changed. Undoubtedly, a culture in which sparkling achievements and insights are available for anyone to reshape makes for a richer intellectual landscape. It would be a shame to limit creativity because a software program can ferret out every reuse of a perfect phrase. Journalism must always be about honesty, clarity, and credibility. Those foundations will not be shaken if we make our definition of plagiarism more complex, mapping a spectrum on which minor infractions fall on one end and wholesale theft on the other. We are still responsible for governing ourselves. Dive into the ocean of ideas, grab the tastiest bits, make creative use of them—but always with generous, plentiful nods to those who came before you. Culture changes constantly. Courtesy and respect are forever.

Marc Fisher is a senior editor at *The Washington Post*.

Louis Menand

Crooner in Rights Spat

Are Copyright Laws Too Strict?

Rod Stewart is being sued over the rights to an image of his own head.

In 1981, a professional photographer named Bonnie Schiffman took a picture of the back of Stewart's head, which was used, eight years later, on the cover of the album "Storyteller." Now a different picture of Stewart's head, also from the back, has been used to promote his Las Vegas act and world tour. Schiffman claims that the resemblance between her photograph and the new image is too close—the legal term is "substantial similarity"—and she is suing for copyright infringement. She is asking for two and a half million dollars.

A copyright is, first and foremost, the right to make a copy. The first products to be protected by copyright—the statutory history begins in Britain, in 1710, with the passage of a law known as the Statute of Anne—were books. Once you buy a book, you can legally do almost anything to it. You can sell it to someone else, you can tear the pages out, you can throw it on a bonfire. God knows you can print terrible things about it. But you cannot make copies of it. The right to do that belongs to the author of the book and his or her heirs and assigns.

As with any right, the right to make a copy is a lot less straightforward than it sounds. As the person who wrote this article, I own the right to make copies of it. Since 1976, in the United States, that right has been born with the article, and there are few formalities still required for me to assert it. The belief that you have irrecoverably forfeited your copyright if you have not sent a copy of your book to the Library of Congress, or put a © on it somewhere, is obsolete.

I have granted *The New Yorker* an exclusive license to the article for a limited period, after which the magazine retains certain privileges (including printing it in a collection of [The] *New Yorker* writings and keeping it on its Web site). If, a year from now, someone else, without my permission, reprints my article in a book called "The Most Thoughtful and Penetrating Essays of 2014," I can complain that my right to make copies is being violated and, if the court agrees with me, legally suppress the book. Theoretically, the court could compel the publisher to pulp all the unsold copies. Although not the author of this piece, you, too, would likely feel that the publisher of "Most Thoughtful Essays" was a bandit, and you would share my sense of righteous indignation.

But suppose that a Web site, awesomestuff.com, ran an item that said something like "This piece on copyright is a great read!" with a hyperlink on the word "piece" to my article's page on *The New Yorker*'s Web site. You wouldn't think this was banditry at all. You would find it unexceptionable.

This is partly because of what might be called the spatial imaginary of the Web. When you click on a link, you have the sensation that you no longer are at a place called awesomestuff.com but have been virtually transported to an entirely different place, called newyorker.com. A visual change is experienced as a physical change. The link is treated as a footnote; it's as though you were taking another book off the shelf. The Web reinforces this illusion of movement by adopting a real-estate vocabulary, with terms like "site" (on which nothing can be built), "address" (which you can't G.P.S.), and "domain" (which is a legal concept, not a duchy).

Some courts have questioned the use of links that import content from another Web site without changing the URL, a practice known as "framing." But it's hard to see much difference. Either way, when you're reading a linked page, you may still be "at" awesomestuff.com, as clicking the back button on your browser can instantly confirm. Effectively, awesomestuff.com has stolen content from newyorker.com, just as the compiler of "Most Thoughtful Essays" stole content from me. The folks at awesomestuff.com and their V. C. backers are attracting traffic to their Web site, with its many banner ads for awesome stuff, using material created by other people.

An enormous amount of Web business is conducted in this manner. Most Web users don't feel indignant about it. On the contrary, most Web users would feel that *their* rights had been violated if links like this were prohibited. Something that is almost universally condemned when it happens in the medium of print is considered to be just how digital media work. Awesomestuff.com might even argue that no one is harmed by the link—that it is doing me and *The New Yorker* a favor by increasing our article's readership at no cost to us. But the publisher of "Most Thoughtful Essays" could say the same thing, and the court would be unmoved.

This almost instinctive distinction between what is proper in the analog realm and what is proper in the digital realm is at the center of a global debate about the state of copyright law. Statutes protecting copyright have never been stricter; at the same time, every minute of every day, millions of people are making or using copies of material—texts, sounds, and images—that they didn't create. According to an organization called Tru Optik, as many as ten billion files, including movies, television shows, and games, were downloaded in the second quarter of this year. Tru Optik estimates that approximately ninety-four percent of those downloads were illegal. The law seems to be completely out of whack with the technology.

The point of Peter Baldwin's fascinating and learned (and also repetitive and disorganized) "The Copyright Wars" (Princeton) is that the dispute between analog-era and digital-era notions of copyright is simply the latest installment of an argument that goes all the way back to the Statute of Anne. The argument is not really about technology, although major technological changes tend to bring it back to life. It's about the reason for creating a right to make copies in the first place.

In the United States, the reason is stated in the Constitution. Article I gives Congress power "to promote the Progress of Science and useful Arts, by securing for limited Times to Authors and Inventors the exclusive Right to their respective Writings and Discoveries." The Copyright Act of 1790 set the length of copyright at fourteen years, renewable for another fourteen, after which the work falls into the public domain.

A right is just the flip side of a prohibition. The thinking behind Article I is that prohibiting people from copying and selling someone else's original work is a way of encouraging the writing of useful or entertaining books, just as awarding a patent is a way of encouraging the invention of useful or enjoyable things. The prohibition operates as an incentive for the protected party. For a limited period—fourteen or twenty-eight years—authors get to enjoy the profits from sales of their books, and this prospect of reward induces people to write.

But Article I makes it clear that the ultimate beneficiary of books and inventions is the public. Copyrights are granted and patents are issued in order "to promote the Progress of Science and useful Arts." This is why the Constitution dictates a limit on the right to make copies. After the term of protection expires, a work cannot be copyrighted again. It becomes a public good. It is thrown into the open market, which allows it to be cheaply reproduced, and this speeds the distribution of knowledge. "Intellectual property is a frail gondola that ferries innovation from the private to the public sphere, from the genius to the commons," as Paul K. Saint-Amour, one of the leading literary scholars of copyright, elegantly describes it.

Drugs make a good analogy (as they so often do). A pharmaceutical company that develops a new medication is rewarded for its investment in R. & D. by the right to market the medication exclusively for a limited period of time. When that period expires, other pharmaceutical companies can manufacture and sell knockoff versions. These generic meds are usually far cheaper than the original, brand-name drug, and the result is an improvement in the public's health.

The United States also found another, and even better, way to speed the distribution of knowledge, and that was not to extend copyright to foreign works. This was not uncommon in the nineteenth century, but the United States was particularly slow to reform the practice. Until 1891, a book published elsewhere could be legally copied and sold here without payment to the author or to the original publisher. "It seems to be their opinion that a free and independent American citizen ought not to be robbed of his right of robbing somebody else," Arthur Sullivan, of Gilbert and Sullivan, complained. Charles Dickens campaigned aggressively against the evils of piracy, to no avail. The loss to British authors was not small. The United States is the world's largest consumer of books. Baldwin says that by the late nineteenth century, the American book market was twice the size of Britain's.

The term of copyright has been expanded in the United States periodically since 1790. In 1831, copyright was made renewable for up to forty-two years from the time of publication; in 1909, for up to fifty-six years. In 1976, the law was rewritten to protect copyright for fifty years after the death of the author, and formalities, like requiring authors to register their copyright, were relaxed. This means that anything and everything is now copyrighted. If you made it, no matter how trivial, you own it, and if someone else copies it you can sue.

Finally, in 1998, protection was increased to life plus seventy years, thanks to the passage of what is known as the Sonny Bono Copyright Term Extension Act, named for the late, great songster turned California congressman. (Works with corporate authorship are protected for a hundred and twenty years after creation or ninety-five years after publication, whichever is first.) This means that copies—and, if Bonnie Schiffman prevails in her lawsuit, imitations—of Schiffman's picture of Rod Stewart's head, which is already thirty-three years old, may be illegal until some time in the twenty-second century.

The Bono Act also altered the term for works still in copyright that were published between 1923 and 1978, increasing it to ninety-five years from the date of publication. (In 1993, the European Union had gone even farther, reviving lapsed copyrights of works by authors who died between 1925 and 1944, as a way of compensating rights holders for sales lost during the Second World War.) In 2003, the Supreme Court, in Eldred v. Ashcroft, rejected a challenge to the constitutionality of this additional award to works already under copyright. The Constitution was explicit in granting Congress the power to set the term of copyright, Justice Ruth Bader Ginsburg wrote, provided that term was a limited one. The Constitution did not define what "limited" meant, and it was not the Supreme Court's business to decide whether Congress had exercised its power wisely.

As a result of the Bono Act, you can publish new English translations of the first four volumes of Proust's "In Search of Lost Time," all of which appeared before Proust's death, in 1922, but the copyright for English translations of the last three will continue to be owned by Random House until 2019. Although James Joyce's "Finnegans Wake" has been in the public domain in Europe since the end of 2011 (seventy years after Joyce died), it will remain under copyright in this country until the end of 2034 (ninety-five years after it was published).

On another stratum of economic value, Mickey Mouse, who made his début in 1928, in an animated picture called "Steamboat Willie," won't come out of copyright until 2024. The Disney Company, which owns rights to a number of valuable but, by the standards of the entertainment industry, ancient cartoon characters, lobbied hard to get the Bono Act passed.

As it happens, Mickey Mouse owes his very existence to a copyright issue. In 1927, Walt Disney created a character called Oswald, the Lucky Rabbit, and was engaged to create a series of animated shorts featuring the character for Universal Studios. During a dispute over compensation, he discovered that Universal owned the rights to Oswald, and that the studio could fire him and make Oswald movies without him. He vowed never to give up his rights again, and created Mickey Mouse.

Courts have been receptive, as well, to claims of "subconscious infringement." Even people who are not pirates can be made to cease and desist, or to pay damages. In 1976, an American court found that George Harrison's "My Sweet Lord" had infringed the copyright on "He's So Fine, " by the Chiffons, which was a hit in 1963. One critic went so far as to observe that the refrain "Hare Krishna" essentially copied the refrain "Doo-lang," in "He's So Fine." Harrison ended up paying five hundred and eighty-seven thousand dollars.

Baldwin joins Saint-Amour, the law professors Lawrence Lessig, Jeanne Fromer, and Robert Spoo, and the copyright lawyer William Patry in believing that, Internet or no Internet, the present level of copyright protection is excessive. By the time most works fall into the public domain, they have lost virtually all their use value. If the public domain is filled with items like hundred-year-old images of the back of Rod Stewart's head, the public good will suffer. The commons will become your great-grandparents' attic.

. . .

As it is, few creations outlive their creators. Of the 187,280 books published between 1927 and 1946, only 2.3 per cent were still in print in 2002. But, since there is no "use it or lose it" provision in copyright law, they are all still under copyright today. Patry, in his recent book, "How to Fix Copyright," notes that ninety-five per cent of Motown recordings are no longer available. Nevertheless, you can't cover or imitate or even sample them without paying a licensing fee—despite the fact that your work is not competing in the marketplace with the original, since the original is no longer for sale. (U.S. law does not protect recorded music made before 1972, but state laws can apply—as the nineteen-sixties group the Turtles are claiming in a lawsuit, for more than a hundred million dollars, against Sirius XM.)

In the case of Motown, at least you know whom to call. In the case of many books and photographs, the rights holders are unknown; in other cases, it's expensive to track down the heirs or the legatees or the firms, possibly no longer in existence, to whom the copyright belongs. And so, for fear of being sued and having their work pulped or otherwise erased from the universe, people avoid the risk. Patry says that the BBC has a million hours of broadcasts in its archives that cannot be used, because no one knows who holds the rights.

Before the Internet, the social cost of this obstacle was minimal. Only a few people had the time and the inclination to travel to where they could see or listen to archived broadcasts. But today, when everything can be made available to the entire world at minimal expense, it seems absurd to hold enormous amounts of content hostage to the threat of legal action from the odd descendant. "That a vast existing cultural patrimony, already paid for and amortized, sits locked behind legal walls, hostage to outmoded notions of property, when at the flick of a switch it could belong to all humanity—that is little short of grotesque, " Baldwin concludes. Yet the odd descendant has the law on her side. She has the power to pulp.

What's the rationale for maximizing protection? The idea of a public domain belongs to the theory that individual rights are intended to promote public goods. The First Amendment protects individual expression, for example, because it's in society's best interest to have a robust debate—not because each person has a right to say what he or she thinks simply by virtue of being human. So the right to make copies was imagined by the Framers as a way to encourage the writing of books by individuals for the good of an educated citizenry. But, if you are a natural-rights person and you think that individual rights are inalienable, then you don't recognize the priority of the public domain. You think that society has no claim on works created by individuals. The right to control one's own expressions, to sell them or not, to alter them or not, is not a political right. It's a moral right, and it cannot be legislated away.

Moral rights give authors control over not just the reproducibility but the integrity of their creations. This control can extend beyond the limits of copyright protection—as in cases where the author has assigned the copyright to someone else, like a publisher, or when the term of copyright has elapsed. Moral right is a recognized legal concept in Europe. Courts there have held, for example, that although the buyer of a work of art may destroy it, he or she cannot deface or otherwise alter it. That right belongs to the artist in perpetuity.

Samuel Beckett's restrictions on the staging of his plays is a well-known example of the exercise of copyright as a moral right. Beckett and his estate consistently refused permission to mount productions of his work—"Endgame" in an abandoned subway station is the classic case, but there are many others—unless Beckett's stage directions were complied with literally. The refusal was not based on any economic consideration; these performances were not copies competing with the originals. It was based on the right of the playwright to protect the integrity of his plays.

A natural-rights person would ask why the law shouldn't treat a book the same way it treats any form of real property. If you own a house or a piece of land, the state sets no time limit on your right to use it. A family can live off the income from real estate or from a trust fund in perpetuity. Why can't Ernest Hemingway's heirs live off the income from his books? Is it fair for people who had no relation to Ernest Hemingway to someday make money selling those books? Should they be able to abridge them, or change the endings, with impunity?

These are the two philosophical rationales for copyright protection. Baldwin calls the limited-term, public-domain conception the Anglo-American conception and the much stricter real-property, moral-rights conception the European conception. The differences began emerging toward the end of the nineteenth century, with the founding of the Berne Union, which was created to regularize international copyright laws. Baldwin attributes the Continental conception of copyright as a moral right to the desire of countries like France and Germany to assert their cultural superiority. Protecting the rights of artists was imagined as a way of rejecting the commercialization and commodification of culture that European countries thought less restrictive copyright laws were designed to facilitate. Europeans thought, in effect, that Americans wanted great literature to fall into the public domain so they could make cheesy movies from it.

Britain joined the Berne Union when it was founded, although, Baldwin says, grudgingly. The United States did not join until 1989. Baldwin thinks that this, along with the adoption, in the nineteen-nineties, of a number of additional regulations stiffening copyright protection, including the Bono Act, marked the triumph of the European model. "Copyright's evolution is often told as a story of American cultural hegemony," he says. "In fact, the opposite is more plausible."

At bottom, the argument about copyright is not really a philosophical argument. It's a battle between interest groups. Baldwin points this out—although, like everyone who takes a position on copyright, he also thinks that his is the philosophically defensible one. In the copyright wars, there are many sets of opposing stakeholders. Much litigation involves corporate entities, which have the financial resources to pursue cases through the courts. In these copyright battles, the main antagonists are the businesses that own copyrighted goods and the businesses that don't.

Let's call the first type of business Hollywood and the second type Silicon Valley. Hollywood, along with the music industry and the publishing industry, which are the other major analog-era corporate interests, makes money by producing and distributing content. Silicon

Valley makes money by aggregating other people's content. Hollywood fears pirates; Silicon Valley fears paywalls. Silicon Valley accuses Hollywood of "monopoly" and "artificial scarcity," and talks about the democracy of the Internet. Hollywood accuses Silicon Valley of "free riding" and "contributory infringement," and talks about protecting the dignity of the artist. But each side is only trying to defend its business model.

Freelancers versus salaried content creators is another interest-group antagonism. Most of the people who are critical of the length of copyright protection today are academics. (Patry is an exception, but he's the senior copyright counsel at Google.) This is probably not unrelated to the fact that academics have almost no financial stake in copyright. The research and writing they do [are] part of their job as employees of universities, or as the recipients of external, usually taxpayer supported grants. They don't depend on sales to survive.

Freelancers, on the other hand, are unhappy with what they regard as the erosion of their right to control copying, which they see, for example, in the legally sanctioned practice of posting "snippets" on sites like Amazon, iTunes, and Google Books. Musicians and other artists tend to regard the Internet as a place where anything goes, an ungovernable Barbary Coast. On the Web, the general rule—known as a "take-down notice"—is that you can post almost anything as long as you take it down when the rights holder complains. No harm, no foul. There are some technical preconditions that the poster has to meet to earn the protection, but this does not seem to freelancers to be a very effective way to discourage copying.

Academics oppose copyright protection for another reason as well. They want access to the research in their fields. In the case of scientific research, much of that access is controlled by giant media companies like Springer, Elsevier, and Wiley. These companies publish academic journals and then charge huge subscription fees to the libraries of the universities that supported the very work they are selling back to them. Baldwin calls it "a notorious rentseeking boondoggle," and many academics have organized to find ways to circumvent it—by starting new journals, or by putting their work online in disregard for the copyright claims of Springer and the rest. It was for trying to open access to the digital compiler of academic journals JSTOR that Aaron Swartz was arrested at M.I.T.

As the Constitution states, the ultimate purpose of copyright protection is the spread of knowledge. A lot of the debate over copyright is carried on using the examples of famous novels and popular songs (as in this article). But people aren't going to stop writing and reading novels, or making and listening to music. The analog-era industries will find—they are already in the process of finding—a sounder business model. For the rest of us, less is at risk. The species can survive without cheaper copies of Mickey Mouse cartoons and "Finnegans Wake." It is hard to write these words, but the species can probably survive without Motown.

Copyright law does not completely shut down the circulation of cultural goods. It protects only expression. Facts, ideas, systems, procedures, methods of operation, and many compilations of data are denied protection. The 1976 copyright act made statutorily explicit something that has always been part of the common law of copyright: the doctrine of fair use. Most copyright litigations are essentially disputes over the proper definition of this concept. In the United States, the meaning of fair use is vague, which is good, because courts can judge each case in its own context, but also bad, because guessing wrong can be very expensive.

Contrary to popular belief, fair use does not dictate a maximum number of copyrighted words that you can quote or lines that you can reprint. Parody is protected under fair use, and so are many educational uses of copyrighted material. The key concept is "transformative copying." You can use someone else's creation if the purpose is to make something new with it.

The problem is that the judicial record is inconsistent. The law on musical sampling is draconian, but restrictions on the right to quote from unpublished works (like J. D. Salinger's letters) have been relaxed. Judicial unpredictability makes for legal anxiety. Professors who copy material for use in class are frequently uncertain whether or not they need to seek permission, which almost always entails paying a fee. If they ask their college's general counsel, they will be told to pay the fee. Any lawyer would give the same answer. Paying a small fee (which, in the case of educational materials, can usually be passed along to the students) is a lot cheaper than facing a lawsuit, even one that you should win.

Lawyers remember that ASCAP once demanded that the Girl Scouts pay royalties for copyrighted songs sung around the campfire, and that Warner Bros., the producer of "Casablanca," went into action when it learned that the Marx Brothers were making a movie called "A Night in Casablanca." (Groucho, in turn, wondered whether Warner Bros. had the rights to the word "brothers.") You think these laws don't affect you? Warner/Chappell Music claims to own the copyright to "Happy Birthday to You." So far, in cases like Eldred, the Supreme Court has leaned to the side of copyright owners. But the Court always takes a while to catch up with the times, so it seems likely that the law will eventually change.

The most fundamental opposition in the copyright wars is between creators and consumers. In parliamentary debates in the nineteenth century, Thomas Macaulay called copyright "a tax on readers for the purpose of giving a bounty to writers." Creators want to sell high, and consumers want to buy low. Almost the minute a popular book falls into the public domain, cheap editions flood the market. A virtual minute after that, a digital edition becomes available online for nothing. This is what Congress had in mind when, in 1790, it restricted copyright to fourteen years with a single term of renewal. It wanted to speed the availability of inexpensive copies.

Freelance cultural producers are only weakly organized, in groups like the Authors Guild and the American Federation of Musicians. That's one reason they are better off assigning copyright to a corporate entity, which has the muscle to protect it. Cultural consumers are not organized at all. They can speak only through their elected representatives, but most of those people will be listening to the money—to the lobbyists for the content industries, new and old, as those industries search for more reliable ways to squeeze profits from the awesome stuff that human beings have created.

Louis Menand has contributed to *The New Yorker* since 1991, and has been a staff writer since 2001.

EXPLORING THE ISSUE

Does the Internet Change the Way We Think of Copyright and Plagiarism?

Critical Thinking and Reflection

1. Consider whether the right of a person to profit from his or her own creative and intellectual endeavors should be protected.
2. Think about how easy digital technology makes it to circumvent the law.
3. Reflect on how moral and ethical issues influence our behaviors as well as legal precedents.
4. Examine your own behavior; when you know something is wrong, do you avoid thinking about the problem because it's easier to choose not to think about it?

Is There Common Ground?

Both of the authors for this issue acknowledge that digital information is different from traditional (sometimes thought of as analog) information. While acknowledging the unique characteristics of remix and mashup culture, each views plagiarism and copyright as issues that are challenged by the presence of digital media tools. Both also assert that by not attributing authorship to original work, the fine line between copyright and plagiarism becomes slippery. And, both agree that correct attribution is a moral responsibility for journalists and people who draw from original content to develop derivative content.

Where the two authors deviate, however, is in their interpretation of whether older laws and practices should be followed, or whether our society is ready for revisiting the essential truths behind ownership of original content and ideas. Each takes a different perspective on how sacrosanct the original rules of practice in journalism and public communication are.

The selections in this issue force us to examine issues of cultural practice, expectations, and moral and ethical principles that challenge laws and, ultimately, the First Amendment, as it has been interpreted for centuries. In this issue, we see how new forms of communication can never be considered in isolation. Instead, every new tool and practice touches other social and legal precedents that warrant careful consideration.

Additional Resources

Roberto Caso and Federica Giovanella, *Balancing Copyright Law In the Digital Age: Comparative Perspectives* (Springer, 2015). This book focuses on the problems in the digital age and how they have been dealt with in the past, as well as how they might be dealt with in the future.

Danielle Nicole DeVoss and Martine Courant Rife, eds., *Cultures of Copyright* (New York: Peter Lang, 2015). This is a collection of edited essays dealing with a wide range of cultural contexts to help interpret copyright issues.

Brian F. Fitzgerald and John Gilchrist, *Copyright Perspectives: Past, Present and Prospect* (Springer, 2015). This book focuses on major international interventions to regularize legal issues behind copyright, like the Berne Convention and the role of the World Intellectual Property Organization (WIPO). Perspectives on digital issues are also included.

Debora Webber-Wulf, *False Feathers: A Perspective on Academic Plagiarism* (Berlin: Springer, 2014). This book examines the problems of academic plagiarism that pre-date the Internet. While focusing primarily on the impact of plagiarism in Germany, the examples are universal to all levels of academic dishonesty.

Internet References . . .

The Center for Media and Social Impact (at American University)

http://www.cmsimpact.org/

Copyright Law of the United States (U.S. Copyright Office)

www.copyright.gov/title17/

The Electronic Frontier Foundation

https://www.eff.org

Plagiarism 101

www.plagiarism.org

Guilda Rostama, "Remix Culture and Amateur Creativity: A Copyright Dilemma" World Intellectual Property Organization

www.wipo.int/wipo_magazine/en/2015/03/article_0006.html

Selected, Edited, and with Issue Framing Material by:
Alison Alexander, *University of Georgia*
and
Jarice Hanson, *University of Massachusetts – Amherst*

ISSUE

Are Copyright Laws Effective in Curbing Piracy?

YES: Brian R. Day, from "In Defense of Copyright: Creativity, Record Labels, and the Future of Music," *Seton Hall Journal of Sports and Entertainment Law* (2011)

NO: Alex Sayf Cummings, from *Democracy of Sound: Music Piracy and the Remaking of American Copyright in the Twentieth Century* (Oxford University Press, 2013)

Learning Outcomes

After reading this issue, you will be able to:

- Understand the reasons why copyright laws exist and understand the challenges presented by technologies that make unauthorized duplication of media product so easy.
- Think about the reasons why copyright laws came about and consider whether the laws should be revised.
- Argue for and against copyright constraints from the perspective of a creative artist, industry representative, and consumer.
- Consider ways in which copyright laws may be changed in the future.
- Identify legal, moral, and ethical considerations that are seminal for a discussion of copyright and unauthorized duplication of media content.

ISSUE SUMMARY

YES: Attorney Brian R. Day addresses the size of the recorded music industry which manufactures and distributes 85 percent of the recorded music in the United States today, and discusses the need for copyright protection and the different business models used by the music industry today. He argues that copyright is essential to the music industry and other media industries because it constitutionally protects the work of artists and their ability to profit from their talents.

NO: Alex Sayf Cummings writes from the perspective of the impact of piracy, bootlegging, and counterfeiting on the music industry and concludes that contemporary copyright legislation is just not adequate to circumvent the ease with which people can download unauthorized copies of musical performances. He warns that copyright is no longer adequate to meet the challenge of digital music today, and warns that the recorded music industry is in danger of becoming obsolete.

Copyright laws in the United States originated in Britain, and were adopted by the colonies as ways to protect the original work of artists, including writers and publishers. A clause in the U.S. Constitution defines copyright as "to promote the progress of science and useful arts." Over the years, copyright laws were modified and changed to fit technologies and social conditions that surrounded the creation of intellectual property, and an international agreement called the Berne Convention attempted to define who the original author of a work might be, in all countries. While these efforts and the debate over whether copyright should be a legal or moral issue (making sure that the originator of a product retains the rights to any profits made by the sale of that product) have gone on for years, nothing has challenged copyright as much as the shift to digital technologies that make it possible to duplicate an original product or artifact in such a way as to ensure that duplicated works are virtually identical to the original.

Music, films, television shows, photocopies of printed materials all can be digitally copied today, inexpensively, and easily. It is often hard to tell the difference between an original media artifact and a duplicated one, and this is where issues of piracy, bootlegging, and unauthorized duplication muddy the copyright water. Even more importantly, file sharing can contribute to the unauthorized duplication of material, bypassing any revenue that the original artists, legal distributors, or promoters might claim.

Undoubtedly, copyright laws have become tangled in web of technological change and the changing social mores. You might clearly state that taking someone's car without their knowledge is stealing, but is it the same thing when you borrow a friend's DVD and burn a copy for yourself? The media industries are worried about protecting their products and profits; new artists hope to make a living off of their music or the films or videos they create, and yet, there is something about the ephemeral nature of digital media that seems to encourage illegal behavior in many situations. Many people claim that they can't afford to buy music or the films they want to see, so they share passwords with friends to "borrow" services, but this is a hollow argument. The Recording Industry Association of America acknowledges that when music files can be purchased inexpensively, the amount of illegal file sharing goes down—but the problem is a sticky one for those industries that would like to retain control of the products they distribute (and the profits they enjoy).

Several alternatives have been suggested to deal with issues of copyright that are hard to pin down. Fair use is a category of copyright law that allows some use of copyrighted materials for purposes of education, parody, commentary, or other non-commercial purposes, but there is a lot of folklore about what constitutes fair use. The Electronic Frontier Foundation and GNU Project both advocate something called "copyleft" which is an alternative to copyright, and allows original creators of media products the right to sign a statement allowing others to modify or use their original works, as long as original authorship is attributed. The Creative Commons is another alternative to copyright, and it too allows for sharing of materials with six different agreements an original author can use to license their material to others with no payment.

But despite these alternatives, copyright is a deeply engrained legal concept that has big consequences for individuals and for countries that engage in unauthorized duplication of original media property. Despite many countries' general adherence to the Berne Convention guidelines, some countries have laws about copyright that are very different than U.S. law. For example, in 2009, the owners of a Swedish company called The Pirate Bay were taken to court for their use of bit-torrent to allow fast, low-cost streaming of music, movies, and more to users around the world. Some of the largest media companies in the world entered into the suit, claiming that The Pirate Bay was engaging in, and fostering, copyright infringement.

In the United States, one of the most important legal precedents occurred in 1984 when the Supreme Court heard a case officially called *Sony Corp. of America v. Universal City Studios, Inc.*, 464 U.S. 417. This became known as "the Betamax Case" and dealt with the capability of the new Video Cassette Recorder (VCR) to download television programs to a video cassette for later viewing. While Universal City Studios claimed that people were violating their copyright by recording programs on their VCRs, the Court decided that since the VCR could be used for other purposes than just downloading television content, the technology would be legal. That precedent has influenced many other court decisions in the United States dealing with the capacity of a new technology to challenge previous laws. In this case, as long as VCRs could be used for personal uses to view content recorded on home camcorders, or rent videos, the technology was allowed to be marketed and used for all purposes, including the home recording of television programs—as long as the user did not sell those recordings for personal profit.

Other technologies that did not have multiple uses did not fare as well. Early MP3 technology was thought to lead one to copyright infringement, and peer-to-peer file sharing technology was made illegal if it "induced" (led someone) to copyright infringement—and there was no other use for the technology but to violate copyright.

In the selections chosen for this issue, the authors acknowledge that copyright is more than just laws—and that historically it has undergone changes that were sometimes in the interest of the public, but more often, in the interest of the corporations that held the copyright. This issue should, however, make you think carefully and critically about what you own and control, and what you think needs to have legal protection. Copyright and the media industries are big problems, but they also reflect the way we think about what should be protected, for whom, and by whom. The social contract we enter into when we use these technologies reflect our own moral sense and the way we as individuals reflect and reproduce social relations.

Brian R. Day

In Defense of Copyright: Creativity, Record Labels, and the Future of Music

Introduction

There is perhaps no group more maligned in the United States (U.S.) music industry than that of the record labels and their collective trade organization, the Recording Industry Association of America. The four major record labels—Universal Music Group, Sony Music Entertainment, Warner Music Group (WMG), and EMI Music—collectively create, manufacture, and/or distribute nearly 85% of prerecorded music in the U.S. today. Recorded music is not unlike other forms of intellectual property in the U.S., where corporate entities own and/or control the rights in works produced by creators. Like venture capitalists, record labels provide upfront capital, and diversify their assets in an effort to recoup their expenditures and earn a profit from a small percentage of successful investments. For this reason, record labels have become distinctly aware of consumers' music preferences in an effort to appeal to distinct music markets and sell their recordings. Record labels have also developed large-scale infrastructure and distribution mediums, including numerous "imprint" labels dedicated to discovering and promoting artists in both mass and niche markets. This investment, however, comes with considerable risk. To be sure, it is estimated that only 10–20% of artists are commercially successful, and that only 5% of new artists will ever generate a profit great enough to cover the losses of all the other unsuccessful artists.

As music production and distribution has transitioned into the digital realm, music and legal commentators increasingly contend that the record label business model is unsustainable and unnecessary. Whereas labels were once critical to the promotion, manufacture, and distribution of physical albums, commentators suggest that recent technologies may have significantly undercut the traditional advantages enjoyed by major labels. In a world of Pro Tools, iTunes, and MySpace, some argue that artists are fully capable of recording, promoting, and licensing their own music.

The consequences that such theories might have upon the music industry, and upon the U.S. system of music copyright as a whole, are profound. If labels are in fact no longer necessary to sustain a healthy music market, the fundamentals of music authorship and copyright ownership in the U.S. may undergo significant transfor-mation. Today, recording contracts between record labels and artists weave a complex web of profit-sharing, recoupment, and upfront advances. In a post-label world, artists (and their management) would control all creative and business aspects of their music, including production, marketing, and distribution. Most importantly, however, artists would own the copyright in the music they record, along with the rights to any and all licensing royalties received therefrom. . . .

The Legal Rights at Issue

Before turning to the substantive considerations involved, it is important to first consider the nature of music copyright in the U.S. today. The rights of the artist, record label, publisher, and songwriter vary greatly, and should be conceptualized independently of one another. Although rights-owners are distinct, their rights are in many ways dependent upon each other given the multifaceted nature of music copyright and distribution. These fundamental considerations are illustrated below.

Virtually all sound recordings embody two separate categories of copyrightable works: the sound recording itself, and the underlying musical work. The copyright in the musical work—the lyrics and melody—belongs to the author or composer, who typically assigns his or her rights to a publisher for purposes of representation. Statutes grant certain exclusive right to musical works, including the right to publicly reproduce, distribute, and perform. Some of the most common licenses obtained as a part of digital music distribution are public performance and mechanical licenses. As the name suggests, a public performance license is necessary to lawfully perform a composition publicly. A mechanical license, on the other hand, is required when a composition is reproduced—in the form of a vinyl record, compact disc (CD), or digital delivery—and/or distributed.

Sound recording copyright, on the other hand, protects the originality of the musical recording itself, as distinct from the underlying written lyrics or melody. Thus, there may be several sound recordings protecting different versions or "covers" of a single musical work. When new artists contract with a record label, they generally sign a recording agreement assigning to the label all copyright interests in the sound recordings they produce. Further,

Day, Brian R. From *Seton Hall Journal of Sports and Entertainment Law*, vol. 21, no. 1, 2011, pp. 61–64, 67–68, 72–74, 90–103 (edited).

the recording agreements usually deem the artists' recordings "works made for hire," thereby automatically vesting copyright ownership in the record label. This arrangement has led to significant controversy, leading some to accuse the labels of signing struggling artists to unconscionable "contracts of adhesion." . . .

The Rise of 360-Deals

After nearly ten years of declining revenues, record labels recently began adding language to recording agreements that require artists to share a percentage of their overall royalty streams—including merchandise, endorsement, and/or tour ticket sales—in return for greater capital investment. These so-called "360-deals" are controversial because they involve record labels in areas where they have never before been involved. Steve Greenberg, the former president of Columbia Records, defended the deals, explaining:

> Say I was considering being the sole investor in a new Italian restaurant being opened by a talented chef. . . . And suppose the chef told me that in exchange for putting up all the money and doing all the work marketing the restaurant, he'd share with me the revenue from the pizza sales—but not the revenue from the sales of pasta, meat, fish, beverages, or anything else on the menu. I can't imagine anyone investing under those terms.

Despite the opposition, 360 provisions have become standard in most new artist recording agreements over the past decade. Some extremely successful artists, including Madonna and Jay-Z, have signed 360-deals with Live Nation, one of the largest concert promoters in the U.S. The multimillion dollar deals not only require the artists to share a percentage of their overall revenues with the company, but also grant Live Nation exclusive touring rights with the artists for the duration of the contractual term. In return, Live Nation provides the artists with stock options and enormous signing bonuses.

Two emerging artists who have signed to the new 360-deals include Lady Gaga and British sensation Little Boots. WMG, who signed Little Boots to a 360 recording-contract, does more than just passively collect from Little Boots's secondary income streams; instead, the label has "specialist teams" dedicated to forming brand partnerships, creating and distributing limited edition merchandise on behalf of the artist, and establishing a global social network to enable fans to view exclusive content and merchandise. The result of such an investment seems to have paid off. Little Boots has enjoyed significant success largely due to her agreement with WMG, topping both the British and European albums charts.

In sum, the 360-deals provide record labels with a greater portion of artist royalties while simultaneously committing the music companies to investments that cover a wide range of an artist's professional activities.

Moreover, because artists traditionally only received royalties for album sales from their record label, the new 360-deals "benefit an artist's longevity and mean there is not the same pressure on an artist to go into the recording studio in order to recoup their heavy investment costs."

Despite the increased investment, some have criticized 360-deals as adverse to artists' interests. Greater upfront investment by the label means that it may take even longer for the artist to realize record royalties. The labels argue, however, that the 360-deals allow for greater investment in new acts, and thus benefit the public as much as they do the artists and labels. By sharing in the proceeds from merchandise, endorsement deals, and touring revenues, record labels are more apt to invest in acts that do not necessarily sell the most recordings. As the chairman of Atlantic Records opined, "[i]f we weren't so mono-focused on the selling of recorded music, we could actually take a really holistic approach to the development of an artist brand. . . . What's the healthiest decision to be made, not just to sell the CD but to build the artist's fan base?" At a time when recorded music sales have plummeted, 360-deals provide the necessary return to ensure that labels invest in a broad range of new talent, which serves the interests of artists, labels, and most importantly, the public. . . .

Commentators suggest that music will continue to flourish in a world without record labels. High-quality music could be produced on home computers, distribution could be accomplished quickly and easily over the Internet, and for the first time artists would own the copyright in their sound recordings. With their newfound rights, artists would be free to give their music away to fans, end the longstanding battle against infringement online, and generate revenues from ancillary markets like merchandise sales or concert tickets. It sounds simple enough. The argument, however, relies on several unfounded assumptions and greatly overlooks many important collateral legal issues. . . .

The ability to effectively enforce intellectual property rights in sound recordings would likely die with the record labels. Without a central entity to collectively manage sound recording copyrights nation-wide, artists would be required to enforce their rights individually. Although it is true that some artists might choose to give up the copyright infringement fights altogether, many others might not. Given the high cost associated with infringement lawsuits, like-minded artists would have to band together to establish an organization, like a record label, with the ability to enforce their rights both online and off. With so many vying interests, it is unlikely, however, that a focused and uniform strategy for intellectual property enforcement could be successfully implemented. Such a system would handicap the enforcement abilities of emerging artists. Without time to exploit their works, new artists would also likely be financially unable to enforce their copyrights. Record labels thus serve the important purpose of collectively enforcing intellectual property rights, which secures royalties for both the label and artist alike. . . .

Songwriters, like recording artists, would also be severely affected by the absence of record labels. Although some artists are also gifted songwriters, many others require the assistance of professional lyricists and composers. Indeed, the largest music publishers in the world are themselves divisions of record labels, which work with the labels to select the appropriate composition for new and established artists.

Without the assistance of labels and their representatives, artists would be forced to find compositions on their own. Many artists might be prompted to write their own songs or invest significant time and energy into independently seeking out songwriters. But many artists may not have the ability to write lyrics or draft melodies, know where to go or what to look for when it comes to songs, or know how to structure a licensing deal if they eventually find a composition they wish to use. To overcome such obstacles, artists could hire management, lawyers, or even establish a collective to negotiate songwriting deals on their behalf. How young and emerging artists would organize such collectives and/or afford such expenses remains unanswered by record label opponents.

Moreover, because exploitation of a sound recording necessarily exploits the underlying musical composition, a songwriter's license to the artist would require the artist to account and pay royalties for every sound recording distributed, regardless of whether payment is received from the end user. In other words, even if an artist wanted to give away her music for free, and chose not to enforce her copyright online, the songwriter would have the right to demand that royalties are paid for each and every reproduction and/or distribution of her work. If the artist obtains a compulsory license under 17 U.S.C. §115, for example, the statute requires that a royalty be paid "for every phonorecord made and distributed in accordance with the license. The practical result of such a system is that in the absence of record label advances and royalties, artists would still be responsible for compensating songwriters at the statutorily prescribed (or privately negotiated) rate. Not surprisingly, many emerging artists may not have the skills or resources necessary to obtain licenses in underlying musical compositions, much less to establish an acceptable accounting procedure. Thus, while a music community without labels might encourage some artists to write their own songs, it might also have the significant effect of undermining songwriting as a stand-alone profession. Indeed, when considering the effects that such an industry change might have, it is important to note that of the top five best-selling songs of all-time worldwide, only one was *co-written* by the artist. . . .

Another popular belief is that even without record sales, most artists will be able to survive on touring revenues alone. This argument, however, mistakes the exception for the rule. In 2009, North American concert revenues totaled $2.8 billion. Given the generous royalties that major artists take away from these concerts, many believe that touring would provide adequate financial support to encourage artistic creation in a world without record labels. According to Pollstar data, however, the top 100 North American music concerts comprised more than 80% of all concert revenues collected in 2009. This means that artists like U2, Bruce Springsteen, Elton John, Britney Spears, Madonna, and Cher took home the vast majority of concert revenues last year, leaving roughly $480 million for division between *every other touring artist in the country* tracked by Pollstar.

Industry expert Donald Passman explains:

> It's difficult to make much money touring until you're a major star . . . . In the beginning . . . you will most likely *lose* money on touring. You'll also get stuck in uncomfortable dressing rooms . . . [a]nd you'll be regularly humiliated, playing to half-empty concert halls, since the audience is coming later to see someone else.

Indeed, the entire purpose of touring for new artists is to generate enough buzz to *sell records*. Passman estimates that new artists can expect to earn about $250 to $1,500 per night playing at local venues for a few months of every year. From this income, the band or artist must pay tour expenses, which even for a small band can total around $10,000 per week. Without tour support from a record label, Passman concludes, "you don't need to be a math genius to see that you're going to lose money . . . [a]nd the longer you stay out the more you're going to lose." Nina Persson, lead singer of Sweden's The Cardigans agrees that "[i]t would be very difficult for me to have made a living just from live music. I would have to travel alone with a guitar and no band or crew to make that work."

Simon Renshaw, manager of the Dixie Chicks, expressed similar concerns with respect to touring, noting that "[t]he live [music] industry is doing great, but without the recording industry to develop new artists and build new talent, that live industry in ten years' time could look radically different." Although it is easy for artists who have built up a loyal fan base to break away from their record label and tour independently, unsigned and emerging artists "generally need the upfront financial support of a music company and the marketing and promotional muscle it can bring to the table." Indeed, the manager of one of the most successful touring acts of all time, U2, does not accept the proposition that touring alone can sustain an artist's career. Paul McGuiness, the manager of U2, explains that "[i]t is a myth that artists can build long-term careers on live music alone. In its latest tour, U2 filled huge stadiums around the world. That is because they have had parallel careers as recording artists and live performers since their inception 30 years ago."

Even today's most popular stars may have difficulty making money from tours. For example, one of music's biggest pop stars, Lady Gaga, has toured nationally and internationally with the backing of a major record label. Her most recent tour sold-out some of the largest venues in the world, including the O2 Arena in London. But neither Lady Gaga nor her record label have seen any profits from the tour so far—in fact, at the time of writing, the tour "ha[d] been losing about $3 million [collectively]."...

Fulfilling the Constitution's Promise

With the business and social realities of the music industry in mind, this portion of the article will consider how the business and legal aspects of the music industry relate, and how these aspects ultimately suggest that record labels continue to play a crucial role in today's copyright structure.

The U.S. Constitution explains that copyright protection exists "[t]o promote the Progress of Science and useful Arts." The U.S. Copyright Office has interpreted this provision to mean that copyright must "foster the growth of learning and culture for the public welfare." In this evaluation, Congress should consider "how much will the monopoly granted be detrimental to the public," and whether granting the exclusive right "confers a benefit upon the public that outweighs the evils of the temporary monopoly."

In order to ensure that copyright owners are sufficiently encouraged to create or invest in new works, however, they must be compensated in some meaningful way for the use of their sound recordings. As discussed above, the U.S. Supreme Court has explicitly provided that the copyright law "celebrates the economic motive," and emphasized the crucial role that economic incentive plays in the American system of intellectual property. In the context of the recording industry, one commentator has noted that without sustainable royalties, "record companies will no longer have an incentive to invest in the creation of new sound recordings or to facilitate the creative efforts of their artists because there will be no market for their prerecorded music." The question then becomes, how has the Internet and advancements in technology affected this basic constitutional assumption?

The argument that technology has drastically reduced the marginal costs of producing additional copies of a work is not a new contention. Indeed, skeptics of copyright protection have long assailed book prices due to the low manufacturing costs expended in the creation of individual copies of a work. Such evaluation, however, overlooks the inherent risk of investment-backed intellectual property. As Judge Posner once observed:

> In the absence of copyright protection, the market price of a book or other expressive work will eventually be bid down to the marginal cost of copying, with the result that the book may not be produced

in the first place because the author and publisher may not be able to recover their costs of creating it. ... The problem of recoupment is magnified, however, by the fact that the author's cost of creating the work, and many publishing costs (for example, editing costs), are incurred before it is known what the demand for the work will be. Because demand is uncertain, the difference between price and marginal cost of the successful work must not only cover the cost of expression but also compensate for the unavoidable risk of failure.

Just as Judge Posner predicted, the illegal digital music marketplace has bid the cost of music down to the marginal cost of copying, which on the Internet is essentially zero. The net result of this marketplace is that creators may not be able to recover the fixed costs associated with investing in risky, new creative works, meaning that the same diversity of music may not be produced in the first instance. With less capital funding, record labels are unable to invest in the same broad array of new artists, resulting in an overall decline in the number of new albums and songs released to the public. As one commentator explained, "[i]t took Bruce Springsteen eight years and five albums to achieve his first top-ten radio hit. Today on the other hand, if a band's first album is not a hit, more often than not, that band is dropped from the label. No second chances.

Part of the resistance to labels and the rigorous protection of sound recording copyright seems to be driven by an anticorporate mentality that has been empowered by the availability of peer-to-peer and similar file-sharing services. Corporate ownership of intellectual property, however, is as old as the American copyright system itself. Indeed, such ownership is common in the film, book, and television industry, as well as other areas of intellectual property. Harvard Professor Zechariah Chaffee Jr. responded best to the general criticism in 1945 when he reflected:

> A publisher may own the copyright [in a work] free and clear, and take all the gross income ....
>
> Then is not the talk of helping authors just a pretense? A vigorous attack of this sort has been widely made on the patent system. Most patents are not owned by the inventors, but by manufacturers, who are often very big corporations. Consequently, it is said that we are betraying the purpose of the Constitution. ... Big business is hiding behind the inventor's skirts. This reasoning seems to me unsound. After the inventor makes his invention *work*, an immense expenditure of money is usually necessary to make it sell. ...
>
> Similar reasoning applies to copyrights. ...
>
> One reason, therefore, for protecting the copyright in the hands of the publisher is to give an indirect benefit to authors by enabling them to get royalties or to sell the manuscript outright for a higher price. A second reason is, that it is only equitable that the publisher should obtain a return on his investment.

In sum, the constitutional call for innovation and for a rich public domain is best served when artists and musicians are not only given the tools necessary to create their works, but also when they are given the creative support, promotional consideration, and funding necessary to connect with a large and diverse public. Given the alternatives, as well as the massive infrastructure set up by the labels, reports of record label irrelevancy have been greatly exaggerated; reports of their death, however, are an entirely different matter.

Conclusion

Today the future of the recording industry is undoubtedly in jeopardy. What is less apparent, however, is that the *music industry's* future might also be at risk. The rise in illegal distribution of music online has resulted in declining record industry revenues for over ten years. Reduced capital has and will continue to result in less investment in new artists.

Those critical of record labels, of the labels' relationship with their artists, and of the role that record labels play in the digital environment, often confuse the issue of "relevance" with the need to protect sound recording copyright. In reality, however, the issues are entirely distinct. If an independent artist chooses to record his or her own music and compete in the music marketplace due to reduced barriers to entry, society is undoubtedly benefited. Greater musical diversity is something that the music and recording industries welcome. It is quite a different position, however, to say that record labels are irrelevant simply *because competition exists,* and therefore, that sound recording copyright is not worth protecting. The latter argument is often not explicitly pronounced by detractors, but seemingly underlies their callous indifference. From a business and legal perspective, record labels are legitimate market participants, and should be allowed to freely and fairly compete in the music marketplace. Neither the size, nor history, nor structure of record labels undermines this fundamental principle.

Despite the evident decline of record companies, a new generation of commentators believes that without content investors, such as record labels, music and art will flourish. Chris Anderson, [author of *The Long Tail*] for instance, has concluded that far from destroying music, peer-to-peer services are actually helping music thrive and improving consumer choice in the digital arena. Others suggest that protection of copyright is meaningless in a world where new artists can survive on concert and merchandise sales alone. But these faith-based theories do not withstand careful analysis. Numerous studies have considered and rejected the proposition that the proliferation of digital music has resulted in changes in consumer music preference or consumption. Moreover, there is significant evidence to suggest that the vast majority of new artists actually *lose* money on touring and make virtually no money in merchandise sales. Without a steady stream of income, emerging artists, professional songwriters, and other intermediaries in the recording industry will be faced with ever-increasing hardships. Many songwriters and artists may forego a career in the music industry altogether on the basis that music is simply no longer a viable primary career. Indeed, with decreased barriers to entry on the Internet, music proliferation may actually prohibit new artists from effectively communicating their works to the public, making it harder than ever to sustain a lasting career in the industry.

Moreover, the threat to copyright and the viability of artistic expression is not isolated to music. The motion picture, television, and book publishing industries are also at risk from acts of digital infringement. As broadband speeds continue to increase, it is only a matter of time before consumers in America's largest cities will be able to download content at a rate of 100 megabits per second. Currently, the Federal Communications Commission is pressuring Internet service providers to make such speeds available to 100 million Americans by 2020. At that rate, a typical 700–800 MB iTunes-quality movie will download to a user's computer in approximately seven to eight seconds. As more and more eBook readers hit the market, the proliferation of illegally downloaded eBooks has increased exponentially. In response, some now argue that book publishers are "irrelevant" and that authors can and should directly distribute their works to the public online. It is not clear, however, that such arguments are accurate when applied to the book publishing industry. Notwithstanding the ability of independent authors to compete alongside publishers online, it is important to distinguish greater market competition from the constitutional issues surrounding copyright protection.

Because copyright's primary *constitutional* purpose is to facilitate a rich public domain by means of economically compensating authors, Congress should carefully balance the needs of content holders with the rights of the public when deciding copyright policy. Record labels continue to serve a crucial role in the music industry, despite recent calls to the contrary. As with music, it is a foregone conclusion that art will continue to exist in our society notwithstanding the rise in infringement and potential collapse of artistic investment. Whether authors and artists will be sufficiently encouraged to produce the same quality and diversity in music content is uncertain at best, and is ultimately the most important question.

Given the immense popularity of label-released *music* today, it is no exaggeration to say that the decline of record labels may be akin to killing the goose that laid the golden egg. As one commentator opined, "the real tragedy of the illegal downloading epidemic," and the one of a world without significant investment in music, is that "we don't even know what we're missing".

BRIAN R. DAY is an Attorney with the firm Orrick, Herrington & Sutcliffe, who received his JD degree from George Washington University Law School.

Alex Sayf Cummings

NO

Democracy of Sound: Music Piracy and the Remaking of American Copyright in the Twentieth Century

Introduction

Like many people, rapper J. Cole is not sure how he feels about music piracy. He praises the bootleggers who copy and sell his mixtapes on the street, but he is impatient with fans who copy his music without paying a dime. As of this writing, "The Autograph" had not been formally put on the market. It was unavailable for sale on iTunes, but one could download it as part of the *Friday Night Lights* "mixtape," a set of electronic files available for free on his website; hear it on college radio; and listen to it on You-Tube. The people who distribute his music make it possible for fans to hear him, yet Cole is irked by fans who ask for his autograph on discs they copied themselves. Is it just a matter of disrespect?

Cole is not the first person to have mixed feelings about piracy. Americans have struggled with the problem of unauthorized reproduction—called "piracy," "bootlegging," or "counterfeiting," among other terms, depending on the circumstances—ever since Thomas Edison etched the first sound waves onto tinfoil in his New Jersey lab. Sound recording opened up a variety of new questions about art, economics, and law. Would a wax cylinder or shellac disc be treated, in legal terms, the same way as a novel or photograph? For much of the last century, the answer was no. Who would own the rights to sound waves—the musicians, singers, or speakers who made the sounds? The producers and engineers who captured the sound and shaped it in the studio? The record label that paid everyone involved? And who was allowed to copy what, and under what circumstances?

Copyright interests are prone to paint copying as a cut-and-dried matter of morality. The Motion Picture Association of America runs an ad before movies showing how pirates take food out of the mouths of set painters and other working-class members of the film industry. Record labels say that listeners, through their wanton copying and file sharing, threaten to kill the goose that lays the golden eggs—the creative artist. It is not surprising that these arguments resonate with much of the public. Copying evokes cheating, plagiarism, and unoriginality. Many people, familiar with the ordinary injustices of everyday life, see piracy as just another example of someone getting rich off another person's work. The artist is a worker, "tryna get a dollar," like anyone else.

Such moral convictions may help to explain the hard shift toward stronger copyright laws in America during the last forty years, but they do not account for the many ways in which people copy and use each other's work every day. American law has long recognized, first informally and later by statute, that a certain degree of copying, categorized as "fair use," is acceptable. A teacher can make copies of a poem to discuss in class. . . . And, of course, copyright in the United States has never been an immortal right. The public domain makes freely available all works produced before a certain date, although the ever-expanding scope of property rights has begun to threaten the existence of such a commons of creativity from the past.

The ethics of copying have vexed people since the early days of the printing press. As printing technology spread throughout Europe in the sixteenth century, the possibility of rapidly manufacturing words and images prompted Europeans to develop what would become modern ideas of ownership and authorship. At first, readers did not necessarily link a particular combination of words to a particular author, and printers circulated texts that mutated and evolved through multiple rounds of copying. Soon, however, economics and the politics of censorship intervened. In England, the Crown developed the idea of copyright, granting only the Stationers' Company, a printers guild, the right to produce texts that were approved by the government. Given the religious and political conflicts then unfolding across Europe, a policy that controlled the proliferation of texts was a good bargain for both the government and the printers. Notably, though, the original copyright did not belong to the author but rather to the printer who published a text. Counterintuitive as it may be, this situation remains familiar to many creative people in today's world, who often do not own the rights to their work.

When Americans began to consider how to run their new country in the 1780s, they looked to the legacy of English copyright for cues. The Constitution made it clear that the federal government had the right to regulate what we would now call "media." In the language of the eighteenth century, it was in the public interest for Congress to "promote the Progress of Science and useful Arts, by securing for limited Times to Authors and Inventors the exclusive Right to their respective Writings." The key elements of English law were there: copyright was not a permanent right, but one that would encourage authors to publish by offering the prospect of profit "for limited Times." The first federal copyright law provided only fourteen years of protection, and was limited to books, maps, and charts. Music was not specifically included in the law until 1831.

Copyright, in short, has always been the creature of shifting political interests and cultural aspirations—always incomplete, always subject to change. The United States in the nineteenth century resisted the idea of recognizing the copyrights of other nations, being content to make the cultural fare of Europe cheaply available to its citizens. New media such as photography and sound recording had to be fitted into laws that were primarily written to address works produced by the printing press. As pirates copied sheet music and, later, records, businesses lobbied to have laws passed to protect their products from reproduction; typically, they then pushed for the new protections to be more stringently enforced. At the same time, different interests in the same "business"—for example, songwriters, record labels, radio stations, and jukebox operators—all had different opinions about how works such as songs and sound recordings should be regulated.

Indeed, sound recording set off conflicts over culture and property that profoundly shaped the course of copyright law in the twentieth century. It introduced a kind of medium that could not be perceived with the naked eye. All previous copyrightable works could be seen, whether words on a page, musical notes, or the lines and colors of a photograph. Sound, however, was mechanized; the listener was separated from the content, which was mediated by the stylus and the Victrola horn. Sound also confounded ideas of ownership by making it possible for the same work, a piece of music or a spoken text, to be produced in multiple versions by multiple artists. A hundred players might perform a Joplin rag in a hundred ways, with different instruments, at different speeds, and in different styles. Was each a distinctive work? Americans wrestled with these questions for almost a century following the invention of recording.

Piracy set all these conceptual problems into sharp relief. The early recording industry was perhaps as chaotic as the early days of printing in Europe. Composers clamored to earn income from the recordings made of their music, while competitors in the "talking machine" business copied each other's products. As recorded music grew into a mass medium in the early twentieth century, a system of major labels that marketed hits to national markets emerged, organized along much the same lines as corporations that manufactured cars or soap. But listeners and collectors experimented with ways of copying recordings, and tiny markets for bootlegs emerged by the 1930s. Americans toyed with different modes of experiencing music, apart from buying a record or listening to one on the radio; they collected, copied, and shared records; bootlegged live performances and radio broadcasts; and sold rare and ephemeral recordings in samizdat fashion. . . .

Piracy as Aesthetics

Copying and property have always functioned in dynamic tension. The music or movie industry may like people to believe that the morality of copyright is absolute and self-evident—"You wouldn't steal a car," they say, so why would you steal a movie?—but history tells us that what is acceptable one day may be wrong the next. What is "free as the air" today, as Justice Louis Brandeis put it in 1918, may be property tomorrow. A vendor may sell t-shirts featuring 50 Cent's face at a flea market in North Carolina without expecting reprisal for using the photographer's intellectual property or the rapper's likeness. The same vendor may run afoul of the law for selling bootleg CDs of his music, even though "Fiddy" himself rose to prominence by hawking borrowed sounds on the streets of Queens and Manhattan.

A degree of copying will always be permissible, within certain limits. As Vaidhyanathan, Demers, and others have taken pains to point out, all creativity involves referencing or riffing off of the ideas of others, whether it means quoting a line or borrowing a chord progression or incorporating a sample from another work. Just as importantly, some uses will always fly under the radar, failing to attract the interest of intellectual property owners who are too busy litigating against more lucrative offenders. The record industry paid little attention to jazz bootleggers until their success revealed the commercial viability of reissues, while hip-hop labels tolerated the use of unauthorized samples on DJ mixtapes as long as the free publicity seemed to justify a policy of benign neglect.

Such skirmishes tend to muddy the lines between the sanctity of property rights and the moral turpitude of piracy. Some copiers are profiteers, but others are not. Businesses and rights owners often seek to squelch unauthorized use of their works, but sometimes they look to piracy for cues about new sources of value and even potential benefits from the circulation of sound. These ambiguities, say critics, mean that intellectual property law itself is fundamentally flawed. Demers, among others, has pressed the case for "transformative appropriation," suggesting that some uses of recorded sound should be permitted under the law as recontextualizing or otherwise changing the works they draw upon, unlike the commercial pirate who merely counterfeits a work that is already widely available. Lee Marshall has argued that bootlegging—meaning, in this case, copying live recordings—should be viewed differently than outright piracy, since bootlegs cater to fans and supplement the market for music with a product that does not already exist. They do no harm, in this view, and they arguably do good by documenting music that would otherwise never be heard again.

. . .

Piracy as Economics

. . . The culture of piracy has been too protean, too varied, and too multifaceted for critics of copyright to easily define some uses as good (sampling in hip-hop) or bad (commercial piracy), or for supporters of property rights to defend their preferred position that all copying is always bad. Battles over piracy have polarized businesses, musicians, politicians, and listeners into camps that admit little in the way of mutual recognition, diminishing the potential for a discussion about how copying and copyright have historically constituted each other. If, as the anarchist philosopher Pierre-Joseph Proudhon said, "property is theft," it may be true that theft is also property—or rather that theft produces the need for property rights. Property only exists as a creature of the contests over resources that produce law and legislation. Piracy prompted record companies, musicians, and music publishers to push for new rights, and its persistence continues to shape how the intellectual property regime evolves, for good and ill.

Piracy also shows the demand for products that the market might not otherwise produce, while pioneering new ways in which music can be distributed and experienced by listeners. Playing records on the radio was, after all, a kind of unauthorized reproduction of sound. The medium not only offered new outlets for sound to be reproduced and heard for "free," it also provided musicians a means for finding audiences and record labels for promoting their recordings, although the industry at first feared that the medium would substitute for record sales, rather than supporting them.

Unauthorized reproduction expanded in the early twenty-first century on a scale that equaled or surpassed even the potential of radio to mass produce sound. Whether in the form of MP3s attached to e-mails, torrents on file-sharing networks, or uploads to YouTube, this ceaseless churning of sound reveals two key points: music is more abundant than ever before, and the demand for it remains huge, despite the flagging fortunes of the record industry. The thirteen labels that filed suit in 2010 for $75 trillion based their figure on collecting damages for every infringement—that is, counting every time someone downloaded or uploaded a file from Limewire as an offense, just as an earlier pirate might have paid damages for every copy of an unauthorized record pressed and sold. The figure, of course, far outstrips the number of legitimate record sales during the same period, or any period in the history of the record industry. It reflects not just the industry's penchant for exaggerating figures, but the power of new media to make a wider variety of music available at a greater order of magnitude than earlier technologies. Compared to the solitary efforts of a musician

and the mass production of the record-pressing plant, this new media infrastructure is even more prolific.

Piracy, then, heralded a move from mass production to mass reproduction. Pirates always multiplied the offerings of the market, whether they used home disc engravers in the 1930s, custom-pressing services in the 1940s, or a battery of tape decks in the 1970s. Listeners captured opera and jazz performances from the radio and shared them with friends, creating new "products" that neither the radio station nor the performers intended to produce. Sound engineers could make money on the side by leaking tapes of unreleased recordings from sessions with popular performers, and these outtakes—alternative renditions of songs officially released or new compositions that the artist or company chose not to market, for whatever reason—went into circulation, held under the counter at record stores or sold out of the backs of vans next to college campuses. Concert performances became recorded documents and new commodities. These records often took on a plain, unadorned quality that resembled "burnt" CDs, the homemade discs labeled by listeners with Sharpie pens. . . .

By exploiting the productive capacities of new media, pirates and bootleggers threatened to swamp the market with more music, lowering prices and lessening the incentive for labels to sign the stars and hype the hits. The perennial business model of the music industry—scoring one hit for every nine flops—depended on heavily promoting the popular artist to the public, by means both legal (advertising) and illegal (payola). In 1971, the industry seriously worried that the practice of spending over $500,000 to record and market an album could not survive in the face of widespread unauthorized reproduction by consumers and pirate competitors.

Record labels and pirates presented two very different ways of making and distributing music, and scholars have attempted to describe this difference in terms of a broader change in economic production since the 1970s. The twentieth-century recording industry was a perfect example of a Fordist mode of production that relied on economies of scale to provide a standardized product to a mass audience. Advertising was key to creating the celebrity performer with the giant following and platinum record sales. In contrast, piracy exemplifies the new forms of production that emerged in the late twentieth century, organized around small batches of goods that were often customized to fit demand. Toyota, for instance, introduced its just-in-time system that eschewed massproducing parts ahead of time in favor of a leaner, faster system that only produced goods as they were needed.

File-sharing networks function in much the same way—particular, customizable, and flexible, affording greater choice and diversity than is available on the established market for music. Research by Big Champagne, a company that monitors online file sharing, shows that most users have only a few songs by each artist on their computers, but the range of artists runs the gamut from old to new, from Led Zeppelin to Lil Wayne and TI to Tim

McGraw. Some users have dozens or hundreds of songs by a particular artist, while dabbling in the catalogs of numerous musicians who would rarely be heard on the same radio station or found on the same store shelves. The US Government Accountability Office estimated in 2010 that only one in five illegal downloads actually substituted for a potential record sale, which suggests that as many as 80 percent of downloads involved music that users would not otherwise purchase. The system suits both the casual listener, with a broad but shallow interest in many artists, as well as the "completist" who seeks every single work by a particular artist.

Piracy actually anticipated these innovations in production and distribution. Bootlegging in the 1930s and 1940s demonstrated some of the qualities that theorists later attributed to the post-Fordist economy, yet these practices occurred in the heyday of mass media and standardized factory production. Enterprises like the Hot Record Society and Jolly Roger offered consumers more-specialized products, produced in smaller runs than RCA-Victor, a large, vertically integrated firm considered profitable in the 1950s. In this sense, bootlegging prefigured the "Long Tail" concept that former *Wired* editor-in-chief Chris Anderson introduced in 2004. Anderson pointed out how online retailers Amazon and iTunes could afford to make books and music available that would appeal to only a very small number of consumers; whereas traditional stores maximized profit by allocating scarce inventory and shelf space to the biggest selling goods, the lower costs of stocking and distribution enjoyed by iTunes permitted its parent corporation, Apple, to reap additional income by catering to a wide array of small niche interests. Each additional audio file hosted or sold on iTunes poses little marginal cost to the company.

These new business models are only new in the sense that the established music industry has begun only recently—and reluctantly—to embrace them. Businesses such as iTunes provide a greater variety of choices than a Target or Tower Records could manage to stock on their shelves by exploiting economies of scope, answering the complaints long voiced by collectors and other enthusiasts that record labels and retailers saw little to be gained by providing the obscure music that they desired. For much of the twentieth century, piracy fulfilled this demand, making up for the inadequacies of the legitimate market. Similarly, pirates made music and other goods available in the developing world to consumers who otherwise could not obtain them. In both instances, piracy filled in the cracks between official supply and real demand.

The Politics of Information

The record industry has, of course, more often attempted to squelch this demand rather than cater to it. It won political support for punitive antipiracy measures by arguing that government had to protect sectors such as music and film in the interest of promoting economic growth, at a time when manufacturing was beginning to decline in the United States. Judith Stein and other scholars have examined the political ascendance of post-industrial interests in the 1970s and 1980s, documenting how policy makers embraced tax reforms, deregulation, and other programs that benefited industries in the FIRE (finance, insurance, and real estate) sector. The rise of an important political coalition behind intellectual property rights was but one part of this ideological and rhetorical shift toward an "information society" that favored certain kinds of businesses to the diminution of manufacturing.

The idea of an information revolution first appeared in the early 1960s, soon after journalists and scholars began to speculate about a post-industrial society. Promoted by Madison Avenue, the revolution was eventually embraced by academics, policy makers, and technology giants such as IBM. The future of the American economy did not lie in heavy industry and mass production, but, rather, in automation, computers, and the production of information—the copyrights, patents, and other forms of knowledge that made it all possible. While some optimists looked forward to a day when automation allowed Americans to create more with less labor, and thus enjoy greater leisure, the central premise of information politics was the greater importance of information over labor, manufacturing, or any other concerns. This assumption—widely accepted yet rarely questioned—has become an article of faith among academic theorists, as in Manuel Castells's influential formula of the information society as "a specific form of social organization in which information generation, processing, and transmission become the fundamental sources of productivity and power." In an oft-cited 1977 study, economist Marc Uri Porat estimated that 53 percent of Americans already worked in information jobs (according, of course, to his own categorization). If one accepts the premise that information is the key to the entire economy and that a majority of workers' jobs depend on it, then taking measures to protect information or intellectual property makes plain sense.

Only in the 1960s, though, did lawmakers and jurists at every level begin to view the economic imperative of protecting investments made by record labels and other entertainment companies as paramount. A few politicians, such as Rep. Abner Mikva (D-IL) and Sen. Philip Hart (D-MI), questioned whether stronger copyright would actually favor consumers, but skepticism about copyright was much scarcer in the 1970s than before. The change in attitudes occurred as rock music, magnetic tape, and the counterculture set off the bootleg boom of the late 1960s. It was also the result of a subtle shift in the understanding of property rights that had evolved during the long period when sound recordings were not protected by copyright, as jurists sought an alternative rationale for protecting records that focused on the value companies had already invested in producing and popularizing records. The argument for protecting recordings depended on the investment of time, labor, and money into the product itself, not on the concept of a limited incentive that had traditionally shaped copyright. It committed the state to preserving what later generations would call "brand value."

Representatives of a so-called copyright industry pitched stronger property rights as a vital tool for economic development. Movie studios and record labels, in particular, have routinely pressed Congress for stricter protection of their goods. For example, in 1982 Congress considered a bill to stiffen the penalties against piracy of music and movies. The deliberations over copyright infringement occurred against the backdrop of a wrenching recession in 1982, when jobs involving services and information technology were among the only sectors showing signs of growth. Copyright interests positioned their own businesses as vital to the nation's economic well-being. Disney's Peter F. Nolan argued to Congressman Barney Frank (D-MA) that his company depended on a long-term return on its investment in animated films, which it re-released for new audiences of children every few years. Piracy threatened this business strategy. "You can see that a lot of jobs and a lot of investment capital are riding on your bill," he concluded. Politicians increasingly linked strong enforcement of intellectual property rights to the economic health of an emergent information economy, and in the 1990s Bill Clinton made growing "information-based jobs" a key priority of his administration.

The ascendance of intellectual property coincided, ironically, with the success of politicians like Clinton and Ronald Reagan, who decried "Big Government," as well as a substantial expansion of government intrusion into the lives of Americans. This twist in American political culture reflects the strange heritage of the 1960s—a continued tension between the emerging New Right, with its focus on the economic prerogatives of business, and the anarchistic, hedonistic idea of liberation that germinated in the era's counterculture, of which piracy was one exuberant part. The rhetoric of the "free-market" imagined freedom as low taxes and deregulation, while a distinct subculture flourished in Silicon Valley that emphasized liberation through technology, championed by boomer activists such as Richard Stallman and John Perry Barlow, the former Grateful Dead lyricist who helped popularize the slogan "Information wants to be free." Although the conservative freedom agenda has experienced greater legislative success, the free-information movement has found expression through influential outlets like *Wired* magazine and political vehicles such as the Electronic Frontier Foundation (EFF).

In fact, the conservative economic program—known to scholars as "neoliberalism"—has been misunderstood by many of its critics as being fundamentally antistatist. Intellectual property law was only one dimension of an American state that increasingly intervened in citizen's lives during the 1980s and 1990s. In theory, neoliberalism represents the small-government platform of Reagan, Thatcher, and Bush, politicians who espoused the greater virtue and efficiency of the private sector over the state.

In practice, neoliberalism has become a catch-all category for all things opposed by the Left, even as "neoliberal" leaders pursue a jumble of policies seemingly unrelated by a central theme; consider, for example, the administration of President George W. Bush, which endorsed "small-government" policies like tax cuts and privatization while expanding military spending, government surveillance, and federal intervention in education. Neoliberalism often represents "a further blurring of the line between the state and the economy rather than a rolling back of the public sector," journalist Daniel Ben-Ami observed in 2011. "Indeed, in some respects it involves an extension of state involvement in businesses."

Ben-Ami is right not to take rhetoric of small government and free markets at face value. Far from ushering in the death of the state, the neoliberalism of the late twentieth and early twenty-first century pruned the functions of government in some ways, such as social welfare, but bolstered them in others—providing subsidies for favored taxpayers and businesses, protecting sectors such as finance and entertainment, and controlling the bodies of workers and consumers in newly invasive ways. Its policy prescription amounted to "state protection and public subsidy for the rich, market discipline for poor," as Noam Chomsky observed in 1995. Lawmakers passed more stringent penalties for copyright infringement at the same time that laws regulating drugs and immigration became vastly more punitive. People who trafficked in certain goods and services could expect to face years in prison, thanks to mandatory minimum sentencing and other measures designed to "get tough" on crime. Congress considered one of the earliest mandatory minimum bills the same year it passed the seminal Copyright Act of 1976.

Drug dealers and pirates, of course, were likely not the people politicians had in mind when they lauded small business. Indeed, poor communities and people of color have borne the brunt of the push for more aggressive law enforcement, yet few scholars have looked at the intensification of intellectual property law as part of the same repressive zeitgeist. One need look no further than the case of Ousame Zongo, an immigrant from Burkina Faso who in 2003 was shot dead in New York after being wrongly suspected of hiding pirate CDs in a Chelsea storage locker, for confirmation of how real the regime of copyright enforcement has become.

Zongo's murder was remarkable, even atypical of the war on piracy—more the result of racism and a culture of police violence than of overzealous copyright enforcement, perhaps. Yet it speaks to the tragic futility of a debate that has raged from the days of piano rolls and wax cylinders to global struggles over trade, the Internet, and intellectual property rights. Political action put the state squarely behind the protection of copyright by the 1970s, and law enforcement has labored to curb piracy without ever fully stopping it. Unauthorized reproduction continues—not just online or in Pakistan or Nigeria, but on the counter of an Atlanta gas station that sells clearly bootlegged copies of Nicki Minaj CDs for $3.99 a piece, in full view of the police officers who frequent the store. When a friend tells me about some new music she has, she says I can "steal" it from her, meaning I can connect a USB drive to her laptop and transfer the files to my own computer. "Stealing" has taken on a humorous and altogether ordinary connotation in the context of music. Piracy is, of course, less amusing when a man senselessly loses his life in the quest to protect the record industry's property rights and revenue.

Like the War on Drugs, the war on piracy has fallen far short of its goals. The gap between laws and norms is especially disquieting, as Lawrence Lessig has argued. Despite strong legal sanctions against drug use, studies suggest that Americans are more likely to smoke marijuana than citizens of the Netherlands, with its notoriously permissive drug laws. The behavior lacks the social stigma that policy makers might have wished for when they passed laws forbidding the production and sale of cannabis. Similarly, strict intellectual property laws did not deter millions of Americans from copying music, file sharing, or buying bootleg CDs. Cynicism about the music industry lingered with the public, as some users of online file sharing continue to express little guilt about piracy, seeing it as a way of "getting back" at record companies. Piracy is a problem that may not be solved by law or moral exhortation.

A compromise remains possible between the desires of listeners and the interests of rights owners, particularly artists. Since 2001 the organization Creative Commons has promoted the use of alternative licenses, which allow artists and companies to opt out of copyright law by permitting others to use their work in any number of carefully defined commercial and noncommercial ways. Another opt-out system prevails on sites such as YouTube, which contain numerous creative works that have not been cleared for use by copyright owners. Rights owners can ask the site's managers to remove their material if they wish. A good deal of live concert footage, TV clips, music videos, and other work remains online in any case, since some artists may not oppose their performances being available and some companies may not notice or care that the material is posted.

Fittingly, the innovations of social media arise, at least in part, from the world of music. Piracy prefigured the emergence of online social networking, as evidenced by the web of relationships through which Grateful Dead fans have recorded, copied, and exchanged tapes since the 1970s. These practices are rooted in an ancient, yet oft-forgotten, dimension of musical experience that is primarily social. People see musicians as part of an audience, sing as part of a choir, listen to records or the radio together, and share music to forge relationships and signify their own tastes and identities. In some ways, the rise of recording diminished these social, interactive aspects of music, in much the same way that recording made individual musicianship less essential for people to be able to

experience music. Music becomes private; one can sit and listen to a record in a room alone, with no presence other than the sound of the absent musicians. Music historian William Howland Kenney argued that this private aspect of recorded music should not be overemphasized, though, as people continued to encounter music as part of a group experience through radio, jukeboxes, and other media.

Yet the music industry has long wished to control how consumers used its products, preferring an ideal relationship in which the purchaser is the only one licensed to enjoy the written or recorded music he purchased. As a congressman summed up the industry's viewpoint in 1906, "The property itself does not carry the right to use it." Music publishers lobbied to deny churches the right to share sheet music with each other in the early twentieth century; labels sought to bar the playing of records on the radio in the 1930s; and the industry later warned consumers that copying and sharing tapes was illegal, even when it was not. If nothing else, piracy has catered to a desire to connect with others through music—a desire that swelled and broke out into the open in the age of Napster and YouTube.

Such networks showed that people could produce, distribute, and consume creative works without the traditional intermediaries of talent scouts, record executives, or broadcasters. Without the help of a label and its promotional budget, obscure artists could cultivate followings by presenting their music online as individual tracks or videos, which circulated through music blogs, social networks, and video hosting sites. These developments undercut much of the rationale for record companies' ownership of recordings, which was based on the notion that money spent on production and promotion created a value that the companies alone deserved to exploit. Songwriters, musicians, radio stations, and other interests had long contested the right of labels to own recordings and act as arbiters of access to music, and they only acquiesced to this right in the face of rising piracy in the 1960s and 1970s. As new forms of music distribution supplant the role of labels, unauthorized reproduction may yet prove to be the undoing of those rights.

Not all artists view sharing as bad. They may want their music to be heard, like the music publishers of the early twentieth century who paid pluggers and vaudeville artists to familiarize audiences with their songs by playing them. Hip-hop DJs sometimes saw bootleggers as the unofficial manufacturers of their work, ensuring that mixtapes ended up on the streets and in the hands of retailers, radio stations, and other important audiences. When the Supreme Court considered the case against the file-sharing network Grokster in 2005, numerous artists on small labels expressed concern that they would lose an outlet for their music. "I look at it as a library," Jeff Tweedy of the band Wilco said, "I look at it as our version of the radio." Wilco freely offered recordings on its website for months before releasing a new album, and, like the Grateful Dead, the band favored taping of concerts by fans. A 2007 study of file sharing tentatively suggested that such networks helped independent musicians overcome their lack of promotion and distribution by making their music more easily accessible. The result was more recordings from independent labels making it onto the charts. "If anecdotal evidence is correct in suggesting that minor labels have utilized file-sharing networks to popularize their albums," the study's authors surmised, "then the majors have an added incentive to fight file sharing." For a small artist or firm, "piracy" could be just another word for "distribution" or "promotion."

Early in the twenty-first century, the record industry sought to quash competitors such as Limewire, MP3.com, and the maker of the first MP3 player, Diamond Multimedia, each of which offered different vehicles for bringing music to listeners. Some of these firms worked out deals with independent artists and labels, offering free MP3 downloads to curious listeners and valuable exposure to little-known performers. In 1999, MP3.com even began working with the group Emerging Artists and Talent on a deal that would give musicians a 50 percent royalty on any CDs sold through the site, a much higher rate than most artists received from the major labels. However, litigation soon ended these experiments as MP3.com and the file-sharing networks that followed it were steadily dismantled.

A subsequent wave of new enterprises emerged to resolve the conflict between rights owners and file-sharing networks. Online streaming services such as Pandora and Spotify create the same sensation of free music—choosing anything you want, the surprise of getting something for nothing—that Napster once provided, except with the consent of record labels. In Spotify's case, it took two years for the service to clear legal hurdles in the United States after becoming available in Europe. Such services offer a diverse supply of music to listeners as an ad-supported free service or without ads for a monthly fee. If the music industry is the thesis and piracy is the antithesis, social media and online streaming sites offer a kind of synthesis—driven by user choices, and based on a model that does not necessarily involve the sale of a good but instead the provision of a service that makes music readily and widely accessible. The idea of the information economy, as advanced by businesses and politicians, maintained that sound must be protected from theft just as a book on a bookstore shelf is, whether by antipiracy mechanisms or the threat of prosecution. In the emerging media environment of the early twenty-first century, however, selling a disc or even an MP3 may not be the dominant way that people receive and experience music or that artists make money. A new model may look more like radio, offering free access to sound, than the traditional recording industry that manufactured and sold sound as a scarce good.

Such a reorganization of the industry has profound implications not only for how music is produced and distributed, but what kinds of music survive and prosper. For much of the last century, conventional wisdom held that nine out of ten records failed to make a profit. This arrangement meant debt and oblivion for many artists and, for labels, pandering to the lowest common denominator in the hope of scoring a hit. Some independent artists could make a living by setting up their own miniature version of a major label, as folk singer Ani Difranco did with her Righteous Babe Records in the 1990s, yet they still faced the same barriers of access to reaching radio listeners and consumers. A service-oriented music business at least holds the potential for a broader, more diverse array of musicians to find an audience, without relying as much on record labels and hype to survive.

Yet nothing is assured. The likes of Spotify may fail in the marketplace or the courts, and new middlemen may emerge to take advantage of artists in new, innovative ways. Jazz polymath Herbie Hancock expressed this worry amid the Napster controversy in 2001, when the outcome of the RIAA's lawsuits remained unknown. "*Excuse me,*" he declared, "*but* just because record executives give artists a bad deal doesn't mean everyone else can then go and do worse [emphasis in original]." Music blogs that review and distribute free MP3s may exploit the free labor of emerging artists for profit, and companies such as Pandora may take the place of record labels and radio stations as the gatekeepers of popular culture.

Whatever shape the industry itself takes, the history of recorded sound suggests that unauthorized copying and sharing will persist in its own unpredictable and shifting ways. In 1995 the Clinton administration hoped to stop copying entirely, worrying that "just one unauthorized uploading of a work onto a bulletin board . . . could have devastating effects on the market for the work," yet the idea of preventing any item from ever being shared is unrealistic in the context of a culture and an economy that thrive on the unencumbered communication of ideas and expression. . . .

Uncritical support for intellectual property rights places private interests high above those of the public. When an individual's or corporation's right to maximize profit becomes the only goal of public policy, any stake the broader community may hold in the vast store of human creativity, whether music, art, writing, or technology, disappears from view. Hence the odd argument that copyright should last forever, or almost forever—a rightful inheritance that should endure like a family heirloom or estate. In such a scenario, we would have to seek out the descendants of Shakespeare for permission to perform *All's Well that Ends Well*. The value that culture holds for other artists, seeking inspiration and borrowing ideas, for students seeking affordable access to music and literature, or for any citizens to draw on the legacy of the past appears irrelevant. Copyright interests in the late twentieth century supposed that people should not learn, feel, or experience any expression without money changing hands. Pirates suggested otherwise.

Piracy was present throughout the history of the record industry, a fact of life that was ignored, accepted, or resisted, depending on the circumstances. In its various permutations, from the jazz era to the heyday of rock and the rise of hip-hop, unauthorized reproduction pointed the way to different ways of making and enjoying sound, a nascent set of productive relations that grew in tension with mass culture and copyright law. Lawmakers and judges recast copyright as a bulwark against a rising tide of piracy since the 1950s, yet stronger property rights failed to thwart the industry's pirate nemesis—and the traditional sectors of the music business stumbled into an unprecedented decline in the early years of the twenty-first century. Music remains as abundant as ever, as file sharing and new businesses provide access to a broader range of music than was available to most people for most of the industry's history. Piracy might not kill music, but history may record that it killed the twentieth-century record industry.

ALEX SAYF CUMMINGS is a Faculty Member at Georgia State University, where he teaches and researches the history of law, media, and society. His work focuses on ideological transformation in American culture in the Information Society.

EXPLORING THE ISSUE

Are Copyright Laws Effective in Curbing Piracy?

Critical Thinking and Reflection

1. Do you think that our current copyright laws are obsolete? If so, what other business models might exist to allow artists to make a profit (or a living) from their creative work?
2. How are the business and legal aspects of media industries related and/or interrelated?
3. Is copyright a legal, or a moral protection for artists?
4. If file sharing services could operate with no restrictions, would we need to be concerned about controlling personal information about ourselves (like our health profiles, job histories, or financial records)? Would personal information be protected when there are technologies available that can download any digital content easily?
5. What new technologies or business practices have forced changes in the copyright laws in the United States?

Is There Common Ground?

The authors of these selections would agree that the law establishing copyright has been challenged by new technologies, business practices, and social conditions for centuries, but they differ on how "inviolable" the law should be. Both agree too, that there is a moral component of what undergirds the principle of copyright.

New technologies that lead one to violate copyright, consciously or not, have taken the problem of ease of duplication of media product to a new level that is confusing and challenges traditional law. Some scholars argue that traditional copyright is no longer enforceable, and that old laws should be completely re-envisioned with an eye toward current digital technologies and distribution systems, but to totally revise legal statutes could create chaos for the industries and the economy of those industries. As these authors indicate, interventions may be needed, but a part of the solution may be in educating the public about the law, and reasonable pricing of media product to reduce violations of the law.

Create Central

www.mhhe.com/createcentral

Additional Resources

Ronan Deazley, Martin Kretschmer, and Lionel Bently, eds., *Privilege and Property: Essays on the History of Copyright* (Open Book Publishers, 2010)

Roberta R. Kwall, *The Soul of Creativity: Forging a Moral Rights Law for the United States* (Stanford University Press, 2010)

Lee Marshall, *Bootlegging: Romanticism and Copyright in the Music Industry* (Sage Publications, 2005)

David J. Moser and Cheryl L. Slay, *Music Copyright Law* (Cengage Learning, 2012)

Internet References . . .

Electronic Frontier Foundation (EFF)

www.eff.org/

Jessica Litman, "Lawful Personal Use," *Texas Law Review*, (vol. 85, 1989), pp. 1871–1920.

www-personal.umich.edu/~jdlitman/papers/LawfulPersonalUse.pdf

Kal Raustiala and Chris Sprigman, "How Much Do Music and Movie Piracy Hurt the U.S. Economy?" *Freakonomics.com* (January 12, 2012)

http://freakonomics.com/2012/01/12/how-much-do-music-and-movie-piracy-really-hurt-the-u-s-economy/

Recording Industry Association of America "Who Music Theft Hurts," (October 28, 2013)

www.riaa.com/physicalpiracy.php?content_selector=piracy_details_online

U.S. Copyright Office, "Copyright and Fair Use" (2012)

www.copyright.gov/fls/fl102.html

Unit 5

Media Business

*I*t is important to remember that media industries are businesses and that they must be profitable in order to thrive. Changes in ownership rules have resulted in a new group of media companies and corporations. Newspapers may be the first major industry to fail. Most have retooled and have focused on smaller, targeted audiences. In this section we discuss what has changed in traditional media outlets, and whether some of those changes are really good for the artists who participate in them. Are some forms of media, like print journalism, able to survive in such a highly competitive marketplace? Does media consolidation make sense? These questions lead us to ask what media will be available to us in the future. Are there evolving models of business for the digital age? What aspects of law, regulation, and business practices have come together to change the nature of the media "playing field"? How likely are new services to survive? Is the era of mass media now over?

Selected, Edited, and with Issue Framing Material by:
Alison Alexander, *University of Georgia*
and
Jarice Hanson, *University of Massachusetts—Amherst*

ISSUE

Is Streaming the Future of the Music Industry?

YES: **Joan E. Solsman**, from "Attention, Artists: Streaming Music Is the Inescapable Future. Embrace It," CNET News (2014)

NO: **Charles Arthur**, from "Streaming: The Future of the Music Industry, Or Its Nightmare?," *The Guardian* (2015)

Learning Outcomes

After reading this issue, you will be able to:

- Better understand how streaming has changed the distribution system for music.
- Understand the impact on industries as more technologies use wireless, digital forms.
- Consider how important revenue is to the ongoing maintenance of an industry.
- Better judge the impact of music piracy.
- Consider how business models influence what type of content becomes available to us.

ISSUE SUMMARY

YES: Journalist Joan E. Solsman discusses the rise of streaming services like Pandora and Spotify, and identifies three business models that are emerging from the number of streaming services. Her article shows how divergent the forms of distribution for music have become, and the impact on artist revenue for some of those new services.

NO: Journalist Charles Arthur discusses some of the same streaming services, but identifies how little profit many of them are making because consumer tendency to download free music cuts into the revenue of many of the emerging services.

When an industry is forced to change because of new technology or new business practices, the term used to describe the event is *disruption*. The disruption to the traditional recorded music industry has been monumental in scope and suggests that other media technologies may well be disrupted themselves, as digital technology makes it easier to share, distribute, and even illegally access content that had previously tightly controlled the distribution to maximize revenue. In these two selections that explore the disruptive aspects of streaming music services, we get a sense that the recorded music industry is in for even more disruption as different streaming services compete against

each other for customers, and as revenue models change the way we access music.

The recorded music industry has changed more than any other media-related industry because the shift to digital distribution of music has resulted in a variety of new formats for delivery. Streaming content over the Internet is inexpensive and highly accessible. In part, the biggest challenge for the recorded music industry today is the illegal piracy of signals that are possible through some forms of downloading content. Although there have been many attempts to curb this type of piracy of content, streaming technologies all tend to challenge our traditional concepts of copyright, ownership, and fair compensation for the artists whose content is digitally distributed.

The music industry faced its first challenge to the traditional business model (in which record labels controlled the content of those artists who had signed with their companies) in 1998, when 19-year-old Shawn Fanning developed a free Internet-based, peer-to-peer (P2P) service called Napster that allowed people to share music files through MP3 technology. By 2001, Fanning had been taken to court by the Recording Industry Association of America (RIAA) for copyright infringement, and Napster was shut down. Fanning then sold the logo and name to Roxio, a company that legally sold music through the Internet, and since that time, the recording industry has been in flux and new business models have emerged to promote musicians and music. The former record companies have not given up hope that they could survive the technical shift to digital music and have come up with a number of new services and methods of distributing content, but this plethora of competition has also presented a number of challenges to artists and the industry.

Of course, we can't even talk about streaming without commenting on how the same technologies can be used to pirate content. When this happens, no one in the recording industry makes a profit (except perhaps the pirates themselves, through the sale of their music libraries). So although the two selections in this issue focus on commercial streaming services, we should remember that the same technology can undermine the profit motive within an industry as well.

One of the biggest challenges for commercial services is that streaming services often pay artists different types of royalties for music that someone streams over their service. Some artists receive fractions of a penny for each download of their music, while more established artists may make a bit more—but rarely more than a penny per download. And if an artist's music is being streamed by different companies, those companies are likely to have different scales of royalties. The result is an extremely complicated system of reporting the number of songs streamed, by which companies, and at which rates.

At the same time, some services have actually helped new artists become known. Companies like SoundCloud, BandCamp, and even the re-imagined MySpace (for example) have developed services that allow artists to freely share with each other, and introduce new artists to music aficionados. Despite these possible uses of streaming technology to open the market to new artists, some established artists feel that they no longer can allow their music to be streamed at all, because of the potential loss of revenue that can affect best-selling artists. Singers like Taylor Swift, David Byrne, and Radiohead (for example) have all chosen not to license

their music to streaming services, and Jay-Z launched a service called Tidal, which pays the highest royalties possible to artists. No matter how you look at it, the number of services and the complicated structure of payment to artists have changed the nature of the music industry forever.

Streaming is an important distribution form, since it is highly likely to affect film and television content as well. Many of the companies that are already streaming music now have some video and gaming services, like The Pirate Bay, and many more have plans to roll out video and interactive gaming services in the near future. So the upset in the recorded music industry is very likely to affect film, television, and gaming industries as well.

The media industries are, after all, businesses that cannot thrive for long if they don't make a profit, and performing artists need to be able to control the distribution of their own material. In many ways, the shift from physical records or CDs to streaming music has created an even larger market for artists to go on the road, perform live, and make the bulk of their income from ticket sales and the sale of merchandise when they do perform live. Those high prices to attend a live concert are, in part, due to the relative lack of income generated by streaming technology and the sharing of free content among users.

If you think about other media industries also affected by the changes to the music industry, you start to see how one major change impacts another. Radio and airplay of music are still possible, but royalty payments for radio may be very different from streaming services targeting individual consumers. Many artists license their work for other forms of media, such as when their songs are used in films, or even for the theme songs of television programs. One of the first groups to make a significant income from licensing their previously recorded material was They Might Be Giants, who licensed their song "You're Not the Boss of Me" for the popular TV show *Malcolm in the Middle*, which ran from 2001 to 2006. And the Canadian group Bare Naked Ladies began the trend of establishing their own record label so that they could better control the distribution of their music and how it might be used by other media forms.

As you read these selections, it may be helpful to think about issues of copyright and who (or which jobs) are actually affected by streaming, as well as the technologies that disrupt established industries. The corner "mom-and-pop" record store is no longer the mainstay of any community, and all of the people who were involved in the promotion, distribution, and marketing of traditional recorded music have seen their jobs disappear or radically change. As time passes, we may see that streaming is only a small part of music distribution, or, perhaps we may see streaming become the major distribution form for all sorts of media content.

YES

Joan E. Solsman

Attention, Artists: Streaming Music Is the Inescapable Future. Embrace It

Music's Bedrock Business will be Selling Access to Streams, Not Ownership of Tunes. So What Does That Mean for the Artists You Love? It Should be Music to Their Ears.

Eric Hutchinson long cherished his alphabetized treasury of CDs, but when he began gravitating to streaming-music sites like Pandora, he packed his music collection into four suitcases. That all fits in a pocket now, he remembers thinking, as he shoved the suitcases into a taxi to take to a secondhand CD store.

If you subscribe to the anti-Spotify gospel of Taylor Swift, Hutchinson's actions should strike fear in the hearts of artists: a music lover moving from money-making purchases to the feels-like-free universe of streaming tunes. The only wrinkle: Hutchinson is a musician himself.

A recording artist for more than a decade, Hutchinson is headlining a 30-date cross-country tour, playing theaters that can accommodate 1,000 or more people. The singer-songwriter also listens to 7 to 10 hours of streaming music a week. "The model is not perfect yet for sure, but the more people stream, it's an exciting time to be making music as a result," he said.

The rise of streaming services like Spotify and Pandora is spurring a fundamental change in how the industry makes money, from selling ownership of music to selling access to it. This shift fogs the career path for artists: Beside complicating royalties, it hasn't been around long enough to prove it can sustain careers. Plus, stars looking down from on high—like Swift, Radiohead's Thom Yorke and The Talking Heads' David Byrne—proclaim the model cheapens music and rips musicians off. But artists who look past the high-profile preaching will find that streaming actually levels the playing field, giving more musicians than ever a fighting chance.

Maybe that's what Swift is afraid of. The pop star made herself the poster girl for the anti-streaming set this month, yanking her entire catalog off Spotify just as her album "1989" pulled off the best debut-week sales of any

record in 12 years. Her life's work shouldn't be the guinea pig in an experiment that doesn't fairly compensate creators, she said.

But the streaming takeover is inevitable. In the US, streamed music accounted for 27 percent of music sales in the first half of the year, up from just 3 percent in 2007 and 15 percent in 2012, according to the Recording Industry Association of America. Streaming sales have nearly surpassed sales from physical music—mostly CDs—which stand at 28 percent. Digital downloads made up the biggest chunk at 41 percent of total revenue, but both downloads and physical sales are dwindling.

"Will subscription and access models be the de facto way that the majority of people will end up consuming music at some point in the future? Yes, 100 percent, I'm absolutely convinced that that will be the case," said Rob Wells, the head of global digital business at the world's biggest record-label company, Universal Music Group, who added that downloads and physical purchases aren't going away.

And being paid for sound recordings has never been how artists really make bank. Albums and singles are essential, but the boon for the musician was the merchandise, touring and sponsorships, or that 30-second snippet of song in a national commercial. Streaming actually bolsters those, but it's not easy getting people to take a leap of faith that something so different will work.

"When you've got this new system, you're asking people to learn," said Lars Murray, Pandora's head of label relations. "It's human nature to not want to reset the table."

The Curse of Complications

The biggest stumbling block for artists is that the streaming-music future complicates a business that's already baffling in its complexity.

For one, the blanket term "streaming music" applies to a diverse lineup of services, all of which pay musicians and songwriters differently.

There are three main models. The ad-supported product like Pandora, the Internet's biggest online radio service, pays royalties mostly determined by the US government or government-related bodies. Another category is on-demand, paid-subscription services, such as Apple's Beats Music. You pay a monthly fee for all-you-can-eat listening from a catalog of millions of songs. These services pay royalties based on confidential licensing deals with rights holders, such as labels. The third is a hybrid of the two, like Spotify, which offers a free, ad-supported option and a paid tier with privileged features like offline listening on your phone.

Other platforms defy those categorizations. SoundCloud, an audio YouTube, lets anyone upload and listen to sound files. SoundCloud hit 250 million registered users late last year, on par with Pandora.

Confused yet? Try to untangle the knot of royalties in the music world. Royalties before streaming were already dizzying, with payments for physical products differing from those for performances. Now every kind of streaming service pays different rates to different people under different circumstances in different countries—and many of these rates aren't public.

An artist looking at the sum of her royalty checks from streaming for the year will mostly see a reflection of her contract—not a full picture of what streaming services pay to rights holders. In addition, the royalty rates for a stream of a single song are much smaller than for the purchase of a single song. That's where people like Swift cry foul.

A Leap of Faith

Artists' top criticism of the streaming-music future is that it just won't pay as well. Swift's label, Big Machine, put a number to that argument Wednesday: $496,044. That's how much the label received for US streams of Swift's music in the last 12 months. That's much smaller than the $6 million a year Spotify founder and Chief Executive Daniel Ek said an artist of Swift's stature was on track to earn.

The consensus response to this complaint: just wait until streaming goes mainstream.

"When the CD was three years old, people were complaining that you couldn't build a career on CD sales," said Charles Caldas, chief executive of Merlin, a group that represents more than 20,000 independent labels worldwide. "It took years for that format to get to scale."

While a per-song payment for a download is much higher than the per-song payment of a stream, downloads are a onetime deal. That makes streaming the gift that keeps on giving. "Revenues look small because there are relatively few subscribers," said Alex Pollock, who has handled tour accounting for bands like Coldplay, Maroon 5 and the Beastie Boys. "But if you buy into the concept that subscriber base will continue to grow, the money will grow exponentially."

Evidence is building that streaming services, particularly subscription, will pay material sums to the industry as they get bigger. Spotify, for example, will pay out more [than] $1 billion to rights holders this year, double its payments of 2013.

"Spotify is the single biggest driver of growth in the music industry, the No. 1 source of increasing revenue, and the first or second biggest source of overall music revenue in many places," Ek wrote Tuesday.

The Opportunity for the Open-Minded

While streaming does complicate the business side for artists, it also gives musicians unprecedented power. Streaming puts global distribution to a massive audience at the fingertips of social-savvy artists, at the same time technology made it easier to record a song on a shoestring budget.

Alina Baraz last year recorded a song on her laptop and uploaded it to SoundCloud. "I remember sitting on my couch and realizing that today is going to be the day I release my first song," she said. Over the year, she's accumulated 29,000 followers and had her most popular song played 2.8 million times. She connected with a producer in Denmark through the platform, with whom she collaborates through Skype, email and shared audio files.

"I don't know how I knew that SoundCloud would be the best opportunity for me, but I don't think anything else would have suited," she said.

Soundcloud co-founder Eric Wahlforss said streaming creates a path for more people like Baraz. "Being a musician was never easy, especially if you're doing music that doesn't appeal to a huge audience," he said. "This is a way to make it sustainable for a larger part of musicians than it has before."

True, but the 2.8 million streams of Baraz's songs are 2.8 million times she gave away her music. As painful as it may be for artists to accept that their invaluable music may not be what listeners want to pay for, the big money doesn't stem from the recordings themselves anyway—it comes from things like concerts.

"It started off you would tour to support an album," Pollock said of legacy bands like his client Depeche Mode.

"That's now shifted to putting out an album to create a reason to justify a tour."

Live performance revenue is the biggest money-maker in the business, and it's getting bigger. Live music sales are expected to grow to 64 percent of the US music industry by 2018, from 59 percent share last year, according to PwC's entertainment and media outlook.

Another perk of streaming: it can tell artists where they'll probably pack venues. After Pandora showed Hutchinson the top 10 cities that listen to him most, he was surprised to see the list include[s] places like Seattle, where he gets less radio play. He made sure to put it on his tour. High-priced VIP tickets sold out weeks in advance.

Streaming music platforms are also allowing artists to widen their "merch table" to include intangible experiences such as selling a one-on-one Skype chat with a fan. Smule, the music-app maker behind Sing Karaoke, has begun a program of promotional partnerships with artists. Emerging artist Todd Carey, for example, offered a contest to Smule-app users: upload a cover of his single for the chance to win an iPad. Because people ended up buying his music to practice, the business effect was immediate and obvious, said manager Jason Spiewak. Carey went from selling 100 or so singles a week to a thousand-plus, and his views on YouTube and social following jumped.

None of these forms of making money—contests, concerts, VIP experiences—are new for musicians, but streaming music puts them within reach of more independent and emerging artists. "Engagement is the most important thing," Spiewak said. When thousands of people interact with his client's music, "if we can convert 1 percent of those people to be ticket holders, for an independent artist like Todd, that's a win," he said.

Carey isn't a solitary case. Indie-label group Merlin surveyed a subset of its members this summer and found that nearly half saw streaming revenue increase more than 50 percent in 2013 from a year ago, while the number of those reporting sales increases in downloads fell. Though

Swift argues streaming perpetuates a perception that music has no value, 73 percent of indie labels surveyed were optimistic about the future of their business as they watched their streaming sales increase.

Previously, "those with institutional money could buy the storefronts, and it was easier to herd consumers," Merlin's CEO Caldas said. The stream and the download changed that. "That's why independents perform better in a digital world."

The Freedom of the Streaming-Music Future

Singer-songwriter Hutchinson, who personified today's morphing listening habits, also embodies the journey of an artist as the world shifts to streaming and subscriptions. Signed to Madonna's Maverick Records in 2005 only for the label to collapse and freeze his album in the middle of its creation, he put out his next record on his own. Its top-selling single went gold.

This year, he released his latest album, "Pure Fiction," through a label-services business that doesn't touch the master rights to his recordings—that lets artists keep more control of their work and retain more of their royalties, including the revenue they bank from streaming services.

Now when people approach him and say they were just listening to his music on Spotify or Pandora, Hutchinson takes no notice that they didn't say they heard him on the radio, on iTunes or on CD.

"I only hear the first half of the sentence: 'I was just listening to you.'"

JOAN E. SOLSMAN is a senior writer for CNET who specializes in digital media coverage. She formerly wrote for *The Wall Street Journal* and *Dow Jones Newswires*. She is based in New York.

Charles Arthur

Streaming: The Future of the Music Industry, Or Its Nightmare?

If you wonder what the person next to you on the bus or train wearing headphones and looking at their mobile screen is listening to, it is probably the new radio—a streaming service.

According to the music business body, the British Phonographic Industry (BPI), Britons streamed 14.8 bn tracks last year, almost double the 7.5 bn of 2013, as internet connectivity improves and becomes pervasive.

Compared to buying music downloads, streaming services have a number of advantages. Listeners can range over millions of tracks—the "universal jukebox," create and share playlists socially, discover new artists effortlessly through "artist radio," and listen anywhere (even downloading temporarily for times when their smartphone gets no signal).

This year Apple is expected to muscle in on the scene using the Beats brand it bought for $3 bn (£2 bn) in May 2014, as is Google's YouTube, which last November launched a paid-for, ad-free music and video streaming service, YouTube Music Key.

Snapchat, best known for its self-destructing photos and videos that are a hit with teenagers, is also planning a music feature, according to emails leaked as part of the hack of Sony Pictures. A partnership with the music video service Vevo could be incorporated into future versions—which surely helped the Silicon Valley darling raise another $485m, valuing it at more than $10 bn, in the past few weeks.

Sometimes it seems as if everyone is planning a music streaming service, just as a decade ago everyone down to HMV and Walmart offered music downloads.

But unlike downloads, musicians do not universally love streaming.

At the start of November, Taylor Swift removed her new album and back catalogue from Spotify and the other streaming services, having complained in a Wall Street Journal column in July: "Valuable things should be paid for. It's my opinion that music should not be free."

Ed Sheeran, Beyoncé and Coldplay have used similar tactics, offering CDs and digital downloads for sale before putting them on streaming services—the opposite of the way radio has been used for promotion for decades.

Yet streaming revenues are rising fast, according to the BPI's figures: they have zoomed from zero in 2007 to £76.7m in 2013. Data released by the Entertainment Retailers Association and BPI this week suggested whole-sale streaming revenues were £125m for 2014. (The ERA reported streaming revenues of £175m, but typically its values show a 40% retail markup over the BPI's wholesale figures.) The problem with streaming services, though, is that they seem remarkably ineffective at persuading people to hand over their money. If they are the new radio, well, who pays to listen to the radio? And unlike radio, advertising cannot cover the cost of the service.

Spotify, for example, is available to nearly 1.1 billion internet users around the world, yet it can claim only 12.5 million paying users and 50m ad-supported accounts. So only 1% of potential subscribers actually pay. Another service, Deezer, claims to be in 182 countries, giving it about as many potential users (and payers) as Spotify; in mid-2013 it reported 16 million monthly active users, and 5 million subscribers.

The US-only Pandora claims 250 million users, but only 3.3 million paying its $5 a month subscription.

Mark Mulligan of Midia Consulting[,] who has a long track record watching the music business, reckons there are only about 35 million paying subscribers world-wide for all streaming services, out of more than a billion potential users.

Mulligan thinks the problem is the price. Even before the digital revolution, the average person spent less than £5 a month on music, with most spending accounted for by a small number of big buyers. Cutting subscription prices would entice many more to pay, he thinks, easily making up for lost revenues. "I've been banging the pricing drum for so long the stick has broken," he said recently. "Unfortunately there was pitifully little progress in 2014, with label fears of cannibalising 9.99"—the price of a standard album, in dollars or euros, on iTunes—"dominating thoughts." Something needs to change. The figures suggest streaming is eating into digital downloads rather than CD sales: its revenue growth is almost exactly matched by a fall in digital download revenues, now at their lowest level since 2011. In the US, Nielsen SoundScan has confirmed the same pattern, with paid song downloads down 12% in 2014, from 1.26 bn to 1.1bn, while song streaming rocketed from 106 bn to 164 bn.

There's another difficulty: streaming services tend to lose money.

Pandora, the market-listed US streaming service, hasn't made an annual profit since it floated in 2011. Spotify still records losses—even though it is expected to seek a flotation this year.

The main problem is that for each song streamed, the service has to pay a set amount to the record labels; the more songs streamed, the greater the payment, creating a cost barrier that never shrinks. Spotify says it pays out 70% of its revenues to artists.

That could be about to change with the arrival of Apple. Its acquisition of Dr Dre's Beats was seen as a defensive move after a dramatic fall in iTunes music downloads and revenues. "Apple had to address streaming," Syd Schwartz, a former EMI Music executive, told Rolling Stone in May.

When Apple introduces Beats Music outside the US, it could galvanise the market. Music industry figures are eager to see what effect it could have because data suggest iPhone owners are typically higher spenders (and so easier to convert to paying subscribers) than the average smartphone buyer. "We've reached a very interesting point where there are important changes to come," a BPI spokesman said. "It seems that we're moving towards a time of people understanding that streaming is the future."

Apple is understood to be seeking lower per-song payments from the music labels, so it can offer lower subscription rates. Google's paid-for YouTube Music Key service launched in November with a six-month free trial and a discounted £7.99-a-month cost (down from £9.99). Mulligan expects that discount to continue, and pricing tiers to fall in line.

Yet YouTube itself might be a key obstacle to boosting subscriptions, because it is unofficially the world's largest ad-supported music streaming service. Teenagers use it to find songs and related artists exactly as they do the normal streaming services. (Snapchat's user demographic is a perfect match for that sort of service—which Vevo may seek to capitalise on.) When Swift removed her content from streaming services, it created a media uproar—but all her songs, including new album 1989, could still be found on YouTube.

Mulligan thinks artists and labels will have to swallow their pride and accept the world of change—and lower payments.

"The whole 'changing download dollars into streaming cents' issue continues to haunt streaming though," he said. "With streaming services struggling to see a route to operational profitability the perennial issue of sustainability remains a festering wound. The emerging generation of artists such as Avicii and Ed Sheeran who have never known a life of platinum album sales will learn how to prosper in the streaming era. The rest will have to learn to reinvent themselves, fast—really fast."

CHARLES ARTHUR was *The Guardian*'s technology editor for nine years and is now a contributing writer for that online service based in the United Kingdom. He writes on technology, business, science, and health.

EXPLORING THE ISSUE

Is Streaming the Future of the Music Industry?

Critical Thinking and Reflection

1. When an industry is *disrupted*, are there new opportunities for people to work in the industries, or are those opportunities fewer in number? What types of jobs are most likely to change?
2. When technology can be used for legal purposes, but also illegal purposes, should there be guidelines, regulations, or laws to punish those who circumvent the legal uses?
3. How reliant are we on other technology industries when we stream music? For example, how important is the Internet? How important is your smartphone carrier? Or even, how important is electrical energy to your ability to stream music?
4. Have you ever considered whether streaming music actually costs you more than the purchase of a CD? Think about the amount of money that a subscription service costs, and whether you use it enough to pay for the cost of the service?
5. Many streaming services include a number of advertisements. Does this change your listening enjoyment or the price you are willing to pay for services that don't include ads?

Is There Common Ground?

Both of the authors' perspectives in this issue acknowledge that streaming is an important part of today's music industry, but each has a different perspective on whether streaming will ultimately make enough money to sustain the business models that are currently emerging. But even though media industries continue to evolve as new distribution services emerge, the smaller companies are often acquired by the bigger firms. If streaming continues at the rate projected by each of these journalists, what might be the future of recorded music?

"Hit" records are almost a rare commodity now, as the music industry focuses on "micro-hits" and local distribution rather than the mass distribution, which created a "hit-machine" in earlier days. Although new business models are emerging, we can expect others also to rise over time. Is this type of disruption likely to become the norm in other media industries too?

Additional Resources

Greg Bensinger, "Amazon Launches Music-Streaming Service," *Wall Street Journal* (June 12, 2014). This article discusses the business behind Amazon's development of a streaming service that will also affect sales for other branches of the Amazon business.

Greg Kot, *Ripped: How the Wired Generation Revolutionized Music* (Scribner, 2009). This book takes an early look at streaming services starting with Napster, and discusses how the traditional music industry has had to adapt to digital distribution.

Donald S. Passman, *All You Need to Know About the Music Business*, 8th ed. (Simon and Schuster, 2012). Taking a long-view perspective, Passman provides advice to musicians who want to break into the music industry.

Bob Stanley, *Yeah, Yeah, Yeah, Yeah: The Story of Pop Music from Bill Haley to Beyonce* (W.W. Norton, 2014). In this historical document of the explosive growth of pop music since the 1960s, Stanley addresses distribution forms and the flow of music from one country to another.

Internet References . . .

BMI, "Types of Copyright"

www.bmi.com/licensing/entry/types_of_copyrights

Pharrell's advice for today's artist . . . beware

https://www.youtube.com/watch?v=MrFPWE2TnrM

Recording Industry Association of
America (RIAA)

www.riaa.com

U.S. Copyright Office, "Copyright and the
Music Marketplace" (February 2015)

copyright.gov/policy/musiclicensingstudy/copyright
-and-the-music-marketplace.pdf

Selected, Edited, and with Issue Framing Material by:
Alison Alexander, *University of Georgia*
and
Jarice Hanson, *University of Massachusetts—Amherst*

ISSUE

Should We Oppose Media Consolidation?

YES: Mark Cooper, from "Testimony before the U.S. Senate Judiciary Committee, Subcommittee on Antitrust, Competition Policy, and Consumer Rights," U.S. Senate (2010)

NO: Brian L. Roberts and Jeff Zucker, from "Testimony before the U.S. Senate Judiciary Committee, Subcommittee on Antitrust, Competition Policy, and Consumer Rights," U.S. Senate (2010)

Learning Outcomes

After reading this issue, you will be able to:

- Understand how the rapidly changing media industries are influencing media consolidation.
- Evaluate the pros and cons of media consolidation.
- Consider the impact of globalization on restructuring within media industries.
- Distinguish between profit and public interest rationales for media structure.

ISSUE SUMMARY

YES: Mark Cooper, Director of the Consumer Federation of American Research, argues that allowing the merger of the largest cable network and the nation's premiere video content producers and distribution outlets will alter the structure of the video marketplace, resulting in higher prices and fewer choices for the consumer. Such consolidation of the marketplace is not in the best interests of the American public.

NO: Brian L. Roberts and Jeff Zucker, then Presidents of Comcast and NBC, respectively, argue that the merged firms will benefit consumers through the investment in innovation of both content and delivery mechanisms. Such a merger will allow this merged unit to compete more effectively in the increasingly global video market.

Since the 1980s, the U.S. media industries have undergone a shift in the technology through which media are distributed and the regulatory philosophy through which media are viewed by government and the public. At the same time, changing national and global economies presented other challenges. Even while media corporations were subject to extreme pressures for financial performance, they were experiencing a decline in viewer loyalty and an increase in sources of media that led to market fragmentation. Pressure to create more profitable corporate entities and changes in the ownership rules made by the Telecommunications Act of 1996 opened the market for substantial restructuring in which acquisitions, mergers, and divestitures abounded. The restructuring of the U.S. media industry is still very much underway. It is easy to expect that media industries will continue to respond to financial performance demands with ongoing efforts to consolidate, cluster properties, gain market power within local and regional operational areas, and capture synergies through vertical and horizontal integration.

Concentration in media industries, particularly in the newspaper, radio, and television industries, is controversial. As part of the 1996 Telecommunications Act, Congress mandated that the Federal Communication Commission (FCC) review its broadcast ownership rules. Protests about loosening ownership rules focused on the problems of a concentrated media system, particularly journalism, being defined by commercial and corporate concerns. Individuals such as Robert McChesney argue that if a few corporate giants dominate communications and information media, these conglomerates will have the ability to affect public opinion and the national and global agenda. They may use their power to advance corporate agendas. Public policy should focus on how to maintain a balance of viewpoints and should be concerned with issues of diversity, localism, and quality. Individuals such as Benjamin Compaine point to vibrant media industries that are constantly reshaping themselves in this challenging economic and technological environment. The ability to converge has allowed the media to reshape in order to meet the ever-changing demands of the media environment. Compaine argues that consolidated media markets allow for better quality of content.

Who is right? The answer is not easy. Eli Noam in *Media Concentration and Ownership in America* summarizes some of his research into media concentration. Did concentration rise? It depends on the comparison year, which suggests that concentration levels vary over time. This would not be unexpected in such a competitive and technologically challenging industry. Overall mass media sector concentration is lower than the legal standards for anti-trust merger guidelines that the Department of Justice uses. Generally, American information and media industries are oligopolistic in structure, meaning that a few firms dominate the industry. The top five media firms accounted for about 26 percent of the sector. This is substantially lower than the telecom and IT sectors, where the top five companies held an aggregate share of 61 percent and 43 percent, respectively. What influence does this have on diversity of voices, localism, and quality? The studies show conflicting results. In some markets, larger corporations have improved the local newspaper. In others, consolidated radio markets have moved to automated programming, with very little if any local content.

One fact, ignored in the above discussion, is that the playing field has inescapably changed. The growth of the Internet has created new distribution channels for new content providers. It has created industry giants such as Google, Apple, Netflix, Facebook, and Twitter, none of which are traditional media companies, but all of whom are moving into aspects of that arena. How does the government regulate them? The FCC was charged with overseeing broadcast licensing. Its power comes from the simple premise that if given a license to use the public airwaves, broadcast companies must operate in the pubic interest. Currently, it regulates interstate and international communications by radio, television, wire, satellite, and cable from a public interest perspective. It has little control over the new Internet giants. The Department of Justice (DOJ) evaluated the merger in the context of antitrust laws, which allow mergers to be prohibited if they reduce competition in the marketplace. The DOJ can prosecute cases where monopolistic practices are impeding competition, as the DOJ famously did with AT&T and Microsoft. But beyond broadcast stations or impeding competition, the federal government has little power to regulate the free market.

From this background, the present issue emerges. In 2009, General Electric (GE) and Comcast Corporation proposed a merger of GE's NBC Universal (NBCU) with Comcast. This was described as a vertical merger that would combine the content production expertise of NBC with the content distribution network of Comcast. Comcast would own 51 percent and thus be manager of the new company. The proposed merger required both DOJ and FCC approval. Comcast is the largest cable system operator in the United States; over the years it expanded into entertainment and communication products ranging from owning several cable channels to providing Internet and voice products for its customers. NBC was the first major broadcast network in the United States. It evolved over the years into a development, production, and distribution entity, creating and providing programming for its own outlets and others. In 2009, NBC was in the last place among the major broadcast networks. All networks were experiencing difficulties as cable and other distribution platforms fragmented the media audience. Although NBCU is primarily known as a television network, NBCU owns CNBC, MSNBC, and other cable channels; the Spanish-language broadcast network Telemundo, a group of 25 owned and operated (O&O) NBC television stations in most of the largest markets in the United States and 15 Telemundo O&Os; Universal Pictures, a digital media group; and parks and resorts.

In February 2010, Roberts and Zucker testified before a Senate Judiciary Subcommittee on Antitrust, Competition Policy, and Consumer Rights in favor of the merger. They argued that the vertical synergy of merging the largest cable network with NBCU's content and distribution outlets would benefit consumers. Cooper argued that the merger would result in higher prices and fewer consumer choices. In 2011, the FCC and DOJ approved the merger. In 2013, Comcast bought out the 49 percent of the old NBCU still owned by GE. What are the outcomes of the merger? Roberts is now Chairman and CEO of Comcast Corporation, which includes ownership of NBCU. Zucker left NCBU in

2010 and is now serving as President of CNN Worldwide. Steve Burke, previous president of Comcast Cable, is now CEO of NBC Universal. Comcast's stock price was up nearly 26 percent in fiscal year 2013. Whether the public interest concerns of those who opposed this merger will emerge is both more difficult to assess and more difficult to disentangle from the ongoing torrent of change currently roiling media industries.

YES ⤺

Mark Cooper

Testimony before the U.S. Senate Judiciary Committee, Subcommittee on Antitrust, Competition Policy, and Consumer Rights

... The merger of Comcast and the National Broadcasting Company (NBC) is a hugely complex undertaking, unlike any other in the history of the video marketplace. Allowing the largest cable operator in history to acquire one of the nation's premier video content producers will radically alter the structure of the video marketplace and result in higher prices and fewer choices for consumers. The merging parties are already among the dominant players in the current video market. This merger will give them the incentive and ability to not only preserve and exploit the worst aspects of the current market, but to extend them to the future market.

Comcast has sought to downplay the impact of the merger by claiming that it is a small player in comparison to the vast video universe in which it exists. It has also glossed-over the fact that this merger involves the elimination of actual head-to-head competition. Finally, it has argued that existing protections and public interest promises will prevent any harms that might result from the merger. All three claims are wrong.

Neither Comcast's regurgitation of market shares and counts of outlets and products nor its public interest commitments begin to address the fundamental public policy questions and competitive issues at stake in this merger. Nor can the merger of these companies be viewed separately from the products they sell. NBC and Comcast do not sell widgets. They sell news and information and access to the primary platforms American use to receive this news and information. Control over production and distribution of information has critical implications for society and democracy. As a consequence, the merger of these two media giants reaches far beyond the economic size of the merging parties to the very content consumers receive and how they are permitted to access it.

Finally, if the size and scope of this merger is not sufficient to give you pause, the past actions of the acquiring party should. Comcast has raised cable rates for consumers every year and is among the lowest ranked companies in terms of customer service. Comcast is the frequent subject of program access complaints of competing video providers as well as of discriminatory carriage complaints by independent programmers. Finally, Comcast is on record lying to a federal agency regarding whether they blocked Internet users' access to a competing a video application for anti-competitive purposes. These past practices do not bode well for future competition if Comcast is allowed to acquire NBC. Further, Comcast's lack of candor in past proceedings cast[s] doubt on the prudence of relying on Comcast's voluntary public interest commitments as a means of addressing the anti-consumer impacts of this merger.

The goal of mega-mergers such as this is to cut costs and increase revenues. The most direct path to those outcomes are firing workers and raising prices. Cutting jobs is hardly a laudable goal in the current environment, but the primary "synergy" that mergers produce is the ability to reduce employment by sharing resources between the commonly held companies. To expect the opposite to happen here based on the evidence-free assertions of Comcast would be foolhardy. Simply put, this merger is about higher prices, fewer choices, and lost jobs.

The Biggest Gets Bigger (and Stronger)

Comcast is the nation's largest cable operator, largest broadband service provider and one of the leading providers of regional cable sports and news networks. NBC is one of only four major national broadcast networks, the third largest major owner of local TV stations in terms of audience reach, an icon of local and national news production and the owner of one of a handful of major movies studios.

As large as Comcast is nationally, it is even more important as a local provider of video services. Comcast is a huge entity in specific product markets. It is the dominant multi-channel video programming distributor (MVPD) in those areas where it holds a cable franchise, accounting, on average for over half of the MVPD market. It is the dominant broadband access provider in the areas where it has a cable franchise, accounting for over half of that market. This dominance of local market distribution platforms is the source of its market power. The merger will eliminate competing distribution platforms in some of its markets and will give Comcast control over strategic assets to preserve and expand its market power in all of its markets.

Broadcasters and cable operators are producers of goods and services that compete head-to-head, including local news, sports, and advertising. In addition, NBC and Comcast are also suppliers of content and distribution platforms, which are goods and services that complement one another. In both roles there is a clear competitive rivalry between them. For example, in providing complementary services, broadcasters and cable operators argue about the price, channel location and carriage of content. The merger will eliminate this natural rivalry between two of the most important players in the multi-channel video space, a space in which there are only a handful of large players.

These anticompetitive effects of the merger are primarily what antitrust practice refers to as horizontal effects. They are likely to reduce competition in specific local markets—head-to-head competition in local video markets, head-to-head competition for programming viewers, head-to-head competition for distributions platforms. The merger will raise barriers to entry even higher through denial and manipulation of access to programming and the need to engage in two-stage entry. The merger will increase the likelihood of the exercise of existing market power within specific markets, and will increase the incentive and ability to raise prices or profits.

The fact that some of the leverage is brought to bear because of the link to complementary products (i.e., is vertical in antitrust terms), should not obscure the reality that the ultimate effects are on horizontal competition in both the distribution and programming markets. The merger would dramatically increase the incentive and ability of Comcast to raise prices, discriminate in carriage, foreclose and block competitive entry and force bundles on other cable systems. The merger enhances the ability of Comcast to preserve its position as the dominant local MVPD, reinforce its ability to exercise market power in specific cable or programming markets and extend its business model to the Internet.

We raise these concerns about the merger based on eight specific anticompetitive effects that the merger will have on the video market. . . .

Higher Prices, Fewer Choices, Less Competition

(1) **This merger will reduce choice and competition in local markets.** The merging parties currently compete head-to-head as distributors of video content, in local markets. Because broadcasters own TV stations, they compete with cable in local markets for audiences and advertisers—especially in the production and distribution of local news, and local and political advertising. This merger eliminates this head-to-head competition in 11 major markets where NBC owns broadcast stations and Comcast operates a cable franchise. These 11 markets account for nearly a quarter of U.S. TV households.

This merger also eliminates a competitor for local and political advertising. In fact, in 2006 NBC told the Federal Communications Commission that local cable operators present the single biggest threat to broadcasters in terms of securing local and political advertising.[1] Now that NBC is looking to merge with Comcast, the potential elimination of this local competition has been conveniently ignored. But federal authorities cannot and should not ignore the fact that a merger between Comcast and NBC is likely to cause a significant decline in competition in local advertising markets and excessive domination by the merged company. Not only will advertisers lose an important option, but the merger will be to the detriment of other local broadcasters—particularly smaller, independent ones—who are already facing ad revenue declines in an economic downturn. A stand-alone broadcaster will not be able to offer package deals and volume discounts for advertising across multiple channels the way that Comcast/NBC will be able to do post-merger. That means other local broadcasters will have less money to produce local news and hire staff. To compete, rival broadcasters will have two options: fire staff and reduce production of local news and information; or consolidate in order to compensate for market share lost to the new media mammoth.

(2) **This merger removes an independent outlet and an independent source of news and information.** These two companies compete in the video programming market, where Comcast's regional sports and news production compete with NBC's local news and sports production. By acquiring NBC, Comcast's incentive to develop new programming would be reduced. Instead of continuing to compete to win audience, it just buys NBC's viewers. Where two important entities were producing programming, there will now be one.

(3) The merger will eliminate competition between Comcast and NBC in cyberspace. NBC content is available online in a variety of forms and on different websites and services. Most prominently, of course, NBC is a stakeholder in Hulu—an online video distribution portal that draws millions of viewers. Comcast has put resources into developing its own online video site—"Fancast"—where consumers can find content owned by the cable operator. The merger eliminates this nascent, head-to-head competition.

Moreover, Comcast is the driving force behind the new "TV Everywhere" initiative. This collusive venture—which we believe merits its own antitrust investigation—would tie online video distribution of cable content to a cable subscription and pressure content providers to restrict or refrain from online distribution outside of the portal. This is a disaster for video competition. The proposed merger strengthens Comcast's hand in this scheme by increasing their market power in both traditional and online video distribution. Comcast is clearly attempting to control the distribution of the video content it makes available on the web by restricting sales exclusively to Comcast cable customers. It does not sell that content to non-Comcast customers. By contrast, NBC has exactly the opposite philosophy—or at least it did. Through Hulu, NBC is competing for both Comcast and non-Comcast customers by selling video online that is not tied to cable. NBC also has incentives to make its programming available in as many points of sale as possible. Merger with Comcast will put an end to that pro-competitive practice.

(4) The merger will provide Comcast with greater means to deny rivals access to Comcast-controlled programming. Comcast already has incentive to undermine competing cable and satellite TV distributors by denying them access to critical, non-substitutable programming, or by extracting higher prices from competitors to induce subscribers to switch to Comcast. Post-merger it will have a great deal more content to use as an anticompetitive tool. Comcast has engaged in these anticompetitive acts in the past and by becoming a major programmer it will have a much larger tool to wield against potential competitors. Moreover, Comcast has opposed, and is currently challenging in court, the few rules in place that would prevent it from withholding its programming from competing services.

(5) The merger will provide greater incentive for Comcast to discriminate against competing independent programmers. Comcast already has a strong incentive to, and significant track record of, favoring its own programming over the content produced by others with preferential carriage deals. Post-merger it will have a lot more content to favor. The current regulatory structure does not appear sufficient to remedy the existing problem and cannot be expected to address the resulting post-merger threat to independent programmers. The econometric analysis of program carriage indicates there is a great deal of discrimination occurring already. The fact that the FCC is continually trying to catch up with complaints of program carriage discrimination is testimony to the existence of the problem and the inability of the existing rules to correct it.

(6) The merger will stimulate a domino effect of concentration between distributors and programmers. The new combination will create a major asymmetry in the current cartel model in the cable industry. It brings together a large cable provider with a huge stable of must-have programming *and* the largest wireline broadband platform in America. Very likely, this will trigger more mergers and acquisitions because it changes the dynamics of the market. But there will be no positive competitive outcomes resulting from this change.

This merger signals that the old, anticompetitive game is still on—but with a twist. Like all other cable operators, Comcast has never entered the service territory of a competing multi-channel video program provider, allowing everyone to preserve market power and relentlessly raise prices. But Comcast's expanded assets and especially its new leverage over the online video market will give it a substantial edge against its direct competitors in its service territory. The likely effect of the merger will be for other cable distribution and broadband companies to muscle up with their own content holdings to try and offset Comcast's huge advantage. In other words, there is only one way to deal with a vertically integrated giant that has must-have content and control over two distribution platforms—you have to vertically integrate yourself. This merger would send a signal to the industry that the decades old game of mutual forbearance from competition will be repeated but at the next level of vertical integration that spills over into the online market. Watch for AT&T and Verizon to be next in line for major content acquisitions. When that happens, it will be extremely difficult for any company that is merely a programmer or merely a distributor to get into the market. Barriers to entry to challenge vertically integrated incumbents will be nearly unassailable. The only option may be a two-stage entry into both markets at the same time—which is an errand reserved only for the brave and the foolish.

(7) By undermining competition, this merger will result in higher prices for consumers. Comcast already raises its rates every year for its cable subscribers, and prices are likely to rise further after the merger. By weakening competition, Comcast's market power over price is strengthened, but there are also direct ways the merger will push the price to consumers up. Comcast will have the opportunity and incentive to charge its competitors more for NBC programs and force competitors to pay for less desirable Comcast cable channels in order to get NBC programming—those added costs will mean bigger bills for cable subscribers. Furthermore, the lack of competitive pressure that has failed to produce any appreciable downward pressure on cable rates since 1983, will not discipline Comcast from raising its own rates.

(8) **This merger will result in higher prices for consumers through the leveraging of "retransmission rights."** Through its takeover of local NBC broadcast stations, Comcast will also gain special "retransmission consent rights," which allow stations to negotiate fees for cable carriage of broadcast signals. These rights will enable Comcast to leverage control over must-have local programming and larger bundles of cable channels to charge competing cable, telco and satellite TV providers more money for content. Additionally, once Comcast acquires a broadcaster, it will have the means and incentive to raise retransmission rights payments for NBC-owned stations. This will be reinforced by two factors. First, as the owner of NBC, Comcast profits from the retransmission payments it receives and does not lose from the retransmission payments it makes, which are passed through to consumers. Second, Comcast can charge competitors more for local NBC programming, and will be able to exploit asymmetric information. Cable operators do not publish what they pay for retransmission; broadcasters do not publish what they get. Because of Comcast's superior bargaining power, it will ask for more and pay less.

A Comcast/NBC Merger Should Not Be Allowed to Proceed

The merger has so many anti-competitive, anti-consumer, and anti-social effects that it cannot be fixed. Comcast's claim that FCC oversight will protect the public is absurd. The challenges that this merger poses to the future of video competition cannot be ignored, or brushed aside by reliance on FCC rules that have yet to remedy current problems and, thus, are ill-equipped to attend to the increased anticompetitive means and incentives that will result from Comcast's acquisition of NBC. The FCC rules have failed to break the stranglehold of cable to-date; there is no reason to believe they

will be better able to tame the video giant that will result from this merger.

Further, any suggestion that the public interest commitments Comcast has made will solve these problems is misguided. Temporary band-aids cannot cure long-term structural injuries. Comcast's promises lack substance and accountability. More importantly, the commitments do not begin to address the anticompetitive effects of the merger. Many of Comcast's commitments amount to little more that a promise to obey the law. Where they go beyond current law, they largely fall within the company's existing business plans. Anything beyond that is meager at best, and in no way substitutes for the localism and diversity that a vigorously competitive industry would produce.

Over the past quarter century there have been a few moments when a technology comes along that holds the possibility of breaking the chokehold that cable has on the multi-channel video programming market, but on each occasion policy mistakes were made that allowed the cable industry to strangle competition. This is the first big policy moment for determining whether the Internet will function as an alternative platform to compete with cable. If policymakers allow this merger to go forward, the prospects for a more competition-friendly, consumer-friendly multi-channel video marketplace will be dealt a severe setback.

I urge policymakers to think long and hard before they allow a merger that gives the parties incentives to harm competition and consumers, while increasing their ability to act on those incentives. This hearing should be the opening round in what must be a long and rigorous inquiry into a huge complex merger of immense importance to the American people. It should be the first step in a review process that concludes the merger is not in the public interest and should not be allowed to close.

Note

1. NBC Media Ownership Comments, FCC Docket 06-121 (filed Oct. 2006).

Mark Cooper is Director of Research at the Consumer Federation of America, a consumer advocacy organization that lobbies on a number of consumer issues. In addition to the research conducted for this organization, he is the author of the book *Cable Mergers and Monopolies*.

Brian L. Roberts and Jeff Zucker

 **NO**

Testimony before the U.S. Senate Judiciary Committee, Subcommittee on Antitrust, Competition Policy, and Consumer Rights

Mr. Chairman, and Members of the Subcommittee, we are pleased to appear before you today to discuss Comcast Corporation's ("Comcast") planned joint venture with General Electric Company ("GE"), under which Comcast will acquire a majority interest in and management of NBC Universal ("NBCU"). . . .

The new NBCU will benefit consumers and will encourage much-needed investment and innovation in the important media sector. How will it benefit consumers? First, the new venture will lead to increased investment in NBCU by putting these important content assets under the control of a company that is focused exclusively on the communication and entertainment industry. This will foster enhanced investment in both content development and delivery, enabling NBCU to become a more competitive and innovative player in the turbulent and ever changing media world. Investment and innovation will also preserve and create sustainable media and technology jobs. Second, the transaction will promote the innovation, content, and delivery that consumers want and demand. The parties have made significant commitments in the areas of local news and information programming, enhanced programming for diverse audiences, and more quality educational and other content for children and families. And finally, Comcast's commitment to sustain and invest in the NBC broadcast network will promote the quality news, sports, and local programming that have made this network great over the last 50 years. . . .

The new NBCU will advance key policy goals of Congress: diversity, localism, innovation, and competition. With Comcast's demonstrated commitment to investment and innovation in communications, entertainment, and information, the new NBCU will be able to increase the quantity, quality, diversity, and local focus of its content, and accelerate the arrival of the multiplatform, "anytime, anywhere" future of video programming that Americans want. Given the intensely competitive markets in which Comcast and NBCU operate, as well as existing law and regulations, this essentially vertical transaction will benefit consumers and spur competition, and will not present any potential harm in any marketplace.

NBCU, currently majority-owned and controlled by GE, is an American icon—a media, entertainment, and communications company with a storied past and a promising future. At the heart of NBCU's content production is the National Broadcasting Company ("NBC"), the nation's first television broadcast network and home of one of the crown jewels of NBCU, NBC News. NBCU also has two highly regarded cable news networks, CNBC and MSNBC. In addition, NBCU owns Telemundo, the nation's second largest Spanish-language broadcast network, with substantial Spanish-language production facilities located in the United States. NBCU's other assets include 26 local broadcast stations (10 NBC owned-and-operated stations ("O&Os"), 15 Telemundo O&Os, and one independent Spanish-language station), numerous national cable programming networks, a motion picture studio with a library of several thousand films, a TV production studio with a library of television series, and an international theme park business.

Comcast, a leading provider of cable television, high-speed Internet, digital voice, and other communications services to millions of customers, is a pioneer in enabling consumers to watch what they want, when they want, where they want, and on the devices they want. Comcast is primarily a distributor, offering its customers multiple delivery platforms for content and services. Although Comcast owns and produces some cable programming channels and online content, Comcast owns relatively few national cable networks, none of which is among the

30 most highly rated, and, even including its local and regional networks, Comcast accounts for a tiny percentage of the content industry. The majority of these content businesses will be contributed to the joint venture. The distribution side of Comcast (referred to as "Comcast Cable") is not being contributed to the new NBCU and will remain under Comcast's ownership and control.

The proposed transaction is primarily a *vertical* combination of NBCU's content with Comcast's multiple distribution platforms. Antitrust law, competition experts, and the FCC have long recognized that vertical combinations can produce significant benefits. Experts and the FCC also have found that vertical combinations with limited horizontal issues generally do not threaten competition.

The transaction takes place against the backdrop of a communications and entertainment marketplace that is highly dynamic and competitive, and becoming more so every day. NBCU—today and post-transaction—faces competition from a large and growing roster of content providers. There are literally hundreds of national television networks and scores of regional networks. These networks compete not only with each other but also with countless other video choices—both for consumers' attention and for distribution on various video platforms. In addition, content producers increasingly have alternative outlets available to distribute their works, free from any purported "gatekeeping" networks or distributors. . . .

Competition is fierce among distributors as well. Consumers in every geographic area have multiple choices of multichannel video programming distributors ("MVPDs") and can obtain video content from many non-MVPDs as well. In addition to the local cable operator, consumers can choose from two MVPDs offering direct broadcast satellite ("DBS") service: DirecTV and Dish Network, which are now the second and third largest MVPDs in America, respectively. Verizon and AT&T, along with other wireline overbuilders, are strong, credible competitors, offering a fourth MVPD choice to tens of millions of American households and a fifth choice to some. Indeed, as competition among MVPDs has grown, Comcast's nationwide share of MVPD subscribers has steadily decreased (it is now less than 25 percent, a share that the FCC has repeatedly said is insufficient to allow an MVPD to engage in anticompetitive conduct). . . .

Consumers can also access high-quality video content from myriad other sources. Some households continue to receive their video through over-the-air broadcast signals, which have improved in quality and increased in quantity as a result of the broadcast digital television transition. Millions of households purchase or rent digital video discs ("DVDs") from one of thousands of national, regional, or local retail outlets, including Walmart, Blockbuster, and Hollywood Video, as well as Netflix, MovieCrazy, Café DVD, and others who provide DVDs by mail. High-quality video content also is increasingly available from a rapidly growing number of online sources that include Amazon, Apple TV, Blinkx, Blip.tv, Boxee, Clicker.com, Crackle, Eclectus, Hulu, iReel, iTunes, Netflix, Sezmi, SlashControl, Sling, Veoh, Vevo, Vimeo, VUDU, Vuze, Xbox, YouTube, and many more. These sites offer previously unimaginable quantities of professionally produced content and user-generated content that can be accessed from a variety of devices, including computers, Internet-equipped televisions, videogame boxes, Blu-ray DVD players, and mobile devices. In addition, there is a huge supply of user-generated video content, including professional and quasi-professional content. . . .

The combination of NBCU and Comcast's content assets under the new NBCU—coupled with management of the new NBCU by Comcast, an experienced, committed distribution innovator—will enable the creation of new pathways for delivery of content to consumers on a wide range of screens and platforms. The companies' limited shares in all relevant markets, fierce competition at all levels of the distribution chain, and ease of entry for cable and online programming ensure that the risk of competitive harm is insignificant. Moreover, the FCC's rules governing program access, program carriage, and retransmission consent provide further safeguards for consumers as do the additional public interest commitments made by the companies to the FCC.

At the same time, the transaction's public interest benefits—particularly for the public interest goals of diversity, localism, competition, and innovation—are substantial. Through expanded access to outlets, increased investment in outlets, and lower costs, the new venture will be able to increase the amount, quality, variety, and availability of content more than either company could on its own, thus promoting *diversity*. This includes content of specific interest to minority groups, children and families, women, and other key audience segments. . . .

In addition, Comcast and NBCU have publicly affirmed their continuing commitment to free, over-the-air broadcasting. Despite a challenging business and technological environment, the proposed transaction has significant potential to invigorate NBCU's broadcasting business and expand the important public interest benefits it provides to consumers across this country. . . .

Moreover, combining Comcast's expertise in multi-platform content distribution with NBCU's extensive content creation capabilities and video libraries will not only result in the creation of more and better programming—it will also encourage investment and innovation that will accelerate the arrival of the multiplatform, "anytime, anywhere" future of video programming that Americans want. This is because the proposed transaction will remove negotiation friction that currently inhibits the ability of Comcast to implement its pro-consumer vision of multiplatform access to quality video programming. Post-transaction, Comcast will have access to more content that it can make available on more outlets, including the new NBCU's national and regional networks and Comcast's cable systems, video-on-demand ("VOD") platform, and online platform. . . .

The past is prologue: Comcast sought for years to develop the VOD business, but it could not convince studio distributors—who were reluctant to permit their movies to be distributed on an emerging, unproven platform—to provide compelling content for VOD. This caution, though understandable in light of marketplace uncertainty, slowed the growth of an innovative and extremely consumer-friendly service. Comcast finally was able to overcome the contractual wrangling and other industry resistance to an innovative business model when it joined with Sony to acquire an ownership interest in Metro-Goldwyn-Mayer ("MGM"). This allowed Comcast to "break the ice" and obtain access to hundreds of studio movies that Comcast could offer for free on VOD. Thanks to Comcast's extensive efforts to foster the growth of this new technology, VOD has gone on to become extremely popular. . . .

The formation of the new NBCU will remove negotiation impediments by providing Comcast with control of a rich program library and extensive production capabilities that Comcast can use to develop novel video products and services that will be offered to consumers across an array of distribution platforms. There is every reason to believe that the transaction proposed here will create a pro-consumer impetus for making major motion pictures available sooner for in-home, on-demand viewing and for sustainable online video distribution—which, as the FCC has observed, will help to drive broadband adoption, another key congressional goal.

As noted above, the risk of competitive harm in this transaction is insignificant. Viewed from every angle, the transaction is pro-competitive.

First, combining Comcast's and NBCU's programming assets will give rise to no cognizable competitive harm. Comcast's national cable programming networks account for only about three percent of total national cable network advertising and affiliate revenues. While NBCU owns a larger number of networks, those assets account for only about 9 percent of overall national cable

network advertising and affiliate revenues. In total, the new NBCU will account for only about 12 percent of overall national cable network advertising and affiliate revenues. The new NBCU will rank as the fourth largest owner of national cable networks, behind Disney/ABC, Time Warner, and Viacom—which is the same rank that NBCU has today. Because both the cable programming market and the broader video programming market will remain highly competitive, the proposed transaction will not reduce competition or diversity, nor will it lead to higher programming prices to MVPDs or consumers or higher advertising prices.

Even after the transaction, approximately six out of every seven channels carried by Comcast Cable will be unaffiliated with Comcast or the new NBCU.

Second, Comcast's management and ownership interests in NBCU's broadcast properties raise no regulatory or competitive concern. While Comcast will own both cable systems and a stake in NBC owned and operated broadcast stations in a small number of Designated Market Areas ("DMAs"), the FCC's rules do not prohibit such cross-ownership, nor is there any policy rationale to disallow such relationships. The prior cross-ownership prohibitions have been repealed by actions of Congress, the courts, and the FCC. . . .

Third, the combination of Comcast's and NBCU's Internet properties similarly poses no threat to competition. There is abundant and growing competition for online video content. Although Comcast operates a video site, called Fancast, and NBCU holds a 32 percent, non-controlling interest in Hulu, a site that provides access to certain online video content, the leader in online viewing (by far) is Google (through YouTube and other sites it has built or acquired), with nearly 55 percent of online video viewing. This puts Google well ahead of Microsoft, Viacom, and Hulu (all of which are in low- or mid-single digits) and even farther ahead of Fancast (currently well below 1 percent). There are countless other sites that provide robust competition and near-infinite consumer choice. . . .

Finally, a vertical combination cannot have anticompetitive effects unless the combined company has substantial market power in the upstream (programming) or downstream (distribution) market, and such circumstances do not exist here. As noted, the video programming, video distribution, and Internet businesses are fiercely competitive, and the proposed transaction does not reduce that competition. The recent history of technology demonstrates that distribution platforms are multiplying, diversifying, and increasingly rivalrous. . . .

In any event, there is a comprehensive regulatory structure already in place, comprising the FCC's program access, program carriage, and retransmission consent rules, as well as an established body of antitrust law that provides further safeguards against any conceivable vertical harms that might be presented by this transaction.

Although the competitive marketplace and regulatory safeguards protect against the risk of anticompetitive conduct, the companies have offered an unprecedented set of commitments to provide assurances that competition will remain vibrant. Moreover, the companies have offered concrete and verifiable commitments to ensure certain pro-consumer benefits of the transaction. In addition to the commitment to continue to provide free, over-the-air broadcasting, mentioned previously, the companies have committed that following the transaction, the NBC O&O broadcast stations will maintain the same amount of local news and information programming they currently provide, and will produce an additional 1,000 hours per year of local news and information programming for various platforms. . . .

Comcast will commit voluntarily to extend the key components of the FCC's program access rules to negotiations with MVPDs for retransmission rights to the signals of NBC and Telemundo O&O broadcast stations for as long as the FCC's current program access rules remain in place. Of particular note, Comcast will be prohibited in retransmission consent negotiations from unduly or improperly influencing the NBC and Telemundo stations' decisions about whether to sell their programming, or the terms and conditions of sale, to other distributors. . . .

The companies also have committed that Comcast will use its On Demand and On Demand Online platforms to increase programming choices available to children and families as well as to audiences for Spanish-language programming. . . .

As Comcast makes rapid advances in video delivery technologies, more channel capacity will become available. So Comcast will commit that, once it has completed its digital migration company-wide (anticipated to be no later than 2011), it will add two new independently owned and operated channels to its digital line-up each year for the next three years on customary terms and conditions. . . .

We have proposed that these commitments be included in any FCC order approving the transaction and become binding on the parties upon completion of the transaction. A summary of the companies' commitments is attached to this statement.

In the end, the proposed transaction simply transfers ownership and control of NBCU from GE, a company with a very diverse portfolio of interests, to Comcast, a company with an exclusive focus on, and a commitment to investing its resources in, its communications, entertainment, and information assets. This transfer of control, along with the contribution of Comcast's complementary content assets, will enable the new NBCU to better serve consumers. The new NBCU will advance key public policy goals: diversity, localism, competition, and innovation. Competition, which is already pervasive in every one of the businesses in which the new NBCU—and Comcast Cable—will operate, provides abundant assurance that consumer welfare will be not only safeguarded but increased. Comcast and NBCU will succeed by competing vigorously and fairly. . . .

BRIAN L. ROBERTS is Chairman and CEO of Comcast Corporation, which has evolved into a vertically integrated global corporation with the acquisition of NBC Universal. Jeff Zucker is currently President of CNN Worldwide. At the time of his testimony, he was President and CEO of NBC Universal.

EXPLORING THE ISSUE

Should We Oppose Media Consolidation?

Critical Thinking and Reflection

1. Does concentration affect media access, localism, and availability? What evidence have you seen in your local area to support or reject the concerns about localism, diversity, and quality content in a concentrated market? Do you, for example, have any bookstores left in your home town? If many have closed, is that a result of consolidation or of a changing distribution system? Have you seen changes in the national market that might have resulted from consolidation? As a media consumer, do you have fewer choices or poor quality media products in your community?
2. Both the First Amendment and the power of the FCC set a context for news in this country. Previous FCC Chairman Mark Fowler once famously quipped that "television is just a toaster with pictures." Deregulation has been a consistent governmental theme for broadcast since the 1980s. Is it time to give up on public interest notions and simply let the marketplace rule?
3. Do you think that the FCC and DOJ were correct in allowing this merger to go through? What would you decide? Why?

Is There Common Ground?

The historical tension between the public interest paradigm and the current focus on the industry's economic and financial performance is an important issue. How the public and policymakers address this issue could have significant impact on the direction in which the industry develops in the next few decades. If media companies are viewed as private enterprises whose primary responsbility is to attract consumers and generate profits for stockholders, deregulation and consolidation will continue and media markets will be controlled by an ever-smaller number of players generating whatever type of content sells best. If, however, the pendulum of regulatory philosophy and public pressure begins swinging back toward the view that the media have a responsibility to serve the public interest commensurate with the special legal protections accorded to media, a return to more regulation on industry stucture and behavior is likely to follow.

The arguments in the two testimonies are even more narrowly focused. Although giving a nod to issues of public interest, Cooper mainly argues for the anti-competitive and anti-consumer results of the merger. Thus, the questions he raises are whether this merger reduces choice and raises prices for consumers. To simplify, both parties share

an important bit of common ground: the important issue is that of the effects of competition in the marketplace and the influence on consumers. Comcast asserts that there will not be negative consequences; Cooper asserts that there will. It is interesting and disturbing that neither party devotes much time to the public interest requirements that both these firms face.

Additional Resources

Robert McChesney and John Nichols, *The Death and Life of American Journalism: The Media Revolution That Will Begin the World Again* (Nation Books, 2011)

Eli Noam, *Media Ownership and Concentration in America* (Oxford University Press, 2009)

Robert Picard, *The Economics and Financing of Media Companies,* 2nd ed. (Fordham University Press, 2010)

Jeff Ulin, *The Business of Media Distribution: Monetizing Film, TV and Video Content in an Online World* (Focal Press, 2009)

Harold Vogel, *Entertainment Industry Economics: A Guide for Financial Analysis* (Cambridge University Press, 2010)

Internet References . . .

Bloomberg News

www.bloomberg.com/news/2012-12-25/merger-made
-comcast-strong-u-s-web-users-weak.html

Bureau of Economic Analysis

www.bea.gov

Business Insider

www.businessinsider.com/these-6-corporations
-control-90-of-the-media-in-america-2012-6

**Federal Communications Commission
(FCC)**

www.fcc.gov/mergers

**New America Foundation: Is Media
Consolidation in the Public Interest?**

http://mediapolicy.newamerica.net/blogposts
/2013/is_media_consolidation_in_the_public
_interest-78469

Unit 6

UNIT

Life in the Digital Age

*P*redictions of a world that is increasingly reliant upon media and communication technologies have generally provided either utopian or dystopian visions about what our lives will be like in the future. New media distribution technologies present new options for traditional ways of doing things. Not too many years ago, people were talking about the possibility of an information superhighway. Today, people talk about Facebook and Twitter. Although we are still learning how electronic communication may change our lives and the ways in which we work and communicate, many questions have not changed. Will new ways of communication change the way individuals interact? Will we find ways to protect the individual in this arena? Will the weakest members of society be protected? How will we know about new information? Will everyone have access to the services and technologies that enable more immediate information exchange? What will new technologies mean to us as individuals as we live in the information age?

Selected, Edited, and with Issue Framing Material by:
Alison Alexander, *University of Georgia*
and
Jarice Hanson, *University of Massachusetts—Amherst*

ISSUE

Do Social Media Enhance Real Relationships?

YES: **Zeynep Tufekci**, from "Social Media's Small, Positive Role in Human Relationships," *The Atlantic* (2012)

NO: **Sherry Turkle**, from "The Flight from Conversation," New York Times Sunday Review (2012)

Learning Outcomes

After reading this issue, you will be able to:

- Discuss the fundamental differences between the two perspectives.
- Evaluate your own behaviors to become more critical of your own patterns.
- Project beyond your age group to consider the influence of social media on middle age and senior adults.
- Defend your own perspective on this issue.

ISSUE SUMMARY

YES: Tufekci argues that social media is a counterweight to the many factors that separate people and a testament to peoples' ongoing desire to connect with each other. Rather than displacing connections, social media is enhancing it in more ways than were ever possible. With social media some become even more social; some have felt awkward but more free online; others find communities of interest that go far beyond the limitations of their current environment. Social media adds, rather than subtracts, from connections.

NO: Turkle argues that social media provide the illusion of connection. Her perspective comes from hundreds of interviews that often describe a lonely environment in which technology trumps authentic communication. People can become confused about whether technology brings them closer together or further apart. Her question is straightforward: Is technology offering us the lives we want to lead?

We've all had the experience of people checking emails during a meeting, texting in the car next to us, playing games or checking Facebook in the back of the classroom or walking across campus with eyes glued to their phone. Most of us have seen people texting their friends during a concert or sporting event, seemingly more involved in that interaction than in the spectacle in front of them. How can individuals be absent from the reality that surrounds them? What are the consequences of obsession with absent others? How do relationships that develop and/or grow through mediated means fare?

Many worry that interpersonal, face-to-face communication is being sacrificed to mediated communication. Interpersonal communication has long been considered the bedrock of linguistic development, as well as the primary means of socialization. Relationships also develop through interaction, and previously that interaction has been through face-to-face communication. Yet the move away from an oral tradition came long ago with the invention of writing. Since then the ways in which communication can be mediated by technology have only increased.

When people move through their environment with their attention on their mobile device, are they missing out on the possibilities of interpersonal communication? The simple "Yes" answer is only partly true. As Tufecki observes, there are many factors that separate people. Although missing out on face-to-face communication, they are often involved in distance or mediated communication with important others. She also points out that social media may enable better communication for those who are anxious or feel socially inept, or it may enable the isolated to find communities beyond their communities of place.

Sherry Turkle develops a complex analysis of this deceptively simple issue question. In *Alone Together* she says "Technology proposes itself as architect of our intimacies." It offers solutions to vulnerabilities around loneliness and intimacy, and provides an entirely new playing field on which to work out our connections. It is, as her initial sentence implies, a different landscape in which the illusion of intimacy and friendship replaces actual conversation. Are we content with that substitution?

Every generation consumes media that defines them. Perhaps your grandparents were a part of either the radio or television generation; your parents, were probably part of either the television or Internet generation. Digital technology has afforded the ability to be mobile and has changed the conditions of interaction as well as of content consumption. Our favored forms of media may well shape what we think is important and where we go to find

out news, information and entertainment, as well as to connect with others. Technologies evolve so quickly, it is often hard to remember what life was like without them.

These articles remind us that human behaviors sometimes change when technology is introduced. It is important to remember that new technologies are almost always met with opposition, based on their perceived ability to cause adverse change. Current discourse about the impact of technology has moved far beyond the debate of simply "positive" or "negative" qualities of some communication forms. The distancing of activities beyond the interpersonal realm is increasingly viewed as an alienating effect of technology. As we adopt social media and the many new media opportunities the future will bring, we need to continue to pay attention to the effects that may result. Social media are a wonderful way to communicate with others inexpensively and in real time, but the substitution of face-to-face communication often brings problems too. Only by examining the social uses of social media can we retain positive social behaviors that are necessary for socialization and survival in a more fully technologized world. As we live our lives in this changing world, we need to become aware of how easy it is to let technology do the work of relationships, and how important it is to exercise those actions that make us a part of a civil and connected society.

YES

Zeynep Tufekci

Social Media's Small, Positive Role in Human Relationships

It's just one factor in modern life that can increase connection in a world divided by the vagaries of capitalism, the disengagement of television, and the isolation of suburban sprawl.

A few years ago I had an interview for a job at one of the leading academic departments in my field. Maybe because I knew that I wasn't likely to be offered the job, I saw the day as a relaxed opportunity to meet people carrying out interesting research. My comfort with the day was shaken, however, when a faculty member showed me ongoing research on avatars—bots—designed to interact with (and provide therapy for) human children with autism. I squirmed. I squinted. I tried to voice my discomfort. I lost my voice. I turned away. I was shaken for the rest of the day and on my way back. That flickering image of the bot we'd one day turn our children over to still haunts me.

. . .

I don't discount the appeal of automating such therapy. Working with children with autism is difficult, tiring work, especially since the social rewards—the smile, the eye-contact, the hug, the thank you—that make most of us tick are few and far between. I've never tried such an endeavor; I'm in no position to judge anyone.

Still the barely-pixelated, realistic face of the "therapist" talking on the screen scares me because it is indeed an indicator of one possible future. Much of what ails our modern life is exactly because we reduce the value of a human being to a number, say salary or consumer power. And the first to be thrown overboard tend to be the elderly, the disabled, and anyone not integrated tightly into the global supply-chain. This phenomenon, coupled with the growing powers of automation and artificial intelligence which promises to make replacing human beings even cheaper, means there is a very important conversation we need to be having—but that conversation is not about the effects of social media.

That might not have been apparent to those who picked up their Sunday *New York Times* to find Sherry Turkle's latest essay arguing that social media are driving us apart. If anything, social media is a counterweight to the ongoing devaluation of human lives. Social media's rapid rise is a loud, desperate, emerging attempt by people everywhere to connect with *each other* in the face of all the obstacles that modernity imposes on our lives: suburbanization that isolates us from each other, long working-hours and commutes that are required to make ends meet, the global migration that scatters families across the globe, the military-industrial-consumption machine that drives so many key decisions, and, last but not least, the television—the ultimate alienation machine—which remains the dominant form of media. (For most people, the choice is not leisurely walks on Cape Cod versus social media. It's television versus social media).

As a social media researcher and a user, every time I read one of these "let's panic" articles about social media (and there are many), I want to shout: Look at TV! Look at commutes! Look at suburbs! Look at long work hours! That is, essentially, my response to Stephen Marche's "Facebook Is Making Us Lonely," which ran in *The Atlantic* magazine.

And then, please, look at the extensive amount of data that show that social-media users are having more conversations with people—online and off!

What evidence we do have does not suggest a displacement of one type of conversation (offline) with another (online). All data I've seen say that people who use social media are either also more social offline; or that they have benefited from social media to keep in touch with people they otherwise could not; or that many people find fellows, peers and like-minded individuals they otherwise could not find. In other words, texting, Facebook-status updates, and Twitter conversations are not displacing face-to-face socializing—on average, they are making them stronger. Social media is enhancing human connectivity as people can converse in ways that were once not possible. Surveys also show that most families think social media enhance their family life—they can stay in touch better, more frequently. (Obviously, there are many complex impacts and not every person is going to "average" impacts.)

In other words, the people Turkle sees with their heads down on their devices while on a train somewhere are . . . connecting to people they deem important in their lives. They are not talking to bots.

Why would they be talking to bots? People tend to hate talking to bots. Anyone who's active on social media would see that. And social media is certainly easy to dismiss from afar. But close up, it's alive and brimming with humanity (and all the good and bad that comes along with that). And, as with all conversational settings, social media does not make much sense taken out of the context. (Ever seen verbatim transcripts of face-to-face conversations? They are almost incomprehensible even though they make perfect sense in the moment.)

One other category that is often overlooked are people who are either not that comfortable at some aspects of face-to-face conversation but find online interaction to be liberating. It's not that these people are not seeking human contact. It's just that they find it hard to make that initial connection. They are the people who don't dominate conversations, the people who appear shy, are less outgoing, who feel nervous talking to new people. Sometimes it's because they are different from the people around them.

From Arab Spring dissidents who were minorities in their communities to my students from a variety of backgrounds, from gay teens in rural areas to just people who feel awkward when in company of new people, I've heard the sentiment again and again that new communication tools are what saved their (offline) social lives.

So far, I've talked about two categories of—those who were already social and who are becoming even more social offline as a result of offline connectivity, and those who have felt awkward offline and who are benefiting from online socializing. What I've not seen in the data I look at extensively (national surveys, qualitative research and other accounts) are significant number of people who were otherwise able and willing to be social face-to-face and are now lost to their devices. It is true that the rise of the Internet may result in some people feeling more isolated than before, but those will likely be the people who do not or cannot use these new tools to engage their social ties. Such people, who reluctantly socialize via online methods due to skill or cost or personal disposition may well find themselves *left out* of conversation.

One twist is that as people are increasingly able to find people based on interests—rather than interacting in the old manner with people with whom they happen to be in the same geographic proximity—people who depended on geographic proximity or family ties to provide social connectivity may indeed find themselves at a disadvantage if they are not able to develop their own networks. This is certainly a disruption and involves a certain kind of loss; however, it is hard to argue that it is all negative.

Finally, I've previously argued that some people may be "cyberasocial," that is, they are unable or unwilling to invoke a sense of social presence through mediated communication, somewhat similar to the way we invoke language—a fundamentally oral form—through reading, which is a hack in our brain. I suspect such people may well be at a major disadvantage similar to the way people who could not or would not talk on the telephone would be in late 20th century.

. . .

In sum, social media is propelling transitions and disruptions in the composition of social networks. Increasingly, what used to be a given (social ties you inherited by the virtue of where you lived or your familial ties) is now a task (social ties based on shared interests and mutual interest). Surely, there will be new winners and losers. None of this, however, indicates a flight from human contact.

Is there a qualitative loss, then? Maybe. Such a subjective argument cannot be refuted with all the data showing people are just as much, if not more, connected now compared with most of 20th century. My sense is that what qualitative loss there is happens to be less so than many other forms of conversation avoidance. In fact, I can't count the number of times I was disturbed upon entering a house—especially in Turkey where this is common—because the television was glaring. Most people use the TV exactly like that—a conversation killer. At least, if people are texting, they are texting a human being. Similarly, I doubt that anyone has not seen how a person can open the newspaper at the kitchen table to block out conversation.

Take the much-maligned teenagers. What have we done to them? First, we move to the suburbs. So, they can't get around unless they drive (which is pretty dangerous). Parents often only take them to organized activities where the activity—hockey, violin, debate club—dominates, not the leisurely social conversation with each other adolescents naturally crave. Or they can hang out at . . . shopping malls. I need not say more about soul-killing.

And then when teenagers attempt to break out of this asocial, unnatural, and bizarre prison constructed of highways, no-recess time, and isolated single-family homes by connecting to *each other* through social media, we "tsk-tsk" them on how they don't know how to actually talk, or that they are narcissists because now we can see their status updates. Hint: Not much new going on here except teenage behavior is now visible thanks to technology and everyone else seems to have forgotten what it was like to be that age. And, yeah, mom and dad, sometimes they want to talk to their peers and not to you. That is not new. It's not even your fault. It's called being a teenager. A bit of a pain, perhaps, but the kids are neither the smartest, nor the dumbest, nor the most narcissistic, nor the most non-conversationalist generation ever.

Or consider the elderly—the most poignant example Turkle raises. Data say they are now online in growing numbers. Why? So they can talk to people. Old classmates. Grandchildren. Each other. I've heard of many similar stories from people with disabilities: Social media allow them to connect in a world which does not otherwise allow them easy access. The fact that, rather than being separate "real" and "virtual" worlds, online and offline spheres are integrated is exactly why people can attempt to break away from the constraints in their offline lives by hacking their connectivity through online interaction. Can't be close to your family because your job took you to the other end of the planet? You can still share updates on Facebook. Your government is censoring news of your protest? You can

tweet photos of it. You cannot find people interested in a particular kind of music which moves you? Surely, there is a community.

. . .

I concur with Sherry Turkle and others that there needs to be a deep and serious conversation about valuing each other—as humans, nothing more or less. And perhaps the impact of these rapidly evolving technologies on the "least among us" (as modern economic structures define them) is the correct place to start this conversation. However, to the degree this discussion can take place, it will mostly be because social media allow for such broad and deep conversations *among* the masses, who are reading and sharing rather than being lectured at and advertised to from their television screens.

ZEYNEP TUFEKCI is a fellow at the Center for Information Technology Policy at Princeton University, an assistant professor at the School of Information and Department of Sociology at the University of North Carolina, and a faculty associate at the Harvard Berkman Center for Internet and Society. She writes on social impacts of technology.

Sherry Turkle  **NO**

The Flight From Conversation

We live in a technological universe in which we are always communicating. And yet we have sacrificed conversation for mere connection.

At home, families sit together, texting and reading e-mail. At work executives text during board meetings. We text (and shop and go on Facebook) during classes and when we're on dates. My students tell me about an important new skill: it involves maintaining eye contact with someone while you text someone else; it's hard, but it can be done.

Over the past 15 years, I've studied technologies of mobile connection and talked to hundreds of people of all ages and circumstances about their plugged-in lives. I've learned that the little devices most of us carry around are so powerful that they change not only what we do, but also who we are.

We've become accustomed to a new way of being "alone together." Technology-enabled, we are able to be with one another, and also elsewhere, connected to wherever we want to be. We want to customize our lives. We want to move in and out of where we are because the thing we value most is control over where we focus our attention. We have gotten used to the idea of being in a tribe of one, loyal to our own party.

Our colleagues want to go to that board meeting but pay attention only to what interests them. To some this seems like a good idea, but we can end up hiding from one another, even as we are constantly connected to one another.

A businessman laments that he no longer has colleagues at work. He doesn't stop by to talk; he doesn't call. He says that he doesn't want to interrupt them. He says they're "too busy on their e-mail." But then he pauses and corrects himself. "I'm not telling the truth. I'm the one who doesn't want to be interrupted. I think I should. But I'd rather just do things on my BlackBerry."

A 16-year-old boy who relies on texting for almost everything says almost wistfully, "Someday, someday, but certainly not now, I'd like to learn how to have a conversation."

In today's workplace, young people who have grown up fearing conversation show up on the job wearing earphones. Walking through a college library or the campus of a high-tech start-up, one sees the same thing: we are together, but each of us is in our own bubble, furiously connected to keyboards and tiny touch screens. A senior partner at a Boston law firm describes a scene in his office. Young associates lay out their suite of technologies: laptops, iPods and multiple phones. And then they put their earphones on. "Big ones. Like pilots. They turn their desks into cockpits." With the young lawyers in their cockpits, the office is quiet, a quiet that does not ask to be broken.

In the silence of connection, people are comforted by being in touch with a lot of people—carefully kept at bay. We can't get enough of one another if we can use technology to keep one another at distances we can control: not too close, not too far, just right. I think of it as a Goldilocks effect.

Texting and e-mail and posting let us present the self we want to be. This means we can edit. And if we wish to, we can delete. Or retouch: the voice, the flesh, the face, the body. Not too much, not too little—just right.

Human relationships are rich; they're messy and demanding. We have learned the habit of cleaning them up with technology. And the move from conversation to connection is part of this. But it's a process in which we shortchange ourselves. Worse, it seems that over time we stop caring, we forget that there is a difference.

We are tempted to think that our little "sips" of online connection add up to a big gulp of real conversation. But they don't. E-mail, Twitter, Facebook, all of these have their places—in politics, commerce, romance and friendship. But no matter how valuable, they do not substitute for conversation.

Connecting in sips may work for gathering discrete bits of information or for saying, "I am thinking about you." Or even for saying, "I love you." But connecting in sips doesn't work as well when it comes to understanding and knowing one another. In conversation we tend to one another. (The word itself is kinetic; it's derived from words that mean to move, together.) We can attend to tone and nuance. In conversation, we are called upon to see things from another's point of view.

FACE-TO-FACE conversation unfolds slowly. It teaches patience. When we communicate on our digital devices, we learn different habits. As we ramp up the volume and velocity of online connections, we start to expect faster answers. To get these, we ask one another simpler questions; we dumb down our communications, even on the most important matters. It is as though we have all put ourselves on cable news. Shakespeare might have said, "We are consum'd with that which we were nourish'd by."

And we use conversation with others to learn to converse with ourselves. So our flight from conversation can mean diminished chances to learn skills of self-reflection. These days, social media continually asks us what's "on our mind," but we have little motivation to say something truly self-reflective. Self-reflection in conversation requires trust. It's hard to do anything with 3,000 Facebook friends except connect.

As we get used to being shortchanged on conversation and to getting by with less, we seem almost willing to dispense with people altogether. Serious people muse about the future of computer programs as psychiatrists. A high school sophomore confides to me that he wishes he could talk to an artificial intelligence program instead of his dad about dating; he says the A.I. would have so much more in its database. Indeed, many people tell me they hope that as Siri, the digital assistant on Apple's iPhone, becomes more advanced, "she" will be more and more like a best friend—one who will listen when others won't.

During the years I have spent researching people and their relationships with technology, I have often heard the sentiment "No one is listening to me." I believe this feeling helps explain why it is so appealing to have a Facebook page or a Twitter feed—each provides so many automatic listeners. And it helps explain why—against all reason—so many of us are willing to talk to machines that seem to care about us. Researchers around the world are busy inventing sociable robots, designed to be companions to the elderly, to children, to all of us.

One of the most haunting experiences during my research came when I brought one of these robots, designed in the shape of a baby seal, to an elder-care facility, and an older woman began to talk to it about the loss of her child. The robot seemed to be looking into her eyes. It seemed to be following the conversation. The woman was comforted.

And so many people found this amazing. Like the sophomore who wants advice about dating from artificial intelligence and those who look forward to computer psychiatry, this enthusiasm speaks to how much we have confused conversation with connection and collectively seem to have embraced a new kind of delusion that accepts the simulation of compassion as sufficient unto the day. And why would we want to talk about love and loss with a machine that has no experience of the arc of human life? Have we so lost confidence that we will be there for one another?

WE expect more from technology and less from one another and seem increasingly drawn to technologies that provide the illusion of companionship without the demands of relationship. Always-on/always-on-you devices provide three powerful fantasies: that we will always be heard; that we can put our attention wherever we want it to be; and that we never have to be alone. Indeed our new devices have turned being alone into a problem that can be solved.

When people are alone, even for a few moments, they fidget and reach for a device. Here connection works like a symptom, not a cure, and our constant, reflexive impulse to connect shapes a new way of being.

Think of it as "I share, therefore I am." We use technology to define ourselves by sharing our thoughts and feelings as we're having them. We used to think, "I have a feeling; I want to make a call." Now our impulse is, "I want to have a feeling; I need to send a text."

So, in order to feel more, and to feel more like ourselves, we connect. But in our rush to connect, we flee from solitude, our ability to be separate and gather ourselves. Lacking the capacity for solitude, we turn to other people but don't experience them as they are. It is as though we use them, need them as spare parts to support our increasingly fragile selves.

We think constant connection will make us feel less lonely. The opposite is true. If we are unable to be alone, we are far more likely to be lonely. If we don't teach our children to be alone, they will know only how to be lonely.

I am a partisan for conversation. To make room for it, I see some first, deliberate steps. At home, we can create sacred spaces: the kitchen, the dining room. We can make our cars "device-free zones." We can demonstrate the value of conversation to our children. And we can do the same thing at work. There we are so busy communicating that we often don't have time to talk to one another about what really matters. Employees asked for casual Fridays; perhaps managers should introduce conversational Thursdays. Most of all, we need to remember—in between texts and e-mails and Facebook posts—to listen to one another, even to the boring bits, because it is often in unedited moments, moments in which we hesitate and stutter and go silent, that we reveal ourselves to one another.

I spend the summers at a cottage on Cape Cod, and for decades I walked the same dunes that Thoreau once walked. Not too long ago, people walked with their heads up, looking at the water, the sky, the sand and at one another, talking. Now they often walk with their heads down, typing. Even when they are with friends, partners, children, everyone is on their own devices.

So I say, look up, look at one another, and let's start the conversation.

SHERRY TURKLE studies the relationship between people and technology. She is a professor in the Science, Technology and Society Program at MIT and founder of the MIT Initiative on Technology and Self. She is the author of *Alone Together: Why We Expect More From Technology and Less From Each Other*.

EXPLORING THE ISSUE

Do Social Media Enhance Real Relationships?

Critical Thinking and Reflection

1. Is there a difference between face-to-face and mediated communication? What is/are these difference(s)?
2. Is one mode of communication better than the other? What is the appropriate balance?
3. Create an imaginary other who exhibits the worst of alienating social media behaviors. How would you talk with him/her about his/her behavior?
4. As in most things, the answer lies in finding the appropriate balance. What would that look like for you?

Is There Common Ground?

Interestingly, there is less common ground than one might think initially because this is an issue of values rather than of fact. Those who find the reliance on mediated communication to be harmful believe that isolation from the immediate environment impoverishes the individual over time. Those who disagree find that mediated communication offers the opportunity to interact with those who mean the most to us and with whom we most enjoy communicating. To the claim that social media connect us to those we care about the most, the reply is that it does so by isolating the individual from other experiences and closing off an important part of a world of experience.

As indicated by the fourth critical thinking and reflection question above, the common ground is probably in finding an appropriate balance. By now, you have certainly figured out that some of the issues are about appropriate behavior (is it rude to take a cell call in a restaurant?), some are about safety (texting while driving being the most obvious offense), and some are rooted in the life choices that are implicated in the social media versus interpersonal decisions we all make. Turkle's reading challenges us to think beyond the surface of this issue to look at how media structure our life. To paraphrase an earlier question: Is this the life we ordered?

Additional Resources

Danah Boyd, *It's Complicated: The Social Lives of Networked Teens* (Yale University Press, 2014).

Brian S. Butler and Sabine Matook, *Social Media and Relationships* (Wiley Online Library, 2015).

Jose van Dijck, *The Culture of Connectivity: A Critical History of Social Media* (Oxford University Press, 2013).

Stephan Marche, "Is Facebook Making Us Lonely?" *The Atlantic* (May 20, 2012).

Sherry Turkle, *Reclaiming Conversation: The Power of Talk in a Digital Age* (Penguin Press, 2015).

Internet References . . .

Pew Research Center on Internet, Science & Tech

www.pewinternet.org/topics/social-networking
/pages/12/
www.pewinternet.org/2014/02/20/couples-the
-internet-and-social-media-2/

Psychology Today

https://www.psychologytoday.com/blog/positively
-media/201305/seven-myths-about-social-media
-and-relationships

TED Talk by Sherry Turkle

https://www.ted.com/talks/sherry_turkle_alone
_together?language=en

Selected, Edited, and with Issue Framing Material by:
Alison Alexander, *University of Georgia*
and
Jarice Hanson, *University of Massachusetts—Amherst*

ISSUE

Can Digital Libraries Replace Traditional Libraries?

YES: **Robert Darnton**, from "A World Digital Library Is Coming True!" *The New York Review of Books* (2014)

NO: **Jill Lepore**, from "The Cobweb: Can the Internet Be Archived?," *The New Yorker* (2015)

Learning Outcomes

After reading this issue, you will be able to:

- Think about the future of information access and the number of forms it could take.
- Evaluate whether the traditional model of publication and the dissemination of research is viable.
- Consider the options for digital storage of material; the lifespan of e-content; and how we may need to develop new search strategies.
- Think about the role of the library as a place for learning and as a community resource.
- Reflect on what it means when valuable information is not appropriately stored for future generations.

ISSUE SUMMARY

YES: Harvard University Library Director Robert Darnton suggests that a new model of publishing scholarly work may need to be created to preserve ideas in electronic form. The traditional library, he says, relies on a financial model that is no longer sustainable. The result, he suggests, is to continue to convert scholarly research to digital data and for libraries to specialize and cooperate in their lending processes.

NO: Historian and Harvard University Professor Jill Lepore examines the efforts to collect digital information—particularly websites—through the Internet Archive, but provides frightening data on how incomplete the archive of digital data is, why that happens, and what consequences occur because of incomplete records of digital data.

Electronic repositories of information are libraries of a sort, but the traditional library, complete with books, stacks, periodicals for browsing, and reference books for consultation, may be changing. The ability to convert print into electronic form is revolutionizing the publishing industries, and nowhere is this more important than in academic and scholarly libraries, where new ideas are collected and preserved for anyone to consult. The basis of the traditional "borrowing" library is that of making work available to all. And yet, as business models of academic (and popular) publishing begin to favor the lower cost of electronic publishing, we fear that something may be lost. Whether it is the joy of coming across something you didn't expect as you peruse the stacks in a library, or the ease of access in what appears to be a World Wide Web of "everything"—we know there are situations in which information we suspect is out there, but just may not be found. Whether we don't use the right keywords to access what we want, we experience "click fatigue" and give up, or whether the information is buried or has been dumped, information access and information availability is changing.

According to the Director of the Harvard Library, Robert Darnton, we only need to look at the high cost of producing academic journals to understand that the budgets of traditional libraries can't keep pace. It is more cost-effective to change the model of publishing so that specialized libraries are in charge of types of information, and that trained librarians become sleuths to help us find what we're looking for. In this article, Darnton discusses the role of academic publishing and suggests that a new model would be for the author to pay for publishing, and then later, after the initial period of time has passed, the work become that of public domain in a more open system. While students may not realize this, many colleges and universities have a "publish or perish" culture in which faculty members must, by contract, continue to do research that adds to general knowledge. In these "publish or perish" institutions, the quality of the journals in which you publish (i.e., the quality of the peer-reviewed journals) is often the arbiter of solid, quality work. But the cost for libraries to subscribe to the many academic journals is a problem for budgets, and therefore, Darnton envisions a different model for the dissemination of scholarly work and a different structure for institutions (like libraries) to access that information.

On the other hand, Jill Lepore investigates the *Internet Archive*, an electronic library of Web-based information that references a significant amount of the Web, but not all of it. In examining the evolution of the *Archive*, she shows how much digital information has already been lost and what the implications are for original material that was published in electronic form. Her evaluation of the content of the *Archive* is frighteningly inaccurate and incomplete, despite the best efforts of the staff of the Internet Archive to be as thorough as they can be with information that proliferates at such incredible speed.

The publishing industry is experiencing a shift in the way it does business in the same way the recording industry has already experienced a revolution in the way it records and distributes music. Scholarly libraries are specifically concerned with material that chronicles our history and culture, but even the popular press is not immune to shifting to an electronic form. Project Gutenberg is the oldest digital library of public domain books (those for which a copyright is not active) and already has made more than 50,000 items available to the public at no charge.

Once the digitization of books and periodicals became technologically possible, the number of ways people read information also began to shift. Certainly electronic text that is available online can be read on any computer or smartphone, but electronic copies of both popular and scholarly books can be downloaded to any number of tablets or electronic reading devices. Amazon is a commercial company that has benefitted greatly from electronic books, in part because it started as an online bookstore that easily had a distribution system in place for the browsing, ordering, and financial aspects of delivering traditional books to readers, but also because it marketed the Kindle reader, which encouraged users to request the electronic form of the book. The portability of the e-reader is a valuable feature for the casual reader, but it doesn't necessarily serve the purpose of someone who is conducting research and engaging with electronic text for that reason.

The term *information literacy* is increasingly being used with regard to the way users of electronic text evaluate the credibility of the author and the statements being made. With today's technology, the writer of a blog can produce and "publish" content on the Web that looks so professionally produced that the reader may have a hard time separating fact from opinion. The proliferation of opinions online makes it more difficult for people to weigh the merits of an argument. Often, when people search for information online they look for something that confirms their own belief system, and think, therefore, that what they are reading is proof of their own preconceived notions. What this means, though, is that the more we recognize the potential for electronic text to mislead, or provide opinion rather than fact, the more we need some arbiters of judgment.

We should also remember that libraries in communities also serve a special function. Often they are the community centers for people. Not only are books and popular periodicals available, many libraries serve important social functions too. Literacy programs, locations for voting, discussion groups for people who like to talk about current events, literature, or any subject really, often take place in the cultural center that is the traditional library.

As you think about the issues raised by these authors, you might want to think about the range of libraries and the way they function in a number of contexts. From the academic library to the local public library, we've formed certain expectations of what the institution does, and what it means in our lives. Will the shift to more digital distribution of information radically change our concept of the library? Will traditional libraries be able to continue to exist and offer services to the public? Like other industries and institutions in the midst of technological change, the library is likely to undergo change. How important might those changes be?

YES ⤹

Robert Darnton

A World Digital Library Is Coming True!

In the scramble to gain market share in cyberspace, something is getting lost: the public interest. Libraries and laboratories—crucial nodes of the World Wide Web—are buckling under economic pressure, and the information they diffuse is being diverted away from the public sphere, where it can do most good.

Not that information comes free or "wants to be free," as Internet enthusiasts proclaimed twenty years ago. It comes filtered through expensive technologies and financed by powerful corporations. No one can ignore the economic realities that underlie the new information age, but who would argue that we have reached the right balance between commercialization and democratization?

Consider the cost of scientific periodicals, most of which are published exclusively online. It has increased at four times the rate of inflation since 1986. The average price of a year's subscription to a chemistry journal is now $4,044. In 1970 it was $33. A subscription to the *Journal of Comparative Neurology* cost $30,860 in 2012—the equivalent of six hundred monographs. Three giant publishers—Reed Elsevier, Wiley-Blackwell, and Springer—publish 42 percent of all academic articles, and they make giant profits from them. In 2013 Elsevier turned a 39 percent profit on an income of £2.1 billion from its science, technical, and medical journals.

All over the country research libraries are canceling subscriptions to academic journals, because they are caught between decreasing budgets and increasing costs. The logic of the bottom line is inescapable, but there is a higher logic that deserves consideration—namely, that the public should have access to knowledge produced with public funds.

Congress acted on that principle in 2008, when it required that articles based on grants from the National Institutes of Health be made available, free of charge, from an open-access repository, PubMed Central. But lobbyists blunted that requirement by getting the NIH to accept a twelve-month embargo, which would prevent public accessibility long enough for the publishers to profit from the immediate demand.

Not content with that victory, the lobbyists tried to abolish the NIH mandate in the so-called Research Works Act, a bill introduced in Congress in November 2011 and championed by Elsevier. The bill was withdrawn two months later following a wave of public protest, but the lobbyists are still at work, trying to block the Fair Access to Science and Technology Research Act (FASTR), which would give the public free access to all research, the data as well as the results, funded by federal agencies with research budgets of $100 million or more.

FASTR is a successor to the Federal Research Public Access Act (FRPAA), which remained bottled up in Congress after being introduced in three earlier sessions. But the basic provisions of both bills were adopted by a White House directive issued by the Office of Science and Technology Policy on February 22, 2013, and due to take effect at the end of this year. In principle, therefore, the results of research funded by taxpayers will be available to taxpayers, at least in the short term. What is the prospect over the long term? No one knows, but there are signs of hope.

The struggle over academic journals should not be dismissed as an "academic question," because a great deal is at stake. Access to research drives large sectors of the economy—the freer and quicker the access, the more powerful its effect. The Human Genome Project cost $3.8 billion in federal funds to develop, and thanks to the free accessibility of the results, it has already produced $796 billion in commercial applications. Linux, the free, open-source software system, has brought in billions in revenue for many companies, including Google. Less spectacular but more widespread is the multiplier effect of free information on small and medium businesses that cannot afford to pay for information hoarded behind subscription walls. A delay of a year in access to research and data can be prohibitively expensive for them. According to a study completed in 2006 by John Houghton, a specialist in the economics of information, a 5 percent increase in the accessibility of research would have produced an increase in productivity worth $16 billion.

Yet accessibility may decrease, because the price of journals has escalated so disastrously that libraries—and also hospitals, small-scale laboratories, and data-driven enterprises—are canceling subscriptions. Publishers respond by charging still more to institutions with budgets strong enough to carry the additional weight. But the system is breaking down. In 2010, when the Nature Publishing Group told the University of California that it would increase the price of its sixty-seven journals by 400 percent, the libraries stood their ground, and the faculty, which had contributed 5,300 articles to those journals during the previous six years, began to organize a boycott. . . .

In the long run, journals can be sustained only through a transformation of the economic basis of academic publishing. The current system developed as a component of the professionalization of academic disciplines in the nineteenth century. It served the public interest well through most of the twentieth century, but it has become dysfunctional in the age of the Internet. In fields like physics, most research circulates online in prepublication exchanges, and articles are composed with sophisticated programs that produce copy-ready texts. Costs are low enough for access to be free, as illustrated by the success of arXiv, a repository of articles in physics, mathematics, computer science, quantitative biology, quantitative finance, and statistics. (The articles do not undergo full-scale peer review unless, as often happens, they are later published by conventional journals.)

The entire system of communicating research could be made less expensive and more beneficial for the public by a process known as "flipping." Instead of subsisting on subscriptions, a flipped journal covers its costs by charging processing fees before publication and making its articles freely available, as "open access," afterward. That will sound strange to many academic authors. Why, they may ask, should we pay to get published? But they may not understand the dysfunctions of the present system, in which they furnish the research, writing, and refereeing free of charge to the subscription journals and then buy back the product of their work—not personally, of course, but through their libraries—at an exorbitant price. The public pays twice—first as taxpayers who subsidize the research, then as taxpayers or tuition payers who support public or private university libraries.

By creating open-access journals, a flipped system directly benefits the public. Anyone can consult the research free of charge online, and libraries are liberated from the spiraling costs of subscriptions. Of course, the publication expenses do not evaporate miraculously, but they are greatly reduced, especially for nonprofit journals, which do not need to satisfy shareholders. The processing fees, which can run to a thousand dollars or more, depending on the complexities of the text and the process of peer review, can be covered in various ways. They are often included in research grants to scientists, and they are increasingly financed by the author's university or a group of universities.

At Harvard, a program called HOPE (Harvard Open-Access Publishing Equity) subsidizes processing fees. A consortium called COPE (Compact for Open-Access Publishing Equity) promotes similar policies among twenty-one institutions, including MIT, the University of Michigan, and the University of California at Berkeley; and its activities complement those of thirty-three similar funds in institutions such as Johns Hopkins University and the University of California at San Francisco.

The main impediment to public-spirited publishing of this kind is not financial. It involves prestige. Scientists prefer to publish in expensive journals like *Nature*, *Science*, and *Cell*, because the aura attached to them glows on CVs and promotes careers. But some prominent scientists have undercut the prestige effect by founding open-access journals and recruiting the best talent to write and referee for them. Harold Varmus, a Nobel laureate in physiology and medicine, has made a huge success of *Public Library of Science*, and Paul Crutzen, a Nobel laureate in chemistry, has done the same with *Atmospheric Chemistry and Physics*. They have proven the feasibility of high-quality, open-access journals. Not only do they cover costs through processing fees, but they produce a profit—or rather, a "surplus," which they invest in further open-access projects.

The pressure for open access is also building up from digital repositories, which are being established in universities throughout the country. In February 2008, the Faculty of Arts and Sciences at Harvard voted unanimously to require its members (with a proviso for opting out or for accepting embargoes imposed by commercial journals) to deposit peer-reviewed articles in a repository, DASH (Digital Access to Scholarship at Harvard), where they can be read by anyone free of charge.

DASH now includes 17,000 articles, and it has registered three million downloads from countries in every continent. Repositories in other universities also report very high scores in their counts of downloads. They make knowledge available to a broad public, including researchers who have no connection to an academic institution; and at the same time, they make it possible for writers to reach far more readers than would be possible by means of subscription journals.

The desire to reach readers may be one of the most underestimated forces in the world of knowledge. Aside from journal articles, academics produce a large numbers of books, yet they rarely make much money from them. Authors in general derive little income from a book a year or two after its publication. Once its commercial life has ended, it dies a slow death, lying unread, except for rare occasions, on the shelves of libraries, inaccessible to the vast majority of readers. At that stage, authors generally have one dominant desire—for their work to circulate freely through the public; and their interest coincides with the goals of the open-access movement. A new organization, Authors Alliance, is about to launch a campaign to persuade authors to make their books available online at some point after publication through nonprofit distributors like the Digital Public Library of America, of which more later.

All sorts of complexities remain to be worked out before such a plan can succeed: How to accommodate the interests of publishers, who want to keep books on their backlists? Where to leave room for rights holders to opt out and for the revival of books that take on new economic life? Whether to devise some form of royalties, as in the extended collective licensing programs that have proven to be successful in the Scandinavian countries? It should be possible to enlist vested interests in a solution that will serve the public interest, not by appealing to altruism but rather by rethinking business plans in ways that will make the most of modern technology.

Several experimental enterprises illustrate possibilities of this kind. Knowledge Unlatched gathers commitments and collects funds from libraries that agree to purchase scholarly books at rates that will guarantee payment of a fixed amount to the publishers who are taking part in the program. The more libraries participating in the pool, the lower the price each will have to pay. While electronic editions of the books will be available everywhere free of charge through Knowledge Unlatched, the subscribing libraries will have the exclusive right to download and print out copies. By the end of February, more than 250 libraries had signed up to purchase a pilot collection of twenty-eight new books produced by thirteen publishers, and Knowledge Unlatched headquarters, located in London, announced that it would soon scale up its operations with the goal of combining open access with sustainability.

OpenEdition Books, located in Marseille, operates on a somewhat similar principle. It provides a platform for publishers who want to develop open-access online collections, and it sells the e-content to subscribers in formats that can be downloaded and printed. Operating from Cambridge, England, Open Book Publishers also charges for PDFs, which can be used with print-on-demand technology to produce physical books, and it applies the income to subsidies for free copies online. It recruits academic authors who are willing to provide manuscripts without payment in order to reach the largest possible audience and to further the cause of open access.

The famous quip of Samuel Johnson, "No man but a blockhead ever wrote, except for money," no longer has the force of a self-evident truth in the age of the Internet. By tapping the goodwill of unpaid authors, Open Book Publishers has produced forty-one books in the humanities and social sciences, all rigorously peer-reviewed, since its foundation in 2008. "We envisage a world in which all research is freely available to all readers," it proclaims on its website.

The same goal animates the Digital Public Library of America, which aims to make available all the intellectual riches accumulated in American libraries, archives, and museums. As reported in these pages, the DPLA was launched on April 18, 2013. Now that it has celebrated its first anniversary, its collections include seven million books and other objects, three times the amount that it offered when it went online a year ago. They come from more than 1,300 institutions located in all fifty states, and they are being widely used: nearly a million distinct visitors have consulted the DPLA's website (dp.la), and they come from nearly every country in the world (North Korea, Chad, and Western Sahara are the only exceptions).

At the time of its conception in October 2010, the DPLA was seen as an alternative to one of the most ambitious projects ever imagined for commercializing access to information: Google Book Search. Google set out to digitize millions of books in research libraries and then proposed to sell subscriptions to the resulting database. Having provided the books to Google free of charge, the libraries would then have to buy back access to them, in digital form, at a price to be determined by Google and that could escalate as disastrously as the prices of scholarly journals.

Google Book Search actually began as a search service, which made available only snippets or short passages of books. But because many of the books were covered by copyright, Google was sued by the rights holders; and after lengthy negotiations the plaintiffs and Google agreed on a settlement, which transformed the search service into a gigantic commercial library financed by subscriptions. But the settlement had to be approved by a court, and on March 22, 2011, the Southern Federal District Court of New York rejected it on the grounds that, among other things, it threatened to constitute a monopoly in restraint of trade. That decision put an end to Google's project and cleared the way for the DPLA to offer digitized holdings—but nothing covered by copyright—to readers everywhere, free of charge.

Aside from its not-for-profit character, the DPLA differs from Google Book Search in a crucial respect: it is not a vertical organization erected on a database of its own. It is a distributed, horizontal system, which links digital collections already in the possession of the participating institutions, and it does so by means of a technological infrastructure that makes them instantly available to the user with one click on an electronic device. It is fundamentally horizontal, both in organization and in spirit.

Instead of working from the top down, the DPLA relies on "service hubs," or small administrative centers, to promote local collections and aggregate them at the state level. "Content hubs" located in institutions with collections of at least 250,000 items—for example, the New York Public Library, the Smithsonian Institution, and the collective digital repository known as HathiTrust—provide the bulk of the DPLA's holdings. There are now two dozen service and content hubs, and soon, if financing can be found, they will exist in every state of the union.

Such horizontality reinforces the democratizing impulse behind the DPLA. Although it is a small, non-profit corporation with headquarters and a minimal staff in Boston, the DPLA functions as a network that covers the entire country. It relies heavily on volunteers. More than a thousand computer scientists collaborated free of charge in the design of its infrastructure, which aggregates metadata (catalog-type descriptions of documents) in a way that allows easy searching.

Therefore, for example, a ninth-grader in Dallas who is preparing a report on an episode of the American Revolution can download a manuscript from New York, a pamphlet from Chicago, and a map from San Francisco in order to study them side by side. Unfortunately, he or she will not be able to consult any recent books, because copyright laws keep virtually everything published after 1923 out of the public domain. But the courts, which are considering a flurry of cases about the "fair use" of copyright, may sustain a broad-enough interpretation for the DPLA to make a great deal of post-1923 material available for educational purposes.

A small army of volunteer "Community Reps," mainly librarians with technical skills, is fanning out across the country to promote various outreach programs sponsored by the DPLA. They reinforce the work of the service hubs, which concentrate on public libraries as centers of collection-building. A grant from the Bill and Melinda Gates Foundation is financing a Public Library Partnerships Project to train local librarians in the latest digital technologies. Equipped with new skills, the librarians will invite people to bring in material of their own—family letters, high school yearbooks, postcard collections stored in trunks and attics—to be digitized, curated, preserved, and made accessible online by the DPLA. While developing local community consciousness about culture and history, this project will also help integrate local collections in the national network.

Spin-off projects and local initiatives are also favored by what the DPLA calls its "plumbing"—that is, the technological infrastructure, which has been designed in a way to promote user-generated apps or digital tools connected to the system by means of an API (application programming interface), which has already registered seven million hits. Among the results is a tool for digital browsing: the user types in the title of a book, and images of spines of books, all related to the same subject, all in the public domain, appear on the screen as if they were aligned together on a shelf. The user can click on a spine to search one work after another, following leads that extend far beyond the shelf space of a physical library. Another tool makes it possible for a reader to go from a Wikipedia article to all the works in the DPLA that bear on the same subject. These and many other apps have been developed by individuals on their own, without following directives from DPLA headquarters.

The spin-offs offer endless educational opportunities. For example, the Emily Dickinson Archive recently developed at Harvard will make available digitized copies of the manuscripts of all Dickinson's poems. The manuscripts are essential for interpreting the work, because they contain many peculiarities—punctuation, spacing, capitalization—that inflect the meaning of the poems, of which only a few, badly mangled, were published during Dickinson's lifetime. Nearly every high school student comes across a poem by Dickinson at one time or other. Now teachers can assign a particular poem in its manuscript and printed versions (they often differ considerably) and stimulate their students to develop closer, deeper readings. The DPLA also plans to adapt its holdings to the special needs of community colleges, many of which do not have adequate libraries.

In these and other ways, the DPLA will go beyond its basic mission of making the cultural heritage of America available to all Americans. It will provide opportunities for them to interact with the material and to develop materials of their own. It will empower librarians and reinforce public libraries everywhere, not only in the United States. Its technological infrastructure has been designed to be interoperable with that of Europeana, a similar enterprise that is aggregating the holdings of libraries in the twenty-eight member states of the European Union. The DPLA's collections include works in more than four hundred languages, and nearly 30 percent of its users come from outside the US. Ten years from now, the DPLA's first year of activity may look like the beginning of an international library system.

It would be naive, however, to imagine a future free from the vested interests that have blocked the flow of information in the past. The lobbies at work in Washington also operate in Brussels, and a newly elected European Parliament will soon have to deal with the same issues that remain to be resolved in the US Congress. Commercialization and democratization operate on a global scale, and a great deal of access must be opened before the World Wide Web can accommodate a worldwide library.

ROBERT DARNTON is the Carl H. Pforzheimer University Professor and Director of the University Library at Harvard University. His primary area of research is eighteenth-century France, but he also writes extensively about print culture.

Jill Lepore
 **NO**

The Cobweb: Can the Internet Be Archived?

Malaysia Airlines Flight 17 took off from Amsterdam at 10:31 A.M. G.M.T. on July 17, 2014, for a twelve-hour flight to Kuala Lumpur. Not much more than three hours later, the plane, a Boeing 777, crashed in a field outside Donetsk, Ukraine. All two hundred and ninety-eight people on board were killed. The plane's last radio contact was at 1:20 P.M. G.M.T. At 2:50 P.M. G.M.T., Igor Girkin, a Ukrainian separatist leader also known as Strelkov, or someone acting on his behalf, posted a message on VKontakte, a Russian social-media site: "We just downed a plane, an AN-26." (An Antonov 26 is a Soviet-built military cargo plane.) The post includes links to video of the wreckage of a plane; it appears to be a Boeing 777.

Two weeks before the crash, Anatol Shmelev, the curator of the Russia and Eurasia collection at the Hoover Institution, at Stanford, had submitted to the Internet Archive, a nonprofit library in California, a list of Ukrainian and Russian Web sites and blogs that ought to be recorded as part of the archive's Ukraine Conflict collection. Shmelev is one of about a thousand librarians and archivists around the world who identify possible acquisitions for the Internet Archive's subject collections, which are stored in its Wayback Machine, in San Francisco. Strelkov's VKontakte page was on Shmelev's list. "Strelkov is the field commander in Slaviansk and one of the most important figures in the conflict," Shmelev had written in an e-mail to the Internet Archive on July 1st, and his page "deserves to be recorded twice a day."

On July 17th, at 3:22 P.M. G.M.T., the Wayback Machine saved a screenshot of Strelkov's VKontakte post about downing a plane. Two hours and twenty-two minutes later, Arthur Bright, the Europe editor of the *Christian Science Monitor*, tweeted a picture of the screenshot, along with the message "Grab of Donetsk militant Strelkov's claim of downing what appears to have been MH17." By then, Strelkov's VKontakte page had already been edited: the claim about shooting down a plane was deleted. The only real evidence of the original claim lies in the Wayback Machine.

The average life of a Web page is about a hundred days. Strelkov's "We just downed a plane" post lasted barely two hours. It might seem, and it often feels, as though stuff on the Web lasts forever, for better and frequently for worse: the embarrassing photograph, the regretted blog (more usually regrettable not in the way the slaughter of civilians is regrettable but in the way that bad hair is regrettable). No one believes any longer, if anyone ever did, that "if it's on the Web it must be true," but a lot of people do believe that if it's on the Web it will stay on the Web. Chances are, though, that it actually won't. In 2006, David Cameron gave a speech in which he said that Google was democratizing the world, because "making more information available to more people" was providing "the power for anyone to hold to account those who in the past might have had a monopoly of power." Seven years later, Britain's Conservative Party scrubbed from its Web site ten years' worth of Tory speeches, including that one. Last year, BuzzFeed deleted more than four thousand of its staff writers' early posts, apparently because, as time passed, they looked stupider and stupider. Social media, public records, junk: in the end, everything goes.

Web pages don't have to be deliberately deleted to disappear. Sites hosted by corporations tend to die with their hosts. When MySpace, GeoCities, and Friendster were reconfigured or sold, millions of accounts vanished. (Some of those companies may have notified users, but Jason Scott, who started an outfit called Archive Team—its motto is "We are going to rescue your shit"—says that such notification is usually purely notional: "They were sending e-mail to dead e-mail addresses, saying, 'Hello, Arthur Dent, your house is going to be crushed.'") Facebook has been around for only a decade; it won't be around forever. Twitter is a rare case: it has arranged to archive all of its tweets at the Library of Congress. In 2010, after the announcement, Andy Borowitz tweeted, "Library of Congress to acquire entire Twitter archive—will rename itself Museum of Crap." Not long after that, Borowitz abandoned that Twitter account. You might, one day, be able to find his old tweets at the Library of

Congress, but not anytime soon: the Twitter Archive is not yet open for research. Meanwhile, on the Web, if you click on a link to Borowitz's tweet about the Museum of Crap, you get this message: "Sorry, that page doesn't exist!"

The Web dwells in a never-ending present. It is—elementally—ethereal, ephemeral, unstable, and unreliable. Sometimes when you try to visit a Web page what you see is an error message: "Page Not Found." This is known as "link rot," and it's a drag, but it's better than the alternative. More often, you see an updated Web page; most likely the original has been overwritten. (To overwrite, in computing, means to destroy old data by storing new data in their place; overwriting is an artifact of an era when computer storage was very expensive.) Or maybe the page has been moved and something else is where it used to be. This is known as "content drift," and it's more pernicious than an error message, because it's impossible to tell that what you're seeing isn't what you went to look for: the overwriting, erasure, or moving of the original is invisible. For the law and for the courts, link rot and content drift, which are collectively known as "reference rot," have been disastrous. In providing evidence, legal scholars, lawyers, and judges often cite Web pages in their footnotes; they expect that evidence to remain where they found it as their proof, the way that evidence on paper—in court records and books and law journals—remains where they found it, in libraries and courthouses. But a 2013 survey of law- and policy-related publications found that, at the end of six years, nearly fifty percent of the URLs cited in those publications no longer worked. According to a 2014 study conducted at Harvard Law School, "more than 70% of the URLs within the Harvard Law Review and other journals, and 50% of the URLs within United States Supreme Court opinions, do not link to the originally cited information." The overwriting, drifting, and rotting of the Web is no less catastrophic for engineers, scientists, and doctors. Last month, a team of digital library researchers based at Los Alamos National Laboratory reported the results of an exacting study of three and a half million scholarly articles published in science, technology, and medical journals between 1997 and 2012: one in five links provided in the notes suffers from reference rot. It's like trying to stand on quicksand.

The footnote, a landmark in the history of civilization, took centuries to invent and to spread. It has taken mere years nearly to destroy. A footnote used to say, "Here is how I know this and where I found it." A footnote that's a link says, "Here is what I used to know and where I once found it, but chances are it's not there anymore." It doesn't matter whether footnotes are your stock-in-trade. Everybody's in a pinch. Citing a Web page as the source for something you know—using a URL as evidence—is ubiquitous. Many people find themselves doing it three or four times before breakfast and five times more before lunch. What happens when your evidence vanishes by dinnertime?

The day after Strelkov's "We just downed a plane" post was deposited into the Wayback Machine, Samantha Power, the U.S. Ambassador to the United Nations, told the U.N. Security Council, in New York, that Ukrainian separatist leaders had "boasted on social media about shooting down a plane, but later deleted these messages." In San Francisco, the people who run the Wayback Machine posted on the Internet Archive's Facebook page, "Here's why we exist."

The address of the Internet Archive is archive.org, but another way to visit is to take a plane to San Francisco and ride in a cab to the Presidio, past cypresses that look as though someone had drawn them there with a smudgy crayon. At 300 Funston Avenue, climb a set of stone steps and knock on the brass door of a Greek Revival temple. You can't miss it: it's painted wedding-cake white and it's got, out front, eight Corinthian columns and six marble urns.

"We bought it because it matched our logo," Brewster Kahle told me when I met him there, and he wasn't kidding. Kahle is the founder of the Internet Archive and the inventor of the Wayback Machine. The logo of the Internet Archive is a white, pedimented Greek temple. When Kahle started the Internet Archive, in 1996, in his attic, he gave everyone working with him a book called "The Vanished Library," about the burning of the Library of Alexandria. "The idea is to build the Library of Alexandria Two," he told me. (The Hellenism goes further: there's a partial backup of the Internet Archive in Alexandria, Egypt.) Kahle's plan is to one-up the Greeks. The motto of the Internet Archive is "Universal Access to All Knowledge." The Library of Alexandria was open only to the learned; the Internet Archive is open to everyone. In 2009, when the Fourth Church of Christ, Scientist, decided to sell its building, Kahle went to Funston Avenue to see it, and said, "That's our logo!" He loves that the church's cornerstone was laid in 1923: everything published in the United States before that date lies in the public domain. A temple built in copyright's year zero seemed fated. Kahle hops, just slightly, in his shoes when he gets excited. He says, showing me the church, "It's *Greek!*"

. . .

When Kahle was growing up, some of the very same people who were building what would one day become the Internet were thinking about libraries. In 1961, in

Cambridge, J. C. R. Licklider, a scientist at the technology firm Bolt, Beranek and Newman, began a two-year study on the future of the library, funded by the Ford Foundation and aided by a team of researchers that included Marvin Minsky, at M.I.T. As Licklider saw it, books were good at displaying information but bad at storing, organizing, and retrieving it. "We should be prepared to reject the schema of the physical book itself," he argued, and to reject "the printed page as a long-term storage device." The goal of the project was to imagine what libraries would be like in the year 2000. Licklider envisioned a library in which computers would replace books and form a "network in which every element of the fund of knowledge is connected to every other element."

In 1963, Licklider became a director at the Department of Defense's Advanced Research Projects Agency (now called DARPA). During his first year, he wrote a seven-page memo in which he addressed his colleagues as "Members and Affiliates of the Intergalactic Computer Network," and proposed the networking of ARPA machines. This sparked the imagination of an electrical engineer named Lawrence Roberts, who later went to ARPA from M.I.T.'s Lincoln Laboratory. (Licklider had helped found both B.B.N. and Lincoln.) Licklider's two-hundred-page Ford Foundation report, "Libraries of the Future," was published in 1965. By then, the network he imagined was already being built, and the word "hyper-text" was being used. By 1969, relying on a data-transmission technology called "packet-switching" which had been developed by a Welsh scientist named Donald Davies, ARPA had built a computer network called ARPANET. By the mid-nineteen-seventies, researchers across the country had developed a network of networks: an internetwork, or, later, an "internet."

Kahle enrolled at M.I.T. in 1978. He studied computer science and engineering with Minsky. After graduating, in 1982, he worked for and started companies that were later sold for a great deal of money. In the late eighties, while working at Thinking Machines, he developed Wide Area Information Servers, or WAIS, a protocol for searching, navigating, and publishing on the Internet. One feature of WAIS was a time axis; it provided for archiving through version control. (Wikipedia has version control; from any page, you can click on a tab that says "View History" to see all earlier versions of that page.) WAIS came before the Web, and was then overtaken by it. In 1989, at CERN, the European Particle Physics Laboratory, in Geneva, Tim Berners-Lee, an English computer scientist, proposed a hypertext transfer protocol (HTTP) to link pages on what he called the World Wide Web. Berners-Lee toyed with the idea of a time axis for his protocol, too. One reason it was

never developed was the preference for the most up-to-date information: a bias against obsolescence. But the chief reason was the premium placed on ease of use. "We were so young then, and the Web was so young," Berners-Lee told me. "I was trying to get it to go. Preservation was not a priority. But we're getting older now." Other scientists involved in building the infrastructure of the Internet are getting older and more concerned, too. Vint Cerf, who worked on ARPANET in the seventies, and now holds the title of Chief Internet Evangelist at Google, has started talking about what he sees as a need for "digital vellum": long-term storage. "I worry that the twenty-first century will become an informational black hole," Cerf e-mailed me. But Kahle has been worried about this problem all along.

"I'm completely in praise of what Tim Berners-Lee did," Kahle told me, "but he kept it very, very simple." The first Web page in the United States was created at SLAC, Stanford's linear-accelerator center, at the end of 1991. Berners-Lee's protocol—which is not only usable but also elegant—spread fast, initially across universities and then into the public. "Emphasized text like this is a hypertext link," a 1994 version of SLAC's Web page explained. In 1991, a ban on commercial traffic on the Internet was lifted. Then came Web browsers and e-commerce: both Netscape and Amazon were founded in 1994. The Internet as most people now know it—Web-based and commercial—began in the mid-nineties. Just as soon as it began, it started disappearing.

And the Internet Archive began collecting it. The Wayback Machine is a Web archive, a collection of old Web pages; it is, in fact, *the* Web archive. There are others, but the Wayback Machine is so much bigger than all of them that it's very nearly true that if it's not in the Wayback Machine it doesn't exist. The Wayback Machine is a robot. It crawls across the Internet, in the manner of Eric Carle's very hungry caterpillar, attempting to make a copy of every Web page it can find every two months, though that rate varies. (It first crawled over this magazine's home page, newyorker.com, in November, 1998, and since then has crawled the site nearly seven thousand times, lately at a rate of about six times a day.) The Internet Archive is also stocked with Web pages that are chosen by librarians, specialists like Anatol Shmelev, collecting in subject areas, through a service called Archive It, at archive-it.org, which also allows individuals and institutions to build their own archives. (A copy of everything they save goes into the Wayback Machine, too.) And anyone who wants to can preserve a Web page, at any time, by going to archive .org/web, typing in a URL, and clicking "Save Page Now." (That's how most of the twelve screenshots of Strelkov's

VKontakte page entered the Wayback Machine on the day the Malaysia Airlines flight was downed: seven captures that day were made by a robot; the rest were made by humans.)

I was on a panel with Kahle a few years ago, discussing the relationship between material and digital archives. When I met him, I was struck by a story he told about how he once put the entire World Wide Web into a shipping container. He just wanted to see if it would fit. How big is the Web? It turns out, he said, that it's twenty feet by eight feet by eight feet, or, at least, it was on the day he measured it. How much did it weigh? Twenty-six thousand pounds. He thought that *meant* something. He thought people needed to *know* that.

Kahle put the Web into a storage container, but most people measure digital data in bytes. This essay is about two hundred thousand bytes. A book is about a megabyte. A megabyte is a million bytes. A gigabyte is a billion bytes. A terabyte is a million million bytes. A petabyte is a million gigabytes. In the lobby of the Internet Archive, you can get a free bumper sticker that says "10,000,000,000,000,000 Bytes Archived." Ten petabytes. It's obsolete. That figure is from 2012. Since then, it's doubled.

The Wayback Machine has archived more than four hundred and thirty billion Web pages. The Web is global, but, aside from the Internet Archive, a handful of fledgling commercial enterprises, and a growing number of university Web archives, most Web archives are run by national libraries. They collect chiefly what's in their own domains (the Web Archive of the National Library of Sweden, for instance, includes every Web page that ends in ".se"). The Library of Congress has archived nine billion pages, the British Library six billion. Those collections, like the collections of most national libraries, are in one way or another dependent on the Wayback Machine; the majority also use Heritrix, the Internet Archive's open-source code. The British Library and the Bibliothèque Nationale de France backfilled the early years of their collections by using the Internet Archive's crawls of the .uk and .fr domains. The Library of Congress doesn't actually do its own Web crawling; it contracts with the Internet Archive to do it instead.

The church at 300 Funston Avenue is twenty thousand square feet. The Internet Archive, the building, is open to the public most afternoons. It is, after all, a library. In addition to housing the Wayback Machine, the Internet Archive is a digital library, a vast collection of digitized books, films, television and radio programs, music, and other stuff. Because of copyright, not everything the Internet Archive has digitized is online. In the lobby of the church, there's a scanning station and a listening room: two armchairs, a coffee table, a pair of bookshelves, two iPads, and two sets of headphones. "You can listen to anything here," Kahle says. "We can't put all our music on the Internet, but we can put everything here."

Copyright is the elephant in the archive. One reason the Library of Congress has a very small Web-page collection, compared with the Internet Archive, is that the Library of Congress generally does not collect a Web page without asking, or, at least, giving notice. "The Internet Archive hoovers," Abbie Grotke, who runs the Library of Congress's Web-archive team, says. "We can't hoover, because we have to notify site owners and get permissions." (There are some exceptions.) The Library of Congress has something like an opt-in policy; the Internet Archive has an opt-out policy. The Wayback Machine collects every Web page it can find, unless that page is blocked; blocking a Web crawler requires adding only a simple text file, "robots.txt," to the root of a Web site. The Wayback Machine will honor that file and not crawl that site, and it will also, when it comes across a robots.txt, remove all past versions of that site. When the Conservative Party in Britain deleted ten years' worth of speeches from its Web site, it also added a robots.txt, which meant that, the next time the Wayback Machine tried to crawl the site, all its captures of those speeches went away, too. (Some have since been restored.) In a story that ran in the *Guardian*, a Labour Party M.P. said, "It will take more than David Cameron pressing delete to make people forget about his broken promises." And it would take more than a robots.txt to entirely destroy those speeches: they have also been collected in the U.K. Web Archive, at the British Library. The U.K. has what's known as a legal-deposit law; it requires copies of everything published in Britain to be deposited in the British Library. In 2013, that law was revised to include everything published on the U.K. Web. "People put their private lives up there, and we actually don't want that stuff," Andy Jackson, the technical head of the U.K. Web Archive, told me. "We don't want anything that you wouldn't consider a publication." It is hard to say quite where the line lies. But Britain's legal-deposit laws mean that the British Library doesn't have to honor a request to stop collecting.

. . .

In 2002, Kahle proposed an initiative in which the Internet Archive, in collaboration with national libraries, would become the head of a worldwide consortium of Web archives. (The Internet Archive collects from around the world, and is available in most of the world. Currently, the biggest exception is China—"I guess because we have materials on the archive that the Chinese government would rather not have its citizens see," Kahle says.)

This plan didn't work out, but from that failure came the International Internet Preservation Consortium, founded in 2003 and chartered at the BnF. It started with a dozen member institutions; there are now forty-nine.

. . .

The plan to found a global Internet archive proved unworkable, partly because national laws relating to legal deposit, copyright, and privacy are impossible to reconcile, but also because Europeans tend to be suspicious of American organizations based in Silicon Valley ingesting their cultural inheritance. Illien told me that, when faced with Kahle's proposal, "national libraries decided they could not rely on a third party," even a nonprofit, "for such a fundamental heritage and preservation mission." In this same spirit, and in response to Google Books, European libraries and museums collaborated to launch Europeana, a digital library, in 2008. The Googleplex, Google's headquarters, is thirty-eight miles away from the Internet Archive, but the two could hardly be more different. In 2009, after the Authors Guild and the Association of American Publishers sued Google Books for copyright infringement, Kahle opposed the proposed settlement, charging Google with effectively attempting to privatize the public-library system. In 2010, he was on the founding steering committee of the Digital Public Library of America, which is something of an American version of Europeana; its mission is to make what's in libraries, archives, and museums "freely available to the world . . . in the face of increasingly restrictive digital options."

Kahle is a digital utopian attempting to stave off a digital dystopia. He views the Web as a giant library, and doesn't think it ought to belong to a corporation, or that anyone should have to go through a portal owned by a corporation in order to read it. "We are building a library that is us," he says, "and it is ours."

When the Internet Archive bought the church, Kahle recalls, "we had the idea that we'd convert it into a library, but what does a library look like anymore? So we've been settling in, and figuring that out."

From the lobby, we headed up a flight of yellow-carpeted stairs to the chapel, an enormous dome-ceilinged room filled with rows of oak pews. There are arched stained-glass windows, and the dome is a stained-glass window, too, open to the sky, like an eye of God. The chapel seats seven hundred people. The floor is sloped. "At first, we thought we'd flatten the floor and pull up the pews," Kahle said, as he gestured around the room. "But we couldn't. They're just too beautiful."

On the wall on either side of the altar, wooden slates display what, when this was a church, had been the listing of the day's hymn numbers. The archivists of the Internet have changed those numbers. One hymn number was 314. "Do you know what that is?" Kahle asked. It was a test, and something of a trick question, like when someone asks you what's your favorite B track on the White Album. "Pi," I said, dutifully, or its first three digits, anyway. Another number was 42. Kahle gave me an inquiring look. I rolled my eyes. Seriously? But it is serious, in a way. It's hard not to worry that the Wayback Machine will end up like the computer in Douglas Adams's "Hitchhiker's Guide to the Galaxy," which is asked what is the meaning of "life, the universe, and everything," and, after thinking for millions of years, says, "Forty-two." If the Internet can be archived, will it ever have anything to tell us? Honestly, isn't most of the Web trash? And, if everything's saved, won't there be too much of it for anyone to make sense of any of it? Won't it be useless?

The Wayback Machine is humongous, and getting humongouser. You can't search it the way you can search the Web, because it's too big and what's in there isn't sorted, or indexed, or catalogued in any of the many ways in which a paper archive is organized; it's not ordered in any way at all, except by URL and by date. To use it, all you can do is type in a URL, and choose the date for it that you'd like to look at. It's more like a phone book than like an archive. Also, it's riddled with errors. One kind is created when the dead Web grabs content from the live Web, sometimes because Web archives often crawl different parts of the same page at different times: text in one year, photographs in another. In October, 2012, if you asked the Wayback Machine to show you what cnn.com looked like on September 3, 2008, it would have shown you a page featuring stories about the 2008 McCain-Obama Presidential race, but the advertisement alongside it would have been for the 2012 Romney-Obama debate. Another problem is that there is no equivalent to what, in a physical archive, is a perfect provenance. Last July, when the computer scientist Michael Nelson tweeted the archived screenshots of Strelkov's page, a man in St. Petersburg tweeted back, "Yep. Perfect tool to produce 'evidence' of any kind." Kahle is careful on this point. When asked to authenticate a screenshot, he says, "We can say, 'This is what we know. This is what our records say. This is how we received this information, from which apparent Web site, at this IP address.' But to actually say that this happened in the past is something that we can't say, in an ontological way." Nevertheless, screenshots from Web archives have held up in court, repeatedly. And, as Kahle points out, "They turn out to be much more trustworthy than most of what people try to base court decisions on."

You can do something more like keyword searching in smaller subject collections, but nothing like Google searching (there is no relevance ranking, for instance), because the tools for doing anything meaningful with Web archives are years behind the tools for creating those archives. Doing research in a paper archive is to doing research in a Web archive as going to a fish market is to being thrown in the middle of an ocean; the only thing they have in common is that both involve fish.

. . .

The footnote problem, though, stands a good chance of being fixed. Last year, a tool called Perma.cc was launched. It was developed by the Harvard Library Innovation Lab, and its founding supporters included more than sixty law-school libraries, along with the Harvard Berkman Center for Internet and Society, the Internet Archive, the Legal Information Preservation Alliance, and the Digital Public Library of America. Perma.cc promises "to create citation links that will never break." It works something like the Wayback Machine's "Save Page Now." If you're writing a scholarly paper and want to use a link in your footnotes, you can create an archived version of the page you're linking to, a "permalink," and anyone later reading your footnotes will, when clicking on that link, be brought to the permanently archived version. Perma.cc has already been adopted by law reviews and state courts; it's only a matter of time before it's universally adopted as the standard in legal, scientific, and scholarly citation.

Perma.cc is a patch, an excellent patch. Herbert Van de Sompel, a Belgian computer scientist who works at the Los Alamos National Laboratory, is trying to reweave the fabric of the Web. It's not possible to go back in time and rewrite the HTTP protocol, but Van de Sompel's work involves adding to it. He and Michael Nelson are part of the team behind Memento, a protocol that you can use on Google Chrome as a Web extension, so that you can navigate from site to site, and from time to time. He told me, "Memento allows you to say, 'I don't want to see this link where it points me to today; I want to see it around the time that this page was written, for example.'" It searches not only the Wayback Machine but also every major public Web archive in the world, to find the page closest in time to the time you'd like to travel to. ("A world with one archive is a really bad idea," Van de Sompel points out. "You need redundancy.") This month, the Memento group is launching a Web portal called Time Travel. Eventually, if Memento and projects like it work, the Web will have a time dimension, a way to get from now to then, effortlessly, a fourth dimension. And then the past will be inescapable, which is as terrifying as it is interesting.

Jill Lepore writes regularly for the *New Yorker*, but also is the Chair of the History and Literature Department at Harvard University. Her specialty is American History, and she has written a number of books. Her first book, *The Name of War*, won the Bancroft Prize and her 2005 book, *New York Burning*, was a finalist for the Pulitzer Prize.

EXPLORING THE ISSUE

Can Digital Libraries Replace Traditional Libraries?

Critical Thinking and Reflection

1. Though it may be odd to think that academic researchers may have to pay to be published, what benefit would there be to humanity if this model of publication of scholarly work were adopted?
2. What is necessary to keep us from experiencing information overload, and information relativity?
3. If we lose the original sources of some of our laws and policies, how can we continue to build a system of rational decision making?
4. Libraries and collections of information often exist for the public good. What would happen if libraries of some types of information were privatized?
5. Community and academic libraries often are much more than repositories of printed materials. What other functions do libraries serve?

Is There Common Ground?

Both of the authors for this issue recognize the role of digital media in shaping and reshaping concepts about publishing, books, and libraries. As critics of American culture, they understand the relationship among publishing houses, the role of the academic press, and the costs of maintaining current collections of printed material. The most common fear they both project is a future in which valuable original material is lost or relegated to a space where no one will ever see it again.

They differ, however, in what the future of the library will be in American culture. Electronic print is very different than the traditional print market, and while students may not always understand the nature of the commitment to published research that many academics share, the idea that some work will not be published because of the cost is frightening. Even more frightening though is that it may be published, only to be lost or misplaced because keywords no longer can index the information in an organized, rationale way.

Certainly, the cost of books and periodicals will affect academic and public libraries, but it is important for any civilization to build upon the repository of laws, regulations, and research that advances our shared knowledge of our surroundings and the really important chronology of what matters to humanity. The selections in this issue remind us that as technology and distribution forms change, we need to pay attention to the important information that can be lost or misplaced along the way.

Additional Resources

Ashley Dawson, "DIY Academy: Cognitive Capitalism, Humanist Scholarship, and the Digital Transformation," in *The Social Media Reader*, edited by Michael Mandiberg (New York: New York University Press, 2012, pp. 257–274). In this book chapter, the author discusses the open source model for academic publishing.

Laura Mandell, *Breaking the Book: Print Humanities in the Digital Age* (Hoboken, New Jersey, 2015). In this book, the author examines the relationship readers have with traditional print versus the electronic version of the word.

Alexander Starre, *Metamedia: American Book Fictions and Literary Print Culture After Digitization* (Iowa City, IA, 2015). The author compares the aesthetics and format of traditional books and digital books, and the experience of reading different formats.

Richard Thompson, *Merchants of Culture: The Publishing Business in the Twenty-first Century,* 2nd ed. (London: Plume, 2012). In this book, Thompson discusses the changing business models of the publishing industry.

Internet References . . .

American Library Association (ALA)

www.ala.org/

Net Literacy

www.netliteracy.org/?gclid=Cj0KEQiAjpGyBRDgrt-
LqzbHayb8BEiQANZauhy7OzKjxDhyIyMnLBATttrUW-
dURv7y9NPC7U4bX1AggaAvn48P8HAQ

Project Gutenberg

www.gutenberg.org/

Public Broadcasting Service (PBS), "Literacy Link" for Adults

http://litlink.ket.org/

Selected, Edited, and with Issue Framing Material by:
Alison Alexander, *University of Georgia*
and
Janice Hanson, *and University of Massachusetts—Amherst*

ISSUE

Will the Benefit Be Worth the Cost
for the Internet of Things?

YES: **Shawn Dubravac**, from *Digital Destiny: How the New Age of Data Will Transform the Way We Work, Live, and Communicate,* Regnery Publishing (2015)

NO: **Federal Trade Commission,** from "Internet of Things: Privacy and Security in a Connected World," FTC Staff Report (2015)

Learning Outcomes

After reading this issue, you will be able to:

- Describe the Internet of Things.
- Analyze what benefits it will bring to individuals, business, and society.
- Analyze what problems it will bring to individuals, business, and society.
- Compare your conclusions from the two analyses presented to decide your stance on this issue.

ISSUE SUMMARY

YES: Dubravac sees a new era in which digital devices and services transform our lives. They will transform our individual lives, solve some major problems for humankind, and improve our access to products and services.

NO: "The Internet of Things: Privacy and Security in a Connected World" contains reports of staff members who participated in an FTC workshop that discussed the potential security risks to personal safety inherent in the Internet of Things.

Technological innovation means vastly different things to different people. Often as a society we embrace new technology as a savior. It will change lives, solve individual and social problems, and bring about a better world. Television, when it began entering American homes in the 1950s, was hailed as the "new family hearth" that would bring families together, encourage communication, and provide family-friendly entertainment. When educational television first started, some posited that it would be the death knell for the educational system, replacing bricks and mortar with educational television in the home.

Just as some embrace innovation, others worry about consequences. The phenomenon of "moral panics" has been seen across centuries. Novels, radio, records, and comic books were all castigated for their negative effects, and often described as ruining the moral fiber of our children. You can probably see similar moral panics today. Sometimes the promise is not fulfilled. Computers supposedly rang in the age of the paperless office. My messy office desk is a testament to that missing benefit for me. Aspects of the interconnected world afforded by computer systems and the Internet are privacy and security issues. Clearly the government can access our data or even our interactions. Surely other governments can spy on us, as we surely spy on them. At the individual level, identity theft is rampant and can be devastating to individuals. A few years ago, there was a move in the health industry to put records online. Many worried about security of what could be very sensitive health information. We have all become reluctantly aware of the massive amount of information that is available on each of us. The Internet of Things adds to that concern.

But what is the Internet of Things? Wikipedia describes the Internet of Things (IoT) as a "network of physical objects or things embedded with electronics, software, sensors, and network connectivity, which enable these objects to collect and exchange data." Other definitions add that this very importantly includes the ability to send and receive data without requiring human interaction. Because we are all inherently egocentric, it is important to realize that these networks will be in factories, healthcare facilities, energy grids, and transportation. Data will no longer be created solely by people; it will also be created by things. Marr in a Forbes blog from 2015 addresses what he calls mind-boggling facts about this phenomenon. For example, he says that in 2015 we will have 4.9 billion connected things; by 2020 predictions are that those numbers will exceed 50 billion. The IoT is estimated to have a total economic impact of up to $11 trillion by 2025. Marr ends by noting that less than 0.1 percent of all the devices that could be connected to the Internet are in fact connected.

Dubravac is an optimist. He paints a vibrant picture of what the Internet of Things will enable. We can envision so many possibilities. Holograms in our living rooms, holodecks for video gamers, access to all entertainment media when we want it, where we want it, and exactly what we want. Homes that include connected refrigerators that tell us what we need to buy and remind us of food expiration dates, driverless cars, security systems that use biometrics for access, computing in a virtual environment. Sounds like science fiction, but at least some of this will come true over the years. The following selection is from a book that takes a comprehensive look at this new world and which includes a discussion of some of the problems that can emerge.

In November of 2013, the Federal Trade Commission (FTC) held a workshop on the Internet of Things in which workshop participants discussed the changes that will occur due to the growing connectivity of devices. This workshop brought together academics, businesses, and advocacy groups to explore the privacy and security issues of these evolving technologies. In January of 2015, the FTC staff report on the workshop was released and as you will read, it focused extensively on issues of security in a highly networked world. The report prompted some dissension among FTC members. Commissioner Wright thought the staff report calls for broad legislation without adequate evidence for this approach. Identifying potential costs and benefits should come before proposals that could have major impact on consumers. Commissioner Ohlhausen sees no need yet for baseline privacy legislation and notes an overreaction in the call for companies to delete valuable data.

We cannot dismiss issues of security and privacy. At the national and global level, WikiLeaks provides one example of how data can be compromised. Issues about whether the National Security Agency (NSA) in the United States has violated constitutional provisions requiring warrants for wiretapping reveals the power of our government to monitor citizens. Many sites have been hacked, sometimes compromising personal information of credit card holders. One individual has quipped, "There are only two kinds of firms: ones who have been hacked and ones who don't know they've been hacked."

To paraphrase Dubravac: What does it mean for us as humans when the whole world has gone digital? To understand its potential, we need to understand its basics. At the most basic level, digital is data. You may have heard the term *big data*. It refers to the enormous amount of data that is now available. Think about the cameras that now run on streets and in businesses and that can capture and retain huge amounts of data. Consider the data collected on consumers that guide many business decisions. The possibility of analyzing such amazing stores of information is exciting. Surely we can find cures for many illnesses, track down violent criminals, and in general correlate information from around the world. If this seems amazing to you now, imagine when that data is multiplied as the Internet of Things evolves.

YES ↵   **Shawn Dubravac**

Digital Destiny: How the New Age of Data Will Transform the Way We Work, Live, and Communicate

. . . Intrigued by this rather simple observation—that the world had gone completely digital—I asked myself the question that led to the book you are reading: What does it mean for us—for human beings—when everything is digital? Is it just a curious trend, like a fashion, changing the way things look, but having little real impact on how we live? Certainly it is more than that. Could it be like the invention of the telephone or the television—game-changing products that forever altered the way human beings receive and provide information? We're getting close, but those are only two products. Of course their impact was revolutionary, but also isolated: you could step away from the television or hang up the phone.

My thinking was still too narrow. Remember, I told myself, *everything* will be digital, not just a few products. So, really, we're talking about something on a larger scale . . . something like the advent of electricity . . . ah-ha! I finally felt like I was getting to the essence of the change before us. My simple question had begun to open horizons I hadn't considered. The truly immense scope of digital began to unfold. Digital technology wasn't only going to change what we did and how we did it. It was evolving in a way that would completely transform how cultures are structured and redefine societal norms.

When Thomas Edison invented the world's first light bulb, it was an extraordinary moment. But we're talking about just a single light bulb. How would that change civilization? Were people's homes suddenly wired? Did power stations just spring up over night? Could anyone have had any realistic notion that one day *everything* would be electric? Indeed, as my CEO Gary Shapiro noted in his best-selling book *Ninja Innovation: The Ten Killer Strategies of the World's Most Successful Businesses*, Edison's true revolutionary innovation was the Pearl Street power station in Manhattan, which provided the current needed to power the light bulbs: "The reason the Pearl Street station was so important—and why Edison would have failed had he not created it—is that the electric light bulb couldn't replace the gas lamp as the primary source of lighting until the entire electrical system was created to sustain it. Otherwise, Edison would have been just the guy who had created a cool, but useless, gadget. In other words, inventing the light bulb was not the end for Edison; it was only the beginning."

. . .

The Internet of Me!

"[The Internet of Everything] will be five to ten times more impactful than the whole Internet revolution has been so far."
—John Chambers (Cisco) 2014 CES keynote address

At the 2014 International CES (Consumer Electronics Show) I noticed a product that was quite unique. It seemed to encapsulate the whole history of digitized data in one convenient item. Was this, I wondered, the product that would revolutionize the home and finally make good on all the promises and expectations of the much-vaunted Internet of Things?

Considering that the product in question was a crock-pot, the answer was obvious: unlikely.

While we might say there are already plenty of digital crock-pots on the market today, they are only digital in the sense that they have a digital interface; otherwise, they are very analog, everyday crock-pots. This one being showcased at CES, however, allowed remote monitoring and control via one's smartphone. The accompanying app told the user the temperature and the elapsed cooking time and allowed adjustments. This new crock-pot is literally part of the so-called Internet of Things. It is digital. It is "connected." It is sensorized.

My tongue-in-cheek praise should not be interpreted as veiled skepticism about this particular product—or of any digital device to come. At the same CES, I also saw Kolibree's smart toothbrush, a digital toothbrush that can track how long you brush, what teeth you clean well, and which teeth could use a little more attention. Revolutionary? Perhaps. The Internet of Things has to start somewhere, and we should applaud those companies who are taking the early risks.

Indeed, these items are just the first of what will be a horde of digital items coming to store shelves—or online outlets—near you. The day will come when not only will you own a digital crock-pot, but the crock-pot will "communicate" with your driverless car to make sure dinner is piping hot the moment you enter the house. As you're getting ready for bed, still full from your amazingly delicious (and perfectly cooked) crock-pot meal, your digital toothbrush will let you know that you've neglected your back molars the last two times brushing and that they have an excess of plaque.

Or not. Maybe digital crock-pots and toothbrushes will never catch on. While you'll certainly be living in a house full of connected items, it's still guesswork which ones will be digitized and online and which ones won't. The experimentation taking place today is most importantly helping to determine which devices and use case scenarios make sense to digitize and connect and which ones don't.

What we do know is that by 2020, according to the IDC "Digital Universe" report, there will be around 30 billion connected things." Your home will be connected—not in the way we think of connected homes today, with a cord running to a central modem or even through Wi-Fi connecting a few key computing products—but through hundreds of everyday objects, running independently but communicating with each other.

The purpose of all these connected things—if we can identify a single unifying theme—will be to transform the home into an extension of yourself, or your family. The home, via its devices, will assume many of the daily tasks, annoying chores, and myriad other activities we now perform manually. In the home of the future you will even be able to create the very products you buy online.

. . .

A Day in the Life . . .

Now, what does all this talk about the future of the Internet have to do with the home? Good question. First, it makes sense that the place where you spend most of your time will be the place where the Internet of Things—connected objects with sensors—will be highly operational. Second, the trend we see the Internet taking is the same trend that will play out in the home: a progression toward near-universal customization. In their book *The New Digital Age: Transforming Nations, Businesses, and Our Lives*, authors Eric Schmidt and Jared Cohen write of this future, "You'll be able to customize your devices—indeed, much of the technology around you—to fit your needs, so that your environment reflects your preferences."

That's all the Internet of Things really is—yet another step toward removing the distance and the friction between data and action. Connected objects capture and analyze the data in a quantity and at a speed that human beings could never match—and then they will act on it, removing the human element from the equation.

So what will this look like in practice? Well, let's create a day in the life of our future selves . . .

6:42 a.m.: Your alarm goes off. Is it strange that your alarm went off at the forty-second minute and not the fortieth minute? Not if your alarm knows your sleep cycles and wakes you during your lightest moment of sleep, a much more natural way to wake up than being shocked awake when you might be in deep REM sleep. Gently, the ambient lighting in your bedroom turns on, brightening at the same rate that your eyes can adjust. At the same moment, your shower turns on as well—adjusting the water temperature to match your personal preference, which it has learned. After you shower, your calendar matches the day's events with options in your wardrobe, prompting you with different options and predicting your preferences among the choices presented.

7:30 a.m.: Your coffee is fresh and waiting for you, brewing based upon past behavior and sensor data from throughout your home. You arrive in the kitchen and are prompted with several breakfast choices. The option with the highest rank uses the last of the strawberries because your refrigerator sensed that they were about to go bad. As you eat, you glance through the day's news on one of several screens around you, your favorite news sites arranged in the order you like to read them, with news stories chosen to match your interests. Or maybe you prefer the television in the morning, in which case the TV program delivers the news in the way you prefer: sports first, then weather, then local, and finally national and foreign. Or perhaps the stories are delivered to you in an order derived from the number of friends or colleagues who have "liked" or "recommended" them. A ding from your watch lets you know precisely when you need to leave if you're going to make your 8:30 appointment—relying on a real-time feed from traffic monitoring systems like Waze or future systems relying on V2V and V2I, discussed in the previous chapter. You step into the garage where your driverless car is already on, with the inside temperature adjusted perfectly to the outside weather and your personal preference. It zips away while you continue reading the news or perhaps take the time to return some emails or make some calls. You didn't have to worry about turning off lights, turning the thermostat up or down, or checking whether you have enough food for dinner. As devices in your home were digitized, sensorized, and connected, those tasks were turned into data, and algorithms are now automating them on your behalf. Your pantry and refrigerator know which products are running low and which ones need to be re-ordered—which they do without your involvement.

Work Day: While at work, you're alerted at various times of the day about your home's activities. These tasks are all likely taken care of without your involvement, but you are given the option to override the automation. It rained the night before so your sprinkler system won't turn on at its normal time today—unless you decide to override the computerized recommendation, a choice you'll have with several other assorted options today. A package arrives at the house (via drone?), and you sign for it remotely. Your entertainment system tells you the next season of your favorite show is ready for streaming, while your calendar automatically, dynamically, and continuously updates itself for your evening commute to ensure that you aren't late to your daughter's soccer match or your son's baseball game. You can decide what you'll have for dinner, but nothing comes to mind. Your home recommends a few options based on what's in the pantry and refrigerator as well as your dietary and health needs and fitness goals.

5:39 p.m.: You leave the office in your driverless car after a long, hard day. You don't relax quite yet because you still have a few more emails to send and a call to make. Your wearable body sensors know that you have heightened anxiety and alert your home (and your other family members). When you eventually walk through the door, the lights are set at a relaxing level, while your favorite music is already playing. If you set your dinner to cook in the morning before you left (in a connected crock-pot, no less), it is ready and waiting.

9:00 p.m: After you've watched highlights from the evening baseball or football game, you get an alert that your body is more tired than you realize and that going to sleep now would align with your body's needs, based upon your calendar of events for the next day. You don't fight it and crawl into bed.

You'll notice that throughout this scenario I'm intentionally avoiding predicting the details of specific "connected" objects and their functions. But with this sketch you can begin to understand how the home of the future will function: decisions driven by data. In the mind of science fiction writers and popular imagination a generation or two ago, these tasks were performed by androids. While I have no doubt that we'll see human-form robots in some way in our digital future, I'm less certain that they'll be doing stuff for us in the home. We don't need them. Through the Internet of Things and connected devices, the home will look and feel much like homes do today, but it will function as an extension of ourselves. Robots, as we imagine them, don't have much of a place in this scheme. That said, will your refrigerator be a robot? Is your driverless car a robot? Those are far more relevant questions. In the sense that these objects will be automated things capable of independent operation, even communication, then yes, they'll be robots. But we shouldn't expect that the home of the future will have a robotic maid, like Rosie from the Jetsons.

Rather, the home, through its connected objects, will be attuned to our individual preferences, of both mind and body. The Internet will be there, but in the background, like a power source—funneling the data from one object to the next in a continuous flow. We likely will have some sort of PC, but so many other objects will replace the need to use this PC for Internet activities as we do today: reading the news, paying bills, checking bank statements, indulging our interests, interacting on social media. These things will be compartmentalized, separated from one another, as opposed to mashed together the way they are today whenever we go "online."

From Scarcity to Abundance

Our digital destiny will have a big impact in other areas as well. Digital is moving through the entertainment industry like a bulldozer, leveling structures that have been in existence for decades. Nothing is going to stop the bulldozer, but that doesn't mean something won't try to get in its way.

Since the days of the ancient poets and playwrights, one characteristic has defined entertainment for mankind: scarcity. In ancient times, the cost of paper and the written word precluded an abundance of poets and writers. Only the best where published—and only the best have come down to us thousands of years later. So too with playwrights. There were only so many festivals and theater productions each year at which playwrights could showcase their skills. Only the best competed against one another in ancient Athens, and only the best created works survive to this day.

It has been no different in modern times. Of the thousands of books that are submitted to publishers every year, only a fraction ever see print. Of the thousands of screenplays that get written, only a fraction become movies. There is a limited amount of shelf space in the bookstores and theaters in the world. Only the best make it there; the rest are never seen.

In an analog world we attempted to overcome these constraints by increasing the volume of whatever the scarce resource was. So we went from single-screen theaters to dual-screen theaters to multiplexes with ten or more screens. In publishing, the Internet eliminated some of the scarcity of the bookshelf, but as long as publishers were still using printers and paper and ink, there remained a scarcity of resources. In either case, the scarcity was perhaps improved, but it remained a scarcity.

In an analog world, the limiting factors of scarcity dictate the choices individuals make. Consumers only see and read what has already been decided by an elite class of publishers and producers to be the best (or at least the most profitable). These elite gatekeepers determined what was on our shelves, on our television screens, and in our theaters. Consumers did dictate which of those works that made it past the gatekeepers would be successful, but they were starting from a selection that had already been greatly winnowed by others.

In his seminal 2004 *Wired* article "The Long Tail," which he expanded into a book, Chris Anderson called this winnowing process "the tyranny of lowest-common-denominator fare," by which he meant that economics—not quality—determined what we know as popular culture. Scarcity dictated what theater and bookstore owners would stock. If a product couldn't pay its shelf-space "rent," it was discontinued. Of course this doesn't mean that the product in question wasn't good or popular with some—it just wasn't popular *enough.*

The same is true for analog radio and television. There are only so many stations, and each can broadcast only a set number of hours of programming. "[T]he tyranny of lowest-common-denominator fare" demands that in such a world only those programs that attract the most ears or eyeballs will be broadcast.

Of course the problem is, as Anderson wrote, that "everyone's taste departs from the mainstream somewhere." Whatever movie is the biggest summer hit, whatever book is No. 1 on the *New York Times* best-seller list, or whatever television show gets the best Nielsen ratings week after week. Everyone loves something that wasn't a commercial success. But in an analog world, where scarcity dictates what is available for sale, you can't read, watch, or listen to the non-hit.

Digital removes scarcity from the equation. With no physical limitations, digital libraries can carry anything and not hurt their revenue—in fact, sales increase. In an analog world, stocking a non-hit CD means that you consequently stock one less hit CD—you're losing money by catering to fewer customers. But in the digital world, your shelf space "rent" essentially drops to close to zero. You can carry both, attracting both customers, because your shelf space is limitless.

. . .

Much of this is old news. Physical entertainment—even digital physical entertainment including DVDs and CDs—will succumb eventually to the digital bulldozer, just as Anderson predicted. Unable to compete against a business model whose "shelf-space costs" are zero, not to mention unable to carry the variety consumers have come to expect, physical distributors and their products find themselves drowning in a world of digital, streaming abundance.

. . .

A Look Ahead

The future of the entertainment industry, in whatever medium we're talking about, is one of a dizzying array of possibilities:

Creation: Digital creates a mechanism for a feedback loop between content creator and content producer. Historical content creation relied on small focus groups to determine how different scenes might play in front of larger audiences. For example, in places like Las Vegas and Austin there are testing centers for content because Las Vegas and Austin are considered "average" America. As I pointed out earlier, content was historically made for averages. Digital changed that, and digital is changing it further. Now content creators can see changes in preferences materialize in real time.

One obvious way creators do this today is through social networks. When a television show displays a hashtag at the bottom of its program, its primary purpose is marketing, to create a "trending" topic on Twitter and foster a community; but its secondary purpose is for the creators to mine what fans of the show think about the episode. Do they like this character? Do they like that story line? What do they think will happen next week? Creators use this real-time feedback to help guide the future of the show.

And it's a practice that will only expand as the two-way communication between creators and viewers grows. Whether it's through social networks or some other medium, creators are going to want to be as close to their viewers' thoughts as possible—not just to determine if what they've done is working but also, as we have seen, to determine the future direction of the show.

Amazon recently released pilots for a number of series under consideration for original content production. The company let its entire user base dictate its future production investments—much as Netflix is able to determine the tastes and demographics of its users and craft a show it knows they will like. The metrics and digital data available to aid creation are set to explode as we digitize greater swaths of our everyday lives.

In short, the wall separating creators from viewers is getting thinner and more transparent every year. There will come a day when the wall disappears entirely and viewers will be taking and active role in the direction of their favorite shows.

Discovery: Today Netflix offers recommendations of movies you might like based upon some basic demographic details it has about you combined with your viewing habits and the viewing habits of its millions of other users. This is a huge leap forward from where we were. Digital is almost always at the root of recommendation engines. But this is just the beginning. As we increasingly digitize our physical space, the number of inputs into these recommendation and discovery engines increases exponentially. Imagine—not too many years from now—that you have a few friends over and you want to watch something you'll all enjoy. In the analog world you flipped through whatever was being pushed out across a few channels. The advent of cable opened up the choice but didn't help with the decision. Then Netflix came along and began offering recommendations, but those recommendations are based on your viewing habits which might be—and likely are—different from everyone else's in the room.

But now imagine that the Netflix home screen taps into other data sources in addition to your viewing habits. Perhaps it can also see the viewing habits of your friends by identifying them through their phones (which all have the Netflix app). It can pull data from the camera built into the bezel of your television and know how many people are in the room. It can see if you are lying down or standing up. It can pull weather-related information from your Nest thermostat and know how cold it is inside and what the weather is like outside. It might also pull in very personal information about you and your friends using your fitness trackers, such as how active you've been today. It might use heart rate and blood pressure to determine if you are excited or depressed. Then pulling in all of these diverse digital streams of data, it might be able to make movie recommendations that fit the people in the room and conform to your environment. . . . We stumbled over these decisions in the past. Serendipitous discovery will still happen in the future, but it can also be significantly augmented by digital data.

. . .

Niche corners: Today, millions of viewers tune into Twitch to watch others play video games. Yes, you read that correctly. There is a site that thrives on letting people watch others play video games. And YouTube has become a key destination when people are looking for "how-to" videos. There is literally no topic too obscure or mundane to have a devoted following. Go ahead, pick an obscure skill and search YouTube for it. See how many hits you get in return. Pentak Silat—a martial art from certain Southeast Asian island nations—yields 140,000 hits. Even out-of-date skills get hits. "Conjugating Latin" yields 1,400 hits. "Adjusting the tracking on a VCR" yields 764 hits. "Reading neumes"—useful if you want to learn Gregorian chants—yields 78 hits. It would probably help to know Latin for this last one too, so check out the Latin videos you found in the above-mentioned search. This is all going to explode even further. The Internet, and particularly the new Internet, is a perfect vehicle for bringing together people from all over the globe, people who are otherwise strangers, to share in their one unifying passion. Indeed, the social networks of the future will coalesce around these communities, catering to niche audiences. We already see this today with online book, hobby, and gaming clubs. The ability to indulge one's interests and passions will be no farther than a click or voice prompt away. Whether universal sites like Facebook or Twitter will split apart on account of this process or not, they will almost certainly lose their dominance as people choose to customize their social circles even more intimately. So instead of having one Facebook feed for all of your friends, you will have a feed for each of your niche communities.

. . .

The Next Phase

As we digitize greater swaths of our physical environment we will see completely new and previously unconsidered challenges. Need will help us find a path through the chaos. At the same time, we will receive the benefit of new services that we never imagined possible. The future looks bright. We will eventually look at these unimaginable innovations and wonder how we ever lived without them.

In our march forward we will influence the digital environment and digital data will continue to influence us, how we live and communicate, and ultimately who we are. In the end we will get to decide what our destiny looks likes in this new paradigm.

It is worth asking what the next phase of our digital transformation will look like. Where will need drive us to use digital data next? Isn't that what this whole book has been about, you ask? Yes, but I'm speaking about our near-future, the months and years immediately ahead. Curating that data, sifting it, finding the gems that allow us to remove yet another barrier will be where the next great innovations will occur.

As Edward O. Wilson wrote in his 1998 book *Consilience*, "Thanks to science and technology, access to factual knowledge of all kinds is rising exponentially while dropping in unit cost. It is destined to become global and democratic. Soon it will be available everywhere on television and computer screens. What then? The answer is clear: synthesis. We are drowning in information, while starving for wisdom. The world henceforth will be run by synthesizers, people able to put together the right information at the right time, think critically about it, and make important choices wisely."

Indeed, digital data will change the way we live, and not just the basic functions of living. It will change every aspect of our daily lives: how we live, work, and communicate. Mobile phones provide a modern and contextual example. They've given rise to new forms of communication and even helped the development of new "languages" as texting and other messaging services have evolved. Smartphones redefine geographic space; now you can have a "live" conversation with someone who is miles away or shop at a retailer while you are physically standing within the confines of a competing store. Space has shrunk to the size of our mobile phones. Digital data, in its many manifestations on the horizon, will further shrink distance in all its varied forms as we isolate the valuable data—the gems—from the noise.

As the Greeks connected the stars in the night sky to find patterns, shapes, and things, so too we will look at the stars in the digital universe and create something out of nothing. This is one part of our digital destiny with which we have little direct experience as of yet. Our devices—from smartphones to laptops and PCs—are already becoming "smarter," in that they better understand what we need; but what we see today will pale in comparison to what we will make possible tomorrow.

The fact is that most of us still understand the Internet as a single entity—a giant labyrinth one enters from thousands of different points. From there, we scrape through the darkness grasping at these valuable points of light. Search is just the most advanced way we have devised to make sense of the Internet. But, as I've argued, search is failing us even now, as the digital universe expands through the billions of billions of connected devices that are coming our way.

Using search as we understand it to navigate this abyss won't just be more difficult; it will literally be impossible. The whole nature of the Internet will shift from a community of web sites to an ocean of data. But through our devices and other digital objects, we will be able to find the lights. We just won't have to do it ourselves. Our devices and other digital objects will deliver a curated experience providing settings that fit our moods, recommendations that meet our needs, and the distinctiveness of an experience perfectly measured for the individual. This curation is made possible only through the five pillars of digitized data that I laid out in the earlier chapters of this book—ubiquitous computing, explosion of digitized devices, universal connectivity, digital data storage, and sensors.

If we step back and look at our lives abstractly, we see that decisions we make are not made exclusively by us in isolation, but are shaped by the interactions we have with the technology we use. Most modern cars either won't start until the seat belt is engaged or will provide an (often painfully annoying) indication that the seat belt isn't engaged after the vehicle is started. Either we engage the seat belt and stop the incessant beeping or we "endure" the beeping and continue to drive without the seat belt engaged. The technology exerts its influence on us in either case.

The influence of technology is growing, as we already see from the devices of today. Our devices empower us to make decisions and choices that were once unavailable. For instance, technology allows us to contact someone whom we might otherwise not have contacted. That's technology influencing our decisions. Our future, and the decisions we make then, will see even more influence from the digitization of data that is now taking place—but unlike in my seat belt example, much of this influence will be less visible to us. The digitization of data began with revealing unobservable data, making the invisible visible. That is but the first step. Our digital destiny will fully take hold when this newly visible data fades into the background and begins making decisions on our behalf. Once again data will seem invisible, but the influence of digital data will be immense.

. . .

Shawn Dubravac is chief economist for the Consumer Electronics Association and has taught at several business schools. He is a widely cited technologist.

FTC Staff

Internet of Things: Privacy and Security in a Connected World

Executive Summary

The Internet of Things (IoT) refers to the ability of everyday objects to connect to the Internet and to send and receive data. It includes, for example, Internet-connected cameras that allow you to post pictures online with a single click; home automation systems that turn on your front porch light when you leave work; and bracelets that share with your friends how far you have biked or run during the day.

Six years ago, for the first time, the number of "things" connected to the Internet surpassed the number of people. Yet we are still at the beginning of this technology trend. Experts estimate that, as of this year, there will be 25 billion connected devices, and by 2020, 50 billion.

Given these developments, the FTC hosted a workshop on November 19, 2013—titled *The Internet of Things: Privacy and Security in a Connected World*. This report summarizes the workshop and provides staff's recommendations in this area.[1] Consistent with the FTC's mission to protect consumers in the commercial sphere and the focus of the workshop, our discussion is limited to IoT devices that are sold to or used by consumers. Accordingly, the report does not discuss devices sold in a business-to-business context, nor does it address broader machine-to-machine communications that enable businesses to track inventory, functionality, or efficiency.

Workshop participants discussed benefits and risks associated with the IoT. As to benefits, they provided numerous examples, many of which are already in use. In the health arena, connected medical devices can allow consumers with serious medical conditions to work with their physicians to manage their diseases. In the home, smart meters can enable energy providers to analyze consumer energy use, identify issues with home appliances, and enable consumers to be more energy-conscious. On the road, sensors on a car can notify drivers of dangerous road conditions, and software updates can occur wirelessly, obviating the need for consumers to visit the dealership. Participants generally agreed that the IoT will offer numerous other, and potentially revolutionary, benefits to consumers.

As to risks, participants noted that the IoT presents a variety of potential security risks that could be exploited to harm consumers by (1) enabling unauthorized access and misuse of personal information; (2) facilitating attacks on other systems; and (3) creating risks to personal safety. Participants also noted that privacy risks may flow from the collection of personal information, habits, locations, and physical conditions over time. In particular, some panelists noted that companies might use this data to make credit, insurance, and employment decisions. Others noted that perceived risks to privacy and security, even if not realized, could undermine the consumer confidence necessary for the technologies to meet their full potential, and may result in less widespread adoption.

In addition, workshop participants debated how the long-standing Fair Information Practice Principles (FIPPs), which include such principles as notice, choice, access, accuracy, data minimization, security, and accountability, should apply to the IoT space. The main discussions at the workshop focused on four FIPPs in particular: security, data minimization, notice, and choice. Participants also discussed how use-based approaches could help protect consumer privacy.

1. Security

There appeared to be widespread agreement that companies developing IoT products should implement reasonable security. Of course, what constitutes reasonable security for a given device will depend on a number of factors, including the amount and sensitivity of data collected and the costs of remedying the security vulnerabilities. Commission staff encourages companies to consider adopting the best practices highlighted by workshop participants, including those described below.

First, companies should build security into their devices at the outset, rather than as an afterthought. As part of the security by design process, companies

Federal Trade Commission. "Internet of Things: Privacy and Security in a Connected World," FTC Staff Report, January 2015.

should consider (1) conducting a privacy or security risk assessment; (2) minimizing the data they collect and retain; and (3) testing their security measures before launching their products. Second, with respect to personnel practices, companies should train all employees about good security, and ensure that security issues are addressed at the appropriate level of responsibility within the organization. Third, companies should retain service providers that are capable of maintaining reasonable security and provide reasonable oversight for these service providers. Fourth, when companies identify significant risks within their systems, they should implement a defense-in-depth approach, in which they consider implementing security measures at several levels. Fifth, companies should consider implementing reasonable access control measures to limit the ability of an unauthorized person to access a consumer's device, data, or even the consumer's network. Finally, companies should continue to monitor products throughout the life cycle and, to the extent feasible, patch known vulnerabilities.

2. Data Minimization

Data minimization refers to the concept that companies should limit the data they collect and retain, and dispose of it once they no longer need it. Although some participants expressed concern that requiring data minimization could curtail innovative uses of data, staff agrees with the participants who stated that companies should consider reasonably limiting their collection and retention of consumer data.

Data minimization can help guard against two privacy-related risks. First, larger data stores present a more attractive target for data thieves, both outside and inside a company—and increases the potential harm to consumers from such an event. Second, if a company collects and retains large amounts of data, there is an increased risk that the data will be used in a way that departs from consumers' reasonable expectations.

To minimize these risks, companies should examine their data practices and business needs and develop policies and practices that impose reasonable limits on the collection and retention of consumer data. However, recognizing the need to balance future, beneficial uses of data with privacy protection, staff's recommendation on data minimization is a flexible one that gives companies many options. They can decide not to collect data at all; collect only the fields of data necessary to the product or service being offered; collect data that is less sensitive; or de-identify the data they collect. If a company determines that none of these options will fulfill its business goals, it can seek consumers' consent for collecting additional, unexpected categories of data, as explained below.

3. Notice and Choice

The Commission staff believes that consumer choice continues to play an important role in the IoT. Some participants suggested that offering notice and choice is challenging in the IoT because of the ubiquity of data collection and the practical obstacles to providing information without a user interface. However, staff believes that providing notice and choice remains important.

This does not mean that every data collection requires choice. The Commission has recognized that providing choices for every instance of data collection is not necessary to protect privacy. In its 2012 Privacy Report, which set forth recommended best practices, the Commission stated that companies should not be compelled to provide choice before collecting and using consumer data for practices that are consistent with the context of a transaction or the company's relationship with the consumer. Indeed, because these data uses are generally consistent with consumers' reasonable expectations, the cost to consumers and businesses of providing notice and choice likely outweighs the benefits. This principle applies equally to the Internet of Things.

Staff acknowledges the practical difficulty of providing choice when there is no consumer interface and recognizes that there is no one-size-fits-all approach. Some options include developing video tutorials, affixing QR codes on devices, and providing choices at point of sale, within set-up wizards, or in a privacy dashboard. Whatever approach a company decides to take, the privacy choices it offers should be clear and prominent, and not buried within lengthy documents. In addition, companies may want to consider using a combination of approaches.

Some participants expressed concern that even if companies provide consumers with choices only in those instances where the collection or use is inconsistent with context, such an approach could restrict unexpected new uses of data with potential societal benefits. These participants urged that use limitations be considered as a supplement to, or in lieu of, notice and choice. With a use-based approach, legislators, regulators, self-regulatory bodies, or individual companies would set "permissible" and "impermissible" uses of certain consumer data.

Recognizing concerns that a notice and choice approach could restrict beneficial new uses of data, staff has incorporated certain elements of the use-based model into its approach. For instance, the idea of choices being keyed to context takes into account how the data will be used: if a use is consistent with the context of the interaction—in other words, it is an expected use—then a company need not offer a choice to the consumer. For uses that would be inconsistent with the context of the interaction (i.e., unexpected), companies should offer clear and conspicuous choices. In addition, if a company collects a consumer's data and de-identifies that data immediately and effectively, it need not offer choices to consumers about this collection. Furthermore, the Commission protects privacy through a use-based approach, in some instances. For example, it enforces the Fair Credit Reporting Act, which restricts the permissible uses of consumer credit report information under certain circumstances. The Commission also applies its unfairness authority to challenge certain harmful uses of consumer data.

Staff has concerns, however, about adopting a pure use-based model for the Internet of Things. First, because use-based limitations are not comprehensively articulated in legislation, rules, or widely-adopted codes of conduct, it is unclear who would decide which additional uses are beneficial or harmful. Second, use limitations alone do not address the privacy and security risks created by expansive data collection and retention. Finally, a pure use-based model would not take into account consumer concerns about the collection of sensitive information.[2]

The establishment of legislative or widely accepted multistakeholder frameworks could potentially address some of these concerns. For example, a framework could set forth permitted or prohibited uses. In the absence of consensus on such frameworks, however, the approach set forth here—giving consumers information and choices about their data—continues to be the most viable one for the IoT in the foreseeable future.

4. Legislation

Participants also discussed whether legislation over the IoT is appropriate, with some participants supporting legislation, and others opposing it. Commission staff agrees with those commenters who stated that there is great potential for innovation in this area, and that IoT-specific legislation at this stage would be premature. Staff also agrees that development of self-regulatory programs designed for particular industries would be helpful as a means to encourage the adoption of privacy- and security-sensitive practices.

However, in light of the ongoing threats to data security and the risk that emerging IoT technologies might amplify these threats, staff reiterates the Commission's previous recommendation for Congress to enact strong, flexible, and technology-neutral federal legislation to strengthen its existing data security enforcement tools and to provide notification to consumers when there is a security breach. General data security legislation should protect against unauthorized access to both personal information and device functionality itself. For example, if a pacemaker is not properly secured, the concern is not merely that health information could be compromised, but also that a person wearing it could be seriously harmed.

In addition, the pervasiveness of information collection and use that the IoT makes possible reinforces the need for baseline privacy standards, which the Commission previously recommended in its 2012 privacy report. Although the Commission currently has authority to take action against some IoT-related practices, it cannot mandate certain basic privacy protections—such as privacy disclosures or consumer choice—absent a specific showing of deception or unfairness. Commission staff thus again recommends that Congress enact broad-based (as opposed to IoT-specific) privacy legislation. Such legislation should be flexible and technology-neutral, while also providing clear rules of the road for companies about such issues as how to provide choices to consumers about data collection and use practices.[3]

In the meantime, we will continue to use our existing tools to ensure that IoT companies continue to consider security and privacy issues as they develop new devices. Specifically, we will engage in the following initiatives:

- **Law enforcement:**
  The Commission enforces the FTC Act, the FCRA, the health breach notification provisions of the HI-TECH Act, the Children's Online Privacy Protection Act, and other laws that might apply to the IoT. Where appropriate, staff will recommend that the Commission use its authority to take action against any actors it has reason to believe are in violation of these laws.

- **Consumer and business education:**
  The Commission staff will develop new consumer and business education materials in this area.

- **Participation in multi stakeholder groups:**
  Currently, Commission staff is participating in multistakeholder groups that are considering guidelines related to the Internet of Things, including on facial recognition and smart meters. Even in the absence of legislation, these efforts can result in best practices for companies developing connected devices, which can significantly benefit consumers.

- **Advocacy:** Finally, where appropriate, the Commission staff will look for advocacy opportunities with other agencies, state legislatures, and courts to promote protections in this area.

Notes

1. Commissioner Wright dissents from the issuance of this Staff Report. His concerns are explained in his separate dissenting statement.
2. In addition to collecting sensitive information outright, companies might create sensitive information about consumers by making inferences from other data that they or others have already collected. A use-based model might not address, or provide meaningful notice about,

sensitive inferences. The extent to which a use-based model limits or prohibits sensitive inferences will depend on how the model defines harms and benefits and how it balances the two, among other factors.
3. Commissioner Ohlhausen does not agree with the recommendation for baseline privacy legislation. *See infra* note 191.

THE FEDERAL TRADE COMMISSION is charged to protect consumers in the commercial sphere. This report is the result of a workshop held to assess the risks and benefits of the emerging Internet of Things. This report, created by FTC staff, was designed to summarize the recommendations of the workshop and staff.

EXPLORING THE ISSUE

Will the Benefit be Worth the Cost for the Internet of Things?

Critical Thinking and Reflection

1. What do you think are the most exciting innovations you would like to see evolve as the Internet of Things becomes a reality? Which innovations will be most important?
2. What consequences concern you most? Which will be most important?
3. Technology will always move forward. What can be done to assess the costs or to mitigate the issues?

Is There Common Ground?

Technological determinism theorizes that media technology shapes how individuals and ultimately society think and how we process information. This perspective gives rise to the famous quote from McLuhan that "the medium is the message." Whether these new technologies rewire our brain, Dubravac is optimistic that these technologies will allow us to shape a brave new world. The FTC Staff Report is much more pessimistic, citing the many risks, particularly the risks to the security of personal information.

Realistically the common ground is that both perspectives are true: there will be benefits and there will be costs. Weighing them is the difficult issue. Predictions of the consequences of media innovation are rarely correct. Will consumers have the interest and the income to indulge in the many innovations to come? Will the "digital divide" be increased? Will everyone have a smart house, and a smart car, and a smart communication system?

These innovations can and will change our lives. But part of that change will be the risks associated with having so much private data "out there" in the world. As dissenters note, we may not yet have enough information to assess the risks, but we certainly know they will exist.

Additional Resources

Emanuel Delgado, *The Internet of Things: Emergence, Perspectives, Privacy and Security Issues* (Hauppauge, New York: Nova Science Pub Inc., 2015).

Samuel Grignard, *The Internet of Things* (Cambridge, Massachusetts: MIT Press, 2015).

Philip N. Howard, *Pax Technica: How the Internet of Things May Set Us Free or Lock Us Up* (New Haven, Connecticut: Yale University Press, 2015).

Joel Stein, "Your Data, Yourself," *Time* (March 21, 2011).

Bruce Sterling, *The Epic Struggle of the Internet of Things* (London, Moscow: Strelka Press, 2015).

Internet References . . .

The Globe and Mail

www.theglobeandmail.com/report-on
-business/rob-magazine/the-future-is-smart
/article24586994/#introduction

The Guardian

www.theguardian.com/technology/2015/mar/30/internet
-of-things-convenience-price-privacy-security

Siemens

www.siemens.com/innovation/en/home/pictures
-of-the-future/digitalization-and-software/internet-of
-things-facts-and-forecasts.html

Techradar

www.techradar.com/us/news/world-of-tech/future
-tech/six-things-you-should-know-about-the-internet
-of-things-1289157

Wikipedia

https://en.wikipedia.org/wiki/Internet_of_Things